Fifth Edition
Parenting in Contemporary Society

Fifth Edition

Parenting in Contemporary Society

Pauline H. Turner
University of New Mexico

Kelly J. Welch
Kansas State University

PEARSON

Boston Columbus Indianapolis New York San Francisco Upper Saddle River
Amsterdam Cape Town Dubai London Madrid Milan Munich Paris Montreal Toronto
Delhi Mexico City Sao Paulo Sydney Hong Kong Seoul Singapore Taipei Tokyo

Editorial Director: Craig Campanella
Editor in Chief: Dickson Musslewhite
Publisher: Karen Hanson
Editorial Assistant: Christine Dore
Director of Marketing: Brandy Dawson
Executive Marketing Manager: Kelly May
Marketing Assistant: Janeli Bitor
Director of Production: Lisa Iarkowski
Senior Managing Editor: Karen Carter
Associate Managing Editor: Liz Napolitano
Senior Operations Supervisor: Megan Cochran
Art Director, Cover: Anne Bonanno Nieglos
Cover Designer: Ilze Lemesis
Cover Image: © Brocreative/Fotolia
Media Director: Brian Hyland
Supplements Editor: Mayda Bosco
Full-Service Project Management and Composition: Laserwords Maine
Printer/Binder: R. R. Donnelley VA
Cover Printer: R. R. Donnelley VA

Credits and acknowledgments borrowed from other sources and reproduced, with permission, in this textbook appear on page 342.

Copyright © 2012, 2001, 1996 by Pearson Education, Inc. All rights reserved. Manufactured in the United States of America. This publication is protected by Copyright, and permission should be obtained from the publisher prior to any prohibited reproduction, storage in a retrieval system, or transmission in any form or by any means, electronic, mechanical, photocopying, recording, or likewise. To obtain permission(s) to use material from this work, please submit a written request to Pearson Education, Inc., Permissions Department, One Lake Street, Upper Saddle River, New Jersey 07458, or you may fax your request to 201-236-3290.

Many of the designations by manufacturers and sellers to distinguish their products are claimed as trademarks. Where those designations appear in this book, and the publisher was aware of a trademark claim, the designations have been printed in initial caps or all caps.

Library of Congress Cataloging-in-Publication Data

Turner, Pauline H.
 Parenting in contemporary society / Pauline H. Turner, Kelly J. Welch. —5th ed.
   p. cm.
 Rev. ed. of: Parenting in contemporary society / Tommie J. Hamner, Pauline H. Turner. 3rd ed. 1996.
   ISBN-13: 978-0-205-37903-3
   ISBN-10: 0-205-37903-6
  1. Parenting, 2. Parenting—Study and teaching, 3. Families, 4. Child rearing. I. Welch, Kelly. II. Hamner, Tommie J., 1932- Parenting in contemporary society. III. Title.
  HQ755.8.H35 2012
  649'.1--dc23
                          2011024628

10 9 8 7 6 5 4 3 2 1

PEARSON

www.pearsonhighered.com

ISBN-10: 0-205-37903-6
ISBN-13: 978-0-205-37903-3

CONTENTS

Preface xv

PART I Parenting: Concepts, Challenges, and Changes

Chapter 1 Parenting in Perspective 1

Childbearing Trends: Who's Having Babies? 2
- Who Are America's Parents? 2

Having Children: Now, Later, or Never? 5
- The Perceived Value of Children 5
- The Appeal of Parenthood 6
- Gay Men and Lesbians: Deciding to Have Children 7

Family Size: Lots of Tots? Or No Kids, No Thanks? 7
- Draining Mom and Dad: The Resource Dilution Hypothesis 8
- The Quiverfull Movement: "Don't You Know What Causes That?" 9
- Childfree by Choice 9
- Delayed Childbearing 11

Change Over Time: Parenting Is a Process 12
- Mothering 12
- Fathering 16
- Coparenting: Go Team! 19
- Conflict and the Transition to Parenthood 20

Parent Education 21
- Early Parent Education Efforts 22
- A Rebirth 22

Chapter 2 The Changing Nature of Parenting: Infancy and Early Childhood 29

Parenting Infants and Toddlers 30
- The Parent–Infant Relationship 30
- Parenting Involvement with Infants and Toddlers 31
- Theories of Child Development 32

Trust, Attachment, and Reciprocity 35
- Establishing Basic Trust 35
- Attachment: An Emotional Bond 37
- Developing Reciprocity 39

Brain Development and Infant Stimulation   40
   Brain Development: Wiring the Brain   40
   Providing Infant Stimulation: The Parents' Roles   42
Parents and Toddlers: Parents are Protectors   42
   Coping with Growing Autonomy: "Me do it!"   42
   Providing Learning Experiences: Self-Help Skills and Toilet Learning   44
   Social and Intellectual Learning   45
Parents and Preschool Children: Parents are Nurturers   46
   The Styles of Parenting   47
   Discipline and Punishment: One and the Same?   50
Building Self-Concept, Initiative, and Learning   51
   Developing a Self-Concept   52
   Developing a Sense of Initiative   52
   Providing Learning Experiences   53
Programs for Parents of Infants, Toddlers, and Preschoolers   54
   Home Visitation   54
   Head Start   55

Chapter 3 The Changing Nature of Parenting: Middle Childhood and Adolescence   61
Parents and School-Age Children: Parents are Encouragers   62
   Childrearing Practices   62
   School Adjustment   63
   Attachment and Middle Childhood   64
Middle Childhood: Developing Industry and Mastering Friendships   65
   "Will You Be My Best Friend?": Friendships and Chumships   65
   Developing a Sense of Industry   67
   Building a Healthy Self-Concept   67
   Providing Learning Experiences   68
'Tweens: Special Challenges of Preadolescence   70
   Characteristics of Preadolescence   70
   Family Experiences and the Preadolescent   70
   Exit Parents, Enter Friends   70
Parents and Adolescents: Parents as Guides, Supporters, and Monitors   71
   Parenting Styles   71
   Parent–Adolescent Conflict   72

Adolescents' Perceptions of Parents 73
Establishing an Identity, Autonomy, and Intimacy 73
  Adolescents' Friendships and Romantic Relationships 74
  Experiencing Gender Differences in Friendships 74
  Culture/Ethnicity and Friendship 76
Adolescents and Contemporary Issues 76
  Sexual Behaviors: Experiencing a Wide Range in Attitudes and Behaviors 76
  Consequences of Adolescent Sexual Behaviors 78
  Teenage Pregnancy 78
  Sexually Transmitted Infections 80
  The Influence of Parents 81
  Adolescent Substance Use 82
  Bullying 83
Programs for Parents of School-Age Children and Adolescents 86
  Parent Involvement in the Schools 86
  Chapter I Programs 86
  Programs for Parents of Adolescents 87

Chapter 4 The Changing Nature of Parenting: Later Life 93
The Family Life Cycle 94
Parents and Their Adult Children 95
  Adult Children Living At Home: Doubling Up 96
  Adult Children Living Away from Home 99
  Intergenerational Ties 100
  The Parent–Adult Child Relationship in Late Adulthood 101
  Extended Family Experiences 102
Grandparenting 102
  Characteristics of Today's Grandparents 103
  Styles and Experiences of Grandparenting 104
Parenting, Round II: Grandparents as Parents 105
  How Do Parenting Grandparents Fare? 106
  How Do Grandchildren Fare? 107
  Stepgrandparenting 107
Providing Care for Elderly Parents 108
  Parent Care 109
  Stressors Associated with Caregiving 110

PART II Parenting: Diversity in Today's Families

Chapter 5 Effective Strategies for Contemporary Parents 117

Successful Parenting: Communication is the Foundation 118
   Communication: Interconnecting Family Relationships 118
   Cornerstones of Communication 120
Systematic Training for Effective Parenting 123
   The Goals of Misbehavior 123
   Reflective Listening and Open Responses 124
   Effective Talking 124
Correcting Behavior: Discipline or Punishment? 125
   Natural and Logical Consequences 125
   Assertive Discipline 126
Other Effective Successful Parenting Models 127
   The National Extension Parent Education Model 127
   Partners for Fragile Families 128
   Growing Together 128
   Parent Programs' Strengths and Limitations 129
   Outcomes and Effectiveness 131
Successful Parenting: Willing to Forgive 132
   Forgiving: The Individual Level 132
   Forgiving: The Relationship Level 133
   Communicating Forgiveness: A Family Process 133
   Barriers and Benefits 134

Chapter 6 Contemporary Parenting: Diversity and Change 137

Parenting in Cultural Contexts 138
   Collectivist Cultures 138
   Individualistic Cultures 139
Understanding Today's Parents 139
   The Nuclear Family 140
   The Nuclear Family in History 140
   The Expanding Family Landscape 142
Contemporary Families 145
   African American/Black Caribbean Families 145
   Latino American Families 147

Asian American Families 149
Native American/Alaska Native Families 151
Arab American Families 154
How Do Children Learn About Their Racial/Ethnic Identities? 154
Government's Role: Policies for Families 155
Poverty 156
Social Welfare 158
Poverty, Social Welfare, and Parenting Behaviors 159

Chapter 7 Parenting in Single-Parent Families and Stepfamilies 165
Single-Parent Families 166
Single Parents: Deficits or Strengths? 166
Single-Parent Mothers 167
Single-Parent Fathers 170
The Aftermath of Divorce: Transitions 173
The Binuclear Family 173
Former Spouse Relationships 174
Divorced Moms 174
Divorced Dads 175
How Divorce Affects Children and Adolescents 176
The Negative Effects of Divorce 176
Children's and Adolescents' Adaptation 177
The Passage of Time 178
The Legal Aspects of Divorce: Child Custody and Support 181
Spousal Support 181
Child Support 181
Child Custody 183
Living, Loving, and Parenting in Post-Divorce Families 184
Challenges for Single Parents 185
Changes in Household Finances 185
Changes in Residence 185
Changes in Boundaries 185
Changes in the Emotional Environment 186
Transitions to Repartnering 187
Stepfamilies Today 187
Common Challenges for Children 189

Chapter 8 Parenting and Work: A Balancing Act 197
    Working Families: The Transformation of American Homes 198
        A Portrait of Contemporary Dual-Earner Couples 198
        Service Men and Women 200
    Couples and Work: Just Trying to Make Ends Meet 201
        Dual-Earner Couples and Family Well-Being 202
        Work Hours and Family Life: Shift Work 203
        The Demands of Overtime 204
        Opting Out: Stay-at-Home Moms 205
        Leaving the Workforce: Stay-at-Home Dads 205
    The Balancing Act: Juggling Family Life And Work 206
        Conflicting Demands: Heartstrings versus Purse Strings 206
        Juggling Parenting and Household Chores 208
        Childcare 210
        It's Just No Fun Anymore: Leisure Time and Parenthood 210
    Ten Strategies for Family, Parenting, and Work Balance 211
        Value Family 211
        Strive for Partnership 211
        Derive Meaning from Work 211
        Maintain Work Boundaries 211
        Be Focused and Productive at Work 212
        Prioritize Family Fun 212
        Take Pride in Dual Earning 212
        Live Simply 213
        Learn to Say "No" 213
        Value Time 213

PART III Parenting: Risks and Alternatives

Chapter 9 Parenting in High-Risk Families 217
    The Crisis of Family Violence 218
        Domestic Violence 219
        The Victims 220
    Parents Who Abuse Their Children 222
        Types of Child Abuse and Neglect 223
        Who Batters or Abuses? 225
        Family Characteristics 225

Community Characteristics and Lack of Social Support   227
The Effects of Abuse on Children   227
    The Effects of Physical Abuse and Neglect   228
    The Effects of Child Sexual Abuse   228
    The Effects of Family Abuse   229
    Reporting Abuse   230
    Support for Abusive Parents   230
Homeless Families   231
    Who Are the Homeless? What the Numbers Say   231
    Homelessness and Temporary Shelters   232
    Characteristics of Homeless Parents   233
    Characteristics of Homeless Children   233
    Support for Homeless Families   235

Chapter 10 Parenting Children with Exceptionalities   239

Having a Child With Disabilities   240
Types of Exceptionalities   242
    Physical Disabilities   242
    Intellectual Disability   243
    Learning Disabilities   245
Other At-Risk or Disabling Conditions   248
    Prematurity   249
    Prenatal Substance Use   249
Challenges for Families with Exceptional Children   250
    Stress and Family Environment   250
    Parent–Child Relationships   252
    Resilient Children   255
Support and Empowerment for Parents with Exceptional Children: Best Practices   255
    Be Empathic and Foster Hope   256
    Recognize Families as Experts and Enhance Their Self-Efficacy   256
    Enhance Family Access and Offer Family Networking   256
    Encourage Effective Problem-Solving and Coping Skills   256

Chapter 11 Alternatives to Biological Parenthood   261

The Experiences of Adoptive Parents   262
    Who Adopts?: Characteristics of Adoptive Parents   262
    Intrafamily Adoptions   263

Gay and Lesbian Adoption   263
The Experiences of Adopted Children   265
   Children with Special Needs   265
   Transracially Adopted Children   265
   Outcomes of Adoption   266
   Children's Coping Strategies   267
Adult Adoptees: The Search for Birth Parents   268
The Adoption Process   269
   Initial Information   269
   Preparation   269
   The Family-in-Waiting   269
   The Placement   269
   It's Final!   270
When Conception Fails: Infertility   270
   Women and Infertility   270
   Men and Infertility   270
   Treating Infertility   271
   The Psychological Impact of Infertility   273
Foster Parenthood   273
   The Children   274
   The Foster Parents   277
   Foster Care and the Biological Parents   277

Chapter 12   Alternatives for Childcare and Early Education   283
Types of Care and Education   284
   Caregiver in the Home   284
   Family Childcare   284
   Center-Based Care and Education   288
Infant Care: Different Decades, Different Issues   289
Quality Early Care and Education   291
   Assisting Parents in Selecting Quality Programs: Licensure   291
   Assisting Parents in Selecting Quality Programs: Important Factors to Consider   292
   Assisting Parents in Selecting Quality Programs: Income and Childcare Quality   293
   The State of Union: Overall Quality of U.S. Childcare   293
Effects of Early Care and Education   294
   Effects on Cognitive Development   294

Effects on Emotional Development 295
Effects on Social Development 295
Parental Satisfaction with Childcare 296
The Future 297
Other Preschool Programs 298
School-Age Children in Self-Care 299
Readiness for Self-Care 300
Effects of Self-Care 300
Families of Children in Self-Care 301
After-School Programs 302

Glossary 305
Author Index 315
Subject Index 328
Photo Credits 342

PREFACE

This Fifth Edition of *Parenting in Contemporary Society* is even better than the first four. Based on our belief that there is no "recipe" for effective parenting behavior—but instead that there are a number of strategies, skills, insights, and resources that can assist parents—the topics in this Fifth Edition represent those we believe to be the most current, relevant issues facing today's parents and the professionals who work with them.

Parenting in Contemporary Society provides students with a realistic, engaging, and academically informative discussion about the choices and challenges associated with parenting in today's global society. This Fifth Edition builds on the success of the first four editions and maintains many of its original features. Global changes in this edition include new and expanded numbers of informative graphics and photos, more attention to diversity and multicultural issues, and significantly updated research. Further, chapter lengths have been streamlined and condensed where possible.

This book is written to acquaint upper-level undergraduate and graduate students with parenting in three primary areas: 1) concepts, challenges, and changes; 2) diversity in and among families; and 3) risks and alternatives. To this end, the book is divided into three parts.

Part I Parenting: Concepts, Challenges, and Changes This unit consists of the first four chapters which introduce the concepts of mothering and fathering, address the changing nature of parenting through the life cycle, and the contemporary strategies of parenting that many parents use to assist them in becoming more effective parents. The first chapter presents an in-depth look at the landscape of contemporary mothering and fathering. With significantly updated sources and demographic trends, changes in this Fifth Edition include new discussions about why people today decide to have/not to have children, and about why the transition to parenthood is difficult for most. New coverage also includes a discussion about parenting as a process, and information about mothering, fathering, and co-parenting, as well as gay and lesbian parenting.

Chapters 2, 3, and 4 are companion chapters that discuss the changing nature of parenthood across the life cycle, from infancy through old age. These chapters emphasize the reciprocal nature of parent-child relationships. New discussions in Chapter 2 include in-depth coverage about child development theories, parenting involvement with infants and toddlers, and maternal gatekeeping. We are especially excited to offer new research about ethnic group differences in parenting. Chapter 3 gives considerable attention to contemporary issues adolescents face today, including adolescent sex, teen pregnancy, sexually transmitted infections and HIV/AIDS, substance use, and bullying. This chapter also offers a new, in-depth discussion about the influence of parents on teens' sexual activities (includes coverage about racial/ethnic differences in how parents communicate about sex with their teens). Chapter 4 examines experiences of young adults, parenting in later life, grandparenting, and caring for elderly parents. Including significantly updated trends among aging adults and substantially more diversity coverage, this chapter also discusses the Family Life Cycle as a way to understand the multiple entrances and exits from the family of origin; the need for parents to transition from adult-child interactions to adult-adult interactions with their grown children; new coverage about the revolving door syndrome, where adult children return home after launching, and new coverage about intergenerational ties.

Part II Parenting: Diverse Family Types   This unit discusses diversity in family forms, structures, and experiences. Chapter 5 explores how parents can achieve "success" in parenting, and begins by looking at communication as foundational to parent-child relationships. This chapter also includes a new discussion about communication within different family types: nuclear families, gay and lesbian families, stepfamilies, single-parent families, and cohabiting families. We also examine managing children's misbehaviors and new research that addresses forgiveness as a cornerstone of effective, healthy family relationships. Chapter 6 looks at the different cultural contexts in which parenting occurs, and then addresses characteristics of parenting and parent-child interactions among diverse cultural groups in the United States. We also explore the socioeconomic statuses of today's families and conclude with discussing governmental policies and how they affect families with children. Chapter 7 examines the issues experienced by contemporary single-parent and stepfamilies and some of the unique challenges they face as they raise their children. We also look at the aftermath of divorce as parents strive to co-parent their children, and we conclude with discussing how divorce affects children and adolescents. This revised chapter has an abundance of updated demographic trends, and gives students a solid understanding of the diversity of parenting experiences in the U.S. today. This unit concludes with Chapter 8—with significantly updated resources, we examine the experiences of working families, and the demands faced by military families when a loved one is deployed to Iraq or Afghanistan. We then look at the types of stress and strain families face when they try to juggle work with family life and parenting, and we conclude by discussing the skills effective working families use in their daily lives.

Part III Parenting: Risks and Alternatives   In this unit, we examine parenting in high-risk families, such as with teenage parents, abusive parents, and homeless families. In Chapter 9, we look in-depth at two high-risk parenting family types: abusive or neglectful parents, and homeless parents. We include new coverage about the growing crisis of family violence and of the characteristics of parents who abuse their children, as well as a new, in-depth discussion about the effects of physical abuse and neglect on children, the effects of child sexual abuse, and the effects of family abuse on the community. Chapter 10 explores some of the common types of children's exceptionalities, as well as challenges for families with exceptional children. We also discuss support for parents. Although most people become parents by biologically bearing children, a small percentage of parents do not. We conclude this unit with Chapter 11, which discusses alternative methods of conception, adoption, and the experiences of foster parenting.

Chapter 12, the book's concluding chapter, discusses the different alternatives for childcare and early education available for parents today, as well as self-care and after-school programs for school age children. Before we end our study, we examine the age-old question: Is alternative childcare or early education harmful to a child's development? As with each of the other chapters in this Fifth Edition, the chapter has a significant number of updated resources.

Supplements for the Instructor: The following supplements are available to qualified instructors who have adopted this textbook.

Instructor's Manual and Test Bank (020516501X):   The Instructor's Manual and Test Bank has been prepared to assist teachers in their efforts to prepare lectures and evaluate student learning. For each chapter of the text, the Instructor's Manual offers different types of resources, including detailed chapter summaries and outlines, learning objectives, discussion questions, classroom activities and much more.

Also included in this manual is a test bank offering multiple-choice, true/false, fill-in-the-blank, and/or essay questions for each chapter. The Instructor's Manual and Test Bank is available to adopters at HYPERLINK "http://www.pearsonhighered.com" www.pearsonhighered.com.

MyTest (ISBN 0205020666): The Test Bank is also available online through Pearson's computerized testing system, MyTest. MyTest allows instructors to create their own personalized exams, to edit any of the existing test questions, and to add new questions. Other special features of this program include random generation of test questions, creation of alternative versions of the same test, scrambling question sequence, and test preview before printing. Search and sort features allow you to locate questions quickly and to arrange them in whatever order you prefer. The test bank can be accessed from anywhere with a free MyTest user account. There is no need to download a program or file to your computer.

PowerPoint Presentations (ISBN 0205020658): Lecture PowerPoints are available for this text. The Lecture PowerPoint slides outline each chapter to help you convey sociological principles in a visual and exciting way. They are available to adopters at HYPERLINK "http://www.pearsonhighered.com" www.pearsonhighered.com.

MySearchLab: MySearchLab provides a host of tools for students to master a writing or research project, It provides online access to reliable content for internet research projects, including thousands of full articles from the EBSCO ContentSelect database a complete online handbook for grammar and usage support. a tutorial on understanding and avoiding plagiarism, and AutoCite, which helps students correctly cite sources.

There is no question that the field of parenting education is in a continuous stage of change, and it is our sincere hope that our hard work on this revision helps instructors and students alike stay on the leading edge of these changes.

Although this book is specifically designed as preparation for students who will enter a profession requiring them to work directly with parents, it also provides useful information for students who someday desire to become parents themselves.

As you thumb through the pages of this book, we hope that you'll agree that we have brought your students the most current, relevant information about the social and emotional aspects of parenting, and that we present a sensitive, inclusive, nonjudgmental balance of theory and research. It is our sincere hope that you find this to be a natural partner to your course, and that your students discover a resource to help them make informed professional and personal decisions about parenting.

We are indebted to all the members of our families who so patiently endured the writing of this Fifth edition. Kelly is especially thankful to her husband, David, who provided encouragement and support every step of the way, and who has successfully transitioned to his new role of stay-at-home dad!

We also acknowledge with much praise and many thanks the folks who made this Fifth edition possible: Karen Hanson, Pearson Education Publisher extraordinaire(!); Maggie Brobeck, Pearson Production Project Manager (who unflinchingly got this revision to the finish line!); and Christine Dore, Editorial Assistant, Pearson Education (who is incredibly adept at managing several hundred minute details at once!). I'd also like to thank Kateland Welch (LMFT) who did the tedious work of compiling the glossary. Thank you for your attention to detail, Katie! Each of you truly made this process an enjoyable experience!

Again, we sincerely hope that you enjoy reading and teaching from this book. We have worked so diligently to try to incorporate the necessary changes to reflect parenting in the 21st century, and have given our best to ensure that issues facing parents today are included. At the end of the day, we hope that students are presented a realistic picture of parenting in contemporary society, and that they hold in their hands a book that is relevant to their lives!

Our very best to you!

Pauline H. Turner

Kelly J. Welch

Chapter 1
Parenting in Perspective

Across the pages of time and history, children were considered a vital, necessary segment of society because they were needed to ensure the survival of the culture or race—they were viewed as necessary economic assets for society's continuation and as the manual labor needed to bring about that continuation. Although the challenges of parenting today are vastly different from those of parenting many years ago, contemporary parents still face unique demands as they raise their children.

Children the world over represent their culture's future, and because of this, society expects parents to do a good job and create healthy, productive citizens (Lerner, Noh, & Wilson, 2004). To be sure, parenting a child is a monumental task! Bringing a child into a family, either by birth, adoption, or foster parenting, is probably the biggest decision a couple or a woman will ever make.

Throughout our course of study together, we explore what it means to be a mother or a father and to parent, and what the parenting role requires at different stages of infant, child, and adolescent development. We also look at contemporary issues that today's parents face, such as parenting in diverse and high-risk families and juggling parenting with other responsibilities such as work.

As with any other human service field, knowing what to expect about parenting and equipping ourselves with knowledge and expertise prepares us to rise to the challenges. This book provides people in, or desiring to enter, the helping professions with information about effectively working with parents. It also assists prospective parents and those who are already parents in exploring the concepts of parenting so that they might develop the skills necessary for effectiveness in their roles.

We start our intriguing study by taking a look at childbearing trends—who are America's parents? We next examine the distinctions between parenthood and parenting. We then explore the concept of parenting education by looking at past education efforts, assess the present, and look briefly at the challenges for the future.

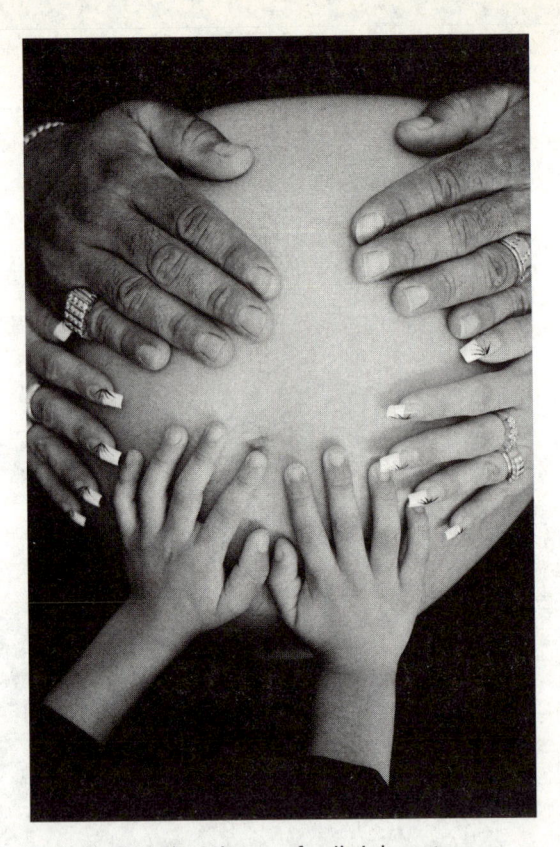

Each time a baby is born, a family is born too.

CHILDBEARING TRENDS: WHO'S HAVING BABIES?

Parents are the foundations that influence a child's development and well-being from birth into early adulthood, and they play instrumental roles in stimulating and shaping a child's cognitive, social, and emotional development (Solomon-Fears, 2008). Because of the tremendous influences parents exert on a child's development, let's take a look at the childbearing trends in the United States today: Who's having babies, and how old are America's parents?

Who Are America's Parents?

Each year, the population of the United States increases by the addition of slightly more than 4 million babies (Centers for Disease Control and Prevention, 2005). The **crude birthrate** is the number of childbirths per 1,000 women per year. These figures are tracked worldwide; in general, the crude birthrate in economically disadvantaged countries is higher than in more economically advantaged countries. In less economically developed countries, such as Niger, Uganda, Kenya, and Pakistan, the crude birthrate is significantly higher than in richer countries. In 2007, the crude birthrate in the United States was 14.2 (per 1,000 women) (National Vital Statistics Report, 2008).

The **fertility rate** is the average number of live births per woman, in a given population, per year. The U.S. fertility rate in 2005 was 2.08 (Centers for Disease Control and Prevention, 2005). Similar to crude birthrates, countries that are less economically advantaged tend to have higher fertility rates. It is important to note, however, that fertility rates also indicate religious, cultural, and ethnic norms. For example, because of their strong ties to families, Latinos tend to have more children than whites do; this is referred to as *familism*. The one-child policy in China—a practice that encourages late marriages and late childbirths, and mandates only one child per couple in urban areas—is a cultural norm that accounts for China's and Taiwan's low fertility rates. For any given country, a fertility rate of 2.1 is considered to be the *replacement level* of fertility. By tracking the crude birthrate from year to year, as well as the fertility rates, demographers are able to see certain childbearing trends, such as the age of birth mothers.

What is the current teen birthrate? Are women waiting until they are older to have children? Are there more babies born to single women than to married women? Answers to these questions can be found by looking at birth certificate data—the registered births.

TRENDS AMONG TEENAGERS In Chapter 9, we explore the experiences of teen parenting in depth. Here, it is necessary to understand today's trends associated with this age group.

In 2004, the birthrates for U.S. teenage mothers reached an historic low. With a decrease of 33 percent since 1991, the overall rate of teen births in 2004 was 41.2 births per 1,000 women aged 15 to 19 (Centers for Disease Control and Prevention, 2005). These trends were encouraging because they indicated that teens were either adhering to abstinence pledges, or that they were practicing safer methods of sex. Sadly, the teenage birthrate in the United States rose in 2006 for the first time since 2001. Between 2005 and 2006, the birthrate for teens (aged 15 to 19) rose 3 percent, from about 41 births per 1,000 to nearly 42 births per 1,000 (Centers for Disease Control and Prevention, 2008). The largest increases were seen among African American/Black Caribbean teens, who experienced an increase of 5 percent. Hispanic teens saw a 2 percent rate increase, white teens had a 3 percent rate increase, and American Indian/Alaska Native teens had a 4 percent increase (Centers for Disease Control and Prevention, 2008).

Although it is too early to determine if these data indicate that a new trend in teen childbearing is on the horizon, it is concerning to see these notable changes after 15 years of decreasing childbearing trends. As Figure 1.1 shows us, the birthrate among U.S. teens is twice the average for other developed countries.

TRENDS AMONG UNMARRIED PARENTS Nonmarital births are widespread, and they touch families of all different races and ethnicities, income classes, religious groups, and demographic areas. In 2006, a record 38.5 percent of all U.S. births were nonmarital births (Solomon-Fears, 2008). Births to unmarried partners can be first or subsequent births; they can occur to a woman who has never been married, as well as to divorced or widowed women. Furthermore, a woman with children may have had one or more within marriage, and other births outside of marriage. And, because U.S. demographers do not consider gay or lesbian partnerships to be "marriages," births to these couples are considered to be "nonmarital" births.

Teen Birth Rates in Developed Countries: 2007–2008
(Births per 1,000 females ages 15–19)

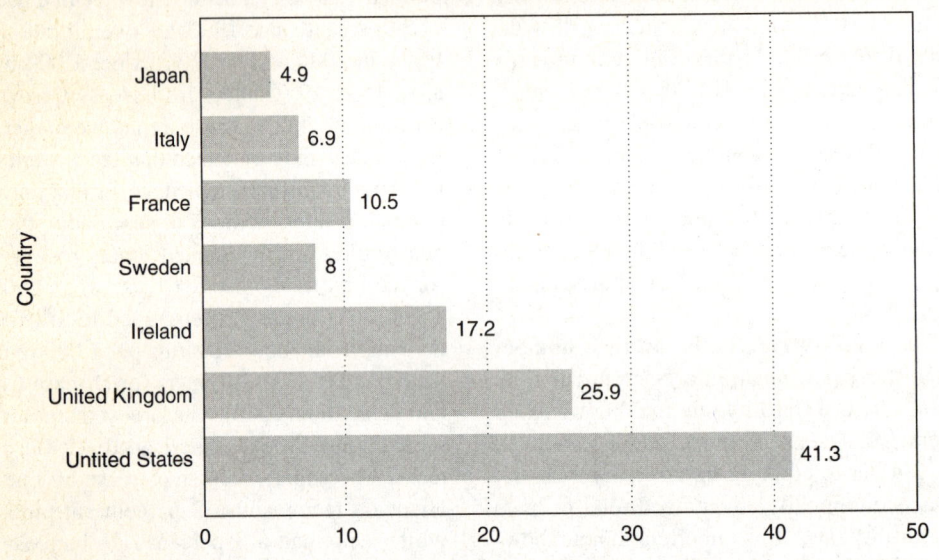

Country	Rate
Japan	4.9
Italy	6.9
France	10.5
Sweden	8
Ireland	17.2
United Kingdom	25.9
Untited States	41.3

FIGURE 1.1 Teen birthrates in developed countries.
The birth rate among U.S. teenagers is twice the average for all developed countries.

Source: Based on data from United Nations, UN Statistics Division (2010). Available: http://www.unstats.un.org/unsd/mdg/SeriesDetailaspx?srid=761 [2010, September 11].

A number of factors are associated with the unprecedented rates of births that occur outside of marriage. These include (Solomon-Fears, 2008):

- Marriage postponement—there is an increase in the median age at first marriage
- Childfree movement—there is decreased childbearing among married couples
- Increased divorce rates
- Increased numbers of cohabiting couples
- Increased sexual activity outside of marriage
- Improper use/lack of contraceptive methods
- Participation in risky behaviors that often lead to sex, such as alcohol and drug use

When considering all of these factors, the birth trends of unmarried partners may very well continue, and may even further increase. Certainly, these trends will continue to reshape the landscape of American family life and experiences.

PREGNANCY AT DIFFERENT AGES In the past, women in their 20s were thought to be at the peak of their childbearing years and have historically accounted for the most births. What are today's trends? In 2006, among women aged 20 to 24, the birth rate dipped to an all-time low, with 92.8 births per 1,000 women (U.S. Census Bureau, 2006). These data may reflect the overall trend of women who delay childbearing to pursue educational endeavors. In line with historical trends, in 2006, among women aged 25 to 29, the birth rate was the highest of any age group, with 104.6 births per 1,000 women. These data appear to support the idea that women in their 20s are in their peak childbearing years (see Figure 1.2).

Do you want children? At what age did you come to your decision—have you wanted to have/not have children for as long as you can remember, or have you only recently come to this decision? And when is the "right time" to become a parent?

Birth Rate (Per 1,000 Women) by Age of Mother:

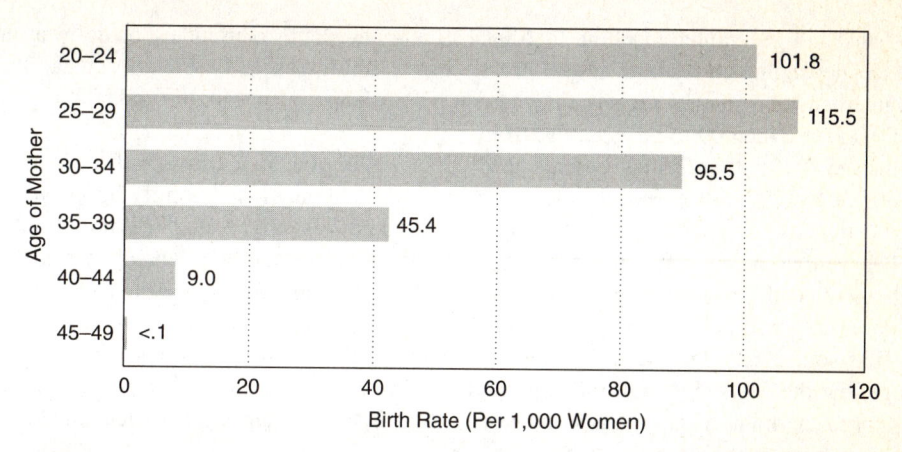

- 20–24: 101.8
- 25–29: 115.5
- 30–34: 95.5
- 35–39: 45.4
- 40–44: 9.0
- 45–49: <.1

FIGURE 1.2 Birthrates among all age groups.
Historically, women in their 20s were considered to be in their peak childbearing years. Although more and more older women are bearing children today, women in their 20s still account for the largest percentages of births.

Source: Welch, *Family Life Now*, 2e. (2010). Boston: Allyn & Bacon. p. 320. Data source: Centers for Disease Control and Prevention, Division of Vital Statistics (2005c).

HAVING CHILDREN: NOW, LATER, OR NEVER?

The decision to become a parent is a very complex issue because it includes a number of interrelated components. For instance, do we have a child because of the subjective value societies place on them, or because of personal, intrinsic reasons—or both? Do we have children because society *expects* us to?

Since the 1970s, researchers have attempted to document the various needs that children fulfill for adults; they have also tried to better understand how adults perceive the value of children (see Hoffman & Hoffman, 1973). Over the past three decades, researchers have discovered that people most often desire to have children because of the psychological satisfactions they offer to parents, the social ties children offer as adults age, and their economic value (such as tax breaks) (for a complete review, see Lawson, 2004). On the other hand, the lack of desire to become a parent has been associated with adults who place greater importance on self-fulfillment, leisure time, relationship quality, career advancement, and greater financial freedom (Seccombe, 1991).

Two main approaches have been taken by social science researchers to understand the attitudes and motivations associated with becoming a parent: the perceived value of children and the appeal of parenthood.

The Perceived Value of Children

Most studies and theories about the motivation to become a parent center on the perspective that there are perceived rewards and costs associated with parenthood (Lawson, 2004). Many of us engage in a cost–benefit analysis when we choose our life partners, and we do the same when we decide whether to have children. For example, some research suggests that one of the rewards of having children is that they meet some of our basic psychological needs (such as love and affection), and this is what motivates peoples' desires to have children (Al-Fadhli & Smith, 1996; Yamaguchi & Fergusson, 1995). Some adults may evaluate the costs (such as substantial decreases in personal time and freedom and substantial increases in financial responsibilities) and decide against having children. The amount that parents spend in rearing a child varies according to income level, marital status, and geographic location. In 2008, for instance, depending on parents' annual gross income, in urban areas it costs parents anywhere from $190,000 to $406,000 to raise a child from birth to the age of 17; in rural areas, parents need from $130,000 to $277,000 to raise a child to the age of 17 (Lino & Carlson, 2009). If prospective parents believe that the net value of having children is greater than the costs associated with having children, they will be motivated to become parents (Lawson, 2004). On the other hand, if they judge that the costs outweigh the benefits, they will forgo the mommy/daddy track and seek other sources to meet their needs, such as turning to nieces and nephews for psychological need fulfillment not met by having their own children.

The Perceptions of Parenting Inventory (PPI) helps people determine the rewards and costs they associate with having children (Lawson, 2004). This inventory assesses the rewards and costs associated with parenting by examining study participants' responses to different factors:

- *Enrichment:* In this category, the inventory asks participants to consider such things as, "Caring for the child would bring me happiness" and "Parenting the child would make me a better person."
- *Continuity:* When assessing this category, individuals respond to statements such as, "The child would carry my family name" and "I look forward to being a grandparent someday."
- *Isolation:* This potential cost addresses concerns such as, "I would have less time doing what I enjoy."
- *Commitment:* "Parenting the child would be a neverending responsibility" and "The child would be dependent on me" are items that assess the commitment required to parent.
- *Instrumental costs:* Financial concerns and other costs, such as "Parenting the child would be emotionally and physically exhausting" are addressed in this cost category.
- *Perceived support:* This category ascertains to what extent family and friends are available to provide support, by asking such things as, "My friends and family would help me care for the child."

As you look through these items, which ones do you most strongly agree with? Most strongly disagree with? It's important to note that your answers may change across time. For example, you may not want to have a child at this point in time because of the financial and emotional costs; however, when your circumstances change you may decide that the benefits of having children outweigh these particular costs.

The Appeal of Parenthood

We have all probably had experiences where we see children having a temper tantrum at the grocery store and go limp as a wet noodle when an exasperated parent tries to pick the child up to get him or her out of the store as fast as possible. And under our breath we have probably said, "I will *never* have children!" Certainly, there are times when having children doesn't seem like a very appealing thought! Despite the fact that all of us have probably not wanted children at one time or another, there is some evidence that there are certain psychosocial factors that are related to the appeal of parenting, particularly that of early childhood experiences.

A number of studies have attempted to show that our early experiences with our parents, such as parental nurturance, discipline, and attention, are significantly related to the motivation to parent. For example, some research has demonstrated that bad memories of our childhood experiences have accounted for unique variances in why some men and women choose to have children, and others do not (Gerson, 1980, 1985, 1986). These experiences underlie what is known as the **family projection process** (Bowen, 1966). This process stresses that the appeal of having children is the result of finding a way to satisfy our individual unmet needs from childhood. Stated another way, people who become parents do so because they feel that they were not given enough love, attention, or support as a child. Their own children, then, serve to enact their internalized unsatisfactory childhood experiences—parents have children to give them what they themselves never had as a child. It's important to note, however, that other research has shown that as individuals enter their 30s they feel less dependent on childhood memories in making important life choices, such as having children (Gerson, Posner, & Morris, 1991).

Gay Men and Lesbians: Deciding to Have Children

Although the number of planned families by gay men and lesbian women has been steadily growing in recent years, little research has been undertaken to understand the motivations of gays and lesbians to become parents (Bos, van Balen, & van den Boom, 2004). While certainly the existing research concerning the perceived value of children and the appeal of parenthood applies to homosexual parents as well to heterosexual parents, some have ventured to try to determine if gays and lesbians have additional, different motivations to become parents.

In a study of 178 lesbian families and 100 heterosexual families in the Netherlands, the researchers discovered a number of findings when comparing the two groups (Bos et al., 2004):

- *Experience of parenthood:* There were no significant differences between lesbian biological mothers and heterosexual mothers on parental competence, feeling parental burdens (stress), and the desires to become parents.
- *Quality of the couple's relationship:* Overall, there was no significant difference between lesbian and straight couples' relationship satisfaction. However, lesbian mothers were more satisfied with their partner as a co-parent than heterosexual mothers were with their husbands as co-parents. In comparison to heterosexual fathers, lesbian co-parents were significantly more satisfied with their couple relationship.
- *Justification of parenting:* Lesbian mothers, more so than heterosexual mothers, felt a greater need to justify the quality of their parenting to others.

- *Synchronicity:* Lesbian couples were more likely than straight couples to share childcare responsibilities and household duties; this synchronicity may account for the higher levels of relationship satisfaction.

The emergence of planned gay fatherhood and lesbian motherhood is indicative of broad social change that is taking place in our society, and societies around the world. Regardless of their sexual orientation, people are questioning existing parenting norms and are finding ways to create families (Berkowitz & Marsiglio, 2007). Examining the experiences of gay men and lesbians gives us an important opportunity to accept them into the parenting mainstream.

The decision to have a child or forego childbearing is a crucial—and irrevocable—decision that warrants careful and thoughtful attention. The next question is: How many children do you desire to have?

FAMILY SIZE: LOTS OF TOTS? OR NO KIDS, NO THANKS?

A recent Gallup Poll of 1,000 U.S. adults revealed that slightly over half of those surveyed indicated that two children is the "ideal" family size; about one-fourth said that three children were ideal (see Figure 1.3). The ideal family size trends change over time, and reflect cultural and societal changes. For instance, there is a sharp decline in the perceptions of ideal family size between the 1960s and the 1970s. This trend may reflect the advent of the birth control pill in the 1960s, which gave women more control over their fertility; this increased control may have, in turn, shaped attitudes about ideal family size.

In many ways, the U.S. is considered to be a pronatalist society. **Pronatalism,** or **natalism,** is an ideology that embraces childbearing. Pronatalist attitudes and beliefs are prevalent in the United States (Brooks, 2004). For instance, when a woman or a couple gives birth to just one child and says, "no more," or she/they decide to forego having children altogether, sometimes people aren't sure how to respond. Is she infertile? Are they selfish?

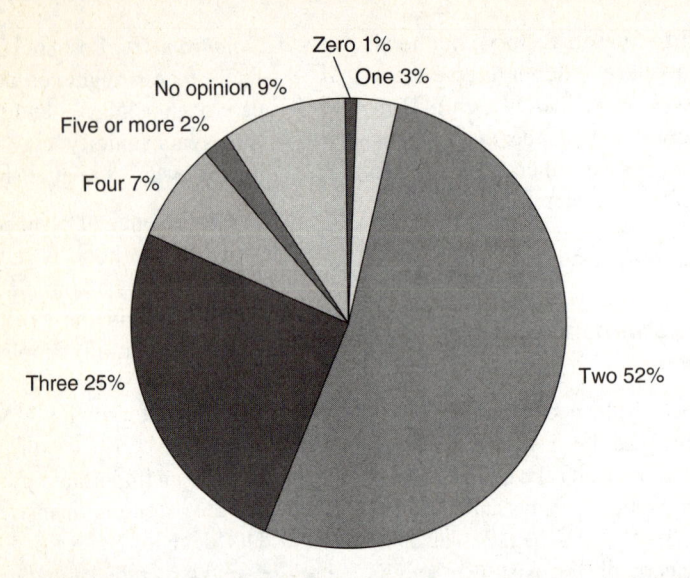

FIGURE 1.3 Ideal family size.
Source: Based on data from Carrol (2007).

Zero 1%
One 3%
Two 52%
Three 25%
Four 7%
Five or more 2%
No opinion 9%

Antinatalist countries discourage childbearing. An example of this would be China, where each couple is allowed to have only one child.

Do parents only have so much to give to their kids? One theory maintains that parents' resources are limited, and become depleted when additional children are added to the family.

Draining Mom and Dad: The Resource Dilution Hypothesis

Parental time, energy, and resources are limited, and the **resource dilution hypothesis** theory contends that parents' finite resources become diluted when spread over a larger number of children (Blake, 1981). A number of studies in the 1980s and 1990s seemed to support this theory when the researchers discovered that a child in a large household receives less attention than a child in a smaller household, and this lack of attention later affected the educational level the child attained (see Strohschein, Gauthier, Campbell, & Kleparchuk, 2008, for a complete review). Other studies have similarly shown that maternal attention is greatest for firstborn children, and less for subsequent siblings, and that mothers reduce positive interactions with their older children following the birth of another. With these results in mind, you may be thinking, "Wow, family size *does* matter—I really should only have one child!" But new research may contradict these prior findings.

Researchers from Canada recently surveyed over 13,000 parents and found that, because the relationship of a parent to each child is unique, effects of family size need to be studied differently than they were in the past (Strohschein et al., 2008). In their current study, the investigators looked at two different areas of parenting: positive interaction (the extent to which parents are responsive to their children's needs) and consistent parenting (the frequency with which parents set boundaries and establish standards for appropriate behavior). Using these two factors, they wanted to determine how parenting practices change when new children are added to the family system. In their long-term study, the researchers discovered that "parents do not so much *dilute* their resources when a new child is added . . . [more accurately] they act to deploy their resources differently" (Strohschein et al., 2008, p. 681). Instead of draining resources away from other children, as prior studies suggested, this new body of research seems to indicate that when new siblings are added to the family, parents employ a "managerial approach" to parenting—they shift, reallocate, and reorganize their resources to ensure that every family member's needs are met. When parenting our children, we referred to this as "zone" parenting, rather than "man-to-man" parenting.

It's impossible to determine the "ideal" family size because it is a uniquely personal decision that is affected by many factors. Today, there is an emerging trend that needs to be addressed when discussing family size: the Quiverfull Movement.

The Quiverfull Movement: "Don't You Know What Causes That?"

Large families are considered unusual in the United States (Arnold, 2005). While more common in the past, families with more than six children are so rare today that the census no longer tracks this data (Hartill, 2001). But with the Quiverfull Movement, today an increasing numbers of parents are having as many as 20 children.

The **Quiverfull (QF) Movement** is a pronatalist belief that is practiced among some evangelical Protestant Christian couples in the United States, as well as some Catholics and Mormons, and also has some adherents in Canada, Australia, New Zealand, and England. Foregoing all forms of birth control as a matter of principle and personal choice, a QF couple is motivated to have many children because of a desire to be obedient to what they believe are commands in the Bible. Citing Biblical passages such as "be fruitful and multiply" and "blessed is the person who has a quiver full of children," adherents to the Quiverfull Movement maintain an "open willingness" to joyfully receive and not thwart however many children are bestowed upon them (Campbell, 2003).

But how does religion affect a person's fertility? Some earlier research suggested that there are three conditions that produce religious effects on fertility: (1) the religion promotes norms about fertility-related behaviors, such as the use of birth control; (2) the organization is able to enforce conformity to these norms (either through social influence or through sanctions); and (3) when religion is a very important part of a person's individual identity (McQuillan, 2004). A recent study of 7,600 nationally representative subjects to identify what determines differences in rates of fertility among some religious groups confirms the earlier research (Hayford & Morgan, 2008). The researchers found that women for whom religion is an important facet in daily life have higher fertility intentions compared to nonreligious women.

Though some may disagree with QF couples' choices to have large numbers of children, it is important to consider whether they—just as other diverse family forms—should be afforded the same social support as other diverse families are.

Childfree by Choice

The **childfree-by-choice** trend is certainly nothing new as a quick glance at A-list celebrities shows: Kim Cattrall, Stockard Channing, Jay Leno, Steve Martin, George Clooney, and Oprah Winfrey all have opted to remain childfree. Even Dr. Seuss, the infamous children's book author, was childfree by choice. But the "no kids, no thanks" trend is moving beyond the borders of Hollywood and extending to U.S.A. mainstream. Today, about one-in-five women ends her childbearing years without having a child, compared to one-in-ten in the 1970s (Pew Research Center, 2010). This no-kids trend is not isolated to the United States. One body of research from Australia estimated that one in five women in the childbearing years opted to not have children (Merlo & Rowland, 2000).

To date, there has been little empirical research in family studies, sociology, or psychology that examines the motives of women and men who are voluntarily childless; however, there are a few studies that help us understand why people opt to remain childfree. For example, one body of research found that there are certain categories or groups among those who elect not to become parents. These groups include those who are certain they do not want children; those who are certain they do not want children at this point in their lives; those who are ambivalent to having children; and those who feel the decision was made for them because of health reasons or lack of a partner (Cartwright, 1999).

The reasons people remain childfree are as many and varying as those reasons people opt to become parents. Rathus and Nevid (1992) found in their study of hundreds of couples that there are various reasons why individuals and couples opt for the no-kids track: having more time with one another; the freedom from the responsibility of raising children; financial freedom; being able to devote more time to careers; and concerns about worldwide overpopulation.

Other research found that beyond individual factors ("micro" factors), social ("macro") factors, such as the increase in women's education levels and their participation in the job market, "compete with raising children" (Weston & Qu, 2001). Changing social values, decreasing importance of religion, access to legal abortion, and effective contraceptives also alter childbearing. These research findings indicated that those who choose to be childless do so because of their dislike of children, choice of lifestyle, lack of interest in children and parenting, or a belief that the world is too dangerous for children.

Similar to Rathus and Nevid, other studies similarly found that financial security and job security are also factors closely linked to an individual's decision to become a parent (MacKay, 1994; McDonald, 2000; Wooden, 1999). An additional study appears to confirm the findings from prior research. Sociologist Kristin Park (2005) analyzed the motives of 23 childless men and women. Through in-depth interviews, she found that women believed parenting would conflict with their careers and/or leisure activities. The women also indicated that they lacked a "maternal instinct," or they were generally uninterested in children. Men, more than women, believed that parenting required too many sacrifices, including great financial expense. Both men and women indicated that they felt their personalities were not suited to parenting.

Other research into childlessness categorizes childless women in the following groups (Baum, 1999):

Hedonists: These women are not willing to, nor do they have a desire to, sacrifice money, energy, time, or themselves in rearing children.

Emotional: Some women who choose not to become parents have no "maternal instincts"; these women report that they have no emotional connection or feelings toward babies or children.

Idealistic: These women indicate that they feel the world is not a safe place to bring a child into. They also feel that the world's resources are limited and they raise environmental concerns in their decision not to have children.

Practical: Women in this category desire to remain childfree for practical reasons, such as educational or career goals.

Though to some it may appear that women remain childfree for selfish reasons, this is not necessarily the case. Couples must be honest when assessing whether or not to become parents. Some people feel their lives are complete and full without children. Others choose to be childfree because of unfortunate circumstances, and in these instances, the decision can be a painful one. For instance, a close friend of mine desperately desired to be a mother but because she is a genetic carrier of a fatal type of muscular dystrophy, she opted to remain childless. Other couples may not consciously decide not to have children—they simply fall into childlessness.

Delayed Childbearing

While some couples remain childfree by choice and other couples are childless for medical or physiological reasons that prohibit them from becoming pregnant, some couples perhaps have every intention of becoming parents but for one reason or another parenthood eludes them. As Lisa, a colleague of mine, explains, "Before we became engaged, Kirk and I knew we wanted children—it was something we held in common. He comes from a very large family, and I come from a family with three other siblings. Our plan was to have our first child by the age of 30, but our business was really taking off and we thought we had plenty of time. We began trying [to conceive] when we were 35 or so and found out we had infertility problems. We tried fertility treatments for a few years with no success . . . so now we find ourselves in our mid-40s without children. Totally not planned. But even though it's not what we planned, we're very content with our lives right now."

Sociology professor Jean Veevers (1980) sought to determine how couples like Lisa and Kirk become a childless couple. This study defined four specific stages involved in delayed childbearing decision making:

1. *Postponing Childbearing for a Definite Period of Time:* Couples in this first stage intentionally delay childbearing in order to achieve certain goals they have set for themselves, such as meeting educational goals. Like Lisa and Kirk, perhaps they want to devote their attentions to their careers or give the business time to get established.
2. *Postponing Childbearing for an Indefinite Period of Time:* "We'll eventually get around to having children." In this stage of decision-making, couples' reasons for not having children become more and more unclear and perhaps even indefinable to even themselves. For whatever reasons, they feel that the timing is "just not right."
3. *Weighing the Pros and Cons of Being Parents:* During this stage of decision making, couples deliberate the costs and benefits associated with parenthood.
4. *Coming to Terms with Being Childless:* It is at this point that couples realize they have become childless by default. Like Lisa and Kirk, many couples may have intended to become parents, but numerous postponements in their decision making essentially made the decision for them.

While subsequent infertility and significantly increased risks of deleterious outcomes for the baby are associated with delayed childbearing in women, there are several bodies of empirical research that suggest childbearing among older parents is advantageous to children. For example, University of Maryland sociology professor Steve Martin (2002) found through his review of the literature that both economic and psychosocial (social and emotional) benefits for the child are associated with delayed childbearing. He cites a number of studies that indicate that the older a woman is when she has her first child, the greater the economic benefit to both herself and her baby. Findings further indicated that women who postpone childbearing are more likely to stay in the workforce throughout retirement eligibility, and as a result, they have distinctively higher earning potential than early childbearers. Women who postpone childbearing are also better able to find quality childcare because of their earnings. Quality childcare in turn increases the woman's work productivity and earnings potential greatly reduces "lost career time." In addition to being born into a higher income bracket, children born to older parents have better access to educational opportunities. Children of older parents also suffer fewer financial consequences if their parents divorce.

Children of older parents also experience psychosocial benefits. For instance, older parents have stronger and more reliable social support networks than younger parents, providing more stability for the entire family to cope with the inevitable stressors that accompany childrearing (Martin, 2002). The quality of the mother–child relationship is higher compared to mother–child relationships of younger mothers. For example, older mothers tend to be more positive about parenting and show less anger and frustration in parenting, while older fathers tend to be very involved in their children's lives, though they are not as physically active in play as are younger fathers. Older fathers are also more likely than younger fathers to share household tasks following the birth of a baby. And finally, because of having already experienced many significant life experiences, older parents are less likely than younger parents to experience depression, loss of self-esteem, or feelings of incompetence in parenting. Martin concludes that while older parents may experience fatigue and a lack of energy, their increased maturity seems to outweigh these negative psychosocial outcomes.

CHANGE OVER TIME: PARENTING IS A PROCESS

For those who are to become parents, there are no words to convey the excitement they will feel the first time they hear the baby's heartbeat, or hear their baby's first cries and first words. When a parent sees a baby's first smile the sense of love, responsibility, and commitment is palpable. But the thrills move beyond infancy. Watching children grow, learn, discover, and uncover this world at every stage of their development is both entertaining and exciting (except for driver's education—that would fall into the "frightening and scary" category!). To watch them move from the rambunctious, rough-and-tumble years of childhood to the young men and women they become fills parents with a sense of pride, and at times apprehension as their grown children enter the real world on their own. But that growth from infancy to manhood or womanhood involves a tremendous process of not only individual growth and change, but growth and change in the parents and in their relationship.

Parenting has been defined as the process or state of being a parent (Brooks, 1991). Lerner, Castellino, Terry, Villarruel, and McKinney (1995) suggest that parenting is a *process,* a course of events that evolve and change over time. This process includes nourishing, protecting, and guiding a child through the course of his or her physical, social, emotional, and intellectual development (Brooks, 1991). In this process, parenting is a continuous series of interactions between parent and child, and these interactions change both partners.

Parenting brings new challenges, experiences, and trials into the family system. As children grow, parents grow, too. This parenting process meets both the biological needs of the children and, at the same time, the needs of the society in which children are socialized. Indeed, two of the base goals of parenting are to meet the **survival needs** of infants, which include the provision of food, shelter, safety, security, and love; and to meet the **socialization needs** of children, which encompasses ensuring they become productive, contributing members of society. Parent educator and author Chris Theisen (2004) notes that there are eight essential parenting responsibilities:

1. Providing a safe environment
2. Providing basic needs
3. Providing self-esteem
4. Teaching children morals and values
5. Developing mutual respect
6. Providing effective and age-appropriate discipline
7. Being involved in the child's education
8. Knowing the child by communicating with him or her

Given the sheer importance of parenting, then, it is of little wonder that so much empirical attention focuses on parenting. Family practitioner Virginia Satir once observed, "Parents teach in the toughest school in the world—the school for making people."

Mothering

In societies across the globe, women are expected to become mothers by certain culturally determined ages, and this expectation creates pressures for them to bear children. Thus, becoming a mother is considered to be a normative developmental stage for women in all cultures. In the broadest sense, **mothering** is defined as a process whereby someone performs the relational and logistical work of caring for others (Arendell, 2000). With this definition, we can see how someone—a woman or a man—could "mother" someone who is not a child, such as an aging parent or a sibling who has a disability; we can also "mother" a friend or a loved one who is in need. However, in most societies women are expected not only to be the bearers of children, but to nurture, care for, and socialize them as well—mothers are expected to "mother" the children in society (Arendell, 2000).

Girls and boys are socialized to fulfill roles that are determined and defined by their cultures; though each society's roles are unique, motherhood is one of the few roles assigned to women that appears to be universal, and the experience of motherhood today remains a central part of many women's identities (Arendell, 2000). For example, in a study of 1,200 parents, women identified themselves as mothers more often than they identified themselves by their occupation or career or their marital status; on the other hand, fathers identified themselves by their occupation and not by their status as fathers (Rogers & White, 1998). Even though today women fill multiple roles, such as provider and caregiver to aging parents, they are also expected to simultaneously "nurture, schedule, taxi, and feed their families"—and to do it all well (Medina & Magnuson, 2009). Because of these multiple demands and expectations, some researchers believe that the standards for "good mothering" are escalating (Douglas & Michaels, 2004, cited in Medina & Magnuson, 2009).

Sharon Hays, a professor of sociology and women's and gender studies, examined the social construction of motherhood in the latter part of the 20th century. From her scholarly works, she coined the term **intensive mothering** to reflect the mothering roles and expectations that have been evolving since the 1980s, when women flooded the workplace (Hays, 1996). The **intensive mothering ideology** is the Western cultural belief that a mother should give of herself unconditionally, and focus all of her time, energy, money, love, support, and every other resource she has on raising her children. If she works outside of the home, she is expected to make up the time with her children that is "lost" at work. Furthermore, intensive mothering is expected of mothers even if a father is present in the home, if he is employed, and if they share equally in household and childrearing tasks. As this ideology shows us, the cultural expectation of mothers today is clear: The well-being of children is the responsibility of the mother, and she is to respond to their needs before those of her own or of her husband (or partner). Of course, this means that women who fall short of this cultural ideal do not fit today's social construction of "good mothers" (Medina & Magnuson, 2009). In Chapter 8 we explore the stressors associated with mothers' multiple roles and the pressures they feel in trying to adhere to the intensive mothering standard.

The transition to motherhood is a major developmental life event for most women because it requires women to restructure their goals, behaviors, and responsibilities (Mercer, 2004). The **theory of maternal role attainment (MRA)** speaks to the fluid, continual, fluctuating processes associated with becoming a mother (Rubin, 1967). According to this theory, women actually begin adopting roles associated with motherhood during their pregnancies, such as bonding emotionally with the growing baby. While pregnant, a woman also begins to observe the behaviors of *mother models* she has in her environment (such as her own mother, grandmothers, and friends); as her pregnancy continues, she adopts those behaviors she believes would be ideal for her and her child, and she rejects behaviors she judges as inappropriate for herself. Through pregnancy, and after the birth of her child, she continues to construct an "ideal" image of herself as mother; she then adopts roles that support this ideal image.

There are a number of factors that influence MRA. These include (Mercer, 1986):

- The age of the mother
- Socioeconomic background
- Social stress and support
- Temperament
- Self-concept
- Childrearing beliefs and attitudes
- Role strain
- Perception of the infant

Particularly important to MRA is the woman's relationship with her own mother. For example, one body of research demonstrated that mothers' current relationships with their mothers were recreated in their relationships with their infants (Kretchmar & Jacobvitz, 2002). Other research found that pregnant mothers' attitudes and memories about their mothers influenced their prenatal attachment to their babies, and that mothers' memories of how accepting/rejecting their own mothers were also influenced their ability to adopt motherhood roles (Crockenberg & Leerkes, 2003; Priel & Besser, 2001).

"Motherhood" is a developmental process that is influenced by many factors, and one that unfolds over time—she affects and is affected by her child, by her spouse or partner, by her past experiences in her own childhood, and by her relationship with her mother.

Research suggests that there are also certain behavioral and attitudinal traits of mothers and certain environmental conditions that mothers can provide to enhance the optimal development and competence of their children. In the sections that follow, we briefly examine some empirical studies that explore mothering and its effects on children; throughout our study together, we expand upon this discussion.

ATTACHMENT From the 1970s through the 1990s, a significant amount of attention was given to mothering during infancy. The healthy bonding process of mothers to infants seems to make possible a healthy attachment of infant to mother. In some of the now-classic studies on attachment, it was discovered that an infant becomes optimally attached to only one person at a time (the concept of *monotropy*), and that person is usually the mother.

John Klaus and Marshall Kennell (1982) maintained that the original parent–infant attachment is so crucial it influences the quality of all future bonds to others. They believed that the following principles contribute to the mother's early attachment to her baby:

- Close skin-to-skin contact with the infant for the first 45–60 minutes following birth
- The infant's response to the mother by some signal, such as body or eye movement
- Witness of the birth process by mothers in a state of alertness
- The difficulty a mother has attaching herself to an infant when she is under stress

This attachment research emphasized the dangers of separation of mother and infant, especially during the last half of the first year, when the attachment process is paramount to an infant's development. In the 1990s the issue of the impact of early and prolonged out-of-home childcare on infant–mother attachment resurfaced (Belsky, 1991). We explore the multiple aspects of childcare at length in Chapter 12.

MATERNAL INVOLVEMENT There are a number of positive characteristics of mothering; these are presented in Table 1.1. High levels of observed maternal positive involvement (such as affectionate contact and verbal stimulation) during the first 2 years of life forecast low levels of children's behavior problems at age 4, and maternal acceptance and responsiveness during the infant/toddler years predict high levels of empathy at age 10 (Belsky, Youngblade, Rovine, & Volling, 1991). Conversely, children who experience rejecting parental care and/or who fail to identify with their parents experience higher levels of depression in adolescence and lower levels of ego development in early- to middle adulthood (Dubow, Huesmann, & Eron, 1987). These findings show us that the effects of emotionally supportive or unsupportive care may extend well beyond childhood.

COMPLIANCE The seeds of compliance, cooperation, or antisocial behavior are sown in early childhood. For example, in one study, mothers of preschoolers who proactively engage their young children in interesting materials before they started to play with off-limits objects induce more compliance than do mothers who simply reject in every instance their children's handling

TABLE 1.1 Positive characteristics of mothering.

INFANCY/TODDLERHOOD
  Healthy bonding
  Nurturance
  Acceptance
  Sensitivity
  Consistent and prompt responsivity
  Provision of appropriate play materials
  Avoidance of restriction and punishment
  High degree of verbal and physical interaction

PRESCHOOL
  Nurturance
  Acceptance
  Sensitivity
  Allowance of exploration/expression
  Reasoning and inductive discipline
  Use of elaborated language and teaching strategies
  Setting limits

SCHOOL AGE
  Nurturance but not restrictiveness
  Stimulation but not directiveness
  Responsiveness but not control

behavior, aggression with peers, and low self-esteem as the child reaches school age and adolescence.

LANGUAGE DEVELOPMENT Research shows that the words mothers speak to their young children are picked up by them. For example, young children are tuned in to the qualities of **motherese,** the special speech register adults use when talking to children, consisting of short simple sentences, frequent repetitions, high pitch and exaggerated pitch contours, and emphasis on the here and now. Researchers have also discovered significant correlations between children's language gain and mothers' *verbal input* (number of utterances, noun phrases per utterance, number of "wh-" questions, and other kinds of questions and directives), *verbal prodding* (accepting the child's language and asking questions that demand sentences as answers), and *simple expansions* of children's utterances (Clarke-Stewart, 1988).

CHILD DEVELOPMENT KNOWLEDGE Mother's knowledge about child development and concepts of childrearing appear to have positive outcomes for children. One longitudinal study of low birth weight, preterm infants sought to determine the effects of maternal knowledge of child development and concepts of childrearing on the quality of the home environment and child cognitive and behavioral outcomes; data were collected from birth to 36 months (Benasich & Brooks-Gunn, 1996). The researchers found:

- Measures of maternal knowledge of child development and concepts of childrearing at 12 months predicted home environment, number of child behavior problems, and child IQ at 36 months (to a small but significant extent).
- Maternal knowledge was associated with home environment over and above socioeconomic status.
- Maternal knowledge continued to be important in the structuring of the environment when the child was 3 years old.

something that is forbidden (Holden & West, 1989). Mothers who are skilled in following their toddlers' leads in play have children who are more responsive to and compliant with maternal directions (Rocissano, Slade, & Lynch, 1987). Mothers who engage in direct control strategies and frequently reprimand their preschoolers are more likely to have children who defy them, whereas agemates whose mothers use indirect and persuasive strategies (such as explanations) are more likely to negotiate with their mothers in the face of conflict (Kuczynski, Kochanska, Rodke-Yarrow, & Girniss-Brown, 1987).

Considered together, these studies suggest that age-appropriate, sensitive care that fosters long-term harmony in adult–child relationships and maintains children's inherent motivation to cooperate with the desires of adults (especially parents) reduces the likelihood of noncompliant

This study suggests that maternal knowledge about child development and concepts of childrearing provides a pathway through which the home environment is structured by the mother, which, in turn, influences child outcomes.

THE RECIPROCAL NATURE OF MOTHERING

Perhaps the most important point regarding mothering is that maternal behaviors at every age level of the child are affected by the child's behavior and temperament. In other words, the relationship is always reciprocal. Classic research demonstrates that infants differ from the moment of birth (Brazelton, 1969; Chess & Thomas, 1973). Some babies cry a lot, others cry a little. Some are easy to soothe, others are difficult. Some eat and sleep well, others seem to demonstrate rhythmicity with great effort.

Picture the mother of an "easy" baby who cries little, sleeps soundly, is socially responsive, and thrives. If she is awakened only once a night to feed her baby, it appears obvious that she will have energy and enthusiasm for mothering and will interact with her baby in positive ways. Compare that picture with one of a mother who is awakened at 12:00 A.M., 2:00 A.M., and 4:00 A.M. for feedings, and even after the feedings, the baby continues to cry and to fuss, despite her best efforts to soothe the baby. She becomes anxious and communicates that anxiety to her infant through her tone of voice, rigid body, and facial expressions. A vicious cycle is set into motion, and her maternal behavior will be far from enthusiastic or energetic.

Fathering

Like motherhood, the social construction of fatherhood continues to change over time. Among America's first families in Colonial Williamsburg in the 17th century, for example, British immigrants brought the traditional patriarchal family structure to Virginia. The **patriarchal family structure** included the father figure, who was considered to be the authority over his entire household—wife, children, dependent kin, servants, slaves, and apprentices. This family structure served to preserve the wealth and power of the patriarch's household and the family's lineage. When fathers died, they willed their land and property to their sons, ensuring that the family's wealth remained within the family. Daughters typically inherited servants and livestock, rather than land or money. Within this family structure, fathers were all-powerful and served as the unquestioned, oftentimes uncaring, ruler (Lamb, Pleck, Charnov, & Levine, 1987). In this era, men were charged with the responsibility of their children's moral and spiritual development, and because of this, discipline was their responsibility. The early father–child relationship was typically emotionally distant and correctional; it also lacked warmth, nurturing, and affection because these behaviors were associated with parental indulgence, which was thought to ruin the character of the children (Pleck & Pleck,

The social construction of fatherhood continues to change over time. Today it's not uncommon for fathers to pitch in with childrearing and household tasks, such as meal preparation.

TABLE 1.2 Factors that influence fathering.

CONTEXTUAL FACTORS

Institutional practices	Employment opportunities	Economics
Race/ethnicity	Resources and challenges	Cultural expectations
Social support		

FATHER FACTORS

Role identification	Employment characteristics	Skills
Commitment	Psychological well-being	Relations with own father
Knowledge		Residential status

CHILD FACTORS

Attitude toward father	Behavioral difficulties	Temperament
Gender	Age	Developmental status

MOTHER FACTORS

Attitude toward father	Employment characteristics	Support of father
Expectations of father		

CO-PARENTAL RELATIONSHIPS

Marital status	Dual vs. single earner	Mutual support
Custodial arrangements	Relationship commitment	Conflict
Cooperation		

Source: Doherty, W., Kouneski, E., & Kouneski, M. (1998). Responsible fathering: An overview and conceptual framework. *Journal of Marriage and the Family,* 60, 277–292.

1997). Patriarchal parenting continued in the United States until the mid-18th century.

With the rise of industrialism and urbanization in Western cultures, the social construction of fatherhood began to change. As fathers moved their work into factories and away from the home, mothers' roles expanded to include moral teacher and disciplinarian (Pleck & Pleck, 1997). Historians note that the separation of the workplace from the home life created two opposing trends that are still in existence today: *father absence* and *father involvement* (Rotundo, 1993). Some men, for instance, withdraw emotionally, psychologically, and physically from their children because their work requires that they are absent from their families; on the other hand, the decline of patriarchy has given men "permission" to display more warmth, nurturing, and intimacy with their children, allowing them to be more involved.

FATHER INVOLVEMENT As Table 1.2 shows us, today, modern fathers tend to fall somewhere between these two opposing fatherhood types, even though they are still not quite as involved as mothers in the lives of their children (Wall & Arnold, 2007). In one study, the researchers discovered that fathers spend about 1.5 hours on a weekday and about 3 hours on a weekend day with their children who are under the age of 13, while an earlier study demonstrated that fathers have shown levels of engagement ranging from 2 to 2.8 hours per day (Pleck, 1997; Yeung, Sandbert, Davis-Kean, & Hofferth, 2001). On the whole, fathers today spend about one-third of their time with preschoolers, whereas mothers spend about two-thirds of their time with their tots (Silver, 2000).

Despite the amount of time spent with children, though, few fathers take primary responsibility for their children's nurturing and other needs; however, in comparison with mother involvement, father involvement (time spent with the family) increased to 67 percent of the time mothers spent with the family on weekdays, and to 87 percent of the time mothers spent with the family on weekends (Hofferth, 2001; Yeung et al., 2001).

Some of the most influential bodies of research on father involvement comes from studies that advanced a three-part model of paternal involvement (Lamb, Pleck, Charnov, & Levine, 1985; Lamb et al., 1987). This multidimensional view of paternal involvement, now seminal in guiding father-involvement research, shows us the various ways in which fathers are involved with their children (for a full review, see Brown, McBride, Shin, & Bost, 2007):

1. *Interaction (engagement):* Consists of direct, one-on-one father/child activities, such as playing and feeding.
2. *Accessibility:* The father is physically and/or psychologically available to the child when not directly interacting.
3. *Responsibility:* The father assumes responsibility for the child's welfare, education, and care, such as making childcare arrangements or knowing when the child has a pediatrician appointment. Being "responsible" does not necessarily include direct interaction with the child, but responsibility includes concern and/or contingency planning.

Lamb and colleagues (1987) proposed a four-component model of the determinants of father involvement: motivation, skills and self-confidence, support, and institutional factors. They noted that the psychological importance of work to the father's sense of identity, as well as the objective constraints associated with the workplace, may be crucial to his level of involvement. Fathers' attitudes toward parenting and work are important correlates of their involvement. Other new bodies of research incorporate the *quality* of father care into their conceptualizations of father involvement (Lamb, Chuang, & Cabrera, 2003; Marsiglio, Amato, Day, & Lamb, 2000).

ATTACHMENT Throughout much of the research history of attachment, the primary focus has been on mother–child attachment (Brown et al., 2007). Although original attachment research (Bowlby, 1988) suggested that there is a hierarchy of sorts with attachment (i.e., the primary caregiver is at the top—typically the mother), we now better understand that an infant's attachment relationships with the mother and father develop independently (Schoppe-Sullivan et al., 2006). It appears as though children develop attachments to fathers in ways and rates similar to how they develop attachment to mothers, and that these attachments exist independently of mother–child attachments (for a full review, see Brown et al., 2007).

Father–child attachment and father sensitivity is significant across a child's lifespan. Children who experience secure attachments with their fathers (see Brown et al., 2007):

- Tend to exhibit fewer behavior problems (Verschueren & Marcoen, 1999).
- Experience greater sociability (Lamb, Hwang, Frodi, & Frodi, 1982).
- Have higher quality peer relationships (Parke, 2002).
- Have higher levels of cognitive and socioemotional competencies in later childhood and adolescence (Carson & Parke, 1996; Fagan & Iglesias, 1999).

PLAYMATE AND SOCIALIZER Infants tend to direct more playful behaviors toward their fathers than toward their mothers. Such patterns of infant behavior suggest that the roles of attachment figure and playmate are conceptually distinct. Data provide support for the contention that the infant–father relationship is more centrally concerned with affiliative needs (i.e., felt security). The father, as socializer and playmate, provides the infant with social and cognitive stimulation that is qualitatively distinct from that provided by the mother (Bridges, Connell, & Belsky, 1988).

Theoretical and empirical work suggests that the father–child relationship is a particularly important influence on the child's social relationships outside the family. For example, paternal physical activity with preschool children is related to the children's positive social attributes as reported by teachers, particularly for boys. Studies with other age groups have found that paternal characteristics are related to the emotional quality of social interactions between infants and strangers and later with important members of the adolescent's social networks. Fathers, in essence, teach their children how to "get along" with friends and strangers outside the family. Through physical play with the father, a child learns how to interpret the affective communications of the parent as well as how her own emotional signals influence the behavior of the parent. This ability to interpret affective behaviors of interactive patterns correctly and to influence others through emotional signals is considered to be a major source of social competence (Bridges et al., 1988).

THE RECIPROCAL NATURE OF FATHERING
Like maternal behaviors, paternal behaviors must be viewed in the context of reciprocity; that is, at every age level, the child's behavior influences the father's behavior. Fathers have been found to be less responsive to and affectionate toward their infants and young children who are perceived by them and by their mothers to be temperamentally difficult. Fathers are likely to use coercive measures in response to the frustration of a problem child (Simons, Whitbeck, Conger, & Melby, 1990).

It can no longer be said with any degree of conviction that fathers are the forgotten contributors to child development. First it seems clear that fathers do not necessarily take, and have not necessarily taken in the past, a back seat to mothers in exerting a positive and powerful influence over their children—their influence has simply been less visible and less studied. Research indicates that children develop best when their fathers (as well as their mothers) combine warmth and nurturance with strength, protection, and specified limits. The combination of providing discipline with warm affection seems to facilitate creativity, independence, generosity, and sensitivity. It can be concluded that fathers undeniably play an important role in child development from infancy through childhood and that the role of fathering has changed considerably over time.

If we use a family systems approach to understanding parenting, we can see that the mothers and fathers together create a subsystem in the family—the parent subsystem. Every day, parents are faced with decisions and challenges about how to bring up their children and how to most effectively parent them. When fathers and mothers share parenting responsibilities and when they agree on parenting decisions—when they coparent—all family members benefit.

Coparenting: Go Team!

How parents negotiate their childrearing beliefs and share in everyday parenting responsibilities is referred to as **coparenting;** in essence, it is the support parents provide to one another in the raising of their children (Gable, Crnic, & Belsky, 1994). Joint parenting is important to children's well-being because it creates a home environment that fosters their growth and development. While most research concentrates on heterosexual parents who are married or divorced, coparenting also applies to others who are jointly raising children, such as grandparents, gay men, and lesbians.

Coparenting can best be thought of as an alliance between parents (Gable et al., 1994). It is a significant component of parenthood because partners can turn to one another for support when they are faced with the stressors and demands of raising children. In a very real way, coparenting is an extension of the couple's relationship, and it is just as an important process in family living as is communication, love, intimacy, or sex. That's not to say that coparenting is easy to achieve, however. When a new baby or a child arrives on the scene, partners have to find ways to expand their interactions to include the new addition—but at the same time, they have to set limits on these interactions so as to maintain a healthy couple relationship. Stated another way, they have to remember that their role as a couple is just as important (if not more so) as their role of parents. This is sometimes easier said than done! In general, there are three types of coparenting: supportive, unsupportive, and mixed (Belsky, 1990). These are presented in Table 1.3. As you can see, there is a wide range in ways in which parents work to raise their children.

Coparenting strategies are important to a child's overall development and well-being, because they provide predictability and stability in family rules, practices, and discipline for children. For example, numerous studies have linked positive coparenting to children's emotional well-being and academic success (among others, McHale, Rao, & Krasnow, 2000; Schoppe, Mangelsdorf, & Frosch, 2001). Supportive coparenting has also been associated with older children's well-developed self-regulatory abilities (Brody, Flor, & Neubaum, 1998). While many of the studies of coparenting in the United States have focused on white, middle-class samples, research on urban Chinese families and Japanese families has demonstrated that both parents' involvement in daily, meaningful caregiving is linked to academic success and greater child empathy; when parents have conflict in their coparenting, children are more likely to act out and to display anxious behaviors (McHale et al., 2000; Ogata & Miyashita, 2000).

Despite what family and social scientists currently understand about coparenting, much still needs to be learned about the relationship between effective and ineffective shared parenting and its impact on children.

Conflict and the Transition to Parenthood

The transition to parenthood is difficult for most people. In the past, researchers have concentrated on the *individual* factors that may lead to conflict in relationships during pregnancy, and have ignored the importance of the *relational dynamics* of marital dissatisfaction and symptoms of depression (Salmela-Aro, Aunola, Saisto, Halmesmaki, & Nurmi, 2006). Thus, results of such studies concluded that the changes in the couple's relationship following pregnancy and during the transition to parenthood were due to such things as a woman's depressed mood, rather than due to the systems nature of their relationship (see, e.g., Campbell et al., 1991).

To illustrate the importance of examining the couple's relationship, and not just the individual, researchers from Finland studied the

TABLE 1.3 Coparenting styles.

Supportive coparenting. Parents directly or indirectly agree with each other by promoting the same general message to the child (such as sticking to the agreed-on curfew and not changing it without consent of the other parent). It also occurs when one parent directly asks the other for assistance with an issue that involves the child (such as helping with discipline).

Unsupportive coparenting. This occurs when one parent subtly—or not so subtly—undermines the other parent's efforts (such as changing curfew without consulting with the other parent). It also takes place when one parent interrupts the interactions of the other parent and child (such as following a divorce), when one parent is openly critical of the other's parenting styles or parenting activity, or when a parent ignores the other parent's request for assistance with a child's needs.

Mixed coparenting. In this type of coparenting, one or both parents' responses are mixed—sometimes they support one another, sometimes they don't.

Source: Welch, *Family Life Now*, 2e (2010). p. 360.

experiences of 320 women and their partners through pregnancy and into the early months of parenthood (Salmela-Aro et al., 2006). They discovered that, in those couples who reported high levels of conflict, the struggles and disagreements that were present during the transition to becoming parents was already a part of the couple's relationship. In other words, depressive symptoms and marital dissatisfaction during pregnancy were common to the couple's relationship during pregnancy—these characteristics didn't suddenly appear as the couple became parents, as earlier studies suggested.

The researchers also found a decrease in marital satisfaction during the transition to parenthood among couples who reported high levels of marital satisfaction during early pregnancy. The investigators speculated that this is because prepregnancy "happy" couples have taken time to nurture their relationships, and that as pregnancy/parenting demands increase over time, their attention shifts from their relationship to the baby.

Other research that examined 293 Dutch couples explored relationship quality during pregnancy and the early months of pregnancy (Kluwer & Johnson, 2007). Based on the assumption that adding a new member to the family system is accompanied by drastic and dramatic changes in a couple's relationship, this study looked at conflict frequency during pregnancy. This study found:

- More frequent conflict during pregnancy was related to lower levels of relationship quality across the transition to parenthood.
- Lower levels of relationship quality during pregnancy were linked with more conflict during pregnancy.
- Frequent conflict is likely to determine declines in relationship quality during the early months of parenthood.

These findings are very important to our understanding of parenting life because they show us that the couples' marital discord and distress stemmed from problems that *existed during pregnancy*—not necessarily because of the *transition to parenthood*. It may very well be that the first childbirth isn't what elicits marriage troubles, but instead, that the troubles have always been there and are just highlighted once the baby arrives. Some couples may be more vulnerable to a difficult transition to parenthood than others (Kluwer & Johnson, 2007).

Finally, other evidence suggests that in couples who do not live together, who are unhappy with their partner, or who perceive their relationship to be a negative experience, couples experience increased anxiety and depression during pregnancy and the early months of parenting (Figueiredo et al., 2008). All of the empirical findings are important because they suggest that *both* members of the couple need to be supported during pregnancy, in order to prevent or lessen the stressors associated with the transition to parenting.

PARENT EDUCATION

Table 1.4 shows us that there are a number of factors that determine the quality of parenting. Given these, it's no surprise that many people turn to parent education to better themselves in the important role of parenting.

TABLE 1.4 Determinants of parenting behavior.

Child Characteristics
    Personality
    Mood
    Activity level

Parent Characteristics
    Mental health
    Psychological resources
    Family of origin

Cultural Context
    Socioeconomic status
    Level of education
    Marital relationship
    Social-support network
    Mass media

The concept of parent education has existed for a long time, and has been used in this country as early as the 1920s. Recently, the term **parent education** has been used to include a variety of experiences to assist persons who are already parents to be more effective in their roles as well as to educate individuals who plan to become parents in the future.

Early Parent Education Efforts

At the beginning of the 20th century, many "experts" in the area of child study began to appear. During the decade of the 1920s, dramatic changes took place in the professional and public attitudes toward childcare practices. The parent education movement, transformed into a "well-organized social movement" (Schlossman, 1976, p. 10), reached millions of people for the first time. Many programs and publications appeared, reflecting a new interest in the scientific aspect of childcare and parenting skills. The impact of science was noted by the disappearance of references to the Deity in the literature. Whereas mothers of the late Victorian era had put their faith in the Bible, the mothers of the 1920s relied on scientific information on nutrition and good habits to help them solve childrearing problems. The vigorous interest in parent education during the 1920s was affected by the breaking down of the social and moral codes that had guided the behavior of the middle class for generations.

Furthermore, there was great confidence in the ability of science to solve problems in all aspects of life (Schlossman, 1983). As the movement grew and as parenthood brought increasing frustration, the number of parent education organizations increased. Between the 1930s and 1970s, contemporary parenting programs emerged. These efforts at family intervention were numerous and varied but were aimed primarily at changing parents' behavior rather than assessing parents' effects on children's development (Clarke-Stewart, 1988).

A Rebirth

In the 1960s and 1970s, and again in the 1990s, a renewed interest in parenting, combined with social and cultural changes in society, early-intervention research, certain political movements (such as civil rights, women's rights, and gay and lesbian rights), federal legislation, and increased interest on the part of parents themselves, served as the impetus for parent education. A proliferation of programs emerged, and many were totally or partially funded by the federal government.

1980s: PARENT EDUCATION IS BENEFICIAL TO MOTHERS During the 1980s, research continued to demonstrate that parent education was beneficial to both parents and children. Outcomes reported for parent education included:

- Mothers' caregiving became more sensitive and their interactions with infants more developmentally appropriate as a result of participation in parent education programs
- Mothers improved in social skills
- Mothers can be successful at teaching cognitive skills to their children
- Mothers gained confidence in and insight into the parenting role
- Mothers became more accepting, understanding, and trusting of their children

One shortfall of these studies is that none of the studies in the 1980s assessed the changes with long-term effects on children's behavior and competence.

1990s: PARENT EDUCATION IS NECESSARY TO ADDRESS SOCIAL CHANGES In the 1990s, parent education programs were numerous and varied and were deemed as critical as ever because of the changing structure and function of American families and the increased pressure on these families. In the 1990s, the United States saw an increase in the number of teenage pregnancies and parents; an increase in the number of nonmarital childbirths; an increase in the number of gay and lesbian parents; more women as major wage earners in their families; and the reduction of the amount of time parents could devote to parenting. Furthermore, reports from early-intervention studies underscored the importance of parents in facilitating their children's development; as a result, researchers' interests in family influences on child development and contributions of social support systems to the quality of childrearing illustrated the benefits of parent education.

There are, however, criticisms about some parent education programs. Some critics, for example, claim that simply providing parents information about children's development and teaching parenting as a collection of skills is not likely to affect deeper, critical parental perspectives. Others have pointed out that typical programs are successful with only a narrow range of parents, that broader individual and family outcomes are rarely addressed, and that such programs fail to reflect newer, more complex and comprehensive perspectives of family and human development. Such criticisms have generated alternative ways of thinking about parent education, which we address throughout our study.

THE FUTURE It remains to be seen what is on the horizon for parent education. It is likely that programs will have a broad focus aimed at changing the lives of parents and children. A continuation of comprehensive, community-based family support programs and parent education and involvement will be a part of these efforts—a significant part, we hope. As President Barack Obama told Congress in 2009, "There is no program or policy that can substitute for a mother or father who will attend parent–teacher conferences or help with homework or turn off the TV, put away the video games, read to their child. Responsibility for our children's [futures] must begin at home."

Research clearly shows that participation and involvement in parent training and the effects and effectiveness of parent training programs depend on various traits and circumstances of the parents: their education, race/ethnicity, attitudes and beliefs, personalities, goals, degree of social support, and stress.

Summary

We have covered a lot in this chapter, from gaining an understanding of the current trends in childbearing, to the factors that go into the decision to have children, to discussing the distinctions between mothering and fathering, to past and current parent education programs.

How we parent our children significantly impacts who they become. In addition, the changing landscape of who can parent—married couples, single mothers, single fathers, grandparents, gay and lesbian parents—further requires that today's family professional fully recognizes the responsibilities associated with parenthood. It is also important to understand that parenting behaviors result from a complex network of variables that includes mothering and father characteristics, child characteristics, and the social context of families. In our study together, we explore in-depth parents' ever-evolving roles and the accompanying changing nature of parenting, contemporary strategies to becoming a more effective parent, and understanding diversity in families today.

References

Al-Fadhli, H. M., & Smith, J. C. (1996). Assessing the impact of violence on motivation for parenthood among blacks and whites. *Journal of Negro Education, 65*(4), 424–433.

Arendell, T. (2000). Conceiving and investigating motherhood: The decade's scholarship. *Journal of Marriage and the Family, 62,* 1192–1207.

Arnold, L. B. (2005). Don't you know what causes that?: Advice, celebration, and justification in a large families bulletin board. *Communication Studies, 56*(4), 331–351.

Baum, F. (1999). Cross-national trends in childlessness. Australian National University Research School of Social Sciences. *Working Papers in Demography, 73.*

Belsky, J. (1990). Children and marriage. In F. Fincham and T. Bradbury (Eds.) *The psychology of marriage: Basic issues and applications* (pp. 172–200). New York: Guilford.

Belsky, J., & Rovine, M. (1990). Patterns and marital change across the transition to parenthood: Pregnancy to three years postpartum. *Journal of Marriage and the Family, 52*(1), 5–19.

Belsky, J., Youngblade, L., Rovine, M., & Volling, B. (1991). Patterns of maternal change and parent–child interaction. *Journal of Marriage and the Family, 53*(2), 487–498.

Benasich, A., & Brooks-Gunn, J. (1996). Maternal attitudes and knowledge of child-rearing: Associations with family and child outcomes. *Child Development, 67,* 1186–1205.

Berkowitz, D., & Marsiglio, W., (2007). Gay men: Negotiating procreative, father, and family identities. *Journal of Marriage and Family, 69*(2), 366–381.

Blake, J. (1981). Family size and the quality of children. *Demography, 18,* 421–442.

Bos, H. M. W., van Balen, F., & van den Boom, D. C. (2004). Experience of parenthood, couple relationship, social support, and child-rearing goals in planned lesbian mother families. *Journal of Child Psychology and Psychiatry, 45,* 755–764.

Bowen, M. (1966). The use of family theory in clinical practice. *Comprehensive Psychology, 7,* 345–374.

Bowlby, J. (1988). *A secure base: Parent–child attachment and health human development.* New York: Basic Books.

Brazelton, T. B. (1969). *Infants and mothers: Differences in development.* New York: Dell.

Bridges, L., Connell, J., & Belsky, J. (1988). Similarities and differences in infant–mother and infant–father interaction in the strange situation: A component process analysis. *Developmental Psychology, 24*(1), 92–100.

Brody, G., Flor, D., & Neubaum, E. (1998). Coparenting processes and child competence among rural African-American families. In M. Lewis & C. Feiring (Eds.), *Families, risk, and competence* (pp. 227–243). Mahwah, NJ: Erlbaum.

Brooks, D. (2004). The new red-diaper babies. *The New York Times,* (December 7, 2004), Retrieved May 7, 2011 from http://www.nytimes.com/2004/12/07/opinion/07brooks.html?_r=1&oref=login&oref=login&hp.

Brown, G. G., McBride, B. A., Shin, N., & Bost, K. K. (2007). Parenting predictors of father–child attachment security: Interactive effects of father involvement and father quality. *Fathering, 5*(3), 197–219.

Campbell, N. (2003). *Be fruitful and multiply.* San Antonio, TX: Vision Forum.

Campbell, S. B., Cohn, J. F., Flanagan, C., Popper, S., & Myers, T. (1991). Course and correlates of postpartum depression during the transition to parenthood. *Development and Psychopathology, 4,* 29–47.

Carroll, J. (2007). Americans: 2.5 children is "ideal" family size. Roughly one in three say ideal family size include three or more children. Retrieved: June 6, 2011 from http://www.gallup.com/poll/27973/americans-25-children-ideal-family-size.aspx.

Carson, J. L., & Parke, R. D. (1996). Reciprocal negative affect in parent–child interactions and children's peer competency. *Child Development, 67,* 2217–2226.

Cartwright, R. (1999, Autumn). Childless or childfree? *Journal of Fertility Counseling.*

Centers for Disease Control and Prevention. Division of Vital Statistics. (2005). Births: Preliminary data for 2004. *National Vital Statistics Report, 54*(8). Retrieved August 2, 2009, from www.cdc.gov/nchs/data/nvsr/nvsr54/nvsr54_08.pdf.

Centers for Disease Control and Prevention. (2008). Births, marriages, divorces, and deaths: Provisional data for July 2007. *National Vital Statistics Reports, 56,* 14.

Chess, S., & Thomas, A. (1973). Temperament in the normal infant. In J. Westman (Ed.), *Individual differences in children* (pp. 83–103). New York: Wiley.

Clarke-Stewart, K. (1988). Parents effects on children's development: A decade of progress? *Journal of Applied Developmental Psychology, 9*(1), 41–84.

Crockenberg, S. C., & Leerkes, E. M. (2003). Parental acceptance, postpartum depression, and maternal sensitivity: Mediating and moderating processes. *Journal of Family Psychology, 17,* 80–93.

Doherty, W., Kouneski, E., & Kouneski, M. (1998). Responsible farming: An overview and conceptual framework. *Journal of Marriage and the Family, 60,* 277–292.

Dubow, E., Huesmann, R., & Eron, L. (1987). Childhood correlates of adult ego development. *Child Development, 58*(3), 859–869.

Fagan, J., & Iglesias, A. (1999). Father involvement program effects on fathers, father figures, and their head start children: A quasi-experimental study. *Early Childhood Research Quarterly, 14,* 243–269.

Figueiredo, B., Field, T., Diego, M., Hernandez-Reif, M., Deeds, O., & Ascenio, A. (2008). Partner relationships during the transition to parenthood. *Journal of Reproductive and Infant Psychology, 26*(2), 99–107.

Gable, S., Crnic, K., & Belsky, J. (1994). Coparenting within the family system: Influences on children's development. *Family Relations, 43,* 380–386.

Gerson, M. J. (1980). The lure of motherhood. *Psychology of Women Quarterly, 5*(2), 207–218.

Gerson, M. J. (1985). *Hard choices: How women decide about work, career, and motherhood.* Berkley: University of California Press.

Gerson, M. J. (1986). The prospect of parenthood for women and men. *Psychology of Women Quarterly, 10,* 49–62.

Gerson, M. J., Posner, J. A., & Morris, A. M. (1991). The wish for a child in couples eager, disinterested, and conflicted about having children. *American Journal of Family Therapy, 19*(4), 334–343.

Hartill, L. (2001). Life with a supersized family. *Christian Science Monitor.* Retrieved January 12, 2009, from www.csmonitor.com/2001/0910/p15sl-lifp.html.

Hayford, S. R., & Morgan, S. P. (2008). Religiosity and fertility in the United States: The role of fertility intentions. *Social Forces, 86*(3), 1163–1189.

Hays, S. (1996). *The cultural contradictions of motherhood.* New Haven, CT: Yale University Press.

Hofferth, S. L. (2001). *Race/ethnic differences in father involvement in two-parent families: Culture, context, or economy.* Paper presented at the Urban Seminar on Fatherhood, Harvard University, Cambridge, MA.

Hoffman, L. W., & Hoffman, M. L. (1973). The value of children to parents. In J. T. Fawcett (Ed.), *Psychological perspectives on population* (pp. 19–76). New York: Basic Books.

Holden, G., & West, M. (1989). Proximate regulation by mothers: A demonstration of how differing styles affect young children's behavior. *Child Development, 60*(1), 64–69.

Klaus, M., & Kennell, J. (1982). *Parent–infant bonding.* St. Louis, MO: Mosby.

Kluwer, E. S., & Johnson, M. D. (2007). Conflict frequency and relationship quality across the transition to parenthood. *Journal of Marriage and Family, 69,* 1089–1106.

Kretchmar, M. D., & Jacobvitz, D. B. (2002). Observing mother–child relationships across generations: Boundary patterns, attachment, and the transmission of caregiving. *Family Processes, 41,* 351–374.

Kuczynski, L., Kochanska, G., Rodke-Yarrow, M., & Girniss-Brown, D. (1987). A developmental interpretation of young children's noncompliance. *Developmental Psychology, 23*(1), 1–8.

Lamb, M. E., Chuang, S. S., & Cabrera, N. (2003). Promoting child adjustment by fostering positive paternal involvement. In R. M. Lerner, F. Jacobs, & D. Wertlieb (Eds.), *Handbook of applied developmental science* (Vol. 1, pp. 211–232. Thousand Oaks, CA: Sage.

Lamb, M. E., Hwang, C. P., Frodi, A. M., & Frodi, M. (1982). Security of mother– and father–infant attachment and its relation to sociability with strangers in traditional and nontraditional Swedish families. *Infant Behavior and Development, 5,* 355–367.

Lamb, M. E., Pleck, J. H., Charnov, E. L., & Levine, J. A. (1985). Paternal behavior in humans. *American Zoologist, 25,* 883–894.

Lamb, M. E., Pleck, J. H., Charnov, E. L., & Levine, J. A. (1987). A biosocial perspective on paternal behavior and involvement. In J. B. Lancaster, J. Altaman, A. Rossi, & R. L. Sherrod (Eds.). *Parenting across the lifespan: Biosocial perspectives* (pp. 11–42). New York: Academic.

Lawson, K. (2004). Development and psychometric properties of the Perceptions of Parenting Inventory. *Journal of Psychology, 138*(5), 433–455.

Lerner, R., Castellino, D. R., Terry, P. A., Villarruel, F. A., & McKinney, M. H. (1995). A developmental contextual perspective on parenting. In M. H. Bornstein (Ed.), *Handbook of parenting: Biology and ecology of parenting* (Vol. 2, pp. 285–309). Hillsdale, NJ: Erlbaum.

Lerner, R., Noh, E. R., & Wilson, C. (2004). *The parenting of adolescents and adolescents as parents: A developmental contextual perspective.* Retrieved August 12, 2004, from http://parenthood.library.wisc.edu/Lerner/Lerner.html.

Lino, M., & Carlson, A. (2009). *Expenditures on children by families, 2008.* U.S. Department of Agriculture, Center for Nutrition Policy and Promotion (Misc. Publication No. 1528–2008). Retrieved March 27, 2010, from www.cnpp.usda.gov/Publications/CRC/crc2008.pdf.

MacKay, H. (1994). *DINKs.* Lindfiled, NSW, Australia: MacKay.

Marsiglio, W., Amato, P., Day, R. D., & Lamb, M. E. (2000). Scholarship on fatherhood in the 1990s and beyond. *Journal of Marriage and the Family, 62,* 1173–1191.

Martin, S. P. (2002). *Delayed marriage and childbearing: Implications and measurement of diverging trends in family timing.* College Park: University of Maryland, Department of Sociology, and Maryland Population Research Center.

McDonald, P. F. (2000). Low fertility in Australia: Evidence, causes, and policy responses. *People and Place, 8*(2), 6–21.

McHale, J., Rao, N., & Krasnow, A. (2000). Constructing family climates: Chinese mothers' reports of their coparenting behavior and preschoolers' adaptation. *International Journal of Behavioral Development, 24,* 111–118.

McQuillan, K. (2004). When does religion influence fertility? *Population and Development Review, 30*(1), 25–56.

Medina, S., & Magnuson, S. (2009). Motherhood in the 21st century: Implications for counselors (practice and theory). *Journal of Counseling and Development, 87*(1), 90–98.

Mercer, R. T. (1986). *First-time motherhood: Experiences from teens to forties.* New York: Springer.

Mercer, R. T. (2004). Becoming a mother versus maternal role attainment. *Journal of Nursing Scholarship, 36*(3), 226–232.

Merlo, R., & Rowland, D. (2000). The prevalence of childlessness in Australia. *People and Place, 8*(2), 21–32.

National Vital Statistics Report. (2008). Births, marriages, divorces, and deaths: Provisional data for June 2007. *National Vital Statistics Report, 56*(12).

Ogata, K., & Miyashita, K. (2000). Exploring links between father's participation in family chores, child's empathy, family function, and father's identity development. *Japanese Journal of Family Psychology, 14,* 15–27.

Park, K. (2005). Choosing childlessness: Weber's typology of action and motives of the voluntarily childless. *Sociological Inquiry, 75*(3), 372–402.

Parke, R. D. (2002). Fathers and families. In M. Bornstein (Ed.), *Handbook of parenting: Vol. 3. Being and becoming a parent* (2nd ed., pp. 27–73). Hillsdale, NJ: Erlbaum.

Pew Research Center (2010). *More women without children* (June 25, 2010). Retrieved May 7, 2011 from: http://pewresearch.org/pubs/1642/more-women-without-children.

Pleck, E. H., & Pleck, J. H. (1997). Fatherhood ideals in the United States: Historical dimensions. In M. Lamb (Ed.), *The role of the father in child development* (pp. 33–48). New York: Wiley.

Pleck, J. H. (1997). Parental involvement: Levels, sources, and consequences. In M. Lamb (Ed.), *The role of the father in child development* (pp. 66–103). New York Wiley.

Priel, B., & Besser, A. (2001). Bridging the gap between attachment and object relations theories: A study of the transition to motherhood. *British Journal of Medical Psychology, 74,* 85–10.

Rathus, S. A., & Nevid, J. S. (1992). *Adjustment and growth: The challenges of life* (5th ed.). Fort Worth, TX: Harcourt Brace Jovanovich.

Rocissano, L., Slade, A., & Lynch, V. (1987). Dyadic synchrony and toddler compliance. *Developmental Psychology, 23*(5), 698–704.

Rogers, S. J., & White, L. K. (1998). Satisfaction with parenting: The role of marital happiness, family structure, and parents' gender. *Journal of Marriage and the Family, 60*(2), 293–308.

Rotundo, E. A. (1993). *American motherhood.* New York: Basic Books.

Rubin, R. (1967). Attainment of the maternal role. Part 1. *Nursing Research, 16,* 237–245.

Salmela-Aro, K., Aunola, K., Saisto, T., Halmesmaki, E., & Nurmi, J.E. (2006). Couples share similar changes in depressive symptoms and marital satisfaction anticipating the birth of a child. *Journal of Social and Personal Relationships, 23*(5), 781–803.

Schlossman, S. (1976). Before home start: Notes toward a history of parent education. *Harvard Educational Review, 46*(3), 436–467.

Schlossman, S. (1983). The formation era in American parent education: Overview and interpretation. In R. Haskins & D. Adams (Eds.). *Parent education and public policy* (pp. 7–36). Norwood, NJ: Ablex.

Schoppe, S. J., Mangelsdorf, S. C., & Frosch, C. (2001). Coparenting, family process, and family structure: Implications for preschoolers' externalizing behavior problems. *Journal of Family Psychology, 15,* 526–545.

Schoppe-Sullivan, S. J., Diener, M., Mangesldorf, S. C., Brown, G. L., McHale, J. L., & Frosch, C. F. (2006). Attachment and sensitivity in family context: The roles of parent and infant gender. *Infant and Child Development, 15,* 367–385.

Seccombe, K. (1991). Assessing the costs and benefits of children: Gender comparisons among childfree husbands and wives. *Journal of Marriage and the Family, 53,* 191–202.

Silver, C. (2000, Summer). Being there: The time dual-earner couples spend with their children. *Canadian Social Trends, 57,* 26–29.

Simons, R., Whitbeck, L., Conger, R., & Melby, J. (1990). Husband and wife differences in determinants of parenting: A social learning and exchange model of parenting behavior. *Journal of Marriage and the Family, 52*(2), 375–392.

Solomon-Fears, C. (2008). Nonmarital childbearing: Trends, reasons, and public policy interventions. *CRS Reports for Congress.* Retrieved August 2, 2009, from http://ftp.fas.org/sgp/crs/misc/RL34756.pdf.

Strohschein, L., Gauthier, A. H., Campbell, R., & Kleparchuk, C. (2008). Parenting as a dynamic process: A test of the resource dilution hypothesis theory. *Journal of Marriage and Family, 70,* 670–683.

Theisen, C. (2004). *The parent coach plan: Eight parenting responsibilities.* Retrieved March 26, 2009, from www.parentcoachplan.com.

U.S. Census Bureau. (2006). *How many mothers?* Retrieved November 5, 2009, from www.cdc.gov/nchs/data/nvsr/nvsr54/nvsr54_02.pdf.

Veevers, J. E. (1980). *Childless by choice.* Toronto: Butterworth.

Verschueren, K., & Marcoen, A. (1999). Representation of self and socioemotional competence in kindergartners: Differential and combined effects of attachment to mother and father. *Child Development, 70,* 183–201.

Wall, G., & Arnold, S. (2007). How involved is involved father?: An exploration of the contemporary culture of fatherhood. *Gender and Society, 21*(4), 508–527.

Weston, R., & Qu, L. (2001, Autumn). Men's and women's reasons for not having children. *Family Matters, 58,* 10-15.

Wooden, M. (1999). Job insecurity and job instability: Getting the facts straight. *BCA Papers, 1*(1), 14–18.

Yamaguchi, K., & Fergusson, L. R. (1995). The stopping and spacing of childbirths and their birth history predictors: Rational choice theory and event history analysis. *American Sociological Review, 60,* 272–289.

Yeung, W. J., Sandbert, J., Davis-Kean, P., & Hofferth, S. (2001). Children's time-use with fathers in intact families. *Journal of Marriage and the Family, 63*(1), 136–154.

Chapter 2
The Changing Nature of Parenting: Infancy and Early Childhood

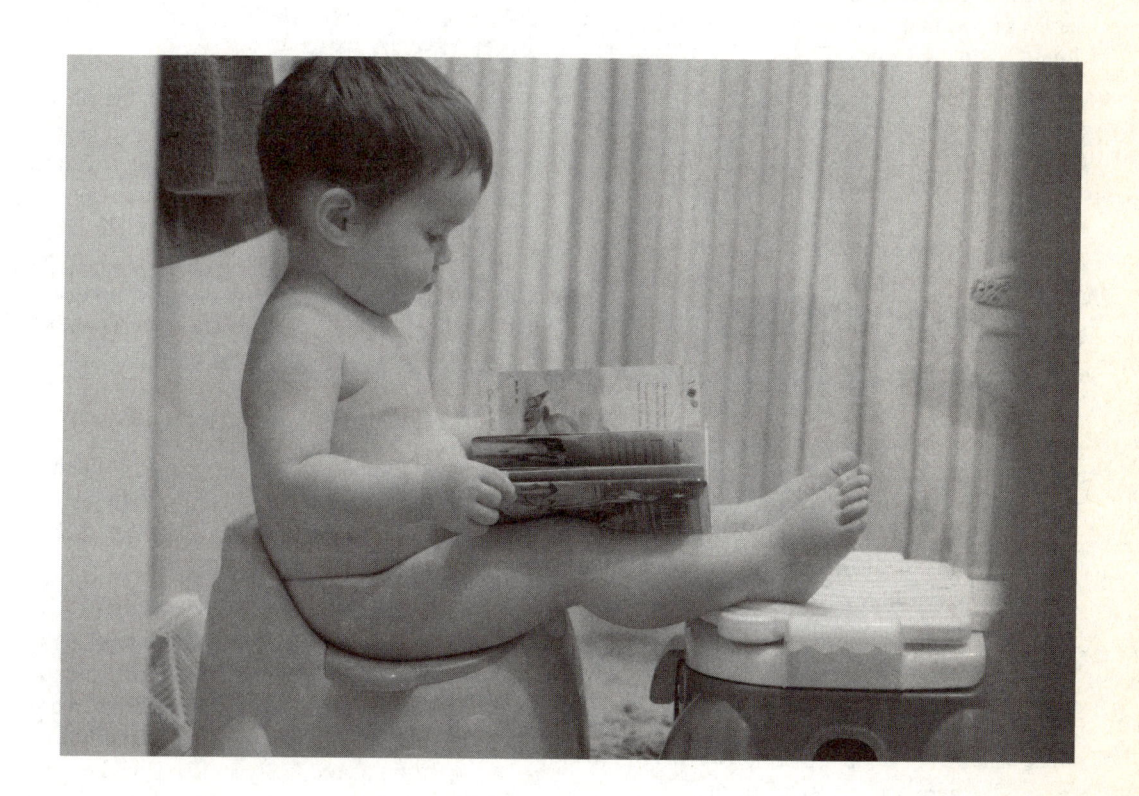

There is no question that how parents parent is fundamental to optimal developmental and health outcomes for the child (Blake, 1954). The **parent–child relationship** refers to the emotional and physical connection between a parent and his or her child; it includes attributes such as emotional cohesion (closeness), parental influence on the child's development, attachment, and parental investment in the child's well-being (Lutz, Anderson, Riesch, Pridham, & Becker, 2009). Through their parenting styles and behaviors, parents also serve as important social influences for their children (Cassidy & Conroy, 2006).

The manner in which parents interact with and guide their children influences children's development in more ways than are immediately visible (such as behavior and school performance). Consider the interaction and relational patterns between you and your parent(s) or primary caregiver. Did these experiences allow you to feel that you were worthy of affection and love? Or instead, did your early parent–child experiences cause you to feel shame, guilt, and doubt, resulting in fear of intimacy, fear of abandonment, betrayal, and rejection in your adult relationships? As we are growing up, our interactions with our parents convey to us our worth—our purpose—as individuals, and this perception influences our ability to relate to others on an intimate level the remainder of our lifespan.

Given the ups and downs of parenting and the inherent adjustments that must be made as a result of children's demands, given its uncertainty, given the fact that no two children are alike, and given the fact that no two people (or parents) experience parenting in the same way, is it really possible to prepare professionals and future parents for what one developmentalist (Carter & McGoldrick, 1999) describes as "one of the most definitive stages of life"? Probably not. Nevertheless, we can address those issues we know impact children's healthy development.

In this chapter, we briefly explore the different theories of child development. We then examine in depth the significance of infants' and toddlers' abilities to develop trust and attachment with their parents or caregivers, and the importance of infant stimulation in the development of trust. We then turn our attention to parents' roles as protectors and nurturers as they adjust to their child's growing autonomy through toddlerhood and provide an environment rich for social and intellectual learning. We conclude our study in this chapter by taking a look at programs for parents of infants, toddlers, and preschool children.

PARENTING INFANTS AND TODDLERS

The term **caregiver** has been used in the literature to refer to the person or persons responsible for providing primary care of the infant or young child. Initial caregiving consists primarily of the provision of life support and protection. The pregnancy, the infant's physical appearance, and the baby's helpless movements all contribute to maintaining the caregiving system. There are a number of factors that affect caregiving experiences.

The Parent–Infant Relationship

At least three major factors appear to influence relationships between parents and their babies (Eiden, Teti, & Corns, 1995; Fox, 1995):

1. *The past*—the quality of the parents' own early experiences. What type of care did each parent receive as babies or toddlers?
2. *The present*—the conditions of the parents' present condition, such as the parents' marital stability, presence of marital conflict, job security, health, daily stressors, and so on.
3. *The infant*—the characteristics of the infant him- or herself.

Some studies have also shown that the infant's behavior is related to the mother and father's expectations. What do parents believe the baby can do?

Other research has shown that the more difficult the child is temperamentally, the less responsive the mother is likely to be. A classic longitudinal study described *easy babies, difficult babies,* and *slow-to-warm-up babies* (Thomas & Chess, 1977). A description of the different temperaments of babies is based on nine traits, which are thought to be largely innate. For example, difficult babies tend to cry a lot and have irregular schedules. It is tough to soothe them and they do not adapt easily to new people and situations. These babies do not fare well with impatient, unresponsive mothers, and may, in fact, contribute to their mothers' impatience and unresponsiveness. Goodness of fit does not occur between mother and baby, and **synchrony**—reciprocal, mutually rewarding interactions—is difficult to achieve.

Babies also contribute to the parent–child interaction by their state of awareness, such as whether they are sleeping, awake, drowsy, or alert. They further affect interactions by the types of signaling they demonstrate through vocalizing, touching, or looking, as well as by the amount of attention they seek. It seems obvious, then, that the infant is no mere passive recipient of stimulation who is controlled by the adults in his or her environment. Rather, babies are active participants in their own development, and their unique manners of participation are a critical factor in the kind of parenting they receive.

Competent caregiving lays the foundation for social interactions, reciprocal communication and signaling, and the development of special skills during the period of infancy. But one question still needs to be answered: Do mothers and fathers equally contribute to caring for their babies?

Parenting Involvement with Infants and Toddlers

Historically—*and still today*—much of the responsibility for caregiving and childrearing rests on the mother's shoulders, a pattern seen in industrialized and nonindustrialized societies alike. Traditional gender roles in Western cultures are based on the belief that mothers (or women in general) have an innate ability that allows them to nurture and care for infants and children better than men do. From diapers to discipline, from empty bottles to emotional support, from daycare to dating dilemmas, mothers seem to be the predominant advisors and guides. They are also the ones doing the laundry, the cleaning, the grocery shopping, and the daily scheduling. In many households, mothers put in twice as much time as fathers when it comes to childrearing (among many, Bianchi, 2000; Cohen, 1993; McBride & Mills, 1993; Pleck, 1997).

Even couples who have an egalitarian (equal) relationship prior to the arrival of a baby tend to fall back into traditional gender roles once the new baby arrives. Melissa Milkie, a sociologist and researcher of women's issues, examined 234 married couples about their attitudes toward marital roles and childrearing (Milkie, Bianchi, Mattingly, & Robinson, 2002). These researchers

There is more going on here than the simple act of comforting a baby. While the parents interact with their infant, the baby reciprocates with interactions of her own.

found that although the parents asserted that both should be equally responsible and equally involved in parenting, caregiving, and childrearing, mothers consistently reported higher levels of involvement for themselves than did their husbands. In particular, mothers expressed significantly higher levels of involvement in the areas of child discipline and providing emotional support for their children.

Fathers perceived their involvement in parenting (discipline, emotional support, play, monitoring, caregiving) at much higher levels than the mothers reported, resulting in what the researchers term an **ideal–actual gap.** When mothers viewed the fathers' parenting involvement as less-than-ideal (not equal to their own involvement), their relationships were found to have higher levels of stress. When women felt that discrepancies existed between their roles as disciplinarians and those same roles of their husbands—when they felt they were more involved than their husbands—they reported higher levels of dissatisfaction due to perceived unfairness. Similarly, child and adolescent psychologist and childrearing expert Ron Taffel (1994) discovered that although his study participants reported a fairly equal divide over childrearing tasks, when lists were compared the division was more along the lines of the woman doing about four times more than her husband.

Studies such as these speak to a broader point: Despite the efforts of the 20th and 21st centuries to more actively involve fathers in childcare and childrearing, we cannot escape the ways we have been socialized. Several research studies investigating the division of family work and parental responsibilities (see Chapter 8) showed that women's socialization—and the inherent cultural notion that she will always be the better parent—makes it difficult for the mother to relinquish her traditional role (for a comprehensive review, see Baxter, Hewitt, & Haynes, 2008). This is described as **maternal gatekeeping.**

Women and men today may anticipate and expect their parenting involvement to be equal, but socialization and established ways of thinking make it very easy to fall into traditional gender roles once the first baby arrives. Suddenly, this egalitarian relationship no longer exists, challenging preset expectations, raising stress levels, and giving rise to feelings of unfairness. As a result, conflict ensues and marital satisfaction plummets. We explore these difficulties at length in Chapter 8.

Of course, just when parents believe they have figured out the ins and outs of parenting, the child passes into a new phase of growth and development (with its own uncharted territory)! In the next section, we briefly look at theories of child development.

Theories of Child Development

There are several theories that seek to explain and understand child development. In general, there are four theories of child development: psychoanalytic, learning, cognitive, and sociocultural. Each theory offers its own unique contribution to our understanding of how and why children develop the way that they do. (See also Table 2.1.)

PSYCHOANALYTIC THEORIES The "grandfather of psychology," Sigmund Freud (1856–1939), developed his **psychoanalytic theory,** which focused on the personality development of children. In his view, development takes place through a series of **psychosexual stages,** in which sensual energy or satisfaction is focused on one particular part of the body. For example, during the **oral stage** (from birth to about age 1), the focus of sensual energy is the mouth and the tongue; the emphasis for personality development is thus centered on breastfeeding. In the **anal stage** (ages 1 to 3), the focus of the sensual energy is associated with potty training, particularly with respect to the anus.

In the **phallic stage** (ages 3 to 6), Freud believed children were intensely interested in the physical differences between men and women. He also maintained that the focus of the sensual energy during this stage was the genitals, and believed that children engaged in self-stimulation of their genitals to derive pleasure. In the **latency phase** (ages 7 to 11), according to psychoanalytic theory, the sensual energies subside for a time, and during the final stage, or **genital stage** (ages 12 and beyond), people developed mature sexual interests in the opposite

TABLE 2.1 Ages and stages of child development.

Age	Cognitive Stage	Social and Emotional Stage
0–1	Cries to signal needs; vocalizes, babbles, coos; says first words; interested in picture books	Recognizes family members; shows anxiety when separated from parents; fearful of strangers; likes to be tickled and touched; wants parents in sight
1–2	Has vocabulary of 8 to 20 words; identifies objects in books; makes animal sounds	Can play alone with toys; likes to be read to; will comfort others in distress; enjoys pretend play; shows affection
2	Uses 2-to 3-word sentences; sings; names toys, animals, people; enjoys stories and rhymes; enjoys simple make-believe	Possessive of parents' attention; can show beginning of independence; shy around/doesn't share with others
3	Uses 5-to 8-word sentences; listens actively to stories/songs; pretends to read; names colors; counts to 2 or 3	Seeks adult attention; helps with chores; engages in solitary play, but with others nearby; doesn't share; likes to laugh and be silly
4	Is imaginative, loves to make believe: uses complex sentences; counts to 10 or higher; understands categories (small, big, tall); very inquisitive and curious	Likes to engage in cooperative play with others; shares; cooperates; obeys simple instructions; loves to love others
5	Uses complex sentences of 10 or more words; enjoys storytelling, tracing, drawing, writing, coloring; counts; has good attention span; can memorize	Seeks adults' approval; embarrassed by own mistakes; understands relationships among people; likes to give to others; shares and takes turns; enjoys playing with friends
6–8	Reads; understands time of day and days of week; increased attention span; problem-solving capabilities increase; begins logical thinking	Friends become very important; wants to do everything well; easily hurt by criticism; still self-centered, but begins to see others' points of view; gender-centric
9–11	Reads; daydreams about future; logic becomes solidified; begins abstract thinking; begins to think about justice and ethics	Friendships become very important, consuming as much as 40 percent of their time; empathy toward others continues
12–14	Engages in abstract thought; able to think about hypothetical situations; able to think about the future	More mature friendships; friendship groups become larger and now include friends of opposite sex; embarrassed by parents

Source: Welch, *Family Life Now*, 2e. (2010). Boston: Allyn & Bacon. p. 367.

sex. The experiences through these stages—particularly through age 5—shape a child's personality for an entire lifetime. Freud's psychoanalytic theory also emphasized the role of the unconscious and held that most of people's actions, behaviors, and emotions are the result of these drives that lie below a person's level of awareness.

Erik Erikson (1902–1994) developed his own psychoanalytic theory based on Freud's original work (we explore aspects of Erikson's theory at length in this chapter, as well as in the next). Unlike Freud's theory, Erikson developed eight stages that spanned a person's entire lifetime. He also believed that, while early childhood experiences are crucial in shaping a person's personality, later events in life could alter the influence of the earlier experiences.

LEARNING THEORIES In general, **learning theories** emphasize the role of the environment, such as the home, school, community, and peers, in shaping a child's development. In other words, all behavior is learned from environmental influences. According to learning theories, parents play a significant role in who their children ultimately become. There are several learning theorists.

B. F. Skinner (1904–1990) believed that children learn behaviors through a series of rewards and punishments, and this series is called **operant conditioning. Rewards** reinforce behavior and increase the likelihood that the behavior will occur again. For example, if a child is praised for making his bed, it is likely that he will repeat that behavior. If, on the other hand, a child is criticized because he did not do a good job or make his bed perfectly, it is not likely that he will repeat the behavior. **Punishments** decrease the likelihood that a behavior will be repeated. According to Skinner, operant conditioning is the way that parents guide, shape, and mold the behaviors they desire of their children.

John B. Watson (1878–1958) promoted his theory of **classical conditioning,** which proposes that people make associations between two events. For example, babies open their mouths and smack their lips when their parent puts them in a highchair, or when their parent opens a jar of baby food. Conditioning (opening their mouths or smacking their lips) has taken place because the babies make the association between one event (being put in a highchair) and the other event (hearing their food source being opened). Similarly, some children (and college students!) cringe, become panicked, or get sick to their stomachs when an exam is handed out.

Have you ever been told that you sound just like your mother or father? Or that one of your behaviors is just like that of your mother or father, or another family member? Albert Bandura's (1925–) **social learning theory** focuses on how children acquire behaviors. He believed that the acquisition of behaviors and personality traits are the result of observing others, and that we then imitate the behaviors we observe. For example, parents model certain gender roles, their children observe these modeled behaviors, and they subsequently acquire the same or similar behaviors. As Bandura once noted, "Of the many cues that influence behavior, at any point in time, none is more common than the actions of others."

COGNITIVE THEORIES Cognitive theories focus on how children think and how they understand their world. The focus of childhood development is not centered on personality development but on children's thinking and reasoning. A 4-year-old will comprehend and reason about his parents' divorce differently than will his 10-year-old brother; a 10-year-old will comprehend and reason about his parents' divorce differently than will his 15-year-old sister. Jean Piaget (1896–1980) advanced the most widely recognized cognitive development theory, which comprised four sequential stages.

Piaget maintained that as children progressed from stage to stage, they applied their current thinking and reasoning capabilities to new experiences. Unlike behaviorist theorists who believed that children were passive learners, Piaget believed that children actively seek to understand their environment.

SOCIOCULTURAL THEORIES Unlike the previously mentioned theories that stated that children proceed from one stage of development through the next, **sociocultural theories** propose that children do not progress through any stages. Instead, children's development is thought to occur as a result of direct interaction with their culture—that the values, goals, and expectations of their culture significantly shape and mold them. Thus, "development" means different things to different children in different cultures; what is considered developmentally appropriate for a child in one culture may not be considered so in another culture. The pioneer of sociocultural theory is Russian-born psychologist, Lev Vygotsky (1896–1934), who believed that parents are children's primary teachers. According to Vygotsky, parents who are sensitive to their child's development sense when the child is ready to learn new tasks and skills, and they engage their children in different activities to help their child develop these new skills. For example, whether it is a Maya mother teaching her daughter to make tortillas, or whether it is an American mother teaching her son to measure flour and sugar to make cookies, each parent is teaching her child new skills—and cultural values at the same time.

Sociocultural theories maintain that our external social worlds—our unique cultures—shape our individual development.

Studying children and their development is a fascinating field of study. While each theory has a different explanation of how and why children develop the way they do, each one helps us better understand the complexities of children's development. In the next section, we take a closer look at how a basic sense of trust is fostered in babies and toddlers.

TRUST, ATTACHMENT, AND RECIPROCITY

The degree to which a child comes to trust the world, other people, and him/herself depends to a considerable extent on the quality of care an infant receives. The baby whose needs are met when they arise, whose discomforts are quickly removed, and who is cuddled, fondled, played with, and talked to develops a sense of the world as a safe place to be and of people as helpful, dependable, and trustworthy.

Establishing Basic Trust

Erik Erikson (1963) described the stages of the life cycle and the psychosocial development of the ego, as presented in Table 2.2. Erikson conceived of each stage as being marked by a developmental issue, or "crisis." The first of these stages, occurring from birth to about 1 year, is defined as **trust versus mistrust.**

When care is consistent and accepting, trust is fostered in the baby. If, however, the care is inconsistent, inadequate, and rejecting, children develop a basic mistrust, an attitude of fear and suspicion on the part of the infant toward the world in general and toward people in particular. This trust carries through to every subsequent stage of development. Erikson did not believe, though, that the problem of basic trust versus mistrust was resolved once and for all during the first year of life; rather, it arises again at each successive stage of development. If basic physical and emotional needs are not met, the child feels somehow empty, cheated, at a loss, and ill at ease with others and with him- or herself.

CRYING: BABY'S COMMUNICATION The newborn comes equipped with one major means of communicating with others in the environment—crying. At first, parents must guess what the baby is attempting to communicate with his or her cries. Is he hungry? Is she cold? Wet? Lonely? Parents check diapers, feed the baby, change its position, rock it, and sometimes in desperation, drive the baby around town—whatever they can think of to relieve the infant's distress. Sometimes new parents get it right, sometimes they do not, but one thing is certain: they are at the mercy of the baby's cries.

Fortunately, it is not long before parents begin to distinguish a hunger cry from a tired cry, or an I-need-my-diaper-changed cry from a cry

TABLE 2.2 Erikson's Developmental stages.
Influential psychologist Erik Erikson formulated the Eight Stages of Man developmental theory. According to Erikson, a person is in a continuous state of development from the cradle to the grave.

Stage	Age	Developmental Task
Trust vs. Mistrust	Infancy, 0–24 months	Child develops a belief that his or her caregivers will provide a secure and trustful environment.
Autonomy vs. Shame and Doubt	Toddlerhood, 2–4 years	Child develops a sense of Independence and free will; feels shame if he or she doesn't use the free will appropriately.
Initiative vs. Guilt	Early Childhood, 4–6 years	"The Age of Acquiring": Child learns to explore his or her environment and acquires a newfound set of skills; feels a newfound sense of initiative and accomplishment.
Industry vs. Inferiority	Middle Childhood, 7–12 years	"The Age of Mastery": Child masters the skills acquired during early childhood.
Identity vs. Role Confusion	Adolescence, 13–21 years	Teen develops a sense of who he or she is in comparison to others (sense of "self"); develops a keen sense of role expectations.
Intimacy vs. Isolation	Young Adult, 22–35 years	Develops ability to give and receive love; begins to consider long-term relationships, marriage, and parenting as realistic options.
Generativity vs. Stagnation	Middle Adulthood, 36–65 years	Develops interest in giving of himself or herself to younger generations by helping them lead meaningful lives and by caring for them.
Integrity vs. Despair	Older Adulthood, 65+ years	Desires to find meaningful and personal gratification with the life he or she has lived.

Source: Welch, *Family Life Now,* 2e. (2010). Boston: Allyn & Bacon. p. 150.

of pain. Soon, parents are able to attend to their baby's cries with less trial-and-error attempts to soothe the infant. But how much attention should be given when a baby cries? And how quickly should a parent respond? If we don't respond quickly, will our baby develop a sense of mistrust?

Nearly 40 years ago, researchers found that infants who have an early history of delay on the part of the mother in responding to crying tend later to cry for longer periods than do infants with a history of less delay (Bell & Ainsworth, 1979); the consistency and promptness of maternal response during the first 3 months (or its absence) affects the pattern of later infant crying. Furthermore, the researchers discovered that infants whose cries had been neither ignored or responded to with undue delay developed modes of communication other than crying. So, a baby whose experience has been that his mother responds to his signals with consistency and promptness learns to expect that signaling—and, later, communication—is potentially successful in producing a desired or intended result, and not merely that there will be a response to crying. It is important to note that although fathers were not involved in this classic study, it is reasonable to assume that the study's conclusions would apply to them as well.

Some theories of child development, such as learning theories, propose that if a mother or father attends to crying too often, the infant's behavior is reinforced and will cry more.

However, research indicates that prompt attention to crying during the early months is one way of facilitating the basic trust that Erikson believed to be so important. Additionally, the repeated pattern of infant crying and parental responding is critical for the development of early communicative skills and secure attachments (Green, Gustafson, & McGhie, 1998).

MAINTAINING A PREDICTABLE ENVIRONMENT
Equally important as prompt, consistent attention to the infant's needs is the maintenance of an orderly, predictable environment. The infant at birth does not view him- or herself as a separate entity from others in the environment. In fact, at first, everything and everyone is an extension of the baby. A critical task of infancy, then, is to develop a sense of self and of others as separate from self. This task is related in a complex way to establishing a sense of basic trust.

In the beginning, much of the infant's world is centered on physiological needs. If fed when hungry, changed when wet, helped to sleep or rest when tired, and cared for by the same few people the baby recognizes as significant, then the infant's day-to-day environment becomes predictable, orderly, and consistent. The baby comes to know that certain things happen at certain times and that familiar people come when a cry is elicited. The baby also learns to recognize, too, the particular patterns of responses of his or her special caregivers—their tones of voice, their scents, and the way their bodies feel when held closely. All of these consistent, predictable subtleties help the baby learn that he or she can depend on others.

Trust is also built from the child's own behavior; that is, a baby begins to view herself as competent by her ability to act on her environment and her success in eliciting certain responses from her caregivers. If, however, the infant is cared for by a number of people, if there is no predictability in her feeding, sleeping, or being played with, and especially if there is abuse or neglect, then her sense of basic trust in herself as competent and others as dependable is impeded.

Profoundly related to a sense of trust during the first year is the security of attachment the infant develops for his mother, father, and other primary caregivers.

Attachment: An Emotional Bond

Attachment refers to the special bond that the infant forms with significant adults in his or her life. It is best described as an emotional or affectional bond that ties or binds the child to the parent or primary caregiver (Bowlby, 1988). Some experts regard attachment as encompassing the totality of the infant–parent relationship, expressed in a range of interactive contexts (Pederson & Moran, 1996). In order to describe the enduring, lasting patterns of interpersonal relationships from the cradle to the grave, John Bowlby (1980) developed the **attachment theory** based on his observations of parent–child interactions. With the premise that all babies need nurturance in order to survive, Bowlby asserted that in the process of providing for these survival needs, newborns form a type of bond—an attachment—with their caregivers (typically the mother and/or father). Bowlby's attachment theory puts forth the idea that it is from this close affectional and emotional bond that children derive a sense of security, a trusting sense that the world, and the interpersonal relationships we encounter along the way, is a safe place to be.

Because of the importance of these early human relationships, Bowlby, along with prominent researcher Mary Ainsworth and her associates, asserted that the attachment behaviors that take place throughout infancy ultimately direct, shape, and mold our personality. Consequently, these behaviors in turn significantly direct, shape, and mold the interpersonal attachment relationships we experience later on as children, adolescents, and adults (Ainsworth, Belhar, Waters, & Wall, 1978).

Some researchers believe that attachment may begin even earlier. They suggest that the emotional and affectional bonds actually begin during pregnancy, well before birth takes place

(Klaus, Kennell, & Klaus, 1995). Although researchers may not all agree on the exact time attachment occurs, they do agree that the ability to form and experience an emotional attachment to a parent(s) or caregiver in the earliest days and months of life is, in effect, a predictor of an individual's ability to form interpersonal (and love) relationships in the future.

Biological and environmental factors work together to facilitate the infant's attachment to significant others. Maternal sensitivity and responsivity are the central features that appear to foster secure attachment:

- *Maternal sensitivity:* **Sensitivity** is the mother's ability to perceive the infant's signals accurately and the ability to respond to them promptly and appropriately (DeWolff & van Ijzendoorn, 1997).
- *Maternal responsivity:* **Responsivity** refers to the degree to which mothers respond to their baby's cries, how affectionate and tender they are, how positive their behaviors are, and how often they interfere in their baby's ongoing behaviors (Isabella & Belsky, 1991).

Other variables that seem to affect security of attachment are mutuality and synchrony, stimulation, positive attitude, and emotional support (DeWolff & van Ijzendoorn, 1997). The child's temperament and gender also affect attachment—insecure attachment is a greater likelihood in boys (Fox, 1995).

ATTACHMENT TYPES There are three major categories or classifications of attachment: secure, secure-avoidant, and insecure-resistant. Researchers determine a baby's attachment type by using a laboratory setting referred to as the *Strange Situation.* The infant's response to the stress induced by being separated from his or her parent is used to assess the security of attachment (Ainsworth et al., 1978).

Infants rated as **secure** use their parents as a secure base (i.e., returning to them periodically when exploring a new situation) from which to explore the novel environment, and the parent's response to the infant's signals is appropriate and predictable—the parent and the child's behaviors are in harmony. Secure infants seek comfort from their parents when distressed, such as upon the parent's return after separation in the Strange Situation (Pederson & Moran, 1996). These children typically continue to develop healthily, both cognitively and emotionally.

Insecure-avoidant infants tend to be relatively independent of their parents and display little proximity seeking (the tendency to reduce distance from the attachment figure in times of distress). Typically, parents display inconsistent behavior, being at times attentive to their infants' signals and at others times inattentive. Infants may actively seek comfort from their parents, but when they are successful at gaining attention, they become fussy and hostile (Pederson & Moran, 1996). Overinvolved and intrusive parents also foster insecure ambivalence by leading their infants to develop defenses whereby they shut down from within. Insecure-avoidant behavior, then, is a self-protecting strategy for parental insensitivity and intrusiveness. This attachment style may be associated with poor social development later on.

Infants classified as **insecure-resistant** have parents who are underinvolved. The parent's behavior is unresponsive, such as delay in responding to the infant's cries. These infants tend to be distressed by separation from the parents in the Strange Situation and to seek contact during reunion, but appear to be inconsolable (Steele, Steele, & Fonagy, 1996).

Recently, a fourth category of attachment has been added. **Disorganized** attachment describes infants who do not fit into any of the three major classifications. This type of attachment is considered to be a risk factor for aggressive behavior, and for concurrent and subsequent psychopathology (van Ijzendoorn & Bakermans-Kranenburg, 2003).

ATTACHMENT ACROSS GENERATIONS A relatively recent line of research has investigated the transmission patterns across generations. Using the *Adult Attachment Inventory (AAI),* mothers' or fathers' relationships with their own parents or primary caregivers during their early childhood are assessed. Parents are then asked to describe their relationship with their parents and to provide specific memories, such as experiences of rejection, distress, hurt, loss, abuse, and separation. Parents are classified into the secure or one of the insecure groups, depending on the clarity, coherence, completeness, and orderliness of their narratives.

One study found a significant relationship between both mothers' and fathers' attachment and their infants' attachment classifications (between secure and autonomous and between insecure-avoidant and dismissing) (Steele et al., 1996). The study's results also showed an apparently greater influence of the mother as opposed to the father upon infant–parent attachment. Another study found similar results. In nearly three-fourths of the dyads, there was a match between mother–child attachment classifications of secure/insecure (Eiden et al., 1995). These data lend support to the notion of the intergenerational transmission of attachment patterns.

The importance of secure attachment cannot be overstated. As the infant's first primary socioemotional relationship, our secure attachment with our parent(s) and caregivers lays the foundation for future positive relationships with peers, siblings, romantic partners, spouses, and ultimately, our own children. The quality of the parent–child relationship during the first year plays the primary role in this important process.

Developing Reciprocity

The parent–infant system is reciprocal in nature, with the behavior and characteristics of one influencing the behavior and characteristics of the other. Much more has been written about mother–infant reciprocity than father–infant; however, the same sort of reciprocity can be developed between a father and his infant and between any other caregiver and an infant.

Reciprocity is the degree of positive or negative involvement at given points during interaction (Brazelton, Koslowski, & Main, 1974). Similar concepts are those of synchrony and mutuality. *Synchrony* refers to the extent to which the parent–infant interaction is reciprocal and mutually rewarding. On the other hand, asynchronous interactions are those that are represented by one-sided, unresponsive, or intrusive behavioral exchanges. *Mutuality* includes positive exchanges in which parent and infant attend to the same thing, mutual gazing, parents' skillful modulation of babies' arousal, and active maintenance of the interaction (DeWolff & van Ijezendoorn, 1997). Reciprocity appears to be brought about by a process of mutual adaptation between parent and child. Both learn to recognize cues, signals, or patterns of specific behaviors and characteristics of each other in numerous situations. This sort of mutual adaptation begins in the prelinguistic phase and, in time, allows each partner to communicate to the other his or her involvement in the interaction.

Both mother (and father) and infant contribute to the maintenance of an optimal level of reciprocity. For example, sensitive mothers provide appropriately timed stimulation for their infants; that is, they take cues from the infant—whether the baby is alert or drowsy, what stimuli the baby is attending to, and what signals the infant is sending. These mothers are neither intrusive nor unresponsive. They respond contingently to the baby's behavior. They reduce or stop stimulation when appropriate, to allow the infant a brief period to withdraw and reestablish equilibrium. By the same token, babies seek stimulation when they desire it, they create or prolong pleasant situations, and they avert their gaze or turn their heads when stimulation is too overwhelming. Thus, the two partners work together to regulate the reciprocal interaction.

The development of reciprocity and the goodness of fit during the first 6 months of life facilitate the infant's learning to separate him- or herself from others in his or her environment. The infant learns which behavior patterns represent "Mommy" and thereby can distinguish her from others in the environment. Reciprocity fosters a sense of competence in that the child learns that he or she can influence how others behave toward him or her. During the last half of the first year, the infant's behaviors signal a preference for particular types of responsiveness instead of generalized responsiveness. He begins to anticipate his mother's actions in response to his own and initiates interactive sequences or alters interaction the mother has initiated in order to better suit his own needs and devices. The development of a system of communication is determined to a large extent by the manner in which the mother responds to the infant's signals in the earlier months.

It appears that the development of reciprocity in the early months and the maintenance of reciprocal relationships in the later months are both critical to healthy development. It is clear that both mother (or father) and infant either facilitate or impede this progress. Either an unresponsive baby or an unresponsive parent can interfere with the development of reciprocity, as can an overly intrusive mother who seldom gives her infant opportunity to initiate interaction.

Along with establishing basic trust, developing secure attachments, and using reciprocity, to give babies the best start in life parents and caregivers must also effectively stimulate their infants.

BRAIN DEVELOPMENT AND INFANT STIMULATION

Only within the later part of the 20th century was significant attention given to any aspect of infant care other than caring for physical needs. But with the influence of Piaget, the development of infant childcare centers, and bodies of research concerning the importance of the first 2 or 3 years of life, today more emphasis is placed on optimal experiences during the infancy period. The most exciting and revealing research has been conducted by neuroscientists and focuses on brain development of fetuses, infants, and children.

Brain Development: Wiring the Brain

The electrical activity of young brain cells actually changes the physical structure of the brain. Over the first few months of life, the connections between brain cells take place at a rapid rate. These connections reach their peak at about age 2, and remain at that level until about age 10 (see Figure 2.1). Spontaneous bursts of electrical activity strengthen some connections, and those not reinforced by activity become weak and atrophy.

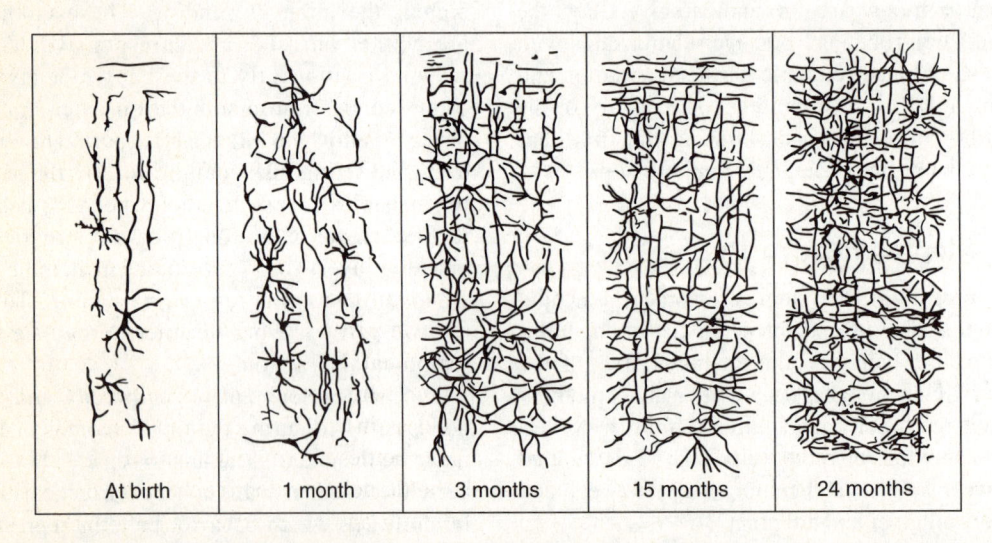

FIGURE 2.1 Experience by experience, the connections between brain cells are built. These connections change the physical structure of the brain, and literally wire the brain for a child's future learning.

Source: Feldman, *Development Across the Life Span*, 6e. (2011). Boston: Pearson. p. 115.

What triggers these bursts of electrical activity? Sensory experiences and stimulation. Children who experience these bursts have brains that thrive, while those who are deprived of stimulating environments have brains that suffer. For example, children who do not play much or who are seldom touched by their parents or caregivers have been found to develop brains as much as 30 percent smaller than normal for their age (Nash, 1997). It is repeated positive experiences that wire a child's brain—for vision, for emotions, for language, for movement—by providing a variety of experiences, including interesting things to look at; loving and responsive care; talking, singing, and reading; and space and objects to explore.

Beginning at about age 10, the brain discards or prunes its weakest connections, preserving those that have been strengthened by repeated experiences, either positive or negative. For example, early experiences of stress form some sort of template around which later brain development is organized. Additionally, infants reared by depressed mothers show significantly reduced activity in the area of the brain that serves as a center for happiness and joy. Sad experiences produce sad brains (Nash, 1997). These findings emphasize the importance of early experiences and their impact on later development. It places an enormous responsibility on parents and other primary caregivers of infants to provide appropriate, timely, and reciprocal stimulation.

Parents provide stimulation in two ways: by structuring the environment to facilitate sensorimotor activities and by interacting directly with their infants. Babies are born with sensory equipment that helps them to attend to every stimuli.

VISION It is now known that infants can see from the moment of birth, but their focus and coordination are immature. Visual stimulation should consist of bright colors, light-and-dark contrasts (stripes, bull's-eye patterns, and geometric shapes), objects that move, and contoured surfaces. Although familiarity is important in the early months, within 5 or 6 months infants seem to prefer attending to moderately complex stimuli.

The human face is a favorite object for attention: It is contoured, it moves, and it talks. Close face-to-face gazing and vocalizing provide opportunities for significant visual, auditory, and even tactile stimulation. Frequent changes in position—from back to stomach, from crib to blanket on the floor, and from infant swing to a parent's lap—provide infants with different vantage points of vision and the variation they seek. The infant's room should have pictures, mobiles, collages, and other items that can be moved and changed frequently as the infant seeks novelty and variation.

HEARING For auditory stimulation, vocalizing (such as imitating coos and babbles, talking, singing) is of utmost importance. The amount and the type of language used in the home during the period of infancy is a critical factor in the child's later intellectual development. Exposure to music (all types), daily sounds in and out of the house, and reading regularly to the baby all help to provide auditory stimulation. It should be emphasized, however, that control of noise and distraction is important. Infants who are bombarded with noise (constant TV, radio, shouting, and general commotion) learn to tune out the distractions and may have difficulty later in auditory discrimination.

TOUCHING Of all the types of sensory stimulation, tactile (touch) stimulation seems to be the most important for healthy development. The sense of touch is the most highly developed sense at birth, having functioned prenatally longer than the other senses. Holding, cuddling, stroking, rocking, and movement are essential to the infant. Caregivers can provide tactile stimulation while feeding and changing the baby, as well as in other routine activities. Adults who prop bottles or who put their babies to bed with a bottle not only deprive the baby of a sense of warmth and closeness, but also deprive them of critical visual, auditory, and tactile stimulation. Toys that have varied textures (soft, slick, fuzzy, flexible, rigid) also provide diverse tactile experiences.

Providing Infant Stimulation: The Parents' Roles

Throughout infancy, much of the parents' role centers on providing an interesting, stimulating environment for their babies. If parents provide such an environment, the infant's learning will be self-initiated.

On examining Piaget's description of the growth of intelligence during the period of infancy, it becomes even more clear that the environment does not mold the child's behavior by simply imposing itself on a passive infant. Rather, the infant seeks contact with his environment—he searches for environmental events to happen and seeks increased levels of stimulation and excitation. The infant interprets events in his environment and gives them meaning, and consequently produces specific behaviors (Piaget, 1952).

The sensitive caregiver encourages action cycles with the infant by observing her moods, knowing what is interesting to her and learning what her skills are, giving her a chance to practice the familiar, and then challenging her to extend her skills in new directions with moderately novel materials and behaviors.

It is important, then, to balance the infant's day with self-initiated, independent activities for which the parent has set the stage, and with interactive exchanges. An effort should be made to keep these interactions spontaneous, fun, and consistent with the needs of both parent and child, striving for high mutuality. Remembering always that quality of stimulation is more important than quantity, infant stimulation should be varied, appropriately timed, linked to the infant's actions, and presented in a context of basic trust.

Each phase of the parent–child interaction can alter the status of a child so that during the subsequent phase of interaction the child stimulates the parent in a different way or reacts differently to parent behavior. In turn, parents discover that previous behaviors are no longer appropriate, and they are faced with finding new ways of guiding and interacting with the child.

PARENTS AND TODDLERS: PARENTS ARE PROTECTORS

As a child becomes mobile, the role of parents gradually takes on the new dimension of protector. The once dependent, "helpless" infant is transformed into an active, tireless, curious toddler. Suddenly he can see the top of the table, reach the magazines, flush toys down the toilet, drink from the pet's bowl, eat the dog's or cat's food, and perform a host of other activities that are fascinating to his growing curiosity. These behaviors are related to the fact that the toddler no longer needs hands to assist with getting around—he is now free to feel and touch and explore things that are attractive. Of course, this means that as protectors, parents must provide the safest environment possible for toddlers to exercise their growing independence and increased capacity for learning. Table 2.3 presents those things parents can do to accident-proof their homes and yards.

Coping with Growing Autonomy: "Me do it!"

The years from 1 to 3 constitute for the child a declaration of independence (Brazelton, et al., 1974). Stage 2 in Erikson's theory of psychosocial development is described as **autonomy versus shame and doubt.** The child takes pride in her new accomplishments of walking and climbing, opening and closing, dropping, pushing and pulling, and holding on and letting go. She now wants to do everything for herself.

If parents recognize the young child's need to do what he is capable of doing at his own pace and in his own time, the toddler develops a sense that he can control his muscles, his impulses, himself, and, not insignificantly, his environment. The phrase, "Me do it!" is familiar to most parents who have developed the endless patience required to let the child dress himself in the morning, pour his own milk, or put away his toys. Erikson believed, however, that if caregivers are impatient and do for the child what he is capable of doing himself, they reinforce a sense of shame

TABLE 2.3 Accident-proofing the home.
As protectors, parents must provide the safest possible environment for toddlers to exercise their growing autonomy and increased capacity for learning.

The Home: Should be accessible to the child to expand her space and possibilities for learning.
Experts suggest that parents crawl on the floor, to view and experience the room as the baby/toddler does:

- Remove anything that's breakable, fragile, or precious
- Remove furniture with sharp corners (such as coffee or end tables)
- Put safety devices in electrical outlets
- Place gates across entrances and exits to stairways (and other places that might pose danger)
- Remove all cords to blinds or draperies (look for all entanglement hazards)
- Do not hang pictures on the wall above the child's crib
- Put locks on all cupboards (it's helpful to leave one cupboard for the baby's exploration, such as the cupboard with the plastic/metal bowls and lids)
- ALL cleaning supplies, shampoos, medications, and toiletries should be placed in cabinets that are inaccessible to a child

The Yard: Many parents are quite mindful of their home's safety, but sometimes neglect to "child-proof" the yard and play area:

- Fences and gates should be secure
- Outdoor equipment should be safe and in good repair
- Children should be supervised at all times! Never, ever leave a child alone to play outdoors, even if just for a few minutes

and doubt. When caregiving is consistently overprotecting or critical or harsh and unthinking, the child develops an excessive sense of doubt about his abilities to control his world and himself and develops shame with respect to other people.

Evidence shows that resistant and angry child behavior peaks during the second year and then begins its decline thereafter. In fact, mothers and fathers have been shown to react more positively to 12-month-olds than to 18-month-olds, and parents' self-rated enjoyment of parenting declines from 18 to 24 months. Many parents resist their toddlers' strivings for autonomy, and/or they have limited skills in managing effectively the child's emerging developmental advances (Belsky, Woodworth, & Crnic, 1996). Studies show that about 65 percent of parent–child interactions at age 2 are parental prohibitions, and parents interrupt their toddlers every 6–8 minutes to induce them to change their behavior (Baumrind, 1996).

This striving for autonomy in toddlers is often coupled with open negativism toward the parents. With toddlers' no's they establish themselves as separate from their parents. They learn what parents expect of them and how parents will act in response to them. Parents can minimize setting themselves up for a "no" from the child by phrasing statements in the form of *expectations* rather than *choices* when choices are not intended. For example, if a parent expects the toddler to go to bed, he should not say, "Do you want to go to bed?" Instead, he should say, "It's bedtime."

SETTING LIMITS There is no question that once children become mobile, parents must set firm limits and enforce them consistently in a loving manner. Either extreme in the setting of limits at this stage interferes with healthy development.

The most important limits have to do with the child's own safety and well-being. The newfound freedom of the toddler carries with it potential danger, making the setting and maintenance of limits necessary. The other purpose of parental control at this point is to make it possible for the child to know how and when to control herself. Erikson (1963) believed that a lasting sense of goodwill and pride derives from a sense of self-control without loss of self-esteem.

TEMPER TANTRUMS More severe forms of negativism are manifested by toddlers in their frequent temper tantrums. These occur normally because toddlers' wishes and desires for independence are thwarted. They are perpetuated by the parents who either force a contest of wills or give in to toddlers' desires. Neither technique is appropriate. Contests of wills may be avoided by making expectations simple, clear, and consistent. When children test these expectations (and they will—often!), parents can assist cooperation by reinforcing verbal requests by physical contact (such as taking the child by the hand and leading him in the desired direction), modeling the expected behavior for the child, and offering realistic choices so that he can exercise his independence—what kind of juice he wants, which book he wants to read, or which shirt he wants to wear.

If all this fails and a tantrum ensues anyway, then the worst possible behavior is for the parent to give in to the child's wishes, if it is clear that those wishes are inconsistent with the limits the parent has already set. Consistent failure to pay attention to tantrum behaviors usually serves to reduce its occurrence. Parents fail to reinforce it not only by not giving in, but also by withdrawing attention from the tantrum and refusing to allow the child to harm himself, others, or property. It may be necessary to remove the child from the immediate environment in order to remove reinforcing agents.

Belsky, Grossmann, Grossmann, and Scheuerer-Englisch (1996), in their research with families and their firstborn male toddlers, identified a group of families who seemed to have more difficulty than others managing their children. The families in the "most troubled" group were more likely to rely on basic control techniques (directives and prohibitions) and least likely to couple these control efforts with guidance (simple declaratives accompanied by reasons or explanations). Their children were found the most defiant and subsequently experienced the most escalation of negative affect by parents. Furthermore, these children demonstrated more aggression and acting out, and their parents reported more daily hassles.

These investigators found that, in addition to low socioeconomic status, families likely to be "most troubled" were characterized by more support for and less interference with the fathers' work; had both mothers and fathers who were less social, more negative, and less friendly; and had both mothers and fathers who were least satisfied with the social support they were receiving.

The authors raised the important question of whether trouble in the second year forecasts further trouble in childrearing. Some experts speculate that the parent–child interaction during toddlerhood represents a critical period for patterns that persist in the future. If such is the case, it seems that parents with toddlers should be targeted for family support and parent-education programs that might offset future problems.

Although autonomy is a necessary stage of healthy development, it can sometimes be frustrating—for both parent and child. Even though parents can feel threatened and ill equipped to handle their toddler's negativism and lack of compliance, they should recognize that this is expected, healthy development. By finding an appropriate balance between too little and too much independence, they can facilitate their toddler's self-control without causing the child to lose his or her self-esteem.

Providing Learning Experiences: Self-Help Skills and Toilet Learning

For a child to develop optimally, parents must provide a wide variety of experiences in a safe environment. The most important learning experiences for the toddler are those of self-discovery and those that are intellectual in nature. The role of the parent in discovery learning is to structure the environment so that discovery can take place—that is, the parent provides the materials and the experiences and interacts with the child in verbal and physical ways.

SELF-HELP SKILLS The first area in which a parent can provide learning experiences for the toddler is in **self-help skills.** For example, before a child can walk, she indicates a readiness to feed herself. Even though the result is often that less ends up in her mouth than on her face, hair, and highchair, it is necessary that parents pick up on the child's cues that she is ready, despite the fact that the toddler's coordination may not be equal to her desire for independence! Some parents may give the toddler a spoon or some finger food and alternate feeding her with their own attempts. This gets the job done and allows the child to be involved in the interaction and practice her budding skills.

Somewhat later the child repeats his "Me do it!" in connection with dressing. A compromise may be reached between parent and child by allowing the child to do simple things, such as pulling up his pants and putting on his socks. Simple clothing that the child can manipulate (large buttons, no straps, shoes that slip on) makes the task easier for the child—and saves the parent a lot of frustration. Pants that can easily be pulled up and down are especially important during the toilet-training phase.

TOILET LEARNING In the United States, toilet training perhaps causes parents more frustration than any other experience of early childrearing. Parents indicate a desire for more information on the subject (Gross & Tucker, 1994). In our society, there is no urgency in accomplishing toilet training; we can wait for a child to learn at his or her own pace.

The child indicates to his caregiver that he is ready for assistance in learning to control his bodily functions, first by demonstrating regularity in bowel movements and later in frequency of urination, followed by the child's understanding that dirty or wet pants are related to an act that he himself has performed. Finally, language skills to communicate the need to go to the bathroom signal the readiness for transition from diapers to training pants, at least during waking hours. If parents are alert to these cues, assist the child by providing simple clothing and accessibility to toileting facilities, and have infinite patience, the process usually proceeds smoothly (but perhaps not quickly by parental standards). A positive, reinforcing, patient attitude on the part of the parent helps a child to gain a sense of autonomy. On the other hand, a critical, harsh, impatient attitude promotes a sense of doubt and shame and a loss of self-esteem.

The developmental step of toileting should be treated like all others: Parents should wait for the child to learn at her own pace. If it is treated differently from the child's other tasks, then undue emphasis is placed on it. If it becomes a focus for attention, the child may use it for rebellion and negativism, and the child's determined strength almost always wins.

The child's motivation and autonomy are of primary importance to any real success in toilet training. Viewing toileting as a learning experience within the context of acceptance, the child gains pleasure and excitement from mastering each step herself.

Social and Intellectual Learning

Aside from encouraging independence in self-help skills as learning experiences for the toddler, there are four other areas of learning that are critical during this period: the acquisition of social skills, language, the development of curiosity, and the formation of the roots of intelligence.

In the first area, toddlers need exposure to interactions with other children their own age. Frequently, parents choose to place toddlers in a play group or a childcare center at this time so children can learn basic social skills, such as waiting one's turn, sharing toys and equipment, delaying gratification, and getting along well in groups.

Children who do not have play-group or childcare experiences during toddlerhood need the opportunity to interact with their peers. Oftentimes, however, children treat their peers as objects, not people, especially in the beginning stages of association. The "No, mine!" protest that is familiar to all of us further emphasizes the immaturity of the toddler's understandings of social interactions. The child's grabbing, pulling, biting, and hitting are in part due to egocentricity and in part due to lack of language skills that older children use when cooperating in play.

The learning of appropriate social skills requires a patient adult who recognizes the child's immature level of development and therefore does not place too many demands on him or her to "be nice" or to "share the toys." Parents and educators in the know duplicate toys and activities to minimize conflict over any special one. They also use distraction and offer alternatives, and most importantly, model appropriate social behavior for the child.

An extremely important event in the life of a toddler is the rapid development of language. From 18 months to 3 years, the average vocabulary of a child leaps from approximately 20–22 words to 900 words! Naturally, the child understands far more words than he or she uses. The parent's role in language development includes:

- Labeling familiar objects and events
- Expanding on the child's telegraphic speech
- Reinforcing language attempts
- Modeling

Numerous studies indicate that a child's development is correlated closely with the quality and quantity of language used in the home. Furthermore, children learn early language from adults, not from other children. The degree to which parents talk *with* the child, ask/answer questions, read to the child, and consider language as a valued tool for intellectual development relate to early language facilitation in the child.

The development of curiosity and the formation of the roots of intelligence during the toddler stage are related closely to language development. Even before the toddler has the language to ask questions, he demonstrates his curiosity by using the senses of touch, taste, smell, vision, and hearing. These senses, coupled with the ability for independent locomotion, provide important cues about his expanded world and assist him in the formation of basic concepts related to color, shape, size, weight, distance, and causality. As he acquires greater language facility, he is able to expand his concepts by attaching labels to them. For example, a toddler with a basket full of objects from around the house can learn something about size, shape, and cause-and-effect relationships. With the parent's verbal interaction, she is also learning that a particular word stands for a particular object. Besides, she is probably having a lot more fun than a toddler whose mother tries to teach her the alphabet or how to use the computer.

As in earlier infancy, there should be a balance between self-initiated and self-sustained activities by the child, in addition to parent–child interactions. In this way, the child controls much of his own learning within a framework provided by the parent.

PARENTS AND PRESCHOOL CHILDREN: PARENTS ARE NURTURERS

Nurturance is affectionate care and attention. This definition aptly describes the chief role that parents assume as their children move into the preschool period. Although the child's environment still must remain safe and protective, preschool children do not need the constant watchful eye of parents that was so necessary for infants and toddlers. To discover the optimal amount of supervision without interference, assistance without indulgence, and warmth and love without suffocation is difficult for many parents. They find that their need to be needed is still very strong, and some find it difficult to meet that need in a way that is healthy for both themselves and their children.

Warmth refers to a parent's emotional expression of love. Children of parents with warmth and empathy are more motivated to participate in cooperative strategies, and these parental characteristics are associated with children's internalization of moral values. On the other hand, a predominance of parental negative mood and facial expressions is associated with defiance and hostile aggression in children (Baumrind, 1996).

It is likely that a child's perception of the emotional climate that exists within the home is of far greater consequence in healthy development than the specific behaviors of the parent. Consistency also in the kind of discipline used by parents, how it is administered, and in what context seem to be more influential in facilitating healthy development than the specific type of discipline used (Baumrind, 1996). If parents have not agreed already on the goals and values they have for their children, it is critical that some agreement be reached at this point. Belsky and his associates (1996) reported that spousal disagreements about childrearing attitudes and values when children were 3 years old predicted both child behavior problems 2 years later and marital dissolution 7 years after that. Other research shows that such disagreements forecast psychological and behavioral development when children are as old as 18.

Each parent is different and interacts with the child in ways that are unique to his or her own style, but consistency in making and enforcing rules, as well as a common agreement as to whether discipline will be permissive, authoritative (democratic), or authoritarian offers the young child the consistency that is vital to his or her growing sense of competence. In essence, children need to know that behavior approved by Mom is also approved by Dad. They need the comfort that parents respond with consistency—both within the individual parent and between the parents.

A strong love relationship between parents at this time further facilitates their roles as nurturers of their children. Respect for each other and respect for their children as individuals creates a positive emotional climate in the home. Additionally, the love and respect parents have for one another is an effective tool for facilitation of the identification process in the late preschool period.

One major consideration in providing nurturance is knowing how to establish limits and achieve responsible behavior in young children without threatening their sense of autonomy and initiative.

The Styles of Parenting

Research psychologist Diana Baumrind (1927–) asserted that normal parenting centers on the issue of control and that parents' primary roles are to influence, teach, and control their children. Based on her observations of parent–child interactions, Baumrind believed that there are two specific dimensions of childrearing: parental warmth or responsiveness/affection/supportiveness toward the child, and parental control or how demanding or restrictive the parents are toward their child (also referred to as behavioral control). In examining these two dimensions, Baumrind (1991) identified four parenting styles. Each of these parenting styles reflects different patterns of parental values, practices, and behaviors.

UNINVOLVED PARENTING Uninvolved parents are typically low in responsiveness, warmth, and affection, and they are low in parental control or demands. Parents may both reject and neglect their children. Not all parents who are uninvolved are neglectful or rejecting; some are simply detached and uninterested in their children's lives. For example, while some parents may meet their child's basic needs (shelter, clothing, education, food), they may not offer praise for a child's efforts or compliment the child's accomplishments. In essence, there are few meaningful and inclusive family interactions.

There are a number of negative consequences of uninvolved or disengaged parenting for children and adolescent well-being. Across all racial and ethnic groups, for example, there are reports of increased substance use and abuse, higher rates of delinquency, poorer school performance, and negative psychological well-being

(Pittman & Chase-Landsdale, 2001; Samaniego & Gonzales, 1999; Steinberg et al., 1994).

Recent research further suggests that disengaged parenting styles, when combined with families who live in dangerous or socially disorganized neighborhoods, are linked with increased later-life delinquency in African American and Latino boys (Roche, Ensminger, & Cherlin, 2007). There is also an association of uninvolved/disengaged parenting with increased school problem behavior and depression among African American youth, particularly when mothers are not involved in their children's parenting. This evidence is clear and convincing: The stakes of uninvolved or detached parenting are profound among African Americans, particularly among males.

PERMISSIVE PARENTING Also referred to as *indulgent* parents, **permissive parents** demonstrate high levels of warmth, affection, and responsiveness toward their children, and also show adequate to high levels of parent–child communication. This parenting style does not place high demands on children, nor do parents attempt to control their children's behavior; children's behavior is mostly self-regulated. Baumrind refers to these parents as *lenient* and *nontraditional*.

Similar to uninvolved or disengaged parenting, children of parents who set no boundaries and who do not provide behavioral regulations experience higher levels of depression, poorer school performance, poorer psychological adjustment and well-being, and greater use of substances (Pittman & Chase-Landsdale, 2001; Samaniego & Gonzales, 1999; Steinberg et al., 1994). Parents who engage in high levels of **autonomy granting,** such as parents who do not monitor the children's time, also put their children at risk for elevated depression; this is particularly true for Asian females and African American males (Radziszewska, Richardson, Dent, & Flay, 1996). In high-risk (i.e., low-income/low-education), dangerous neighborhoods and communities, permissive parenting is associated with later school problem behavior and poor school performance (Roche et al., 2007).

AUTHORIT*ARIAN* PARENTING According to Baumrind, **authoritarian parents** are "obedience- and status-oriented, and expect their orders to be obeyed without explanation" (1991, p. 62). To put it another way, authoritarian parents are very demanding and controlling with their children, but at the same time not very responsive, warm, or affectionate toward their children. This type of parenting style is characterized by rigid rules of behavior, which children are expected to follow with no questions asked; it is often referred to as *punitive parenting*. Parent–child communication is very low, and there is no room for compromise. Power is the key player.

Across all racial and ethnic groups, this type of restrictive, punitive parenting is associated with increased emotional problems (such as anxiety), psychological problems (such as depression), and increased behavioral problems (Eamon & Mulder, 2005; Grogan-Kaylor, 2005; McLeod & Nonnemaker, 2000). When parents use corporal punishment (spanking or hitting), children and adolescents exhibit more incidences of problem behaviors; however, this is found more among whites and Latinos than it is among African Americans (Lansford et al., 2004). Corporal punishment also appears to be more strongly associated with behavior problems in boys than it is in girls (Grogan-Kaylor, 2005). Interestingly, punitive/restrictive parenting is associated with *increases* in depression, delinquencies, and problem behaviors for African American males who live in safe neighborhoods/communities, but it is linked with *decreases* in these for blacks who live in dangerous neighborhoods. We discuss the possible reasons for these findings a bit later in this chapter.

AUTHORIT*ATIVE* PARENTING With this parenting style, parents are responsive while demanding certain behavioral standards. This style of parenting does not use shame, withdrawal of love, or guilt (as might authoritarian parents) to control behavior. **Authoritative parents** set clear boundaries for their children's behavior, but they are flexible and will change these boundaries if the situation warrants, such as later in adolescence when children experience even more autonomy. Authoritative parents are warm and responsive, and they encourage parent–child communication. Children are expected to follow the rules of the house, but are still allowed to be autonomous. With this style, parents use a balance of power and reason.

Of all of Baumrind's parenting styles, authoritative parenting provides children with a balance of control and warmth, which yields the best outcome for children's health and well-being in the areas of social competence and psychosocial development. A number of research studies consistently demonstrate that:

- Children reared by authoritative parents exhibit more social competence than do other children (Amato & Folwer, 2002; McClun & Merrell, 1998; Steinberg & Morris, 2001).
- Both boys and girls reared by authoritative parents exhibit lower levels of problem behavior across all stages of the lifespan and across all ethnic groups (Jackson, Henriksen, & Foshee, 1998; Kim, Hetherington, & Reiss, 1999).
- Children reared by authoritative parents are better able to balance the demands of conforming to others' expectations with their own needs for uniqueness and autonomy (Durbin et al., 1993; Shucksmith, Leo, Hendry, & Glendinning, 1995).
- Both boys and girls tend to perform better in school if they are reared by authoritative parents—this higher level of performance is seen from preschool throughout early adulthood (Brooks-Gunn & Markman, 2005; Chen & Kaplan, 2001).
- Effective parenting skills further the growth of a child's social and communication skills, as well as their ability to concentrate on tasks and at school (Connell & Prinz, 2002; Lamb-Parker, Boak, Griffin, Ripple, & Peay, 1999).

When parents are warm, sensitive, and responsive to their child's needs, they foster a wide range of interpersonal development in children, from the development of a healthy sense of self, to a sense of belonging and well-being, to high levels of self-esteem (Harvard Family Research Project, 2006).

ETHNIC GROUP DIFFERENCES IN PARENTING

Research demonstrates that race and ethnicity influence parenting styles. In a landmark, large-scale study of approximately 10,000 adolescents representing four ethnic groups (African American, white, Hispanic, and Asian American), the researchers found that the *authoritative* parenting style was the most common among white families and least common among Asian Americans; it was also more common among married biological parents than it was among single parents or stepfamilies (Steinberg, Mounts, Lamborn, & Dornbusch, 1991). The study also showed that parenting styles differ by social class. Authoritative parenting was more common among middle-class parents than among working-class parents, with the exception of Asian American parents, who demonstrated authoritarian parenting styles.

Subsequent research has found that *parenting goals,* such as raising children so they will succeed in college and in their careers, are tied to parenting styles (Cheah & Rubin, 2004). Parenting goals are influenced by the parents' cultural values. For example, Asian American parents may raise their children with the authoritarian parenting style because they believe it helps to maintain their cultural identity; African American parents may do so because they are "keenly aware of the degree to which social forces such as racism may impede their children's achievement of educational, economic, and social success…. They [believe] that adopting an authoritarian parenting style will enhance their children's potential for success" (Boyd & Bee, 2009, p. 224). The link between this parenting style and child outcome variables such as self-control suggest that it is effective for African Americans (Broman, Reckase, & Freedman-Doan, 2006). It is important to note, however, that not *all* African American parents adopt this parenting style—parenting styles are as unique as each individual.

These studies show us that there are *culturally specific* processes that underlie parents' behaviors and communication. The reality of parenting is that it is an experience comprised of interconnected, multiple processes that are affected by the parents' race/ethnicity, cultural beliefs, income level, and living environment. Much more work needs to be done to fully understand the interplay of cultural/parenting contexts and parenting, because these studies can serve as a launching pad for family life education programs and public policies to strengthen family life (Cebalo et al., 2008).

Discipline and Punishment: One and the Same?

One of the major concerns that parents of young children face is how much or how little to discipline their children. In our society, the terms *discipline* and *punishment* are often used interchangeably. **Discipline** refers to one who receives *instruction* from another. When the word is used correctly, then, a system of discipline should imply a broad positive system of guidance of the young child, with particular methods of **punishment**—most often physical in nature—being only a minor aspect (if any) of that total discipline system.

INDUCTIVE DISCIPLINE *Inductive discipline* focuses on encouraging the young child to take into account the potential effects of his behavior on other people and on himself when making decisions about what he will and will not do. This approach is most often combined with an authoritative parenting style. The inductive parent emphasizes process goals, stressing the "how" rather than the "what" of behavior. This is in contrast to a parent telling a child that certain behaviors are good and others are bad, which is more likely to produce unnecessary feelings of guilt and shame.

It is important to show children why their present behavior pattern is inappropriate, show them how to act instead, and demonstrate the expectation that they will change their behavior in the desired direction. Parents who use inductive disciplinary techniques often have children who are less likely to violate prohibitions than other children are.

NATURAL AND LOGICAL CONSEQUENCES Ruydolf Dreikurs was noted for his approach to discipline through the use of natural and logical consequences (Dreikurs, & Grey, 1968), and this approach is still widely used today. **Natural consequences** are those that occur naturally from the behavior, such as a child who refuses to eat goes hungry. **Logical consequences** are those that are assigned by the parent to express the reality of the social order, not of the person. For example, a child who disturbs the rest of the family at mealtime is given the choice to settle down or to leave the table.

There are advantages of using natural and logical consequences (Dinkmeyer, McKay, & Dinkmeyer, 1997):

- It holds children (not parents) responsible for behavior.
- It allows children to make their own decisions about what courses of action are appropriate.
- It permits children to learn from the natural or social order of events, rather than forcing them to comply with the wishes of people.

When using this type of discipline, parents must separate the deeds from the doer—the parent's actions must be based on respect for the child as a person separate from his or her deeds. The parent should also be firm in following through with the consequences, yet kind in the tone of voice used to discipline the child. Encouragement is implicit in this approach. Children eventually learn to accept responsibility for their own behavior in a way that conveys mutual respect and avoids power struggles.

SPANKING Spanking is a common occurrence in families with young children, and fathers typically spank less than mothers do (Day, Peterson, &

McCracken, 1998). Well over 61 percent of mothers of preschool children report spanking their children, with a mean of about three spankings per week (Giles-Sims, Straus, & Sugarman, 1995).

The strongest and most consistent predictors of parental spanking are the personal characteristics of the parents (such as young age and conservative religious ideology) and perceived characteristics of the child (such as whether the child is difficult) (Day et al., 1998). Other characteristics lead to wide variations in the incidence and intensity of spanking behaviors. African American mothers, for instance, spank more than other mothers (Giles-Sims et al., 1995). Rural mothers, young mothers, and Protestant mothers spank more than urban, older, and Catholic mothers.

These findings are important for us to understand because spanking can pose a serious threat to the well-being of children: It increases the chances of both physical aggression and delinquency and is associated with depression, spousal abuse, and reduced occupational achievement in adulthood (Giles-Sims et al., 1995). Thus, when a parent deems it necessary to administer physical punishment (spanking), several conditions should be met. These are summarized for us in Table 2.4. As you can see, if parents use spanking judiciously and concentrate on achieving compliance with their standards by using explanations, reason, and external reinforcement, it may be possible to obtain obedience and self-correction without stimulating self-punitive reactions.

One of the major disadvantages of spanking or other forms of corporal punishment is that normally they serve as a vehicle for the release of parental feelings as opposed to helping the child learn appropriate behavior. But even more problematic, the parent models aggressive, angry behavior for the child and, in effect, tells the child that it is all right for a person to hit another person when he or she becomes angry. If the parent remains calm and focuses on the behavior of the child instead of the child him- or herself, the child's self-respect is not damaged in the process of facilitating acceptable behavior.

BUILDING SELF-CONCEPT, INITIATIVE, AND LEARNING

One of the most significant results of nurturance during the preschool period is the building of a healthy self-concept in young children. Self-concept is believed to be intimately related to the

---

TABLE 2.4 Administering physical punishment.
When a parent or caregiver decides to administer physical punishment (spanking), several conditions must first be met.

1. *The punishment should immediately follow the act.* Spanking is effective at suppressing rule-breaking behaviors when it is administered without delay. Waiting until Dad or Mom get home from work actually punishes the child all day.
2. *The punishment must be deserved and understood.* When deciding to spank, a parent must take into consideration the contexts of the child's misbehavior. Did she miss her nap because Mom continues to shop? Children need to know exactly what they are being punished for—especially preschool children, who have short memories. An explanation of the misbehavior and punishment work well to result in effective discipline.
3. *The punishment must be related to the act.* The punishment must fit the crime. If a child, for example, colors on the wall, an appropriate punishment is having her help to clean the wall. This way, he associates the punishment with the act, and is less likely to repeat it.
4. *The punishment should be administered in a loving way.* Parents should be loving, calm, and understanding when administering discipline. This sends the message that the child isn't bad, but that the behaviors were unacceptable.

individual's interactions with significant others in his or her social world.

Developing a Self-Concept

Traditionally, the two aspects of the child's self-concept that have been emphasized are a sense of belonging and a feeling of worth. Although these are no doubt critical to the child's overall feeling of self-esteem, the more recent examination of the child's perceived behavioral competencies is consistent with the view of the child as an active participant in her overall development. It appears that the young child's ability to interact successfully with her environment is a vital aspect of her development of a positive self-worth. As you saw earlier, the characteristics of authoritative parents contribute to young children's self-concept. See the summary of parent behaviors that further promote positive self-concepts in Table 2.5.

Abundant evidence also suggests that a child's self-concept is a powerful determinant of his or her behavior. A correlation exists between self-concept and achievement as early as kindergarten, though this relationship becomes more prominent during the school-age period. In fact, a person's chances for success increase as self-esteem increases. Preschool children with poor self-concepts may be overly cautious when attempting new tasks, fearing failure. They may appear anxious, defensive, and withdrawn. Although self-concept changes over the course of development—for better or for worse—the preschool period is a crucial time for observing behaviors that might suggest a poorly emerging self-concept.

Developing a Sense of Initiative

Erikson (1963) described his third stage of psychosocial development as **initiative versus guilt.** This stage has its beginning in the latter part of the third year after the child has attained proficiency in walking and feeding himself. The child's attention, no longer needed to develop and control basic activities (such as in toilet learning), is now free to add a new dimension to his newly achieved muscular autonomy. He now directs his attention toward increasing participation in his social environment, largely his family, but also to other adults and peers.

Whether a child leaves this stage with a sense of **initiative**—a sense that she can accomplish anything before her—depends to a considerable extent on how her parents respond to her self-initiated activities. Children who are given freedom, opportunity, and encouragement to initiate play, to ask questions, and to engage in fantasy play have their sense of initiative reinforced. But at the same time, conscience is beginning to

---

TABLE 2.5 Parenting behaviors that promote positive self-concepts.

The parent . . .
- Shows warmth for, acceptance of, and respect for the child
- Shows concern for and attentiveness to the child
- Provides an environment appropriate for the child
- Allows the child freedom within established structure
- Provides an environment for successful interaction
- Exhibits consistent love, conscientiousness, and security in handling child
- Maintains high nurturance, high control, and high demands
- Has clear expectations
- Makes firm demands coupled with understanding
- Has a positive self-concept

develop, and the child begins to understand the difference between right and wrong and pleasing and displeasing his parents. If he thinks that his play is bad or dangerous or that his questions are a nuisance, he may develop a sense of guilt over self-initiated activities. This guilt may persist through later life stages.

Children who successfully resolve the conflict between initiative and guilt learn to control their behavior and respect social conventions and moral responsibilities. At the same time, they do not lose their psychological freedom to assume initiatives and the responsibilities that come with them. Conversely, children who fail to resolve this conflict successfully tend to emerge with overly strong and inflexible consciences that inhibit them from taking initiative in ambiguous situations in which they are not sure that they are safe from disapproval.

Providing Learning Experiences

Much of what we have discussed—methods of discipline, the building of a healthy self-concept, and developing initiative—can hardly be separated from providing optimal learning experiences. A child who is nurtured, who is given freedom to initiate, and who feels good about herself as a person and a family member is inspired to learn. A young child learns from every event in which she participates, from her peers, her play, and her everyday interactions with her environment. Warmth, nurturance, and responsiveness are prerequisites for effective learning experiences during the preschool years.

In addition to a positive social and emotional climate that facilitates the natural learning process, other aspects of the home environment enhance the learning process of young children. For example, research shows that parents' educational level shows a strong relationship to children's IQ, and some studies have found a same-sex relationship. That is, mothers' educational level correlates with their daughters' IQ, and fathers' educational level correlates with sons'. Other aspects of the home environment that affect children's cognitive development and later school success include the amount of reading materials available (and read!), variety in daily stimulation, and provision of appropriate play materials.

Through play, young children learn in a way that no one can teach them. Play is the major vehicle for learning during the early childhood years, and preschoolers like to "mess and manipulate." They learn about their physical world by touching, examining, testing, exploring, evaluating, and imagining.

Today, many parents and preschool teachers introduce children to computers during this stage of development. When children are able to start the computer, load the software, and interact with the software without continued adult help, they probably are interested and ready for computers. However, computers should be used like any other activity with preschool children—as a choice among many in which children can participate. A sensible "take it or leave it" attitude by parents of preschool children is warranted. Children will become computer literate either when they become interested or when they are required to do so in an academic setting later on.

Perhaps the most important ingredient for learning experiences is people. A loving, caring adult who is available to the child to answer his questions, to engage him in imagination and fantasy, to introduce him to new words and ideas, and to pick up on his cues of curiosity cannot be replaced by dozens of toys. The adult who structures the environment so that learning occurs, who allows the child freedom and encouragement for exploration, and who interacts with him in a warm, accepting manner provides the most important learning experiences of all.

Adults can scaffold children's learning by anticipating the child's developmental readiness for new ideas and experiences and responding at the appropriate time. Lev Vygotsky talked about the child's **zone of proximal development,** the small area just beyond a child's demonstrated level of development that a child can move toward with adult guidance. Adults sensitive to children's cues can extend children's development into that proximal zone.

PROGRAMS FOR PARENTS OF INFANTS, TODDLERS, AND PRESCHOOLERS

There is no consensus about the most effective form or timing of parent education. It seems, however, that parent education programs for the parents of very young children are particularly important for two reasons. First, it is assumed that a person is most motivated when he or she *is* a parent or is about to become a parent. Also, parents have a more realistic orientation to some of the problems of parenthood than potential parents have and will reap more benefits from a program that is directed toward their current needs. Second, the emphasis that has been placed on the importance of the environmental experiences for brain development in the early years and their implications for the child's further development suggest the need for early intervention and support for parents. In fact, when it comes to education programs, the earlier the better, the longer the better, and the more consistent the better.

In the sections that follow, we take a brief look at two types of parent education programs that support the needs of parents as children develop from infants to preschoolers: home visitation programs and Head Start.

Home Visitation

Recently there has been renewed interest in home-visiting programs for new parents, which currently serve a variety of populations and achieve many different goals. **Home visitation** is not a single, specific, uniformly defined service; rather, it is a strategy for service delivery—it brings various services to a family rather than requiring the family to come to the service provider(s). Programs primarily target pregnant women and/or families with young children up to 3 years of age.

The goals of the programs range from a single goal, such as preventing low birth weight, to multiple goals, such as promoting a child's physical health and cognitive development. Still others take an even more comprehensive approach, seeking to address the needs of other family members. Some programs target specific populations, such as pregnant teens or families at risk for child abuse and neglect, whereas other programs are universal, or open to any family who wishes to participate (Gomby, Larson, Lewit, & Behrman, 1993). One such example of a universal program is *Parents as Teachers,* which is widely used across the country. Though not empirical, evaluations of the Parents as Teachers program indicate that both parents and children benefit—children, by demonstrating advanced academic skills once they are in school when compared with nonparticipants, and parents, by being involved more than nonparticipant parents in their children's schooling. We discuss this program at length in Chapter 5.

There are several impediments to the success of education and support programs for parents of infants (McKim, 1987):

- *Reluctance of parents:* Some parents do not want to admit that their baby may have a problem; this is compounded by the lack of specialized training of social service and health professionals who may imply to the parents that the baby is okay.
- *Working parents are not accommodated:* Oftentimes, programs do not accommodate working parents.
- *Lack of infant care:* Many programs do not make provisions for the care of infants while the program is in session.
- *Varying needs:* Parents of different socioeconomic levels may have different needs; it is well known that **SES, or socioeconomic status,** is an important variable in the relationship between parenting knowledge and the quality of stimulation in the home (Parks & Smeriglio, 1986).

TABLE 2.6 Developing programs for infants and toddlers.

The following issues need to be considered when developing programs for parents of infants and toddlers:

1. Training professionals to be sensitive to and skillful in counseling about the daily issues and adjustments of parents and young infants.
2. Designing long-term programs that emphasize the psychological aspects of parenting children during the first 3 years of life.
3. Considering the particular needs of parents of different racial, ethnic, and SES backgrounds in developing program content.
4. Designing programs that have immediate relevance for age-related development.
5. Using delivery methods (such as Webinars, DVDs, on-line sessions, and community outreach) that reach a broader range of parents, particularly those who are in the most need.

In order for programs to be effective, then, several factors need to be considered in developing and implementing programs for parents of infants and toddlers. These are summarized in Table 2.6. As you can see, both short- and long-term planning are necessary in order for home service programs to be effective and have lasting impact.

Head Start

Parent involvement and/or parent education was a requirement of the federally funded preschool programs in the late 1960s through the 1970s. More than any other program of the Johnson Administration's War on Poverty in 1965, Head Start translated the parent-participation principle into specific guidelines. The **Head Start** program is a program of the U.S. Department of Health and Human Services. It provides comprehensive education, health (such as vision and hearing screenings), nutrition, and parenting education/involvement services to low-income children and their families.

Each year, Head Start state programs enroll about 1.1 million preschoolers (U.S. Department of Education, 2010). Two national studies, the Head Start Impact Study (U.S. Department of Health and Human Services, 2003) and the Family and Child Experiences Survey (FACES; Administration for Children and Families, 2008) reveal that consistently, Head Start offers effective, quality programming. The Head Start Impact Study found statistically significant positive impacts for 3- and 4-year-olds in prereading, prewriting, and vocabulary.

Formalized parent education programs in conjunction with other forms of parent participation and involvement have always been an essential component of Head Start. Since Head Start was the only early-intervention program to survive the federal budget cuts of the 1990s, few formalized parent-education programs for parents of young children currently exist. But, given that the years before a child reaches kindergarten are of the utmost importance in influencing learning for later life, in 2009 President Barack Obama established the Presidential Early Learning Council. Through the *Early Childhood Initiative,* the Obama Administration supports comprehensive services and education for children, ages birth to 5 years. Together, the U.S. Department of Education and the U.S. Department of Health and Human Services are working "to ensure that our children have a strong foundation in both the educational and the social-emotional domains that provide children with the preparation they need to enter kindergarten ready for success" (U.S. Department of Education, 2010). Today, educational services, such as high-quality language, literacy, and prereading activities, are offered to low-income families, prisons that house women and children, and migrants. Also, childhood education, adult education, parenting education, and literacy programs are becoming integrated. The goal is "family literacy" programs that service both parents and children.

Because the early childhood years are so important for laying the foundation for later development, and because parenting today is so complex, careful, well-planned programs that support and enhance parents' roles are essential.

Summary

No doubt parents face many responsibilities and challenges in providing the best possible environment for their children: Parenting infants, toddlers, and preschool children is a challenging task! During the first 6 years of life, a child evolves from a "helpless" infant to a curious toddler, to an intrusive preschooler who seems to have boundless energy. It is undeniable that parents are the most influential people in the lives of these children, and early parental influences are felt for many years to come.

In this chapter, we have come to better understand the processes by which infants acquire trust, attachment, and reciprocity, all crucial elements for their present and later social, emotional, and cognitive development. Infants, toddlers, and preschoolers—active participants in their environments—best experience all of their early learning if they have parents or caregivers who are warm, responsive protectors and nurturers. With this foundation firmly in place, children move on to middle childhood where they master the skills they first acquired in the first 6 years of their lives.

References

Administration for Children and Families. (2008). *Head Start FACES: 2003: Recent trends in program performance. Fifth Progress Report.* Washington, DC: U.S. Department of Health and Human Services.

Ainsworth, M. D. S., Blehar, M. C., Waters, E., & Wall, S. (1978). *Patterns of attachment: A psychological study of the strange situation.* Hillsdale, NJ: Erlbaum.

Amato, R. P., & Fowler, F. (2002). Parenting practices, child adjustment, and family diversity. *Journal of Marriage and Family, 64*(3), 703–716.

Baumrind, D. (1991). The influence of parenting style on adolescent competence and substance use. *Journal of Early Adolescence, 11*(1), 56–95.

Baumrind, D. (1996). The discipline controversy revisited. *Family Relations, 45,* 405–414.

Baxter, J., Hewitt, B., & Haynes, M. (2008). Life course transitions and housework: Marriage, parenthood, and time on housework. *Journal of Marriage and Family, 70,* 259–272.

Bell, S. M., & Ainsworth, M. D. (1979). Infant crying and maternal responsiveness. *Child Development, 43,* 1171–1190.

Belsky, J., Grossmann, K., Grossmann, K., & Scheuerer-Englisch, H. (1996). Continuity in parent–child relationships from infancy to middle childhood and relations with friendship competence. *Child Development, 67,* 1437–1454.

Belsky, J., Woodworth, S., & Crnic, K. (1996). Trouble in the second year: Three questions about family interaction. *Child Development, 67,* 556–578.

Bianchi, S. M. (2000). Maternal employment and time with children: Dramatic change or surprising continuity? *Demography, 37,* 401–414.

Blake, F. G. (1954). *The child, his parents and the nurse.* Philadelphia: Lippincott.

Bowlby, J. (1980). *Attachment and loss: Attachment* (Vols. 1–3). New York: Basic Books.

Bowlby, J. (1988). *A secure base.* London: Routledge.

Boyd, D., & Bee, H. (2009). *Lifespan development* (5th ed.). Boston: Allyn & Bacon.

Brazelton, T. B., Koslowski, B., & Main, M. (1974). The origins of reciprocity: The early mother–infant interaction. In M. Lewis & L. Rosenblum (Eds.), *The effect of the infant on its caregiver* (pp. 49–76). New York: Wiley.

Broman, C. L., Reckase, M. D., & Freedman-Doan, C. R. (2006). The role of parenting in drug use among black, Latino, and white adolescents. *Journal of Ethnicity in Substance Use, 5*(1), 39–50.

Brooks-Gunn, J., & Markman, L. B. (2005). The contribution of parenting to ethnic and racial gaps in school readiness. *Future of Children, 15*(1), 139–168.

Carter, B., & McGoldrick, M. (1999). *The expanded family life cycle: Individual, family, and social perspectives* (3rd ed.). Boston: Allyn & Bacon.

Cassidy, C. M., & Conroy, D. E. (2006). Children's self-esteem related to school- and sport-specific perceptions of self and others. *Journal of Sport Behavior, 29*(1), 3–26.

Cebalo, R., Chao, R. K., Hill, N. E., Le, H., Murry, V. M., Pinderhughes, E. E. (2008). Excavating culture: Summary of results. *Applied Developmental Science, 12*(4), 220–226.

Cheah, C. S. L, & Rubin, K. H. (2004). Comparison of European American and mainland Chinese mothers' responses to aggression and social withdrawal in preschoolers. *International Journal of Behavioral Development, 28,* 83–94.

Chen, A., & Kaplan, H. B. (2001). Intergenerational transmission of constructive parenting. *Journal of Marriage and Family, 63*(1), 17–31.

Cohen, T. F. (1993). What do fathers provide? Reconsidering the economic and nurturant dimensions of men as parents. In J. C. Hood (Ed.), *Men, work, and family* (pp. 1–22). Newbury Park, CA: Sage.

Connell, C. M., & Prinz, R. J. (2002). The impact of childcare and parent–child interactions on school readiness and social skill development for low-income African American children. *Journal of School Psychology, 40*(2), 177–193.

Day, R., Peteron, G., & McCracken, C. (1998). Predicting spanking of younger and older children by mothers and fathers. *Journal of Marriage and the Family, 60,* 79–94.

DeWolff, M., & van Ijzendoorn, M. (1997). Sensitivity and attachment: A meta-analysis on parental antecedents of infant attachment. *Child Development, 68*(4), 571–591.

Dinkmeyer, D., McKay, G., & Dinkmeyer, D. (1997). *The parents' handbook* (A part of the complete STEP Program). Circle Pines, MN: American Guidance Service.

Dreikurs, R., & Grey, I. (1968). *A new approach to discipline: Logical consequences.* New York: Hawthorne.

Durbin, M., DiClemente, R., Siegel, D., Krasnovsky, F., Lazarus, N., & Camacho, T. (1993). Factors associated with multiple sex partners among junior high school students. *Journal of Adolescent Health Care, 14,* 202–207.

Eiden, R., Teti, D., & Corns, K. (1995). Maternal working models of attachment, marital adjustment, and the parent–child relationship. *Child Development, 66,* 1504–1518.

Erikson, E. H. (1963). *Childhood and society* (2nd ed.). New York: Norton.

Fox, N. (1995). Of the way we were: Adult memories about attachment experiences and their role in determining infant–parent relationships: A commentary on Ijzendoorn (1995). *Psychological Bulletin, 117*(3), 404–410.

Giles-Sims, J., Straus, M., & Sugarman, D. (1995). Child, maternal, and family characteristics associated with spanking. *Family Relations, 44,* 170–176.

Gomby, D., Larson, C., Lewit, E., & Behrman, R. (1993). Home visiting: Analysis and recommendations. *Future of Children: Home Visiting, 3*(3), 6–22.

Green, J., Gustafson, G., & McGhie, A. (1998). Changes in infants' cries as a function of time in a cry bout. *Child Development, 69*(2), 271–279.

Grogan-Kaylor, A. (2005). Corporal punishment and the growth trajectory of children's antisocial behavior. *Child Maltreatment, 10,* 283–292.

Gross, D., & Tucker, S. (1994). Parenting confidence during toddlerhood: A comparison of mothers and fathers. *Nurse Practitioner, 19*(10), 25–34.

Harvard Family Research Project. (2006). *Family involvement makes a difference in school success.* Retrieved August 2, 2009, from http://www.hfrp.org.

Isabella, R., & Belsky, J. (1991). Interactional synchrony and the origins of infant–mother attachment: A replication study. *Child Development, 62*(2), 373–384.

Jackson, C. Henriksen, L., & Foshee, V. A. (1998). The authoritative parenting index: Predicting health risk behaviors among children and adolescents. *Health Education Behavior, 25*(3), 319–337.

Kim, J. E., Hetherington, E. M., & Reiss, D. (1999). Associations among family relationships, antisocial peers, and adolescents' externalizing behaviors: Gender and family type differences. *Child Development, 70,* 1209–1230.

Klaus, M. H., Kennell, J. H., & Klaus, P. H. (1995). *Bonding: Building the foundations of secure attachment and independence.* Boston: Addison-Wesley.

Lamb-Parker, F., Boak, A. Y., Griffin, K. W., Ripple, C., & Peay, L. (1999). Parent–child relationship, home learning environment, and school readiness. *School Psychology Review, 28,* 413–425.

Lansford, J. E., Deater-Deckard, K., Dodge, K. A., Bates, J. E., & Pettit, G. S. (2004). Ethnic differences in the link between physical discipline and alter adolescent externalizing behaviors. *Journal of Child Psychology and Psychiatry, 45,* 801–812.

Lutz, K. F., Anderson, L. S., Riesch, S. K., Pridham, K. A., & Becker, P. T. (2009). Furthering the understanding of parent–child relationships: A nursing scholarship review series. Part 2: Grasping the early parenting experience, the insider view. *Journal for Specialists in Pediatric Nursing, 14*(4), 262–283.

McBride, B. A., & Mills, G. (1993). A comparison of mother and father involvement with their preschool age children. *Early Childhood Research Quarterly, 8,* 457–477.

McClun, L. A., & Merrell, K. W. (1998). Relationship of perceived parenting styles, locus of control orientation, and self-concept among junior high age students. *Psychology in the Schools, 35*(4), 381–390.

McKim, M. (1987). Transition to what? New parents' problems in the first year. *Family Relations, 36,* 22–25.

McLeod, J. D., & Nonnemaker, J. M. (2000). Poverty and child emotional and behavioral problems: Racial/ethnic differences in processes and effects. *Journal of Health and Social Behavior, 41,* 137–161.

Milkie, M. A., Bianchi, S. M., Mattingly, M. J., & Robinson, J. P. (2002, July). Gendered division of childrearing: Ideals, realities, and the relationship to parent well-being. *Sex Roles: A Journal of Research,* pp. 31–39.

Nash, M. (1997, February, 3). Fertile minds. *Time,* pp. 49–56.

Parks, P., & Smeriglio, V. (1986). Relationships among parenting knowledge, quality of stimulation in the home, and infant development. *Family Relations, 35,* 411–416.

Pederson, D., & Morgan, G. (1996). Expressions of the attachment relationship outside of the Strange Situation. *Child Development, 67,* 915–927.

Piaget, J. (1952). *The origins of intelligence in children* (M. Cook, Trans). New York:

Pittman, L. D., & Chase-Lansdale, P. L. (2001). African American adolescent girls in impoverished communities: Parenting style and adolescent outcomes. *Journal of Research on Adolescence, 11,* 199–224.

Pleck, J. H. (1997). Paternal involvement: Levels, sources, and consequences. In M. E. Lamb (Ed.), *The role of the father in child development* (pp. 66–103). New York: Wiley.

Radziszewska, B., Richardson, J. L., Dent, C. W., & Flay, B. R. (1996). Parenting style and adolescent depressive symptoms, smoking, and academic achievement: Ethnic, gender, and SES differences. *Journal of Behavioral Medicine, 19,* 289–305.

Roche, K. M., Ensminger, M. E., & Cherlin, A. J. (2007). Variations in parenting and adolescent outcomes among African American and Latino families living in low-income, urban areas. *Journal of Family Issues, 28*(7), 882–909.

Samaniego, R. Y., & Gonzales, N. A. (1999). Multiple mediators of the effects of acculturation status on delinquency for Mexican American adolescents. *American Journal of community Psychology, 27,* 189–210.

Shucksmith, J., Leo, B., Hendry, L. B., & Glendinning, A. (1995). Models of parenting: Implications for adolescent well-being within different types of family contexts. *Journal of Adolescence, 18,* 253–270.

Steele, H., Steele, M., & Fonagy, P. (1996). Associations among classifications of mothers, fathers, and their infants. *Child Development, 67,* 541–555.

Steinberg, L., Lamborn, S. D., Darling, N., Mounts, N. S., & Dornbusch, S. M. (1994). Over-time changes in adjustment and competence among adolescents from authoritative, authoritarian, indulgent, and neglectful families. *Child Development, 65,* 754–770.

Steinberg, L., & Morris, A. S. (2001). Adolescent development. *Annual Review of Psychology, 52,* 83–110.

Steinberg, L., Mounts, N., Lamborn, S., & Dornbusch, S. (1991). Authoritative parenting and adolescent adjustment across various ecological niches. *Journal of Research on Adolescence, 1,* 19–36.

Taffel, R. (1994). *Why parents disagree: How men and women parent differently and how we can work together.* New York: Morrow.

Thomas, A., & Chess, S. (1977). *Temperament and development.* New York: Brunner/Mazel.

U.S. Department of Education. (2010). *Prepare my child for school: Early childhood education.* Retrieved April 11, 2010, from www.ed.gov/parents/earlychild/ready/resources.html.

U.S. Department of Health and Human Services. (2003). *Building futures: Head Start Impact Study.* Washington, DC: Author.

van Ijzendoorn, M. H., & Bakermans-Kranenburgy, M. J. (2003). Attachment disorders and disorganized attachment: Similar and different. *Attachment and Human Development, 5,* 313–320.

Chapter 3

The Changing Nature of Parenting: Middle Childhood and Adolescence

The interaction patterns established during the early years continue to influence children as they grow and develop throughout middle childhood and adolescence. Previously the child was in a situation of total physical and psychological dependency, now the school and adolescent years are marked by critical developmental periods during which the child becomes increasingly self-sufficient and independent.

In this chapter we explore parents' shifting roles as their children become more autonomous throughout middle childhood, preadolescence, and adolescence. We also examine some psychosocial developmental milestones, such as the development of industry and an identity separate from that of the parents', and the formation of peer groups. We then turn our attention to contemporary issues adolescents face today, including adolescent sex, teen pregnancy, sexually transmitted infections, substance use, and bullying. We conclude our study by examining parenting programs.

PARENTS AND SCHOOL-AGE CHILDREN: PARENTS ARE ENCOURAGERS

As a child develops from infant to toddler to preschooler to school age, the parent's role changes from protector to nurturer, and finally, to encourager. With growing competencies and an emerging sense of individuality, the child gradually decreases conformity to parents and increases conformity to peers. In this section, we first look at the importance of parenting styles in middle childhood. We then examine how parenting styles affect a child's school performance and sense of industry. Finally, we discuss children's increasing dependence upon their peers, and the significance of these relationships in lifespan development.

Parents continue to serve as strong models and reinforcing agents for their children's behaviors, but the range of behaviors and attitudes to which children are exposed on entering school becomes far greater. Parents may find themselves applying different consequences for behavior simply because they are either more effective or more suited to the child's developmental level. For example, withholding privileges becomes a common technique for achieving desired behavior for many parents, whereas isolation for undesirable behavior may become less common. Reasoning and explanation may be used more frequently simply because the parent believes the child of school age is more capable of responding to such techniques than the toddler or the preschooler.

Childrearing Practices

There are three major categories of childrearing practices, which are presented in Table 3.1; each parenting style has certain effects on children (Hoffman, 1970). These practices are still cited in contemporary discussions of parenting styles, and seem especially applicable to school-age children.

As you can see, both power-assertion and love-withdrawal techniques are punitive in nature. Furthermore, power assertion is not associated with positive conscience development, whereas induction, at least for mothers and children, shows a positive relationship with conscience development. Parents who use love-withdrawal techniques likely produce more anxious children who are more susceptible to adult influence than other children are.

Other research found that parents' use of inductive, as opposed to power-assertive, discipline is related to children's prosocial behavior (Krevans & Gibbs, 1998). Children of inductive parents are more empathic, and more empathic children are more prosocial. The one component of inductive discipline that is most strongly related to children's prosocial behavior is the expression of disappointment. Only for those children who scored high on empathy does guilt predict prosocial behavior. Girls are found to be more empathic and more prosocial than boys.

TABLE 3.1 Types of childrearing practices.

POWER ASSERTION

Attempts to control children by exercising power of a superior nature, either physical or control of resources (spanking, deprivation of privileges/objects, grounding, withholding meals, or threats of punishment)

LOVE WITHDRAWAL

Direct expression of anger and/or disapproval without use of power; love is conditional on child's behavior

INDUCTION

Provision of reasons or explanations to describe desirable behavior; emphasis of impact of behavior on self and others

Source: Based on Hoffman, M. L. (1970). Moral development. In P. Mussen (Ed.), *Carmichael's manual of child psychology* (Vol. 2, 3d ed.). New York: Wiley.

All parents, however, do not use inductive techniques, even when their children are school age. For example, in their investigation about spanking as a discipline strategy, the researchers found that spanking is a common occurrence in families (Day, Peterson, & McCracken, 1998). The researchers also found that:

- Boys are spanked more frequently than girls, and mothers spank more frequently than fathers.
- Children older than age 7 are spanked less frequently than younger children.
- Black mothers, but not black fathers, tend to spank more frequently than white mothers.
- Parents who view the child as competent and not difficult spank less.

Furthermore, certain parental attributes (such as poor mental health, lower educational level, older age, and conservative religious orientation) predicted greater use of spanking. Usually, as parents acquire greater experience in childrearing, they are more likely to demonstrate alternative forms of firm control, such as reasoning or the deprivation of privileges, which diminish the need for spanking as a disciplinary style. These researchers estimate that 2 to 5 percent of parents use harsh physical punishment even when the child gets older, and these are the parents who should be targeted for intervention.

School Adjustment

It appears that parenting styles and practices during middle childhood have far-reaching impacts on children's school experiences. For example, one study of 585 parent/children pairs sought to determine the impact of supportive parenting on children's school adjustment over a 7-year period; children and parents were assessed when the children were 5 years old, when they were in kindergarten, and in every grade thereafter through grade 6 (Pettit, Bates, & Dodge, 1997). Parental proactive teaching, calm discussion in disciplinary encounters, warmth, and interest and involvement in the child's peer activities are parenting aspects that predict children's behavioral, social, and academic adjustment in both kindergarten and grade 6. Each kindergarten adjustment outcome is associated with multiple supportive parenting variables, which then predict changes in children's academic performance from kindergarten to grade 6. These predictive relationships suggest that early positive and supportive parenting qualities might play a distinct role in promoting children's school adjustment.

In this study, supportive parenting also appears to buffer some of the developmental risks associated with early family adversity.

Supportive parenting is most strongly related to child adjustment in grade 6 for those children who had been reared in single-parent and/or low-socioeconomic-status families in their early years. This finding suggests that supportive parenting may serve as a protective factor against the risks associated with certain types of family adversity.

Parenting style also relates to school adjustment, academic achievement, and self-concepts. Using family reports and observations over a 3-year period, researchers examined family factors relating to children's adjustment during the middle-school years (Bronstein et al., 1996). Children and parents were assessed when the children were in the fifth, sixth, and seventh grades. Results showed that supportive and aware parenting, characterized by affection, approval, attentiveness, responsiveness, guidance, and receptivity to emotions, is associated with fifth-grade girls' and boys' more positive self-concept, higher academic achievement, and greater popularity with their peers, as well as with lower incidence of psychological and behavioral problems in the following year. In addition, the relationship between the positive parenting measures and adjustment outcomes appear to be stable over time; that is, parenting a first grader similarly correlates with the same adjustment measures obtained in the seventh grade.

As predicted, more problematic parental behaviors also are associated with negative adjustment outcomes. Parenting practices are related to eventual improvements in girls' and boys' adjustment over the transition to middle school, including better academic performance, decreased incidence of psychological and behavior problems, and increased peer popularity. Aware parenting is particularly salient for boys, in that it appears to be associated with decreased externalizing behavior, whereas for girls, it appears to serve as a buffer against a decline in self-esteem. Problematic parenting behaviors tend to be associated with negative changes in adjustment over time for both boys and girls.

Attachment and Middle Childhood

Secure attachment to parents, established during infancy, seems to have long-term effects on children's behavior. One body of research examined school-age attachment, mother-child interaction, and maternal self-reports in explaining teacher-reported behavior problems; participants were 121 children (ages 5 to 7) and their mothers (Moss, Rousseau, Parent, St. Laurent, & Saintonge, 1998). Results suggest that school-age attachment significantly predicts teacher-reported behavior problems at the transition to school and 2 years later. When compared with the secure group, insecure-attachment groups are more likely to manifest behavior problems. Insecure controlling/other and younger ambivalent children are more likely to demonstrate higher levels of externalizing and other problem behaviors. Additionally, these researchers found that problem behaviors during the early years continue into the school years. The findings support previous studies of associations between disorganization and behavior problems.

Another study tested several hypotheses relating children's attachment security during the preschool years to their perceptions of emotional support from their mothers and best friends, and to socioemotional adaptation during middle childhood (Booth, Rubin, & Rose-Krasnor, 1998). Results indicate that attachment security is related to the children's ranking of their mothers as sources of support relative to other members of the support network. Children who are securely attached in the preschool years (i.e., who experience their mothers as a supportive presence) are likely, in middle childhood, to view their mothers as important sources of emotional support. Insecurely attached girls are more likely to turn to sources of support outside their immediate families than were girls who are securely attached.

Parenting style during middle childhood is necessary for children's healthy development and adjustment. Promoting mutual respect while gradually encouraging greater independence and self-discipline are important goals at this time because school-age children enter Erikson's fourth stage of psychosocial development.

MIDDLE CHILDHOOD: DEVELOPING INDUSTRY AND MASTERING FRIENDSHIPS

The elementary school years present a tremendous opportunity for social and emotional growth. The school-age child shows unceasing energy toward investing all possible efforts in producing. She works incessantly on expanding bodily, muscular, and perceptive skills as well as on expanding knowledge of the world around her. Questions such as, "How is this made?" "How does this work?" "Why do things work the way they do?" dominate a child's days. With a sense that she can accomplish anything and everything, the child feels a strong need for accomplishment and wards off failure at almost any cost. The child's peers become far more significant to her, and she tries to relate to and communicate with them. Acceptance by peers is critical for a child's ego development.

"Will You Be My Best Friend?": Friendships and Chumships

For children in about first grade through sixth grade, the initiation and formation of peer groups increases, as does the significance of these relationships to the child's developing sense of self. As children move through elementary school, more and more of their time is spent interacting with same-sex peers. Be it a whispered secret during recess or a quick pickup game of basketball after school, childhood friendships provide children great companionship and an opportunity to disclose their innermost secrets, wishes, and fears. In addition, childhood peer relationships afford children a "safety net" of sorts that allows them to practice and rehearse their new relational roles.

The formation of peer groups is a multistep process. An academic who studied the formation of friendships, D. C. Dunphy (1963), in a classic study examined adolescent friendship development in urban areas. The earlier stages of friendship development described by Dunphy are found during the school years:

Childhood chumships play a key role in a child's developing sense of self and ego development.

- **Stage One: Pre-Crowd Stage.** From about kindergarten through fifth grade, during this stage of friendship development, isolated unisex peer groups exist in the form of *cliques,* small groups of four to nine members. Spontaneous, shared activities provide the opportunity to relate personally. Boys tend to join larger groups and enjoy doing activities together, while girls tend to join smaller, more intimate groups. These peer group types dominate the school years. It is not uncommon to see these types of peer groups on a school playground, where boys are excluding girls from their pickup football game at recess, or where girls forbid boys to listen in on their "girl talk." Members are attracted to one another on the basis of similar interests, neighborhoods, schools, or religions. Boys' groups are often larger and more stable than girls' groups (Atwater, 1992).
- **Stage Two: The Beginning of the Crowd.** Still same-sex in nature, peer groups toward the end of sixth grade/beginning of seventh grade begin to shift to *crowds,* which consist of ten or more members. Crowds are essentially a collection of cliques—membership in cliques is required to belong to the crowd (Atwater, 1992). Crowd activities such as after-school dances and sporting events provide preadolescents the chance to "practice" interacting with the opposite sex, alleviating the uneasiness that often comes with opposite-sex relationships. For instance, Kateland may have a crush on Danny, yet she flirts with all of the other boys in her friendship crowd. In this way, she practices her newfound intimacy skills on others, without the risk of being rejected by Danny if she flirts with only him.
- **Stage Three: The Crowd in Transition.** During the end of junior high (eighth or ninth grade) and throughout high school, peer groups are seen as in transition. During this time, smaller cliques are formed within the larger crowd. The pairing off of male and female couples, typically seen sooner in early maturing boys and girls, drives the crowd into transition. While the crowd may still hang out together for certain events, such as going to a movie or to a school basketball game, they more frequently begin to prefer to interact with the smaller group of friends, and begin to exclude others from the emerging smaller clique.
- **Stage Four: The Fully Developed Crowd.** The fully developed crowd is composed entirely of opposite-sex cliques; no longer are the same-sex friendship affiliations dominant as they were throughout elementary school and the early years of junior high. Stage four peer groups exist only long enough for members to learn or to be socialized into those characteristics needed for adult relationships, such as sharing intimate thoughts and feelings, and interdependence.
- **Stage Five: Crowd Disintegration.** As adolescents mature into adulthood and take on adult responsibilities, such as a job or pursing a college degree, and as they become involved in serious intimate relationships, crowd-type friendship groups begin to disintegrate. Often the support of friends is replaced by an intimate partner with whom young adults now share and disclose, and with whom they are perhaps sexually involved. Friendship groups consequently become more loosely associated. Over time, many find their spouse or life mate to be their "best" friend, though they still hold on to one or two close friends.

Other researchers have since found peer group formation to be similar to Dunphy's original 1960s study of peer group formation (Atwater, 1992; Paul & White, 1990).

What is it that makes friendship so special or so different from other kinds of relationships in our lives? Recent research has shown that friendships, unlike family relationships, provide us more feelings of freedom, closeness, and pleasure; we are also able to experience higher levels of self-disclosure with our friends than we do with our families (Mendelson & Kay, 2003; Rybak & McAndrew, 2006). Also, friendships are often quite emotionally rewarding, because the sharing that takes place between friends fosters the growth and development of empathy. **Empathy** is the capacity to understand another's circumstances or situation, and the ability to feel or express emotional concern for another person. It is believed that the experiences of empathy are what lead to a greater sensitivity—and emotional bond—to each other, both in friendships and in any other intimate relationship (Rybak & McAndrew, 2006).

As you can see from Dunphy's study, as children grow through childhood and enter adolescence, their dependence on their parents for intimacy lessens and they turn to "chumships" for support. It is also interesting to note how the changes in friendships are associated with life transitions. Some researchers have discovered that maintaining and adapting friendships throughout these life changes help buffer the stress associated with major transitions, such as going away to college or getting married (Brooks, 2002; Oswald & Clark, 2003). It is important to understand these developmental changes in peer group structures and the significance of friendships, because each type of friendship group (intimate relationships) throughout life affect a person's psychosocial development in all subsequent stages of life. During childhood, intimate friendships contribute to the child's establishment of industry.

Developing a Sense of Industry

At about the age of 6, children enter the fourth stage of Erikson's (1963) theory of psychosocial development, **industry versus inferiority.** This stage ends at about age 11.

The child's feeling of competence at this stage is the belief that he or she is capable and able to do meaningful tasks. It includes taking on projects and tasks because of a basic interest in doing them, and in working to complete them to achieve satisfaction (a sense of industry) from the results. When the child's use of his expanding skills and competencies meets with success, when he receives support and approval from parents, peers, and teachers, then he develops a sense of **industry.**

On the other hand, there is a pull toward an earlier level of lesser production. As a child, he has fears of **inferiority**—a persistent sense of inadequacy or a feeling that he is of lower status than others. Because of this inferiority, he tries to overcome by diligently engaging in opportunities to learn by doing. If there are repeated experiences of failure and disapproval, feelings of inferiority dominate.

Since children strive to accomplish a sense of industry, they are work-oriented. Attention should be given, both at home and at school, to the establishment of positive work habits. Erikson believed that many of the attitudes toward work and work habits that are exhibited later in life are formed during this developmental period. It is therefore important that both parents and teachers provide many opportunities for the child to succeed at a variety of work experiences. In doing so, they also further the formation of their children's healthy self-concepts.

Building a Healthy Self-Concept

There are three basic dimensions of self-concept: a *sense of belonging* (the individual perceives himself as part of a group and is accepted and valued by the other members of that group); a *sense of worth* (the individual perceives himself as a "good" or worthy person); and a *sense of competence* (the individual perceives that he is successful at doing things well). Parenting style and the quality of interactions between parents and children are significantly related to the child's development of a healthy self-concept.

There has been much discussion concerning the relationship between children's self-concept and academic achievement. Parental attitudes and behaviors—as well as the quality of the parent-child relationship—begin early to have a strong impact on how the child views herself. The school-age child's sense of self is very much a reflection of the success of her interactions with others, especially her parents. For example, there is ample evidence to suggest that positive self-concept is related to high academic achievement during the school-age years (Chapman, Lambourne, & Silva, 1990). On the other hand, low self-concept and low academic achievement interact and negatively feed back on each other. Since parental acceptance and support seem to be relevant factors in the child's self-concept, this dimension of parent behavior should be related to the child's academic performance.

In the view of himself, a child plays a role, too. Children behave in ways consistent with the ways they see themselves. If a child feels he is worthless, he will expect others to treat him as worthless. Since children cannot be viewed as simply mirror images of external events but as active, striving, learning individuals, self-esteem represents the child's unique organization of his own genetic makeup, the evaluations made of him by significant adults, and the feedback he receives from his world. There seems to be a downward trend in self-concept as children enter school because of the increased sources of evaluations by teachers and peers, but by fifth grade the trend climbs upward. Because the school-age child is more independent and increasingly in charge of himself, more and more evaluations of behavior are self-evaluation, and a larger percentage of his rewards are self-rewards. It seems important, then, for parents to help children identify their strengths and reward themselves for those while minimizing negative evaluations of weaknesses.

To this end, researchers examined the direct and indirect associations among general family relationships, school-focused parent–child interactions, child personal characteristics, and school adjustment with 161 fourth- and seventh-grade children, their parents, and teachers (Ketsetzis, Ryan, & Adams, 1998). Results indicate that child characteristics (exclusive of self-esteem) are directly associated with school adjustment. However, a variety of parent–child interaction factors and family-life factors also are found to predict adjustment indirectly. Overall, parental pressure decreases self-esteem, but parental support increases it.

The researchers concluded that excessive parental pressure for school success is associated with decreased levels of children's self-esteem, frustration tolerance, and intellectual effectiveness. Another study confirmed that parental support enhances children's self-esteem (Franco & Levitt, 1998). These researchers further found that parental support contributes indirectly to the quality of the child's best friendship, which, in turn, contributes further to self-esteem.

The role of the parent in developing a healthy self-concept in the child during middle childhood, just as in infancy and early childhood, remains crucial. Even though the child has a structured learning environment in school, the home continues to be an important learning laboratory.

Providing Learning Experiences

With a growing sense of industry, children work to expand both their body skills and their perceptual skills. The role that parents play in structuring the home environment to permit these capacities to develop and in assisting and encouraging the child to pursue relevant out-of-home, out-of-school activities is extremely important.

The significance of play during middle childhood cannot be overemphasized, since it provides the child with situations in which he or she can test him- or herself, work out feelings, experiment with roles, learn rules and expectations, and develop and practice skills that will be important for adult life in society. Many of these goals are achieved by play involving peers or by team efforts.

OUT-OF-HOME LEARNING EXPERIENCES Aside from peer-group interaction within the normal course of a school day, children have an opportunity to achieve group status as well as to broaden their scope of learning through organized out-of-home activities, such as sports, music or dance, scouting troops, and church activities.

Clearly there are both advantages and disadvantages to children being involved with such activities. The advantages are relatively obvious, as they allow children to:

- Associate and identify with unrelated adults who are important socializing agents for them.
- Extend their peer interactions beyond the classroom, making friendships with others from a variety of cultural backgrounds.
- Spend time with other children who share their interests.
- Develop and practice their growing bodily and perceptual skills within the context of a group setting.
- Learn to play by rules and how to be good winners and good losers.

The disadvantages may not be quite so obvious to parents. First, many parents fall into the "more is better" trap or the "my child is busier than your child" syndrome when planning for the child's out-of-home activities. In their desire to develop well-rounded children, some parents over-enroll their children in activities, so that there is little time left for meaningful interaction or for children to pursue other interests.

The second major disadvantage is that parents may actually coerce children to be involved in an activity simply because the parents themselves enjoy it. A typical example is the athletic father who almost literally forces his son into sports. When children are not genuinely interested in an activity, the activity will not provide effective learning experiences for them. Finally, the competitive aspect of organized sports may overshadow their inherent learning potential. Parents need to examine the competitive aspects of such organized groups and identify the potential for positive development that accompanies them.

IN-HOME LEARNING ACTIVITIES Two types of family activities that provide valuable learning experiences for school-age children are those that are planned and organized (such as camping or going to a museum) and those that are unplanned or spontaneous (going on a picnic, kicking a soccer ball in the yard, reading together). Activities give families opportunities to share common interests, to be together away from a usually hectic home schedule, and to share new experiences.

Parents who make arrangements for their children to be involved in an array of enriching social and cultural experiences during the elementary years have children who perform better on achievement tests and who are rated as more task-oriented and better adjusted by their teachers. In addition, parental involvement with children is consistently related to child competence throughout the child's development.

Issues that commonly divide parents and their school-age children are television viewing and playing video games—when, how often, and what kind. Clearly how these activities influence children is an issue that has attracted much attention in recent years. For example, studies have indicated that the effects of television watching are evident in children's play and fantasy behavior as well as in everyday behavior and personal interactions. However, mediating factors such as personality characteristics, IQ, and social class begin to interact with television viewing during the preschool period and continue to do so into school age. Although some of the child's behaviors that appear to be related to television are negative—that is, aggression or sex-role stereotypes or standards—others may be positive, such as indicating greater knowledge of public affairs and current events. Common sense dictates that video games be monitored (for content) and regulated (for frequency) by parents. Whatever rules parents make about television watching and video games should be reasonable and enforceable.

The school-age years continue to be an important stage during which learning experiences outside the school play a crucial role in the child's development. Parents enhance learning by creating a home environment that is conducive to learning, by helping the child select extracurricular activities that promote overall adjustment and development, and by helping the child achieve a mix of peer and family activities that is acceptable to both parents and children.

'TWEENS: SPECIAL CHALLENGES OF PREADOLESCENCE

Preadolescence is a period of transition between childhood and adolescence, roughly spanning the years between 9 and 13. This transition period is the one about which the least is known. One thing is clear—the role parents play during this period of development is crucial but confusing and sometimes unstable, vacillating between encourager and counselor. Obviously, because peer identification is paramount, preadolescents still need their parents' encouragement to interact with their peers that was so necessary during middle childhood.

Characteristics of Preadolescence

Awkwardness, restlessness, and laziness are common characteristics of preadolescents as a result of rapid and uneven growth. Accompanying behaviors may include excessive criticism, unpredictability, rebellion, and lack of cooperation in the home setting. These on-and-off behaviors may result in rejection of adult standards, and they make the parenting role a difficult one. In addition to encouragement, parents need to understand the physical and emotional changes that are about to come and understand and accept peer-group pressure.

Counseling the child, without undue pressure, in the move toward greater independence and increased responsibility is a role that parents begin to assume and one that will flourish as the child moves into adolescence. Condemnation of the child's choice of friends (inevitably, ones who are rejected by the parents), nagging about keeping appointed meal times and failure to do chores, and "talking down" as one might do to a younger child are nonproductive forms of parental behavior. Warmth, affection, a sense of fairness, and, most of all, a sense of humor and being a good sport are necessary for parents to survive.

Family Experiences and the Preadolescent

Preadolescents appear to be particularly vulnerable to family disruption. Researchers examined aspects of the family experience of white males at age 10 as predictors of police arrest by age 17. They found clear evidence that experiencing a stepfamily or a single-parent family in preadolescence is associated with a substantially higher risk of arrest, even after controlling for other key predictors (Coughlin & Vuchinich, 1996). Children in these families were more than twice as likely to be arrested by age 14 as were children with two biological parents in residence.

But the effects of family problem solving differ markedly across family structure. In stepfamilies, effective problem solving in preadolescence reduces the odds of arrest by about half; in families with two biological parents, there is no significant effect. However, in single-parent families, ineffective problem solving more than doubles the risk of arrest in adolescence. It could be that negative mother–son relationships following divorce create the basis for adolescent problem behavior.

Good parent–child relations and discipline practices have significant protective effects. In the next section, we take a look at the significance of peers during preadolescence.

Exit Parents, Enter Friends

Preadolescence represents a transition from the adult code of the parent to the peer code—a transition from dependence to independence, which will ultimately lead the child at adolescence into identity formation. The group phenomenon, or clique and gang formation, during preadolescence is essential to the child's later functioning as a citizen in society. However, the more the "gang" character is subversive of certain adult standards, the more thoroughly it is enjoyed by the child. In many cases, then, the peer code may be diametrically opposed to the adult code. Some examples include the values of cleanliness, good grades in school, obedience to adults, dress codes and hairstyles, and dirty jokes and/or language. What is labeled "good" or "bad" behavior by parents may be labeled exactly the opposite by peers. Often the peer-group behavior or code is unspoken but nevertheless strongly implied.

The change from adult code to peer code is not an easy process for a child, and it may be accompanied by conflict. Although the preadolescent wants and needs to be admired and respected by his friends, he is still loyal to his family and does not want to be misunderstood by them or make them unhappy. On the other hand, if he pleases his parents and they accept him, he may run the risk of being called a "sissy" or a "coward" by his friends.

Perhaps the most difficult adjustment that parents must make when their children are preadolescents is that of understanding and accepting the child's rejection of adult standards and her loyalty to peers. Although most parents *want* their children to be independent, they wish it could be done less painfully. They wish they could impart the wisdom of experience to their children. Parents may feel guilty because they think that they have failed—otherwise the child would not reject them. The child, in turn, may feel guilty because she does love her parents but cannot bear to lose face with her friends. The resolution of this crisis is an important factor in parent–child relationships at this time. A satisfactory resolution will determine, to some extent, how parents deal with the so-called midlife crisis.

PARENTS AND ADOLESCENTS: PARENTS AS GUIDES, SUPPORTERS, AND MONITORS

Because of the developmental characteristics of adolescents, parents must once again change their roles. Parents struggle with finding the appropriate guidance techniques, yet the effects of past parent–child interactions and childrearing practices carry into adolescence. Parental support appears to be one of the most important characteristics at this stage of development, relating positively to cognitive development, conformity to adult standards, moral behavior, internal locus of control, self-esteem, instrumental competence, and academic achievement. The greater the degree of parental support, the greater the adolescent's social competence (Gecas & Seff, 1991). The converse also seems to be true: Lack of parental support is related to negative socialization outcomes for teenagers, such as low self-esteem, delinquency, deviance, drug abuse, and other problem behaviors. Support includes general sustenance, physical affection, companionship, and sustained contact (Weiss & Schwarz, 1996).

Parenting Styles

The benefits of authoritative parenting that accrue before adolescence continue throughout the teen years. One study examined the relationships of six parenting styles (authoritative, democratic, nondirective, nonauthoritarian-directive, authoritarian-directive, and unengaged) to adolescent behavior in four domains: personality, adjustment, academic achievement, and substance use (Weiss & Schwarz, 1996). Adolescents from authoritative homes appear to receive the most or second-most favorable scores in all areas assessed, but the differences are not statistically significant. Nondirective parenting results in almost as many positive outcomes as authoritative parenting. Unengaged parenting style is associated with the following characteristics: more nonconformity, maladjustment, domination, selfishness, lack of originality, and high consumption of alcohol.

Teens from authoritarian-directive homes are particularly weak in academic aptitude and achievement compared with children from nondirective or authoritative homes. Democratic and nondirective parenting seem to be more effective for daughters than for sons, suggesting that sons may require more rules and limit setting than daughters to reach their full potential.

Another study found that authoritative parents are the most successful in fostering personal and social responsibility in adolescents, without limiting their emerging autonomy (Glasgow, Dornbusch, Troyer, Steinberg, & Ritter, 1997). Adolescents exposed to nonauthoritative parenting styles are less inclined than adolescents with authoritative parents to view their academic achievements as the products of their own capacities and persistence. These students are more apt to emphasize either external causes for high school grades or low ability as the cause of poor grades.

Although authoritative parenting is characterized by a high degree of support and autonomy-granting in particular areas, it also is characterized by a certain amount of control. However, different types of control have different outcomes. Authoritarian or *coercive control*—based on threats, force, or physical punishment—has negative consequences, whereas authoritative or *inductive control* has positive outcomes. Failure to distinguish between these two types of control has resulted in much confusion and inconsistency on the part of parents.

Much of the conflict and stress of parent–adolescent interactions revolves around the issue of control, since teens usually want greater freedom and parents usually seek greater control. Parents have more influence over adolescents when they express a high level of support and exercise inductive control. In fact, by articulating clearly the societal or welfare concerns that complex issues raise, authoritative parents are likely to facilitate adolescents' understanding of the limits or boundaries of their personal restrictions. These parents maintain clear boundaries between moral, conventional, and personal issues, whereas authoritarian parents treat both moral and conventional issues as obligatory and legitimately subject to parental authority (Smetana, 1995).

Some authoritarian parents continue to use corporal punishment with adolescents. One body of research found that parental corporal punishment during adolescence increases the probability of approving violence against one's spouse in adulthood, experiencing depression as an adult, and elevated levels of marital conflict (Straus & Yodanis, 1996). These three factors, in turn, lead to increased risk of physically assaulting one's spouse, regardless of age, socioeconomic status, ethnicity, and whether one had witnessed violence between one's own parents. Also, there is evidence for the continuity in parent–child relationships from adolescence into young adulthood—the history of the parent–child relationship with respect to control and conflict set the stage for either intergenerational solidarity or a lack of solidarity in adulthood (Aquilino, 1997).

Parent–Adolescent Conflict

The degree of parent–adolescent conflict varies from culture to culture and from family to family. Culturally, conflict is greater in periods of rapid social change; familially, conflict is greater when there is a high degree of parental power and authority. Other factors that contribute to conflict include expression of sexuality or the postponement of sexual expression, experimentation with alcohol and drugs, confusion about the adolescent's economic role, increasing independence from the family and yielding to peer pressure, the failure of schools to fulfill the adolescent's needs, pressure to choose a life occupation, and discord between parents and/or dysfunctional parental behavior. More specific differences occur between parents and teenagers in the areas of assuming responsibility, curfews, use of the car, academic performance, tidiness, dress and grooming, choice of friends, and so on.

Parental interest and involvement in the adolescent's activities, but not intrusion, seem crucial in preventing and resolving conflict. Simple attitudes and behaviors, such as the following, facilitate the teenager's perception of parental interest and involvement: knowing the names of the teenager's friends; being interested in where they go and what they do; welcoming friends into the home; participating (when appropriate) in school, athletic and social events; and showing tolerance for contemporary styles of dress, music, and harmless teen activities.

Parents can reduce conflict by being warm, accepting, nurturant, supportive, and autonomy-granting. When conflict does occur between parents and children, many parents try to resolve the conflict by exerting more power or control. Usually, this approach is counterproductive, resulting in more conflict.

A more effective approach for resolving conflict is to engage in joint decision making and to show respect for the opinions of teenagers. Mutual understanding and respect between parents and children, reasonable and consistent rule enforcement, as well as interest and involvement in the teen's activities, will facilitate resolution of minor differences and minimize conflict. Larger issues of morality or ideology may be more difficult to resolve.

Adolescents' Perceptions of Parents

As we emphasized earlier, the teenager's *perceptions* of the parents' attitudes and behaviors are as important as the actual attitudes and behaviors. Several studies have shown that there may be discrepancies between what actually occurs and the teenager's perception, as well as discrepancies between reported perceptions of the parents and reported perceptions of the adolescents.

In general, adolescents tend to perceive lower levels of intimacy and independence, greater differences in characteristics, and slightly higher levels of conflict with their parents than parents themselves perceive, but some evidence shows consistency between parents' and adolescents' perceptions. In one study, both mothers and fathers who perceived themselves as more competent parents had adolescents who reported more competent parenting (warm, accepting, and helpful) (Bogenschneider, Small, & Tsay, 1997). Positive affect by adolescents toward parents is associated with better psychological functioning of adolescents, whereas negative affect is associated with problematic psychological functioning. Another study found that older adolescents tend to have more positive and fewer negative feelings about their mothers than about their fathers (Phares & Renk, 1998).

Several studies indicate that relationships with the father are crucial for the healthy development of both adolescent boys and girls. Boys who receive less than adequate affection from fathers are less secure, less self-confident, and more distant from their fathers. Perceived parental hostility or mistreatment by young adolescents in one study predicted internalizing behaviors for both boys and girls and externalizing behaviors in boys. In fact, the influence of actual parental hostility and adolescent awareness of conflict frequency on psychological distress was entirely mediated by the adolescent's perception that she was being treated in a hostile fashion by her parents (Harold & Conger, 1997). Therefore, adolescents' perceptions of parental behavior and attitudes of both mothers and fathers have direct effects on their own behavior.

The adolescent period of human growth and development is a time of many transitions for the teen. Along with the physical changes that take place during puberty come changes in teens' cognitive capabilities, as well as growth and change in the social and emotional areas. Angela Huebner (2000), a family practitioner and professor of child development, provides a thorough discussion of these psychosocial changes. The following key points highlight her findings.

ESTABLISHING AN IDENTITY, AUTONOMY, AND INTIMACY

In order to experience healthy intimate relationships in later stages of adult development, an individual must first have a strong sense of **identity,** or the sense of "who" he or she is (Erikson, 1963). Adolescent friendships play a key role in the adolescent's social, emotional, and relational development.

The questions "Who am I?" and "Why am I on Earth?" occupy an adolescent's thoughts, and over the course of the adolescent developmental period, teens incorporate their beliefs, values, and opinions of influential others (parents, peers, teachers) into their own identities. At the same time, adolescents begin the process of **individuation**—that is, forming an identity that is separate from that of their family of origin.

This developmental process of individuation affects the development of intimacy, because as teens open up and disclose with their peers, it helps them clarify their own thoughts and emotions, and thus helps them better define their own uniqueness (German, 2002). As teens share with their peers and the significant others in their lives, they develop a deeper understanding of not only themselves, but of others as well. Intimate friendships are more common during adolescence because teens feel that it's safer to reveal their thoughts and feelings to friends rather than to family (Berndt & Savin-Williams, 1990). In essence, teens feel that since others their same age are going through similar experiences, they are better able to relate. The outcome of this process is that as adolescents approach the transition to early adulthood, they have a clearer sense of their values, beliefs, and relationship expectations. This enhanced sense of identity promotes intimacy.

Teens must also develop **autonomy,** which refers to not only establishing a sense of independence, but also becoming a self-governing person within the context of relationships. Adolescents must begin to take responsibility for their actions and decisions that affect themselves and, in many cases, those around them. For instance, if an adolescent chooses to have unprotected sex, he or she must realize that this decision may carry associated risks, such as acquiring a sexually transmitted infection or resulting in an unwanted pregnancy, and that these risks don't just affect them, but their partner and both families as well.

As we have seen, as we develop throughout our early childhood and our school years, our peers become increasingly important to us, and also to the formation of our capacity for intimacy. Perhaps more than at any other time in our life-course development, it is during adolescence that friends are most significant. Through friendships we learn to be open and honest, to self-disclose, to share empathy, and to trust.

Adolescents' Friendships and Romantic Relationships

As we progress through adolescence and approach early adulthood, our friendships move from same-sex group interactions, to mixed-sex interactions to coupling or pairing off, to eventually having only a select, few friends. For example, preadolescents spend about an hour or less per week interacting with the opposite sex, but by the 12th grade, boys spend about 5 hours a week with the other sex; girls spend about 10 hours per week with boys (Richards, Crowe, Larson, & Swarr, 1998).

Romantic relationships also become increasingly important to the lives of adolescents, and they fulfill a number of adolescents' needs (Furman, 2002). For example, while 10th graders rely primarily on close friends for emotional support, by 12th grade romantic partners become a major source of support (Furman & Buhrmester, 1992). Romantic relationships also contribute to a person's identity formation, the development of peer relationships, the transition to adulthood, and the development of sexuality (Furman, 2002). These relationships, however, do not fulfill the same functions that adult romantic relationships do. Although adults, for instance, turn to one another for caregiving and emotional support, adolescents still turn to their peers—not the romantic partner—for such support (Furman, 2002). Although these functions develop over time, the need for affiliation with another and sexual needs are met first in adolescent romantic relationships.

Experiencing Gender Differences in Friendships

How do male friendships differ from female friendships? As you saw from Dunphy's (1963) study, as children mature their peer groups shift in gender preference. As the shifts in gender preference occur, other discrepancies between males and females emerge:

- Females attach more emotional importance to their friends than do males (Lempers & Clark-Lempers, 1993).
- Men are less expressive and supportive toward friends than women are (Bank & Hansford, 2000; Burleson, 2003).
- Men are less likely to turn to their friends in times of trouble than women are (Rubin, 1986).

- Females more strongly emphasize mutual understanding, security, and mutual exploration of interests than do males (Kuttler et al., 1999).
- More so than males, females discuss family problems and activities, dreams, fears, personal problems, and secrets (Johnson & Airies, 1983).
- Males emphasize activity and achievement in their group friendships; they show less interest in reciprocity/mutuality and support/caring than do girls (Thorne, 1986).
- Males discuss sports and hobbies more so than females (Johnson & Aires, 1983).

Researchers believe that the differences found between male and female friendship experiences are due to socialization patterns, or **gender typing** (Johnson & Airies, 1983; Kuttler, LaGreca, & Prinstein, 1999). Male socialization tends to emphasize the establishment and maintenance of achievement, while female socialization tends to emphasize the importance of the establishment and maintenance of interpersonal relationships. Recent empirical study revealed that gender typing affects the type of communication between friends (Basow & Rubenfeld, 2003). For example, women are more likely to try to resolve a problem, offer sympathy, and share a similar story as a response to a friend with a problem, while men are more likely to try to resolve the problem, tell the friend not to worry, or change the subject in a similar circumstance (Basow & Rubenfeld, 2003). There are also gender differences in feelings and emotions in response to being given advice from a friend—women are more likely to feel comforted and grateful when advice is offered by a friend, whereas men are more likely to feel angry and hurt.

Emerging research suggests that there is still much to learn about friendships, particularly in the area of cross-sex friendships. **Cross-sex friendships (CSFs)** are friendships between opposite-sex peers. For many decades, CSFs were viewed by researchers as potential romantic attractions between partners and not as friendships (Bleske-Rechek & Buss, 2000). Today, however, empirical study is beginning to view CSFs as qualitatively different from both romantic relationships and same-sex friendships in four distinct areas: defining the relationship, managing sexual attraction, establishing equality, and managing the interference of other friends and family (i.e., pushing the cross-sex friends to pursue dating) (Lenton & Webber, 2006).

A number of recent studies show us that:

- Men have more CSFs than women do (Reeder, 2003). This may be because men view the friendship as a potential gateway to sexual interaction; it may also be because men are more comfortable sharing their thoughts and feelings with a woman and not a man.
- Men may gain intimacy from their female friends (West, Anderson, & Duck, 1996).
- Women may gain protection from their male friends (Bleske-Rechek & Buss, 2000).
- CSFs may be a mate-acquisition strategy for women (Bleske-Rechek & Buss, 2001).
- Some men and women may use CSF as a way to become exposed to more opposite-sex people, thus increasing their chances of meeting a romantic partner (Monsour, 2002).
- More single people have CSFs than married people (Lenton & Webber, 2006).
- "Feminine" people (both men and women) report having more female than male friends; "masculine" people (both men and women) report having more male friends (Reeder, 2003).

All of these recent findings are interesting because they point to potential societal changes in how and why we select the friends that we do, and to changes in how we select potential mates. Much more study needs to be done to understand the multiple factors associated with CSFs, and to understand the benefits of these relationships to the development of friendships.

Considering the intrinsic diversity within contemporary society, another question remains to be answered: How do cultural differences influence adolescent friendships?

Culture/Ethnicity and Friendship

Despite the fact that the United States is rich in cultural diversity, scant research exists that examines the influences of culture and/or ethnicity on friendship formation.

In a study of the formation of adolescent friendships, researcher Caryn Dolich (2005) examined three cultures in an attempt to determine whether cultural differences affect males' and females' friendships. She compared the differences in aspects of friendship among Moroccan, European, and American adolescents. Dolich found that within all of the cultures, females reported higher ratings of the importance of intimacy and companionship than did males. In addition, she found that among the cultures, females discussed personal and daily events/trivial issues more frequently than males did. Consistent with prior research (such as Johnson & Airies, 1983), females among the three cultures in Dolich's study developed more intimate and personal relationships than males did. However, unlike the results found in previous research, the males in Dolich's study did report that they discuss with some frequency such things as intimacy, family relationships, dating, and sex with opposite-sex friends. Dolich's study did not determine whether culture ultimately influences the experience of friendship during adolescence.

The **contact hypothesis** puts forth the idea that negative stereotypes (prejudices) about other groups exist because of the lack of contact and interaction between racial groups (Allport, 1958). Given that college and university campuses are often the most racially and ethnically diverse environments that most students have experienced, does this mean that the college environment translates into a more diverse friendship network?

Some studies have shown that greater diversity in junior high and high school does foster the development of relationships across racial and ethnic lines, and that intergroup contact leads to improved racial attitudes (Duncan, Boisjoly, Levy, Kremer, & Eccles, 2003; Quillian & Campbell, 2003; Sacerdote & Marmaros, 2005) and lessens negative stereotypes (Pettigrew & Tropp, 2006).

As you can see from our discussion, there are differences in how each gender experiences intimate relationships with others. Cultural and ethnic differences also appear to enrich the adolescent and young adult developmental periods. Within these friendships, adolescents establish their unique identities and intimacy.

ADOLESCENTS AND CONTEMPORARY ISSUES

We commonly tend to identify puberty as the time when sexual maturation occurs, the time when we are "awakened" sexually. Although some children may experience their first heterosexual or homosexual interpersonal attraction around the age of 10 (Harrison, 2003), and though they may begin masturbation as early as the first or second grade (Weinstein & Rosen, 2006), most of us become more aware of our sexuality—and desire to act on these new feelings and sensations—during early adolescence.

As the adolescent experiences changes in cognition and thought processes, his or her *need for intimacy* changes. As they individuate, find their own identities, and are given more freedom, adolescents' *capacities to have intimate and sexual relationships* change. This, too, is seen in the formation and maintenance of peer relationships. And as they undergo the physiological changes associated with puberty, they have a new way in which to *be intimate* with others.

Sexual Behaviors: Experiencing a Wide Range in Attitudes and Behaviors

Young people are engaging in sexual activity—and their attitudes about sexuality and sexual expression are becoming increasingly open-minded. Adolescent sex and sexuality are of great interest to social science researchers and demographers because often the behaviors put adolescents at risk for a number of health concerns, such as unwanted pregnancies, violence, and sexually transmitted diseases (O'Donnell et al., 2006).

There is an encouraging downward trend in the number of students who report having sex before the age of 13. For example, recent research reports that sexual intercourse among preadolescents has declined from about 10 percent in 1991 to about 6 percent in 2007; about 2 percent of sexually active teens had their first sexual intercourse experiences at age 11 (Sexuality Information and Education Council of the United States, 2009). However, youth of color remain at the highest risk for early sexual intercourse. As Figure 3.1 shows us, both blacks and Latinos report having sex before the age of 13 in larger numbers than white preteens do (Sexuality Information and Education Council of the United States, 2009). Teens in the United States have sex at much younger ages than those in other countries do. For example, in Mexico, the average age of virginity loss (first sexual intercourse) is between 17 and 18, and in Asian countries, such as China, Thailand, and Indonesia, young adults do not become sexually active until about the age of 19 or 20 (Durex, 2007).

In 2007, nearly one-half (48 percent) of all teens ages 15 to 19 had ever had sexual intercourse, and about 15 percent had had sex with at least four persons (Centers for Disease Control and Prevention, 2008a). The likelihood of being sexually active increases by about 11 percentage points each year (Centers for Disease Control and Prevention, 2008b):

- 20.1 percent of ninth graders have had sexual intercourse
- 30.6 percent of tenth graders have had sexual intercourse
- 41.8 percent of eleventh graders have had sexual intercourse
- 52.6 percent of twelfth graders have had sexual intercourse

During the teenage years, oral sex is more common than sexual intercourse. Among teenagers, oral sex is common because many teens consider it to be more socially acceptable than vaginal sex (Halpern-Felsher, Cornell, Kropp, & Tschann, 2005; Lindberg, Jones, & Santelli, 2008). The numbers of teens having oral sex appear to support this notion. A nationwide study of 2,271 teens found that more teens had engaged in oral sex than vaginal sex (55 percent vs. 50 percent). Although oral and vaginal sex tend to go hand-in-hand, over one-fourth of virgins reported engaging in oral sex (Lindberg et al., 2008). Generally speaking, white teens tend to engage in oral sex more than Latinos, blacks, and Asians do (Rosenbaum, 2009).

Some researchers believe that the high percentages of teens having oral sex are a result of the increase in the number of teens who are pledging to remain virgins until marriage because

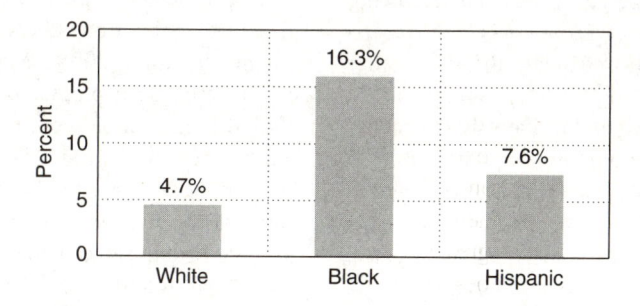

FIGURE 3.1 High school students that had sexual intercourse before age 13.
Age of first sexual experiences vary by race and ethnicity. African American/Black Caribbean and Latinos are at risk for having sexual intercourse before age 13.

Source: Based on data from SIECUS (2009).

they believe it is a "safe" alternative to the dangers associated with intercourse (Bruckner & Bearman, 2005; Halpern-Felsher et al., 2005; Rosenbaum, 2009). In fact, some teens are unaware of *any* health risks associated with oral sex (Halpern-Felsher et al., 2005; Hoff, Greene, & Davis, 2003). They also believe they are still "technically virgins" if they have had oral sex, but not vaginal intercourse. Adolescents also experiment with anal sex. One study showed that approximately 11 percent had engaged in anal sex with someone of the opposite sex (Lindberg et al., 2008).

There is also an increasing trend among preteens and adolescents to engage in recreational—not relational—sex (Wallace, 2007). This casual sex is referred to as **hooking up.** To date, no studies have assessed just how many adolescents engage in hooking up, or the regularity with which it takes place. But as one high schooler noted, "Sex with a friend, sex with a stranger, sex in private, sex in public; it all boils down to just having fun. It's no big deal" (Wallace, 2007). Or is it?

Consequences of Adolescent Sexual Behaviors

While there are obvious consequences of sexual behaviors for any age group, such as acquiring a sexually transmitted infection (STI) or experiencing an unwanted pregnancy, there are other consequences that also affect this age group. In a recent study that wanted to identify the physical, social, and emotional consequences of 275 high schoolers (all about age 14) who engaged in oral and/or vaginal sex for the first time, students reported on a number of items, such as "I got in trouble with my parents after I had sex," "I got a bad reputation," and "I feel bad about myself" (Brady & Halpern-Felsher, 2007). Figures 3.2a and 3.2b show the percentages of adolescents who reported various positive and negative consequences of sexual behavior. General findings of this study include:

- Students believe that oral sex is associated with fewer negative consequences than vaginal sex.
- Students who only had oral sex were less likely to feel guilty or used, having their relationship get worse, and getting in trouble with their parents.
- Girls were twice as likely as boys to report feeling bad about themselves following a sex act, and almost three times as likely to report feeling used.
- Boys were twice as likely to report an increase in their popularity after reporting their sexual activities to friends.

It is clear that there are significant medical and social consequences of adolescent sex, but as this study shows us, teenagers do feel that there are some positive consequences of having sex. These are somewhat concerning findings because experiencing positive outcomes, such as an increase in popularity, may encourage sexual behavior—making it difficult to convince teens (particularly boys) that there is a negative side with potential life-changing outcomes (Brady & Halpern-Felsher, 2007).

Teenage Pregnancy

During the next 12 months, 1 million teenagers will become pregnant and nearly 500,000 will give birth—about one every minute (Alan Guttmacher Institute, 2008). Making up one-fourth of all unintended pregnancies each year in the United States, adolescent birthrates continue to remain higher than similar birthrates in other Western or developed countries. Adolescent birth and abortion rates are twice as high as those found in Great Britain and Canada, and five times higher than those found in Sweden and France (Alan Guttmacher Institute, 2008).

Births to teen moms are linked to a host of critical issues: poverty, overall child health and well-being, births to unmarried women, responsible fatherhood, sexuality and health concerns, education/school failure, child abuse and neglect, and

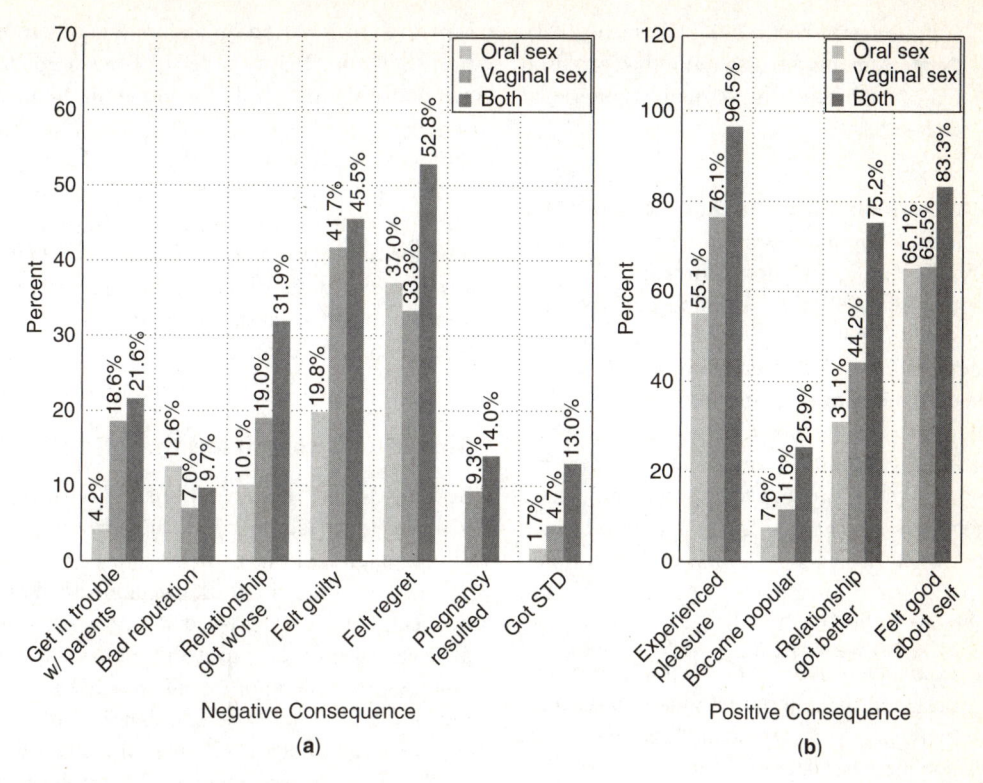

FIGURE 3.2 Consequences of adolescent sexual behaviors.
Source: Based on Brady & Halpern-Felsher (2007).

other risky behaviors, such as drug and alcohol use and abuse and crime (National Campaign to Prevent Teen Pregnancy, 2008). Without question, teen mothers face a range of developmental risks.

IMPACTS OF TEEN PREGNANCY ON THE MOM
Teen parents and their babies start out with many disadvantages. When the head of the family is an adolescent girl, both the teen parent and her child are at increased risk for medical, psychological, developmental, and socioemotional problems.

- *Medical/Psychological.* The medical risks for adolescent mothers and their babies are significant, especially for younger adolescent mothers (10- to 14-year-olds). For example, their risk of dying during labor and birth is two to four times higher for women at age 17 than it is for women who have children in their 20s (Alan Guttmacher Institute, 2004).
- *Developmental.* Research consistently shows that adolescent mothers struggle when trying to form and maintain stable interpersonal relationships and family life (Larson, 2004; Lehrman, 2001; Quinlivan, Tan, Steele, & Balck, 2004). Many of these teen parents continue their dependency on family members rather than shift to more independence and autonomy (Hanson, 1992).
- *Socioeconomic.* About half of all teen moms, and over three-fourths of all unmarried teenage mothers, receive welfare within 5 years of the birth of their first baby; about 80 percent of teen parents eventually depend on welfare for their economic support (Alan

Guttmacher Institute, 2004; Klerman, 2004). Teenage moms are also more likely to drop out of high school than their nonpregnant counterparts.

INTERVENTIONS FOR ADOLESCENT PARENTS
The National Organization on Adolescent Pregnancy, Parenting, and Prevention (2008) notes that given that "all children need healthy, nurturing, stable relationships and to experience the protective factors during early childhood...[and] given the competing dynamics of adolescence and the demand of parenthood, it is incumbent upon families, communities, and society to provide supportive [structures] to teen parents to ensure their children grow healthy and safe and reach school ready to learn." To this end, a national campaign to reduce teen pregnancy should include the following:

- *Comprehensive School-Based Programs* designed to keep the pregnant and/or parenting adolescent in school and on track to complete her degree.
- *Comprehensive Family Support Services* designed to help parents of the pregnant and/or parenting teen to develop parenting skills and coping skills.
- *Expansion of Government Programs* designed to improve the medical and psychosocial health and well-being of pregnant and parenting teens and their offspring.
- *Comprehensive Community Programs* designed to enhance adolescents' parenting skills and support the unique needs of teen mothers and fathers and to provide early education for at-risk infants and children.

In 2007, then–U.S. Senator Barack Obama (D-IL) introduced a bill to reduce teen pregnancies in minority communities. The *Communities of Color Teen Pregnancy Prevention Act of 2007* seeks to strengthen community-based intervention efforts for teen pregnancy services, and to establish a comprehensive national database to provide culturally and linguistically sensitive information on teen pregnancy reduction. Senator Obama noted, "Teen pregnancy can derail the plans of students with dreams of achieving professional success, and it's hitting minority communities particularly hard. Pregnancies in African American and Latino communities remain inexcusably high. We must develop innovative approaches to strengthen our community support networks and services to educate our teens about pregnancy and provide them with every chance to succeed in school and beyond."

Sexually Transmitted Infections

Sexually transmitted infections (STIs) also pose a threat to an adolescent's health and sexual development. In the United States, as many as 26 percent—one in four—of adolescent girls between the ages of 14 and 19 are infected with at least one sexually transmitted disease; even among girls who reported only one lifetime partner, the STI prevalence was nearly 21 percent (Centers for Disease Control and Prevention, 2009). African American/Black Caribbean teen girls are most severely affected—nearly half of them are infected with an STI.

Today, two-thirds of all sexually transmitted infections are found in young adults under the age of 25, and almost half of the 19 million diagnosed cases of STIs each year in the United States are among young men and women aged 15–24 (Centers for Disease Control and Prevention, 2009); more than 65 million people in the United States currently have an STI (Montgomery et al., 2008). In the United States alone, medical costs associated with STIs are estimated at nearly $15 billion annually, and more than $8 billion is spent each year to diagnose and treat STIs, which does not include the costs associated with the treatment of HIV (American Social Health Association, 2009).

The HIV/AIDS pandemic is also a major threat to public health, both in the United States and abroad. Today 1.1 million people in the United States are living with HIV (Centers for Disease

Even though today's students associate some positive outcomes with sexual behaviors, such as becoming more popular, there is no question that adolescent sex carries with it a number of negative—and potentially life changing—consequences.

Control and Prevention, 2009; Johnson-Mallard et al., 2007). Furthermore, adolescent males today are disproportionately infected with HIV (Centers for Disease Control and Prevention, 2009a).

Despite these alarming trends, in a survey of over 80,000 late adolescents and college students, only 36 percent used a condom during vaginal intercourse, and only 28 percent used a condom during oral sex (National College Health Assessment, 2008). And, nearly three times as many coeds did not use a condom during anal intercourse (14 percent) compared to those who did (5 percent). These trends are important because they tell us that, even though many students have had sexual and health education, and even though they know they *should* use a condom every time to protect themselves, they *do not*.

The Influence of Parents

Though parents rarely provide the type and accuracy of sexuality information and education that school health programs do, they still influence their children in critical ways. For instance, several bodies of research suggest that adolescent sexual initiation is delayed if parents monitor and supervise their children's activities; there is also a decrease in sexual risk behavior (Capaldi, Crosby, & Stoolmiller, 1996; Romer, Black, Ricardo, Reigelman, Kalgee, Galbraith et al., 1994). Warm and responsive parenting styles are also associated with delayed sexual initiation in adolescents, as well as a decrease in the likelihood that a teen will engage in frequent sexual intercourse when they do become sexually active (Jaccard, Dittus, & Gordon, 1998; Miller, Forehand, & Kotchick, 1999; Resnick, Bearman, Blum, Bauman, Harris, Jones et al., 1997). When parents disapprove of adolescent sexual activity, teens are less likely to engage in sexual behaviors, and if they do become sexually active, they tend to have fewer sex partners (Jaccard et al., 1996).

Interestingly, verbal communication between parents and adolescents appears to have little or no effect on whether a teen decides to initiate sexual activity (Kaiser Family Foundation, 2004). Research shows this is due to several reasons:

- Sexual communication is infrequent and limited, and includes only certain family members, such as between mothers and daughters (Rosenthal & Feldman, 1999).
- Parents have incomplete or inaccurate information (Eisenberg, Bearinger, Sieving, Swain, & Resnick, 2004).
- Communication about sex often doesn't happen until after the teen has become sexually active (Eisenberg et al., 2004).
- Parents and teens don't agree on what should and should not be discussed (Shtarkshall, Santelli, & Hirsch, 2007).

There are also racial and ethnic differences in how parents communicate about sex with their teens. Research reveals that Hispanic and African American/Black Caribbean teens have the closest relationships with their mothers, and black teen girls are the most comfortable discussing sexual topics; sexual communication is lower among Hispanics and black groups than in white groups (Somers, 2006).

As family practitioners continue their sexuality research efforts, we will come to learn more about adolescent sexuality development and subgroup differences, and will ultimately be able to devise approaches that best equip and empower teens to make healthy lifestyle choices.

Adolescent Substance Use

Adolescents use tobacco, alcohol, marijuana, stimulants, and other illicit drugs at alarming rates. In fact, children are introduced to a variety of drugs in elementary school, and the availability of drugs has become widespread. Despite the efforts to restrict young people's access to drugs and to keep schools and neighborhoods safe, one of the most pressing societal problems today is the combination of drugs and violence that threatens the lives and well-being of our children.

The use of substances by teenagers can be conceptually perceived as one strategy to cope with adverse circumstances associated with inadequate family structure or lack of positive familial relationships. One study found positive relationships between harsh/inconsistent parenting and adolescent tobacco use, and negative relationships between nurturant/involved parenting behaviors and adolescent tobacco use (Bynum, 2000). Though tobacco use may not necessarily lead to drug use, it appears to be part of a general syndrome of problem behavior that predicts increased risk for developmental difficulties throughout adolescence (Mclby, Conger, Conger, & Lorenz, 1993).

Several studies have examined family variables that relate to substance use by teens. One significant risk factor for alcohol use is a drinking problem in the family. Equally important to the modeling function, parental support and responsiveness are key factors in preventing alcohol abuse. When adolescents perceive lower levels of family support, higher levels of alcohol consumption and cigarette use—as well as greater incidence of delinquent activity and depressive symptoms—are found (Bogenschneider, Wu, Raffaelli, & Tsay, 1998; Windle & Miller-Tutzauer, 1992). Lower family social support is perceived when the primary caregiver feels anxious and overly burdened by parental responsibilities (Windle & Miller-Tutzauer, 1992). The best predictor of adolescent drug use was lack of bonding with the mother, followed by family drug problems (Bahr, Maughn, Marcos, & Li, 1998). Religious involvement also may be a protective factor that decreases the chance of adolescent substance use.

Several studies have examined the effects of family structure on adolescent substance use. One study found that after controlling for race/ethnicity, family structure did not predict regular drinking or deviance (Barnes & Farrell, 1992). On the other hand, another body of research found significantly higher levels of use of cigarettes, alcohol, and marijuana for children in nonintact families (Flewelling & Bauman, 1990). Similarly, a longitudinal study found that adolescents who experienced a divorce during adolescence had greater involvement with drugs than children who had experienced a divorce before adolescence and those who lived in intact families. When mothers remarried, female adolescents increased their drug involvement and male adolescents decreased their use (Needle, Su, & Doherty, 1990).

Furthermore, adolescents in father-custody families showed significantly heightened risk of drug use, even after controlling for the effects of several demographic characteristics, family income, and residential mobility (Hoffman & Johnson, 1998). These data seem to suggest that the relationship between teen substance use and family structure is a complex one—depending on the gender of the child, the gender of the custodial parent, when the family disruption occurs, and whether the custodial parent remarries.

Important as family variables are, several studies suggest that the strongest predictor of drug use for adolescents is the extent to which their friends consume drugs, because friends make drugs available to one another, they model drug use, and peer-group norms sometimes favor drug use (Bauman & Ennett, 1994). Additionally, the role of drug use in friendship formation (selection) and attributing one's own behavior to the behavior of friends (projection) are factors that demonstrate the link between peers and substance use. Research confirms that adolescents who use drugs tend to have close friends who also use drugs (Bahr et al., 1998). Peer orientation, then, is a significant predictor of both drinking and other drug behavior, and it interacts with aspects of parenting.

Research also discovered that parenting practices influence adolescents' orientation toward peers, and that experiences in both the parent and the peer domains influence the likelihood that teens will engage in substance use (Bogenschneider et al., 1998). For example, when mothers report higher levels of responsiveness, adolescents report lower orientation to peers, which in turn results in lower rates of substance use. Furthermore, when mothers are less disapproving of adolescent alcohol use in certain circumstances (e.g., as long as drinking and driving do not occur), maternal responsiveness is associated with less substance use. However, when mothers disapprove of adolescent alcohol use in *every* circumstance, maternal responsiveness is associated with more substance use. The researchers concluded that there is a mutual, contingent, and interactive parent–peer linkage for adolescent substance use.

When the parent–child relationship is difficult, however, teenagers are likely to withdraw from the family and rely more heavily on the influence of peers. Adolescents who value peer opinions, as opposed to those of their parents, for important life decisions and values are at high risk for alcohol abuse, illicit drug use, and other problem behaviors (Barnes & Farrell, 1992). Drug-using adolescents are more likely to interact frequently with their friends and to be distant from their parents than nonusers are.

It appears, then, that adolescent personality attributes, parental attitudes and behaviors, and peer orientation all have an impact on drug use. Most drug-prevention programs focus on the negative consequences of ingesting drugs. However, more broadly based programs that combine information with a focus on resisting peer influences and decreasing psychological distress are needed. The success of these programs is due primarily to enhancing an adolescent's ability to resist passive social pressure (e.g., social modeling and overestimation of peer use) rather than to teaching refusal skills to combat active social pressure (i.e., explicit drug offers from friends).

Bullying

In January 2010, 15-year-old Irish immigrant Phoebe Prince hanged herself. For nearly 3 months on a daily basis, the Massachusetts high school student endured verbal assaults, vicious text and email messages, demeaning Facebook posts, and threats of physical harm. The day before her suicide, students threw soda pop cans at her while taunting and yelling at her. The relentless bullying, perpetrated by fellow classmates, was an attempt to make it impossible for Phoebe to go to school. Nine students now face charges for criminal bodily injury, stalking, harassment, and civil rights violations. The obvious question remains to be answered: Where were the adults?

A growing common phenomenon in schools across the nation and abroad, **bullying** is defined as a "power differential in which one or more youth repeatedly use aggressive strategies to dominate and cause harm to others of relatively lower status" (Farmer et al., 2010). In other words, bullying isn't about power—it's about the abuse of power. *Direct bullying* includes any type of physical abuse or violence; the intent is to physically harm someone (U.S. Department of Health and Human Services, 2007). *Indirect bullying* involves trying to affect someone negatively, through verbal or emotional abuse and harassment (such as ignoring/excluding someone, laughing/taunting, hurting someone's feelings, showing dislike or disdain). Indirect bullying also takes place when others witness the abuse but do not report it. When the bullying takes place in an electronic format (such as texting, email, or Facebook), it is referred to as **cyberbullying** (Hinduja & Patchin, 2009).

Because incidences are greatly under-reported, we do not know for certain just how many bullying victims there are. In one national U.S. Department of Health and Human Services (2007) poll of 1,200 boys and girls (ages 9 to 13), for every 100 children, an average of:

- Eight are bullied every day.
- Seven are bullied every week.
- Thirty-three are bullied every once in a while.

Another study of 2,200 middle schoolers examined bullying tactics and prevalence rates. The researchers found that nearly 30 percent were victimized by bullies; the victims reported that the most common bully tactic was that the bully told lies or spread false rumors and tried to get others to dislike them (Hinduja & Patchin, 2009). The most common type of cyberbullying was posting something offensive online (23.1 percent).

As with the case of Phoebe Prince, bullying is linked with suicidal ideation: Children, youth, and adolescents who are bullied have significantly increased rates of suicidal thoughts, attempts, and completed suicides (for a full review, see Hinduja & Patchin, 2009). Repeated peer harassment and bullying increase victims' feelings of depression, lower self-esteem and self-worth, and create hopelessness, helplessness, and isolation/loneliness. Because of the increase in the number of cyberbullying-related suicide completions in recent years, researchers have coined the term **cyberbullicide** to describe suicides that are influenced by online harassment and aggression (Hinduja & Patchin, 2009).

THE BULLIES Several bodies of research indicate that there are three primary categories of those affected by bullying (Perren & Alsaker, 2006; Solbere, Olweus, & Endresen, 2007; Veenstra et al., 2005):

- Bullies, but not victims
- Victims, but not bullies
- Those who are both bullies and victims

Bullies possess common characteristics (for a full review, see Farmer et al., 2010). In kindergarten, bullies tend to be more physically and verbally aggressive than their classmates, they are impulsive and easily frustrated, and they lack empathy. Interestingly, oftentimes they have strong leadership skills and a larger peer group than those who are not involved in bullying. When boys bully, they use physical behaviors; when girls bully, they use words.

These characteristics appear to persist through sixth grade, and about one-half of bullies are well integrated into their classroom and peer structures, and despite their aggressiveness they are quite popular. Contrary to popular belief, then, not all bullies are socially isolated or rejected. The one consistent characteristic in bullies is that they almost always have aggressive personalities and hot temperaments. When bullies were asked why they pick on one particular person and leave another alone, the most common response is that the victim "provoked" them (Frisen, Jonsson, & Persson, 2007).

While bullying does appear to peak in grades 4 through 7, it doesn't disappear altogether; rather, bullying is replaced by sexual harassment in later grades. Most acts of bullying occur on school grounds (at recess, in the cafeteria, in the hallways while changing classes, in bathrooms, on the school bus). In almost all of these venues, there is no adult supervision.

THE BULLIED In general, bully victims tend to have fewer friends/playmates, are somewhat socially isolated, and have fewer social skills (see Farmer et al., 2010). Other bodies of research indicate that children who are bullied are "different"—in appearance (facial features, weight, height, hygiene), clothing, behaviors, or speech (Erlin & Hwang, 2004). Recent research confirms these findings. In a study of 119 adolescents, students were asked, "Why do you think children and adolescents are bullied?" (Frisen et al., 2007). The most common reason reported by adolescents was the victim's appearance (40 percent), followed by the victim's behavior (such as being shy or insecure) (36 percent).

Bullying is *not* a normal part of growing up. The effects of bullying are significant, and may be long-lasting. Victims of bullies experience (U.S. Department of Health and Human Services, 2007):

- Anxiety
- Loneliness
- Low self-esteem
- Depression
- Social withdrawal
- Increased absenteeism
- Poor academic performance

Sadly, oftentimes when children inform an adult that they are the victims of bullying, they are advised by teachers and/or parents to work it out with the offender.

PARENTS AND TEACHERS Today, many adults still believe that bullying is a normative experience in childhood and adolescence; some even maintain that bullying "builds character." The U.S. Department of Health and Human Services (2007) notes that a number of adults and teachers tacitly accept bullying because they themselves experienced it (either as an offender or a victim) when they were younger.

Furthermore, research reveals that adults are barely aware of the bullying that occurs in their schools (Frisen et al., 2007). And, when adolescents were asked what makes bullying stop, only 14 percent of study participants indicated that bullying stops when teachers intervene. They have little confidence in adults' abilities to stop the violence (Frisen et al., 2007). Even in the case of Phoebe Prince, some teachers and school administrators knew that she was repeatedly bullied and harassed—and did nothing to protect her.

Schools can intervene by using such approaches as (Watkins, 2000):

- Pairing students so they go to and from areas in school using the buddy system.
- Monitoring "bully-prone" areas in the school.
- Displaying written behavioral expectations; expectations contract signed by students, parents, and teachers.
- Applying consistent consequences for those students who do not comply.
- Pairing victim-prone students with older student mentors.

As with any other area of physical and emotional health, parents are a child's first and best educator about the dangers of bullying. Parents and school personnel must always take bullying as the serious threat that it is. If a child reports being bullied, adults should validate (not marginalize) the child's experiences (U.S. Department of Health and Human Services, 2007). They should also immediately speak to the child's teachers, coaches, and other school administrators, and request that those in authority at the school be aware of who the bullies are in the school, and who the bullies' victims are. Parents should also request that their child is not left unsupervised (during lunch, recess, in the restroom, in the school hallways). Waiting to see if the behaviors change or decrease is not advisable because bullying behaviors persist over time.

Parents can also do their part by making sure their children understand that it is never permissible to taunt, tease, or bully another person, no matter how "harmless" the child or adolescent thinks the behavior is. Adults should also reinforce to youth that watching bullying occur is the same as condoning it, and that bullying *hurts* (U.S. Department of Health and Human Services, 2007).

Of course, the ideal time to teach children about bullying is before they experience it. Dinnertime conversations can include such questions as, "Do you ever see anyone putting down your friends or picking on someone?" and "What do you do when you see that happen?" Although parents cannot protect their children 100 percent of the time, they can buffer their children from bullying by instilling confidence, social skills, and empathy in them.

PROGRAMS FOR PARENTS OF SCHOOL-AGE CHILDREN AND ADOLESCENTS

The older the child, the fewer the programs that exist for parents. Therefore, parent-education programs for those with infants and preschool children far outnumber programs for those with school-age children. As a society we have assumed that parents with young children need more support and assistance than those with older children. We also have assumed that parent behaviors and attitudes are resistant to change and we should therefore focus on early parental behavior. Although a variety of agencies—including churches, mental-health clinics, and family-counseling agencies—have made sporadic attempts at education for parents of school-age children, the most consistent efforts have been through the public education system.

Parent Involvement in the Schools

Efforts to involve parents in school programs are not new. Since the founding of the National Congress of Mothers in 1897, which became the PTA (Parents and Teachers Association) in 1924, attempts to create links between home and school have been evident. A variety of approaches have been used, including parent–teacher conferences, involving parents in fundraising and open houses, and utilizing parents as volunteers in the classroom and as tutors either at home or in the school. These activities have been most successful with middle-class mothers, with little involvement of fathers or working-class parents, except in Chapter I programs (see following discussion). It has been assumed that this kind of involvement contributes to greater adjustment and achievement of children and improved attitudes on the part of parents.

Even so, parent involvement in the schools has left much to be desired, sometimes reaching the point of hostility between parents and school personnel. It is not unusual for teachers to complain that parents have little interest in their children, leaving the business of childrearing to the schools, and, on the other hand, to resent parents' intrusion into the classroom. Parents, too, may insist that teachers are poorly prepared and assert their perceived parental rights to determine school curricula. Of course, the success with which these issues are resolved varies from teacher to teacher, school to school, and district to district. The rebirth of the "back to basics" movement of the 1980s, however, resulted in state legislation allowing home education and a greater proportion of parents educating their children at home because of dissatisfaction with both the content of public school curricula and the degree of parental input into curriculum decision making. The issue of parental versus institutional rights in public education is far from resolved.

The importance of parent involvement in the schools has reemerged in recent years as public schools have been increasingly attacked for their failure to educate children properly. However, since much of the emphasis has been placed on the early-childhood period, few successful models have been implemented and tested. Professionals and parents alike are nonetheless renewing their interest in finding ways to work together for the benefit of school-age children.

Chapter I Programs

Public schools are eligible to receive Chapter I funds under the Elementary and Secondary

Education Act to develop stimulating and remedial education for low-income children in order to achieve the goals of grade-level proficiency of children, education for their parents, and greater involvement of parents in the education of their children. Many of these programs exist throughout the country, and activities vary according to the needs of the parents in the community where the program is located. Parents and teachers collaborate on the design and implementation of Chapter I programs. The goal of Chapter I programs is to equip parents to become more effective partners in their children's educational experience (Turner, Hamner, & Orell, 1993).

There are four major capacities in which parents have been involved: (1) as observers or learners, (2) as participants in school activities, (3) as volunteers in the classroom, and (4) as participants on school advisory committees. The major purpose of involving parents as observers or learners is to enable them to increase their understanding of themselves, their children, and/or the school program. These efforts have been most successful when parents perceive that the information offered is vital to learning, or to their child's interests, or when the programs are aimed specifically at parent interests and needs.

In general, there has been a low level of involvement of parents in the school advisory committees of Chapter I programs. Often administrators have not encouraged participation at this level, and confusion has existed over role responsibilities. The effects of such participation, where it has occurred, on student achievement, on the school program, and on the parents themselves have not been definitively shown by the research.

Programs for Parents of Adolescents

Given the difficulties that many parents face at this particular stage in the life cycle, it is ironic that so few formalized parent-education programs exist specifically for parents of adolescents. It is true that many of the contemporary strategies of parenting described in Chapter 5 can be used with adolescents as well as with younger children. However, the majority of programs that use these strategies involve parents of children younger than adolescents. One thing is certain given the issues teens face today: Parents of adolescents are in critical need of some form of education, whether it be discussion groups, development of skills in behavior management, or an emphasis on maintaining positive communication.

Much of what currently exists for parents of adolescents is therapeutic in nature. Clinics sponsor parent–adolescent counseling sessions *after* the child is in trouble; mental-health agencies require parents and teenagers to participate in drug-abuse programs *after* the child's achievement begins to lag. There seems to be very little preventive parent education available anywhere. Parents do have a rather wide selection of printed materials to choose from regarding the characteristics of adolescence and suggestions for positive parent–adolescent interaction—newspaper articles, paperbacks, popular magazines, and so on. But there seems to be a void in preparing parents for the changes that will occur in their own lives and those of their children when they reach adolescence.

Programs for parents of adolescents should focus on the biological and psychological changes occurring at this stage of development and ways to facilitate healthy development. Helping parents to fulfill more effectively their roles as counselors by, for example, practicing communication skills and developing a balance between freedom and responsibility for their children would seem to be helpful. Talking with other parents about current teenage trends in music, dress, and leisure activities may help parents to be more accepting. Making an effort to get acquainted with the parents of children's friends can provide a support network. Clearly there is a need for programs that are preventive in nature if parents are to facilitate successfully their offspring's transition from child to adult.

Summary

Our study so far is showing us that parenting is a complicated, evolving, reciprocal process. During the school years, children become exposed to many new experiences, and these necessitate adaptive parenting styles. Encouragement seems to be a crucial parental characteristic as children develop a sense of industry and a healthy self-concept.

Central to youth's development is the formation of peer groups. Today, teens face numerous pressures, from having sex to using substances. Children, preteens, and adolescents also face bullying on a regular basis. Healthy peer groups, along with positive communication with parents who assume the roles of guides, supporters, and monitors, seem to be necessary ingredients to minimize the threat of these problems.

References

Alan Guttmacher Institute. (2004). *U.S. teenage pregnancy statistics: Overall trends, trends by race and ethnicity, and state-by-state information.* Washington, DC: Author.

Alan Guttmacher Institute. (2008). Abortion and women of color: The bigger picture. *Guttmacher Policy Review, 11*(3). Retrieved March 13, 2010, from http://www.guttmacher.org/pubs/gpr/11/3/gpr110302.html.

Allport, G. W. (1958). *The nature of prejudice.* Garden City, NY: Doubleday.

American Social Health Association. (2009). *HIV and AIDS overview: 2009.* Retrieved March 13, 2010, from www.ashastd.org/lern/lern_hiv_aids_overfirew.cfm.

Aquilino, W. (1997). From adolescent to young adult: A prospective study of parent–child relations during the transition to adulthood. *Journal of Marriage and the Family, 59,* 670–686.

Atwater, E. (1992). Peers. *Adolescence, 3,* 151–153.

Bahr, S., Maughn, S., Marcos, A., & Li, B. (1998). Family, religiosity, and the risk of adolescent drug use. *Journal of Marriage the Family, 60,* 979–992.

Bank, B. J., & Hansford, S. L. (2000). Gender and friendship: Why are men's best same-sex friendships less intimate and supportive? *Journal of Social and Personal Relationships, 7,* 63–78.

Barnes, G., & Farrell, M. (1992). Parental support and control as predictors of adolescent drinking, delinquency, and related problem behaviors. *Journal of Marriage and the Family, 54*(4), 763–776.

Basow, S. A., & Rubenfeld, K. (2003). Troubles talk. *Sex Roles: A Journal of Research, 48*(3/4), 183–188.

Bauman, K., & Ennett, S. (1994, September). Peer influence on adolescent drug use. *American Psychologist,* pp. 820–822.

Berndt, T. S., & Savin-Williams, R. C. (1990). Friendship and peer relations. In S. S. Feldman & G. R. Elliot (Eds.), *At the threshold* (pp. 277–307). Cambridge, MA: Harvard University Press.

Bleske-Rechek, A., & Buss, D. M. (2000). Can men and women just be friends? *Journal of Social and Personal Relationships, 7,* 131–151.

Bogenschneider, K., Small, S., & Tsay, J. (1997). Child, parent, and contextual influences on perceived parenting competence among parents of adolescents. *Journal of Marriage and the Family, 59,* 345–362.

Booth, C., Rubin, K., & Rose-Kransor, L. (1998). Perceptions of emotional support from mother and friend in middle childhood: Links with social-emotional adaptation and preschool attachment security. *Child Development, 69*(2), 427–442.

Bogenschneider, K., Wu, M., Raffaelli, M., & Tsay, J. (1998). Parent influences on adolescent peer orientation and substance use: The interface of parenting practices and values. *Journal of Marriage and the Family, 69*(6), 1672–1688.

Brady, S. S., & Halpern-Felsher, B. L. (2007). Adolescents' reported consequences of having oral sex versus vaginal sex. *Pediatrics, 119*(2), 229–237.

Bronstein, P., Duncan, P., D'Ari, A., Pieniadz, J., Fitzgerald, M., Abrams, G., et al. (1996). Family and parenting behaviors predicting middle school adjustment. *Family Relations, 45,* 415–426.

Brooks, R. (2002). Transitional friends?: Young people's strategies to manage and maintain their friendships during a period of repositioning. *Journal of Youth Studies, 5,* 449–467.

Bruckner, H., & Bearman, P. (2005). After the promise: The STD consequences of adolescent virginity pledges. *Journal of Adolescent Health, 36*(4), 271–278.

Burleson, B. R. (2003). The experience and effects of emotional support: What the study of cultural and gender differences can tell us about close relationships, emotion, and interpersonal communications. *Journal of Social and Personal Relationships, 10,* 1–23.

Bynum, R. (2000, January 29). High school smoking drops. *Albuquerque Journal,* p. A12.

Capaldi, D., Crosby, L., & Stoolmiller, M. (1996). Predicting the timing of first sexual intercourse for at-risk adolescent males. *Child Development, 67,* 344–359.

Centers for Disease Control and Prevention. (2008a). Births, marriages, divorces, and deaths: Provisional data for July 2007. *National Vital Statistics Reports, 56,* 14.

Centers for Disease Control and Prevention. (2008b). Teen birth rate rises for the first time in 15 years. Atlanta, GA: Author. Retrieved September 2, 2009, from www.cdc.gov/nchs/pressroom.html.

Centers for Disease Control and Prevention (2009). Division of STD Prevention (DSTDP). Atlanta, GA: Author. Retrieved September 2, 2009, from www.cdc.gov/std/.

Chapman, J., Lambourne, R., & Silva, P. (1990). Some antecedents of academic self-concept: A longitudinal study. *British Journal of Educational Psychology, 60,* 142–152.

Coughlin, C., & Vuchinich, S. (1996). Family experience in preadolescence and the development of male delinquency. *Journal of Marriage and the Family, 58,* 491–501.

Day, R., Peterson, G., & McCracken, C. (1998). Predicting spanking of younger and older children by mothers and fathers. *Journal of Marriage and the Family, 60,* 79–94.

Dolich, C. (2005). *Male–female sex differences in cross-sex and same-sex adolescent friendships.* Retrieved Septembe 10, 2009, from http://students.haverford.edu/cdolich/final%paper.htm.

Duncan, G. J., Boisjoly, J., Levy, D. M., Kremer, M., & Eccles, J. (2003). *Empathy or antipathy? The consequences of racially and socially diverse peers on attitudes and behaviors.* Working Paper Series. Chicago, IL: Joint Center for Policy Research.

Dunphy, D. C. (1963). The social structure of urban adolescent peer groups. *Sociometry, 26,* 230–246.

Durex (2007). *Global sex survey.* Retrieved December 19, 2008, from www.about.com.

Eisenberg, M. E., Bearinger, L. H., Sieving, R. E., Swain, C., & Resnick, M. D. et al. (2004). Parents' beliefs about condoms and contraceptives: Are they medically correct? *Perspectives on Sexual and Reproductive Health, 26*(2), 50–57.

Erikson, E. (1963). *Childhood and society.* New York: Norton.

Farmer, T. W., Petrin, R. A., Robertson, D. L., Fraser, M. W., Hall, C. M., Day, S. H., et al. (2010). Peer relations of bullies, bully-victims, and victims: The two social worlds of bullying in second-grade classrooms. *Elementary School Journal, 110*(3), 364–392.

Flewelling, R., & Bauman, K. (1990). Family structure as a predictor of initial substance use and sexual intercourse in early adolescence. *Journal of Marriage and the Family, 52*(1), 171–181.

Franco, N., & Levitt, M. (1998). The social ecology of middle childhood: Family support, friendship quality, and self-esteem. *Family Relations, 47,* 315–321.

Frisen, A., Jonsson, A. K., & Persson, C. (2007). Adolescents' perception of bullying: Who is the victim? Who is the bully? What can be done to stop bullying? *Adolescence, 42*(168), 749–761.

Furman, W. (2002). The emerging field of adolescent romantic relationships. *Current Directions in Psychological Science, 11*(5), 177–180.

Furman, W., & Buhrmester, D. (1992). Age and sex differences in perceptions of networks and social relationships. *Child Development, 63,* 103–115.

Gecas, V., & Seff, M. (1991). Families and adolescents: A review of the 1980s. In A. Booth (Ed.), *Contemporary families: Looking forward, looking back* (pp. 208–225). Minneapolis, MN: National Council on Family Relations.

Glasgow, K., Dornbusch, S., Troyer, L., Steinberg, L., & Ritter, P. (1997). Parenting styles, adolescents' attributions, and educational outcomes in nine heterogeneous high schools. *Child Development, 68*(3), 507–529.

Halpern-Felsher, B., Cornell, J. L, Kropp, R. Y., & Tschann, J. M. (2005). Oral versus vaginal sex among adolescents: Perceptions, attitudes, and behavior. *Pediatrics, 115*(4), 845–851.

Hanson, S. L. (1992). Involving families in programs for pregnant teens: Consequences for teens and their families. *Family Relations, 41,* 303–311.

Harold, G., & Conger, R. (1997). Marital conflict and adolescent distress: The role of adolescent awareness. *Child Development, 68*(2), 333–350.

Harrison, T. W. (2003, March 1). Adolescent homosexual concerns regarding disclosure. *Journal of School Health, 73,* 107-112.

Hinduja, S., & Patchin, J. W. (2009). Cyberbullying research summary: Cyberbullying and suicide. *Cyberbullying and Suicide.* Retrieved April 23, 2010, from www.cyberbulling.us.

Hoff, T., Green, L., & Davis, J. (2003). *National survey of adolescents and young adults: Sexual health knowledge, attitudes, and experiences.* Menlo Park, CA: The Henry J. Kaiser Family Foundation.

Hoffman, J., & Johnson, R. (1998). A national portrait of family structure and adolescent drug use. *Journal of Marriage and the Family, 60,* 633–645.

Hoffman, M. (1970). Moral development. In P. Mussen (Ed.), *Carmichael's manual of child psychology* (3rd ed., Vol., 2, pp. 261–359). New York: Wiley.

Huebner, A. (2000, March). *Adolescent growth and development.* Virginia Cooperative Extension, Publication No. 350–850.

Jaccard, J., Dittus, P., & Gordon, V. (1998). Parent–adolescent congruency in reports of adolescent sexual behavior and in communications about sexual behaviors. *Child Development, 69*(1), 247–261.

Johnson, F. L., & Airies, E. J. (1983). Conversational patterns among same-sex pairs of late-adolescent close friends. *The Journal of Genetic Psychology, 142,* 225–238.

Johnson-Mallard, V., Lengacher, C. A., Kromrey, J. D., Campbell, D. W., Jevitt, C. M., Daley, E., et al. (2007). Increasing knowledge of sexually transmitted infection risk. *Nurse Practitioner, 32*(2), 26–32.

Kaiser Family Foundation, National Public Radio, and John F. Kennedy School of Government. (2004). *Sex education in America: General public/parents survey.* Menlo Park, CA: Kaiser Family Foundation.

Ketsetzis, M., Ryan, B., & Adams, G. (1998). Family processes, parent–child interactions, and child characteristics influencing school-based social adjustment. *Journal of Marriage and the Family, 60,* 374–387.

Klerman, L. V. (2004). *Another chance: Preventing additional births to teen mothers.* Washington, DC: National Campaign to Prevent Teen Pregnancy.

Krevans, J., & Gibbs, J. (1998). Parents' use of inductive discipline: Relations to children's empathy and prosocial behavior. *Child Development, 67,* 3263–3277.

Kuttler, A. F., LaGreca, A.M., & Prinstein, M. J. (1999). Friendship qualities and social-emotional functioning of adolescents with close, cross-sex friendships. *Journal of Adolescent Research, 9*(3), 339–366.

Larson, N. C. (2004). Parenting stress among adolescent mothers in the transition to adulthood. *Child and Adolescent Social Work Journal, 21*(5), 457–476.

Lehrman, G. (2001). *The history of private life: Courtship in early America.* The Gilder Lehrman Institute of American History. Retrieved June 4, 2008, from http://yalepress.yale.edu.

Lempers, J. D., & Clark-Lempers, D. S. (1993). A functional comparison of same-sex and opposite-sex friendships during adolescence. *Journal of Adolescent Research, 8*(1), 89–108.

Lenton, A. P., & Webber, L. (2006). Cross-sex friendships: Who has more? *Sex Roles: A Journal of Research, 54,* 809–820.

Lindberg, L. D., Jones, R., & Santelli, J. S. (2008). Noncoital sexual activities among adolescents. *Journal of Adolescent Health, 43*(3), 231–238.

Melby, J., Conger, R., Conger, K., & Lorenz, F. (1993). Effects of parental behavior on tobacco use by young male adolescents. *Journal of Marriage and the Family, 55*(2), 439–454.

Mendelson, M. J., & Kay, A. C. (2003). Positive feelings in friendship: Does imbalance in the relationship matter? *Journal of Social and Personal Relationships, 20,* 101–116.

Miller, K., Forehand, R., & Kotchick, B. (1999). Adolescent sexual behavior in two ethnic minority samples: The role of family variables. *Journal of Marriage and the Family, 61,* 85–98.

Monsour, M. (2002). *Women and men as friends: Relationships across the lifespan in the 21st century.* Mahwah, NJ: Erlbaum.

Moss, E., Rousseau, D. Parent, S., St. Laurent, D., & Saintonge, J., (1998). Correlates of attachment at school age: Maternal reported stress, mother-child interaction, and behavior problems. *Child Development, 69*(5), 1390–1405.

National Campaign to Prevent Teen Pregnancy. (2008). *National data.* Retrieved November 29, 2009, from http://www.thenationalcampaign.org/national-data/default.aspx.

National College Health Assessment. (2008). *Reference group data report.* Retrieved August 1, 2009, from http://www.acha-ncha.org/reports_ACHA-NCHAoriginal.html.

National Organization on Adolescent Pregnancy, Parenting, and Prevention. (2008). Retrieved December 1, 2009, from www.healthyteennetwork.org.

Needle, R., Su, S., & Doherty, W. (1990). Divorce, remarriage, and adolescent substance use: A prospective longitudinal study. *Journal of Marriage and the Family, 52*(1), 157–169.

O'Donnell, L., Steuve, A., Wilson-Simmons, R., Dash, K., Agronick, G., & JeanBaptiste, V. (2006). Heterosexual risk behaviors among urban young adolescents. *Journal of Early Adolescence, 26*(87), 87–109.

Oswald, D. L., & Clark, E. M. (2003). Best friends forever?: High school best friendships and the transition to college. *Journal of Social and Personal Relationships, 10,* 187–196.

Paul, E. L., & White, K. M. (1990, Summer). The development of intimate relationships during late adolescence. *Adolescence,* 375–400.

Perren, S., & Alsaker, F. (2006). Social behavior and peer relationships of victims, bully-victims, and bullies in kindergarten. *Journal of Child Psychology and Psychiatry, 47,* 45–57.

Pettigrew, T. F., & Tropp, L. R. (2006). A meta-analytic test of intergroup contact theory. *Journal of Personality and Social Psychology, 90,* 751–783.

Pettit, G., Bates, J., & Dodge, K. (1997). Supportive parenting, ecological context, and children's adjustment: A seven-year longitudinal study. *Child Development, 68*(5), 908–923.

Phares, V., & Renk, K. (1998). Perceptions of parents: A measure of adolescents' feelings about their parents. *Journal of Marriage and the Family, 60,* 646–659.

Quillian, L., & Campbell, M. E. (2003). Beyond black and white: The present and future of multiracial friendship segregation. *American Sociological Review, 68,* 540–566.

Quinlivan, J. A., Tan, L. H, Steele, A., & Black, K. (2004). Impact of demographic factors, early family relationships, and depressive symptomatology in teenage pregnancy. *Australian and New Zealand Journal of Psychiatry, 38*(4), 197–208.

Reeder, H. M. (2003). The effect of gender role orientation on same- and cross-sex friendship formation. *Sex Roles: A Journal of Research, 49,* 143–152.

Resnick, M. D., Bearman, P.S., Blum, R.W., Bauman, K.E., Harris, K.M., Jones, J. et al. (1997). Protecting adolescents from harm: Findings from the National Longitudinal Study on Adolescent Health. *Journal of the American Medical Association, 278*(10), 823–832.

Richards, M. H., Crowe, P. A., Larson, R., & Swarr, A. (1998). Developmental patterns and gender differences in the experiences of peer companions during adolescence. *Child Development, 69,* 154–163.

Romer, D., Black, M., Ricardo, I., Feigelman, S., Kalgee, L., Galbraith, J. et al., (1994). Social influences on the sexual behavior of youth at risk for HIV exposure. *American Journal of Public Health, 84*(6), 977–985.

Rosenbaum, J. E. (2009). Patient teenagers?: A comparison of the sexual behavior of virginity pledgers and matched nonpledgers. *Pediatrics, 123*(1), e110–e120.

Rosenthal, D. A., & Feldman, S. S. (1999). The important of importance: Adolescents' perceptions of parental communication about sexuality. *Journal of Adolescence, 22*(6), 835–851.

Rubin, L. (1986). On men and friendship. *Psychoanalytic Review, 73,* 165–181.

Rybak, A., & McAndrew, F. T. (2006). How do we decide whom our friends are? Defining levels of friendship in Poland and the United States. *Journal of Social Psychology, 146*(2), 147–163.

Sacerdote, B., & Marmaros, D. (2005). *How do friendships form?* NBER Working Paper W11530. Retrieved November 1, 2009, from www.ssrn.com/abstract=776569.

Sexuality Information and Education Council of the United States (SIECUS). (2009). Retrieved August 19, 2009, from www.siecus.org.

Shtarkshall, R. A., Santelli, J. S., & Hirsch, J. S. (2007). Sex education and sexual socialization: Roles for educators and parents. *Perspectives on Sexual and Reproductive Health, 39*(2), 116–120.

Solbere, M. E., Olweus, D., & Endresen, I. M. (2007). Bullies and victims in school?: Are they the same pupils? *British Journal of Educational Psychology, 77,* 441–464.

Somers, C. L. (2006). Parent–adolescent relationships and adolescent sexuality: Closeness, communication, and comfort among diverse U.S. adolescent samples. *Adolescence, 41*(161), 15–38.

Straus, M., & Yodanis, C. (1996). Corporal punishment in adolescent and physical assaults on spouses in later life: What accounts for the link? *Journal of Marriage and the Family, 58,* 825–841.

Thorne, B. (1986). Girls and boys together…but mostly apart: Gender arrangements in elementary schools. In W. W. Hartup & Z. Rubin (Eds.), *Relationships and development* (pp. 167–184). Hillsdale, NJ: Erlbaum.

Turner, P., Hamner, T., & Orell, L. (1993). *Children and their families in New Mexico.* Albuquerque: New Mexico First.

U.S. Department of Health and Human Services. (2007). *Stop bullying now.* Retrieved April 23, 2010, from www.stopbullyingnow.hrsa.gov.

Veenstra, R., Lindenburg, S., Oldenhinkel, A. J., De Winter, A. F., Verhulst, F. C., & Ormel, J. (2005). Bullying and victimization in elementary schools: A comparison of bullies, victims, and bully/victims, and uninvolved preadolescents. *Developmental Psychology, 41,* 672–682.

Wallace, S. G. (2007, March 1). Hooking up, losing out? The new culture of teen sex and how to talk to your campers about it. *Camping Magazine.* Retrieved March 13, 2010, from http://www.acacamps.org/campmag/0703wallace.php.

Watkins, C. E. (2000). *Protecting against bullying throughout the life cycle.* Retrieved April 23, 2010, from www.ncpamd.com/Bullying_thru_life_cycle.htm.

Weinstein, E., & Rosen, E. (2006). *Teaching about human sexuality and family: A skills-based approach.* Belmont, CA: Thomson Wadsworth.

Weiss, L., & Schwarz, C. (1996). The relationship between parenting types and older adolescents' personality, academic achievement, adjustment, and substance use. *Child Development, 67,* 2101–2114.

West, L., Anderson, J., & Duck, S. (1996). Crossing the barriers to friendships between men and women. In J. T. Wood (Ed.), *Gendered relationships* (pp. 111–127). Mountain View, CA: Mayfield.

Windle, M., & Miller-Tutzauer, C. (1992). Confirmatory factor analysis and concurrent validity of the perceived social support family measure among adolescents. *Journal of Marriage and the Family, 54*(4), 777–787.

Chapter 4

The Changing Nature of Parenting: Later Life

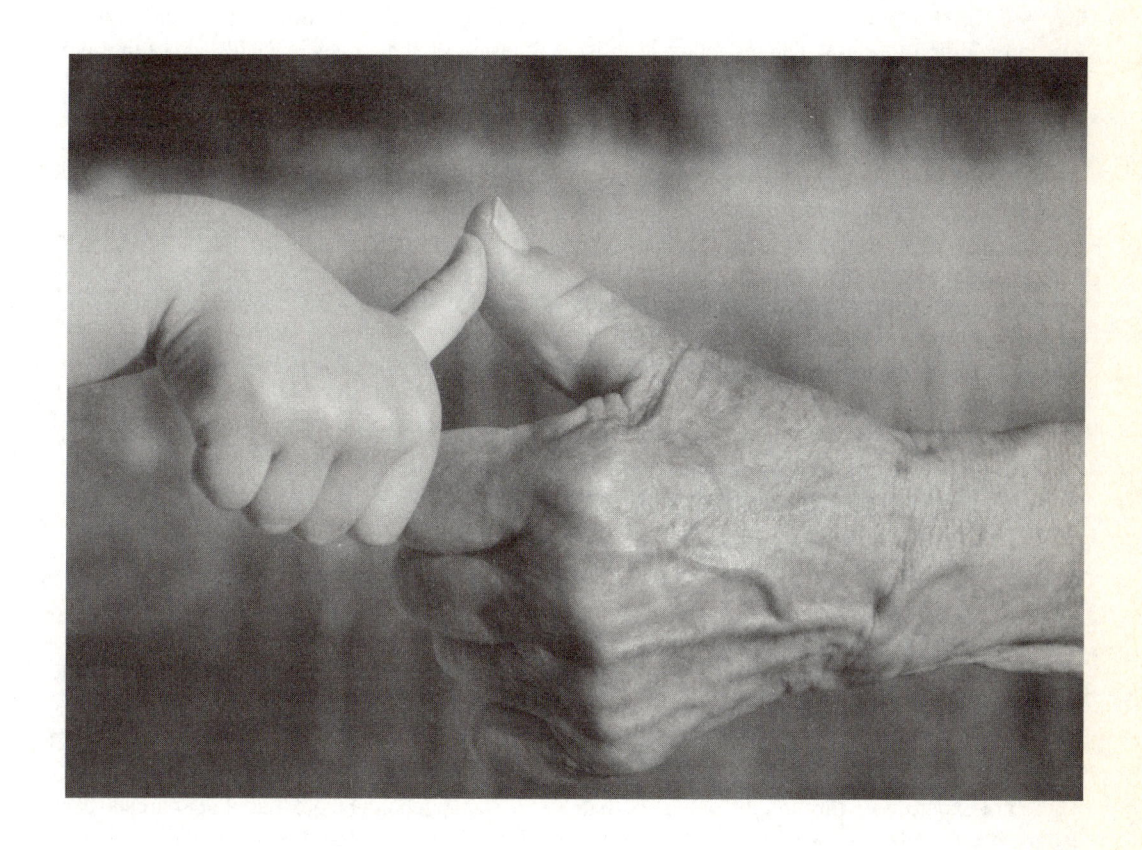

The traditional concept of the role of parenthood spans the period from the birth or adoption of the first child through the adolescent period of the last child. Parenting, then, has been thought of as a 20- to 30-year commitment. Recent social changes, such as the economic crisis and skyrocketing unemployment rates that swept the U.S. in 2009, have contributed to an expanded conception of parenthood. These changes have resulted in children remaining in the parental home longer and, for some adult children, returning to live, at least for a brief period.

In addition to these changes, our nation is moving into an unprecedented time in its history: By the year 2030, there will be 72 million people (roughly 20 percent of the population) over the age of 65 living in the United States—more than ever before (He, Sangupta, Velkoff, & DeBarros, 2005). With this increase in later-age adults, many grandparents adopt the roles of caregiving for their grandchildren. Finally, greater longevity also contributes to increased responsibility of middle-aged adults who provide assistance and care to their elderly parents. All of these phenomena have a significant impact on the changing nature of parenting, both for parents and for children. This chapter examines experiences of young adults, parenting in later life, grandparenting, and caring for elderly parents. But first, let's take a look at the *Family Life Cycle*, a model that helps us understand the normative developmental tasks families navigate.

THE FAMILY LIFE CYCLE

There are experiences throughout our lives that establish a foundation for our ability to parent someday. Integral to these experiences is our family of origin. As you have learned throughout our study so far, we do not develop in isolation! Every phase of our development is affected by, intersected by, and overlapped with the developmental cycle of our family, and our family development is influenced by the multiple cultural contexts that surround it. The **Family Life Cycle** comprises multiple entrances and exits from the family of origin. For example, a young adult leaving for college is an exit, while the formation of a new family of origin as children marry is an entry. Families with young children experience multiple entries with their new family members, while families in later life experience multiple exits, such as when family members die. Along with the changes in the *structure* of the family come certain *emotional transitions* and *related changes* in the family status that are needed to move on developmentally.

The cycle of family growth and transition consists of challenges in each stage of family life that cause us to develop or gain certain relational skills (Neighbour, 1985):

- *Pairing/marriage:* In this stage, individuals fuse as a couple. They must then leave their families of origin and establish goals, roles, and values as a new couple.
- *Childbearing:* Although not all couples have children, many do. In this developmental stage, couples must realign their roles and share each other with children. There may be role ambiguity and role strain/conflict (such as wife, woman, mother).
- *School-age children:* In this stage, parents nurture their children, and at the same time be a spouse. While providing a secure emotional and physical environment for their children, parents must also balance the demands of work.
- *Family with adolescents:* This family developmental stage is punctuated with their adolescent children's boundary-testing. The adolescent, in attempting to form an identity separate from that of her parents, begins much social and sexual exploration, resulting in issues of control versus freedom, power struggles, and rebellion.
- *Family as a launching ground:* As adolescents leave the nest, some parents may view the empty nest as loss, while others view it as new opportunity. Some parents rediscover each other, while latent marital conflict may surface among others.

- *Middle years:* This stage may be marked by simultaneously caring for their children and their aging parents. The middle years are oftentimes fulfilling for middle-aged adults as they realign their marital roles.
- *Aging:* In this developmental stage, aging adults deal with bereavements as they lose their siblings, spouse, and friends to death.

Developing these skills helps us work through the changes associated with family life; at the same time, we develop abilities we will someday carry into our own relationships. Of course, few make these transitions seamlessly and sometimes families' relationships are painfully stretched as they experience job loss or financial problems, severe illness, or the death of a loved one. Family development is, certainly, a multifaceted molding process as change occurs both inside and between family members. Whether you are a parent or child, brother or sister, bonded by blood or love, your experiences through the family life cycle affect who you are and who you become.

It is important to note, however, that there are criticisms of the family life cycle. Specifically, the family life cycle has been criticized because it ignores the varying family constellations (such as families of color, gay/lesbian families, or intergenerational/extended families). In short, deviations or differences from a "traditional" family are ignored by the family life cycle. It also assumes that *all* families of origin share a common group identity, ignoring the fact that many today have departed from the previously common progression of family life. Finally, the model has been criticized because it is child-centric—it assumes that all families have children. Prominent family life educators Betty Carter and Monica McGoldrick address these inadequacies of the family life cycle in their book, *The Expanded Family Life Cycle* (2005). They note that today students need to think about human development and the life cycle in a way that reflects society's shifts to a more diverse and inclusive definition of "family."

PARENTS AND THEIR ADULT CHILDREN

Some parents look forward to launching their children, while others do so with much trepidation and doubt. Still others do not successfully manage the transition to an **empty nest**—the home with no children—well at all. Table 4.1 presents the changes that occur in the family system that accompany the empty nest. As you can see, significant changes take place in the family members' roles, as well as in the relationships with the now-grown children. While lifespan development courses emphasize the earlier years of parenting and the significance of the parent–child relationship during the early years, preschool years, and school years of a child's life, too often much is left unsaid about the importance of the parent–adult child relationship.

When a child enters into early adolescence, an important turning point is reached in the parent–child relationship. It is during this phase of development that parents and children alike establish intimacy levels that will, to a very large extent, define their subsequent *parent–adult child* relationship. This developmental stage of the family life cycle brings important questions to the forefront, such as how do adolescent children affect the well-being of their parents? Because children come of age during this period of family development and eventually leave the nest (and perhaps return to the nest again and again), what impact does this have on midlife parents?

In many families, children's entry into adolescence coincides with the parents' transition to midlife. As young adolescents strive for increased independence and autonomy, they often begin to challenge their parents' authority. Meanwhile, parents encounter their own developmental tasks associated with midlife, such as caring for their aging parents and preparing for retirement. These normative life-course events introduce many challenges into the family system, as parents are forced to play simultaneous roles as caretaker and parent. But typically, marital satisfaction and stability increase as children enter into their

TABLE 4.1 Developmental tasks associated with the empty nest.
As parents begin to empty the nest, there are common struggles that most couples encounter.

- **Change in roles/loss of roles.** When children leave, it's not uncommon for parents to feel a void once their parenting role is diminished or lost. Some parents try to fill this void with volunteering or other activities. Parents also need to shift to the role of parent of *adult* children.
- **Marital issues.** Raising children requires so much time, energy, and attention that sometimes children are a diversion that keeps parents from working on problems in their marriage. When children leave the nest, the diversion is no longer there. Parents need to re-examine their goals as a couple as they enter the second half of their marriage.
- **Career change.** Frequently, emptying the nest coincides with changes in one or both parents' careers. While men may be thinking of early retirement, women who entered the workforce later because of childrearing responsibilities may be just reaching a peak in their careers.
- **Caregiving shifts.** Typically, as children leave the home, parents find that their own parents need more care and attention. Caregiving responsibilities don't lessen—they simply shift to a different generation.
- **Relationships with children.** For many parents, accepting their children as adults is difficult; other parents accept that their children are adults and require less advice and support. What is more important to mid-life parents, however, is *how* children leave the nest: Are the parents and children on good terms?

Source: Welch, *Family Life Now*, 2e. (2010). Boston: Allyn & Bacon. p. 532.

adolescent years (Swensen, Eskew, & Kohlhepp, 1981; Veroff, Douvan, & Kulka, 1981; Wu & Penning, 1997). This increase is likely because conflicts over childrearing issues decline.

It is also during these middle years of the family life cycle that parents and children begin to renegotiate their relationship, parents begin to reflect back on their parenting experiences, and "accept their life choices, relate to their children, and adjust to 'how [the children] have turned out'" (Lemme, 2006, p. 274). These reflections about their success or failure as parents greatly affect the parents' purpose in life, their self-acceptance, and thus their well-being.

Although recent attention has been given to adult development, little has been given to parenting young adult children. Adult children are considered to be those 18 years of age or older, married or single, living in or out of the parental home. The time at which "young adult children" cease to be young is clearly debatable. For convenience's sake, young adult children referred to here are those between 18 and 29 years of age. In the United States, coming of age is not noted by any particular rite of passage, but becoming eligible at age 18 to vote and for military service signify in our society legal status as an adult. By law parents are no longer responsible for their offspring after their 18th birthdays. For many, however, parenting continues for years to come, even until death of the parent or the child. There are few norms governing familial relationships in adulthood, but adult parenting usually is characterized by more equal relationships between parents and children (Atkinson & James, 1991).

Adult Children Living At Home: Doubling Up

In the past, it has been the practice in the United States for young adults to leave the parental home in their late teens or early twenties to establish homes of their own or to attend college. Beginning in the 1980s and continuing until the present, more and more young adults have been living with their parents than at any other time since 1940, when the aftermath of the Depression resulted in a high unemployment rate, thus prohibiting young people from becoming financially independent.

Based on recent trends, it seems that for many families today the parenting career is extended, either because the launching stage is postponed, or because it resumes again after a brief empty-nest period. This phenomenon is referred to as the *cluttered nest* or the *elastic nest*. Today, adult children as coresidents are known as the **boomerang generation** (Atkinson & James, 1991; Mitchell & Gee, 1996). Very recently, a new term—**revolving door syndrome**—was coined to describe the returning of young adult children. The economic downturn in 2009 drove young adult children home in record numbers: Today, nearly 53 percent of America's 18 to 24 year olds live with their parents (Mykyta & Macartney, 2011). U.S. Census Bureau demographers are now referring to this trend as **doubling up,** or households that include at least one extra adult that is not a spouse or cohabiting partner (Mykyta & Macrtnery, 2011).

So common and widespread is the trend of adult children returning home after launching, in 2010 President Barack Obama's Healthcare Reform legislation mandated that single, adult children are to be covered under their parents' health insurance plans until the age of 26; before this, adult children were no longer covered under their parents' insurance after the age of 21 or 23. Furthermore, not only are adult children remaining at home longer or returning after college, but also they are more likely to return after their first and subsequent departures (Mitchell & Gee, 1996).

There are several reasons for adult children remaining and returning home: increased age at first marriage; economic circumstances, such as the high cost of living and high youth unemployment rates; the need for more education for career placement; lack of financial aid for postsecondary programs or college; ambivalence about the capacity to assume adult roles; and increase in divorce (Mitchell & Gee, 1996). But are some adult children more likely to return home than others?

Empty nest? Today, it's becoming so common for adult children to move back in with their parents for a period of time that the term "empty nest" is being replaced with the term **"revolving door syndrome."** Have you experienced moving back home after having achieved independence? Was it a positive or negative experience?

WHO LIVES AT HOME? The most typical adult child who resides at home is one who is continuing schooling at a college or university or at a vocational school within commuting distance of the parental home. There are, however, young adults who are not in school who continue to live at home, most of whom are employed or seeking employment. In either case parents are faced with the task of interacting with offspring over whom they have little control and who generally have a different lifestyle from that of their parents. The rules and regulations that governed the period of adolescence and the nature of interactions are no longer appropriate, but daily proximity forces intrusion of one lifestyle on the other. The need for independence among young adults is widely recognized, but the need for independence on the part of middle-aged parents often is ignored (Thompson & Walker, 1984).

One body of research examined the life-course transitions of children leaving and returning home and the impact of parental family structure on the timing of these events (Goldscheider & Goldscheider, 1998). This study's results showed that living in any form of nontraditional family, such as a stepfamily, reduced the likelihood of young adults leaving home for college and increased the likelihood of leaving home early and not returning. Those who left home to form a family via cohabitation or single parenthood were less likely to return. The researchers assert that the timing of "nest-leaving" and the reasons for leaving home reflect parental investment in children. Having two parents in a stable family structure, having parents with more resources, and having fewer siblings appear to facilitate children's mature launch into adulthood. Adult children who have had different experiences during childhood, particularly disruptions during adolescence (such as parents' divorce and/or remarriage), often leave home at an early age any way they can and are likely to move into relationships that provide less support and less stability.

RELATIONSHIP SATISFACTION AND CONFLICT
What happens to parents' relationship satisfaction when adult children move back home? One study found several parent and child variables associated with marital satisfaction among parents with coresiding adult children. For example, parents are 10 times more likely to experience marital satisfaction if the child returns home only once, rather than three or more times; they are also more willing to accept one or two returns, but a pattern of bouncing back and forth strains family relationships and diminishes marital satisfaction for the parents (Mitchell & Gee, 1996).

The researchers also found that parents are more satisfied with their marriages when children left home to become independent, presumably permanently, than when they left home temporarily for work or school. Parent–adult child relationships are also important. Parents, for instance, are significantly more satisfied with their marriages when the returned children had excellent relationships with their mothers than when they had poor relationships; father–child relationships do not predict marital satisfaction. Another national survey found that parental satisfaction with the coresidence of their adult children (ages 19 to 34) is highly related to the degree of parent–child conflict (Aquilino, 1991).

A number of other factors also affect parents' relationship satisfaction when adult children move back home. For example, while the age of the adult child doesn't appear to affect parents' satisfaction, the child's progress in the transition to adulthood is a strong force in shaping parent–child relationships (Aquilino, 1991). Parental satisfaction seems to be highest when parents are involved with adult children in pleasurable activities and when adult children are more self-sufficient (Mitchell & Gee, 1996). Interestingly, parents with more education and higher incomes report more negative effects of coresidence of adult children than parents with less education and income. It may be that this stems from middle-class parents' higher expectations for self-development and life opportunities during their midlife stage (Aquilino, 1991; Aquilino & Supple, 1991).

Using Erikson's framework, most parents of young adult children are completing their stage of **generativity** and moving toward the final stage of **integrity versus despair.** At the same time, their offspring are seeking to achieve a sense of *intimacy,* beginning to think about establishing their own homes and families. As a result, conflicts are not surprising. In fact, one study found that 42 percent of the middle-aged parents surveyed report serious conflicts with at least one of their resident adult children (Clemens & Axelson, 1985), and another study reported that only one-quarter of the parents approve of their adult children moving in with them (Aquilino & Supple, 1991).

FINANCES: WHO PAYS FOR WHAT, AND WHEN? The related issue of financial aid raises conflicts. Does the adult child pay rent? Does she contribute to the purchase of food? Does she pay for her own health and car insurance? Has she begun a savings account? What kind of financial assistance does she get from her parents, if any?

Most parents expect some financial contribution from their live-in children if they are employed full time, but one study found that children's room-and-board payments did not affect parental satisfaction with coresidence (Aquilino, 1991). Financial issues seem to be related both to whether the young adult is employed or is in school and to the economic status of the parents. Many parents, if they are willing and able, subsidize their children's room and board as well as their tuition and books as long as they are actively pursuing an education. Some parents place a time limit on these kinds of subsidies.

COMING AND GOING: NEED TO KNOW? The issue of rules and regulations looms large for many families with adult children at home. To what extent do parents have a right to know where their children are, when they will be home, and whom they are with? Should parents set down rules about dress, socializing with friends, use of parents' possessions, and the use of alcohol and drugs?

Many parents feel the need to apply rules that make their own lives more comfortable, yet they feel guilty that they are not accepting their child's level of maturity and sense of responsibility. Creating an atmosphere of peaceful coexistence while maintaining mutual respect is often difficult. There actually is no magic solution to this dilemma. Each party must be sensitive to the feelings and expectations of the other, and, no doubt, all must make compromises.

Adult Children Living Away from Home

When children leave home to establish independence and to begin their own careers and families, parental concern and worries do not stop—there is no such thing as a "postparental" period (Aldous, 1985). Nevertheless, children may still be dependent on parents economically and/or emotionally. Parents, too, may have difficulty in resolving their emotional dependency on their children, because when a parent has parented for 20 or more years, it is difficult for them to change roles and not parent. Despite this, it has been speculated that emotional dependencies are more balanced in adulthood than in early parent–child relationships when the child is more dependent on the parent (Thompson & Walker, 1984). Still later an imbalance may occur in the other direction as aging parents become more dependent—physically, economically, and psychologically—on their mature children.

The nature of the relationships between parents and their adult children depends to some extent on the marital status of the parent(s) and the marital and parental status of the children, but the results of studies show inconsistencies. One body of research reported that parents and daughters are more involved with each other's lives than are parents and sons (Aldous, 1985). However, parents may show greater concern for their divorced children/grandchildren than for their other adult children who are not divorced. Parents are also more likely to provide childcare for these grandchildren, to give comfort to their own divorced children, and to help them with housework.

Other studies have shown that divorced children receive less support from parents and experience more strain in relationships with them than married children (Umberson, 1992). For example, parental divorce and remarriage are associated with significantly less social, instrumental, and financial support to adult children (White, 1992). The reduced financial support to adult children might be accounted for by the lower earnings and assets, and greater obligations of divorced parents, but the reduced support in other areas appears to be the result of lower parent–child solidarity. It seems, then, that structural circumstances influence the quality of relationships and the degree of intergenerational transfers between adult children and their parents (Umberson, 1992).

Transfer of aid or assistance among the generations is never really symmetrical because almost always it is transferred from parent to child. Only by grown children transferring to their own children is there any balancing of material and emotional investment. Transfer of aid was examined in two generations of mother–daughter relationships; most of the youngest generation of daughters (who were university students) were single (Thompson & Walker, 1984). The investigators found that nonreciprocity existed in the transfer of aid: The mothers essentially were the givers, and the daughters were the receivers. Some research reported greater closeness and reciprocity of aid between mothers and their young adult daughters when the mothers were widowed as opposed to married. It may be the family member in the nonreciprocating position (receiving but not giving help) who avoids contact with kin.

Our discussion so far has shown us that relationships between mature adults and their adult children, whether the children are living at home or not, are complex and little understood. There is great diversity in the degree and extent of contact and in the transfer of aid, goods, and services. Because of this, few generalizations can be made, and few guidelines can be established. Therefore it appears that an interesting and promising area of research would be the relationship between parents and their adult children.

As adults age through later adulthood, intergenerational ties become increasingly important because these relationships often provide the foundation for intimacy throughout the aging process (Fingerman, 2001). In the section that follows, we explore the importance of multigenerational relationships, and how relationships change as we age.

Intergenerational Ties

Intergenerational ties refer to the relationships between family members across multiple generations, and these relationships are indeed important to us as we age. In everyday language, the term *generation* describes people who were born during the relatively same time period (such as the "baby boomer" generation). When discussing intergenerational relationships, however, the term *generation* is used to describe family members who are "on the same rung of the family ladder," or who are related to one another either biologically or through adoption. Most intergenerational relationships are offshoots of the parent–child relationship, though biological ties are not a necessary prerequisite in order for someone to experience a sense of family, kinship, and intimacy (Fingerman, 2001). For example, sometimes after many years with a stepmother or stepfather, the "step" aspect of the relationship becomes less significant and the relationship becomes as meaningful as those between biological parents and their children.

Similarly, older African American adults frequently do not distinguish "kin" along biological lines; for instance, it is common for nieces, nephews, godchildren, or even younger adults who are not blood or otherwise related to fill the role of an adult child for older African American males (Johnson, 1999). **Fictive kin** are people who are not biologically related to someone, but who fulfill a family role. Among African American/Black Caribbean families, fictive kin are important sources of emotional support, as well as support in meeting the elderly's needs (MacRae, 1992). As African Americans/Afro-Caribbeans age, they tend to enjoy warmer relationships with their adult children, brothers, sisters, young children, and fictive kin than aging white Americans do (MacRae, 1992). Aging Hispanic and Asian families also experience

Adults' relationships with their parents are affected by their gender, geographical distance, their parents' marital status, and their culture.

extended kin and fictive kin relationships more often than white families do. Importantly, later in the developmental life course, intimacy "may exist between individuals who *define themselves* as parent and offspring" (Fingerman, 2001, p. 23, emphasis added). Of the many different and varying interpersonal intimate relationships we form throughout our lives, none is as important to some people as the relationship between parent and child.

The Parent–Adult Child Relationship in Late Adulthood

As parents age and begin to experience physiological and cognitive changes, their roles within the family change also. The parent–adult child relationship is central to the lives of the elderly: Aside from having their adult children there to provide care when needed, having warm and close relationships with their children provides aging parents a sense of well-being (Pinquart & Soerensen, 2000). According to developmentalist Karen Fingerman (2001), four primary factors influence intimacy between older adults and their adult children: gender, geographical distance, a parent's marital status, and culture.

- *Gender:* Gender plays a significant role in the intimacy levels of the elderly and their grown children. Women, for example, tend to express greater emotional intensity than do men in their intergenerational ties (Fingerman, 2001; Troll & Fingerman, 1996). Subsequently, elderly mothers and their adult daughters and daughters-in-law experience greater intimacy than do fathers and sons.
- *Geographical distance:* One national survey indicated that 63 percent of elderly parents see at least one of their children weekly (Crimmins & Ingegneri, 1990). Of the 11,000 senior citizen respondents in the national study, only 20 percent noted that they see their children once per month (or less).
- *Parent's marital status:* The older parent's marital status also influences the quality of intimacy between elderly parents and their children. Widowed or single older people (particularly women) frequently turn to their grown children or grandchildren for companionship and emotional support.
- *Culture:* Culture and ethnicity are key determinants in how intergenerational relationships develop and how intimacy

is fostered within these relationships. In the United States, for example, involvement in the aging parent's daily life is not supported by American culture, whereas in Japan and other Asian cultures such involvement is a dominant belief. These cultural differences may explain in part the discrepancies seen in the research as it relates to the impact of adult–child involvement in aging parents' lives, such as in India and among Latino Americans.

But clearly, while the "intimacy parents and offspring share in late life does not involve the close sense of oneness they could derive from a romantic partner" (Fingerman, 2001, p. 31), older adults take pleasure in these intergenerational ties.

Extended Family Experiences

In 2008, the U.S. Census Bureau indicated that nearly 9 percent of American households included grandparents and children under the age of 18 living in the same home, and 2.5 million grandparents assumed responsibility for most of the children's basic needs (food, shelter, clothing) of their grandchildren (U.S. Census Bureau, 2008b).

The **extended family** is typically defined as a family unit where two or more generations of close family relatives live together in one household. There are three common extended family configurations (Barbour, Barbour, & Scully, 2005):

1. A mother and father with children (may be married or not), with one or more grandparents.
2. Mother and father with children (may be married or not), with at least one unmarried sibling of the parents, or another relative, such as a cousin.
3. A divorced, separated, or never-married single parent with children, in addition to a grandparent, sibling, or other relative.

This type of extended or multigenerational family structure remains today an integral part of the lives of many families, and particularly in families of color. For example, families with African American roots often experience close-knit, multigenerational family groups—in addition to parents and children, family members are often grandparents. Today, about 30 percent of African American/Black Caribbean children is in an extended family configuration (U.S. Census Bureau, 2008b). Similarly, Latino American and Asian American families are often characterized by an extended family form; slightly under one-fourth of Hispanics and Asian American children live in an extended family, as compared to about 18 percent of white children (U.S. Census Bureau, 2008b).

Today, some of the most enjoyable, enriching intergenerational relationships the aging experience are with their grandchildren.

GRANDPARENTING

Grandparents are more prevalent today than ever before, partly due to the fact that the average life expectancy in the United States is anywhere from 68 to 80, depending on a person's race and gender (He et al., 2005). In the United States today, 3 in 10 adults (about 70 million) are grandparents; about 54 percent of grandparents are under the age of 65 (U.S. Census Bureau, 2008a). The passage to grandparenthood is often referred to as a *countertransition* because it is brought about by the transition of another family member (an adult child having children) (Pruchno & Johnson, 1996). Thus, unlike other adult roles, grandparenthood is not self-initiated or voluntary.

Becoming a grandparent is an exciting time for most people (Somary & Stricker, 1998). As adults enter their middle years, they begin to take on several new roles, such as in-law, grandparent, and caregiver to their aging parents. In the United States, while some parents become grandparents in their 30s (Szinovacz, 1998), typically most do so while in their 40s (about one-third), and about one-half of women become grandparents while in their 50s. And, as you will see a bit later in this chapter, today a significant number of grandparents assume the parenting role.

Overall, grandparenting experiences appear to be immensely satisfying—92 percent of survey respondents expressed high levels of satisfaction with their grandparenting role (Kaufman & Elder, 2003; Segatto & Di Filippo, 2003). Studies show that grandparents wish to see their grandchildren on a frequent basis, and these relationships often have positive outcomes on grandchildren's development (Adkins, 1999).

Until very recently there has been little theoretical foundation for the dynamics of grandparenthood, but the topic is stimulating interest in both the scholarly and the popular areas. Perceptions about grandparents have changed radically over the years. The perception of the grandmother, for example, in the late 1800s was one of a kindly, elderly, somewhat frail, gray-haired woman sitting in a rocking chair by the fire. Today grandmothers range in age from their thirties to their hundreds, and the "typical" grandmother is a middle-aged active woman, most likely dressed for work or working out at the gym. There is no uniform, consistent picture of grandparents because there is great diversity.

Characteristics of Today's Grandparents

Several variables are identified that seem to affect grandparenting experiences. The first of these is *gender*. Women outlive men by about 8 years, so that the oldest member of the family lineage is likely to be female. Therefore, most grandfathers are likely to be married, and a greater proportion of grandmothers are likely to be widowed. Perhaps that is the reason that grandmothers have been studied in more depth than grandfathers have.

Another factor that influences grandparent–grandchild relationships is the *geographical distance* separating them. Proximity is one of the strongest predictors of the grandparent–grandchild relationship. Evidence suggests that movement of older people to retirement communities reduces in-person contact between grandparents, their adult children, and grandchildren. The boomerang generation of adults might maintain or strengthen their relationships with grandparents by virtue of living with parents who facilitate extended intergenerational involvement.

Ethnicity is another factor related to grandparenting style. Research on intergenerational living arrangements, expectations, and circumstances of custodial grandparents emphasizes the need to examine ethnicity and social class in studies of grandparenting. For example, there is some evidence that **acculturation**—the adoption of mainstream values, language, and practices—creates a cultural gulf between generations in Hispanic families. Spanish-language compatibility between grandparents and grandchildren predicts the amount of contact between them, underscoring the importance of cultural affinity in structuring intergenerational relations.

Studies of white grandparents have focused on describing different types of grandparents and examining the meaning of the grandparent role, whereas studies of black grandparents have focused on grandparents as parent substitutes. Grandparenting seems to have a more central role for African American/Afro-Caribbean men than for male members of other ethnic groups, and grandparenthood is more important to rural black grandfathers than to rural white grandfathers (Pruchno & Johnson, 1996).

Grandmothers are central to the childrearing system of many black families, and they play a critical role in childrearing and parenting support, with grandmother involvement being a common response to family transitions and family crises, such as teen pregnancies, drug addiction, incarceration, or physical or mental illness (Hunter, 1997). Black grandparents rarely demonstrate a passive style of grandparenting, with most having an authoritarian, or influential, style that involves high levels of support and/or a "parentlike" influence. Black children are more likely than white children to view grandmothers as more influential in teaching lessons about life, morality, the importance of learning, and religion.

Finally, family disruption, especially the *divorce* of adult children, is shown to have substantial, often profound, effects on grandparents. Divorce may alter the normative, voluntaristic nature of the grandparent role, and the nature, type, and amount of interaction may either significantly increase or decrease.

Today, grandparent roles are ambiguous, in both form and function. In fact, there is no one-size-fits-all grandparent role because there are many ways to be a grandparent (Giarrusso, Silverstein, & Bengtson, 1996).

Styles and Experiences of Grandparenting

Just as there are different parenting styles, there are different styles of grandparenting. In a classic study by a pioneer in the study of aging, Bernice Neugarten and her colleague K. K. Weinstein (1964) identified five primary styles of grandparenting: formal, fun seeker, remote, involved, and dispenser of wisdom.

In the **formal grandparenting** role, grandparents see their role along common, traditional lines. These grandparents babysit every now and then and indulge their grandchildren on occasion, but when it comes to childrearing and discipline, they play a "hands-off" role; they are content to leave that aspect of parenting to the parents. About one-third of the grandparents practiced this grandparenting style. One study surveyed a representative sample of grandparents and found that over one-half of their research participants had a **companionate relationship** with their grandchildren (Cherlin & Furstenberg, 1985). Similar to the formal relationship, companionate grandparents enjoy warm, loving, and nurturing relationships with their grandkids, though they are happy to send them home when it is time!

Another common style of grandparenting is the **fun seeker**. These grandparents have a relationship with their grandchildren that is characterized by an informal, spontaneous playfulness. On the other hand, the distant grandparent has little or no contact with grandchildren and is only involved on occasional holidays or birthdays. This grandparenting style is defined as a **remote relationship**.

Many grandparents today assume the role of parent and are *surrogate* parents; this grandparenting style is described as an **involved relationship**. Overall, African Americans, Asian Americans, Italian Americans, and Hispanics are more likely to be actively involved in their grandchildren's lives than are whites because the sense of family is a core value among these cultures (Cavanaugh & Blanchard-Fields, 2002). Finally, the **dispenser of wisdom** grandparent offers information and advice to their grandchildren—often whether it is asked for or not.

EARLY GRANDPARENTING ROLES Grandparents' roles change as they and their grandchildren develop. Younger grandmothers may fulfill multiple roles, such as caring for their own children, their aging parents, and their grandchildren. They may have neither the time nor the desire to assume the conventional role of grandmother (Emick & Hayslip, 1996). When the grandchildren are young, grandparents may be more supportive and authoritative through providing more caregiving and helping services. As grandchildren enter adolescence, however, these roles and activities give way to mutual assistance, advice giving, and discussion of problems.

LATER GRANDPARENTING ROLES A few studies have examined relationships between adolescent and adult grandchildren and their grandparents. Adolescence, with its emphasis on identity formation, may be a time when contact with grandparents can be especially helpful because grandparents' historical accounts of familial/cultural events might provide a sense of continuity to the adolescent's life by merging her familial past with the future (Creasey & Koblewski, 1991). Although actual contact with grandparents tends to decrease throughout the lifespan, grandchildren's desire for contact over the course of adolescence does not decline; grandparents are still viewed as important attachment figures. A study of older adolescents and their grandparents found that grandparents were not seen as major targets for intimacy and did not provide significant instrumental aid, but grandchildren reported mutual love and respect and very low levels of conflict with their grandparents. The researchers concluded that most grandparents continue to play a relatively active role within their adolescent grandchildren's social networks (Creasey & Koblewski, 1991).

In fact, adult grandchildren report that their relationships with their grandparents are close and enduring, and these ongoing relationships often include high levels of association. When asked to choose a grandparent with whom they had the emotionally closest relationship, respondents in one study were more likely to pick a grandmother—especially the maternal grandmother—than a grandfather, regardless of their own sex. Furthermore, they found that time spent in an extraordinary relationship, such as that of a grandparent acting as surrogate parent for a grandchild, fixed a permanent attachment between the generations. Finally, men and women alike noted that as they had grown to adulthood, they were more likely to appreciate their grandparents (Hodgson, 1992).

An interesting study found that grandparents who had known their own grandparents as children, as opposed to those who had not, participated in more activities with their grandchildren, provided more instrumental assistance, were more likely to play the roles of mentor and companion, felt that they knew their grandchildren better, and were more likely to talk to their grandchildren about problems and plans for the future (King & Elder, 1997). Also, grandparents who lived with a grandparent while growing up were more likely than others to discuss their grandchildren's futures with them.

There are many sociological changes and transitions today that are changing the face of American families. Grandparents raising their grandchildren in extended family formations contribute to the expanding family landscape.

PARENTING, ROUND II: GRANDPARENTS AS PARENTS

Today, about 3 in 10 grandparents are responsible for raising their grandchildren (U.S. Census Bureau, 2008a). Referred to as **kinship care,** grandparents provide a living environment for their grandchildren for a number of reasons, but particularly because parents struggle with substance abuse, mental illness, economic hardship, divorce, domestic violence, and incarceration (Raphel, 2008). Most of these living arrangements are informal, private, and voluntary—the court system and/or the Social Welfare System are typically not involved in these arrangements. Parents commonly retain legal custody and can make decisions regarding their children, although in some cases the grandparents share legal custody; although not common, some grandparents adopt the grandchildren, and the rights of the parents are legally terminated.

The role of grandparents as parents is classified into four categories (Reynolds, Wright, & Beale, 2003):

- *Limited caretaking:* Grandparents have limited contact with their grandchildren, and parents have primary responsibility.
- *Participatory caretaking:* In these situations, grandparents are engaged and involved in their grandchildren's lives, such as taking an active interest in the children's education and their activities. Care may be provided for grandchildren while the parents are at work, but parents have primary responsibility for them.
- *Voluntary caretaking:* Grandparents assume the parental role and responsibilities for raising their grandchildren. Though situations vary, typically these types of caregivers assume the role of grandparents as parents to make sure their grandchildren are in a safe, stable environment in the absence of their parents.
- *Involuntary caretaking:* These grandparents are full-time caregivers of their grandchildren, and most often they have little to no

warning; many times, it is not the grandparents' preference—the situation was more or less thrust upon them. These types of arrangements are often difficult for children because of the unexpected shift in environments and caregivers.

While many grandparents welcome the opportunity to care for their grandchildren, others experience financial, social, and emotional intrusions, as well as an increase in health problems. As one body of research suggests, for many grandparents the role of second parenthood limits their independence and their personal development in mid- to later adulthood (Glass & Hunneycutt, 2002). However, other research suggests that there are rewards, such as getting a chance to raise a child differently, to nurture family relationships, and to receive love and companionship from their grandchildren (Burton, Dilworth-Anderson, & Merriwether-de-Vries, 1995).

Grandparent caregiving is particularly common in low-income, inner-city areas, where between 30 and 50 percent of children are cared for by grandparents (Minkler & Roek, 1996). African American/Black Caribbean grandparents, young grandparents, and grandparents with multiple grandchildren were more likely to be primary caregivers than grandmothers from other groups (Fuller-Thomson, Minkler, & Driver, 1997).

How Do Parenting Grandparents Fare?

How do grandparents fare when they take on the "second round" of parenting? One body of research explored the psychological and relational aspects of grandmother involvement in childcare from the grandmothers' points of view (Gattai & Musatti, 1999). Both paternal and maternal grandmothers describe strong love relationships, or actual bonds, with their grandchildren. They insist that these feelings are unique, different from other feelings of love for their spouses and children. Feeling less responsibility for their grandchildren than for their own children provide these grandmothers free rein to give affection to their grandchildren. Additionally, caregiving elicited memories of caring for their own children and difficulties in reconciling work and childcare, and often the involvement reestablished loose links with their own children.

Grandfathers' roles are minimal—sharing moments of play and walks with the grandchildren and relieving grandmothers when they had household tasks to perform. These grandfathers did not form deep, stable relationships with their grandchildren, and they tended to ignore the children's lack of autonomy and need for care.

DIMINISHED HEALTH Even though most grandparents take the role of parenting willingly, some studies indicate that custodial grandparents have a variety of problems. For example, grandparents have been found to score low on psychological and overall well-being. Many frequently feel depressed or anxious; they suffer from insomnia, hypertension, back and stomach problems, and other conditions that may be caused by the physical demands of the new role (Minkler & Roek, 1996; Pruchno & Johnson, 1996). In another study, more than one-third reported a decline in their health status, and many reported having missed a recent doctor's appointment because of demands of caregiving. Increases in alcohol and cigarette consumption also have been observed (Minkler & Roek, 1996; Pruchno & Johnson, 1996).

ECONOMIC DRAIN Of the grandparents providing care for their grandchildren, nearly 500,000 report income below the poverty line (U.S. Census Bureau, 2008b). There are several reasons for this. First, for younger grandparents, assuming the caregiving role often means quitting a job, decreasing work hours, or making job-related sacrifices that jeopardize their economic situations. Furthermore, retired or nonworking caregivers also frequently suffer financially from the decision to become full-time caregivers because many have no savings as cushions and have to stretch already inadequate Social Security checks even further.

DIMINISHED SOCIAL SUPPORT Besides health and economic costs, grandparents often face diminished social support. Some grandmothers report that parenting responsibilities limit their social roles, isolate them from friends, and give them less time with other family members (Minkler & Roek, 1996). Younger grandmothers who had to quit their jobs and leave behind valued social ties are the most isolated. However, while grandmothers in one study reported a variety of social roles, about one-third reported no contact at all with social or community organizations (Bayder & Brooks-Gunn, 1998).

SERVICE PROGRAMS FOR GRANDPARENTS As interest in grandparent caregiving has grown, community interventions and service programs to assist relative caregiving have increased. Support groups all over the United States provide opportunities to share feelings and concerns while giving and receiving informational support about resources and methods for coping with the new caregiving role. These support groups are of two kinds: informal, which often are held in a grandparent's home, and formal, which are sponsored by a health or social-service agency, a church, a school, or some other organization (Minkler & Roek, 1996).

Comprehensive programs generally offer a range of services, such as individual counseling, parenting classes, and supportive services for children. Peer training, respite care, and legislative advocacy of the rights of grandparents rearing children are among other activities provided. Some programs meet specific needs of parents, such as bus transportation for grandmothers and young children in their care so that they may visit incarcerated mothers or play-therapy sessions for young children prenatally exposed to crack cocaine.

Coalitions have been developed to influence legislative changes needed to address the needs of grandparent-headed families. The Grandparent Information Center in Washington, D.C., provides information and referral for grandparents nationwide. It also publishes a newsletter three times annually and "tip sheets" on how to start support groups, plus other topics of interest (Minkler & Roek, 1996).

How Do Grandchildren Fare?

Little research has focused on the effects on children of being reared by grandparents. Most custodial grandparents assume the care of their grandchildren because of the parents' inability to care for them. Thus, although some studies have shown that some of the children reared by grandparents exhibit behavioral or emotional problems, it is unclear whether these problems result from disturbances in their families of origin or from residence with grandparents. When the child's parent(s) resides with or near the child, both children and adults may suffer role confusion. Too many caregivers may lead to the presumption that someone else has performed a specific childcare duty, and grandchildren may subsequently suffer.

Children reared by grandparents are found to be poorer students academically but less likely to experience behavioral problems in school. In addition, they tend to be physically healthier than were children reared by single biological parents. Children reared by older grandparents appear to be better students than those reared by younger grandparents (Emick & Hayslip, 1996). Overall, children reared solely by their grandparents fare quite well relative to children in families with one biological parent present (Pruncho & Johnson, 1996).

Stepgrandparenting

Only within the past 5 years has attention to *stepgrandparents* been found in the research literature. The high rates of divorce and remarriage in the United States have increased dramatically a child's chances of having both grandparents and stepgrandparents, and sometimes ex-stepgrandparents.

A study of young adult college students assessed relationships with stepgrandparents and found that stepgrandchildren maintained contact with their stepgrandparents beyond high school, and the majority of young people desired more contact (Trygstad & Sanders, 1989). Almost half rated their relationships with stepgrandparents as important, though the relationship strengths were rated as moderate.

Stepgrandchildren perceived the relationship as both personal and social, and they expected little from their stepgrandparents beyond gift-giving. It has been suggested that the older the child is when he becomes a stepgrandchild, the less important the relationship will be. Other variables, such as the prestige of the biological father and the stepfather, distance between stepgrandchildren and their stepgrandparents, acquisition of the stepgrandparents through death or divorce, satisfaction with the remarriage of the biological parent, and maternal or paternal lineage of the stepgrandparents are all related to the stepgrandchild–stepgrandparent relationship (Trygstad & Sanders, 1989).

These young adults had considerably more contact with their grandparents than with their stepgrandparents, and relationships with their grandparents were rated as stronger than those with their stepgrandparents. Additionally, the young adults' expectations of their grandparents exceeded their expectations of their stepgrandparents. It appears that stepgrandparents can play an important role with their stepgrandchildren, but the relationship does not replace the relationship with the children's grandparents (Sanders & Trygstad, 1989).

Grandparent visitation laws, which grant grandparents legal standing to petition for legally enforceable visitation with their grandchildren—even over parental objections—have been passed in all 50 states. The impetus for these statutes was the severing of grandparent–grandchild relationships following the death or divorce of the custodial parent, usually, but not always, the mother. The award of visitation rights depends in most states on a judicial determination of the child's "best interests." Despite the positive role that grandparents can play in facilitating the healthy development of grandchildren, intergenerational conflict as a result of a visitation dispute can victimize grandchildren, and the ensuing long-term consequences are unknown. Clearer guidelines for "best interests" are needed, and more data on what happens in families following a judicial award of visitation privileges is essential (Thompson, Tinsley, Scalora, & Parke, 1989).

Grandparents raising their grandchildren is a growing phenomenon in the United States, and much more study needs to be done so family practitioners understand the unique needs of the grandparents and the children they are parenting. With this knowledge, human service providers, such as teachers, social workers, ministers, and mental health workers, can begin to successfully implement parenting classes and other resources for caregiving grandparents in order to equip them with the necessary skills to best raise their grandchildren.

The final stage in Erickson's stages of psychosocial development occurs when individuals approach old age. This stage, **integrity versus despair,** represents a time in which people reflect on their lives—it is hoped, with a sense of satisfaction. For many, it is at this point in the life cycle that childrearing and parenting demands decrease or cease, and caring for elderly parents increases.

PROVIDING CARE FOR ELDERLY PARENTS

Many people hold the common misconception that elderly people who can no longer "do" for themselves reside in a long-term care facility, such as a retirement home or a nursing home. On the contrary: for every one person who resides in a healthcare facility, there are at least two who live out their remaining years with the help of family caregivers (He et al., 2005). These family members provide the lion's share of medical and personal health assistance, in addition to emotional, spiritual, and financial support.

Being in the middle of two generations—parenting adolescent or younger children while at the same time caring for aging parents—is known as the **sandwich generation,** and presents many challenges to middle-aged adults, as the opening vignette illustrates for us. Being squeezed between two generations is perhaps one of the greatest distinguishing features of families today compared to the family decades ago: "In middle adulthood . . . the family role involves not only giving assistance in both directions in the generational chain, but also shouldering the primary responsibility for maintaining affectional bonds. These responsibilities produce what is sometimes called the mid-life 'squeeze,' and those being squeezed form the sandwich generation" (Boyd & Bee, 2009, p. 433).

Today's longer lifespans present a new challenge to adult children because providing care for aging parents extends the caregiving career by a number of years. In most cases, caregiving is not isolated to a single period in the family life cycle, but instead exists throughout the entire family life cycle. The **caregiving career** makes up those years caregivers tend to dependent children, aging parents, and eventually, dependent husbands or wives (Brody, 1985). If the spouse cannot provide the necessary care, the burden shifts to the adult children (Lemme, 2006).

Parent Care

There is a distinction between the concepts of caregiving and providing aid. **Caregiving** reflects dependence on another person for any activity essential for daily living, including instrumental activities (such as laundry, meal preparation, and certain aspects of healthcare) (Walker, Pratt, & Eddy, 1995). Caregiving encompasses assistance beyond the aid provided to physically and psychologically healthy parents. For example, getting an item from the grocery store is considered to be an intergenerational aid exchange rather than caregiving unless the parents are unable to shop independently. Providing aid to elderly parents is more common than providing care.

Parent care has been conceptualized from a lifespan perspective, likening it to childrearing. In the early part of the lifespan, parents provide the necessities for the child's survival—food, clothing, shelter, love, and guidance. During this time there is an imbalance in the exchange of help in favor of the child, often resulting in parental sacrifices. The child, it is hoped, develops the basic attachment that provides the foundation for later relationships. When the child reaches young adulthood, the exchange of help becomes more balanced, especially if the young adults have children of their own. Middle-aged parents may provide babysitting, help with finances, and so forth, and young adults may assist their parents with transportation, household and yard maintenance, and so forth. In the latter part of the lifespan, the exchange of help often shifts in favor of the elderly parent, when parent caring is essential for survival of the elderly. Viewed this way, parent caring and childrearing become intricately related (Krause & Haverkamp, 1996).

ADULT DAUGHTERS AS CAREGIVERS The caregiving landscape is dominated by women, making daughters and daughters-in-law the most common caregivers. In an examination of national healthcare trends, the National Council on Aging (2005) found that approximately 73 percent of all caregivers are women, with an average age of 46. Additionally, women are more likely than men to miss work or reduce their workload in order to care for a family member or an ailing spouse. Research in early 2000 indicated that nearly 90 percent of caregivers for people with Alzheimer's disease are women (Daire, 2004).

Why is it that women are the more likely caregivers for their aging parents? Developmentalists Helen Bee and Denise Boyd (2009) offer two suggestions. One factor may be that women experience greater emotional closeness to their parents, and consequently feel a greater need to care for them as they age. Another factor may be related to the ways in which women are socialized: Women are typically socialized to be the nurturing parent to their own children; they simply transfer their nurturing to their aging parents.

Because parent care almost always is provided by a daughter, women have been referred to as "women in the middle" (Noelker & Wallace,

1985). These women are more likely to provide care to their mothers so that both the givers and the receivers of this care are overrepresented by women (Marks, 1996). Roles as caregiving daughters and daughters-in-law to dependent older people have been added to their traditional roles as wives, homemakers, mothers, grandmothers, and workers.

One study examined the motivations of adult children for caring for elderly parents (Stein et al., 1998). They found that feelings of obligation are more important than feelings of affection and general attitudes about filial responsibility combined. Overall, women experience greater feelings of obligation than do men. Specifically, female children feel more obligation to maintain contact, to participate in family rituals, to provide assistance, to avoid conflict, and to engage in personal sharing with their parents. Like many other aspects of family relationships, parental obligation is an issue primarily for women.

ADULT SONS AS CAREGIVERS Actually, male caregivers constitute a sizable portion of the total population. About one in seven men is a caregiver, but not all the men in the sample care for elderly parents (Marks, 1996).

There are differences in the way sons and daughters approach caregiving, the roles they play, and the impact of the caregiving experience on their lives. For example, caregiving sons receive more support from their spouses than caregiving daughters do, and they are less likely than daughters to make sacrifices to provide care (Mui, 1995). Daughters who provide care report more neglect of other family responsibilities and more negative effects on their future plans and leisure time than sons report. Married daughters expect little from their husbands, and they view their husbands as supportive as long as they neither resent nor interfere with their caregiving activities (Walker et al., 1995).

OTHER CHARACTERISTICS OF CAREGIVERS There is great variability among caregivers and their experiences. Race, ethnicity, socioeconomic status, education level, marital status, and personality characteristics affect both the caregiver and the person receiving the care. In most cases, family members work together to decide who will help with what in providing various caregiving tasks (Ingersoll-Dayton, Neal, Ha, & Hammer, 2003). Research shows that people who have launched all of their children, are not working outside of the home, and are not married are more likely to provide care for aging parents (Brody, Litvin, Hoffman, & Kleban, 1994).

Caring for aging parents involves multiple tasks (Gatz & Hurwicz, 1990):

- Emotional support
- Personal care (bathing, dressing, toileting, wound care, assisting with mobility or medications)
- Instrumental help (cooking, cleaning, grocery shopping, laundry, lawn care, and such)
- Financial management or financial assistance
- Making decisions about care and arranging any required care by physicians, nursing care, social services, hospice care, and the like.

Caregiving responsibilities exert physical and emotional wear and tear on caregivers. This is called **caregiver burden.**

Stressors Associated with Caregiving

Providing care for aging loved ones is a stressful experience, both for the caregiver and for the entire family system. So stressful is caring for an aging loved one that depression rates for caregivers are between 30 and 50 percent (Lemme, 2006). The more stressful aspects of caregiving include (National Council on Aging, 2005):

- *The transformation of a cherished relationship.* For many caregivers, it is difficult when an interdependent relationship is transformed to a dependent relationship. When the caregiver is an adult child, the caregiving role becomes the overarching aspect of the parent–child relationship.

- *Problematic physical behaviors.* Because the caregiver is responsible for helping a loved one with dressing, bathing, toileting, and communicating, many caregivers feel a great deal of stress from these perpetual responsibilities.
- *Cognitive impairments.* When caregivers are taking care of a cognitively impaired parent, such as those with dementia or Alzheimer's disease, emotional distress is felt greatly by both patient and caregiver.

A number of stressors and rewards are commonly reported by adult child caregivers. Psychologist Mary Ann Parris Stephens (Stephens & Franks, 1999; Stephens, Franks, & Atienza, 1997; Stephens, Townsend, Martire, & Druley, 2001) undertook numerous studies to determine the types of stressors caregivers experience when caring for a loved one. Some of the stressors include:

- Receiving complaints and criticisms from parents
- Uncooperative or demanding parents
- Agitated parents
- Forgetful or unresponsive parents
- Helping with personal care needs
- Managing a parent's financial or legal affairs
- Receiving little help from family or friends

Although caregiving is often difficult and demanding, it also provides many rewards. Stephens's multiple research studies show many rewards, including:

- Knowing the parent is well cared for
- Spending quality time with a parent
- Enjoying the parent's affection and appreciation
- Seeing a parent derive pleasure from small things
- Seeing a parent calm and content
- Experiencing a closer relationship with a parent

The stressors are not isolated to individual caregivers, however. When a parent or family member becomes a caregiver for an elderly parent, not only does it cause stress and strain on the caregiver, but these radiate throughout the entire family system and, in turn, affect the family's balance. This stress causes increased family tensions, reduced time families have to spend together, role conflict and role strain, changes in individual and family lifestyles, and financial strain (Lemme, 2006). And according to Lemme (2006), the tensions created by family caregiving can exacerbate previously existing strengths or weaknesses in the family system.

When the tables turn and middle-aged adults begin to parent their parents, they suddenly take on conflicting roles. In negotiating these competing roles, many adults experience losses associated with providing care to their aging parent. Understanding these losses is key in understanding and coping with the feelings associated with parenting parents (Conway & Conway, 2000).

PARENTS' LOSSES AND NEEDS As parents age and lose their independence, their children notice other gradual losses along the way. In addition to losing their financial stability, for example, they also lose what was once an important social network, an important source of identity. As their aging friends begin to die, their social identity is further eroded. With the loss of their social network, losses associated with physical decline become that much more pronounced. With their vision, hearing, mobility, memory, strength, and independence in jeopardy, many older adults feel that they will lose their usefulness and their worth. Therefore, it is essential that aging parents are shown that they have continued dignity, and that they are still valued and useful to society. Older parents may also need to have their business needs met, such as helping them to pay bills and care for their property. While caring for the parents, adult children also have needs and experience losses, too.

ADULT CHILDREN'S LOSSES AND NEEDS The caregiver—the adult child—experiences losses also. As we have discussed, middle-aged adults lose their time and freedom and take on a number of additional stressors that may affect their own personal health and intimate relationships. As they devote increasing amounts of time to their parents' needs, they are leaving less time to spend with their own spouses and children, or to furthering their careers. By and large parents have been back-ups throughout life, providing for their children's every need. Thus, when they age, "not only are they weakening physically and shrinking physically in size, [they also] shrink in their capacity to help" (Conway & Conway, 2000). As we observe the gradual deterioration and decline in our parents, we realize (often quite suddenly) that our parents are mortal—and that death is an eventuality.

It is important to understand, then, that when adult children assume the role of caregiver for their aging parents, new needs and family challenges emerge (Conway & Conway, 2000). Being the "squeeze" generation often means that in the process of meeting the needs of two generations, the adult children's personal needs are squeezed out and forgotten. Consequently, it is important for sandwiched caregivers to nurture their marital and other intimate relationships by making time to spend with one another. (Conway & Conway, 2000). It's also imperative that adult-children caregivers guard their own mental, emotional, and physical health. This may include learning coping techniques that help buffer the stress associated with caregiving, and doing things that nourish mental health and the physical body. Finally, middle-aged children caring for their parents need to be realistic. A parent may sometimes require "tough love," just as parenting a child does. It is necessary to balance being rational with sensitivity and compassion.

Managing the dual roles of parenting two generations simultaneously brings a variety of conflicting feelings. But if family members understand the legitimate needs of the family members and can make the necessary adaptations and adjustments necessary to meet those needs, then parenting parents while parenting children can be a deeply rich and rewarding life experience.

Summary

Our study in these last three chapters shows us the evolving nature of parenting, how the roles of both parents and children change as each navigates the developmental tasks associated with family living. Once fully dependent infants and young children, across the lifespan we become increasingly more independent, relying less on our parents for support and care. And, over time, many of us gradually become more dependent on our children to care for us in our later years. And the cycle begins again.

Now that you have an understanding of parenting processes across the life course, in the next unit we turn our attention to effective parenting strategies, such as communication and forgiveness, and parenting in diverse cultures. We then explore diverse experiences such as single parents and gay and lesbian parenting.

References

Adkins, V. (1999). Grandparents as a national asset: A brief note. *Activities, Adaptation, and Aging, 24*, 13–18.

Aldous, J. (1985). Parent–adult child relations as affected by the grandparent status. In V. Bengston and J. Robertson (Eds.), *Grandparenthood* (pp. 117–132). Beverly Hills: Sage.

Aquilino, W. (1991). Predicting parents' experiences with co-resident adult children. *Journal of Family Issues, 12*(3), 323–342.

Aquilino, W., & Supple, K. (1991). Parent–child relations and parents' satisfaction with living arrangements when adult children live at home. *Journal of Marriage and the Family, 53*(1), 13–27.

Atkinson, A., & James, D. (1991). The transition between active and adult parenting: An end and a beginning. *Family Perspective, 25*(1), 57–66.

Barbour, C., Barbour, N. H., & Scully, P. A. (2005). *Families, schools, and communities: Building partnerships for educating children.* Upper Saddle River, NJ: Pearson.

Baydar, N., & Brooks-Gunn, J. (1998). Profiles of grandmothers who help care for their grandchildren in the United States. *Family Relations, 47,* 385–393.

Boyd, D., & Bee, H. (2009). *Lifespan development* (5th ed.). Boston: Allyn & Bacon.

Brody, E. M. (1985). Parent care as a normative family stress. *Gerontologist, 25,* 19–29.

Brody, G., Flor, D., & Neubaum, E. (1998). Coparenting processes and child competence among rural African-American families. In M. Lewis & C. Feiring (Eds.), *Families, risk, and competence* (pp. 227–243). Mahwah, NJ. Erlbaum.

Brody, E. M., Litvin, S. J., Hoffman C., & Kleban, M. H. (1995). Marital status of caregiving daughters and co-residence with dependent parents. *The Gerontologist, 27,* 75–85.

Burton, L., Dilworth-Anderson, P., & Merriwether-de-Vries, C. (1995). Context of surrogate parenting among contemporary grandparents. *Marriage and Family Review, 20,* 349–366.

Carter, B., & McGoldrick, M. (2005). *The expanded family life cycle: Individual, family, and social perspectives* (4th ed.). Boston: Allyn & Bacon.

Cavanaugh, J. C., & Blanchard-Fields, F. (2002). *Adult development and aging* (4th ed.). Belmont, CA: Wadsworth.

Cherlin, A., & Furstenberg, F. (1985). Styles and strategies of grandparenting. In V. Bengston and J. Robertson (Eds.), *Grandparenthood* (pp. 97–116). Beverly Hills, CA: Sage.

Clemns, A., & Axelson, L. (1985). The not-so-empty nest: The return of the fledgling adult. *Family Relations, 34*(2), 259–264.

Conway, J., & Conway, S. (2000). *Parenting your parents.* Retrieved May 2, 2009, from www.midelife.com.

Creasey, G., & Koblewski, P. (1991). Adolescent grandchildren's relationships with maternal and paternal grandmothers and grandfathers. *Journal of Adolescence, 14*(4), 373–387.

Crimmins, E. M., & Ingegneri, D. G. (1990). Interaction and living arrangements of older parents and their children. *Research on Aging, 12,* 3–35.

Emick, M., & Hayslip, B. (1996). Custodial grandparenting: New roles for middle-aged and older adults. *International Journal of Aging and Human Development, 43*(2), 135–154.

Fingerman, K. L. (2001). A distant closeness: Intimacy between parents and their children in later life. *Generations, 25*(2), 26–33.

Fuller-Thomson, E., Minkler, M., & Driver, D. (1997). A profile of grandparents raising grandchildren in the United States. *The Gerontologist, 37,* 406–411.

Gattai, F., & Musatti, T. (1999). Grandmothers' involvement in grandchildren's care: Attitudes, feelings, and emotions. *Family Relations, 48,* 35–42.

Gatz, M., & Hurwicz, M. (1990). Are old people more depressed? Cross-sectional data on Center for Epidemiological Studies depression scale factors. *Psychology and Aging, 5,* 284–290.

Giarrusso, R., Silverstein, M., & Bengtson, V. (1996, Spring). Family complexity and the grandparent role. *Generations,* pp. 17–23.

Glass, J. C., & Hunneycutt, T. L. (2002). Grandparents parenting grandchildren: Extent of situation issues involved and educational implications. *Educational Gerontology, 28*(2), 139–161.

Goldscheider, F., & Goldscheider, C. (1998). The effects of childhood family structure on leaving and returning home. *Journal of Marriage and the Family, 60,* 745–756.

Halpren, J., Shroder, M., & Citera, M. (1996). Perceptions by adult children of elderly parents' needs. *Psychological Reports, 78,* 571–577.

He, W., Sangupta, M., Velkoff, V. A., & DeBarros, K. A. (2005). 65+ in the United States: 2005. *United States Census Bureau Current Population Reports* (pp. 23–209). Retrieved April 12, 2009, from www.census.gov/prod/2006pubs/p23-209.pdf.

Hodgson, L. (1992). Adult grandchildren and their grandparents: The enduring bond. *International Journal of Aging and Human Development, 34*(3), 209–225.

Hunter, A. (1997). Counting on grandmothers: Black mothers' and fathers' reliance on grandmothers for parenting support. *Journal of Family Issues, 18*(3), 251–269.

Ingersoll-Dayton, B., Neal, M., Ha, J., & Hammer, J. (2003). Collaboration among siblings providing care for older parents. *Journal of Gerontological Social Work, 40,* 51–66.

Johnson, C. L. (1999). Fictive kin among oldest old African Americans in the San Francisco Bay area. *Journal of Gerontology, 54,* S368–S375.

Kaufman, G., & Elder, G. (2003). Grandparenting and age identity. *Journal of Aging Studies, 17,* 269–282.

King, V., & Elder, G. (1997). The legacy of grandparenting: Childhood experiences with grandparents and current involvement with grandchildren. *Journal of Marriage and the Family, 59,* 848–859.

Krause, A., & Haverkamp, B. (1996). Attachment in adult child–older parent relationships: Research, theory, and practice. *Journal of Counseling and Development, 75,* 83–91.

Lemme, B. (2006). *Development in adulthood* (4th ed.). Boston: Allyn & Bacon.

MacRae, H. (1992) Fictive kin as a component of the social networks of older people. *Research on Aging, 14,* 226–247.

Marks, N. (1996). Caregiving across the lifespan: National prevalence and predictors. *Family Relations, 45,* 27–36.

Minkler, M., & Roek, K. (1996, Spring). Grandparents as surrogate parents. *Generations,* pp. 34–38.

Mitchell, B., & Gee, E. (1996). "Boomerang kids" and midlife parental marital satisfaction. *Family Relations, 45,* 442–448.

Mui, A. (1995). Caring for frail elderly parents: A comparison of adult sons and daughters. *The Gerontologist, 35*(1), 86–91.

Mykyta, L., & Macartney, S. (2011). *The effects of recession on household composition: "Doubling up" and economic well-being.* SEHSD Working Paper Number 2011-4. Retrieved May 7, 2011 from: www.census.gov/hhes/www/poverty/publications/recession-effects.doc.

National Council on Aging (NCOA). (2005). *Caregiver research: The latest news.* Retrieved August 12, 2009, from http://www.ncoa.org/content.cfm?sectionID=379&detail=2044.

Neighbour, R. H. (1985). The family life cycle. *Journal of the Royal Society of Medicine 78*(8), 11–15.

Neugarten, B. L, & Weinstein, K. K. (1964). The changing American grandparent. *Journal of Marriage and the Family, 26,* 299–304.

Noelker, L., & Wallace, R. (1985). The organization of family care for impaired elderly. *Journal of Family Issues, 6*(1), 23–44.

Pinquart, M., & Soerensen, S. (2000). Influences of socioeconomic status, social network, and competence on subjective well-being in later life: A meta-analysis. *Psychology and Aging, 15,* 187–224.

Pruchno, R., & Johnson, K. (1996, Spring). Research on grandparenting: Review of current studies and future needs. *Generations,* 65–70.

Raphel, S. (2008). Kinship care and the situation for grandparents. *Journal of Childhood and Adolescent Psychiatric Nursing, 21*(2), 118–120.

Reynolds, G. P., Wright, J. V. & Beale, B. (2003). The roles of grandparents in educating today's children. *Journal of Instructional Psychology, 30*(4), 316–325.

Sanders, G., & Trygstad, D. (1989). Stepgrandparents and grandparents: The view from young adults. *Family Relations, 38*(1), 71–75.

Segatto, B., & Di Filippo, L, (2003). Relationship and emotions in couples in the retirement and/or empty nest phase. *Eta_Evolutivia, Giunti Firenze.*

Somary, K., & Stricker, G. (1998). Becoming a grandparent: A longitudinal study of expectations and early experiences as a function of sex and lineage. *The Gerontologist, 38,* 53–61.

Stein, C., Wemmerus, V., Ward, M., Gaines, M., Freeberg, A., & Jewell, T. (1998). "Because they're my parents": An intergenerational study of felt obligation and parental caregiving. *Journal of Marriage and the Family, 60,* 611–622.

Stephens, M. A. P., & Franks, M. M. (1999). Intergenerational relationships in later-life families: Adult daughters and sons as caregivers to aging parents. In J. C. Cavanaugh & S. K. Whitbourne (Eds.), *Gerontology: An interdisciplinary perspective* (pp. 329–354). New York: Oxford University Press.

Stephens, M. A. P., Franks, M. M., & Atienza, A. A. (1997). Where two roles intersect: Spillover between parent care and employment. *Psychology and Aging, 12,* 30–37.

Stephens, M. A. P., Townsend, A. L., Martire, L. M., & Druley, J. A. (2001). Balancing parent care with other roles: Inter-role conflict of adult daughter caregivers. *Journal of Gerontology: Psychological Sciences, 56B,* P24–P34.

Swensen, C. H., Eskew, R. W., & Kohlhepp, K. A. (1981). Stage of family life cycle, ego development, and the marriage relationship. *Journal of Marriage and the Family, 60,* 413–425.

Szinovacz, M. E. (1998). Grandparents today: A demographic profile. *The Gerontologist, 38,* 37–52.

Thompson, L., & Walker, A. (1984). Mothers and daughters: Aid patterns and attachment. *Journal of Marriage and the Family, 46*(2), 313–322.

Thompson, R., Tinsley, B., Scalora, M., & Parke, R. (1989). Grandparents' visitation rights: Legalizing the ties that bind. *American Psychologist, 44*(9), 1217–1222.

Troll, L., & Fingerman, K. L. (1996). Parent/child bonds in adulthood. In C. Malestesta-Magai & S. McFadden (Eds.), *Handbook of emotion, adult development, and aging* (pp. 185–205). Orlando, FL: Academic Press.

Trygstad, D., & Sanders, G. (1989). The significance of step-grandparents. *International Journal of Aging and Human Development, 29*(2), 119–134.

Umberson, D. (1992). Relationships between adult children and their parents: Psychological consequences for both generations. *Journal of Marriage and the Family, 54*(3), 664–674.

U.S. Census Bureau. (2008a). *Current Population Survey, 2007 Annual Social and Economic Supplement.* Washington, DC: Author. Retrieved August 20, 2009, from www.census.gov/population/www/socdemo/hh-fam.html.

U.S. Census Bureau. (2008b). Living arrangements of children: Household economic studies. *Current Populations,* P70-114. Washington, DC: Author.

Veroff, J., Douvan, E., & Kulka, R.A. (1981). *The inner American: A self-portrait from 1957 to 1976.* New York: Basic Books.

Walker, A., Pratt, C., & Eddy, L. (1995). Informal caregiving to aging family members: A critical review. *Family Relations, 44,* 402–411.

White, L. (1992). The effect of parental divorce and remarriage on parental support for adult children. *Journal of Family Issues, 13*(2), 234–250.

Wu, Z., & Penning, M. J. (1997). Marital instability after midlife. *Journal of Family Issues, 18*(5), 459–478.

Chapter 5
Effective Strategies for Contemporary Parents

There is no question that children's outcomes in all realms of their development—biological, cognitive, and psychosocial—are linked to a family's childrearing practices (American Academy of Pediatrics, 2002). Because of the eagerness of parents for support and guidance in raising their children, a number of strategies for childrearing have evolved to help parents become more effective. For example, many strategies have been introduced to parents by the publication of books designed specifically for them. Others have been more formalized in the sense that they have been "taught" to parents by professionals. More recently, strategies such as workshops and websites have been developed.

Throughout our study we have come to understand that parents and the family significantly affect children's health and well-being, no matter what the family's structure (married, single-parent, cohabiting, or divorced), the parents' income (single-earner, dual-earner, or poverty), or the parents' education (high school drop-out or college educated). We have also seen that in today's society, there are a number of social changes and stressors that, at times, make effective parenting difficult. But what is a "successful" family or a "successful" parent? And, given individual differences in children and parents alike, is it even possible to define—and achieve—such a thing as "successful" parenting?

In this chapter we explore the aspect of communication as foundational to parent–child relationships. We then take a look at different parenting strategies that some parents may employ to address their children's misbehaviors, and we also look at the difference between discipline and punishment. We conclude by examining a new area of empirical research: the concept of forgiveness as a cornerstone of effective, healthy relationships.

Nurturers. Motivators. Guides. Advocates. Communicators. When each of these parenting roles are done well, parents foster their children's self-worth and self-respect.

responsive, sensitive care. Children's attachment needs are fostered through enduring, cohesive, affectionate parenting (American Academy of Pediatrics, 2002). Throughout our study, we have discussed numerous parenting styles and parenting strategies. In the section that follows we build upon this knowledge base as we explore certain characteristics that successful families and parents have. We start by looking at the importance of family/parent communication.

SUCCESSFUL PARENTING: COMMUNICATION IS THE FOUNDATION

First, it's important to recall from Chapter 2 that all children thrive in homes where there is reliable,

Communication: Interconnecting Family Relationships

All interpersonal relationships—including the parent–child relationship—involve change, and communication is no exception. As relationships with partners and with children grow, change, and develop over time, so too do our communication patterns and behaviors. The communication process is such a critical aspect of our lives that it shapes the family and gives it its distinct identity (Galvin, Bylund, & Brommel, 2008).

When we communicate with our children and partners, we have a joint or reciprocal impact on each other in our exchanges. This dynamic is a **transactional** process in which we *simultaneously affect and are affected by our intimate relations*. When we discuss communication in this context, the focus of the interaction is not on the *words* people speak, but instead on the *interconnectedness* of the relationship.

How parents communicate with their children influences the quality and the content of their relationships. For example, in Chapter 3 you saw the significance of parent–adolescent communication in regard to teens' sexuality and delaying the onset of adolescent sexual behaviors. Because we develop all of our interpersonal (social and relational) communication skills within our family of origin, this is where we build our foundation (whether in healthy ways or unhealthy ways) for communicating to resolve conflict, share intimacy, and express our needs, wants, fears, hopes, frustrations, anger, or desires. When we discuss family and parenting communication we are referring to not just the talk that takes place among couples and parents and their children, but the entire array of communication transactions, such as storying (see Figure 5.1).

Broadly stated, **communication** is the process of making and sharing meanings. Lynn Turner and Richard West (2006), professors and researchers of communication studies, summarize the general concepts of communication:

- **Communication is a transaction.** Communication is a transactional process where parties act simultaneously as senders or receivers of messages. All human behavior is a continuous dialogue.
- **Communication is a process.** Communication is dynamic and ever-changing. Viewed in this way, emphasis is placed on the *process* of meaning-making, rather than on the *outcome* of the exchanges. Each family undertakes the process of meaning-making differently; culture and ethnicity are key in the process of meaning-making.
- **Communication involves co-construction of meanings.** Each person in a relationship speaks a unique language that was acquired from his or her family of origin. The process of communication thus consists of learning the meaning of things—*constructing definitions*—between family members.

Storying is one of the most fundamental ways families create meanings and thus their unique family identity. Growing up, how many times did you hear family stories like "When you were a baby, you ..." or "Ask Shawn to tell you about the time he drove the car through the garage door when he was 4 years old." Family stories tell us how our family came to be, how the family stands behind its members, how the family handles diversity, and what it means to be a Welch, a Carlisle, or a Garcia. Family stories are what give meaning to everyday family life, allowing families to reflect upon their collective experiences (Galvin and others, 2008).

1. Is there a particular holiday, family vacation, or other family event that stands out in your memory? What makes this occasion more memorable than another?
2. Have your memories of this event changed over time?
3. What do you think a nonfamily member would learn about your family from this story?

FIGURE 5.1 Family stories.

Sources: Welch, *Family Life Now*, 2e. (2010). Boston: Allyn & Bacon. p. 86. Based on Galvin and others (2008); International Reading Association (2005); McLaughlin (2005); Wells (1986).

- **Communication involves symbols.** In order to construct meanings or definitions of things, people rely on *symbols* or *codes*. Across cultures, the codes that are used for communication are *verbal* and *nonverbal*. These two broad categories are used to describe how we convey meanings to one another, both in our interpersonal and social relationships.

Of course, given the diversity of today's families, there is no one-size-fits-all communication template. And, since our first experiences with interpersonal relationships occur within our families of origin, our understanding of how families communicate and parent is often narrow (Turner & West, 2006), so we need to widen our knowledge of communication behaviors within a broad range of family types. Do family structures differ in the issues that challenge them? Communication experts help us to see how communication might differ within different family types (Turner & West, 2006).

COMMUNICATION WITHIN NUCLEAR FAMILIES Issues important in today's contemporary families center on communicating about the division of household chores, the effects of work life on family life, and the involvement of men in their children's lives. Men in contemporary nuclear families have increased the amount of time they spend with their children as well as household chores. But spillover—when the stresses associated with work affect home life—tends to increase levels of conflict at home.

COMMUNICATION WITHIN GAY AND LESBIAN FAMILIES In some respects, gay and lesbian partners and parents struggle with relationship issues (such as conflict) and parenting issues (such as childcare) just as heterosexual parents do. But gay fathers tend to receive more support from their families of origin than do lesbian mothers, though self-disclosure of their sexual identity is a difficult communication subject for many.

COMMUNICATION WITHIN STEPFAMILIES Family communication within stepfamily structures most often centers on negotiating roles, communication rules, and the unique family subsystems that are formed when two families merge to form a stepfamily. Families who understand that it takes time for families to "blend" see less family conflict than those families who challenge or resist the process of merging the two families.

COMMUNICATION WITHIN SINGLE-PARENT FAMILIES In families where *collectivism* is endorsed (as in African American, Hispanic, and Asian American families), single parents receive a great deal of support, protection, and emotional reinforcement. In cultures where *individualism* is embraced, as in white families, the family of origin may communicate blame and guilt to the single parent.

COMMUNICATION WITHIN HETEROSEXUAL COHABITING FAMILIES Unique to cohabiting couples is a lack of communication role models for this specific family configuration. Cohabiting couples face greater demands in the areas of roles and support of their family structure.

Cornerstones of Communication

To better understand nurturing communication between couples, parents, and children, it helps to know what forms the basis for effective communication patterns and behaviors. Kathleen Galvin and her colleagues (2008) offer insight into concepts that provide families rewarding and satisfying communication across the developmental life cycle of the family. From their research they outline the key concepts of family-strengthening communication.

USE CONFIRMING MESSAGES AND RESPONSES Confirming *messages/responses* validate those with whom we are communicating. These types of communication are characterized by recognition of the other person, relevant dialogue, and acceptance; all of these show a willingness to

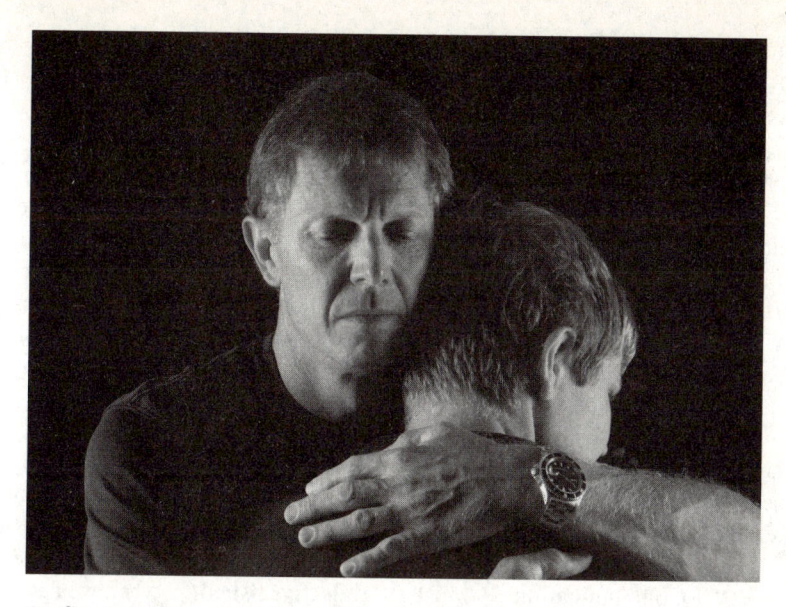

Confirming messages can be verbal or nonverbal, but they always convey positive feelings about the person or the relationship. Does this father need to speak the words, "All is forgiven" or do you think that the child knows his father forgives him? What confirming messages do you observe?

be involved in the relationship (Sieburg, 1973). When we use confirming messages and responses, not only do we acknowledge the other person's presence, but we also suggest we are willing to become involved with that person.

There are two key aspects of confirming messages or responses: recognition and acceptance. *Recognition* essentially consists of confirming or acknowledging—either verbally or nonverbally—another's presence and validates them as a significant, contributing member of the relationship. Such confirmation is an absolute must for family and parent–child relationships. Confirming messages such as, "It was so sweet of you to take the garbage out without me asking you," or "Thank you so much for playing with your little brother while I was on the conference call!" imply acceptance of the other. On the other hand, rejecting responses such as "You're so stupid," or "Oh shut up, you don't know what you're talking about!" serve only to invalidate or reject the family member (Canary, Cody, & Manusov, 2000). Over time the individual feels rejected and that they are of little importance to the family system.

Acceptance simply means that every family member has the sense that they are "all right" (Galvin et al., 2008). On the surface this seems reasonable and easy to achieve. But ethnic and cultural differences affect how we react and respond to those with whom we are communicating. In some cultures, families talk openly and are affectionate, while in other cultures family members are reserved and formal. For everyone, the growth of interpersonal relationships depends on messages that reflect each person's investment in the relationship (Galvin et al., 2008).

COMMUNICATE OFTEN Parent–child and couple relationships can either be enhanced or hindered by the time devoted to—committed to—nurturing the process of communication. According to the Pew Research Forum (2008), 75 percent of the respondents indicated that a lack of time with family was a greater family problem than a lack of money, despite the economic crisis that occurred in the United

States in 2008. Simply stated, if you are not ever together as a family then precious little time exists to nurture the relationship, and this includes the fundamental element of family—communication. It helps if couples and families periodically take an inventory of what is happening in each other's lives and open the lines of communication when taking stock of communication patterns and behaviors. **Family meetings** or weekly family discussions (whether they are formal or informal) provide structure and organization to the family system and allow for meaningful conversation. It is up to the parents to ensure that a safe, trusting atmosphere exists within the home to foster an environment that encourages open, honest communication between parents and the children.

LISTEN ACTIVELY Communication is most effective when **active listening** takes place. When we actively listen, we *hear* what the other person is saying. We are interacting with someone who is important to us. This process is considered an art that connects us to another so we understand not only what others are saying, but what they are feeling, too (Lindgren, 1998). When active listening does not take place, the effects of poor listening can be quite detrimental to a family's communication patterns. Family scientist Herbert Lindgren (1998) describes several styles of poor listening in Table 5.1. Notice that the primary reasons behind poor listening styles tend to be *self*-centered, rather than *other*-centered. And herein lies a base skill in effective, meaningful communication: accurately hearing and receiving the words, meanings, attitudes, feelings, and emotions of the person sending the messages.

Another form of attentive listening is **reflective listening**, when we pay close attention to a person's verbal and emotional (nonverbal) messages, and respectfully acknowledge their

TABLE 5.1 Poor listening styles.

To truly listen to others involves the art of connecting in such a way that you fully understand not only what they are saying but also what they are feeling. Indeed, active listening is a vital, essential skill that is needed in marriages, families, and intimate relationships. Family scientist and practitioner, Herbert Lindgren, notes that ineffective or poor listening often is the result of bad listening habits or styles:

- **The Faker.** Fakers pretend to listen but don't. Their minds wander in and out of the conversation, but they may nod their head or smile as if they are listening.
- **The Interrupter.** Interrupters are more concerned about their own thoughts and feelings than they are with those of others. They seldom allow the other person to finish, or they immediately respond without pausing for much reflection or consideration of what the other has said. They seldom offer an understanding ear.
- **The Intellectual Listener.** Rather than listen relationally, intellectual listeners attend only to the actual spoken words. They ignore nonverbal communication cues and approach the conversation in a rational, logical way, rather than relying on their feelings or emotions.
- **The Self-Conscious Listener.** These listeners are more concerned with their own status and impressing someone than they are with the thoughts, ideas, or feelings of the other. Because they are trying to impress people with whom they are communicating, they do not listen with understanding. Instead, while the other is talking, the self-conscious listener is already forming his or her reply.
- **The Judge and Jury Listener.** These listeners judge the ideas and behaviors of others, letting others know how wrong or incorrect their thoughts and feelings are. In doing so, they do not hear what the other is saying.

Communication is a two-way, transactional process. Both the listener and the speaker have responsibility to make sure the message is understood.

Source: Welch, *Family Life Now*, 2e. (2010). Boston: Allyn & Bacon. p. 89. Based on Lindgren (1998).

perspective. During the course of the communication exchange, we should occasionally seek clarification from family members by saying things such as, "When you said _____, did you mean _____? I want to make sure I understand." Or, "Am I understanding you correctly when you say _____?" By taking time to *repeat in our own words* what we think the message is, we are both clarifying and validating the message we are receiving. While reflective listening exchanges such as these will sometimes result in a family member saying, "You're still not listening, that is not what I mean!" we need to keep in mind that reflective listening is not necessarily aimed at reaching an agreement as much as it is aimed at trying to come to an understanding of the message.

Another effective strategy in resolving conflict is to **reframe** an issue, which means looking at the issue from another perspective. Reframing allows you to see the issue while standing in the shoes of another. Reflective listening and reframing together foster an open, trusting, and caring communication environment.

The next sections discuss some of the contemporary strategies for parenting that are used by schools, agencies, and other groups to help parents become more effective. We begin by first looking at STEP, or Systematic Training for Effective Parenting. This program, founded on healthy family communication, promotes a democratic family atmosphere. Quality, effective parenting is fostered through encouragement, mutual respect, discipline that is consistent with behavior, firm limits, offering choices, making suggestions, and joint decision making by parents and children. As we work our way through the next section, you will see why effective communication strategies are important to the healthy development of children and to the parent–child relationship.

SYSTEMATIC TRAINING FOR EFFECTIVE PARENTING

The principles upon which **Systematic Training for Effective Parenting (STEP)** date to more than 65 years ago, when Alfred Adler, a psychiatrist, conducted open family-counseling sessions. Some of Adler's students came to the United States and established family centers based on his principles. Perhaps Adler's best-known student was Rudolf Dreikurs, who founded Child Guidance and Family Education Association centers in Chicago. Today, teachers and practitioners alike still utilize the STEP program.

The Parent's Handbook (Dinkmeyer, McKay, & Dinkmeyer, 1997a) is the updated version of the STEP program, and discusses essential topics—understanding yourself and your child, understanding beliefs and feelings, encouraging your child and yourself, listening and talking to your child, helping children cooperate, discipline that makes sense, and choosing your approach. In addition, the handbook includes topics on single parents, stepfamilies, cooperation in the family, schoolwork and homework, drugs, violence, and gangs. It also provides at-home activities for parents and family members.

The Goals of Misbehavior

As parents, we all at one point or another ask ourselves (oftentimes in desperation!), *"Why is my child acting like this?!"* Sometimes, all we manage to utter is, "Ugh!" Why *do* children misbehave, especially older children who almost certainly know that a behavior will almost guarantee that he or she will be disciplined? Adler offered an explanation to these questions.

Implicit in Adler's approach to understanding behavior is the notion that behavior serves a purpose and is best understood in terms of its social consequences—observing the parent's reaction to the misbehavior (Dinkmeyer et al., 1997a). The child's response to the parent's attempts at correction serve to reveal the purpose of the misbehavior, which usually stems from the child's major goal in life—to belong. According to these authors, misbehaving children are discouraged because they do not believe they can belong in useful ways; they therefore seek to belong through misbehavior (Dinkmeyer et al., 1997b).

The four categories of misbehavior are seen as "goals" in the sense that the misbehavior achieves something for the child. The first goal, *attention,* is almost universal in young children. If children cannot gain attention in constructive ways, they will seek it in destructive ways, especially if they feel that they can belong only by receiving attention. When this occurs, STEP advises parents to either ignore the misbehavior or pay attention to it in ways the child does not expect.

The second goal is *power.* Children who seek power may feel that they are important only when they are the boss. When children seek power, STEP recommends that parents refrain from becoming angry and disengage themselves from the power struggle. If the struggle for power continues, children may alter their desire and pursue the third goal.

Revenge is a goal that children pursue when they feel they must hurt others as they believe they have been hurt. The child finds a place by being cruel and disliked. Parents need to realize that vengeful behavior stems from discouragement, and they should avoid retaliation. Remaining calm and showing goodwill are necessary to improve the parent-child relationship.

When children continue a war of revenge with their parents, they may sometimes give up and seek to be excused for their misbehavior by displaying the fourth goal, *inadequacy.* These children are extremely discouraged and have given up hope of succeeding. Normally parents, too, feel despair, and children will respond to parents passively or fail to respond at all. When displays of inadequacy occur, parents need to eliminate criticism and focus on the child's strengths and assets, encouraging any efforts to improve.

Since children usually are unaware of their goals, their behavior and intentions toward their parents will change only if parents change their approaches. Before parents can change, it is important for them to understand more about their children and themselves. For example, STEP emphasizes that emotions are based on beliefs, and children learn to use their emotions to achieve one or more of the four goals. Often, beliefs are faulty because interpretations of experiences are inaccurate. Factors that contribute to beliefs are family atmosphere and values, sex roles played by parents, family constellation, and parents' attitudes and behavior toward children. The last factor is a significant one. STEP differentiates between "good" parents, who are so involved with their children that they believe they must do everything for them, and "responsible" parents, who give their children choices and let them experience the results of their decisions.

Reflective Listening and Open Responses

As you saw earlier, the communication process in families is so important, that it literally shapes family members' relationships. Not surprisingly, then, STEP emphasizes communication in effective, responsive parenting. We just saw how reflective listening promotes our ability to ascertain what a child is feeling when she communicates, and how this listening style helps us to analyze a child's "feeling" message and then put the feeling word into a response. For example, if a child laments, "That teacher is unfair! No matter what I do she won't like it!", a parent utilizing reflective listening might respond, "You're feeling angry and disappointed, but don't give up" (Dinkmeyer et al., 1997b).

Similarly, **open responses** acknowledge the child's right to his or feelings by demonstrating that the listener both accepts and understands the feeling and the message. On the other hand, **closed responses** deny children a right to their feelings by demonstrating the listener's unwillingness to accept and understand. When a child cries, "That teacher is unfair!", a parent using closed responses might say, "Her job isn't to be fair, her job is to teach you." This statement not only invalidates the child's feelings, it also indicates that the parent doesn't quite grasp the child's concerns.

Effective Talking

Equally important to listening effectively to children is talking effectively to them. Most parents use ineffective methods of communicating, such as sending a "solution message" or a "put-down message."

The emphasis on "I" messages (a confrontation skill) rather than on "you" messages helps parents to understand that if they give the child a statement of fact about how the parent is feeling in a given situation, they are less likely to be met with resistance and rebellion. For example, when a child has a messy room, a "you" message might be: "You are so lazy; this room is a mess." An alternative "I" message might be: "I get frustrated when I'm trying to keep the house clean and I see that your share hasn't been done." The second alternative avoids implying that the child is "bad" and places the responsibility with the child for modifying his or her behavior.

An "I" statement indicates an individual has a problem, but a "we" statement indicates that someone thinks a relationship has a problem; thus, the use of "we" statements is recommended when the problem is one of mutual concern to parent and child (Burr, 1990). For instance, a parent who is trying to help solve a family dispute about which TV program to watch may observe that the children are being too inconsiderate of one another. A mother might say, "We have a problem bigger than just what program to watch tonight. It's that we're not being considerate of one another."

"We" statements, then, are declarative sentences that try to locate tendencies, patterns, problems, thoughts, feelings, or other experiences in a relationship rather than in a person. These statements usually create less defensiveness and resistance than "I" messages. They foster the cooperative, mutually facilitating aspects of the relationship rather than a somewhat competitive or adversarial situation that leads to defensiveness.

Another area many parents struggle with is discipline. For example, is it harmful to spank a child when he or she misbehaves? There is a difference between *effective* discipline and *appropriate* response (Larzelere & Kuhn, 2005). In the next section we look at how successful parents correct their children's misbehavior.

CORRECTING BEHAVIOR: DISCIPLINE OR PUNISHMENT?

Another key element in the STEP approach is the utilization of natural and logical consequences as an alternative to reward and punishment. The purpose of allowing natural consequences to occur and of designing logical consequences is to encourage children to make responsible decisions, not to force their submission (Dinkmeyer et al., 1997b). There is a difference between correcting a child's negative behaviors and physically and emotionally wounding a child.

Natural and Logical Consequences

Natural consequences are those that occur naturally as a result of behavior. For example, a child who refuses to eat goes hungry or a child who refuses to wear mittens gets cold hands (Dinkmeyer et al., 1997b). **Logical consequences** are those that are imposed as a result of behavior but are logically related to the behavior. They express the reality of the social order and acknowledge mutual rights and mutual respect. For instance, a child who does not put his dirty clothes in the hamper by laundry time might go without her favorite outfit for another week. Several principles are given in STEP to guide the use of natural and logical consequences, and these are presented in Table 5.2.

TABLE 5.2 Exploring alternatives.

Use reflective listening to understand and clarify the child's feelings.
Explore alternatives through brainstorming.
Assist the child in choosing a solution.
Discuss probable results of the decision.
Obtain commitment for the course of action.
Plan a time for evaluation.

Source: Based on Dinkmeyer, D., McKay, G., & Dinkmeyer, D. (1997b). *The parent's handbook.* Circle Pines, MN: American Guidance Service, pp. 89–92.

STEP points out that there are some major differences between applying logical consequences and punishment. Logical consequences (Dinkmeyer et al., 1997b):

- acknowledge mutual rights and mutual respect, whereas punishment expresses the power of personal authority.
- are logically related to misbehavior, whereas punishment rarely is.
- imply no element of moral judgment, whereas punishment tells the child he or she is bad.
- focus on present and future behavior, whereas punishment focuses on what is past.
- are based on goodwill, and punishment is associated with threats or retaliation.
- permit choice, whereas punishment demands obedience.

As we noted earlier, under no circumstances should discipline violate the physical or emotional well-being of children (Canter & Canter, 1985). Given this, some researchers define **discipline** as corrective action designed to help teach children more appropriate behavior—it is not an action designed to make a child hurt (Canter & Canter, 1985).

Assertive Discipline

Lee Canter, a family-child counselor, and Marlene Canter, a teacher, developed the Assertive Discipline strategy. **Assertive discipline** is a structured behavioral management approach designed to help teachers, educators, and parents to positively influence children's behaviors (Canter & Canter, 1985).

The Canters note that assertive discipline is warranted when other approaches fail to work, and that a parent needs to take charge in problem situations and let children know that the parent is the "boss." The central message that a parent should get across is that he or she loves the child too much to let him or her misbehave; therefore, problem behavior must stop. In addition, assertive discipline techniques promote the idea that it is equally important for parents to provide their children with direct and positive feedback when they change the problem behavior. These strategists recognize that many parents are reluctant to "come on strong" with their children, and most do not know how to take charge.

In the Assertive Discipline training program, before parents are taught to implement an assertive discipline plan, the typical inappropriate responses that many parents use are discussed. For example, *nonassertive responses* are inappropriate because parents are not stating clearly what they want the child to do, or they are not reinforcing their words with actions. These responses, then, communicate to the child that parents do not "mean business." *Hostile responses* usually result in negative feelings between parent and child and communicate to the child that the parent is out of control. Once parents learn to recognize inappropriate responses, they are ready to learn how to put an assertive discipline plan into action. The assertive discipline plan has three basic steps: communicate assertively, back up words with action, and lay down the law.

According to the authors, to communicate assertively, a parent must address the child with direct, assertive statements and consistently praise a child throughout the day. The parent must also back up her words with action by using disciplinary consequences for behavior, such as separation, taking away privileges, or grounding. However, the parent should also provide positive support when he "catches the child being good." Laying down the law (a no-nonsense approach that makes it clear that the parent demands the child changes his or her problem behavior) includes setting up a systematic assertive discipline plan.

There are criticisms of the assertive discipline techniques, however. Specifically, although the approach incorporates some positive techniques from other strategies (reinforcement for "good" behavior, utilizing choices, selecting logical consequences, and developing a contract), the emphasis seems to be on a more authoritarian approach. Other criticisms point out (Gartrell, 1987; Hitz, 1988):

1. The model does not facilitate the development of a positive self-concept, especially for young children, 4 to 8 years of age.
2. Desirable behavior is forced through power-assertion techniques rather than through developing responsible behavior rooted in ethical purposes. It appears that children learn only that behavior is good because it is rewarded or bad because it is punished.
3. Positive attitudes are inhibited.
4. Although positive reinforcement is recommended in the model, it is often ineffective and can be coercive and manipulative.

These criticisms may seem harsh, but no data to date have refuted them.

OTHER EFFECTIVE SUCCESSFUL PARENTING MODELS

There are a number of successful parenting models available for parent education today. In the sections that follow, we briefly examine the National Extension Parent Education Model, Partners for Fragile Families, and Growing Together.

The National Extension Parent Education Model

The **National Extension Parent Education Model** was developed by a group of extension specialists to assist parent educators in developing and focusing their parent-education efforts (Smith, Cudaback, Goddard, & Myers-Wall, 1994). The model is not a parenting curriculum but, rather, an overview of parenting essentials.

SELF-CARE Effective parents manage personal stress and their family resources, and they offer support to other parents. They also ask for and accept support from others when needed, recognize their own personal and parenting strengths, and have a sense of purpose in setting childrearing goals. They cooperate with their childrearing partner.

UNDERSTAND It is important that parents observe and understand their children's development, and that they recognize how children influence and respond to what happens around them.

GUIDE Parents must also establish and maintain reasonable limits, and provide their children with developmentally appropriate opportunities to learn responsibility. This includes conveying fundamental values, teaching problem-solving skills, monitoring children's activities, and facilitating and monitoring their contact with peers and adults.

NURTURE Nurturing not only involves parents who ably express affection and compassion for their children, it also includes fostering children's self-respect and hope. This is accomplished when parents listen and attend to their children's feelings and ideas, as well as when they provide for their children's nutrition, shelter, clothing, health, and safety needs. Nurturing might also include providing children with their sense of heritage.

MOTIVATE Much like a coach, parents are their children's motivators. Parents teach children about themselves, others, and the world around them. They stimulate creativity and curiosity, imagination, and the search for knowledge. They create interactive learning conditions, and they help children process and manage information in developmentally appropriate ways.

ADVOCATE Effective parents find, use, and create community resources when needed to benefit their children, and their community's children. They also stimulate social change to create supportive environments for children and families alike. In addition, they build family, neighborhood, and community relationships.

There are a variety of ways to implement this model (see Table 5.3 for suggestions). The curriculum guide for this program includes a description of parent-education resources developed in various states; it also includes ordering information. Materials to assist parent educators

TABLE 5.3 Suggestions for implementing the national extension parent education model.

Parent-education groups	Parent-education resource centers
Newsletters	Radio programs
Home visits	Mentor mother/grandparent programs
Hospital programs	Newspaper articles/tabletop messages
Community forums	Interagency support/collaboration
Support groups	Community coalitions/task forces
Learn-at-home activities	Parent advisory groups
Social-change groups/liberation pedagogy	

Source: Based on Smith, C., Cudaback, D., Goddard, W., & Myers-Wall, J. (1994). *National extension parent education model of critical parenting practices.* Manhattan, KS: Kansas State University.

in developing parenting programs are available through county Extension offices throughout the country. County Extension specialists use these materials with individual parents and with groups of parents in developing more effective parenting skills.

Partners for Fragile Families

Partners for Fragile Families was developed to address young fathers' real experiences (Wilson & Johnson, 1991). This curriculum offers support, information, and motivation on issues involving parenthood, relationships, sexuality, job skills, and becoming self-sufficient. Some sessions are devoted to personal development, including topics such as values, responsibility, and male stereotypes. Other sessions deal with life skills, including communication, decision making, dealing with stress, and coping with discrimination.

As we have learned throughout this text, fathers have a profound influence on their children's development, and one of the greatest strengths of the Partners for Fragile Families program is the content about responsible fatherhood. Topics geared toward supporting inexperienced fathers include fatherhood today, understanding the child-support system, understanding children's needs, a father's influence on his children, coping as a single father, building a child's self-esteem, and helping children learn. Toward the end of the course, the sessions focus on health and sexuality. These discussions deal with men's health, substance abuse, sexuality, and reducing sexual risks.

Growing Together

This program was developed for teen mothers in 1992. Similar to the Partners for Fragile Families program, **Growing Together** is geared toward single, at-risk teenage mothers. The program teaches positive behaviors to young mothers, such as setting goals; seeking help in the family, school, and community; and developing pride in themselves and their new role as parents. It also focuses on practical methods to help teen moms cope with their own needs and those of their infants.

The video/DVD program format consists of topics of interest to teen parents. These include:

- *Just Like You:* Dealing with self-esteem, this content presents ways to develop a solid foundation for the emotional health of the baby and ways to help the mother develop her own self-esteem.
- *Out of Danger:* This outlines and discusses the vulnerability of babies and steps their mothers can take to protect them.

- *Good Food for a Good Start:* This teaches the fundamental principles of proper infant feeding. The session explains and encourages a healthy diet for both the baby and the mother.
- *Strong and Healthy:* Presenting basic information the mother should know about maintaining the infant's health and her own, the program emphasizes a positive approach to healthy living and when to call the doctor in case of illness.
- *What My Baby Can Do:* This session covers physical development, what to expect at each age, and how to foster normal infant development.
- *Feelings, Family, and Friends:* The last session focuses on social and emotional development through positive play activities, interaction with family, and finding support from friends.

As we look at these parenting programs, we can see that most strategies have as their goals the raising of physically and emotionally healthy children. The goals that are implicit in most of the strategies are helping parents and children resolve conflict in ways that assist children in becoming more responsible, providing choices, promoting decision making, being consistent in demands, and emphasizing the needs of parents as well as children. We can also see that modeling of responsible behavior of the child is advocated as a way to foster responsibility in children. We next need to look at the strengths and limitations of these programs.

Parent Programs' Strengths and Limitations

Because of the great diversity in families today, no one parenting education program will be a good fit for each family. As with all other aspects of parenting, many parents find that using different aspects of several parenting programs works best for them. Strategies for parenting described in this chapter share several similarities and some differences.

SIMILARITIES The most obvious similarity is the emphasis on a free-and-equal relationship between parents and children, with the child's needs and feelings respected as being valid and as being highly correlated with behavior. Only in the case of assertive discipline are power-assertion techniques emphasized. Punitive techniques (shouting, threatening, ridiculing, shaming, and physical punishment) are not advocated, whereas inductive techniques, use of encouragement, and development of self-control are emphasized. Parenting behaviors are manifested in a context of warmth, nurturance, and acceptance in all the strategies, again with the exception of assertive discipline techniques, and most strategies recommend imposing certain limits. Communication is seen as the major component of a positive parent–child relationship.

Identifying the causes of children's behavior is emphasized in all the strategies except assertive discipline. STEP, especially, emphasizes that all misbehavior has a goal that is based on faulty beliefs, and parents need to understand the beliefs and identify the goals before they can effectively deal with the behavior. This is why it is so important for parents to have an understanding of developmentally appropriate behavior and to understand how children respond to what happens around them.

DIFFERENCES The major difference among the strategies seems to be the degree of emphasis given to various principles. STEP and assertive discipline stress changing the child's behavior, but the mechanism for doing so is different in each strategy. Assertive discipline uses explicit rewards and punishments to change behavior, whereas STEP focuses on changing children's behavior by the use of natural and logical consequences. Even though other strategies focus less on changing children's behavior, they address the issue through the use of problem-solving sessions or changes in communication techniques.

The use of parental power is the technique that separates assertive discipline techniques from other strategies. Whereas other strategies seek to reduce the power of the parent and to create a more egalitarian relationship, assertive discipline enhances the parent as the powerful authority figure. This strategy also forcefully employs the use of punishment more than other strategies.

Most strategies advocate the use of praise, but the way in which it is used varies. STEP differentiates between praise and encouragement and only recommends the use of encouragement. It is contended that praise focuses only on the outward manifestation of a specific behavior (the product), whereas encouragement focuses on the child's motives and efforts (the process).

Obviously, these similarities and differences in approach result in slightly differing parental behavior in certain situations and in similar parental behavior in other situations.

PROGRAM STRENGTHS It appears that each of the strategies previously described has unique strengths and limitations. In general, the skills described in the strategies are relatively simple for parents to learn. If parents apply them over a period of time with success and see that they actually cause either their children or themselves to change behavior, then they are likely to become encouraged and develop a more positive relationship with their children. In addition, being trained in a specific strategy of parenting may give parents some concrete ideas of how to deal with specific problems in the parent–child relationship. As we have already mentioned, parents are now more isolated from sources of support in parenting than they once were, and many of them are eager for sources of ideas and advice.

Finally, most of the strategies take into account the parents' feelings as well as the children's. Becoming aware of our own anger, discouragement, satisfaction, needs, desires, and concerns may be the first step in becoming a more effective parent. And improving communication between parents and children can be mutually satisfying to both.

PROGRAM LIMITATIONS Strategies for parenting have limitations, both individually and collectively. First, most strategies do not account for either age or sex differences in children. Most research indicates that there are subtle differences in the behavior of boys and girls and differences in the ways both mothers and fathers interact with each sex. Also, although the strategies make some attempt to differentiate between the application of methods for younger children and teenagers, a precise differentiation is absent. Parents need a bit more guidance in understanding the effects of both gender and the developmental level of children in their application of specific methods or skills.

Another assumption that seems to be made by strategists is that a given strategy is applicable equally to all cultures and socioeconomic classes. Clearly, strategies fail to take into account variations in cultural attitudes and values and complex issues related to poverty. In fact, most strategies are oriented to middle-class white families.

In order for any program to be effective, it must address the unique needs of the population it is servicing. Those parenting programs that have been successful use methods designed especially for low-income families—home visits to individualize the support, make up sessions for families unable to be present for all treatment sessions, and financial incentives for completing the program.

Low-income parents are more likely to remain in parent-education programs if family management training is provided first in the sequence of activities. We also know that family practitioners should:

- Focus on very practical skills that parents can immediately implement at home.
- Help parents learn to observe and define specific behaviors to be changed.
- Teach parents to reinforce positive behaviors and to prevent problem situations.
- Teach parents to respond to negative behaviors with nonaversive consequences.

- Teach parents to help children set goals and solve problems.
- Assist parents in establishing family rules, meetings, and traditions.

Some critics contend that parents would probably benefit more from a basic, adequate knowledge of child development than from step-by-step guidelines—contemporary strategies appear to be cookbook approaches even though they are based on solid theoretical perspectives. A parent who relies on a single overall framework might achieve consistency in his or her relationships with children, but chances are that a single approach will not serve the parent adequately in all respects. In addition, the expectation that the specifically prescribed behaviors for parents will result in predictable behavior in children fails to consider the complex nature of the parent–child relationship and other variables that undoubtedly affect that relationship. Therefore, it seems that more emphasis must be placed on putting into the hands of parents child-development literature that is understandable.

Critics of traditional parenting programs note that programs are of help only to parents who do not have many problems with their children, and that such programs tend to decrease the self-confidence of parents who already have problems with their children or who come from the lower economic strata. Although these criticisms have been used to argue against the use of parenting education programs altogether, they also may be used as a rationale for designing alternative programs that are more sensitive to parental needs.

Outcomes and Effectiveness

Several theoretical models have been used and tested to measure outcomes and the effectiveness of parent-education programs. The *phenomenological approach* was used to assess the outcomes of a parent-education program by examining both the structure and the experiences of the participants (First & Way, 1995). This qualitative study used intensive interviews, and the stories participants told were analyzed. These researchers concluded that transformative learning, which helps participants see their lives in fundamentally different ways and to act on those perceptions, occurred. The *cognitive development model* used to design, implement, and evaluate a parent-education program focused on parent development in the areas of parental awareness and interpersonal interaction themes; it also proved to be an effective approach (Thomas, 1996).

Another theoretical model was designed to evaluate a parenting-skills training program focusing on teaching skills to parents and middle-school students to reduce a child's risk for drug and alcohol use (Rueter, Conger, & Ramisetty-Mikler, 1999). The model identified two variables that moderate the benefits that parents might receive from the training: pretreatment skills of parents and life context. The researchers hypothesized that family stress resulting from marital difficulties or financial concerns would reduce the benefits of the program, and that strong preprogram skills (e.g., parental communication, parental negativity, or parent–child relationship quality) would increase benefits. Results were different for mothers and fathers, with fathers responding in the expected direction. However, mothers with the weakest preprogram communication skills and reported marital difficulties benefited the most. These researchers proposed that variables that could mediate program outcomes should be considered when assessing a program.

In many ways, this is where what we have learned throughout our study all comes together, and why it is so important that family practitioners and educators have a firm grasp on the different experiences of today's parents. Our exploration of parenting strategies in this chapter emphasizes why parenting programs need to become more conceptually comprehensive, procedurally interactive, and topically relevant to parental backgrounds and needs. The application of any one-size-fits-all approach is not effective. Instead, an integration of strategies seems necessary.

No one strategy is a cure-all for parent–child relationships. It seems best to take a more eclectic approach to parent education. We should provide parents with a broad base from which to function and allow them more freedom to choose from a number of strategies whose methods the parents feel comfortable with and that seem to be successful for them and their children.

Despite our blue-ribbon efforts, however, sometimes our communication and parenting efforts are ineffective or they fail, and when this happens, conflict or disagreements occur (Anderson & Sabatelli, 2007). While some couples or parents may try to avoid conflict, it is to be expected. And, when a family member hurts or offends another, sometimes it's difficult to let it go. Although the concept of *forgiveness* has received a lot of attention from philosophers, theologians, and poets for years, only as recently as the past decade have social and family scientists begun to explore its necessity for effective family and parenting life. Next we explore forgiveness as a characteristic of successful parenting.

SUCCESSFUL PARENTING: WILLING TO FORGIVE

A Campaign for Forgiveness Research (2008) is a foundation that supports scientific studies that deepen our understanding of forgiveness and how reconciliation takes place. It seeks to answer questions such as, *How does forgiveness improve the human condition? How do we choose to forgive? What are the effects of holding grudges and seeking revenge?* In the social science literature, **forgiveness** is described as a deliberate process that transforms a strong desire for revenge into a positive response (Maio, Thomas, Fincham, & Carnelley, 2008). In other words, forgiveness is a process where the forgiver intentionally moves from negative thoughts, feelings, and behaviors associated with the event to more positive ones (Maio et al., 2008). It is not condoning, excusing, or forgetting what happened. Forgiveness occurs at two different levels: at an *individual* level and at a *relationship* level (Thompson, Snyder, Hoffman, Michael, Rasmussen, Billings, et al., 2005).

Forgiving: The Individual Level

All too frequently, the people that we love the most are the people that we hurt and are hurt by (Fincham, Beach, & Davila, 2004). But how can we move past this inevitable hurt—what motivates us to forgive someone? Why do some people put more effort into forgiveness than others?

When discussing forgiveness at the individual, or *intrapersonal,* level, we first need to recognize that the concept of forgiveness is an internal process—it is primarily for the individual who was hurt, not for the offender. When we forgive someone, we free ourselves from the control of the person who hurt us.

We also need to understand that forgiveness is subjective. We are each taught in our families of origin what behaviors demonstrate/convey forgiveness and unforgiveness; the concept of forgiveness is defined in each home to serve the needs of those particular family members. For example, if your partner had sex with another person while committed to you, would you leave that partner and end the relationship?

Overwhelmingly, most often people respond that yes, they would leave their partner. But every now and then someone might indicate that one of their parents had been cheated on, yet chose to stay in the marriage and work things out. By their example, the couple taught their children that forgiveness is an option in this situation.

Certainly, subjective notions of forgiveness vary from person to person, and from culture to culture. In fact, this has been one of the looming hurdles for investigators who desire to examine the application of forgiveness to certain relationship problems (Silberman, 1995). In addition to the intrapersonal level, forgiveness can be applied differently to situations within the same relationship.

Forgiving: The Relationship Level

The reality of any human relationship is that everyone fights! In order for a relationship to succeed, then, it is important for us to grasp the concept that forgiveness is essential in our relational lives because it can break patterns that would otherwise interfere with—or even destroy—the relationship. When we discuss forgiveness at the relationship level, we are referring to the *interpersonal* level.

Forgiving spouses report more positive outcomes in their relationships because forgiveness is linked to tendencies to behave more positively in the marriage (Fincham et al., 2004; Fincham, Hall, & Beach, 2006). For instance, in one study that examined forgiveness among 72 newly married couples, the researcher found that spouses who were forgiving reported being happier in their marriages than those who did not report high levels of forgiveness (McNulty, 2008). The research also revealed that forgiveness was associated with having less severe marital problems, as well as spouses who behaved less negatively (i.e., bickering, arguing, stonewalling) with each other.

Emerging scholarship suggests that there are a number of factors associated with the interpersonal level of forgiveness. These include conflict resolution skills and the willingness to forgive, overall relationship satisfaction, and commitment to the relationship (Fincham et al., 2004; Kachadourian, Fincham, & Davila, 2005; Younger, Piferi, Jobe, & Lawler, 2004). The rapidly expanding body of forgiveness research shows us that people forgive others both at the intrapersonal and interpersonal levels. But we still must determine *how* people forgive.

Communicating Forgiveness: A Family Process

Forgiveness is an essential family process that is necessary to help family members deal with and heal from the inevitable offenses, hurts, or traumas that take place in relationships (Wade, Bailey, & Shaffer, 2005). If we don't forgive, emotional and relational wounds fester and cause anger, fear, and rage to develop. But how do families and individuals develop the capacity to forgive?

There are many different pathways to forgiveness, and researchers have begun to better understand models of relational forgiveness. For example, Dr. Fred Luskin, a researcher from Stanford University, put forth a model of forgiveness in which people pinpoint their rage, realize that harboring anger is unhealthy, and look at their situation differently so it's not as problematic as they first thought (Luskin, 2003). A recent study found that people contemplate their situation and go through a series of thoughts before considering forgiveness as an option (Knutson, Enright, & Garbers, 2008). The participants' responses, in order of importance, are:

1. I admitted to myself that the person hurt me.
2. I became aware of my anger.
3. I admitted to myself that I felt shamed or humiliated by what the person did.
4. I lost my energy by staying resentful.
5. I thought over and over about what happened.
6. I compared my unfortunate state with my offender's more fortunate state.
7. I realized that I may have been permanently changed by the offense.
8. I realized my ways of handling the problem were not working.
9. I was willing to consider forgiveness as an option.
10. I committed to forgive the person who hurt me.
11. I thought of the [person/situation] in broader and [different] terms.
12. The anger left me.

As you can see, forgiveness is a process that begins with admitting to ourselves that someone hurt us. As we move through the process, we acknowledge that our resentment is consuming us and changing us, and that we have to consider forgiving the offender before the anger can leave us.

Other contemporary research reveals that there are three ways in which we communicate forgiveness: *directly, indirectly,* and *conditionally* (Kelley, 1998):

- **Direct Forgiveness** With **direct forgiveness**, family members or intimate partners clearly, plainly, and directly tell the offender that they are forgiven. Forgivers use statements such as, "We talked about the situation and I told her she was forgiven," and "I let him know that by saying I forgave him so he has no doubts about it" (Merolla, 2008). When using direct forgiveness, people typically use strategies that include discussing the offense and the issues surrounding it, and the forgiver telling the person that they understand (Kelley, 1998).
- **Indirect Forgiveness** Family members or intimate partners communicate **indirect forgiveness** by nonverbal displays (such as a hug, a smile, or eye contact), and by acting as though the transgression never happened—by getting back to normal (Kelley, 1998). Forgivers indicate that, "I forgave him by acting the way we did before the event took place" (Merolla, 2008).
- **Conditional Forgiveness** The third way people forgive is with conditions attached to the forgiveness, which is why it's referred to as **conditional forgiveness**. This type of forgiveness is used when people want relational repair, but they want to make it very clear that repeating certain behaviors will not be tolerated (Merolla, 2008). For instance, a forgiver might say, "I'll forgive you, but you have to stay off the booze," or "If you promise never to do it again, I'll forgive you" (Merolla, 2008).

Clearly, forgiveness is not a process in which the forgiver condones, excuses, or forgets what happened to them (Knutson et al., 2008). For example, it is certainly possible to forgive an absent father, an abuser, or a cheating partner without reconciling with them. As one group of researchers observes, "When forgiveness is properly understood, it occurs from a position of strength, not weakness, because the forgiver recognizes the injustice and labels it for what it is" (Knutson et al., 2008, p. 193).

Finally, forgiveness needs to be understood just as any other process in family living. That is to say, the traits associated with forgiveness change as individuals progress through their lifespans, and as families progress through the family life cycle (Maio et al., 2008).

Barriers and Benefits

The most common roadblocks to forgiveness in intimate relationships center on pride (Baumeister, 2002). First, there are those people who believe that they are entitled to, or deserve, only the good things in life; they view forgiveness as too risky and unfair to them (Baumeister, 2002). These people are referred to as having a strong sense of **narcissistic entitlement**. This is an important finding because as another researcher notes, if someone possesses a sense of entitlement and thus believes that he or she is above forgiving or asking for forgiveness, how can a relationship survive (Exline et al., 2004)?

Another form of a pride-related barrier to forgiveness is **self-righteousness**, where a person can't see his or her own potential for doing wrong or hurting another person. Roy Baumeister, a researcher with Florida State University (2002), found in a series of studies that when people have a sense of self-righteousness, they tend to be less willing to forgive others and are harsher in their judgments of others. Dr. Baumeister observed that following the national tragedy of September 11, 2001, people reported they had less vengeful, unforgiving feelings if they believed the U.S. had committed similar serious acts on other countries in the past (Baumeister, 2002). In other words, low levels of self-righteousness allow people to see that they themselves are capable of committing such acts; as such, they are quicker to forgive or ask for forgiveness.

Finally, some people are afraid to forgive because they think it opens them up to or sets them up for being hurt again (Baumeister, 2002). Although researchers have found very little evidence that forgiving someone increases the chance of being hurt again by the same person, Baumeister's findings suggest that people still worry about the possibility.

Forgiveness is one of the most underutilized family processes that people can use to maintain healthy intimate and family relationships and friendships. Outside of love, forgiveness is perhaps the most important tool available for the longevity of family relationships.

Summary

In an effort to assist parents in becoming more effective in a rapidly changing society, a number of professionals have developed strategies of parent education. Some of the strategies have been developed and packaged so that parents participate in structured training sessions over a given period of time, whereas others are simply outlined in reading and video materials so that parents can be self-taught. All the strategies are designed for "normal" parents and children, providing support rather than crisis intervention.

Contemporary strategies share several similarities, and each has its strengths and weaknesses. Unfortunately, little research exists that tests the long-term effects of change in either parents' or children's behavior as a result of parent training using a particular strategy. Therefore, the effectiveness of these contemporary strategies must be assumed rather than known. Nevertheless, the availability of such resources for parents seems to be a positive force in today's society.

We are, as professionals who work with parents and their children, fortunate to have quality educational programming that we can use to help strengthen today's families. But as we have seen, without healthy communication families will struggle. We've learned that effective communication means listening and hearing *beyond the words*. Sometimes it means hearing with our hearts—listening compassionately—and not with our ears. Productive and healthy communication also involves a basic understanding that everything we say or do affects us, as we simultaneously affect others. And sometimes it means forgiving someone who has offended us or who has deeply wounded us, even though it can be a challenge—and a lot of individual and relational work—to do so. One of the greatest gifts a couple can give their children is to create an environment where each child is valued as a contributing member to the family system.

References

A Campaign for Forgiveness Research. (2008). Retrieved September 26, 2009, from www.forgiving.org.htm.

American Academy of Pediatrics, Committee on Psychosocial Aspects of Child and Family Health. (2002). Coparent or second parent adoption by same-sex parents. *Pediatrics, 109,* 339–240.

Anderson, S. A., & Sabatelli, R. M. (2007). *Family interactions: A multigenerational developmental perspective* (4th ed.). Boston: Allyn & Bacon.

Baumeister, R. (2002). *Humility, egotism, forgiveness, and the victim role.* Retrieved September 26, 2009, from www.forgiving.org.htm.

Burr, W. R. (1990). Beyond I-statements in family communication. *Family Relations, 39*(3), 266–273.

Canary, D. J., Cody, M. J. & Manusov, V. (2000). *Interpersonal communication: A goals-based approach* (2nd ed.). New York: Bedford/St. Martin's Press.

Canter, L., & Canter, M. (1985). *Assertive discipline for parents* (Rev. ed.). New York: Harper & Row.

Dinkmeyer, D., McKay, G., & Dinkmeyer, D. (1997a). *Leader's resource guide.* Circle Pines, MN: American Guidance Service.

Dinkmeyer, D., McKay, G., & Dinkmeyer, D. (1997b). *The parent's handbook.* Circle Pines, MN: American Guidance Service.

Fincham, F. D., Beach, S. R. H., & Davila, J. (2004). Forgiveness and conflict resolution in marriage. *Journal of Family Psychology, 18,* 72–81.

Fincham, F. D., Hall, J. H., & Beach, S. R. H. (2006). Forgiveness in marriage: Current status and future directions. *Family Relations, 55,* 415–427.

First, J., & Way, W. (1995). Parent education outcomes: Insights into transformative learning. *Family Relations, 44,* 104–109.

Galvin, K. M., Bylund, C. L., & Brommel, B. J. (2008). *Family communication: Cohesion and change* (7th ed.). Boston: Pearson Allyn & Bacon.

Gartrell, D. (1987). Assertive discipline: Unhealthy for children and other living things. *Young Children, 42*(2), 10–11.

Hitz, R. (1988). Assertive discipline: A response to Lee Canter. *Young Children, 43*(2), 25–26.

Kachadourian, L. K., Fincham, F. D., & Davila, J. (2005). Attitudinal ambivalence, rumination, and forgiveness of partner transgressions in marriage. *Personality and Social Psychology Bulletin, 31,* 334–342.

Kelley, D. (1998). The communication of forgiveness. *Communication Studies, 49,* 255–271.

Knutson, J., Enright, R., & Garbers, B. (2008). Validating the developmental pathway of forgiveness. *Journal of Counseling and Development, 86*(2), 193–199.

Larzelere, R. E., & Kuhn, B. R. (2005). Comparing child outcomes of physical punishment and alternative disciplinary tactics. A meta-analysis. *Clinical Child and Family Psychology Review, 8*(1), 1–37.

Lindgren, H. G. (1998). *Listening with your heart as well as your words* (NebGuid 92-1092). Lincoln: University of Nebraska Cooperative Extension.

Luskin, F. (2003). *Forgive for good: A proven prescription for health and happiness.* San Francisco: Harper.

Maio, G. R., Thomas, G., Fincham, F. D., & Carnelley, K. B. (2008). Unraveling the role of forgiveness in family relationships. *Journal of Personality and Social Psychology, 94*(2), 307–319.

McNulty, J. K. (2008). Forgiveness in marriage: Putting the benefits into context. *Journal of Family Psychology, 22*(1), 171–175.

Merolla, A. J. (2008). Communicating forgiveness in friendships and dating relationships. *Communication Studies, 59*(2), 114–130.

Pew Research Forum. (2008). *Inside the middle class: Bad times hit the good life.* Retrieved April 9, 2010, from www.pewsocialtrends.org/pubs/706/middle-class-poll.

Rueter, M., Conger, R., & Ramisetty-Mikler, S. (1999). Assessing the benefits of a parenting skills training program: A theoretical approach to predicting direct and moderating effects. *Family Relations, 48,* 67–77.

Sieburg, E. (1973). *Interpersonal confirmation: A paradigm for conceptualization and measurement.* Paper presented at the annual meeting of the International Communication Association, Montreal, Quebec (April, 1973).

Silberman, S. (1995). *The relationships among love, marital satisfaction, and duration of marriage.* Unpublished doctoral dissertation, Arizona State University.

Smith, C., Cudaback, D., Goddard, W., & Myers-Wall, J. (1994). *National extension parent education model of critical parenting practices.* Manhattan: Kansas State University.

Thomas, R. (1996). Reflective dialogue parent education design: Focus on parent development. *Family Relations, 45,* 189–200.

Thompson, L.Y., Snyder, C. R., Hoffman, L., Michael, S. T., Rasmussen, H.N., Billings, L. S., et al. (2005). Dispositional forgiveness of self, others, and situations. *Journal of Personality, 73,* 313–359.

Turner, L. H., & West, R. (2006). *Perspectives on family communication* (3rd ed.). Boston: McGraw-Hill.

Wade, N. G., Bailey, D. C., & Shaffer, P. (2005). Helping clients heal: Does forgiveness make a difference? *Professional Psychology: Research and Practice, 36*(6), 634–641.

Wilson, P., & Johnson, J. (1991). *Partners for fragile families.* Washington, DC: National Center for Strategic Non-profit Planning and Community Leadership.

Younger, J. W., Piferi, R. L., Jobe, R. L., & Lawler, J. A. (2004). Dimensions of forgiveness: The views of laypersons. *Journal of Social and Personal Relationships, 21,* 837–855.

Chapter 6
Contemporary Parenting: Diversity and Change

Today it is essential that students know the differing arrangements of families because this understanding allows human service providers and other family professionals and educators to more effectively support, value, and work with diverse families (Banks & McGee-Banks, 2002). In essence, **diversity** refers to the broad spectrum of demographic and philosophical differences among people groups within a culture. When we talk about being **diverse**, or about diversity in the United States, we are referring to peoples' differences in age, gender, race, ethnicity, culture, sexual orientation, and religion. When we study people from a diversity perspective, it not only furthers our knowledge about the variances in parenting experiences, but it also helps us to value individuals and groups, free from bias. This then fosters a climate of equity and mutual respect.

In this chapter we first examine the different cultural contexts in which parenting occurs, and we then address characteristics of parenting and parent–child interactions among diverse cultural groups in the United States. We also look at the socioeconomic status of families, which is a key variable in parenting practices. As we conclude the chapter, we briefly explore governmental policies and how they affect families with children.

PARENTING IN CULTURAL CONTEXTS

As we continue our study of contemporary parenting, it is necessary to understand and embrace the idea that we do not develop in isolation. Who we are as human beings—every emotion, fear, thought, and behavior—is somehow linked to the family in which we were raised, both genetically and environmentally. It is also important to understand that there are many areas of parenting that are affected and influenced by the broader culture in which we live, by the many facets of society that surround us. Often these influences are overlooked in the study of the processes associated with parenting practices.

It is important to understand that parenting experiences are determined in large part by how a culture defines its **social identity**, or whether societal goals emphasize the advancement of the group's interests or individual interests. Particularly important is whether the culture defines itself as a *collectivist* culture or an *individualistic* culture, because culturally approved beliefs influence our expectations, experiences, attitudes, and behaviors (Neto, 2007). It profoundly affects the ways we behave and respond to the world.

Collectivist Cultures

In **collectivist cultures**, individuals define their identity in terms of the relationships they hold with others. For instance, if asked the question, "Who are you?", a collectivist is likely to respond by giving the family's name or the region from which they originate (Triandis & Suh, 2002). The goals of the *collective*—the whole society—are given priority over individual needs, and group membership is important (Myers, 2008). In these cultures, members strive to be equal, contributing, beneficial members of the society, and their personal behavior is driven by a feeling of obligation and duty to the society (Johnson, Kulesa, Cho, & Shavitt, 2005; Triandis & Suh, 2002). Collectivist cultures promote the well-being and goals of the collective *group*, rather than the well-being and goals of the *individual*. Because of the desire to maintain harmony within the group, collectivist cultures stress harmony, cooperation, and promoting feelings of closeness (Kupperbusch, Matsumoto, Kooken, Loewinger, et al., 1999).

Latinos, for example, value strong interdependent relationships with their families and they value the opinions of close friends (who, in many cases, are treated as family members); this, in turn, influences how they display and experience emotions, such as love and affection (Casta-eda, 1993; Fernandez-Dols, 1999). Asians, too, accentuate the importance of the collective whole and they therefore emphasize family bonds in their

Collectivist cultures, such as Arab Americans who embrace their Muslim faith, value strong relationships with their families. Their belief systems and relationships reflect the goals of their cultures—not their individual goals.

experiences of love, including extended family members. People's self-concepts, personal goals, expectations of family members, family experiences, and the larger society are inseparable in collectivist societies (Johnson et al., 2005).

Individualistic Cultures

In **individualistic cultures**, where individual goals are promoted over group goals, people define their identity or sense of self in terms of personal attributes, such as wealth, social status, education level, and marital status (Myers, 2008). Unlike in collectivist cultures, *individualists* view themselves as truly independent entities from the society in which they live, and their personal needs and rights guide their behavior, rather than the needs of the society (Johnson et al., 2005). Individualistic cultures, such as America and Europe, promote the idea of autonomy and individuation from the family (Dion & Dion, 1993).

A culture's social identity shapes and directs the attitudes, norms, and behaviors of its members, such as how extended family members are important to Latino and Asian families—these behaviors are the result of how collectivist ideals shape families.

But there are other cultural factors that significantly influence and shape family life experiences and parenting, such as family structure and race/ethnicity.

UNDERSTANDING TODAY'S PARENTS

Variations in parenting attitudes and styles are evident among the diverse cultural groups in the United States, as well as in the diverse family structures in which children are raised today. In nearly all societies the world over, the family is the social unit that is responsible for nurturing, protecting, educating, and socializing children (Barbour, Barbour, & Scully, 2005). Figure 6.1 illustrates for us the types of households in the United States (U.S. Census Bureau, 2008c). As you can see, half of all households today are married-couple families, but there is also great diversity in family forms.

As we explore the nature of contemporary parenting, we use statistics to help us identify current patterns and trends. Though sometimes it's tempting to skip over statistics in our reading, numbers are necessary because they present overall trends and provide us with an instant snapshot of American families in which today's children develop.

In the sections that follow, we first take a look at *nuclear* family forms. We then examine the expanding family landscape in our culture today.

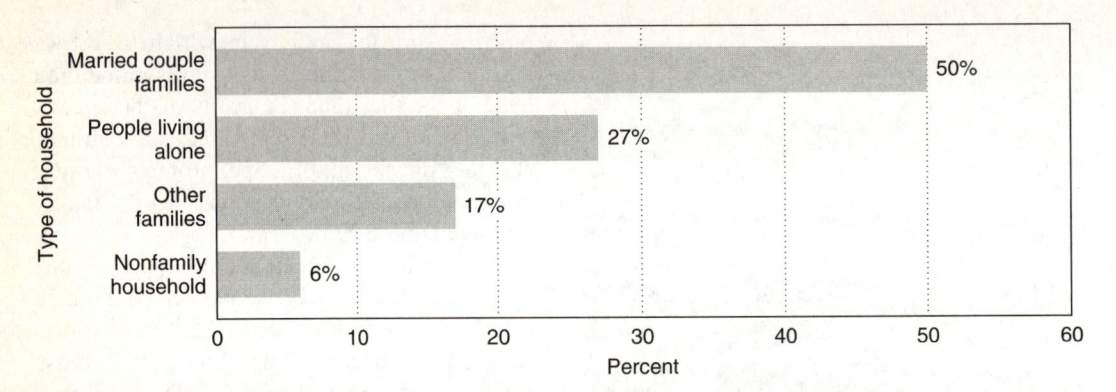

FIGURE 6.1 Types of households in the United States.
Today, there is no such thing as a "traditional" family form in the United States. There is great diversity in the configurations of households.
Source: Based on data from U.S. Census Bureau (2008a).

Bar chart showing:
- Married couple families: 50%
- People living alone: 27%
- Other families: 17%
- Nonfamily household: 6%

(Y-axis: Type of household; X-axis: Percent, 0 to 60)

The Nuclear Family

The **nuclear** family consists of a biological father, a biological mother, and their biological or adopted children. In the truest sense of the definition, nuclear families consist of first-time married parents, their biological or adopted children, and no other family members living in the home. In 2008, the "typical" nuclear family form was found in about two-thirds of the 111 million households (U.S. Census Bureau, 2008c). Figure 6.2 illustrates the family configurations in which American children live today. Notice that while the majority of children live in nuclear families, other family forms show the complexity of contemporary family living and parenting.

Often, the nuclear family is referred to as the *traditional* family. This term carries with it a conventional depiction of the family form and the accompanying family values and traditions. **Family values** is a term that is commonly used today by politicians and TV news reporters, although it may mean different things to different people. Most often, family values refers to a society's paradigm or viewpoint that expects its members to adhere to perceived proper social roles, such as marrying and having children, remaining monogamous and faithful to the marriage partner, and opposing same-sex relationships, marriages, and parenting by gay or lesbian partners. The family values viewpoint also frowns upon births to women outside of marriage. It evokes a certain set of ascribed gender roles; for example, the women fulfill homemaker and mothering responsibilities (the breadmaker role) and the men fulfill the role of primary wage earner (the breadwinner role). This particular family form is also considered a *patriarchy,* wherein the male is dominant and is in charge of most decision making in the family.

The Nuclear Family in History

Historian and author Peter McWilliams (1998) offers insight into the roots of the traditional family. He notes that the modern concept of two adults rearing their children under a single roof grew out of necessity during the Middle Ages, when the minimum number of people required to own and maintain a plot of land was two. In order to multiply their wealth, it was necessary to have others work the land; children were free labor. Thus, in order to have the free labor provided by children, it was economically necessary that one of the adults was a man and the other was a woman—and they were thus paired until death. According to McWilliams, love had nothing to do with the pairing. "Even if a husband and a wife

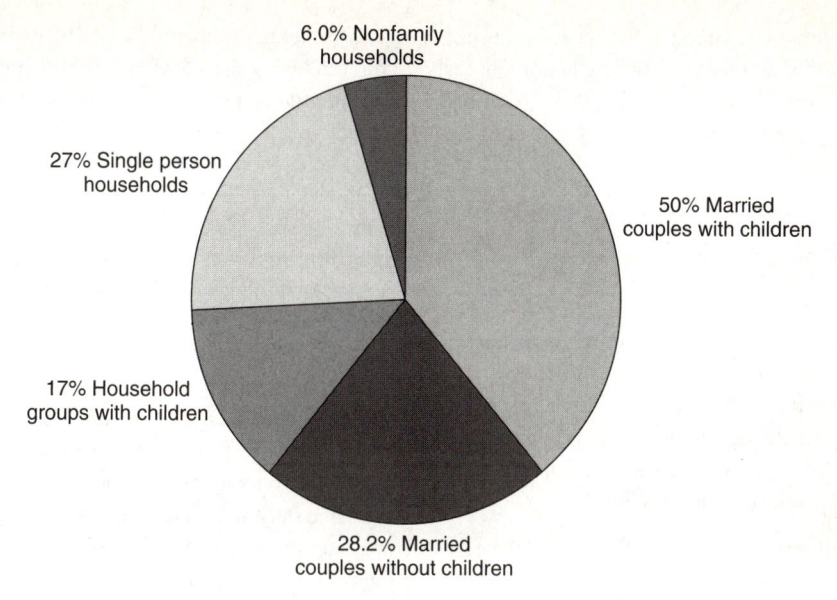

Chapter 6 • Contemporary Parenting: Diversity and Change **141**

- 6.0% Nonfamily households
- 27% Single person households
- 50% Married couples with children
- 17% Household groups with children
- 28.2% Married couples without children

FIGURE 6.2 U.S. household configurations. **Children live in a variety of household types today.***

*(Numbers do not total 100%)
Source: Based on data from U. S. Census Bureau (2008b).

hated each other, all they had to do was wait a little while—with disease, war, childbirth, and an average lifespan of about 35, most marriages lasted less than five years. The departed partner was immediately replaced, and the system continued." Men and older children worked the land and the women tended to the livestock, the crops nearby the home, and to the younger children. Because the system worked so well, the church eventually got involved and, over time, the one man/one woman-for-life theology emerged.

If we were to identify a specific period in American history that the traditional family form was in vogue, we would look at the period of the 1950s in the United States (McWilliams, 1998). The high postwar marriage and birthrates, coupled with a prosperous economy in which a single wage earner could support a family, led to a national perception of the period as a "golden era" for families (McWilliams, 1998).

Through television and the media, families tuned in to watch the idealized image of the American family: the wise, reassuring father who came home from a hard day at the office; the apron-clad homemaker mother (wearing pearls) who offered comfort and support to her hardworking husband and perfect children; the clutter-free, immaculate home and the homogeneous neighborhood. Notes McWilliams (1998), the family life portrayed in the 1950s media was wholesome: there were no single parents (unless the father was a widower, such as with the fathers in *My Three Sons, Andy Griffith,* and *Bonanza*), no infidelities, no divorce, no abuse, no teen runaways, and no prior marriages or children from prior marriages. There was no discussion about religion, politics, or the economy, no one lost his job, there was no gang violence in the neighborhood, no racism, no high-school dropouts, no homosexuality, and no babies born out of wedlock.

Despite TVLand's depiction of the American family during this era, it is questionable whether this idealized image of family really ever existed. Stephanie Coontz (1992, 1999), author and professor of comparative family history, notes the discrepancies of the idealized 1950s "good old days" family form portrayed in the media and the reality of family living during the 1950s:

- About one-quarter of the population lived below the poverty line.
- The number of pregnant brides more than doubled from the 1940s.
- From 1944 to 1955, the number of babies born outside of marriage and placed for adoption rose 80 percent.
- Juvenile delinquency was so prevalent that in 1955 Congress considered nearly 200 bills to address the problem.

As Coontz notes, the 1950s were a dismal time for women, minorities, homosexuals, and any other social group that did not "fit in" with the images typified on the television screen.

The traditional, nuclear family is no longer predominant in the United States. In the new century, 1950s television shows like *I Love Lucy* and *Leave it to Beaver* have been replaced by shows like *The Simpsons, Family Guy, Two and a Half Men, Brothers and Sisters,* and *Modern Family,* which perhaps better reflect the diversity found in today's families.

The Expanding Family Landscape

In the United States today there is no such thing as a "traditional" or "typical" family configuration. In order to better serve today's parents and to help them reach their full potentials, we need to understand the changing compositions of contemporary families, as well as the racial and ethnic compositions of these families.

SINGLE-PARENT FAMILY Single-parent family types can be the result of the choice of the parent or by circumstance; they can result either from divorce, the death of a spouse, or unmarried parenthood. Trends indicate that single-parent households are on the increase in the American family.

Although the majority of the nation's 72 million children live with two parents (either their biological parents, stepparents, or others), the dawn of the new millennium saw an increase in parenting households where there is no spouse. Today it is estimated that 37 percent of families are single-parent families (U.S. Census Bureau, 2006). Over three-fourths of all single-parent households are headed by females (U.S. Census Bureau, 2008c). Slightly over 10 percent of single-parent households are headed by males. There are also racial and ethnic differences among single parents. For example, over one-half of all African American/Black Caribbean children live with their mother only, while only about one-fourth of Hispanic children live only with their mother; among all races, only about 5 percent of children live only with their fathers (Child Trends, 2008).

Understanding these trends in single-parenting experiences is important because as our study will show us in just a bit, single parents oftentimes live in poverty—which in turn affects their children's development. We also explore single parents in depth in Chapter 7.

CHILDLESS/CHILDFREE FAMILY As you learned in Chapter 1, on average, Americans have been having fewer children than in decades past. Couples may consider themselves **childless** if they are unable to conceive or bear children of their own or adopt children. Some couples today prefer to remain **childfree** as a conscious choice. Currently, 20 percent of women between the ages of 40 and 44 do not have children; nearly one-half of all women ages 15 to 44 are childless (U.S. Census Bureau, 2008d).

It is important to note, however, that this is not the first generation of people who are deciding not to have children. Notes Philip Morgan, professor of sociology at Duke University, "Childlessness is not new, [but] in the past it was more closely connected with non-marriage than now. During the depression, many Americans also chose not to have children because they could not afford them. Childlessness levels now are not higher than those in the 1930s" (*When a marriage,* 2005). Morgan adds that there are many factors involved in couples' decision to remain childfree today.

Family practitioners and social scientists differ in their opinions about today's trends in childfree couples. For example, directors of the National Marriage Project David Popenoe and Barbara Dafoe Whitehead (2002) maintain that the decline in the number of children in U.S. households indicates a loss of "child centeredness" in the nation, and that "neighborhoods are less likely to contain children, and that children are less likely to be a consideration in daily life." They attribute this decline to the fact that "the needs and concerns of children—especially young children—gradually may be receding from our consciousness" (p. 24). On the other hand, Dorian Solot and Marshall Miller (2004), authors and founders of the Alternatives to Marriage Project, counter these claims, noting that today we recognize and embrace family diversity and the range of family forms, and thereby accept couples' choices to remain childfree.

STEPFAMILY A stepfamily (or reconstituted family) is formed when, after death or divorce, a parent marries again. A stepfamily is also formed when a never-married parent marries and children from different biological families end up living within the new marriage for part of the time. In short, the presence of a stepparent, stepsibling, or half sibling designates a family as a stepfamily (U.S. Census Bureau, 2008d).

The U.S. Census Bureau recently stopped providing data as they relate to marriage, divorce, and remarriage, so it is difficult to obtain accurate statistics about stepfamilies. But census experts today estimate that one out of three Americans—about 33 percent—is now either a stepparent, a stepchild, a stepsibling, or some other member of a stepfamily (U.S. Census Bureau, 2008d). Although the popular sitcom 1970s television show *The Brady Bunch* portrayed stepfamily living as an emotionally cohesive, trouble-free, happily adjusted family, this idealized concept of the stepfamily form is simply not the norm.

(Because of the complexities of stepfamily living, an entire segment is devoted to this family form in Chapter 7.)

COHABITING FAMILY Unmarried partners who live together in a single household are referred to as **cohabiting** couples. Though once considered a scandalous, uncommon alternative lifestyle, cohabiting before marriage (or instead of marriage) is now *the* prevailing living arrangement of intimate partners—the next step following serious dating. In 2006 there were 5.5 million unmarried heterosexual partner households (over 11 million people) (U.S. Census Bureau, 2006). Data from the National Survey of Family Growth (NSFG) show that over 60 percent of women ages 25 to 39 have cohabitated at least once, nearly doubling the rate from just 7 years earlier (U.S. Department of Health and Human Services, 2006). Furthermore, since 1995 more than two-thirds of men and women who marry for the first time cohabited beforehand (Manning & Jones, 2006). Many of these couples have no plans for eventual marriage. Indeed, some 53 percent of women's first marriages are preceded by cohabitation (Manning & Smock, 2003). Census Bureau statistics indicate that slightly over 5 percent of all children in the United States live with cohabiting parents (U.S. Census Bureau, 2008d). The rates of cohabiting parents vary by race; these data are presented in Figure 6.3. The U.S. Census Bureau currently estimates that in the United States about 11 million people live with their unmarried partner; approximately 10 million of these households consist of unmarried, different-sex partners, while the remaining estimated one million households comprise same-sex couples (U.S. Census Bureau, 2008d).

GAY AND LESBIAN FAMILIES Lesbian and gay families consist of same-sex partners who live together in the same household, and may include either natural-born or adopted children. In America today, there are 780,000 same-sex households representing over a 300 percent increase in same-sex households since 1990 (U.S. Census Bureau,

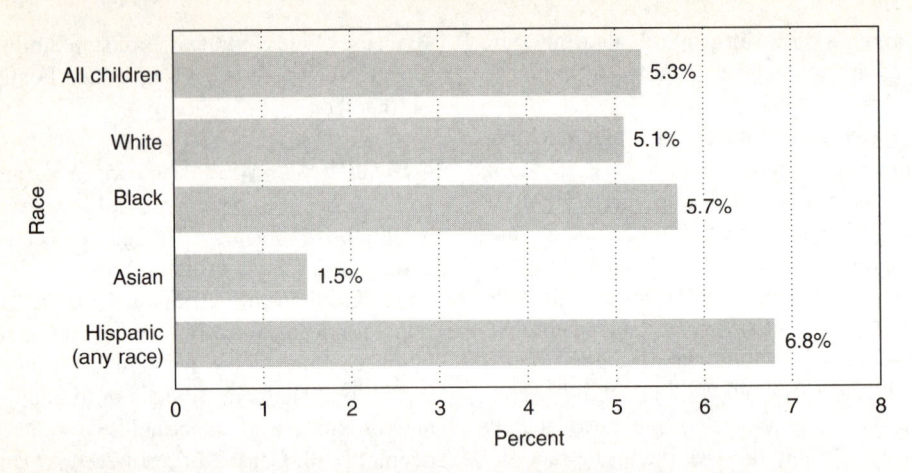

144 Part 2 • Parenting: Diversity in Today's Families

Race	Percent
All children	5.3%
White	5.1%
Black	5.7%
Asian	1.5%
Hispanic (any race)	6.8%

FIGURE 6.3 Percentage of children living with a cohabiting parent, by race. Cohabitation is the prevailing living arrangement of intimate partners before (or instead of) marriage. A number of cohabiting partners have children.

Source: Based on data from U.S. Census Bureau (2008c).

2008d). Census bureau statisticians point out, however, that this increase reflects the fact that same-sex families were previously uncounted, undercounted, or underreported, and not that the numbers of gay or lesbian families have increased significantly (Smith & Gates, 2001). Same-sex family forms may or may not resemble traditional marriage roles, but they often do (with the exception of the legal status granted by the state in which they reside). Today, many same-sex couples pledge a commitment to each another in a public ceremony. Like legally married couples, they share joint responsibility in childrearing. We explore gay and lesbian parenting at length in Chapter 8.

Today in the United States, there are over three-quarters of a million same-sex households.

Our study so far has shown us that in this new century it is hard to encapsulate or sum up the "typical" American family—it simply doesn't exist today in our complex, multifaceted, ever-changing, global society. To get the full grasp of parenting in contemporary society, we now need to examine the racial and ethnic characteristics of today's families.

CONTEMPORARY FAMILIES

Families today are complex and diverse, ranging from traditional two-biological-parent family structures, to single-parent homes, to extended family forms, to households headed by gay or lesbian adults or same-sex couples. There is also greater diversity of racial, ethnic, economic, and religious composition.

As we just saw, when researchers use the terms *diverse* or *diversity,* they are often referring to the racial and/or ethnic attributes of a given population. **Race** refers to a group of people who are distinguished from another group of people, typically by their skin color, ancestry, or genetics. **Ethnicity** refers to a social construction that is used to identify groups of people (commonly, races) who share common cultural traits, such as religion, customs, language, and dress. Furthermore, in the United States today there is an increasing trend in interracial diversity—2.0 percent of the U.S. population (about 6.1 million people) are multiracial (U.S. Census Bureau, 2008d). **Multiracial** individuals can be any combination of races (white, African American/Afro-Caribbean, Asian, Native American/Alaska Native, Pacific Islander, Hispanic, and "any other race") and ethnicities.

Knowing the racial and ethnic composition of U.S. families is important because it aids in our understanding of the complex, changing nature of parenting. Here we briefly examine the racial and ethnic compositions of families so that you have a firm understanding of the diversity within the United States.

African American/Black Caribbean Families

Historically, African American/Black Caribbean families assumed the traditional married-couple family structure, with children born inside the marital union. Today, it is common for black children to be born to a single mother. As Figure 6.4 illustrates, nearly 70 percent of the births to black

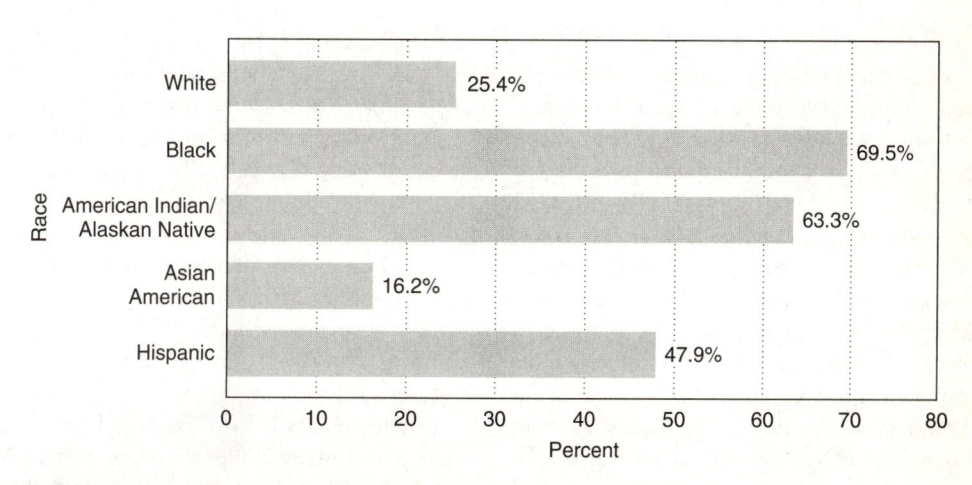

Race	Percent
White	25.4%
Black	69.5%
American Indian/Alaskan Native	63.3%
Asian American	16.2%
Hispanic	47.9%

FIGURE 6.4 Percentage of births to unmarried women, by race: 2006. **The percentage of births to unmarried women.**

Source: Based on data from Child Trends (2008).

women of all ages are to unmarried women (Child Trends, 2008). In comparison to white families where nearly one-fourth of children live with a single parent (most likely a mother), over one-half of black children live in a single-parent home (American Community Survey, 2008). While three-fourths of black children eventually reside in two-parent homes, many of these families are formed with a child who was born outside of the marriage (Barbarin & McCandies, 2003; U.S. Census Bureau, 2008d).

Multigenerational, extended family ties (see Chapter 1) are common among black families. Census Bureau data estimate that about 9 percent of African American/Black Caribbean children live in some type of extended family (Child Trends, 2008). **Multiple mothering**, a practice that involves aunts, cousins, close friends, and fictive kin who provide mothers with a range of modeling and tangible support, is commonplace (Greene, 1995). According to a study by Robert Taylor (2000), characteristics of African American/Afro-Caribbean extended kin include:

- Strong commitment to family and family obligation
- Willingness to allow relatives and close nonrelatives to move into the family home
- Family interactions and get-togethers
- Close system of mutual aid and support

Because of the large numbers of female-headed households among African American/Black Caribbeans, some research suggests that the childrearing and economic support of extended kin is necessary because it is within the extended family networks of grandmothers, grandfathers, aunts, uncles, and cousins that children are cared for, socialized, educated, and have their emotional needs met (Taylor, 2000). About one in three black families is headed by an elderly family member (Smith & Drew, 2002). Of all racial and ethnic groups in the United States, African American/Afro-Caribbean families suffer the highest levels of unemployment and poverty and the lowest median family income—slightly over $30,000 annually (U.S. Census Bureau, 2006). We discuss poverty at length later in this chapter.

AFRICAN AMERICAN/BLACK CARIBBEAN FAMILY PATTERNS There are a number of theories that speak to the diversity and rich cultural heritages of black families. For example, the **New World experience** attributes distinctiveness to American culture rather than to African traditions. The **cultural variant** approach views black families as culturally unique systems. It is also sometimes referred to as the **African heritage theory**, which is based on the assumption that certain African traits have been retained by blacks and are evidenced in kinship patterns, marriage, sexuality, childrearing, and so forth (Hale-Benson, 1986). This theory contends that language, development, interactions, and behavioral patterns of African American/Black Caribbean children differ as a result of growing up in a distinct culture—a culture that has roots in West Africa and/or the Caribbean.

Central to the cultural variant approach is the idea that African culture has survived and has been subtly transmitted through multiple generations, without conscious effort. This is accomplished through **bicultural socialization**, a process wherein both the aspects of African and/or Caribbean heritages and America are integrated. For example, blacks are more likely to socialize children without strict differences determined by the gender of the child and to share in childcare and in decision making about childrearing (Allen & Majidi-Ahi, 1989). Men and women often share household tasks, even though the women still assume a greater share of the responsibility, and men are oftentimes involved in childrearing (Padgett, 1997). Later we explore in depth how children acquire their *racial/ethnic identity*.

Black parents play a crucial role in helping their children learn to participate successfully in society. As in other cultures, male and female African American/Black Caribbean children are reared differently. By the age of 3, most of them are no longer treated as babies. Early independence is valued, and many children assume responsibility for the care of younger siblings. For males the peer group is more important in the socialization process than for females. Male children are socialized into the peer group earlier and more completely than are females. Nevertheless, research emphasizes the gender-role flexibility of African American families as an important adaptive strategy that derives from valuing interdependence among group members (Greene, 1995).

Cultural-specific values of African American/Afro-Caribbean families have also been found in such areas as discipline, expectations regarding age- and sex-appropriate responsibilities, kin network, and awareness of racism. There is special emphasis in childrearing on respect for authority figures; strict discipline; a high value on a variety of responses, abilities, and talents; open receptivity to multiple environmental stimuli; and expression of emotions by both males and females.

PARENT–CHILD INTERACTIONS Because of the emphasis on affective, interpersonal relations and the emotional, people-oriented characteristics of blacks (see Table 6.1), children are likely to grow up to be feeling- and people-oriented and more proficient in nonverbal communication skills than white children are. White children are more likely to be object-oriented, since they have had numerous opportunities to manipulate objects and to discover their properties and relationships.

Additionally, black infants experience considerable human interaction with people of all ages. Babies often are encouraged to feel or to rub the holder's face, and a game of "rubbing each other's face" ensues. Infants and young children often sleep with their parents. There is a rhythm of sleeping and eating, with each activity being of short duration and the pattern repeated frequently.

TABLE 6.1 Characteristics of African American culture that affect childrearing.

Feeling orientation
People orientation
Proficiency in nonverbal communication skills
High degree of human interaction
Biculturation
Multiple environmental stimuli

Verbal communication during infancy may be less important than other types of communication, such as looking deeply into the child's eyes and caressing the baby. Looking into the eyes is used by the mother to impress a point on the child. This is an important characteristic to understand because when black school children refuse to look at their teachers, they may be trying to sever an intense level of communication that is typically shared among their family; the child may also feel that it is disrespectful to an authority figure to look him or her in the eye.

Over the last two decades, a more balanced depiction of African American/Black Caribbean family life has emerged, with growing appreciation of the diversity of these families, in both status and form. Future research should consider the impact of interrelationships among factors that operate at varying levels and potentially manifest themselves through diverse behaviors and phenomena.

Latino American Families

Today, Latinos account for 15 percent of the total U.S. population; this figure does not include the nearly 4 million residents of the U.S. territory, Puerto Rico (U.S. Census Bureau, 2007b). The fastest growing population in the United States because of the large proportion of Latina women of childbearing age, by the year 2020 Latinos are expected to account for nearly one-half of the nation's population growth (Afable-Munsuz & Brindis, 2006).

Latinos place a high value on **familism**, which emphasizes the importance of family life, and close, interdependent relationships among the person, the family, and the community. Typically, familism also stresses the importance of extended family; thus, Latino families are also composed of extended kinship networks (grandparents, aunts, uncles, and cousins). Within this family dynamic, family members are provided clothing, shelter, food, education, and emotional support. Latino families further extend family relationships to fictive, or nonrelated, kin, such as godparents and close friends. Within Latino communities, the well-being of the family takes precedence over the well-being of the individual.

In the United States, about 16 million Latino children reside within families in which at least one parent is an immigrant—foreign-born—or the children are themselves foreign-born (Kids Count, 2007). Today, one out of five U.S. children is living in an immigrant family (Kids Count, 2007). If current immigration levels continue, children in Latino immigrant families will constitute 30 percent of the nation's school population in 2015 (Kids Count, 2007). Latino immigrants and their children commonly live within extended family forms during the first 10 years following immigration (Gonzales, Knight, Morgan-Lopez, Saenz, & Sirolli, 2002). Even as immigrants establish their own households, they do so near their families' homes. Second- and third-generation Latino Americans have even larger extended kin networks than do immigrants (Gonzales et al., 2002).

About 66 percent of Latino children live within two-parent families (Child Trends, 2008). Similar to the experiences of African American/Afro-Caribbean women, births to unmarried Latina women have increased since the 1970s. Nearly one-half of all Latino births are to unmarried women (Child Trends, 2008). Currently, one-fourth of Latino children live in a household with their mothers and have no father present; 4 percent live in a household with their father with no mother present (Child Trends, 2008).

One of the poorest ethnic groups in America today, Latino families earn, on average, about $36,000 per year (U.S. Census Bureau, 2006). The reasons for the high poverty rates among Latinos are varied. Many Latino immigrants may have professional degrees from other countries, but because of the language barrier when they arrive in the United States, they are unable to secure high-paying jobs.

LATINO AMERICAN FAMILY PATTERNS It is important to emphasize that there is no one typical Latino American family. Such factors as education, income, age, geographic location, and time of migration to the United States contribute to a diversity of family types. In fact, time of immigration seems to have a fairly significant impact on the socialization of children (Buriel, 1993).

The home environment of Latino American children varies according to their *generation status*. Shared cultural variables, particularly Spanish-language background and achievement aspirations, vary as a function of generational status. For example, first- and second-generation children often perform better in school than their third-generation counterparts; it is believed this is because immigrant parents (especially mothers) may pass on high aspirations to their children (Buriel, 1993). Also, mothers that are born in Mexico (where children were first- and second-generation immigrants) stress early autonomy, strictness, and productive use of time more than mothers of third-generation children. Fathers of first- and second-generation children are similar to their spouses in areas of autonomy, strictness, and support (Buriel, 1993). The study concluded that a childrearing style resembling responsibility may be crucial in fostering healthy social and academic development in Latino American adolescents because delinquency and school achievement appear to be two serious problems that face third-generation immigrants.

PARENT–CHILD INTERACTIONS Only a few studies have been conducted on the childrearing attitudes and practices of Latino American

TABLE 6.2 Characteristics of Latino American families.

Strong family ties
Migration toward kin networks
Emotional support
Two-parent participation in child rearing
Range of gender roles
Mutual aid, respect, affection
Authoritative, authoritarian, and permissive child-rearing styles
Differences in child rearing according to gender of child
Deference and respect accorded to fathers

parents, and those that exist fail to provide consistent conclusions. Some researchers have concluded that Latino American parents are primarily permissive, whereas others have suggested that traditional values and authoritarian practices are more prevalent.

One writer (Ramirez, 1989) noted that *el amor de madre* (motherly love) is a greater force in Latino American families than wifely love; that is, the parent–child relationship is more important than the spousal relationship. Most homes are child-centered when children are young. Although there is an emphasis on good behavior, much nurturance and protection are provided to young children. There is a basic acceptance of the child's individuality and a relaxed attitude toward achievement of developmental milestones. As children approach the latency period and later (age 5 or so until puberty), parents begin to expect more responsible behavior from children; they are assigned tasks or responsibilities in accordance with their age and ability.

As Table 6.2 shows us, Latino Americans have a number of common ethnic family characteristics, all of which affect parenting. For example, an observational study of predominantly impoverished mothers and their young children found few permissive Latino American mothers, and authoritative and authoritarian mothers were about equal in number. Authoritative parents use rational, issue-oriented discipline techniques and set firm limits within a loving context (Martinez, 1993). Another study examined mothers' parenting and children's adjustment in low-income Mexican immigrant and Latino American families (Dumka, Roosa, & Jackson, 1997). Mothers' supportive parenting was found to partially mediate the effects of family conflict on children's depression. High levels of supportive parenting were linked to low levels of children's depression and low levels of child conduct disorders, whereas high levels of inconsistent parenting were related to higher levels of children's depression and conduct disorder. Furthermore, higher maternal acculturation was related to greater consistency in discipline, which then led to reduced depression in children.

Because Latino Americans are a rapidly growing ethnic group in this country, careful research still needs to be undertaken to give keener insight into these family relationships and parenting styles. Especially important to understand are the ways in which traditional values and intergenerational relationships influence contemporary family relationships and parenting.

Asian American Families

Asian American families come to America from countries including Korea, Japan, China, Taiwan, Vietnam, Cambodia, Sri Lanka, and Indonesia. Each Asian country has a unique culture unto itself, which accounts for the vast cultural and ethnic differences within this racial group in the United States. Like Latino families, Asian American families place greater emphasis on extended kinship ties and the needs of the entire family, rather than on the needs of the individual. About 84 percent of all Asian American children live with both biological parents; only 10 percent live in mother-only families, and about 4 percent live in father-only families (Child Trends, 2008). Today, about 16 percent of Asian women give birth outside of marriage (Child Trends, 2008). With an annual income of slightly over $60,000 per year, Asian American families have the highest median household income of all racial groups in the United States (U.S. Census Bureau, 2006). This is perhaps because Asian Americans have the highest educational qualifications of all ethnic groups in the United States—nearly one-half of all Asian American adults have attained at least a bachelor's degree (U.S. Census Bureau, 2007a).

ASIAN AMERICAN FAMILY PATTERNS The literature on Asian American families is scant in comparison with the research on other cultural and ethnic groups; however, we do know that the time of immigration to the United States seems to affect the degree of acculturation into mainstream American culture, with third- and fourth-generation families demonstrating more similarity to U.S. culture than first- and second-generation immigrants.

Similar to Latino American families, Asian families are child-centric. Within the Asian family structure a greater emphasis is placed on the parent–child relationship than on the husband–wife relationship. In exchange for the undivided loyalty and for sacrifices parents make for their children, Asian American parents expect respect and obedience from their children. Guilt and shame, rather than physical discipline, are used to reinforce the expected behavior of the children (Fong, 2002).

Historically, there was a strong emphasis in traditional Asian society on specific family roles and the proper behavior associated with each. The role structure was vertical and hierarchal, with the father as the undisputed head of the family. The obligations, responsibilities, and privileges of each role were clearly delineated. The father's authority was unchallenged, and he received total respect and loyalty from all family members. In return, he assumed maximum responsibility for the family's social status and economic well-being. The mother was responsible for emotional nurturance of family members and for their psychological well-being, her primary role being to serve her husband and rear the children. Though she was less removed and distant than the father, she was accorded respect by the children. She was discouraged from working outside the home.

In traditional Asian families, there also are gender and birth privileges, with sons more highly valued than daughters. Lineage is passed through the male, whereas females are absorbed into the families of their husbands. The role of female is less rewarding because females do not gain status and respect until they become mothers-in-law (Huang & Ying, 1989; Yau & Smetana, 1996).

Today, these roles have changed radically, and only derivatives of them may be found in Asian American culture. For example, contemporary fathers may be figurative heads of families, with the mother as the driving force and the decision maker behind the scenes. Male/female role distinctions are far less glaring. Some still see the extended family as an important source of social and sometimes financial support, but others see it as a burden and a restriction of autonomy. Because of the collectivist nature of Asian countries, interdependence is the foundation of Asian American families, with group values being more highly valued than individual desires (Huang & Ying, 1989; Miller, Wiley, Fung, & Hui Lang, 1997; Yau & Smetana, 1996).

PARENT–CHILD INTERACTIONS *Filial piety* has governed intergenerational Asian families for centuries. It is a complex system that involves a series of obligations of child to parent—most centrally to provide aid to, comfort to, affection to, and contact with the parent and to bring glory to the parent by doing well in educational and occupational areas, that is, achieving success in the outside world. It means that children are expected to satisfy their parents, to respect and to show reverence for elders in all situations (Kelley & Tseng, 1992; Lin & Liu, 1993). The concept of filial piety, or *hsiao*, is deeply ingrained in Chinese and other Asian cultures, and has served as the moral foundation of interpersonal relationships for centuries (Lin & Liu, 1993).

Overall, Asian parents tend to be warm, affectionate, and lenient toward infants and young children, but once they reach the "age of understanding," discipline becomes much more strict (Kelley & Tseng, 1992). Children are taught mutual dependence, group identification, self-discipline, and good manners, as well as the importance of education. Departure from parental goals is seen as a reflection on the parents; therefore, parents take complete responsibility for the development of their children and are very involved in childrearing. They view the parenting role mainly as one of teacher.

Even though Asian parenting historically has been seen as more authoritarian than mainstream American parenting, some research suggests that authoritarian parenting may be a Western concept that does not accurately depict Asian socialization (Gorman, 1998). In one study, the author found little rule setting for adolescents among the Chinese mothers, suggesting that these mothers did not characterize their roles as including domination and control (Gorman, 1998). These mothers perceived that they were training their children, giving them guidance, and helping them to make good decisions; that is, they provided pertinent information and arguments but left the final decision in their children's hands. This approach is consistent with the Asian cultural value of individual responsibility—expectations for their children are based on mothers' deep desires for children's successful adjustment rather than on a need to dominate their children.

This style of interaction appears to reflect the cultural value of self-sufficiency and the importance of reaching the "age of understanding." This study is important because it helps us to see that Asian American parenting is characterized by an interaction of expectations and filial obligation rather than parental control and child submission. Though the expectations were communicated in subtle ways, they appeared to be understood clearly by the children.

Native American/Alaska Native Families

The terms Native American, American Indian, Alaska Native, and Indian are often used interchangeably. Here, we use the term **Native American/Alaska Native (NA/AN)** to refer to aboriginal peoples of the United States and their descendants, and who maintain tribal affiliation or community attachment. Today, about 2 percent of the total U.S. population reports that they are Native American or Alaska Native (U.S. Census Bureau, 2007a). While about one-fourth of the total U.S. population is under the age of 18, among NA/AN one-third of the population is under the age of 18, making this a young ethnic group (U.S. Census Bureau, 2007a). As with other racial and ethnic groups in the United States, NA/AN communities are culturally diverse, with 561 federally recognized Native entities, and an additional 365 state-recognized American Indian tribes (U.S. Census Bureau, 2007a). Native Americans prefer to be identified by tribal names, such as Wampanoag, Lakota, and Kickapoo (Fleming, 2007); our discussion here is generalized.

In order for us to accurately understand Native American family and parenting experiences, we must be aware of the unique qualities associated with this race. Unfortunately, comparatively little research has been conducted on Native American family life, and especially on Native American parenting. Despite this gap in the empirical literature, however, the Census data do give us insight into some characteristics of Natives. For instance, nearly one-half of all Native American households are married-couple households (see Figure 6.5). Interestingly, nearly 30 percent of households are nonfamily households; this means that a significant number of Native American families are headed by someone other than a parent, such as a grandparent, or even by nonfictive kin. The median income for NA/AN is just under $33,000 per year (U.S. Census Bureau, 2008a).

NATIVE AMERICAN/ALASKAN NATIVE FAMILY PATTERNS The predominance of extended family/nonfictive kin households among NA/AN is a reflection of the cultural roots of this racial group. Native American/Alaska Natives embrace a social identity that stresses the importance of family ties. For example, when they introduce themselves to other Indians, they do so by telling them their maternal heritage, clans, and homelands (Makes Marks, 2007). In contrast to patriarchal societies where people's lineage is determined along *patrilineal* lines (the father's heritage), the roots of NA/AN social and clan relationships are by and large *matrilineal;* that is to say, these societies trace their heritage from a female ancestor to a descendent of either sex. This is also referred to as a *uterine descent.* Within these societies, women are not given power per se because they are women—they are given power because of their status of mother, the power of female as mother.

Indians' spiritual traditions and religious beliefs are also numerous and diverse, and as such, the depth and dynamics of Native Americans' religious experiences are difficult to categorize

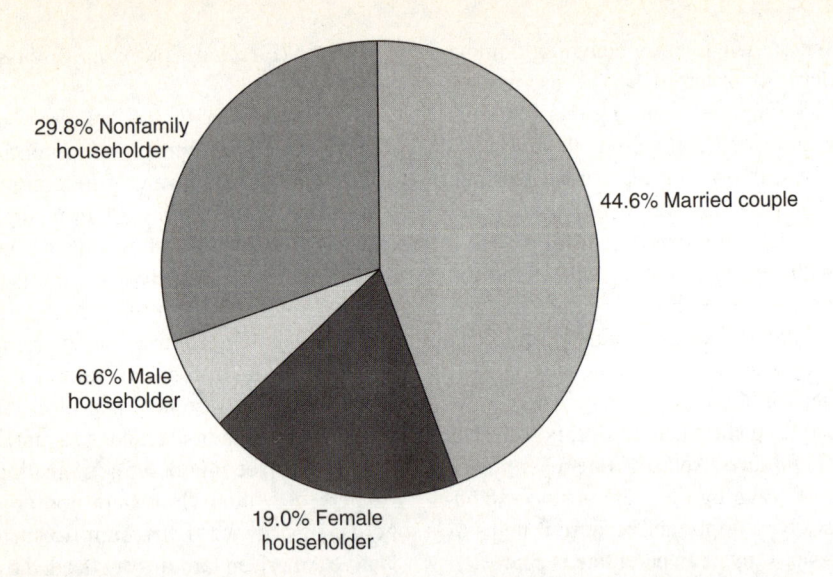

FIGURE 6.5 Characteristics of Native American/Alaska Native households: 2006. Native American/Alaska Native populations are diverse, with 561 federally recognized native entities.

Source: Based on data from U.S. Census Bureau (2006a).

- 29.8% Nonfamily householder
- 44.6% Married couple
- 6.6% Male householder
- 19.0% Female householder

or classify. Even so, there is an underlying or essential principal belief that informs most Indians' spiritual practices: the belief in the existence of unseen powers, that something exists beyond them that is sacred and mysterious (Makes Marks, 2007). Within this belief are embedded tradition, respect, and reverence. But how these religious beliefs shape marital and parenting attitudes, norms, and behaviors is unknown because NA/AN are among the most misunderstood and understudied ethnic group in our culture; this is because they are commonly culturally isolated (Hellerstedt, Peterson-Hickey, Rhodes, & Garwick, 2006).

The traditional Native American family system is vastly different from other extended-family units in this country (see Table 6.3). These networks are structurally open, assume a village-type characteristic, and are usually composed of clans, which include several households of relatives. "Family" is defined by some tribes in terms of household composition, the extended family through second cousins, and clan membership (Carson, Dail, Greeley, & Kenote, 1990). The roles of family members and the structure of the extended family vary across tribes. Traditionally, they live in relational networks that serve to support and nurture strong bonds of mutual assistance and affection. Many engage in the traditional system of collective interdependence, with family members responsible not

TABLE 6.3 Characteristics of Native American families.

High poverty rates
Diverse values, roles, and relationships across tribes
Family is the basic unit of society and community
"Family" includes household residents, extended family, and clan members
Relational networks support and nurture strong bonds of mutual assistance and affection
Elders provide guidance and wisdom
Many individuals participate in childrearing
Living in harmony with nature is valued
Participation in tribal ceremonies and rites of passage
Group-oriented philosophy

only to one another but also to the clan and the tribe (LaFromboise & Low, 1989).

Although the extended-family network is rapidly changing on many reservations, it is still a major factor contributing to family strengths. Guidance and wisdom received from elders facilitate family cohesion and resiliency, and the personal support from extended-family members and the community, especially during times of crisis, contributes immensely to family strengths (Carson et al., 1990).

Native Americans view their extended family as a source of strength and perennial support, offering multiple opportunities for the effective socialization of children, but some feel that the extended-family system is greatly misunderstood by human-service professionals. There have been numerous attempts to impose the traditional Western model of the nuclear monogamous family on Native Americans, but they have struggled continuously to maintain their tribal identities and at the same time their special relationships with the federal government. Generally, Native Americans have not wanted or acquiesced to acculturation and assimilation into mainstream society. Instead of being viewed as a culturally variant but well-functioning society, they have largely received societal ridicule for their resistance to the norms and models of middle-class American society.

PARENT–CHILD INTERACTIONS Perhaps because of the diverse nature of Native Americans, there is little systematic knowledge about parenting styles and how they vary from tribe to tribe. Furthermore, because few widely used developmental tests have been standardized for American Indian populations, we have little insight into the development of NA/AN children. However, childrearing practices are shaped largely by Native worldviews, which regard children as beloved gifts. Time spent caring for, playing with, and admiring children is cherished. Native Americans celebrate milestones in early childhood, such as the first steps, first smile, first word, and so forth, but no pressure is felt over the timing of these events (LaFromboise & Low, 1989).

The most striking difference in childrearing and socialization is the exposure of children to a wide array of persons to whom they can become attached—parents, siblings, aunts, uncles, cousins, and grandparents—thus protecting children and providing them with the assurance of love (Dykeman & Nelson, 1995). Grandmothers and aunts, and in some tribes men, share in childcare. The extended family plays as much a role in childrearing, supervision of children, and the transgenerational transmission of teachings and customs as do parents. Grandparents perpetuate the oral tradition—they are safekeepers of tribal stories. They engage in purposeful activities with grandchildren that are geared toward passing on cultural values and beliefs and educating children about the physical, social, and spiritual world. There also are indirect lines of communication about children's behavior—for example, from the mother to the aunt or uncle—that serve to protect the bonds between parents and youth (Carson et al., 1990; LaFromboise & Low, 1989).

Children are regarded as important to the family and are accorded as much respect as adults—adults rarely hit children. In fact, physical punishment usually is not condoned. Parents more often use facial expressions and other body language to indicate disapproval, or they use social shame (embarrassment). Autonomy is highly valued, and children are expected to make their own decisions and to operate semi-independently at an early age. Parents give children choices and allow them to experience the natural consequences of them. The impact of the child's behavior on others is emphasized. Children are not socialized to expect praise for that which is already required of them; parents reserve praise for special accomplishments. It is these characteristics of parenting that are sometimes perceived as overly permissive or negligent by nontribal social workers.

Native American children demonstrate lower school achievement than most other groups, and they have the highest dropout rate. These problems are due to a number of factors, including health and family problems, geographical distances from schools, absenteeism (sometimes because of tribal ceremonies), and lack of culturally relevant instructional materials and approaches to learning. For example, most teachers focus on verbal instruction, whereas Native children learn better through visual means.

As Indian children enter school, they often feel stranded between two cultures. Many speak a first language other than English, practice an entirely different religion, and hold different cultural values, yet they are expected to perform successfully according to conventional Western criteria. Since these children have grown up with a group-oriented philosophy, striving for individual achievement is foreign to their world outside of school. They prefer anonymity, harmony, and cooperative rather than competitive learning. Because children are likely to feel marginal in both cultures, biculturalism must become an educational priority (Little Soldier, 1992). During the past two decades, NA/AN education has come under increasing tribal control, and there is more emphasis on tribal history, native languages, and increased self-esteem.

Arab American Families

Very little empirical information exists about Arab American families, although their population is increasing in the United States. Coming from countries such as Afghanistan, Israel, Iran, Iraq, Kuwait, Palestine, Saudi Arabia, Syria, and Turkey, the term "Arab American" does not refer necessarily to a racial group as much as it does geographical location and religion, which among Middle Eastern families is very diverse. Arab Americans make up just slightly over 1 percent of the U.S. population, reflecting 22 Arab countries (U.S. Census Bureau, 2007a).

While there is a common perception that most Arab Americans adhere to the Muslim faith, this is not so; about two-thirds of Arab Americans practice the Christian faith, about one-fourth practice the Muslim faith, and the remaining adhere to another faith or have no religious affiliation (Arab American Institute, 2007). This is important to understand because cultural typecasts of Arab American women tend to lump religion (Muslim) and ethnicity into one-and-the-same components of culture, portraying them as veiled Islamic traditionalists who are submissive, secluded in the home, and uneducated (Zahedi, 2007).

But, as sociology professor and researcher Jen'nan Ghazel Read (2003) of the University of California points out, understanding Arab American culture is complicated (2002). On the one hand, as a group, Arab Americans are more highly educated and earn higher incomes than any ethnic or racial group in the United States (Arab American Institute, 2007). On the other hand, Arab religious and cultural customs and rituals reinforce traditional gender roles wherein women raise and nurture the children, and men protect and provide for the family. As a result, many Arab Americans' parenting experiences are strongly shaped by traditional Arab views of honor, modesty, and gender, as well as by the historical values of Islam (Davis & Davis, 1993). Because of these tenets of Islam, heterosexual marriages and nuclear families are expected of devout Muslims (Boellstorff, 2005).

Without a doubt, there is great variation and diversity in our upbringing and our individual experiences with family and parenting. Now, let's look at how children learn about their racial and ethnic identities.

HOW DO CHILDREN LEARN ABOUT THEIR RACIAL/ETHNIC IDENTITIES?

As our earlier discussion showed us, there are racial/ethnic differences in the strategies parents employ to raise their children. Emerging research is beginning to shed even more light on these differences, especially in the distinct parenting challenges with which people of color are faced.

African American/Afro-Caribbeans, Hispanics, Native Americans, Asian Americans, and Arab Americans in this country often experience racism. **Racism** is a belief system that holds that race accounts for differences in human character and/or ability; it results in discrimination and prejudice based on someone's race or ethnic background. Because of the historical disparaging and marginalizing views of people of color, and because of historical racial barriers in equal opportunities, racial and ethnic minority parents are faced with the challenges of insulating their children from the negative consequences of racism. They deal with these challenges by teaching their children how to "navigate and negotiate" the racism terrain through a process referred to as racial/ethnic socialization (Coard, Foy-Watson, Zimmer, & Wallace, 2007).

Racial/ethnic socialization is the way in which families teach children about the social meanings of their race/ethnicity: What does it mean to "be" black, Hispanic, Asian, Native American, or of Arab descent? Oftentimes, this socialization also includes teaching children the consequences of ethnicity and race, such as racism (Brown, Tanner-Smith, Lesane-Brown, & Ezell, 2007). Throughout the socialization process, which is presented in Figure 6.6, children learn about the similarities and differences between races/ethnicities, as well as prejudice and discrimination that some people face. Through intergenerational discussions (which often include storytelling of ancestors' histories), conversations with parents, observations, and modeling, cultural knowledge is transmitted and children learn to "perform" race (Brown et al., 2007). Racial socialization not only teaches children the values and norms associated with their race/ethnicity, but it also shapes attitudes that help them to cope with race-related barriers (Coard et al., 2007). Typically, many white parents don't place importance on discussing racial or ethnic differences with their children (Brown et al., 2007).

Racial/ethnic socialization practices have been linked to a number of positive outcomes in minority children and adolescents (for a comprehensive review of the literature, see Coard et al., 2007; Hughes et al., 2006; Huynh & Fuligni, 2008):

- *Well-developed racial identity:* Children embrace racial and ethnic pride, history, and cultural traditions.
- *Heightened self-esteem:* Children's and adolescents' self-esteem is sensitive to the racial/ethnic messages they receive from their parents. Children who are taught to "blend" with mainstream culture have lower levels of self-esteem because they in some ways deny their heritage.
- *Higher academic functioning:* Positive ethnic identity and high self-esteem are associated with better academic outcomes and higher levels of motivation among children and adolescents.
- *Decreased levels of depression and anger:* The practice of cultural socialization is protective against racial discrimination because children and adolescents develop coping and problem-solving strategies to help buffer racism and deal with prejudice.

Racial/ethnic socialization among minority families is an emerging field of family and social science studies. It is a very complex issue and we have much to learn about the multiple processes associated with this type of socialization, as well as how what children are taught about race influences their lives.

A serious contemporary concern is the growing number of children in the United States, especially younger ones, who live in poverty. In the section that follows, we examine social forces that affect today's parents and families, and the family policies that exist to offer assistance: *poverty* and *social welfare*.

GOVERNMENT'S ROLE: POLICIES FOR FAMILIES

There are a number of social forces that have impact on families and their children, such as being able to afford adequate housing, access to affordable healthcare and quality childcare, access to quality education, being able to work, or living in or above poverty. Broadly speaking, **family policy**

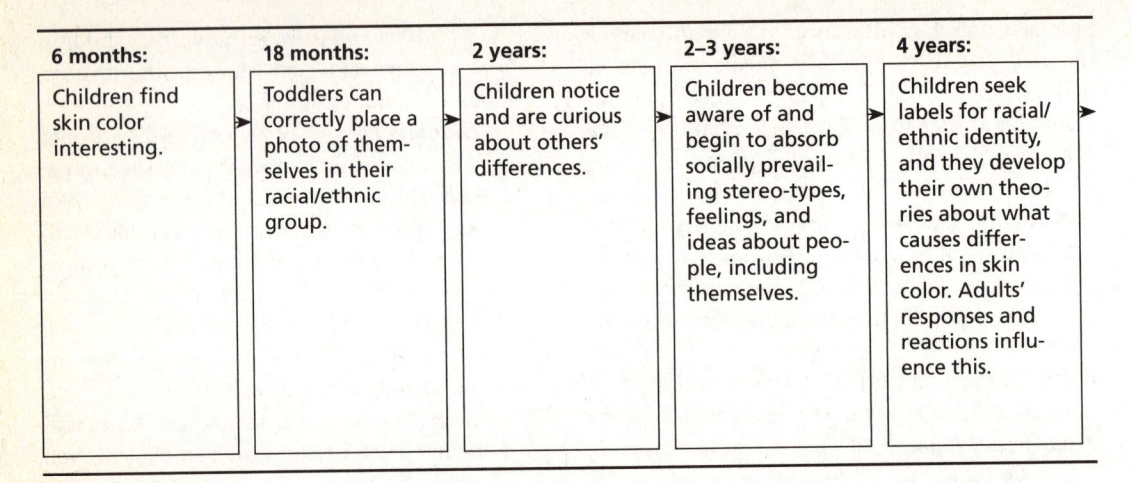

6 months:	18 months:	2 years:	2–3 years:	4 years:
Children find skin color interesting.	Toddlers can correctly place a photo of themselves in their racial/ethnic group.	Children notice and are curious about others' differences.	Children become aware of and begin to absorb socially prevailing stereo-types, feelings, and ideas about people, including themselves.	Children seek labels for racial/ethnic identity, and they develop their own theories about what causes differences in skin color. Adults' responses and reactions influence this.

FIGURE 6.6 The development of racial and ethnic identity.
Racial/ethnic socilization is a process that unfolds across a number of years. How are children taught to "be" their race/ethnicity and what are the social meanings attached to being a member of a racial or ethnic group?

Source: Welch, *Family Life Now*, 2e. (2010). Boston: Allyn & Bacon. pp. 376–377. Based on Katz (1982).

refers to governmental goals and/or programs that seek to support and strengthen families. These programs focus on current social factors that often face parents, such as work, health, education, or the community. Family policies address, for example,

- School readiness and literacy
- After-school programs aimed at keeping children safe
- Parenting and childrearing
- Childcare
- Substance abuse/use awareness programs geared toward youth

Today, federal, state, and local agencies promote social policies that relate to families and communities. The mission of these agencies is to create and distribute research-based educational programs and policies that support parents and families. Centers for family policy are especially crucial today because more and more frequently the welfare and the care of children and families is moving from the federal to the state level. Thus, family policies seek to strengthen families through research, education, and civic involvement.

Poverty

What does it mean to be poor, or to live in poverty? Defining poverty is difficult because it is a complex social issue and because there are different degrees of poverty. Nevertheless, knowing about poverty in the United States is important because those affected by poverty are at risk for hunger, disease, and increased mortality rates. Additionally, poverty among children is associated with lower cognitive abilities and difficulty in school, impaired health and development, and other risks, such as increased exposure to environmental toxins, poor nutrition, parental substance abuse, and trauma/abuse (Webster & Bishaw, 2007).

The **poverty rate** reflects the percentage of people with incomes below the federal government's published **poverty line**. It is necessary to be knowledgeable about poverty trends because these are an indicator of a nation's well-being, and in large part shape many governmental policies. Figure 6.7 shows us percentages of children who live in poverty and household poverty rates for different racial/ethnic groups

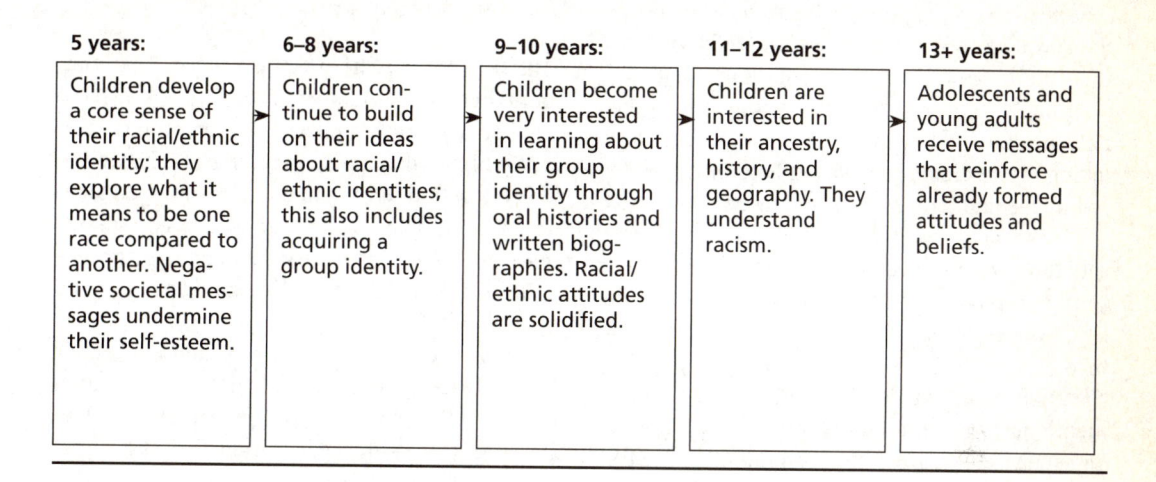

5 years:	6–8 years:	9–10 years:	11–12 years:	13+ years:
Children develop a core sense of their racial/ethnic identity; they explore what it means to be one race compared to another. Negative societal messages undermine their self-esteem.	Children continue to build on their ideas about racial/ethnic identities; this also includes acquiring a group identity.	Children become very interested in learning about their group identity through oral histories and written biographies. Racial/ethnic attitudes are solidified.	Children are interested in their ancestry, history, and geography. They understand racism.	Adolescents and young adults receive messages that reinforce already formed attitudes and beliefs.

in the United States. When comparing male and female heads of households by ethnicity, female householders have the highest percentage of poverty across all ethnic groups, whereas white male householders had the lowest poverty rates. Female-headed households are particularly vulnerable to poverty—the high rates of female-headship among American Indian/Alaskan Native, Hispanic, and African American/Black Caribbean families is why so many children and youth in this country are poor. In 2008, roughly 12 percent of the U.S. population lived in poverty (U.S. Census Bureau, 2008b). Census data reflect that 13 million of America's children live in poverty, roughly 18 percent (U.S. Census Bureau, 2008b).

The term **working poor** refers to people who are working, but who continue to remain

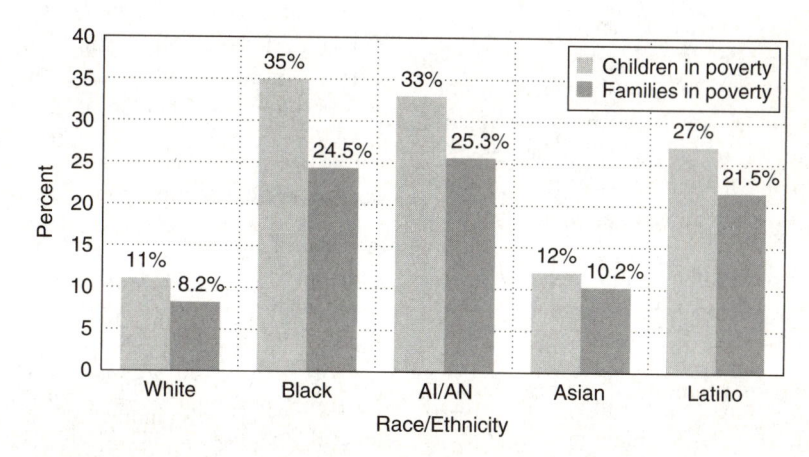

FIGURE 6.7 Children and families in poverty, by race.

Source: Welch, *Family Life Now*, 2e. (2010). Boston: Allyn & Bacon. p. 413.
Based on Annie E. Casey Foundation (2009); U.S. Census Bureau (2008; 2008k).

below the poverty line for their family size. High gas prices, food prices, and healthcare costs often require the working poor to choose between using their income for food or for paying bills, such as their mortgage or rent. As a young married student noted, "Every month is a struggle to make ends meet. I often skip meals for myself or skip taking my medicine so I can put food on our table or buy medicine for my son's earache."

We need to know about the issues surrounding poverty because the numbers of those living in poverty—and, thus, their quality of life—depend on how equally or unequally income is distributed across a society's population. **Socioeconomic status (SES)** is the government's measure of a family's relative economic and social ranking within a community. As SES decreases, physical illness, mental health illness, disability, and mortality increase (Hayen, Lincoln, Moore, & Thomas, 2002). Additionally, SES significantly impacts children's abilities to read and to succeed in school. Families with low SES typically lack many resources, including educational and medical resources that families of higher SES enjoy.

THE RURAL POOR Poverty is experienced in all regions of the United States. Contrary to what some may believe, poverty rates in rural areas are higher than those found in urban areas in every section of the country. **Persistently poor** populations, which are those with continuous poverty rates of 30 percent or higher, are prevalent in the South, West, and Midwest regions of the United States. The U.S. Economic Research Service (ERS; 2009) presents the landscape of the rural poor:

- One in five children in rural areas are poor; these children are referred to as the *forgotten fifth,* because programs/policies to help the poor focus on urban areas.
- Rural children are more likely than urban children to live in extreme poverty, under $11,000 per year for a family of four.
- 57 percent of poor rural children are white; 21 percent are black; 15 percent are Hispanic; and 4 percent are NA/AN.

The plight of those living in rural poverty is often overshadowed by those who live in metropolitan areas—the urban poor.

THE URBAN POOR Because urban areas are more heavily populated than rural areas, the numbers of urban dwellers in poverty are significantly higher than those in rural areas. Likewise, the concentration of ethnic minorities is concentrated more heavily in urban areas. The **ghetto poor** refers to inner-city residents, primarily either black or Hispanic, living at or below the poverty line.

Urban poverty exists in certain pockets or areas of the United States. This was illustrated in 2005 when Hurricane Katrina struck coastline states in the South—the nation saw the tragic plight of those in urban areas who were unable to flee because of their poverty.

WHAT LEADS TO POVERTY? Poverty is not a chronic condition; rather, individuals and families tend to fall below the poverty line in interludes. Factors that can lead to poverty include loss of a job, divorce, illness, disability, and natural catastrophes. Oftentimes, children whose parents divorce live with their mothers, and the loss of family income for the mother after divorce frequently puts the family below the poverty line, even with the ex-spouse's financial support. The term **feminization of poverty** reflects the impact of divorce on mothers and their children (see Chapter 7), and the increasing numbers of unmarried women having children.

Social Welfare

In 1964, President Lyndon B. Johnson delivered a Message to Congress inaugurating a policy that became known as the *War on Poverty.* In this address, he acknowledged the impact of poverty on families throughout the United States. To fight poverty, President Johnson proposed federal legislation that would require federal and state resources to fund a number of social programs and social policies, all in an effort to improve the living quality of the poor. Today, these programs are often referred to as **social**

welfare. By highlighting poverty and making it a national concern, numerous welfare programs were established, all of which continue to exist today:

- *Head Start:* This federal program focuses on educating/assisting preschool children of low-income families so they are better prepared for school.
- *Medicare:* This national healthcare insurance program provides medical benefits for people over the age of 65. People with certain disabilities or major health problems are also eligible for Medicare benefits, regardless of their age.
- *Medicaid:* Medicaid is a federally funded medical benefits program for those who live below the poverty level.
- *Food stamps:* Food stamps are coupons issued by the state welfare agency to low-income people or families for the purchase of certain grocery items.
- *Housing assistance:* Housing assistance is available to low- to moderate-income families to assist them in finding safe and affordable housing.

Johnson's programs worked to reduce poverty and improve life for poor Americans. However, over time, the established welfare policies created an environment of irresponsibility, and even family pathology, in which reliance on welfare was passed from generation to generation. In short, fewer impoverished able-bodied people elected to work, and instead became dependent on governmental assistance.

In 1996, President Bill Clinton signed into law the Welfare and Medicaid Reform Act of 1996, and today needy families receive what is known as *Temporary Assistance for Needy Families (TANF)*. While governmental assistance is still provided to low-income families, it is limited to a maximum of 5 years. Today, assistance is more restrictive, requiring that heads of households work and receive job training and job education. These changes in the social welfare policy provide families the help that they need, but are designed to limit assistance so the recipients become less dependent on the government.

Poverty, Social Welfare, and Parenting Behaviors

A key variable relating to parenting practices is the socioeconomic status of the families. The literature of the 1960s and the early 1970s identified significant differences among lower- and middle-class parents in several areas. Contemporary research has found that the quality of the environment in low-income families is generally lower than for middle- and upper-class families. Fairly consistent differences in parental behavior also have been found.

The impact of poverty on children is mediated by the behavior of adults—how they react to inadequate financial resources structures the consequences of poverty for children. The same level of income or material comfort may be perceived quite differently, depending on whether parents communicate worries about economic insecurity or whether children often are denied objects and experiences because the family lacks money (Garrett, Ng'Andu, & Ferron, 1994; Huston, McLoyd, & Coll, 1994). Nevertheless, a large body of data indicates that poverty has profound effects on parenting, largely because of high levels of stress.

ECONOMIC PRESSURES AND PARENTING

There has been little emphasis in the literature on the parenting behaviors of low-income fathers, but it has been suggested that loss of income for fathers may result in their becoming punitive and unnurturing, which results in children developing socioemotional problems, physical symptoms, and reduced aspirations and expectations. Parents may react to financial stress by overemphasizing obedience, withholding affection, relying on corporal punishment as a means of control, and failing to be responsive to the socioemotional needs of children (Garrett et al., 1994). Using a national sample, one body of research found that the likelihood of punitive parental behavior decreased as household income increased. Parents at low-income levels were especially likely to report behaving in a punitive and unsupportive fashion toward their children (Hashima & Amato, 1994).

Other studies indicate that economic stress may increase conflict and irritability in family interactions, and that aversive behavior toward children is a spillover effect of marital conflict. For example, researchers found that economic pressure is associated directly with parent–adolescent conflicts as well as parents' depressed moods and hostile interactions in the marriage (Conger, Ge, Elder, Lorenz, & Simons, 1994). Both marital conflict and financial conflict were significantly related to parent hostility toward the child.

There is far more emphasis in the literature on the parenting behaviors of low-income mothers and how they affect children. Many studies of diverse samples report that mothers experiencing high emotional stress exhibit diminished nurturance and sensitivity toward their children and, in disciplinary encounters, rely less on reasoning and loss of privileges and more on aversive, coercive techniques. Economic loss has adverse, indirect effects on children's behavior and socioemotional functioning through increasing negative parenting behaviors, which is consistent with the evidence that children of parents who use harsh, punitive, and inconsistent discipline are prone to a number of behavioral and psychological problems (Kalil & Eccles, 1998; McLoyd, Jayaratne, Ceballo, & Borquez, 1994).

EFFECTS ON CHILDREN It has been speculated that low-income mothers employ harsh disciplinary practices at a high rate because of urgent needs to try to prevent their children from becoming involved in antisocial activity, either as victims or as perpetrators. Stress induced by economic disadvantage may lead to increased coercive exchanges between parent and child. Many researchers have found that harsh and punitive parenting is associated with child aggressive behavior, and this relationship holds in diverse cultural groups and with children in five different countries. The stresses of socioeconomic disadvantage may cause a parent to be less attentive to the child's needs and thus less warm toward the child. Some studies have found maternal warmth to be negatively correlated with low socioeconomic status, which is associated with child aggressiveness. Children also may learn aggression from models; violence often is readily observed in low-socioeconomic marital dyads and neighborhoods, and observation of adult conflict is associated with both immediate and long-term adverse effects on children (Dodge, Pettit, & Bates, 1994).

Researchers have found that children in the lowest socioeconomic class received teacher-rated externalizing problem scores significantly above the national mean; more than 60 percent of the low-status children received a score in the clinical risk range at some time during elementary school. In fact, the lower the socioeconomic status, the greater the behavior problems. Impoverished children were more likely than their more advantaged peers to receive harsh discipline from their parents, to observe violence in their extended families and neighborhoods, and to have unstable peer groups and friendships. They received less cognitive stimulation in their home environments; their mothers were less warm and they experienced more life stressors, perceived less social support and greater isolation, and were more likely to believe that aggression is an appropriate and effective way to solve problems. These findings held even when the effects of single parenthood were controlled statistically, revealing their direct relationship to economic disadvantage. Harsh discipline was the strongest predictor of behavior problems (Dodge et al., 1994).

EFFECTS ON ADOLESCENTS Young adolescents from families characterized by lower incomes reported greater maternal rejection, less sense of belonging at school, and greater exposure to major stressful events than their more advantaged peers (Felner et al., 1995). Parental education had a different and more pervasive pattern of association with risk experiences.

Specifically, adolescents from homes in which neither parent had graduated from high school reported more developmentally negative experiences, including higher levels of rejection from both parents, less social support, and less emphasis on intellectual–cultural issues in their families, more negative feelings about school, and heightened levels of exposure to both major and relatively minor stressors. These findings suggested that household employment status and parental educational attainment each had unique influences on children's academic performance and achievement.

Because it appears to inhibit the capacity of families with adolescents to achieve informal social control, poverty increases the likelihood of delinquency. Strong family social controls may serve as an important buffer against structural disadvantage in the larger community. The fundamental causes of delinquency are consistent across time and rooted not in race but in generic family processes—such as supervision, attachment, and discipline—that are systematically influenced by family poverty and structural disadvantage (Sampson & Laub, 1994).

When economic hardship is accompanied by social isolation, parents are more likely to become neglectful of and abusive toward their children. The reported incidence of maltreatment is disproportionately large among families living in poverty, and socially isolated families have higher rates of child abuse than other families do; we address these issues at length in Chapter 9 (Hashima & Amato, 1994). Social support appears to have a positive effect on parenting behavior by making mothers feel less isolated and overwhelmed by their parenting situation, more gratified with the maternal role, and more satisfied with their children (McLoyd et al., 1994).

These studies suggest that there are documented differences between the home environments and the parenting behaviors experienced by poor children and their more economically advantaged peers. Lack of financial resources causes increased stress, leading to negative parenting behaviors, which result in adverse outcomes for children. It's important to note, however, that parenting behavior may be related to other factors, such as education, health status, and biological differences. Additionally, conditions associated with poverty, such as poor neighborhoods, inferior employment, poor health, unstable marriages, and high birthrates, serve to devastate the child's well-being as much as specific parenting behaviors.

Clearly, lower-income parents lack resources in parenting equal to those of other parents—financial, educational, psychological, and medical resources. And this lack of resources surely has some impact on the way in which they interact with their children.

Summary

With the diversity in the United States come vast differences in how we live based on our race, ethnicity, religion, customs, rituals, and beliefs. All of these contribute to unique family and parenting experiences.

But along with the diversity seen among the different races and ethnicities in our society are substantial differences in family structure, parenting, and income. Although the "traditional" family has long been held as the ideal standard in childrearing, we are no longer a society composed primarily of married couples raising their biological or adopted children. And of course, every area of family life—especially parenting—is shaped and influenced by the social contexts that surround us. Today's parents face many issues that affect their family's well-being, and the role of the government is to create family policies that strengthen families through research, education, and civic involvement.

References

Afable-Munsuz, A. & Brindis, C.D. (2006). Acculturation and the sexual reproductive health of Latino youth in the United Sates: A literature review. *Perspectives on Sexual and Reproductive Health, 38*(4), 208–220.

Allen, L., & Majidi-Ahi, S. (1989). Black American children. In J. Gibbs & L. N. Huang (Eds.), *Children of color* (pp. 147–178). San Francisco: Jossey-Bass.

Arab American Institute (2007). Arab Americans: Demographics. Retrieved September 1, 2008, from www.aaiusa.org/arab-americans/22/demographics.

Banks, J. A., & McGee-Banks, C. A. (2002). *Multicultural education: Issues and perspectives* (4th ed.). New York: Wiley.

Barbarin, O. A., & McCandies. T. (2003). African American families. In J. J. Ponzetti, Jr. (Ed.), *International encyclopedia of marriage and family* (2nd ed., Vol. 1, pp. 50–56). New York: Macmillan.

Barbour, C., Barbour, N. H., & Scully, P. A. (2005). *Families, schools, and communities: Building partnerships for educating children.* Upper Saddle River, NJ: Pearson.

Boellstorff, T. (2005). Between religion and desire: Being Muslim and gay in Indonesia. *American Anthropologist, 107*(4), 575–585.

Brown, T. N., Tanner-Smith, E. E., Lesane-Brown, C. L., & Ezell, M. E. (2007). Child, parent, and situational correlates of familial ethnic/race socialization. *Journal of Marriage and Family, 69*(1), 14–26.

Buriel, R. (1993). Childrearing orientations in Mexican American families: The influence of generation and sociocultural factors. *Journal of Marriage and the Family, 55*(4), 987–1001.

Carson, D., Dail, P., Greeley, S., & Kenote, T. (1990). Stresses and strengths of Native American reservation families in poverty. *Family Perspective, 24*(4), 383–400.

Casta-eda, D. M. (1993). The meaning of romantic love among Mexican-Americans. *Journal of Social Behavior and Personality, 8*(2), 257–272.

Child Trends. (2008). *Family structure.* Retrieved August 21, 2009, from www.childtrendsdatabank.org/indicators/59FamilyStructure.cfm.

Coard, S. I., Foy-Watson, S., Zimmer, C., & Wallace, A. (2007). Considering culturally relevant parenting practices in intervention development and adaptation: A randomized controlled trial of the Black Parenting Strengths and Strategies (BPSS) Program. *The Counseling Psychologist, 35*(6), 797–820.

Conger, R., Ge, X., Elder, G., Lorenz, F., & Simons, R. (1994). Economic stress, coercive family process, and developmental problems of adolescents. *Child Development, 65*(2), 541–561.

Coontz, S. (1992). *The way we never were: American families and the nostalgia trap.* New York: Basic Books.

Coontz, S. (1999). *American families: A multicultural reader.* New York: Routledge.

Davis, D. A., & Davis, S. S. (1993). Sexual values in a Moroccan town. In W. J. Lonner & R. S. Malpass (Eds.), *Psychology and culture* (pp. 225–230). Needham Heights, MA: Allyn & Bacon.

Dion, K. L., & Dion, K. K. (1993). Individualistic and collectivist perspectives on gender and the cultural context of love and intimacy. *Journal of Social Issues, 49,* 53–69.

Dodge, K., Pettit, G., & Bates, J. (1994). Socialization mediators of the relation between socioeconomic status and child conduct problems. *Child Development, 65*(2), 649–665.

Dumka, L., Roosa, M., & Jackson, K. (1997). Risk, conflict, mothers' parenting, and children's adjustment in low-income, Mexican immigrant, and Mexican-American families. *Journal of Marriage and the Family, 59,* 309–323.

Dykeman, C., & Nelson, J. (1995). Building strong working alliances with American Indian families. *Social Work in Education, 17*(3), 148–159.

Felner, R., Brand, S., DuBois, D., Adan, A., Mulhall, P., & Evans, E. (1995). Socioeconomic disadvantage, proximal environmental experiences, and socioemotional and academic adjustments in early adolescence: Investigation of a mediated effects model. *Child Development, 66,* 774–792.

Fernandez-Dols, J. M. (1999). Facial expression and emotion: A situationist view. In P. Philippot, R. S. Fledman, & E. J. Coats (Eds.), *The social context of nonverbal behavior* (2nd ed., Vol. 1, pp. 242–261). Cambridge, UK: Cambridge University Press.

Fleming, W. C. (2007). Getting past our myths and stereotypes about Native Americans. *Educational Digest, 72*(7), 51–58.

Fong, T. P. (2002). *The contemporary Asian American experience: Beyond the model minority* (2nd ed.). Upper Saddle River, NJ: Prentice Hall.

Garrett, P., Ng'Andu, N., & Ferron, J. (1994). Poverty experiences of young children and the quality of their home environment. *Child Development, 65*(2), 331–345.

Gonzales, N. A., Knight, G. P., Morgan-Lopez, A. A., Saenz, D., & Sirolli, A. (2002). Acculturation and the mental health of Latino youths: An integration and critique of the literature. In J. M. Contreras, K. A. Kerns, & A. M. Neal-Barnett (Eds.), *Latino children and families in the United States: Current research and future directions* (pp. 45–74). Westport, CT: Praeger.

Gorman, J. (1998). Parenting attitudes and practices of immigrant Chinese mothers and adolescents. *Family Relations, 47,* 73–80.

Greene, B. (1995). African American Families. *National Forum, 75*(3), 29–33.

Hale-Benson, J. (1986). *Black children: Their roots, culture, and learning styles* (Rev. ed.). Baltimore: Johns Hopkins University Press.

Hashima, P., & Amato, P. (1994). Poverty, social support, and parental behavior. *Child Development, 65*(2), 394–403.

Hayen, A., Lincoln, D., Moore, H., & Thomas, M. (2002). Trends in potentially avoidable mortality in NSW. *NSW Public Health Bulletin, 13*(11/12), 226–236.

Hellerstedt, W. L., Peterson-Hickey, M., Rhodes, K. L., & Garwick, A. (2006). Environmental, social, and personal correlates of having ever had sexual intercourse among American Indian youths. *American Journal of Public Health, 96*(12), 2228–2234.

Huang, L., & Ying, Y. (1989). Chinese American children and adolescents. In J. Gibbs & L. N. Huang (Eds.), *Children of color* (pp. 30–66). San Francisco: Jossey-Bass.

Hughes, D., Smith, E. P., Steven, H. C. Rodriquez, J., Johnson, D. J., & Spice. P. (2006). Parents' ethnic-racial socialization practices: A review of research and directions for future study. *Developmental Psychology, 42,* 747–770.

Huston, A., McLoyd, V., & Coll, C. (1994). Children and poverty: Issues in contemporary research. *Child Development, 65*(2), 275–282.

Huynh, V. W., & Fuligni, A. J. (2008). Ethnic socialization and the academic adjustment of adolescents from Mexican, Chinese, and European backgrounds. *Developmental Psychology, 44*(4), 1202–1208.

Johnson, T., Kulesa, P., Cho, Y., & Shavitt, S. (2005). The relationship between culture and response styles: Evidence from 19 countries. *Journal of Cross-Cultural Psychology, 36,* 264–277.

Kalil, A., & Eccles, J. (1998). Does welfare affect family processes and adolescent adjustment? *Child Development, 69*(6), 1597–1613.

Kelley, M., & Tseng, H. (1992). Cultural differences in children rearing. *Journal of Cross Cultural Psychology, 23*(4), 444–455.

Kids Count. (2007). *Data snapshot: One out of five U.S. children is living in an immigrant family.* Retrieved August 21, 2008, from www.aecf.org/KnowledgeCenter/Publications.aspx?pubuid={8661AE11-DBBC-4CBD-92A0-C37DC7AE6D93}.

LaFromboise, T., & Low, K. (1989). American Indian children and adolescents. In J. Gibbs & L. N. Huang (Eds.), *Children of color* (pp. 114–147). San Francisco: Jossey-Bass.

Lin, C., & Liu, W. (1993). Intergenerational relationships among Chinese immigrant families from Taiwan. In H. McAddo (Ed.), *Family ethnicity: Strength in diversity* (pp. 271–286). Newbury Park, CA: Sage

Little Soldier, L. (1992). Working with Native American children. *Young children, 47*(6), 15–21.

Makes Marks, L. F. (2007). Great mysteries: Native North American religions and participatory visions. *ReVision, 29*(3), 29–37.

Manning, W. D., & Smock, P. J. (2003, May 3). Measuring and modeling cohabitation: New perspectives from quantitative data. Paper presented at the annual meeting of the Population Association of America. Minneapolis, Minnesota.

Martinez, E. (1993). Parenting young children in Mexican American/Chicano families. In H. McAdoo (Ed.), *Family ethnicity: Strength in diversity* (pp. 184–192). Newbury Park, CA: Sage.

McLoyd, V., Jayaratne, T., Ceballo, R., & Borquez, J. (1994). Unemployment and work interruption among African American single mothers: Effects on parenting and adolescent socioemotional functioning. *Child Development, 65*(2), 562–589.

McWilliams, P. (1998). *Ain't nobody's business if you do: The absurdity of consensual crimes in a free country.* Los Angeles, CA: Prelude Press.

Miller, P., Wiley, A., Fung, H., & Hui Liang, C. (1997). Personal storytelling as a medium of socialization in Chinese and American families. *Child Development, 68*(3), 557–568.

Myers, D. G. (2008). *Social psychology* (9th ed.). New York: McGraw-Hill.

Neto, F. (2007). Forgiveness, personality, and gratitude. *Personality and Individual Differences, 43,* 2313–2323.

Padgett, D. (1997). The contribution of support networks to household laboring African American families. *Journal of Family Issues, 18*(3), 227–250.

Popenoe, D., & Whitehead, B. D. (2002). *Why men won't commit: Exploring young men's attitudes about sex, dating, and marriage.* New Brunswick, NJ: The National Marriage Project, Rutgers University. Retrieved December 2007 from www.marriage.rutgers.edu.

Ramirez, O. (1989). Mexican American children and adolescents. In J. Gibbs & L. N. Huang (Eds.), *Children of color* (pp. 224–250). San Francisco: Jossey-Bass.

Read, J. G. (2003). The sources of gender role attitudes among Christian and Muslim Arab-American women. *Sociology of Religion, 64*(2), 207–223.

Sampson, R., & Laub, J. (1994). Urban poverty and the family context of delinquency: A new look at structure and process in a classic study. *Child Development, 65*(2), 523–540.

Smith, D. M., & Gates, G. J. (2001, August 22). Gay and lesbian families in the United States: Same sex unmarried partner households: A preliminary analysis of 2000 United States census data. *Human Rights Campaign Report* (p. 2). Retrieved January 3, 2007, from www.urgban.org/UploadedPDF/1000491_gl_partner_households.pdf.

Smith, P. K., & Drew, L. M. (2002). Grandparenthood. In M. Bornstein (Ed.), *Handbook of parenting* (2nd ed., pp. 141–172). Mahwah, NJ: Erlbaum.

Solot, D., & Miller, M. (2004). Affirmation of family diversity. *Alternatives to Marriage Project.* Retrieved October 10, 2007, from www.unmarried.org/family.html.

Taylor, R. (2002). *Minority families in the United States: A multicultural perspective.* Upper Saddle River, NJ: Prentice Hall.

Triandis, H., & Suh, E. (2002). Cultural influences on personality. *Annual Review of Psychology, 53,* 133–160.

U.S. Census Bureau. (2006). *People 18 years old and over, by total money income in 2005, work experience, in 2005, age, race, Hispanic origin, and sex.* Atlanta, GA: Author. Retrieved March 17, 2009, from www.pubdb3.census.gov/macro/032006/perinc/new02_001.htm.

U.S. Census Bureau. (2007a). *American Community Survey: Population 65 years and older in the United States, 2005–2007.* Atlanta, GA: Author. Retrieved August 12, 2009, from http://www.census.gov/Press_Release/www/releases/archives/families-households/009842.html.

U.S. Census Bureau. (2007b). *Income quintiles, 2007.* Atlanta, GA: Author. Retrieved August 26, 2008, from www.pubdb3.census.gov/macro/032007/hhinc/new05_000.htm.

U.S. Census Bureau. (2008a). *American and Alaska Native heritage month: November 2007.* Atlanta, GA: Author. Retrieved September 2, 2008, from www.census.gov/Press_Release/www/releases/archives/facts_for_features_special_editions/010849.html.

U.S. Census Bureau. (2008b). *Asian/Pacific American heritage month: May 2008.* Atlanta, GA: Author. Retrieved March 16, 2010, from www.census.gov/Press-Release/www/releases/archives/facts_for_features_special_eidtions/011602.html.

U.S. Census Bureau. (2008c). *Facts for Features* (CB08-FF.02). Atlanta, GA: Author. Retrieved August 12, 2009, from http://www.census.gov/Press-Release/www/releases/archives/facts_for_features_special_editions/010968.html.

U.S. Census Bureau. (2008d). *Living arrangements of children: Household economic studies. Current populations* (P70-114). Washington, DC: Author.

U.S. Department of Health and Human Services. (2006). *Fertility, family planning, and the health of U.S. women: Data from the 2002 National Survey of Family Growth* (Series 23-25). Hyattesville, MD: National Center for Health Statistics.

U.S. Economic Research Service. (2009). *Rural poverty at a glance.* Retrieved March 18, 2010, from www.ers.usda.gov.htm.

Webster, B. H., & Bishaw, A. (2007). *Income, earnings, and poverty data from the 2006 American Community Survey.* Retrieved August 22, 2008, from www.census.gov/prod/2007pubs/acs-08.pdf.

When a marriage can't make room for daddy. (2005, January 19). *Chicago Tribune.* Retrieved June 25, 2009, from http://www.turnonyourinnerlight.com/ChicagoTribune01192005.htm.

Yau, J., & Smetana, J. (1996). Adolescent–parent conflict among Chinese adolescents in Hong Kong. *Child Development, 67,* 1262–1275.

Zahedi, A. (2007). Contested meanings of the veil and political ideologies of Iranian regimes. *Journal of Middle East Women's Studies, 3*(3), 75–99.

Chapter 7
Parenting in Single-Parent Families and Stepfamilies

Dramatic changes occurred in the marital behaviors of adults in the United States during the decade of the 1970s, and many of the trends have continued into the present. Specifically, the likelihood of marriage has declined or marriage has occurred later, divorce has increased to a record high and then leveled off, and significant changes have occurred in the living arrangements of both adults and children, such as among cohabiting as well as gay/lesbian families. And as you saw in Chapter 6, a significant number of households in the United States are not nuclear families with both biological parents living with their offspring—there has been a gradual, steady increase in the number of nonmarital births in the United States, which reached a record 38.5 percent in 2006 (Solomon-Fears, 2008). Today, 24 percent of children under the age of 18 live in single-parent homes, and over 2 million fathers are the primary caregivers of their children (U.S. Census Bureau, 2010). The percentage of adults and children residing in single-parent or stepfamilies is substantial.

In this chapter, we explore some of the issues experienced by single-parent and stepfamilies and some of the unique challenges they face as they raise their children. We also take a look at the aftermath of divorce as we discuss the many changes that face adults as they strive to effectively coparent their children, and we examine how divorce affects children and adolescents.

SINGLE-PARENT FAMILIES

There are a variety of types of single parents, and no one label is strictly definitive. A single-parent family implies that a mother or a father is parenting primarily alone, but in many cases the noncustodial parent may be highly involved at least part time in childrearing. **Single-parent family** refers to the living arrangements of a family structure consisting of one parent with dependent children living in the same household.

Single parents are not a homogeneous group; they exist in all socioeconomic levels, in all racial and ethnic groups, and in all age groups from younger than 15 to older than 50. Households headed by single parents include impoverished, never-married women or teenage mothers, gay and lesbian parents whose unions are not legally recognized, never-married women who have adopted or borne a child, widows and widowers, and women and men who find themselves single after a marital breakup (Gottfried & Gottfried, 1994). Additionally, many families instantly become single-parent families when a spouse is called to war, or when a spouse dies in combat. The rise in the divorce rate during the last quarter of the 20th century and the increasing number of never-married persons account for most of the single parents in the United States today (Solomon-Fears, 2008).

Regardless of its makeup, each single-parent family has its own unique starting point and its own unique developmental history (Anderson & Sabatelli, 2007). Single parenthood, regardless of its origin, cannot be considered as a single event; rather, it is the process of many events that determines the effects on the adults and children involved. Because mothers with children compose the largest segment of single-parent households, most of our discussion centers on the issues and challenges faced by single mothers. The following sections examine some of these challenges for mothers, fathers, and children.

Single Parents: Deficits or Strengths?

Single parenthood is not a new phenomenon. Throughout history, widows and widowers have reared children alone. But since 1970, the proportion of households made up of married couples with children has decreased while the proportion of households with single parents has increased. According to U.S. Census Bureau demographers, approximately 29 percent of families in the United States are single-parent families (U.S. Census Bureau, 2010). Over three-fourths of all single-parent households are headed by females; about 10 percent of single-parent households are headed by males (U.S. Census Bureau, 2008c). In Chapter 1, we saw the racial and ethnic differences among single parents, and in our study we have discovered that there are a number of reasons why the U.S. is seeing increasing numbers of single parents, such as women getting married later in life, the growth in divorce rates, and an increasing acceptance by society of unmarried childbearing.

Along with the shift in demographic and societal trends, the way researchers are viewing single parenting is changing, too. Throughout the past three decades, two models of single-parent families have been used predominantly.

- **Family Deficit Model:** The *family deficit model* dates back to the 1970s, when single-parent families were far less common than they are today. This model promoted the idea that single-parent households were negative experiences for children for the sole reason that the *family structure was not nuclear* (Marsh, 1990). With the basic assumption that one-parent families are not the ideal family situation for children, much of the research yielded while using this theory supported this (Donahoo, 2004).
- **Risk and Protective Factor Model:** Unlike the family deficit model, which assumes at the outset that the only "ideal" family structure is the traditional nuclear family, the *risk and protective factor model* does not assume at its base that single-parent families are out of the norm (Seifer, Sameroff, Baldwin, & Baldwin, 1992). This model assumes that *every* family form has strengths, or *protective factors,* and weaknesses, or *risk factors.* According to Seifer and his colleagues (1992), protective factors are those factors that positively influence children and lessen the influence and/or impact of any existing *risk factors.* Risk factors are, in essence, the weaknesses in the family system that can have a potentially negative impact on families and children. For example, a family member's employment status, mental health, poverty, educational level, mother's age at first birth, or number of siblings are all factors. Depending on which factors come into play, when risk factors outweigh protective factors, the result most likely will be a negative experience for children; conversely, when protective factors outweigh risk factors, the result will most likely be a positive family experience for children. While single parenting can be a risk factor for children's overall well-being, it is not the *sole predictor* of negative outcomes as suggested by the family deficit model.

As of 2007, approximately 9 percent of all households in the United States were headed by single parents (U.S. Census Bureau, 2008a); of the nearly 13 million children living with single parents, 80 percent live with their mothers. Census Bureau demographers estimate that about 43 percent of the women rearing children by themselves have never been married, and nearly one-third of these families live below the poverty line (Kreider & Fields, 2005).

Single-Parent Mothers

Previous research indicated that single mothers share common concerns, including income inadequacy, role overload, parenting and childcare, social isolation, and emotional and psychological problems (Goldberg, Greenberger, Hamill, & O'Neil, 1992; McLanahan & Booth, 1991; Olson & Banyard, 1993).

SINGLE-PARENT MOTHERS AND POVERTY

A large majority of single women with children of all ages work outside the home in the paid labor force. Employment rates among single female parents have significantly increased since the 1990s, where 44 percent of single mothers worked; in 2003, 54 percent of all single mothers were in the workforce (U.S. Department of Health and Human Services, 2006).

Single parenting affects the economic well-being of women and children. According to the U.S. Census Bureau (2007), a significant number of all households with children headed by mothers live in poverty. Figure 7.1 shows us that nearly one-half of all single-mother families live in economic despair. Black and Hispanic single mothers fare worse than any other group, with a poverty rate of slightly over 50 percent. Furthermore, in a review of the characteristics of over 13 million single mothers, the demographers discovered that 40 percent make less than $10,000 per year (Congressional Caucus on Women's Issues, 2005). Importantly, any spousal support, child support, or public assistance (welfare) the woman receives typically does not come close to offsetting the differences in income between single-mother parents and married parents.

A study sponsored by the Congressional Caucus on Women's Issues (2005) revealed that "single mothers find themselves on a downward slide in their struggle to establish secure and solid footing in the workforce" (Corbett, 2005, p. 2). Other key data from the report reveal that:

- Single mothers are "poor" or "near poor," despite the fact that they work, many of them full time.
- Those who are employed work in low-paying jobs; more often than not, these jobs do not include benefits, such as health insurance.
- More than half of the single mothers did not have education beyond high school.

In this examination of over 13 million single mothers, the Congressional Caucus found that educational attainment is associated with poverty and children's overall well-being. In 2005, about two-thirds of single mothers did not complete high school, or they had no further education after high school; only about 10 percent had completed a bachelor's degree (Congressional Caucus on Women's Issues, 2005). In addition, single mothers are much like many other mothers—they work in low-paying jobs that have few benefits, and provide few opportunities for advancement.

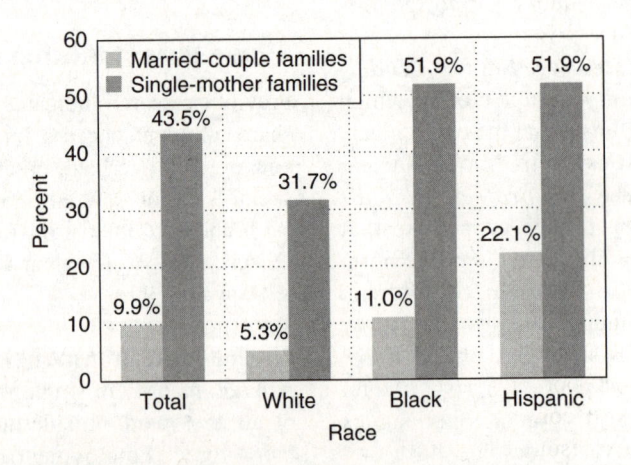

FIGURE 7.1 Percentage of children living in poverty, by family structure and race: 2008.
Single parenting impacts the economic well-being of the family.

Source: Forum on Child and Family Statistics (2010). America's children in brief: key national indicators of well-being, 2010. Available: www.childstats.gov/americaschildren/tables.asp [2010, september 11].

As the Congressional Caucus (2005) notes, local, state, and federal policymakers must begin to develop programs that better serve single mothers. Women's access to educational training, job training, and support programs that provide skills such as life management and work readiness will contribute to women's successes in the workforce.

SINGLE MOTHERS AND CHILDCARE Aside from low wages, a major barrier to employment for most mothers is childcare. Whereas in two-parent families the second parent can provide childcare or share its cost, the single mother has no such support. Thus, she is doubly disadvantaged with respect to earning capacity because her wage rate is lower than that of the higher earner in a two-parent family, and her childcare costs are higher (McLanahan & Booth, 1991). And although a potential second source of income for single mothers is child support from the nonresidential father, most poor mothers do not have a child support agreement; when they do, only about one-third of them receive the full amount. All too often, whatever they receive is not enough to bring women and children out of poverty (Pirog, Klotz, & Byers, 1998). We discuss child support following divorce a bit later in this chapter.

SINGLE MOTHERS AND HEALTH ISSUES Being poor also places single mothers at extremely high risk for anxiety, depression, and other health problems (Simons, Beaman, Conger, & Chao, 1993). Feelings of helplessness and despair are common and understandable (Davies, Avison, & McAlpine, 1997). The findings of one study suggested two routes to poor adjustment among single parents. The first consists of the ramifications of inadequate resources, whereas the second involves the consequences of antisocial orientation; single mothers with little education and low access to social-support networks and those who were under severe economic pressure report both high exposure to negative life events and low social support (Simons et al., 1993). Meager income and economic hardship increases the mothers' likelihood of experiencing negative life events, whereas low education reduces their chances of having access to social-network support. These reduced means serve to increase exposure to stressful events while limiting the availability of important coping resources, the ultimate result being psychological distress.

The current context of single parenthood, however, may be only partially responsible for the mental health of single mothers (Davies et al., 1997). One body of research found that single mothers, whether never married, separated, or divorced, are three times more likely than married mothers to have previously experienced a depressive disorder (Davies et al., 1997). Other researchers suggest that ongoing problems of money, parenting, inadequate and/or dangerous living arrangements, and intimate relationships present daily stressors for single mothers (Olson & Banyard, 1993).

COPING STRATEGIES USED BY SINGLE MOTHERS
Several studies have explored coping strategies used by single mothers to alleviate financial strain, improve their status, and receive support (Driscoll et al., 1999; Edin & Lein, 1996; Hao & Brinton, 1997). About one-third of poor mothers move their families out of poverty by marriage, and another one-third through employment. However, single mothers face a small pool of marriage partners, partly because of the reluctance of males to marry them and partly because many males do not or cannot sustain employment. The latter situation is especially prevalent among African Americans. Evidence indicates that divorced women at higher socioeconomic levels are more likely to marry than poor women. Therefore, women in the most disadvantaged economic situations are the least likely to improve their situations by marriage (Driscoll et al., 1999).

The extended family, especially the single mother's mother, is an important part of the single mother's support system. Living with kin can provide normative supervision and encouragement, potential in-kind transfers (room and board, childcare assistance, housework assistance), and possible role modeling. Also, single mothers who live in a parent's home are significantly less likely to receive public assistance because they receive room and board, childcare, and some additional cash assistance (Folk, 1996). Furthermore, living in a parent's home significantly reduces the household workload for these mothers.

Social support networks also contribute to positive coping by single mothers, and these networks vary by ethnicity. For example, one study noted that white women report having more close friends, interacting with friends more frequently, and relying on friends for advice and social support more often than Latino American women (Schaffer & Wagner, 1996). On the other hand, Latino American women generally have larger extended families, live closer to their relatives, and maintain family relationships more actively than whites through frequent visiting and mutual aid; this results in more internally cohesive support networks. Finally, women who are employed have significantly more friends.

In their study of family support to single African American mothers, researchers found that kin support in the financial, emotional, and childcare arenas was present and functioning for their sample (Jayakody, Chatters, & Taylor, 1993). The majority of mothers live in close proximity to their families, have daily contact with them, and report feelings of closeness to and satisfaction with their families. In this study, about one-quarter of never-married mothers received financial assistance and less than a fifth received childcare assistance. In contrast, the most extensive support provided these mothers was emotional assistance, reported by four out of five mothers. Analysis demonstrated that support, proximity, interaction, and affinity are important in specifying kin networks and their degree of viability. Family satisfaction and the proximity of immediate family are predictors of family assistance.

PARENTING BY SINGLE MOTHERS Since single mothers are vulnerable to stress resulting from a variety of contextual and personal variables, parenting is difficult, and ineffective parenting practices and poor parent–child relationships may result. Numerous studies have linked single mothers' psychological adjustment to their ability to parent (Amato & Booth, 1996; Arditti & Bickley, 1996; Bank, Forgatch, Patterson, & Fetrow, 1993; Barratt, Roach, & Colbert, 1991; Simons et al., 1993). Significant negative correlations were found between psychological symptoms and mothers' organization of the physical and temporal environment, maternal involvement with the child, and the provision of age-appropriate toys.

Other research found that negative life events in the lives of single mothers and inadequate social support were associated with psychological stress that precipitated ineffective parenting (Simons et al., 1993). Another empirical study discovered that single mothers are ineffective in their discipline practices, are more negative, issue more commands, and employ more dominating and hostile styles in interacting with their children (Bank et al., 1993).

Research on children in single-parent and other types of nontraditional families has emphasized that transitions to single-parent, stepparent, and nonparental living arrangements are linked to lower academic performance, lower probability of high school completion, behavior problems, decreased probability of postsecondary education, earlier movement toward residential independence, earlier marriage and subsequent divorce, and cohabitation (Aquilino, 1996). Some of the problems have been attributed to reduced parental involvement and less stringent supervision of children. Educational attainment of mothers appeared to mediate some of the problems of children, especially school achievement.

Single-Parent Fathers

While there is an abundance of literature about single mothers, their income levels, their educational attainment, and their occupational status, virtually none exists about single fathers as household heads. A single-father family is one that consists of an unmarried male and his minor child or children who live in the same household.

Single fathers include widowers, divorced or separated fathers, never-married males, and single adoptive fathers who have primary responsibility for care of their children.

The phenomenon of single-parent fathers is not new, but the incidence of this family type increased significantly in the last quarter of the 20th century. While most single parents are females, the proportion of families headed by single fathers is increasing in the United States, as well as in many other developed countries. According to Census Bureau data, of the approximate 13 million single-parent families in America today, about 2.5 million are headed by men (U.S. Census Bureau, 2008a).

Family and social scientists attribute the increased numbers of single-father households to a variety of reasons. For instance, more judges are awarding custody to fathers in divorce cases, more women are opting to pursue careers rather than seek custody of their children in divorce cases, and today more fathers are seeking joint custody arrangements (this arrangement reduces their monthly child support payments). Still, single-father households constitute only a small percentage of the overall picture of single-parent homes. Poverty rates are higher among single-father households than they are among married-couple households.

Although these family forms are increasing in number, very little research exists to shed light on the unique characteristics of these families headed by fathers. Kirk Bloir (2005) asserts that more fathers are rearing children by themselves as a result of four social factors:

1. Current divorce laws and "gender-neutral criteria" for rearing children have made it easier for fathers to gain custody of their children following divorce than in years past.
2. Mothers may choose to grant the father custody of the children to allow themselves the opportunity to pursue career or personal goals.
3. Divorce courts' are taking a more favorable view of the role of fathers in childrearing, resulting in an increase in joint custody arrangements following divorce.
4. An increase in fathers' willingness to take a more active role in parenting than in years past.

The researcher also notes characteristics that differentiate single fathers from single mothers. These include:

- Single fathers are less likely to live at or below the poverty line (although they tend to be poorer than married fathers).
- They are more likely to be employed.
- They tend to be younger than married fathers, but older than single mothers.
- Single fathers do not have as many children as married fathers, but have more than single mothers.
- They are more likely to live with other relatives in the household.
- Very few single fathers receive child support from the mother, whereas many mothers receive child support from fathers.
- Single fathers tend to suffer more from work–family role conflicts than married fathers or single mothers, such as being late, childcare, missing work, leaving early, or work-related travel concerns.

SOURCES OF STRESS FOR SINGLE FATHERS

The onset of single fatherhood, regardless of the manner in which the status is achieved, produces a psychological crisis for the father and for his children, at least temporarily. Sources of stress for single fathers include negative affect, job/family conflict, financial concerns, and parenting issues.

Although single fathers do experience financial problems, they are better able to realize economic security than single mothers are. Some fathers report that they are unable to work overtime because of parental responsibilities, and other fathers report difficulties with budgeting. Some studies have indicated that financial status is the key to a man's performance and satisfaction as a single father. Other studies have not found income to have a significant direct effect on parent–child relationships or on a variety of parenting experiences. However, job-related problems could have an indirect effect (Grief, 1995).

Potentially, a single father faces a number of problems, many of them psychological. He is at risk for increased adjustment difficulties, depression, lowered self-esteem, anxiety, and loss of influence in making the child feel a part of the family. Additionally, the single father is likely to experience feelings of self-doubt and ambivalence, and a generally diminished sense of importance as a parent (Wilbur & Wilbur, 1988).

One study of the social and emotional well-being of single custodial parents found some differences between single mothers and single fathers. Fathers were more bothered than mothers by high blood pressure and frequent drinking and drug use, whereas mothers seemed more bothered than fathers by insomnia, fatigue, and crying spells (Buehler, 1988).

Single fathers are subject to job/family conflict similar to the ways in which single mothers are. Conflicts between childcare responsibilities and vocational responsibilities are likely to occur. Business trips, job mobility, working hours, earnings, promotions, and relations with coworkers and supervisors may be limited. The problems relating to employment, finances, and childcare tend to interact and to impinge on the family at a time when emotional resources are likely to be at the lowest ebb.

The synchronization of work, supervision of children, and household management seems to be a major problem for most single fathers. For example, they state that they have no chance to shop for bargains, are seldom able to cook economically, and do not have time to perform housekeeping tasks properly. The stress associated with these tasks appears to stem from role overload rather than inability to perform tasks.

PARENTING BY SINGLE FATHERS Relationships with children, childrearing, and childcare present adjustment problems for single fathers (Wilbur & Wilbur, 1988). Some research indicates that initially single fathers seek reassurances from their children to an unhealthy degree. With time, however, most single fathers move past the need to rely on their children for validation (Grief, 1995). The father's level of comfort with parenting depends upon the satisfaction with his social life, not having a religious affiliation, an increased income, rating himself as a good parent, and a positive relationship with his children.

Evidence demonstrates that single fathers can fulfill the primary parenting role satisfactorily, and overall, single fathers report a fairly high level of comfort with their roles (Grief, 1995; Tillitski, 1992). Over time, they show improvement in their skills, but they become more challenged by other problems. Although managing housework and childcare becomes easier as children become more responsible and independent, rearing older children poses new challenges. Adolescent sexuality and peer pressure challenge many parent–child relationships in new ways. Furthermore, loneliness may increase if there are no prospects for marriage.

There is no question that single-parent families face challenges that are unique to their family structures. And although the current U.S. divorce rate is at its lowest since 1975, with about four couples divorcing for every 1,000 who are married (U.S. Department of Health and Human Services, 2009), divorced parents and their children also face challenges they must navigate. There are a number of demands and stressors associated with divorce, but there is a final transition that we must consider—the *aftermath* of divorce. Well after the decision to divorce is made public to family and friends, well after the separation takes place, and well after the legal divorce is finalized, the reconstruction continues.

There is no universal pathway to rebuilding following divorce, and in the sections that follow we discuss the transitions and the ways in which families rebuild their new lives.

Different families' structures bring them certain challenges, which we explore in the context of binuclear families, single-parent families, and remarriage and stepfamilies.

THE AFTERMATH OF DIVORCE: TRANSITIONS

The transition of status from married to divorced often leads to upheaval and disorganization within the family system. To cope with these changes, families must take on the central task associated with the aftermath of divorce—the reorganization of the family. This requires reconstructing the single nuclear family into a *binuclear family,* a process that creates two family systems from one family of origin.

The Binuclear Family

The term **binuclear family** refers to the separate, distinct households that form after marital separation or divorce. This dramatic change in family life reverberates throughout the entire family system, and this turn of events often brings the entire family to new levels of stress and crisis. The two subsystems that have been formed—the maternal (mother) and the paternal (father)—are now the child's family of origin. This restructuring from one central family into two accounts for much of the upheaval and confusion associated with divorce.

Constance Ahrons is a therapist and an internationally recognized lecturer and top professional in the area of divorce. She and her colleague, therapist Roy Rodgers (1987), believe that the major goal of family reorganization centers on establishing healthy patterns of relating within *all* areas of family life. This transformation involves replacing old patterns of interrelating with new patterns, and replacing existing family boundaries with new ones. *Over time, these changes help to redefine the family into a binuclear family.* As the former spouses navigate this rocky transition, they must find a way to establish their independence

There is no question that divorce hurts everyone involved. Although there are a number of stressors associated with the many processes of divorce, how parents continue to parent their children post-divorce largely determines children's outcomes.

while continuing to fulfill their obligations to their children, their families, their friends, and their careers (Ahrons & Rodgers, 1987). According to anthropologist Paul Bohannan (1971), the coparental divorce is the most painful, difficult, and complex aspect of the divorce. To better understand coparenting in the aftermath of divorce, it helps to understand former spouse relationships.

Former Spouse Relationships

Despite the frequency of divorce in today's culture, the ongoing relationship between divorced parents is often marked by bitterness, anger, hurt, and hostility. Former spouse relationships are especially important to consider because the relationship between ex-spouses lays the groundwork and sets the emotional climate for the newly defined binuclear family (Ahrons & Rodgers, 1987).

By any definition, the dissolution of a marriage is a stressful life event. There is no question that **primary divorce stressors**, such as custody arrangements, visitation, and child support, are demanding and that they exert a number of strains on the entire family. **Secondary stressors** are those things that occur following the divorce. In essence, secondary stressors are the "fallout" associated with divorce. For example, hundreds of studies have revealed that divorced individuals experience more depression, are less happy, and are at greater risks for health problems than married individuals are (for a complete review, see Amato, 2000). But are there differences between how women and men experience divorce? Is there such a thing as his-and-her divorces?

Divorced Moms

Divorced women—particularly those who have children—face a number of these experiences, including financial difficulties. In addition, they must contend with role overload when they assume the roles of both mother and father to their children in comparison to divorced men. Financial limitations directly influence things such as housing, food, clothing, transportation, medical care, childcare, and the opportunities for recreational and/or leisure activities (Lynch & Kaplan, 2000).

The lack of these not only has immediate negative impacts on women and their children, but also may have cumulative impacts on the single mother. First, the ongoing stressful conditions associated with divorce exert negative health effects on a person, causing such things as a lowered ability to fight infections and an increased risk of cancer (Wickrama, Lorenz, Conger, & Elder, 2006). Second, the stressors and strains associated with divorce also affect emotional health, and oftentimes mothers experience increased levels of depression, anxiety, stress, self-doubt, and pessimism about the future. For example, after a divorce mothers tend to stay angrier longer and are less likely to forgive than fathers (Bonach, Sales, & Koeske, 2005; Hetherington & Kelly, 2002). Also, the adverse social conditions associated with divorced single motherhood expose mothers to disadvantaged social positions, which include such things as long work weeks and single-handed parenting and childcare—that mothers are oftentimes solely responsible for their children's well-being is especially difficult for divorced moms (Braver, Shapiro, & Goodman, 2006; Wickrama et al., 2006).

In addition to these findings, research reveals another disturbing finding: The demands of single motherhood following divorce are so great that it appears to substantially increase the probability of alcohol abuse in mothers of young children (Williams & Dunne-Bryant, 2006). In a study of nearly 5,000 post-divorce women, the investigators found that among parents of preschool children, women reported greater consumption of alcohol than men did. The researchers attach some caution to these findings because they did not assess the mothers' and fathers' *predivorce* levels of alcohol use. However, they speculate that an increase in mothers' drinking may be the result of social drinking (such as attending more clubs or bars following their divorces), or the result of a decline in social support; feeling alone, women turn to alcohol. Because of the ramification of these findings for children's well-being, family and social scientists need to explore whether mothers are at greater risk of abusing alcohol following divorce.

Divorced Dads

While mothers' difficulties following divorce are commonly due to financial worries and single-handed parenting, divorced dads' greatest stressors are associated with the decreased contact they have with their children (Braver et al., 2006). A number of recent studies show that fathers are more depressed, stressed, and disheartened than mothers after divorce because of their inability to be with their children, and because they miss their children so much (Baum, 2006; Bokker, Farley, & Denny, 2005; Hallman & Deinhart, 2007; Stone, 2007). Oftentimes, the father doesn't have control over how often he sees his children because frequent contact with children may be impeded or altogether prohibited by some former wives who continue to carry hostile, angry, or bitter feelings toward their ex-husbands. For example, about one-third of divorced mothers move the kids 400 to 500 miles away from their fathers within the first 2 years following divorce; this drastically reduces the amount of time fathers can spend with their children (Bailey & Zvonkovic, 2006; Kelly, 2007). Other research also suggests that custodial moms discourage children's contact with their fathers by denying access to the children, by engaging in conflicts or confrontations at the time of picking up the children, and by cutting into the time fathers have with their kids by not having them ready when the father arrives to pick them up (Lehr & MacMillan, 2001; Leite & McKendry, 2002). Many times fathers will reduce or greatly avoid contact with their children in an effort to keep away from the ongoing conflict with their former wives (Hetherington & Kelly, 2002). In addition, some mothers act as **gatekeepers** of their children, but too frequently mothers not only guard the gate—they lock it. A number of recent studies show that many mothers acknowledge that they deny visitation, make it difficult for fathers to see their children, and that they do not intend to share parenting with the father (Cookston, Braver, Griffin, DeLusé, & Miles, 2007; Criddle & Scott, 2005; Henley & Pasley, 2007; Markham, Ganong, & Coleman, 2007).

Children's involvement with their fathers following divorce is important to their development. Studies show that children who experience a warm post-divorce relationship with their fathers have higher self-esteem, fewer behavioral problems, and better social, academic, and cognitive skills (Hetherington, 1991). This appears to be especially true for African American children (McLanahan & Sandefur, 1994). Fathers' involvement in the lives of their children matters because children without fathers are more likely to drop out of high school; become dependent on alcohol or other substances; become delinquent; run away from home; end up in prison; or commit suicide (Parke & Brott, 2003).

Unfortunately, however, divorce often brings with it significant changes in the ways in which fathers parent, particularly the noncustodial father. For example, post-divorce noncustodial fathers are more likely to be permissive in their parenting and take on a recreational, companion role rather than the role of disciplinarian (Furstenberg & Cherlin, 1991). This phenomenon of fathers taking on the "friend" role following divorce is so common that some have labeled noncustodial fathers as "Disneyland Dads." While these fathers are happy to entertain their children, fathers who do not have custody tend to be less sensitive to their children's emotional needs and are less supportive of them in times of crisis and stress (Stewart, 1999). This inability to effectively parent may, in turn, contribute to the amount of contact a father seeks to have with his children following divorce. For instance, some research suggests that many newly divorced dads feel overwhelmed with their new parenting role because their experiences with their children before divorce were most often limited to day-to-day tasks and responsibilities (Pleck, 1997). Because of this lack of parenting skills, many fathers take on the "friend" role. Others may completely withdraw from their children rather than risk being inadequate.

Each year, 1 million children experience the divorce of their parents (U.S. Census Bureau, 2008b). Understandably, much attention has been given to the effects of divorce on children over the past several decades, as divorce is one of the most common stressors experienced by today's children (Shaw & Ingoldsby, 1999). In the section that follows, we take a closer look at how divorce affects children and adolescents.

HOW DIVORCE AFFECTS CHILDREN AND ADOLESCENTS

A substantive body of research shows that divorce has detrimental impacts on both short- and long-term adjustment in children and adolescents. While in some instances divorce is beneficial to children, such as when there is physical, sexual, or emotional violence, in most instances, divorce has some negative effects on children (Cartwright, 2006; Hetherington, 2003; Kelly & Emery, 2003; Wallerstein & Lewis, 2004).

The Negative Effects of Divorce

An abundance of empirical research concludes that children who experience their parents' divorce are at increased risk for certain difficulties. Post-divorce effects on children and adolescents are broken down into three areas: acting out, emotional problems, and problems in school (Shaw & Ingoldsby, 1999). Children **externalize** difficulties through their behavior when they grapple with the inner turmoil, confusion, anger, and hurt they feel in the aftermath of their parents' divorce. Commonly known as **acting out,** children and adolescents externalize their feelings about the divorce, typically through aggressive misbehaviors, noncompliance, disobedience, delinquency, increased absences from school, and increased aggressiveness (Amato, 2000; Fincham, 2002; Hetherington & Kelly, 2002; Stanley & Fincham, 2002). Offspring of divorce are also more likely to become teenage parents and leave home earlier (Hetherington, 2003). It is not surprising that boys exhibit externalizing behaviors more frequently than girls. This may be due to boys' increased vulnerability to stressor experiences in general (Shaw, 1993). This also explains why boys experience greater post-divorce adjustment difficulties than girls (Fincham, 2002).

Internalizing difficulties result in emotional problems such as worry, feelings of unhappiness, anxiety, depression, distress, guilt, and poor self-concept. When compared with children whose parents' marriages are intact, children of divorced families have been shown to have a lower concept of self, as well as a lower sense of well-being, and they also have fewer problem-solving skills (Hetherington, 2003; Gohm, Oishi, Darlington, & Diener, 1998; Parish & Wigle, 1985). Additionally, children of divorced parents report lower levels of intimacy with parents and friends and experience interpersonal relationship problems, including difficulty in trusting others (Fincham, 2002; Hetherington, 2003; King, 2002; Stanley & Fincham, 2002). The correlation between divorce and internalizing problems is especially high for girls (Fincham, 2002; Furstenberg & Allison, 1989; Stanley & Fincham, 2002).

In general, children who experience their parents' separation or divorce have more difficulties in the classroom and performing academically than children who have not had similar experiences (Carlson, 1995). In fact, children from established households headed by one parent or children who live in an established stepfamily perform better academically than those children who have recently experienced their parents' divorce.

Why is this so? To a large extent, the reasons children whose parents are divorcing demonstrate poor academic performance are intrinsically tied to the internalization problems encountered by children of divorced families. The emotional aspects of divorce, such as anxiety, depression, guilt—and possibly aggression—affect the children's ability to concentrate in school, negatively affecting their ability to meet scholastic expectations (Dacey & Travers, 2002). This emotional toll may also affect children's ability to interact socially with teachers and peers.

Shaw and Ingoldsby (1999) point to a body of research that speaks to the fact that children of divorced families often experience a subsequently lower socioeconomic status (SES), which has consistently been linked to poor school achievement. This tends to be the case especially among those children who reside in single-parent families with little interaction with the other parent. Although some children experience great resilience after family dissolution, a significantly large number of children are not as fortunate.

Children's and Adolescents' Adaptation

Individual reactions to divorce vary greatly, but as Table 7.1 shows us, there are common age-related responses when parents divorce. In terms of those aspects that determine how children and adolescents adjust to family reorganization and redefinition, empirical evidence strongly suggests that it is not the divorce *per se* that ultimately influences post-divorce adaptation; rather, there appear to be mediating family process variables that account for children's responses to divorce. Shaw and

TABLE 7.1 Children's reaction to divorce by developmental stage.

Age	Reaction
Infants	Infants may react to their parents' distress by losing their appetites, changing their sleep patterns, or exhibiting changes in other routines, such as being fussy during play time. Parents should try to maintain a daily routine, and relate physically and emotionally to the infant.
Toddlers	Toddlers may react to the absence of the parent by crying more and becoming clingy. They may have trouble eating and sleeping, and they may regress to behaviors they had as infants, such as thumb sucking or needing diapers. Parents should reassure their toddler that they will always love her or him. Regular contact with both parents is essential.
Preschoolers	Preschoolers are often called the "forgotten mourners." They know something is wrong and they grieve the loss of the absent parent, but they do not know how to put their feelings into words. They often blame themselves for their parents' breakup. Parents should reassure them that the children did nothing to cause the divorce, and that they will always be loved. Regular contact with both parents is essential.
School-Aged	Children at this age understand that their parents don't love each other and that they can't live together. Children may fantasize about ways to reunite their parents. They feel a tremendous sense of loss and rejection, and they worry a lot about the future, about who will care for them and what will happen if their remaining parent dies. They may have physical symptoms such as headaches and stomach aches, and they may have problems sleeping. They may show signs of depression, such as withdrawing from friends and activities. Parents need to be good listeners and reassure children that the divorce is not the children's fault. They need to have predictable contact with the absent parent.
Preteens and Adolescents	Although children of this age understand the permanence of divorce, they don't like it, and they don't readily accept it. It is not uncommon for children of this age to act out and become rebellious. Parents need to talk about the adolescent's feelings and concerns, not about the problems the parents are having with their ex-spouses. Parents need to make sure the child's responsibilities are age appropriate and not so demanding that they have to grow up too soon.

Sources: Welch, *Family Life Now*, 2e. (2010). Boston: Allyn & Bacon. p. 462. Based on DeBord (1997); Long & Forehand (2002).

Ingoldsby (1999) outline the interrelated family factors that affect children's and adolescents' long-term adjustment to divorce.

SEPARATION FROM AN ATTACHMENT FIGURE

Recall from Chapter 2 that emotional attachment between a child and a caregiver is critical to a child's development. Central to the concept of attachment is the idea that as a result of this initial attachment, children develop a sense of security and trust, allowing for optimal development. When a child experiences the loss of a primary attachment figure, such as in the case of divorce, it may trigger difficulties in interpersonal relationships, including friendships and love relationships (Hannum & Dvorak, 2004; Hinderlie & Kenny, 2002; McIntyre, Heron, McIntyre, Burton, & Engler, 2003). Shaw and Ingoldsby (1999) recognize that it is difficult to determine conclusively whether these relationship difficulties are due to the separation from the parent, or whether the problems are due to the multifaceted, multidimensional family processes associated with divorce and the resulting family reorganization.

The Passage of Time

Is it true that time heals all wounds? The effects of **temporal influences**, such as the passage of time and the child's age at the time of divorce, may play a role in children's long-term adjustment to their parents' divorce, though there is conflicting evidence. For example, Shaw and Ingoldsby (1999) observe, "as time passes, many of the stressors associated with divorce are lessened in intensity as adults and children adapt to new living situations" (p. 350). Other research offers conflicting findings.

Psychologist Judith Wallerstein devoted more than two decades to studying the effects of divorce on children. In her landmark longitudinal study in the early 1970s of 131 children from dissolved families, she found that one-half to two-thirds of the children in her study carried with them feelings of vulnerability and fear, and noted that for children of divorce, growing up was harder every step of the way than it was for children whose parents did not divorce. In her book, *The Unexpected Legacy of Divorce* (Wallerstein, Lewis & Blakeslee, 2000), Wallerstein discusses a research finding that materialized some 30 years after her research had begun—that children carried with them these same feelings of vulnerability and fear well into adulthood. Notes Wallerstein, "When children of divorce become adults, they are badly frightened that their relationships will fail, just like the most important relationship in their parents' lives failed. Their decisions about whether or not to marry are shadowed by the experience of growing up in a home where their parents could not hold it together" (p. 8).

Recent research appears to confirm Wallerstein's findings. Using data gathered from life-story interviews of 40 young adults, ages 19 to 29, the researcher discovered that while a majority of the study participants were positive about their parents' divorces, the majority also considered that they were currently experiencing negative effects related to their parents' separations (Cartwright, 2006). One study participant discussed her hesitancy to enter relationships:

> "I've never really had any boyfriend from 14 onwards. . . I don't know whether that's a reflection of me and not wanting to because of my parents breaking up. I kind of almost think, I've almost got a bad way of thinking. Like, I don't want to start something if I know it's going to be a waste of time, where it's not going to ever go anywhere, cuz then it's wasting my time, I kind of don't ever open up to anyone, so I think [their divorce] affected me." (p. 132)

THE RELATIONSHIP BETWEEN THE CUSTODIAL PARENT AND THE CHILD Without question, the greatest change to which children and adolescents need to adapt post-divorce is their relationship with their parents. These changes are so significant that researchers have coined the phrase

diminished parenting to describe this new relationship that takes place during the first few years following divorce. Today, an estimated 13.6 million parents have custody of 21.2 million children under the age of 21 while the other parent lived somewhere else; this number represents 26 percent of all children in the United States (Grall, 2007). In 2007, five of every six custodial parents were mothers (84 percent), and one in six were fathers (16 percent). There are also racial and ethnic differences in the numbers of custodial mothers (Grall, 2007):

- *White mothers:* 52.7 percent
- *Black mothers:* 27.8 percent
- *Hispanic mothers:* 16.3 percent

Research has revealed changes in the custodial parent's (most typically the mother) behavior, such as less frequent displays of showing affection, particularly to boys, and less nurturing behavior (Amato, 2000). One body of research shows that the conflict between the custodial parent and the children increases, while their ability to communicate with their children declines (Amato & Rezac, 1994). This study is of particular note because the researchers studied over 12,000 children in all types of single-parent homes. During the first year or so following divorce, many children assume more household responsibilities and often exhibit greater independence. Meanwhile, the custodial parent's parenting becomes more negative and less consistent. Some custodial mothers may become permissive in their parenting style and emotionally dependent upon their children. But there are any number of family process variables (such as economic difficulties or support, the mother's emotional state, her extended family and social support) that contribute to disturbances in parenting.

THE RELATIONSHIP BETWEEN THE NONCUSTODIAL PARENT AND THE CHILD One of the single greatest adjustments required for family reorganization into a binuclear family is that of incorporating a noncustodial parent into the family dynamics. In the United States, it is more than likely that the nonresident parent is the father. The success or failure of this adjustment depends largely on the frequency of visitation the noncustodial parent has with his or her children. On average, about 32 percent of children of divorce have no contact or visitation with their fathers following divorce, but nearly one-fourth of nonresident fathers see their children at least once a week (U.S. Department of Health and Human Services, 2009). For those who do have visitation arrangements, the children spend significantly less time with the nonresidential parent than they did with that parent prior to the divorce. As the length of time increases following the divorce, the amount of time nonresident parents typically spend with their children decreases (Lehr & MacMillan, 2001).

But as with any parent–child relationship, the frequency of contact and the length of visitations are not as important as the quality of the interactions and the relationship between the child and the parent. A strong, intimate relationship with the noncustodial parent, then, bodes well for children's adjustment to a binuclear family, as it appears that good parent–child relationships cushion and shield against the adverse effects of divorce (Davis & Friel, 2001; Lehr & MacMillan, 2001; White & Gilbreth, 2001). One study indicated that as children of divorce became adults, 62 percent of those studied noted that their relationships with their fathers improved or stayed the same over the 20 years since their parents' divorce (Ahrons & Tanner, 2003).

COPARENTING IN BINUCLEAR FAMILIES
It has been said before that it is difficult for suffering parents to be effective parents. While divorced parents understandably have many adjustments of their own to make following the dissolution of their marriage, such as adjusting to custody arrangements and binuclear family parenting, financial support, and relocation, these do not lessen the parents' responsibilities in ensuring the needs of their children are met.

Regardless of the custodial arrangements, the parents' post-divorce relationship greatly influences how they fulfill their parental functions. A recent study supports this. Data drawn from the Binuclear Family study, which followed the lives of 98 pairs of spouses and their children for 20 years, revealed that over half of the participants indicated that their parents got along fairly well now that the children were grown (Ahrons, 2007). Furthermore, one-half of those surveyed reported that their parents now cooperated well in parenting, and another 10 percent believed their parents were friendly. Only 22 percent indicated that their parents were still angry with one another. Several factors affect parenting following divorce:

- *Parents' education level*—Parents with higher education levels tend to engage in higher levels of coparenting than do parents with lower education levels (Cooksey & Craig, 1998).
- *Income level*—Parents in higher SES brackets tend to coparent more effectively than do parents in lower income brackets (Arditti, 1999).
- *Duration of the marriage*—Couples who are married longer are more likely to engage in more cooperative post-divorce parenting (Ahrons & Rodgers, 1987).
- *Time elapsed since the divorce*—If other variables, such as higher education levels and higher SES levels, are present, divorced couples are more apt to effectively coparent over time as "wounds begin to heal" (Furstenberg & Cherlin, 1991).
- *Remarriage of one or both spouses*—Remarriage often negatively impacts former spouses' ability to coparent (Ahrons & Rodgers, 1987).
- *Who initiated the divorce*—Most commonly, the spouse who initiates the divorce is the more cooperative coparent (Duran-Aydingtug, 1995).
- *The legal process of divorce*—If the divorce process involves hostility and conflict or is difficult and protracted, the father tends to be less involved with his children (Madden-Derdich & Arditti, 1999).

While more parents share joint custody of their children following divorce than in past decades, as you saw earlier, significantly more children live with their mothers following divorce

Following divorce, there are a number of legal issues that parents need to sort out, such as child custody and child support payments. Despite parents' hurts, it is essential that they work together to insure their children's best interest are being met.

than with their fathers (Grall, 2007). This distinction is important because family study researchers have determined that there are considerable differences between mothers and fathers and how they fulfill their parental duties and functions following divorce—for example, the majority of custodial mothers carry out their parenting responsibilities in the same way they parented before they divorced (Baum, 2003). And while some fathers also continue to parent in the same way as before they divorced, other fathers' parental involvement increases, and as we saw earlier, others' involvement decreases.

For the past several decades, social norms dictated that because mothers are the more "nurturing" parent, mothers should be awarded custody of the children following divorce. Yet because recent scientific studies have revealed that children fare better when both parents are involved in their growing up, legal and social policies have changed to accommodate the needs of the children (Emery, 1994).

THE LEGAL ASPECTS OF DIVORCE: CHILD CUSTODY AND SUPPORT

Once the decision to divorce has been made, there is much to decide: child custody, community property settlement, child support, and spousal support. In the United States, **family law** establishes policies and regulations to ensure that married or divorced couples fulfill their obligations to each other and to their children. Though specific family laws vary from state to state, these laws were enacted to protect the rights and well-being of all family members, as well as both spouses. There are contractual obligations of marital parties according to family laws (Ventura & Reed, 1998). Like marriage laws, family laws that govern formal separation and divorce proceedings are also intended to ensure that ex-spouses' and children's rights are protected. While these laws do not lessen the emotional toll families endure post-divorce, they do provide a framework for the legal aspects of marital dissolution.

Spousal Support

Historically, spousal support was absolutely essential. Because ex-wives were typically less educated than their husbands, had fewer employment opportunities, and had fewer job skills, women had very little means of supporting themselves and their children. To compensate, ex-husbands were responsible for paying **alimony** to their ex-spouses. Alimony, today more commonly referred to as **spousal support**, is a monetary payment, typically paid monthly, that one spouse pays to the other spouse during and after the divorce proceedings. A great misconception is that spousal support payments are mandatory by law. Not so! Family court judges determine whether or not alimony is to be paid, and their decisions are legally binding.

Spousal support payments are predicated on the assumption that most men and women can provide for themselves following divorce; thus today's support payments are considered to be *rehabilitative* alimony payments, which are short term in nature, rather than *permanent* alimony payments. Rehabilitative payments are based on such things as the length of the marriage, the number of children, and the needs of each ex-spouse (Ventura & Reed, 1998).

Divorce attorneys, family court judges, and divorce mediators help negotiate spousal support settlements. It is sometimes possible for a spouse to opt for a lump-sum alimony payment rather than monthly payments. Spousal support can also be modified if spouses' circumstances change.

Child Support

Whether the parents are married or divorced, spouses have an obligation to provide for their children under 18 years old. Just as with spousal support payments following divorce, **child support** payments are typically paid out as fixed, monthly payments. They may be paid by one or the other spouse, or ex-spouses may split the costs associated with raising children, typically until the children reach their early 20s. The amount assigned to one or both spouses is determined largely by the custody arrangements, and although the child support guidelines (mathematical formulas) vary from state to state, these guidelines are typically percentages of the parents' income. Because of state-to-state variances in the mathematical formula, it is difficult to determine what an "average" monthly child support payment might be. For example, in Texas, child support awards are based on the parent's *gross income,* or the income before federal, state, and local income taxes are deducted. The court will generally follow these guidelines unless the parents agree to a different payment amount (Office of Child Support Enforcement, 2008):

- 20 percent, one child
- 25 percent, two children
- 30 percent, three children
- 35 percent, four children
- 40 percent, five children
- Not less than 40 percent, six children

Special rules apply in cases of split or joint custody, or multiple children in different households. In addition, if the family court believes that the paying parent is not earning as much money as he or she could (given their past employment history or education level), the payment can be based on *earning potential,* the income the parent could potentially earn. This monthly payment is just for the "basics." If children require special education, have medical costs that exceed health insurance benefits, or are involved in extracurricular activities, parents are expected to share these costs equally.

HOW MUCH CHILD SUPPORT IS PAID ANNUALLY?
According to the Office of Child Support Enforcement (OCSE; 2008), a division of the federal government that tracks child support payments, there were 15.8 million child support cases in 2007, in which over $25 billion in child support payments were collected and distributed (OCSE, 2008).

Child support payments are collected in a variety of ways, including withholding wages, intercepting unemployment compensation, and intercepting federal income tax returns. Figure 7.2 shows the methods of child support collection in 2007; 70 percent of all payments collected are through wage withholding. About one-third of custodial fathers are owed child support by their ex-wives (U.S. Census Bureau, 2008b).

DOES EVERYONE PAY? Just because a family court issues a judgment does not mean that spouses pay the court-mandated amount. Some spouses may view child support payments as

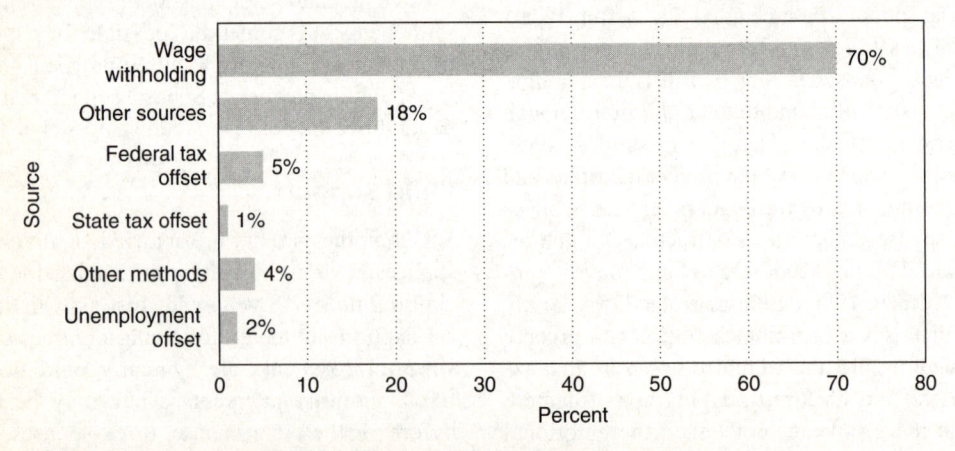

FIGURE 7.2 Total collections received by method of collection, 2007.
The majority of child support payments are collected through withholding wages.
Source: Based on data from Office of Child Support Enforcement (2008).

nothing more than spousal support in disguise. The spouses believe the money will go to support the ex-spouse's lifestyle, and not toward raising the children. Some ex-spouses feel that the amount designated for child support is too great and they subsequently pay an amount they feel is "fair." Conversely, custodial parents often feel that amount awarded is too low, and may go back to family court, sometimes repeatedly, to request modification of the initial decision. Sometimes this is done out of anger or revenge; other times, the request is made out of genuine need.

No matter the reason why people do not pay child support, as of 2007, noncustodial parents owed a staggering $30 billion in late child support payments (OCSE, 2008). Since the turn of this century, about 60 percent of those who owe back (late) child support continue to pay on the debt they owe (OCSE, 2008). The economic hardship of the noncustodial parent forces many divorced parents onto public assistance from the federal government.

Child Custody

Perhaps one of the most grueling aspects associated with divorce is determining child custody arrangements. **Custody** refers to who is responsible for the children's financial, physical, and emotional well-being (Ahrons, 1994). **Legal custody** refers to which parent has the right to make decisions about how the child is reared, such as decisions concerning education or religion. It is common today for parents to be awarded **shared legal custody**, which means that both parents have an equal say in the child's upbringing. Family laws provide several custody options for divorced coparents.

JOINT CUSTODY Parents who have **joint custody** of their children share in the decision making on behalf of their children. They may also share the physical custody of their children. This type of arrangement helps ensure that children receive the benefits of having both parents actively involved in their lives. Three types of joint custody are:

- *Joint legal custody*—both parents share equally in decisions in childrearing, but the child resides primarily with one parent.
- *Joint physical custody*—children spend close to equal time with each parent but one parent has primary legal custody.
- *Joint legal and physical custody*—both parents share equally in decisions and physical custody.

PHYSICAL CUSTODY When a parent is granted **physical custody**, he or she is granted the legal right to have the child live primarily with him or her, making this parent the *custodial parent*. The *noncustodial parent* is granted the right to have child visitations on a schedule determined by the parents, or by the courts if the coparents cannot agree. Today, three out of every four mothers have physical custody (about 74 percent) of the children following divorce (U.S. Census Bureau, 2008b).

SOLE CUSTODY Just as the term implies, **sole custody** means that one parent is the primary parent—legally, physically, or both legally and physically. While this type of custody arrangement was historically awarded to mothers because courts assumed they were the more nurturing parent, today, more states have moved away from this arrangement because it tends to significantly minimize and limit the role of one parent. Even in the event that sole legal and physical custody is awarded to one parent, the other parent is often awarded visitation rights; however, if one parent is deemed unfit for reasons such as substance or alcohol abuse or physical, sexual, or emotional abuse or neglect, he or she may only be awarded *supervised visitation*. In that event, the court requires supervision of the noncustodial parent's visitation by a third party, such as the custodial parent or a representative of a public or private supervisory agency. In extreme cases when a parent is determined by the court to pose a threat to the children, the parent may be denied all parental rights.

BIRD'S NEST This is an alternative to some of the more common custody arrangements just discussed. The bird's nest custody arrangement is joint legal and physical custody with a bit of a twist: rather than have the children move between two different homes, the parents take turns going back and forth to their separate homes. This way, the children are able to remain in the family home. This is the type of custody the reality TV show Kate Plus 8 utilizes. The core distinction of this arrangement is that each parent maintains a separate residence where they reside when it's not their turn to live in the "bird's nest." Sometimes one parent leaves right away when the other parent arrives, or sometimes the family shares a family dinner together or another activity. This is typically the most expensive type of child custody arrangement because parents need to maintain three different residences—the bird's nest and each parent's separate residence.

Living, Loving, and Parenting in Post-Divorce Families

Decades of research indicate that, by and large, the picture of divorce for children isn't usually bright or optimistic. Emerging findings, however, show that Americans are finding newer and better ways to live, love, and parent in a divorce-saturated society. Hetherington and Kelly (2002) found, after studying 1,400 families, that the multiple processes of divorce can result in healing and ultimate fulfillment. Their research addresses six past research findings:

- *Divorce only has two outcomes: Win or lose.* Hetherington and Kelly (2002) maintain that there are a number of different ways that people adjust to divorce, not that the process produces only winners or losers. Each of these patterns of adjusting are not permanent, and will change over time.
- *Children always lose out after a divorce.* Divorce is not a rosy experience for children, but *over time* children demonstrate their resiliency to their parents' divorce.
- *The pathways following divorce are fixed and unchanging: Not so!* According to the researchers, the effects of divorce are not irrevocable. A negative experience can be offset by later positive experiences.
- *Men are the big winners in divorce.* While women experience greater economic losses following divorce, overall they do better emotionally following divorce than do men. Even though women frequently fall into poverty following divorce, this trend is changing as women become better educated, and as federal and state agencies become stricter about enforcing child support payments.
- *The absence of a father is the greatest risk to children.* Indeed, fathers matter. But it's not the mere *presence* of a father that makes a difference. The researchers discovered that involved, supportive mothers can counter the adverse effects of a father's absence.

Divorce presents many disruptions in children's and adolescents' lives. Some of these changes require coping and adaptation beyond their years, and clearly put the child at risk for short- and long-term developmental, academic, and interpersonal problems. The interconnected family and environmental variables influencing youth's adjustment and adaptation to divorce point to the need for effective parenting and coparenting when establishing a binuclear family.

Reorganizing and redefining a family from one nuclear family into a binuclear family is a multifaceted transition that requires tremendous efforts of both parents to ensure the best interests of the children are met. Former spouse relationships that promote collaborative, cooperative shared parenting foster positive parent–child relationships that benefit both the parents and the children.

The divorce transition still involves many challenges, particularly for single mothers. In the next section we explore the difficulties faced by single mothers.

CHALLENGES FOR SINGLE PARENTS

There are significant challenges that face single-parent mothers following divorce, including changes in financial status, changes in residence, changes in boundaries for children, changes in the emotional environment, and post-divorce dating (Anderson & Sabatelli, 2007).

Changes in Household Finances

An interrelated family factor that affects children's and adolescent's long-term adjustment to divorce is the state of family economics before and after divorce. Economic hardship is a post-divorce reality for many families, particularly for women. Part of the legal terms of a divorce is determining child support due the custodial parent (discussed later). Even if the noncustodial parent (usually the father) faithfully pays child support, however, the amount is rarely sufficient to meet the living expenses of the mother and children.

The economic toll of divorce often translates into still more adjustments for children (Amato, 2000). These adjustments may require enduring potentially poorer quality of parenting as the custodial parent must take on more work, and coping with the effects of financial pressures and strains on the family. While some children are more fortunate and are able to remain living in the family home, the financial pressures may mean that they need to make other sacrifices such as forgoing music lessons and/or sports lessons in order to make ends meet.

When economic hardship afflicts single-parent households, other challenges arise for families already struggling to reorganize and redefine themselves following divorce. Because of the interrelated nature of family living, economic hardship then affects every other aspect of family life, including the challenges newly divorced families face.

Changes in Residence

A common expression is that divorce brings with it "new everythings"—a new family structure, a new way of interacting with parents, and perhaps at some point, a new family if one or both parents remarry. In many cases, these transitions include relocating to a new home. Unless the move is within the same neighborhood, a move to a new home introduces other "new everythings," for it also brings new neighborhoods, new peers, new schools, and new teachers.

Recently divorced single parents often find that because of the radical changes in their finances they are no longer able to live in their pre-divorce home (Kelly & Emery, 2003). Quite frequently, in an effort to lessen the strain on the family budget that comes with transitioning to single-parent living, divorced women find that they are forced to sell their homes. Additionally, this transition involves not just an economic rebalancing, but an emotional rebalancing as well (Anderson & Sabatelli, 2007). When recently divorced single parents then move to a different neighborhood and into a less expensive home, they and their children are faced with the harsh reality of a new beginning that redefines the family system (Kelly & Emery, 2003).

Changes in Boundaries

Central to the challenges of post-divorce parenting is the issue of reworking parenting roles. And as Anderson and Sabatelli (2007) note, even for those parents who are willing, strongly desiring of, and firmly committed to parenting cooperatively, divorce is always accompanied by greater separateness and autonomy, along with a decline in interdependence—and this change in the relationship between parents and children adds to the other everyday, ordinary stresses associated with parenting.

In essence, the reestablishment of parenting roles ensures that what was once shared by both parents is now covered independently by each parent. Some tasks associated with establishing new parental roles following divorce include (Graham, 2005):

- Forming new relationships with children that do not include ongoing input, support, and the collaboration from the other parent. Even in the best of circumstances where both parents are actively involved in the children's lives, one parent is still absent from the home.
- Creating a working business relationship with the former spouse that ensures successful completion of childrearing tasks, such as helping children with homework, taking them to after-school activities, or taking them to doctor or dentist appointments.
- Establishing methods of discipline that do not rely on the other parent's input or aid.
- Developing a parenting plan. The parenting plan outlines the rights and responsibilities of each parent and establishes an appropriate working relationship between the parents (for issues regarding the children's health, education, and well-being).
- Communicating clearly and accurately to the other parent those things that are taking place in the child's life. At the forefront of such communication are the child's emotional stability and the protection of the child's best interests. Making these the priority of communication minimizes the children's exposure to ongoing parental conflict and minimizes the temptation to drag the child into the parents' battles.

It is beyond question that the exit of one member from the family system disrupts the balance of the entire system. However, if proper care and attention are given to the re-establishment of parental roles following divorce, over time the family will re-establish itself and find a new reorganized balance.

Changes in the Emotional Environment

There is no other way to state it: Divorce hurts! Managing the emotional climate of the binuclear family is just as important as managing finances and new parenting roles.

A single mother's ability to become sole administrator of the home hinges upon her ability to manage the emotional climate of the newly defined single-parent home. In other words, the mother must assume all authority and responsibility, as well as provide love, understanding, and support. While many single mothers rely on their former spouses, daycare providers, or the children's grandparents to assist them, many mothers decide that if they are the custodial parent, they should have complete authority in whatever decisions are made (Anderson & Sabatelli, 2007; Graham, 2005). This shift in authority allows single mothers to separate from former spouses and gain autonomy. Without this authority, boundaries may not be clear and, all too often children, former spouses and/or grandparents may undermine the mother's efforts and render her ineffective—thus ensuring that inconsistent, dysfunctional parenting roles are established.

According to Anderson and Sabatelli (2007), fathers also have difficulties in managing the emotional tasks of the post-divorce family. Divorced fathers tend to struggle with managing the emotional climate of the home because of a frequent inability to maintain a sense of home and family, even if the father is the noncustodial parent. Typically, when the father is the nonresident parent, he experiences these feelings of loss and he may feel that he has lost control and influence over his children (Kruk, 1991). Fathers will often experience an even greater sense of loss and powerlessness if there remain high levels of conflict between the father and his former wife, if his ex-spouse limits his visitations to his children (in order to exert control over him or punish him), or if the custodial and visitation agreements are not strictly adhered to (Wallerstein, 1998).

About 75 percent of those who divorce will eventually remarry, and today, an estimated one-third of all children in the United States will live in a stepparent home before they reach the age of 18 (Parke, 2007; U.S. Census Bureau, 2006). There are a number of transitions associated with repartnering following divorce.

TRANSITIONS TO REPARTNERING

Stepfamilies are rapidly becoming the most common family structure in the United States (Grall, 2007). Though remarriages are common today, there remains a stereotypical view that these marriages are not as functional as "traditional" marriages (Ganong & Coleman, 2004). To better understand the transitions associated with forming a new family system following divorce, in the following section we examine the stages of the remarriage experience, remarriage stability, and the many characteristics of stepfamilies today.

Stepfamilies Today

As you know, with the dissolution of the nuclear family system because of divorce, two separate family forms emerge, creating a binuclear family. When either one or both of the former spouses choose to remarry, a stepfamily is formed. When one or both of the married partners bring children from a previous relationship into the new marital relationship, the newly merged family is referred to as a **stepfamily**.

While stepfamilies are very common in today's world, there used to be negative undertones associated with the term *stepfamily*, such as the "evil" stepmother who is cruel to her stepchildren, so often portrayed in children's storybooks. Due to the increasing incidence of stepfamilies, there have been attempts over the years to soften the terminology and to use other terms that do not carry the negative connotation, such as "integrated family," "complicated family form," "merged family," or "reconstituted" or "combined family." The alternate term with which most of us are familiar is the term *blended families*. The Stepfamily Association of America (SAA; 2009), however, disagrees with the use of this term, pointing out that when two family systems join together, they do not "blend." Notes the SAA, "A stepfamily does not *recreate* a first family (or, blend into something entirely new with all prior connections severed and the former existence obliterated)." Thus, according to the SAA, to "blend" a family would mean that children and spouses in stepfamilies must lose their identities, their individualities, and their active attachments to the absent parent, to the former first family. All other family forms are defined by the relationship that exists between the parent and child, such as foster, adoptive, single parent, or biological. The SAA holds, then, that it is more accurate and preferred to use the term *stepfamily*. They also assert that implying that two distinct family systems can fold into one sets the new family structure up for unrealistic expectations and "doom" (SAA, 2009).

STEPFAMILY TYPES While the presence of children from a previous marriage defines a stepfamily, the composition of stepfamilies differs. In some instances, members of a stepfamily may or may not live full time within the stepfamily household; in many cases, children are members of *two* stepfamily households. Table 7.2 summarizes the different types of stepfamilies, which are defined by the parent–child relationship. Also, in stepfamilies, children are described in different ways. For example, *siblings* share the same two biological parents, while *stepsiblings* are not biologically related, but have parents who are married to one another. A *mutual child* is the child (or children) who is born to the remarried couple. Some researchers refer to this as the "cement" child, as they are thought to cement the relationship.

STEPFAMILY CHARACTERISTICS Many students often mistakenly assume that stepfamilies are no different than first families since there are two parents in the home who share in the every day tasks of rearing the children. While on the surface

TABLE 7.2 Types of stepfamilies.

Biological mother/stepfather	In this family structure, the household comprises the mother's biological children and her stepchildren (the children of the stepfather).
Biological father/stepmother	In this family form, the household comprises the father's biological children and his stepchildren (the children of the stepmother).
Complex stepfamily	In this type of stepfamily, both partners have children from previous relationships or marriage, although the children may reside in different households.
Joint biological-stepfamily	Within this household, the couple has at least one biological child that is the product of both married parents, and at least one biological child of either parent (meaning the other parent would be the stepparent).

Source: Welch, *Family Life Now,* 2e. (2010). Boston: Allyn & Bacon. p. 475. Based on Stepfamily Association of America (2009).

it may appear that there are not significant differences, the complex combination of roles and relationships makes stepfamily living very different from a nuclear family's, as Table 7.3 shows us.

Certain characteristics distinguish stepfamilies from first families (Parziale & Parziale, 2002).

- ***The stepfamily is born of loss.*** Every stepfamily has one thing in common: they have all faced loss (Wallerstein & Kelly, 1980). Unlike first marriages, a stepfamily is typically born of loss—of a parent or family through death, through divorce, or through desertion.

TABLE 7.3 The ways that stepfamilies and nuclear families differ.

Structural Factor	Typical Stepfamily	Typical Nuclear Family
Number of co-parenting homes	Usually homes linked by legal documents, emotions, finances, genes and ancestry, shared history, responsibilities, and memories	Usually one home
Grandparents (living *and* dead)	Usually six or eight or more	Usually four
Physical and legal child custody	Sole, joint, or split; usually subject to legal decree(s) and often legally contested	Shared; no legal suits or decrees
Spouses' parenting values and styles (e.g., child discipline)	Performed before remarrying and cohabiting; often needs compromising	Evolved together over years; differences are usually less stressful
Caregivers' legal parenting rights and responsibilities regarding minor kids' school/health/custody/etc. (varies by state)	Fewer and less clear rights (stepparents and stepgrandparents); responsibilities more confusing; a legal parenting agreement may exist, which excludes any stepparents	More and clearer rights (bio-parents and bio-grandparents); responsibilities far clearer; no legal documents to enforce or litigate
Last names	Re-wedded bio-mom's names may differ from their kids' names; without adoption, stepsibs have different last names	Adults and kids usually all have the same last name, so less chance of identity and loyalty (priority) confusions
Family-member loyalty, bonding, and cohesion	Initially, pseudo or little among merging families; may or may not improve with time; much more fragile	Generally much stronger throughout the family life cycle; they usually transcend traumas

Source: Welch, *Family Life Now,* 2e. (2010). Boston: Allyn & Bacon. p. 475. Adapted from Geriach (2005).

- ***The family boundaries and roles are ambiguous.*** The frequent entrances and exits of family members from the various stepfamily households, such as stepchildren/stepsiblings coming for or leaving for visitations, may lead to indistinct or blurred boundaries. This ambiguity creates confusion and uncertainty as to who is "in" the family and who is not, and causes doubt about family affiliations. Furthermore, the roles in stepfamilies have no clear, traditionally understood labels, no clear definitions, and no clear expectations (Parziale & Parziale, 2002).
- ***There is a disparity of individual, marital, and family life cycles.*** When two family systems form a stepfamily, an obstacle that all family members face is the fact that they do not share a common history, common traditions, or common life experiences. Compounding these differences is the fact that there will be children with varying developmental needs.
- ***There are several loyalty conflicts.*** Because children have strong emotional ties to their biological parents, their loyalty to the biological parents remains strong. The most common loyalty conflict involves the stepparent whenever children feel that their relationship with their biological parent(s) is threatened as a result of the stepparent joining the family system (Parziale & Parziale, 2002).

All of these changes and expectations are sources of great stress for all involved. Is it any wonder that stepfamily formation and stepfamily life is so challenging?

Common Challenges for Children

Children enter into a stepfamily with a history of loss that is beyond their control. Children tend to respond to this transition with feelings of helplessness and anger. Too often parents mistakenly assume that because children are young they are oblivious to the changes that surround them, or they believe that they will quickly "bounce back." As we have seen throughout this chapter, a child's ability to bounce back is largely dependent upon how they are parented during the turbulent processes of transition—by not only their biological parents, but their stepparents as well. To help children thrive as they transition to stepfamily living, adults must understand the common challenges children face as they enter into this new family system:

- *Loss of Power and Control:* Children lose more than a parent when their nuclear family dissolves; because they have no choice in how the events unfold, they frequently feel a loss of power and control. This sense of powerlessness can be overwhelming for a child. To help children heal, it is imperative that they be given control over some aspect of their new lives. For example, when children are allowed to make small decisions such as how to spend their allowance or about devising new stepfamily rules, this contributes to their feelings of control and minimizes their feelings of helplessness (Kalter, Alpern, Spence, & Plunkett, 1984; Robson, Cook, & Gilliland, 1995).
- *Guilt:* Children often blame themselves for their parents' divorce. They may believe that they were "bad" or "naughty" and that their behavior drove the other parent away; they may believe that they are too "unlovable" or that they are too "expensive" for the parent to care for them; in the case of a deceased parent, they may have "wished" their parent was dead at some point in time. It is crucial that parents engage in honest communication with their children throughout the many processes of divorce and convey to the children that divorce or death is *never* the fault of the child. It is also of the utmost importance that parents assure their children that their parents love them under any circumstances (Warshak, 2000).
- *Loyalty Conflicts:* When a parent remarries, children often feel that if they become close to the new stepparent or if they "love" the

stepparent, they are unfaithful and disloyal to their biological parent—they feel they have betrayed that parent. If divorced parents continue arguing in front of their children or use the children as pawns in the divorce process, this heightens these loyalty struggles. Thus, the rejection of a new stepparent or a new home may be more a reflection of their fear of abandoning their biological parent rather than dislike for the stepparent. It is vital that both parents and stepparents assure (again and again!) the children that it is possible to love many people at the same time and that having a relationship with a stepparent in no way means that they love their biological parent any less (Kheshgi-Genovese & Genovese, 1997).

- *Anger:* It is normal for children to feel angry toward their parents following divorce and during the formation of a stepfamily. The anger may be due to the sense of powerlessness and lack of control they have in the situation, and it may be directed toward a parent who visits infrequently or fails to follow through on promises. The anger may also be a response to a move from the family home, neighborhood, or school. However the child's anger is expressed, it is essential that parents and stepparents reassure the children that it is normal to feel angry, and to feel whatever they have been feeling (Kelly & Emery, 2003; Strohschein, 2005).

Because stepfamilies are structurally and emotionally different than first families, both adults and children have difficulty adjusting and adapting to the changes swept in by divorce (Seymour, Francis, & Steffens, 1995). For adults, adjustment centers on their ability to maintain a close relationship with their new spouse. Children's ability to adapt is largely dependent on how sensitive parents and stepparents are to children's feelings and behaviors. "A little understanding [is] the right foundation for the beginning of a strong stepfamily relationship" (Seymour et al., 1995).

Those who are successful in transitioning their multiple family systems into a cohesive stepfamily system know that, just as with divorce, remarriage involves multiple, simultaneous processes and is accompanied by common struggles faced by both children and adults.

Summary

Divorce hurts. The transitions that take place in life after divorce are no less emotionally confusing or painful than is the process of divorce—it is a broken experience that requires time for family members to pick up all of the pieces, to reassemble, and reorganize their lives. Feelings of despair, disappointment, and helplessness are not uncommon, as it takes years for family members to develop a new orientation to post-divorce life.

The transition to life following divorce involves many processes, which involve emotional, economic, parental, and legal ramifications. For children and adolescents whose parents divorce, there are many negative outcomes. There are also many variables associated with post-divorce outcomes, such as being separated from an important attachment figure, the relationship between the parents and their children, the family's economics, and whether one or both parents remarry. The most critical factor in determining outcomes, however, is the parents' ability to effectively coparent or share parenting.

Although adapting to single-parent life is difficult for mothers, fathers, and children, the most dramatic changes in family life and family structure come about when parents remarry and form stepfamilies. Becoming a stepfamily requires unique tasks for both adults and children—accepting these changes does not happen overnight, but requires years to fully integrate as a family system.

References

Ahrons, C. R. (1994). *The good divorce: Keeping your family together when your marriage comes apart.* New York: HarperCollins.

Ahrons, C. R. (2007). Family ties after divorce: Long-term implications for children. *Family Process, 46*(1), 53–65.

Ahrons, C., & Rodgers, R. H. (1987). *Divorced families: Meeting the challenge of divorce and remarriage.* New York: Norton.

Ahrons, C., & Tanner, J. L. (2003). Adult children and their fathers: Relationship changes 20 years after parental divorce. *Family Relations, 52,* 340–351.

Amato, P. (2000). The consequences of divorce for adults and children. *Journal of Marriage and the Family, 62*(4), 1269–1287.

Amato, P., & Booth, A. (1996). A prospective study of divorce and parent–child relationships. *Journal of Marriage and the Family, 58,* 356–365.

Amato, P. R., & Rezac, S. (1994). Contact with nonresident parents, interparental conflict, and children's behavior. *Journal of Family Issues, 15,* 191–207.

Anderson, S. A., & Sabatelli, R. M. (2007). *Family interactions: A multigenerational developmental perspective* (4th ed.). Boston: Allyn & Bacon.

Aquilino, W. (1996). The life course of children born to unmarried mothers: Childhood living arrangements and young adult outcomes. *Journal of Marriage and the Family, 58,* 293–310.

Arditti, J. (1999). Rethinking relationships between divorced mothers and their children: Capitalizing on family strengths. *Family Relations, 48*(2), 109–119.

Arditti, J., & Bickley, P. (1996). Fathers' involvement and mothers' parenting stress postdivorce. *Journal of Divorce and Remarriage, 26*(1–2), 1–23.

Bailey, S., & Zvonkovic, A. (2003). Parenting after divorce. *Journal of Divorce and Remarriage, 39*(3/4), 59–80.

Bank, L., Forgatch, M., Patterson, G., & Fetrow, R. (1993). Parenting practices of single mothers: Mediators of negative contextual factors. *Journal of Marriage and the Family, 55*(2), 317–384.

Barratt, M., Roach, M., & Colbert, K. (1991). Single mothers and their infants: Factors associated with optimal parenting. *Family Relations, 40*(4), 448–454.

Baum, N. (2006). Post divorce paternal disengagement. *Journal of Marriage and Family Therapy, 32,* 245–254.

Bloir, K. (2005). Single, custodial fathers. *OSU Extension Factsheet, Family and Consumer Sciences.* Columbus: Ohio State University.

Bohannan, P. (1971). *Divorce and after.* New York: Doubleday.

Bokker, P., Farley, R., & Denny, G. (2005). Emotional well-being among recently divorced fathers. *Journal of Divorce and Remarriage, 41,* 157–172.

Bonach, K., Sales, E., & Koeske, G. (2005). Gender differences in co-parenting quality. *Journal of Divorce and Remarriage, 42,* 1–28.

Braver, S., Shapiro, J. R., & Goodman, M. R. (2006). Consequences of divorce for parents. In M. A. Fine & J. H. Harvey (Eds.), *Handbook of divorce and relationship dissolution* (pp. 313–337). Mahwah, NJ: Erlbaum.

Buehler, C. (1988). The social and emotional well-being of divorced residential parents. *Sex Roles, 18*(5–6), 247–257.

Carlson, C. (1995). Working with single-parent and stepfamily systems. In A. Thomas & J. Grimes (Eds.), *Best practices in school psychology* (3rd ed., pp. 1097–1110). Washington, DC: National Association of School Psychologists.

Cartwright, C. (2006). You want to know how it affected me?: Young adults' perceptions of the impact of parental divorce. *Journal of Divorce and Remarriage, 44*(3/4), 125–143.

Congressional Caucus on Women's Issues. (2005). *Chutes & ladders: The search for solid ground for women in the workforce.* Retrieved August 11, 2009, from http://www.womenwork.org/policy/chutes.htm.

Cooksey, E., & Craig. P. (1998). Parenting from a distance: The effects of parental characteristics on contact between non-residential fathers and their children. *Demography, 35*(2), 187–200.

Cookston, J. T., Braver, S. L., Griffin, W., DeLusé, S. R., & Miles, J. C. (2007). Effects of the Dads for Life intervention on interparental conflict and co-parenting in the two years after divorce. *Family Processes, 46*(1), 123–137.

Corbett, M. (2005). U.S. households led by single mothers and displaced homemakers on the rise. *Women's Work.* Retrieved April 7, 2009, from www.womenwork.org.

Criddle, M., & Scott, M. (2005). Mandatory divorce education and post divorce parental conflict. *Journal of Divorce and Remarriage, 62,* 99–111.

Dacey, J., & Travers, J. (2002). *Human development across the lifespan* (5th ed.). Boston: McGraw-Hill.

Davies, L., Avison, W., & McAlpine, D. (1997). Significant life experiences and depression among single and married mothers. *Journal of Marriage and the Family, 59,* 294–308.

Davis, E. C., & Friel, L.V. (2001). Adolescent sexuality: Disentangling the effects of family structure and family contexts. *Journal of Marriage and Family, 63*(3), 669–681.

Donahoo, S. (2004). *Single parenting and children's academic achievement.* Retrieved August 14, 2006, from http://library.adoption.com/pring.php?articleid=3341.

Driscoll, A., Hearn, G., Evans, J., Moore, K., Sugland, B., & Call, V. (1999). Nonmarital childbearing among adult women. *Journal of Marriage and the Family, 61,* 178–187.

Duran-Aydingtug, C. (1995). Former spouse interaction: Normative guidelines and actual behavior. *Journal of divorce and Remarriage, 22,* 147–161.

Edin, K., & Lein, L. (1996). Work, welfare, and single mothers' economic survival strategies. *American Sociological Review, 61,* 253–266.

Emery, R. E. (1994). *Renegotiating family relationships: Divorce, child custody and mediation.* New York: Guilford Press.

Fincham, F. D. (2003). Divorce. In N. J. Salkind (Ed.), *Child development: Macmillan psychology reference series.* Farmington Hills, MI: Macmillan.

Folk, K. (1996). Single mothers in various living arrangements: Differences in economic and time resources. *American Journal of Economics and Sociology, 55*(3), 277–292.

Forum on Child and Family Statistics. (2010). *America's children in brief: Key national indicators of well-being, 2010.* Retrieved September 11, 2010, from www.childstats.gov/americaschildren/tables.asp.

Furstenberg, F. F., & Allison, P. D. (1989). How marital dissolution affects children: Variations by age and sex. *Developmental Psychology, 25,* 540–549.

Furstenberg, F. F., & Cherlin, A. J. (1991). *Divided families: What happens to children when parents part.* Cambridge, MA: Harvard University Press.

Ganong, L. H., & Coleman, M. (2004). *Stepfamily relationships: Development, dynamics, and interventions.* New York: Kluwar Academic/Plenum Press.

Gohm, C. L., Oishi, S., Darlington, J., & Diener, E. (1998). Culture, parental conflict, parental marital status, and the subjective well-being of young adults. *Journal of Marriage and the Family, 60,* 314–319.

Goldberg, W., Greenberger, E., Hamill, S., & O'Neil, R. (1992). Role demands in the lives of single mothers with preschoolers. *Journal of Family Issues, 13*(3), 312–333.

Gottfried, A. E., & Gottfried, A. (1994). *Redefining families: Implications for children's development.* New York: Plenum Press.

Graham, L. (2005). *Resource guide for parenting after divorce.* Manhattan: Riley County District Court, State of Kansas.

Grall, T. S. (2007). Custodial mothers and fathers and their child support: 2005. *Current Population Reports* (P60-234). Washington, DC: U.S. Government Printing Office.

Grief, G. (1995). Single fathers with custody following separation and divorce. Marriage and Family Review, 20(1–2), 213–231.

Hallman, M., & Deinhart, R. (2007). Father's experiences after separation and divorce. *Fathering, 5,* 4–24.

Hannum, J. W., & Dvorak, D. M. (2004). Effects of family conflict, divorce, and attachment patterns on the psychological distress and social adjustment of college freshmen. *Journal of College Student Development, 45*(1), 27–42.

Hao, L., & Brinton, M. (1997). Productive activities and support systems of single mothers. *American Journal of Sociology, 102*(5), 1305–1344.

Henley, K., & Pasley, K. (2006). Coparenting following divorce. In M. Fine & J. Harvey (Eds.), *Handbook of divorce* (pp. 241–262). Mahwah, NJ: Erlbaum.

Hetherington, E. M. (1991). The role of individual differences and family relationships in children's coping with divorce and remarriage. In P. A. Cowan & E. M. Hetherington (Eds.), *Family transitions* (pp. 165–194). Hillsdale, NJ: Erlbaum.

Hetherington, E. M. (2003). Intimate pathways: Change patterns in close personal relationships across time. *Family Relations, 52,* 318–333.

Hetherington, E. M., & Kelly, J. (2002). *For better or worse: Divorce reconsidered.* New York: Norton.

Hinderlie, H. H., & Kenny, M. (2002). Attachment, social support, and college adjustment among Black students at predominantly White universities. *Journal of College Student Development, 43,* 327–340.

Jayakody, R., Chatters, L., & Taylor, R. (1993). Family support to single and married African American mothers: The provision of financial, emotional, and child care assistance. *Journal of Marriage and the Family, 55*(2), 261–276.

Kalter, N., Alpern, D., Spence, R., & Plunkett, J. W. (1984). Locus of control in children of divorce. *Journal of Personality Assessment, 48*(4), 410–414.

Kelly, J. B. (2007). Children's living arrangements following divorce. *Family Process, 46,* 35–52.

Kelly, J. B., & Emery, R. E. (2003). Children's adjustment following divorce: Risk and resiliency perspectives. *Family Relations, 53,* 352–362.

Kheshgi-Genovese, Z., & Genovese, T. A. (1997). Developing the spousal relationship within stepfamilies. *Families in Society, 78*(3), 255–264.

King, V. (2002). Parental divorce and interpersonal trust in adult offspring. *Journal of Marriage and Family, 64*(3), 643–656.

Kreider, R. M., & Fields, J. M. (2005, July). Living arrangements of children: 2001. *United States Census Bureau Current Population Reports* (P70-104). Retrieved January 6, 2006, from www.census.gov/prod/2005pubs/p70-104.pdf.

Kruk, E. (1991). Discontinuity between pre- and post-divorce father–child relationships: New evidence regarding paternal disengagement. *Journal of Divorce and Remarriage, 16*(3/4), 195–227.

Lehr, R., & MacMillan, P. (2001). The psychological and emotional impact of divorce: The noncustodial fathers' perspective. *Families in Society, 82*(4), 373–382.

Leite, R. W., & McKendry, P. C. (2002). Aspects of father status and post-divorce father involvement with children. *Journal of Family Issues, 23,* 601–623.

Lynch, J., & Kaplan, G. (2000). Socioeconomic position. In L. F. Berkman & I. Kawachi (Eds.), *Social epidemiology* (pp. 13–35). New York: Oxford University Press.

Madden-Derdich, D., & Arditti, J. (1999). The ties that bind: Attachment between former spouses. *Family Relations, 48*(3), 243–249.

Markham, M., Ganong, L., & Coleman, M. (2007). Mothers' cooperation in coparental relationships. *Family Relations, 56,* 369–377.

Marsh, H. W. (1990). Two-parent, stepparent, and single-parent families: Changes in achievement, attitudes, and behaviors during the last two years of high school. *Journal of Educational Psychology, 82*(2), 327–340.

McIntyre, A., Heron, R. L., McIntyre, M. D., Burton, S. J., & Engler, J. N. (2003). College students from families of divorce: Keys to their resilience. *Journal of Applied Developmental Psychology, 24,* 17–31.

McLanahan, S., & Booth, K. (1991). Mother-only families: Problems, prospects, and politics. In A. Booth (Ed.), *Contemporary families: Looking forward, looking back* (pp. 405–428). Minneapolis, MN: National Council on Family Relations.

McLanahan, S., & Sandefur, G. (1994). *Growing up with a single parent: What hurts, what helps.* Cambridge, MA: Harvard University Press.

Office of Child Support Enforcement. (2008). *Child support enforcement: FY 2007.* Retrieved February 14, 2009, from www.acf.hhs.gov/programs/cse/pubs/2008/preliminary_report_fy2007/Prelim2007.pdf.

Olson, S., & Banyard, V. (1993). Stop the world so I can get off for a while: Sources of daily stress in the lives of low-income single mothers of young children. *Family Relations, 42*(1), 50–56.

Parish, T. S., & Wigle, S. E. (1985). A longitudinal study of the impact of parental divorce on adolescents' evaluations of self and parents. *Adolescence, 20,* 239–244.

Parke, R. D., & Brott, A. A. (2003). Throwaway dads. In M. Coleman & L. Ganong (Eds.), *Points and counterpoints: Controversial relationship and family issues in the twenty-first century* (pp. 3–13). Boston: Houghton Mifflin.

Parke, M. (2007, May). *Are married parents really better for children?: What research says about the effects of family structure on child well-being.* Couples and married research and policy brief: Center for Law and Social Policy.

Parziale, J., & Parziale, J. B. (2002). *The journey: A traveling guide to Christian stepfamilies.* Tucson, AZ: InStep Ministries.

Pirog, M., Klotz, M., & Beyers, K. (1998). Interstate comparisons of child support orders using state guidelines. *Family Relations, 47,* 289–295.

Pleck, J. H. (1997). Paternal involvement: Levels, sources, and consequences. In M. E. Lamb (Ed.), *The role of the father in child development* (pp. 66–103). New York: Wiley.

Robson, M., Cook, P., & Gilliland, J. (1995). Helping children manage stress. *British Education Research Journal, 21*(2), 165–174.

Schaffer, D., & Wagner, R. (1996). Mexican American and Anglo single mothers: The influence of ethnicity, generation, and socioeconomic status on social support networks. *Hispanic Journal of Behavioral Sciences, 18*(1), 74–86.

Seifer, R., Sameroff, A. J., Baldwin, C. P., & Baldwin, A. (1992). Child and family factors that ameliorate risk between 4 and 13 years of age. *Journal of American Academy of Child and Adolescent Psychiatry, 31*(4), 893–903.

Seymour, T., Francis., C, & Steffens, P. (1995). *Supporting stepfamilies: What do the children feel?* (NF 95-223). Lincoln: University of Nebraska Cooperative Extension.

Shaw, D. S. (1993). Parental functioning and children's adjustment in families of divorce: A prospective study. *Journal of Abnormal Child Psychology, 21*(1), 119–143.

Shaw, D. S., & Ingoldsby, E. M. (1999). Children of divorce. In R. R. Ammerman, C. G. Last, & M. Hersen (Eds.), *Handbook of prescriptive treatments for children and adolescents* (2nd ed., pp. 346–363). Boston: Allyn & Bacon.

Simons, R., Beaman, J., Conger, R., & Chao, W. (1993). Stress, support, and antisocial behavior traits as determinants of emotional well-being and parenting practices among single mothers. *Journal of Marriage and the Family, 55*(2), 385–398.

Solomon-Fears, C. (2008). Nonmarital childbearing: Trends, reasons, and public policy interventions. *CRS Report for Congress*. Retrieved August 2, 2009, from http://ftp/fas.org/sgp/crs/misc/RL34756.pdf.

Stanley, S. M., & Fincham, F. D. (2002). The effects of divorce on children. *Couples Research and Therapy Newsletter, 8*(1), 7–10.

Stewart, S. D. (1999). Disneyland dads, Disneyland moms?: How nonresident parents spend time with their children. *Journal of Family Issues, 20*, 539–556.

Stepfamily Association of America. (2009). *What is a stepfamily?* Retrieved March 15, 2010, from www.saafamilies.org/faqs/fats.htm.

Stone, G. (2007). Father post divorce well-being. *Journal of Divorce and Remarriage, 41*, 139–150.

Strohschein, L. (2005). Parental divorce and child mental health trajectories. *Journal of Marriage and Family, 67*(5), 1286–1300.

Tillitski, C. (1992). Fathers and child custody: Issues, trends, and implications for counseling. *Journal of Mental Health Counseling, 14*(3), 351–361.

U.S. Census Bureau. (2006). *Statistical abstract of the United States* (122nd ed.). Washington, DC: U.S. Government Printing Office.

U.S. Census Bureau. (2007). *Single-parent households showed little variation since 1994 (CB07-46)*. Retrieved August 12, 2009, from http://www.census.gov/Press-Release/www/releases/archives/families_households/009842.html.

U.S. Census Bureau. (2008a). *Current Population Survey, 2007 Annual Social and Economic Supplement*. Retrieved August 12, 2009, from www.census.gov/population/www/socdemo/hh-fam.html.

U.S. Census Bureau. (2008b). *Custodial mothers and fathers and their child support*. Retrieved August 22, 2009, from www.census.gov/Press-Release/www/releases/archives/children/010634.html.

U.S. Census Bureau. (2008c). *Facts for Features* (CB08-FF.02). Retrieved August 12, 2009, from http://www.census.gov/Press-Release/www/releases/archives/facts_for_features_special_editions/010968.html.

U.S. Census Bureau. (2010). *Father's day centennial: June 20, 2010*. Retrieved September 5, 2010, from www.census.gov/newsroom/releases/pdf/cb10-ff11.pdf.

U.S. Department of Health and Human Services. (2006). *Seventh Annual Report to Congress* (A-283). Washington, DC: Author. Retrieved August 12, 2009, from www.acf.hhs.gov/programs/ofa/annualreport7/Appendix/TANF_7th_Report?Appendix/pdf.

U.S. Department of Health and Human Services. (2009). *Noncustodial parents participation in their children's lives: Evidence from the survey of income and program participation*. Retrieved August 12, 2009, from www.hhs.gov.

Ventura, J., & Reed, M. (1998). *Divorce for dummies*. New York: Wiley.

Wallerstein, J. S. (1998). Children of divorce: A society in search of policy. In M. A. Mason, A. Skolnick, & S. D. Sugarman (Eds.), *All our families: New policies for a new century* (pp. 66–94). New York: Oxford University Press.

Wallerstein, J., & Kelly, J. (1980). *Surviving the breakup: How children actually cope with divorce*. New York: Basic Books.

Wallerstein, J., & Lewis, J. M. (2004). The unexpected legacy of divorce: Report of a 25-year study. *Psychoanalytic Psychology, 21*, 353–370.

Wallerstein, J. S., Lewis, J. M., & Blakeslee, S. (2000). *The unexpected legacy of divorce: A 25-year landmark study*. New York: Hyperion.

Warshak, R. (2000). Remarriage as a trigger of parental alienation syndrome. *American Journal of Family Therapy, 28*(3), 229–241.

White, L., & Gilbreth, J. G. (2001). When children have two fathers: Effects of relationships with stepfathers and noncustodial fathers on adolescent outcomes. *Journal of Marriage and Family, 63,* 155–167.

Wickrama K. A. S., Lorenz, F. O., Conger, R. D., & Elder, G.H. (2006). Changes in family financial circumstances and the physical health of married and recently divorced mothers. *Social Science and Medicine 63,* 123–136.

Wilbur, J., & Wilbur, M. (1988). The noncustodial parent: Dilemmas and interventions. *Journal of Counseling and Development, 66*(9), 435–437.

Williams, K., & Dunne-Bryant, A. (2006). Divorce and adult psychological well-being: Clarifying the role of gender and child age. *Journal of Marriage and Family, 68,* 1178–1196.

Chapter 8

Parenting and Work: A Balancing Act

Today, work and family play major roles in the lives of adults. Most Americans come face to face on a daily basis with the demands and challenges of trying to balance work, parenting, and family living. Far too often, there are negative effects when work responsibilities spill over into the family. For example, the global financial crisis that began in the latter part of 2008 with the failures of large financial institutions in the United States rapidly evolved into a crisis for many Americans—adults experienced job losses by the hundreds of thousands, cars were repossessed, families were forced into bankruptcy, and an unprecedented number of homes were lost because families couldn't afford their house payments.

Research indicates that money is a major source of concern for families today, and that there are potentially serious implications when money issues crop up (Dew, 2007; Papp, Cummings, & Goeke-Morey, 2009). And make no mistake about it—because of the interconnected nature of family living, when couples experience money problems, children feel the stress, too. For these reasons, in this chapter we begin our study of work and parenting by looking at the landscape of dual-earner couples, including the demands faced by military families when a loved one is deployed to Iraq or Afghanistan. We then shift our attention to the types of strain and stress families face when they try to juggle work with family life and parenting. To best equip you with the tools for your own family and parent–child relationships, we conclude by exploring the skills effective working families use in their daily lives.

WORKING FAMILIES: THE TRANSFORMATION OF AMERICAN HOMES

Economic stability and the ability of families to meet their daily needs is an important measure of family health and well-being (Allegretto, 2005). As you saw earlier, socioeconomic status (SES) of a family is the government's measure of the family's relative economic and social ranking within a community (Krieger, 2001). Measures of SES typically include the adults' occupation, education level, community/group associations, and income. Other measures may include location of residence and certain home amenities such as a television, computer, telephone, books, and so forth. **Attained SES** refers to the parents' socioeconomic status, while **SES of origin** is the term used when describing a child's family's SES (Krieger, 2001).

As our nation moved into the second half of the 20th century, a number of social/cultural, economic, and political changes occurred that changed the face of American families. These changes include factors such as lowered birthrates and delays in marriage, women's abilities to control their fertility through contraceptives, the legalization of abortion in 1973 and the adoption of no-fault divorce laws, and civil rights legislation in 1965 that banned discrimination. Many of these social and cultural factors propelled women into the workplace. In significant ways, this shift from one-earner families to dual-earner families dramatically changed the face of American families and how we experience family living today.

A Portrait of Contemporary Dual-Earner Couples

Dual-earner couples are defined as marriages or relationships in which both partners work, and workforce participation varies among dual-earner couples. Today, more than half of married couples in the United States are dual-earners (U.S. Department of Labor, 2007). In many such couples one partner works full time while the other partner works part time; in other families, both partners work full time. Many factors influence labor force participation and earnings among dual-earner couples such as education level, urban living, unemployment, and discrimination. There are also racial and ethnic differences in dual-earner couples.

White couples are highly involved in the workforce, and only Asian couples are more likely to be involved in the workforce than whites. One reason for white couples' high participation in the workforce is that they tend to have higher levels of education, which are strongly associated with higher levels of employment. As a result, whites generally earn more than black and Hispanic men and women, even within the same occupation; fortunately, this wage gap is diminishing, especially among women (U.S. Bureau of Labor Statistics, 2008). The median annual income of white families and these higher earnings are associated with enhanced marital quality among whites (we discuss marital quality later in the chapter) (Amato, Johnson, Booth, & Rogers, 2003; U.S. Census Bureau, 2008b).

Educational attainment is a key factor in employment and earnings for black couples. African American/Afro-Caribbean men are the least likely to be employed among each of the ethnic groups while black women are the most likely to be employed. In fact, black men are more than twice as likely to be unemployed than whites. Both black men and women are typically **blue-collar workers**, which means they are highly represented in the service sector (such as sales, office, production, or transportation); as a result, their earnings are generally lower than those employed in **white-collar**, professional occupations (such as attorneys, bankers, or doctors) (U.S. Bureau of Labor Statistics, 2008). Of all racial and ethnic groups in the United States, African American/Black Caribbean families suffer the highest levels of unemployment and poverty and the lowest median family income (U.S. Census Bureau, 2008b).

Asian men and women are more likely than any of the other ethnic groups to be employed in professional positions (U.S. Bureau of Labor Statistics, 2008). Low divorce rates, high education levels, a strong work ethic, self-sufficiency, familism, and high participation in the labor force have led to the "model minority" status for many Asian couples (Taylor, 2002). With an annual income of slightly over $62,000 per year, Asian American families have the highest median household income of all racial groups in the United States (U.S. Census Bureau, 2008b). This is perhaps because Asian Americans have the highest educational qualifications of all ethnic groups in the United States—nearly one-half of all Asian American adults have attained at least a bachelor's degree (U.S. Census Bureau, 2007).

Influenced by Confucian ideology, Asian households are typically patriarchal with well-defined roles. Their cultural traditions and roles tend to provide them with order and stability between work life and family life. Additionally, their collectivist perspective has led to a willingness on the part of many Asian Americans to sacrifice personal needs in order for their families and employees to be successful.

Hispanic couples are similar to Asian couples in that they tend to be patriarchal, familistic, and traditional in their views of men's and women's work roles. Hispanic men are generally highly employed, while Hispanic women tend to have lower employment rates than each of the other ethnic groups (U.S. Bureau of Labor Statistics, 2008). While Hispanic couples are becoming more educated and, therefore, more represented in professional occupations, they are less likely to have completed high school than each of the other ethnic groups. As a result, they are still highly employed in the service sector, resulting in lower earnings than those employed as professionals (Monthly Labor Review, 2004; U.S. Bureau of Labor Statistics, 2008).

One of the poorest ethnic groups in America today, Latino (Hispanic) families earn, on average, about $36,000 per year (U.S. Census Bureau, 2008b). The reasons for the high poverty rates among Latinos are varied. Many Latino immigrants may have professional degrees from other countries, but because of the language barrier when they arrive in the United States, they are unable to secure high-paying jobs. Many immigrants today also face discrimination in the workplace; for example, it is not uncommon in California for field workers to earn as little as $300 per month for their labor (Schlosser, 2001). Furthermore, the transnational (families who are of divided because they live in different countries) and binational (families whose legal citizenship is mixed) status of many Hispanic families has challenged their ability to manage work and family roles (Baca Zinn, & Pok, 2002).

Arab American couples are typically patriarchal and traditional—men are often the family's providers while women are homemakers and raise the children. Arab American men and women tend to be highly educated and are, therefore, well represented in the professional labor force, with higher earnings than the national average. In the United States, Arab Americans with at least a high school diploma number 85 percent (Arab American Institute, 2009). More than four out of 10 Americans of Arab heritage have a bachelor's degree or higher; 17 percent have a post-graduate degree. Today, over two-thirds of Arab American adults are in the labor force, and are employed in a wide array of occupations. Their median annual income is $47,000, but in comparison to overall U.S. workers, more Arab Americans have higher salary ranges (such as incomes of $75,000 per year).

Limited education, high unemployment, divorce, single-mother families, and substance abuse rates have contributed to labor force participation among Native Americans that is varied and sporadic. About three in four married Native Americans are employed, while only about one-half of single female-headed households are employed; this results in higher earnings for those who are married (Taylor, Yellowbird, & Snipp, 2002).

In recent years, families and parents in the United States have been challenged in new ways as service men and women have been deployed overseas due to military engagements in Iraq and Afghanistan. The challenges are many, and all affect the portrait of wage earners in America.

Service Men and Women

The United States military, which comprises the Army, Navy, Air Force, Coast Guard, and Marines, deployed as many as 150,000–200,000 military personnel in 2007 (Congressional Research Service, 2007). While military families deal with stressors that are common to all families, such as parenting concerns, childcare, juggling work

While military families face the same day-to-day struggles and stressors that all working couples face, they also are challenged with unique financial and childcare situations when they are deployed to the wars in Iraq and Afghanistan.

with family, and career decisions, they are also subjected to unique stressors because of the separation from family members (Drummet, Coleman, & Cable, 2003).

PREPARING FOR DEPLOYMENT Until recently, most military personnel had a period of 1 to 2 years between deployments. Recently, however, deployments can often occur in quick succession or tours of duty are extended for prolonged periods of time. For example, during the Gulf War in the early 1990s, single parents and dual-earner couples were mobilized so quickly that these families had only a few hours to find childcare for their children—both immediate childcare and extended childcare while the parent was deployed overseas (Drummet et al., 2003).

Financial worries are of particular concern to deployed military families. What makes the financial picture much worse for so many military families today is that about 8 percent are young and are receiving paychecks for the first time (Varcoe, Emper, & Lees, 2002). Because of this, young couples have not yet learned effective money management skills, and this puts them at significantly higher risk for money troubles during deployment.

FINANCIAL DIFFICULTIES FOR DEPLOYED FAMILIES Today, there are increasing incidents of burgeoning financial difficulties among service families because separations due to deployment oftentimes catch families financially unprepared. In fact, one study of Army families revealed that over two-thirds (64.3 percent) of Army spouses work just to cover basic monthly expenses, such as food and housing (Survey of Army Families IV, 2001).

Among those family practitioners who work with military families to improve their financial well-being, current programs are used that focus on financial situations that are unique to the military. Financial programs for military personnel, such as *Money Sense* and *Financial Fitness,* are preventive educational programs that provide information to service members and their spouses/significant others about ways to manage their financial resources. These types of curricula, especially tailored to the needs of military men and women, teach money management skills and include such things as learning how to budget, how to keep financial records, how to develop healthy spending habits, establishing realistic savings habits, and managing credit card debt. Research demonstrated that financial education as a part of deployment readiness reduced the frequency of families' money problems (Varcoe et al., 2002).

There are, of course, numerous other issues military families face, and we explore those a bit later in this chapter when we look at what it takes for all families to juggle work and family life. Here, it's important to recognize the unique financial situations military families experience, and that family life educators and other family practitioners can provide invaluable resources to these families to assist them during these stressful work-related situations.

COUPLES AND WORK: JUST TRYING TO MAKE ENDS MEET

Economic stability and the ability of families to meet their daily needs is an important measure of family well-being (Allegretto, 2005). **Basic budgets**, or the amount of money families need to manage at the most basic level, must cover expenses including costs associated with housing, food, transportation, childcare, healthcare, clothing, personal care items, school materials, and taxes. However, a significant number of Americans today have difficulty meeting their family's economic needs.

The picture of today's working family in the United States looks something like this (Lazarovici, 2005):

- The average U.S. employee works 1,978 hours each year; this figure represents a 36-hour increase (nearly a full week) since 1990.

- About 65 million women are in the workforce, including three-fourths of mothers of children younger than age 18.
- More than one-fourth of working women spend at least some time of their nights or weekends at work.
- About three-fourths of all employed parents say they have little or no control over their work schedules.
- One-half of all women who are married or who share a household with someone else work different schedules from those of their spouses or partners.
- One-half of working families have childcare expenses; two-income families spend about 16 percent of their earnings on childcare, while single-parent families spend about 19 percent of their earnings on childcare.
- Over 54 million adult employees provide some degree of care for an aging, disabled, or ill family member.

What does it cost for families to make ends meet today? On average nationwide, working families with two parents and two children require an income of $48,778 to meet a basic family budget (Lin & Bernstein, 2008). Budgets for four-person families vary widely by geographic location (Lin & Bernstein, 2008):

- Oklahoma City, OK: $42,106
- Houston, TX: $44,928
- Portland, OR: $48,946
- Fort Lauderdale, FL: $52,287
- Los Angeles, CA: $54,078
- Minneapolis, MN: $58,774
- New York, NY: $68,758

Today, a significant number of American families earn less than the family budget average of $48,778. In the United States, nearly 30 percent of all families make incomes below the family budget level, and over one-half of African American and Hispanic households fall below the family budget level. In many parts of the country, families must be supported by two incomes.

Dual-Earner Couples and Family Well-Being

For both men and women, job status, job complexity, job autonomy, and the number of hours worked are some of the important variables that influence child and family well-being (Perry-Jenkins, Repetti, & Crouter, 2001). **Job status** refers to a type or kind of job that offers some kind of prestige in an organization or community (such as managers or executive officers). **Job complexity** occurs when jobs are at the same time challenging and stimulating, and **job autonomy** happens when employees are allowed a high degree of independence and self-direction. Dr. Maureen Perry-Jenkins and her colleagues' (2001) decade-long review of couples who juggle work with family revealed that when fathers' and mothers' jobs have a high degree of complexity and autonomy, they are more apt to create a positive home environment and show greater warmth in parenting. Job complexity and autonomy are also linked with child outcomes such as enhanced verbal and reading skills and decreases in problem behaviors.

Interestingly, most studies about couples and work focus on the well-being of the *couple,* not well-being at the *family* level (Behnke & MacDermid, 2004). But because of the systems nature of family living—when one family struggles, all others are affected—it is essential that we gain an understanding of how work affects the lives of families. Generally speaking, **family well-being** includes (Behnke & MacDermid, 2004):

- Psychological health, such as low levels of depression and anxiety, high levels of life satisfaction
- High levels of self-esteem, sense of power, and internal locus of control
- Good physical health
- Low behavior/conduct problems, such as alcohol abuse
- Good social support, such as friendships and contact with extended family
- High marital quality
- High marital stability
- Good parent–child relationships

If a family member is struggling at work, or if work conditions are not conducive to a quality family life, then every family member eventually suffers—a family member's occupational well-being is directly related to a good, healthy, comfortable state for the family.

Given the importance of family health and functioning in our lives, it is essential to have an awareness and understanding of the interrelated nature of the workplace and the home. Making work work is easier for some families today because a number of companies offer creative benefits programs (see Figure 8.1). But how do other contemporary families fare?

Work Hours and Family Life: Shift Work

Researchers and family practitioners are interested not only in the total number of work hours that couples put in each week, but they're also interested in how those hours are structured throughout the week (Grosswald, 2004). In many dual-earner families today, one partner works on a schedule that is different from the typical 8:00 A.M. to 5:00 P.M. schedule, and 57 percent of dual-earner couples—over 15 million—have at least one spouse who works nonstandard hours (Davis, Crouter, & McHale, 2006; Presser, 2003). **Shift work** can mean that a partner works nonstandard hours, such as working from 6:00 in the morning until 2:00 in the afternoon, or it could mean working a schedule other than the typical workweek (Monday through Friday in the United States) (Grosswald, 2004). For example, contemporary couples may have a partner that works 12-hour shifts, four times a week, which are common shifts for nurses, emergency personnel, and firefighters.

There are a number of advantages and disadvantages associated with shift work schedules. Potential positive effects of these work schedules

---

Work and family are central to our lives, but finding ways to balance the two is not always easy. How important is it for people to manage work so that they can still enjoy marriage, children, and recreation?

Many corporations are finding out that it is *very* important, so important that some employers are finding ways to provide workers with tools and benefits aiding family life and living. Lancaster Laboratories, a company specializing in laboratory services for the environmental and pharmaceutical industry, was one of the first in a wave of companies to offer family-friendly benefits for employees.

In the mid-1980s, executives at Lancaster Laboratories noticed a continuing theme in the needs assessments of its employees, 60 percent of whom were women: When women were absent from work, it was typically due to problems with daycare. With the number of employees at Lancaster who currently had a family or planned on having one in the near future, the $50 million company knew it had to find a way to retain its workers and to reduce absenteeism.

In August 1986, Lancaster Laboratories Child Care Center opened its doors. The first-of-its-kind on-site daycare had 29 openings, which were quickly filled. Parents soon took advantage of daycare just a few feet away from their job site. Today, the childcare center serves 161 children from infancy to school-age, and even offers summer daycare and kindergarten programs.

The programs are great for working parents, but aside from a spot on *Working Mother's* "Top 100 Companies for Working Mothers" list for 11 years, is it beneficial for employers? Human resources executives at Lancaster Laboratories seem to think so. Turnover remains at around 8 percent companywide, employees skip fewer days of work, and 96 percent of new mothers return to their posts in three months.

Creative benefits programs today are not just for working parents. Taking a job with a company used to mean the standard insurance/company car/401(k) package. But today, more and more companies are offering extras such as on-site fitness centers, concert and sporting event tickets, concierge services, and flex-scheduling. Employers are seeing great value in making sure their employees balance good living and hard working. Having happy workers means keeping a healthy bottom line.

FIGURE 8.1 Making work work for families.

Source: Welch, *Family Life Now*, 2e. (2010). Boston: Allyn & Bacon. p. 412. Based on Powers (2004).

include such things as working fewer days each week, having more family time, and getting more time to be away from the job (for a complete review, see Loudoun, 2008).

However, there are negative impacts of shift work on families. For example, although shift workers may physically have more time to be with their families than standard shift workers do, researchers believe the *quality* of these interactions is significantly less. This is because of the fatigue that intensifies throughout the shift week—some research has revealed that after a shift worker comes home from work and sleeps, he or she has less than 2 hours a day to attend to family duties, household tasks, and to prepare for the next workday. Other studies have demonstrated that shift work significantly impacts family relationships (for a full review, see Davis et al., 2006):

- *Parental Involvement:* There is a "mismatch" in parents' shift schedules and time for children. Overall, studies show that shift workers spend less time with their children than standard, daytime workers do.
- *Marital Conflict:* Sometimes, high stress and work demands associated with shift work lead to increased levels of marital conflict.

With the evolving global economy and the increase in shift work within different industries, much more needs to be understood about the effects of nonstandard work hours on family life. As some family practitioners note, these types of hours make it difficult for parents to create routines, rituals, and family activities—the very things that help to knit family members together and provide the foundation for family closeness (Davis et al., 2006).

The Demands of Overtime

Organizations typically define **overtime** as the hours a person works beyond their normal 40-hour per week schedule (Baird & Beccia, 1980). Working overtime often leads us to feel overworked, burned out—and just plain cranky. But given the systems nature of family living, it's important to keep in mind that these feelings of "enough is enough" not only influence working moms and dads, but it also impacts their families.

Decades of research have shown that long work hours increase workers' perceptions that their jobs interfere with their emotional states, and these, in turn, increase marital tension between spouses (for a complete review, see Crouter, Bumpus, Head, & McHale, 2001). Other studies have demonstrated that when fathers are pressured or stressed at work, they tend to have more conflict with their adolescent children (Crouter, 1995). Finally, research has revealed that wives' overtime work (46+ hours per week) decreases marital interaction and happiness, and increases the potential of divorce (Amato et al., 2003).

While working overtime can be successfully managed in the short term, for many couples it is challenging to manage and balance their family relationships over the long haul, because the amount of time when they can spend time with one another is limited. That's not to say, however, that families can't make it work. As one family practitioner observed, quality time in great quantity is a staple of creating strong family relationships (Defrain, 2000).

COPING WITH UNEMPLOYMENT In the latter part of 2008 and at the start of 2009, a rapidly growing number of Americans experienced job loss due to the U.S. economic crisis, the recession, downsizing, and business restructuring. As Figure 8.2 illustrates for us, the economic picture was bleak for millions of Americans in 2008. Job loss and financial hardship rank among the more severe stressors that families can encounter.

Unemployment is a traumatic situation for families to deal with, and aside from the obvious financial constraints it puts on a family, there are a number of other negative impacts on the family's emotional and physical health. These include (Furstenberg, 1974; Hanisch, 1999; Voydanoff, 1983):

- Family instability
- Decreased family interactions

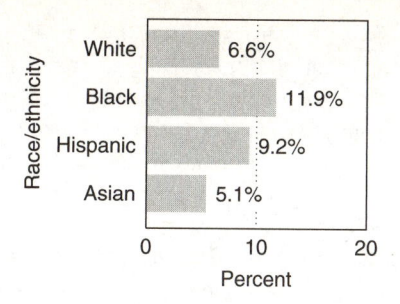

FIGURE 8.2 Unemployment rates by race, 2008. The economic crisis in 2008–2009 left many Americans unemployed.

Source: Based on data from U.S. Census Bureau (2008).

Unemployment rates by race/ethnicity:
- White: 6.6%
- Black: 11.9%
- Hispanic: 9.2%
- Asian: 5.1%

- Increased levels of family violence
- Increased mental hospital admissions

Some research further suggests that being married and having children seems to buffer against the negative impacts of unemployment for women, but tends to have the reverse effect for men (Artazcoz, Benach, Borrelll, & Cortes, 2004). This may be because when women are unemployed, frequently they still have their basic economic needs met by their husbands; periods of job loss also lessen women's multiple demands and allow them greater involvement in family life. The risks of poor mental health for men may be higher than it is for women because of the pressures of traditional patriarchal gender roles, which dictate that men are to protect and provide for their families—certainly, job loss may make them feel that they are not living up to their prescribed role of breadwinner. And, because men are traditionally less involved in the care and nurturing of children, the researchers speculated that these activities can't successfully replace their jobs, as they do with women.

Opting Out: Stay-at-Home Moms

Some mothers have decided that staying at home with their children is how they can best balance personal, partner, and family needs with their partner's work responsibilities. These mothers have opted out of the workforce and choose instead to stay at home and nurture their children; this is referred to **household work**. Of the millions of mothers in the United States today, it is estimated that 5.6 million stay at home and do not participate in the paid workforce (U.S. Census Bureau, 2008a).

The fact that household work is still a critical component of a successful home for dual-earner couples has led some economists to try to place a value on household work. The **opportunity cost method** asks the question, "What would a person be paid in wage labor for 1 hour of household work?" Because what people earn in wage labor varies, this method can tend to skew the real value of household work. An alternative method is the **market alternative cost method**, which estimates the value of household labor by looking at what it would cost in the current market to pay someone to do the household labor the mother performs, such as preparing three meals a day, doing the laundry, caring for the children, and taking care of the home. For example, a group that tracks salaries and wages conducted a recent survey of over 7,000 Internet users. This group valuated a stay-at-home-mom's job and found (Salary.com, 2006):

- If paid, stay-at-home-moms would earn $134,121 annually.
- They work 49.8 hours per week taking care of child and home responsibilities (22 hours are given to household tasks).
- They sleep about 6 hours per night.

Senior Vice President of Salary.com, Bill Coleman, noted that this study "is an eye opener for many people when they see the real market value of the work moms perform."

Of course, moms aren't the only ones who opt to stay at home and care for the children and the home. Today, an increasing number of fathers are doing the same.

Leaving the Workforce: Stay-at-Home Dads

There is also a growing number of men who have decided to stay at home. Stay-at-home-dads are those who have remained out of the labor force for at least 1 year primarily so they can care for their children while their wives work outside of the home. In 2006, there were an estimated 159,000 stay-at-home fathers in the United States; 60 percent have two or more children (U.S. Census Bureau, 2007). For most of these dads, the wife has the better, higher paying job and the couple believed that it would be in the best interest of the family if the father stayed home while the wife worked. This is a good example of how each individual and every family must make a choice that is good, better, or best for them in order to balance work and family successfully.

In today's economic environment, there appear to be three social circumstances that are contributing to the increasing numbers of dads who stay home to care for their children. First, among married fathers, the family's economic considerations make it more appealing for him to stay home than they do for her to do so. Second, today's increased divorce rates have resulted in some fathers becoming their children's primary caregiver; because some fathers have economic security, they may opt to stay at home and care for their children, rather than place the children in childcare. Finally, a number of stay-at-home-dads today are gay men whose partners work outside of the home, while they care for the children and assume household tasks. The prevalence of dads staying at home and opting out of the paid workforce will likely increase as this movement continues, and as social acceptance becomes more widespread and attitudes change.

THE BALANCING ACT: JUGGLING FAMILY LIFE AND WORK

"Come on, we're late!" "Let's *go!*" "Do you have your? (backpack, briefcase, trumpet, book report, science project)?" "Where are my car keys?" "Let's *go!*" Balancing work and family is nothing new. Since the women's movement in the 1960s and the surging flood of women in the workplace the past few decades, working families across the United States engage in similar morning rituals in their dash to get the kids off to school and parents off to work.

After the birth or the adoption of a child, dual-earner families must make numerous adjustments to accommodate the schedules and needs of both spouses and the children. Unlike the traditional homemaker/breadwinner family configurations found in the 1950s, once a baby arrives, contemporary couples must not only incorporate sleepless nights into their daily lives, but they must also find a way to juggle the responsibilities, stressors, and struggles associated with managing the multiple roles of mother/father, employee, and wife/husband.

Conflicting Demands: Heartstrings versus Purse Strings

Sometimes our obligations to our jobs come into direct conflict with the needs of our families. When we take on (or have assigned to us) many roles simultaneously—for example, when the family role demands are incompatible with or conflict with the stresses from the work role—**inter-role conflict** occurs (Hammer & Thompson, 2003). Such conflict can result in increased work absenteeism, intentions to leave the workforce, decreased job satisfaction, decreased family satisfaction, decreased life satisfaction, negative mental and physical health, strain associated with dependent care responsibilities (both childcare and elder care), and increased interpersonal conflict or divorce.

SOMETHING'S GOTTA GIVE: WORK–FAMILY CONFLICT Work–family conflict falls into two specific areas and is bidirectional—the conflict goes both ways (Greenhaus & Beutell, 1985):

- *Time-Based:* **Time-based conflict** takes place when demands from the work domain and the family domain vie for a parent's time and attention. This is the most common type of role conflict found in working families. For instance, a meeting that runs late at work might make Mom late for coaching her son's soccer game. A last-minute business call might make Dad late for a parent–teacher conference.

- *Strain-Based:* **Strain-based conflict** occurs when the demands in one domain make it difficult to carry out effective role performance in another domain. For example, consider a mother who finds it difficult to concentrate on her job or complete her job tasks on time because she is also covering all of the tasks at home while her husband works overtime shifts.

In recognition of the multiple roles with which most American families must now cope, in 1993 the federal government enacted the **Family and Medical Leave Act (FMLA)**. Under the FMLA, federal and state employees and those who work for employers with 50 or more employees are able to take up to 12 weeks of unpaid leave in order to care for an ill child, parent, or spouse, or for one's own serious illness without fear of losing their job, benefits, or status. Unpaid leave can also be taken for the birth or adoption of a child, or when placing a child for adoption or foster care. Both working men and women are protected by this legislation.

Family life is a balancing act. Deciding who will work, who will care for the children, when and how to coordinate schedules, and determining who will transport the children to and from events and activities undoubtedly leads to role conflicts. Commonly, the partner with more flexibility in work schedules is called upon to "pick up the slack" when it comes to trying to balance work and family. Oftentimes, though, this leads to frustration and a feeling of being "used" and "unappreciated." Consider, for example, a mother who is frequently frustrated with her husband after the birth of their first child. Because they both work full time, she feels that he should shoulder more of the childrearing responsibilities. Sleep deprivation for both partners is a daily reality and, as a result, unfortunately so is the cycle of escalating conflict: He feels she should appreciate his efforts more and she believes that she shouldn't have to express appreciation because he was just doing his duty as a father.

Good communication and a willingness to avoid criticism, contempt, defensiveness, and stonewalling are important keys to negotiating work–family role conflicts effectively (Gottman, 1994). When conflicts do arise, learning to calm down, speak without causing defensiveness, and to validate our partner can help us reduce the possibility that these conflicts will harm the successful balancing of our work and family relationships (see also Gottman, 1999).

WORK–FAMILY SPILLOVER/CROSSOVER

Research psychologist Patricia Roehling and her colleague, professor and sociologist Phyllis Moen (2003), conclude that dual-earner couples are vulnerable to work-family conflict, as well as **work–family spillover/crossover**, which occurs when a spouse brings the emotional events and tensions of one environment to the other. This spillover/crossover can occur from *family to work;* for example, if a parent has an argument with a teenager before leaving for work, it can lead to poor concentration at work. In the case of *work-to-family* conflict, a "bad day at the office" for either parent may end up being a bad day for everyone else at home. Work–family spillover/crossover can also have positive individual and family outcomes. Roehling and Moen note that good relationships at home energize people, which in turn improves a person's productivity at work; a great day at work can translate to a great day for everyone else at home. The researchers also note that much scientific study shows that couples who combine work, married life, and family report:

- Levels of well-being are higher for both men and women.
- Women experience less anxiety and depression.
- Women report better physical health and higher self-esteem.
- Husbands are more involved with the children.
- Children have a stronger network of social support and social relationships.
- Two wages allow the couple to more adequately provide for their children.

- Marital satisfaction is high when the woman's employment is consistent with the husband's and wife's gender role beliefs.

Current economic trends indicate that dual-career marriages are here to stay. In addition to promoting the physical well-being and the health of children through shared caregiving, and in addition to ensuring the economic survival of the family, parents are also charged with the tremendous responsibility of fostering their children's optimal growth.

BALANCING IT ALL When our lives are in balance, life just seems better, doesn't it? When it comes to work and family, **balance** can be thought of as the positive psychological state we achieve through regularly meeting our own, others', and our work-related needs. It is the state of equilibrium we feel when these needs—and their accompanying responsibilities—are fulfilled to improve our own well-being, and the well-being of those we love (Harris, 2008).

Perhaps we can think about balance in another way by using the *Triangular Theory of Balancing Work and Family* presented in Figure 8.3 (Harris, 2008). This theory maintains that the interaction of our personal needs, others' needs, and work responsibilities creates ever-changing situations that cause either balance or imbalance in a family. Individuals can choose and change how their needs and responsibilities interact to create greater balance in their relationships and improve subsequent happiness and well-being. In other words, we have a choice in how we attempt to balance our work and family relationships while we at the same time try to meet our own personal needs. When we are out of balance in any of the three areas (personal needs, others' needs, and work needs/responsibilities), we intuitively sense that a change needs to occur; how we approach these changes makes all the difference in how happy and satisfied we are in our relationships. Other research recently demonstrated that family health and **family cohesion**—the extent to which family members feel emotionally close and bonded to one another—is influenced by how well working couples are able to integrate the demands of work and family life (Stevens, Kiger, & Riley, 2006). One of the biggest challenges working couples face is who is going to do the tasks necessary to keep the house running, and when.

Juggling Parenting and Household Chores

During the 1990s, more than 200 research articles addressed the many nuances of the division of household labor. Couples may marry with the intent to share household chores just as they intend to share childrearing. But when children enter into the family system, these intentions often do not become reality. Discrepancies between who does what often becomes a source of recurring conflict. With the majority of mothers today working at least 30 hours a week outside the home, the expectation that they are still responsible for the lion's share of running the household and performing household tasks can become a source of resentment. Sociologist

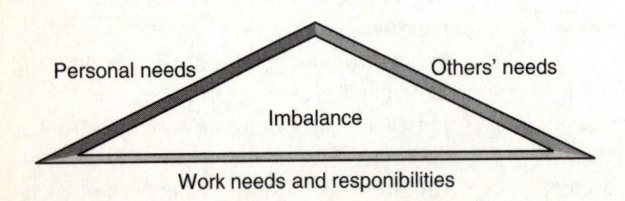

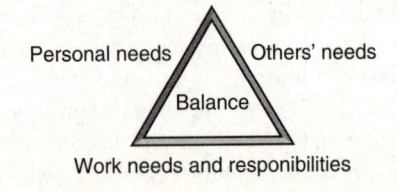

FIGURE 8.3 The triangular theory of balancing work and family.
Source: ©V.W Harris (2008).

Arlie Hochschild (1989) referred to this burden of taking on the dual responsibilities of wage-earner and housekeeper as the **second shift**.

During this second shift, women spend three times as much time performing household tasks as men do, spending 32 hours compared to men's 10 hours (Coltrane, 2000). These tasks include house cleaning, meal preparation, grocery shopping, cleanup after meals, and laundry (Blair & Licther, 1991). Coltrane (2000) refers to these essential tasks as **routine housework** but maintains that "this family work or social reproductive labor is just as important to the maintenance of society as the productive work that occurs in the formal market economy" (p. 1209), that these tasks keep the household, the family, and society going. The author cites numerous studies that indicate that, for the most part, neither women nor men enjoy performing routine household chores. They tend to find occasional **residual tasks**, such as bill paying, yard work, and chauffeuring children, to be more flexible in nature and more enjoyable to carry out.

Like parenting roles, the division of household duties tends to fall along traditional gender roles once a child is born, even if such tasks were previously handled fairly equally (Baxter, Hewitt, & Haynes, 2008). For example, in a study of 2,231 married and cohabiting new parents, the researchers found that the birth of a first child resulted in a dramatic increase in women's housework time—about 6 additional hours a week on average; having additional children continued to increase women's time on household chores. There was no corresponding change in men's housework hours upon the arrival of a child (Baxter et al., 2008).

Coltrane (2000) identifies several factors that contribute to the division of household chores:

- *Women's Employment:* When there are two wage earners in the family, these couples tend to share household tasks more than those couples where only one spouse works.
- *Men's Employment:* Men who work fewer hours outside the home tend to pitch in more around the house and with childrearing responsibilities.
- *Earnings:* Women who earn more money benefit from more shared divisions of household tasks.
- *Education:* In households in which one or both spouses have high education levels (i.e., a college degree or a post-graduate degree), women tend to perform fewer household tasks and are more likely to hire outside help to render services such as house cleaning. Men with high education levels tend to engage in more household labor.
- *Presence of Children:* When children enter the marriage (and change the family dynamic), household labor is less frequently shared evenly between the marital partners and the woman assumes the majority of housework, along with the responsibilities of childrearing.

While gender appears to be an important factor that dictates generally who does what housework and how often, the research does seem to indicate that the division of labor along traditional gender roles is slowly giving way to changing roles of men and women in contemporary society. This is a "ray of hope" for those who struggle with balancing marital and parenting roles because, as Coltrane (2000) concludes, "We now know that when men perform more of the routine household work, employed women feel that the division of labor is fairer, are less depressed, and enjoy higher levels of marital satisfaction" (p. 1226).

The challenges of childrearing go far beyond the stereotypical jokes about changing diapers and getting up in the middle of the night. Childrearing not only demands a realignment of roles within a family but also insists that parents learn how to avoid the potential who-does-what-around-the-house conflicts that may arise. It requires that parents learn how to juggle careers and parenting responsibilities while remaining attentive to the emotional needs of partners and maintaining a strong marriage. Challenging? You bet.

Childcare

In 1940, only 10 percent of children in America lived in a home in which the mother worked outside the home. By 2004, nearly three-fourths of America's children lived in a home in which the mother worked in the paid labor force (U.S. Bureau of Labor Statistics, 2005). With both parents working, parents must weigh options regarding childcare. Some spouses try to work different shifts so that their children spend less time outside of the home in a childcare setting. Consequently, the parents have less time to spend together developing and nurturing their own relationship. Other families have extended family members who are willing to provide childcare. When this option is available, many parents view it as a way for children to receive loving care with trusted family members at a reduced cost. A third option is a childcare center or preschool. Today, many parents are opting for **shared care**, a childcare arrangement in which parents share a babysitter or nanny.

Although children of dual-earner families seem to manifest more positive than negative characteristics, working couples may need help in resolving the conflicts that arise between their professions and their families. Today, families need a strong support network—at the workplace and from spouses, friends, and the extended family.

It's Just No Fun Anymore: Leisure Time and Parenthood

Parenting books, magazines, advice columns, and Internet sites have inordinate quantities of information about how to keep relationships stable and satisfying during a couple's parenting years, but perhaps the best advice offered by these sources is that parents find ways to continue to spend time with each other, without the kids. Despite this advice, however, substantial bodies of research show that, as individuals get married and start families, leisure time is set aside—often at the expense of the couple's relationship satisfaction and happiness (Claxton & Perry-Jenkins, 2008; Lowrey, 2009).

While the majority of parents recognize their need to have "alone time" and to put some excitement into their lives, most have difficulty doing so (Lowrey, 2009). But having healthy families requires that parents are emotionally, spiritually, and physically connected to one another. Making time for themselves is the best gift a couple can give to their children because it increases their relationship satisfaction—and enhances their parenting.

Shared leisure has enduring, positive effects on marriage, and it is particularly beneficial when new couples establish these practices before parenthood (Claxton & Perry-Jenkins, 2008). But instead of just a weekly dinner date, couples' relationships appear to greatly benefit when they keep the excitement in their relationships. With this in mind, couples can:

- *Take a class together:* Learn Italian. Take ballroom dancing lessons. Learn to deep-sea fish. Join a cooking class. The possibilities are endless!
- *Plan an adventure:* Planning a dream-come-true vacation or adventure isn't as important as the actual event. What really matters is the time the couple spends together planning and preparing for it.
- *Get sweaty together:* It'll feel less like a chore and more like a we're-in-this-together moment when you help each other to get your hearts pumping and cheer each other along while you're working out. Or try couples yoga: Twisting your body into pretzel poses will bring you closer together in every way.
- *Romance each other:* Use your imagination!

The whole idea about leisure time for parents is to keep the excitement in their relationship, to remember what it's like to have fun together, and to laugh together. While life can become routine, parents need to work hard to ensure that their relationship does not.

TEN STRATEGIES FOR FAMILY, PARENTING, AND WORK BALANCE

While money doesn't buy happiness, it can definitely provide opportunities for more comfortable daily living, better educational opportunities, healthcare, family vacations, marriage getaways, and other leisure activities. It can also reduce many of the stressors and strains that those who lack economic advantage inevitably endure (Dyk, 2004). Although the demands of balancing work and family can sometimes be draining on a family, research suggests that most employed women and men believe that there are strong benefits to combining work and family, and that the benefits far outweigh the costs (Barnett & Rivers, 1996). Although it takes some effort, it is possible for families to successfully blend and manage these two most important domains in their lives.

In a study that examined the work/family lives of 47 married couples who appear to successfully manage both spheres, the data revealed that these couples structured their lives around 10 major strategies (Haddoc, Zimmerman, Ziemba, & Current, 2001). We discuss these in the sections that follow.

Value Family

Dual-earner couples who make their relationship and their children a priority experience greater satisfaction and well-being in their family relationships (Eyre & Eyre, 2008). Through words and actions, couples who do well at balancing work and family work hard to keep their family as their number one priority, and all of their decisions reflect this priority. Couples can proactively create opportunities for family time and couple time, and during these times can create family rituals and routines—special family times—that are unique to them. Above all, couples need to remember to nurture their relationship: *Strong couples make stronger parents!* Successful couples also emphasize family happiness and well-being over professional responsibilities.

Strive for Partnership

Stressing equality and partnership in the marital relationship is critical to working couples' success. While certainly there are varying degrees of equality among couples, and while there is no doubt that some situations call for greater degrees of partnership than others, partners who possess an overall high degree of equality fare better than those who do not. There appear to be three principal areas where equality is a must: the division of household labor, making decisions together as a couple, and having a "team" mentality. As one partner noted,

> "If I win and she loses, then we both lose. If she wins and I lose, then we both lose. [This belief] has probably made all the difference . . . because you just can't live your life trying to always win. The couple will lose, period."

Derive Meaning from Work

Even if it's not always possible to love their jobs, couples who are successful at balancing work and family note that being able to derive meaning out of what they do is important. For these couples, experiencing enjoyment and purpose from the job brings energy, enthusiasm, and excitement to their lives; it also seems to buffer them against work-related fatigue and burnout.

Maintain Work Boundaries

If couples are able to keep their families as their top priority, it's easier for them to maintain clear—and immoveable—boundaries between their home life and their work life. As the researchers note, couples who are committed to not allowing work to dictate the pace of their lives are better able to compartmentalize their lives, and prevent overlap between their personal and professional lives. As one study participant said, "I think the biggest [strategy] is: When you're at home, you're at home; and when you're at work, you're at work. There's not the crossover. You don't get to think about work unless there's a huge problem."

Be Focused and Productive at Work

Many couples talked about the importance of being productive while at work. They observed that even though they set boundaries, their employers tended to better support their commitment to family if they were efficient while they were on the job.

Prioritize Family Fun

You gotta have fun! Successful working families make a point to enjoy a lot of fun time together as a family. Not only is family fun a way to relax and de-stress, it's also a way that families build emotional connections and create family rituals. Family time together doesn't have to be a costly trip to Disneyworld—it can be an every-Friday-night board game or movie and popcorn night, a spontaneous bike ride on a Saturday, or a quick toss of the Frisbee in the back yard. Of course, a sense of humor goes a long way in buffering the stressors associated with the demands of balancing work and family. Successful families strive to make laughter and humor the general atmosphere in the family.

Take Pride in Dual Earning

Although the reality of family life for many today means that both partners are in the paid labor force, still today some women feel that there are negative societal messages about them working instead of staying home with the children. Couples who successfully balance work and home life adopt

Time together, no matter how limited, helps parents to better balance work and family life. Fun time doesn't have to be an expensive family vacation—it can be something as simple as a day at the city pool together.

the attitude that dual earning is positive for every member of their family, and they refuse to accept negative comments from family or friends. Overall, these couples do not struggle with feelings of guilt, and they didn't fret over spending every spare minute with their children—if they had to sit down to pay the bills, they did so in lieu of playing with the kids. As one parent noted, "I think it's a big benefit for [my son] to have a working mom . . . he's going to grow up understanding that women and men share equally in what's going on, and he's growing up expecting that he's going to share what happens in [his house]."

Live Simply

A number of successful couples have learned to simplify their lives. For example, rather than allowing their children to be involved in as many activities as they wanted to, parents limit each child to one or two activities that they really enjoy doing. Limiting activities in this way helps to minimize the chaos of family living. Couples also note the importance of controlling their finances and living within their budgets as a way to simplify their lives. They also find creative time-saving strategies that make family life more efficient and less complicated. For example, one family helps their children line out their clothes for the entire week; this minimizes the "Where's my other Nike?" and "Where'd you put my belt?" last-minute disorder and confusion in the mornings.

Learn to Say "No"

Keeping a clear sense of priorities helps couples to make decisions that are in the best interest of their marriage, children, families, and careers. Successful couples don't allow the pace of their lives to dictate their schedules—their schedules dictate the pace. As one husband noted, "I view it as my choice. I have control over what I'm going to do. Rather than, 'This schedule is driving me crazy this week!' I remind myself, 'If it's crazy, then I need to make some other choices—I need to say no.'" Couples who balance family life and work well also note the importance of consistent and frequent communication so they can stay on top of their priorities, and to always keep the big picture in mind; this keeps them from getting off track by focusing on things that aren't important.

Value Time

Couples realize that their time together and time with their families is a valuable commodity and a resource to be spent with great care. They are protective of their family time and seldom allow others or other things to get in the way of the time they've carved out for each other. They carefully determine how their time will be best utilized. Couples also find ways to do things together, such as learning to play golf, so that when their kids are grown they have shared interests.

All too often, families struggle with work–family balance, and frequently these difficulties can begin to erode the couple's relationship. These adaptive strategies, individualized to each family's needs, can significantly help couples' abilities to become active participants in creating a successful balance of family and work. Time together, no matter how limited, helps parents to better balance work and family life. Fun time doesn't have to be an expensive family vacation–it can be something as simple as a day at the city pool together.

Summary

Today, balancing the demands of work, parenting, and family is a challenging—but necessary—task for a significant number of American families. In this chapter, we spent some time looking at the differences in work experiences among various racial and ethnic groups. And, although a number of trends were presented, it's important to have an understanding of these trends because they give us a real picture of what's happening in our economic lives today, what a lot of families are up against, and what their day-to-day struggles are. Given the interrelated nature of parenting and family life, it's easy to see how what goes on at work can significantly impact a family's well-being, functioning, and overall health.

Managing complex, multifaceted work/family roles is also a reality for many Americans today. There are a number of ways in which families can ease the stress and strain associated with work, such as keeping their families a priority, managing time more effectively, and carving out time for one another. But today it's just as important to have realistic expectations about trying to balance work, family, and parenting. There will be times when things won't get done around the house—the carpet will be in desperate need of vacuuming, children will be able to drive their Hot Wheels cars through the dust on the furniture and become excited about the "road" they created, and sometimes it will just be easier to put dirty dishes in the dishwasher with the clean ones, and wash them all—again. There will be times when parents fight and yell at one another because they're so overworked and overwhelmed, and just plain tired. That's the reality of balancing work and family. Much like a circus act where the performer is trying to keep a number of plates spinning in the air at the same time, sometimes we can't keep all the plates going. And certainly today, money constraints due to the economic crisis make matters worse.

Can combining work and family really work today? We learned a number of strategies that families who effectively balance the two employ. But above all, it's necessary to keep in mind that we can't possibly control everything. If families keep a sense of humor about the undone housework, if they're willing to revise plans and schedules as necessary to accommodate everyone's needs, and if they communicate often, they can minimize the stressors associated with work and family. Learning to let go of things that won't really matter in the long run is fairly easy to do. When confronted with work/family stressors, ask yourself: "Is this going to make a difference in 5 years?" If not, let it go and focus on the things that *will* make a difference a few years from now.

References

Allegretto., S. (2005, September 1). Basic family budgets: Working families' incomes often fail to meet living expenses around the U.S. *Economic Policy Institute Briefing Paper #165*. Retrieved October 5, 2005, from www.epi.org/content.cfm/bp165.

Amato, P. R., Johnson, D. R., Booth, A., & Rogers, A. (2003). Continuity and change in marital quality between 1980 and 2000. *Journal of Marriage and the Family, 65*(1), 1–22.

Arab American Institute. (2009). Arab American demographics. Retrieved February 1, 2009, from www.aai.org.

Artazcoz, L., Benach, J., Borrell, C., & Cortes, I. (2004). Unemployment and mental health: Understanding the interactions among gender, family roles, and social class. *American Journal of Public Health, 94*(1), 82–88.

Baca Zinn, M., Pok, A. Y. H. (2002). Tradition and transition in Mexican-origin families. In R. L. Taylor (Ed.), *Minority Families in the United States* (pp. 79–100). NJ: Prentice Hall.

Baird, L. S., & Beccia, P. J. (1980). The potential misuse of over-time. *Personnel Psychology, 33*, 557–565.

Barnett, R. C., & Rivers, C. (1996). *She works, he works: How two-income families are happy, healthy, and thriving*. Cambridge, MA: Harvard University Press.

Baxter, J., Hewitt, B., & Haynes, M. (2008). Life course transitions and housework: Marriage, parenthood, and time on housework. *Journal of Marriage and Family, 70*, 258–272.

Behnke, A. O., & MacDermid, S. M. (2004). Family well-being. *A Sloan Work and Family Encyclopedia* entry. Retrieved August 1, 2009, from http://wfnetwork.bc.edu/encyclopeida_entry.php?id=235.

Blair, S. L, & Lichter, D. (1991). Measuring the division of household labor: Gender segregation of housework among American couples. *Journal of Family Issues, 12,* 91–113.

Claxton, A., & Perry-Jenkins, M. (2008). No fun anymore: Leisure and marital quality across the transition to parenthood. *Journal of Marriage and Family, 70,* 28–43.

Coltrane, S. (2000). Research on household labor: Modeling and measuring the social embeddedness of routine family work. *Journal of Marriage and the Family, 62,* 1208–1233.

Congressional Research Service. (2007). *The cost of the Iraq, Afghanistan, and other Global War on Terror Operations since 9/11.* Washington, DC: Author.

Crouter, A. C., Bumpus, M. F., Head, M. R., & McHale, S. M. (2001). Implications of overwork and overload for the quality of men's family relationships. *Journal of Marriage and Family, 63*(2), 404–416.

Davis, K. K., Crouter, A. C., & McHale, S. M. (2006). Implications of shift work for parent–adolescent relationships in dual-earner families. *Family Relations, 55,* 450–460.

Defrain, J. (2000). *Creating a strong family: Qualities of strong families.* Lincoln: University of Nebraska Cooperative Extension, Institute of Agriculture and Natural Resources.

Dew, J. (2007). Two sides of the same coin?: The differing roles of assets and consumer debt in marriage. *Journal of Family and Economic Issues, 28,* 89–104.

Drummet, A. R., Coleman, M., & Cable, S. (2003). Military families under stress: Implications for family life education. *Family Relations, 52,* 279–287.

Dyk, P. H. (2004). Complexity of family life among the low-income and working poor: Introduction to the special issue. *Family Relations, 53*(2), 122–126.

Eyre, R., & Eyre, L. (2008 February, 29). *Balancing work and family.* Logan: Utah State University.

Furstenberg, F. F. (1974). Work experience and family life. In J. O'Toole (Ed.), *Work and the quality of life* (pp. 341–360). Cambridge: MIT Press.

Gottman, J. M. (1994). *What predicts divorce?: The relationship between marital process and marital outcomes.* Hillsdale, NJ: Erlbaum.

Gottman, J. M. (1999). *The marriage clinic: A scientifically based marital therapy.* New York: Norton.

Greenhaus, J. H., & Beutell, N. J. (1985). Sources of conflict between work and family roles. *Academy of Management Review, 10,* 76–88.

Grosswald, B. (2004). The effects of shift work on family satisfaction. *Families in Society, 85*(3), 413–423.

Haddoc, S. A., Zimmerman, T. S., Ziemba, S. J., & Current, L. R. (2001). Ten adaptive strategies for family and work balance: Advice from successful families. *Journal of Marital and Family Therapy, 27*(4), 445–458.

Hammer, L., & Thompson, C. (2003). Work–family role conflict. *A Sloan Work and Family Encyclopedia* entry. Retrieved August 10, 2004, from www.bc/edu/bc)org/avp/wfnetwork/rft/wfpedia/wfpWFRCent.html.

Hanisch, K. A. (1999). Job loss and unemployment research from 1994 to 1998: A review of and recommendations for research and intervention. *Journal of Vocational Behavior, 55,* 188–220.

Harris, V. W. (2008). *The triangular theory of balancing work and family.* Unpublished manuscript, Utah State University, Logan.

Hochschild, A. (1989). *The second shift.* New York: Avon.

Krieger, N. (2001). *Critical perspectives on racial and ethnic differences in health and later life.* National Academic Press, Committee on Population. Retrieved August 30, 2010, from www.darwin.nap.edu/books/0309092116.html.

Lazarovici, L. (2005). *When working women head to the polls, jobs and health care will top their lists.* Retrieved August 11, 2009, from http://www.aflcio.org/aboutus/thisistheaflcio/publications/magazine/0604_wwreport.cfm.

Lin, J., & Bernstein, J. (2008, October). *What we need to get by.* Economic Policy Institute Briefing Paper #224.

Loudoun, R. (2008). Balancing shiftwork and life outside work: Do 12-hour shifts make a difference? *Applied Ergonomics, 39,* 572–579.

Lowrey, C. (2009*). Parenting advice 101: Parents need more than a date night, they need adventure.* Retrieved January 28, 2009, from www.articlesbase.com/parenting-articles.

Monthly Labor Review. (2004, June). *A visual essay: Blacks, Asians, and Hispanics in the civilian labor force.* Retrieved October 11, 2008, from http://www.bis.gov/opub/mir/2004/06/ressum.pdf.

Papp, L. M., Cummings, E. M., & Goeke-Morey, M. C. (2009). For richer, for poorer: Money as a topic of marital conflict in the home. *Family Relations, 58,* 91–103.

Perry-Jenkins, M., Repetti, R. L., & Crouter, A.C. (2001). Work and family in the 1990s. In R. Milardo (Ed.), *Understanding families into the new millennium: A decade in review* (pp. 200–217). Lawrence, KS: NCFR and Alliance Communications Group.

Presser, H. B. (2003). *Working in a 24/7 economy: Challenges for American families.* New York: Russell Sage Foundation.

Roehling, P. V., & Moen, P. (2003). Dual-earner couples. In *Sloan work and family encyclopedia.* Retrieved August 10, 2004, from www.bc/edu/bc_org/avp/wfnetwork/rft/wfpedia/wfpDCEent.html.

Salary.com (2006). *What is mom's work worth?* Retrieved May 8, 2001 from: http://swz.salary.com/MomSalaryWizard/LayoutScripts/Mswl_NewSearch.aspx

Schlosser, E. (2001, Sept./Oct.). Making it work. *Mother Jones,* pp. 68–73.

Stevens, D. P., Kiger, G., & Riley, P. J. (2006). His, hers, or ours?: Work-to-family spillover, crossover, and family cohesion. *Social Science Journal, 43,* 425–436.

Survey of Army Families IV. (2001). Retrieved January 28, 2009, from www.armymwr.com/corporate/docs/planning/SAFIVExutiveSummary.pdf

Taylor, R. (2002). *Minority families in the United States: A multicultural perspective.* Upper Saddle River, NJ: Prentice Hall.

Taylor, R. L., Yellowbird, M., & Snipp, C. M. (2002). Native American families in the United States: Part IV. American Indian families. In R. Taylor, *Minority families in the United States: A multicultural perspective* (pp. 225–249). Upper Saddle River, NJ: Prentice Hall.

U.S. Bureau of Labor Statistics. (2005). Retrieved August 11, 2009, from http:www.census.gov/Press-Release/www/releases/archives/facts_for_features_special_editions/004109.html.

U.S. Bureau of Labor Statistics. (2008). *Highlights of women's earnings in 2007.* BLS Report 2008.

U.S. Census Bureau. (2007). *Income quintiles, 2007.* Retrieved August 26, 2008, from www.pubdb3.census/gov/macro/032007/hhinc/new05_000.htm.

U.S. Census Bureau (2008a). *Household income rises, poverty rate unchanged, number of uninsured down* (CB08-129). Retrieved July 27, 2009, from www.census.gov/Press-Release/www/releases/archives/income_wealth/012528.html.

U.S. Census Bureau (2008b). *State of the union, 2008: By the numbers.* Retrieved August 23, 2008, from www.reuters.com/article/pressRelease/idUS155591+29-Jan-2008+PRN20080129.html.

U.S. Department of Labor. (2007, March 21). *In dual-earner couples, family roles are changing in U.S.* Retrieved August 11, 2009, from http://www.america.gov/st/washfile-english/2007/March/20070321162913berehellek0.6708338.html.

Varcoe, K. P., Emper, N., & Lees, N. (2002). Working with military audiences to improve financial well-being. *JFCS, 94*(1), 33–34.

Voydanoff, P. (1983). Unemployment: Family, strategies for adaptation. In C. R. Figley & H. I. McCubbin (Eds.), *Stress and the family, II: Coping with catastrophe* (pp. 90–102). New York: Brunner/Mazel.

Chapter 9
Parenting in High-Risk Families

No one can predict what tomorrow or the months and years ahead will bring for any given family. The very nature of parenting and family living involves countless complexities and, along with it, inevitable change.

At this point in our study of contemporary parenting, we need to understand there are expected, or *normative,* changes that take place throughout the family life cycle. Some of these changes are considered "vulnerability points," such as getting married; starting a sexual relationship; having a baby; parenting a teenager; juggling dual careers; financial commitments and overcommitments; and caring for aging parents. *Non-normative* life events, or things we cannot predict or anticipate, or things that are not commonly experienced by most families, also bring much disruption to family living. These would include life events such as a child being diagnosed with cancer; unemployment; mothers fighting in combat; or a teenager becoming pregnant.

Numerous factors influence the degree of risk that might be involved in parenting for any particular family or any specific group of families. Risk factors may be related to health, medical, psychological, structural, economic, developmental, or social aspects of family life, or to any combination of these. It is probably accurate to say that some risks exist in every family situation, but many families are able to minimize the risk factors by a network of support systems. Sadly, others are unable to do so with any degree of success.

Certain groups of families attempt to function in relatively high-risk situations and are in greater need of support services than other families. In Chapter 3, we discussed what factors put teenage parents and their children at risk. Here, we examine two more high-risk parenting family types: abusive or neglectful parents and homeless parents. Abusive parents represent a serious risk situation for children and their parents—a risk that is often deadly, at least for the children involved. Homeless parents with children are growing in number, and these families are at risk economically, socially, psychologically, and educationally. These types of families have unique needs and require special kinds of support and intervention services.

Each year in the United States, over 3 million children witness their mothers being abused by her intimate partner.

THE CRISIS OF FAMILY VIOLENCE

Divorce. Poverty. Suicide. Illness. Sexual violence. Mental illness. Family separation because of war. Bankruptcy. Foreclosure. Job loss. Families today are experiencing a wide variety of changes, transitions, and challenges, and are often called upon to confront simultaneous challenges. While entire chapters could be written dealing with each of these family crises, an increasingly widespread social problem in the United States demands our attention: family violence. Today in the United States alone, over 25,000 women will find refuge in a domestic violence shelter as the result of having been severely abused by their male intimate partner; slightly over 19,000 children will have witnessed the violence taking place in their homes (National Network to End Domestic Violence, 2007).

In the following section, we take a close look at the number of family members who were battered in the United States over a 5-year period. It is important to keep in mind that behind the numbers are countless lives that are, undeniably, forever changed because of the violence committed against them. We begin by considering the following experience of a college student (Welch, 2004).

Melanie is a 20-year-old university sophomore. She carries a pretty full class load, she juggles her academic load with her job responsibilities, and she tries to find time to be with her fiancé, friends, and family. She dreads finals week. But Melanie lives with past childhood experiences that make her day-to-day college life tougher to handle than for many students. From the age of 10, her stepfather repeatedly sexually assaulted her. She recalls:

> [W]hen I was in fourth grade, my step-dad one morning before work and after my mom had already left for work sexually molested me at least 30 or 40 times [in my seventh-grade year] . . . it was at least once or twice a week during that time period . . . it was always after my mom went to bed . . . he came into my room and then . . .
>
> . . . Flashbacks still haunt me . . . where I wake up in the middle of the night, curled up in a ball because I'm scared and I can still, after all these years, feel him on my skin . . . it's like, you wake up and you know he's in the room with you. . . . Even though I'm in college now, there are some nights I can't sleep, and I'm still absolutely terrified of someone who is dead.
>
> I'm engaged and my wedding is less than a month away. [Aside from the normal fears of getting married] I also have to deal with, if Danny holds me a certain way, or touches me a certain way, I remember something that Alan did to me . . . it's so unfair that Alan stole that part away from Danny, that there are some things that Danny can't do with me because Alan did them to me. I am absolutely terrified because of what happened to me when I was 10 and then when I was 14. Things like this stay with you . . .

The effects are long-lasting.

Domestic Violence

Violence that takes place in the home is a prevalent, multifaceted social ailment in the United States. Contributing to these assaults are individual factors, such as family of origin patterns, psychopathology, mental illness, and genetic causes; community factors, such as poverty, educational levels, absent or inaccessible family services; and cultural factors, such as media influences.

Domestic violence, or **family violence**, is violence perpetrated against family members by an offender who is related to the victim either biologically or legally, such as by marriage or through adoption (U.S. Department of Justice, 2009). Although most people think of family violence as something that takes place between intimate partners and children, the people who carry out family violence—the **batterers**—include current or former spouses, parents or adoptive parents, legal guardians or foster parents, biological or adopted children, current or former stepchildren, a sibling, grandchildren, grandparents, in-laws, or other relatives, such as aunts, uncles, nephews, and nieces.

Domestic violence is an umbrella term that encompasses any behavior designed to intentionally inflict emotional, sexual, or physical harm. Acts of domestic or family violence may result in harming children, intimate partners (spouse, cohabiting partner, gay or lesbian partner), and/or elderly family members. There are three broad categories of domestic violence:

- *Physical violence* includes such acts as hitting, punching, pushing, slapping, biting, or throwing something at the victim.

- *Emotional violence* includes such acts as controlling the amount of contact a family member has with family and friends, name-calling, constant criticism, threats to leave the partner or throw them out, displays of intense jealousy/accusations that one is being unfaithful, controlling the spending and distribution of money, excessive rule-making, and threats of physical or sexual harm.
- *Sexual violence* includes marital rape (unwanted, forcible sex by a person's marital partner), battering rape (rape along with other acts of physical violence), and forced sexual acts (such as forced oral or anal sex).

Demographers measure family violence in two ways: through survey interviews with the victims, and through statistics gathered by police.

The Victims

While no one is immune from abuse, there are some specific factors that place some at greater risk for experiencing violence than others; for example, women who have less education (especially women who do not attend college), come from lower socioeconomic status, or who are single parents or young teenage parents are more likely to be victims of violence. Also, women who have witnessed a parent being battered are at higher risk of being victims themselves. Generally, women who have low self-esteem, feel a sense of inferiority, are passive, or believe that they are responsible for the batterer's actions are more likely to be abused. When violence is perpetrated against a partner it is referred to as **intimate partner violence (IPV)**.

No gender or racial/ethnic group is immune from family violence, as the data in Figure 9.1 illustrate. While women are victimized more frequently than men, about 15 percent of all acts of IPV are perpetrated against men by women (National Coalition Against Domestic Violence, 2008). In addition, intimate partner violence and family violence cross every socioeconomic and educational level, and every family type including

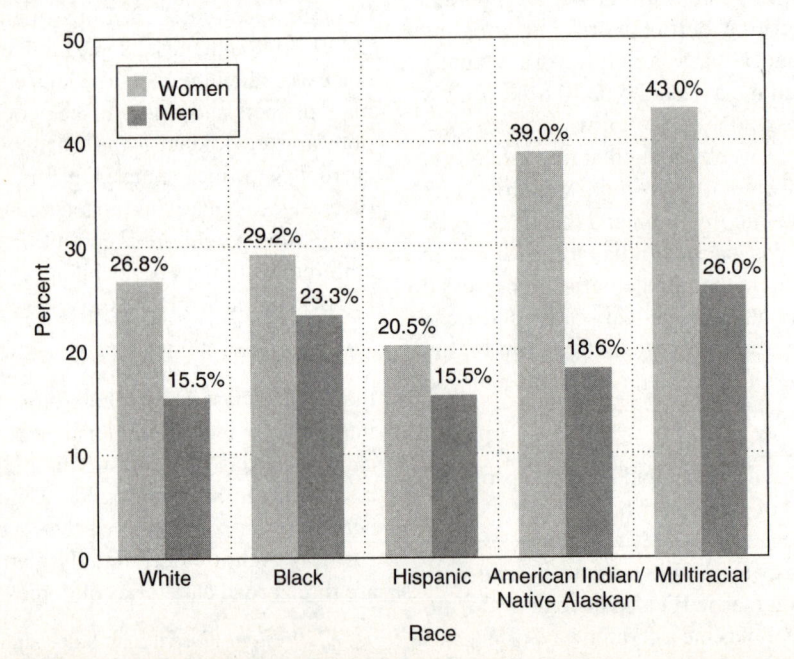

Race	Women	Men
White	26.8%	15.5%
Black	29.2%	23.3%
Hispanic	20.5%	15.5%
American Indian/Native Alaskan	39.0%	18.6%
Multiracial	43.0%	26.0%

FIGURE 9.1 Domestic partner violence by race/ethnicity and gender.
No one is immune from family violence.

Source: Welch, *Family Life Now*, 2e. (2010). Boston: Allyn & Bacon. p. 508. Based on data from Centers for Disease Control and Prevention. (2009, February 8).

married, single-parent, gay, straight, and cohabiting families. For example, each year there are over 6,500 incidents of intimate partner violence among gays, lesbians, bisexuals, and transgender people (Catalan, 2004). In America, one in four women and one in nine men suffers physical and/or emotional violence at the hands of an intimate partner (Centers for Disease Control and Prevention, 2008). Females who are 20 to 24 years of age are at the greatest risk of intimate partner violence (U.S. Department of Justice, 2009); however, as shown in Figure 9.2, women in rural areas seek the services of domestic violence shelters more than those from suburban or urban areas do.

The statistics regarding violence perpetrated at the hands of an intimate partner or a family member are staggering (Durose et al., 2005; National Coalition Against Domestic Violence, 2008; U.S. Department of Justice, 2009):

- *Domestic Violence:* Marital rape accounts for nearly one-fourth of all rapes, and affects over 75,000 women each year; 22 percent of all nonfatal violent victimizations are IPV acts against females age 12 or older; 8 percent of all pregnant women in the United States are subjected to physical violence during their pregnancy; and each year between 3 and 10 million children witness some form of violence in their homes.
- *Dating Violence/Teen Violence:* One in four teen girls in a relationship report being pressured into performing oral sex or having sex against their wishes, and one in five teens report having been hit, slapped, or pushed by a partner.
- *Domestic Murders:* On average, every day in the United States, four women are killed by their intimate partners, and IPV is the leading cause of death among pregnant women in the United States. Intimate partners are responsible for 30 percent of all female homicides each year in the United States, and 5 percent of all male homicides.
- *Violence Against Children:* Physical abuse is the leading cause of death in infants under 4 years of age. A child is abused every 35 seconds in the United States, and each year

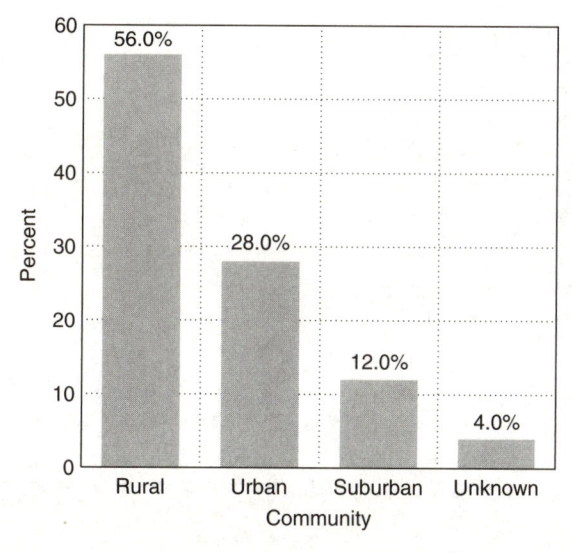

FIGURE 9.2 Primary populations served by domestic violence shelters.
Across the United States, local programs provide support to victims in domestic violence in a variety of communities.
Source: Based on data from National Network to End Domestic Violence (2007).

3 million children experience some type of maltreatment or abuse by a parent/caregiver; sadly, these numbers are believed to be vastly underreported.

Indeed, these trends are alarming. But *why* do people batter? What are the characteristics of those who abuse their family members? We examine these questions in the following section.

PARENTS WHO ABUSE THEIR CHILDREN

The maltreatment or abuse of children by their parents is not a new phenomenon. For example, today many of us would consider allowing or requiring young children to work for long hours in factories, and even "treating children as miniature adults" as child abuse. Yet in previous years these were common practices. Only since the 1960s has child abuse been of such public concern that reporting statutes have been enacted. Currently, all 50 states and the District of Columbia have passed statutory provisions for mandatory reporting of nonaccidental injury or neglect of children (Besharov & Laumann, 1996). Child maltreatment came into public focus because of both the seriousness of the acts and the great extent of the problem, and concern for abused and neglected children has never been more intense in the United States than it is today.

The national Child Abuse Prevention and Treatment Act defines child abuse and neglect as "the physical or mental injury, sexual abuse, negligent treatment, or maltreatment of a child under the age of eighteen by a person who is responsible for the child's welfare under the circumstances which indicate that the child's health or welfare is harmed or threatened thereby" (U.S. Department of Health, Education, and Welfare, 1975, p. 3). It's clear that the spectrum of maltreatment of children has a wide range, as Figure 9.3 illustrates. Both acts of commission and acts of omission are included, so that physical abuse, sexual abuse, and emotional abuse, as well as neglect, are considered maltreatment. Abuse may appear as emotional or nutritional deprivation without

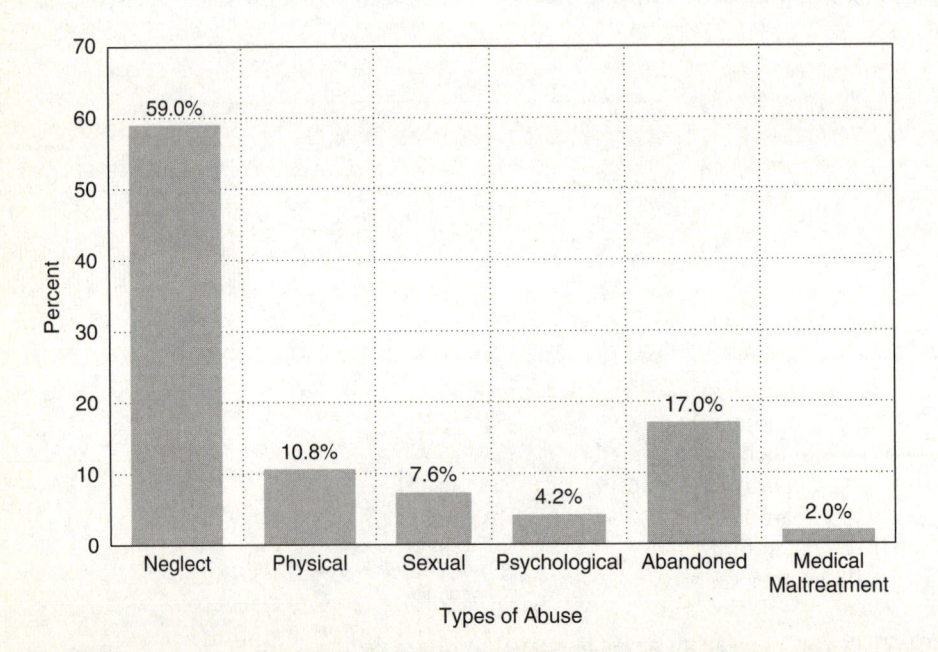

FIGURE 9.3 Types of child abuse and neglect by percent of total abuse.
Source: Based on data from U.S. Department of Health and Human Services (2009).

In the United States, a child is abused or neglected about every 35 seconds by a family member.

any evident physical signs—acts of *omission* (neglect)—or abuse may be incipient or insidious maltreatment, mild deprivation with verbal abuse, and/or premeditated trauma with permanent injury or death—acts of *commission*.

Types of Child Abuse and Neglect

Abuse is an active, hostile, deliberate, and aggressive act carried out by an adult. *Child neglect,* on the other hand, is a more passive type of treatment characterized by a lack of interest in the welfare of the child. Categorizing the various types of abuse is important because it allows those who work with children to more fully understand the scope of the problem. But from the child's standpoint, the classification doesn't make any difference: It is all maltreatment. It is all painful.

NEGLECT Neglect is the omission of the parent(s) to provide for normal growth and development of children, and it has three subcategories: physical neglect, educational neglect, and emotional neglect. *Physical neglect* includes refusal to provide or delay in providing needed healthcare; abandonment; expulsion of the child from the home and other custody issues; inadequate supervision; and other physical neglect, such as inadequate nutrition, clothing, hygiene, and shelter. Physically neglected children frequently are unclean, inappropriately dressed (such as having shoes that are too big or too small), underweight, and in need of medical attention.

Educational neglect includes failure to enroll a child in school, failure to require a child to attend school, and failure to attend to special-education needs. *Emotional neglect* includes inadequate nurturance, domestic violence in the child's presence, permitting substance abuse by the child, and refusal to obtain or delay in obtaining needed psychological care for the child (Cates, Markell, & Bettenhausen, 1995; Martin & Walters, 1992).

PHYSICAL ABUSE Physical abuse is the most often reported. In this case, the parent (or caregiver) inflicts physical injury on the child through beating, whipping, branding, scalding, shaking, or even torture. Common weapons are hairbrushes, belts, sticks, light cords, or whatever is at hand. Frequently cigarette burns or burns caused by scalding water or open flames are inflicted. Gouges in the skin caused by belt buckles, sticks, or other implements are common evidences of physical abuse, as are welts, lesions, and severe bruises. X-rays frequently reveal bone scars where previously unattended breaks have occurred (Cates et al., 1995; Gillmer, 1992).

CHILD SEXUAL ABUSE Much like the sexual abuse of an adult, child sexual abuse involves unwanted sexual contact. **Child sexual abuse (CSA)** is any sexual activity that a child cannot consent to (American Academy of Pediatrics, 2010). In cases of child sexual abuse, the sexual contact is often achieved through force, trickery, or bribery and involves an imbalance in age, size, power, and knowledge. Sexual contact can include fondling of the breasts, buttocks, or genitals; vaginal, anal, or oral intercourse; exhibitionism; forced masturbation or forced viewing of masturbation; obscene gestures or comments; prostitution; or any other sexual activity that is harmful to the child's mental, emotional, or physical welfare (Finkelhor, Ormrod, & Turner, 2009). When these forms of abuse are inflicted on a child by a relative such as a parent, grandparent, uncle, aunt, sister or brother, it is considered **incest**.

Children are greatly affected both physically and emotionally by sexual assault and abuse. Unfortunately, it is not easy to recognize an abused child. Oftentimes children are afraid to tell anyone because they fear they may be blamed, or because the abuser is someone whom they love very much. Also, it often goes unreported or overlooked for long periods of time due to the child's inability to understand what is happening to him or her. CSA is often overlooked because of an adult's inability to notice the signs of abuse or unwillingness, or to admit that the abuse took place (American Academy of Pediatrics, 2010). Table 9.1 presents the physical and emotional signs that a child has been abused.

EMOTIONAL ABUSE When the parent (or adult caregiver) inflicts damage on the child through behaviors other than physical or sexual, this is referred to as **emotional abuse**. These behaviors include systematically ignoring the child;

TABLE 9.1 Signs and symptoms of child sexual abuse.

PHYSICAL	BEHAVIORAL
EMOTIONAL ABUSE AND NEGLECT	
Height and weight significantly below age level	Begging or stealing food
Inappropriate clothing for weather	Constant fatigue
Poor hygiene, lice, body odor, scaly skin	Poor school attendance
Unsupervised, abandoned child	Chronic hunger
Lack of safe and sanitary shelter	Dull, apathetic appearance
Unattended medical or dental needs	Running away from home
Developmental lags	Child reports that no one cares or looks after him
Habit disorders	Sudden onset of behavioral extremes (conduct problems)
Depression	
PHYSICAL ABUSE	
Frequent injuries such as cuts, bruises, or burns	Poor school attendance
Wearing long sleeves in warm weather	Refusing to change clothes for physical education
Pain despite lack of evident injury	Finding reasons to stay at school and not go home
Inability to perform fine motor skills because of injured hands	Frequent complaints of harsh treatments by parents
Difficulty walking or sitting	Fear of adults
SEXUAL ABUSE	
Bedwetting or soiling	Excessive fears, clinging
Stained or bloody underclothing	Unusual, sophisticated sexual behavior/knowledge
Blood or purulent discharge from genital or anal area	Poor school attendance
Difficulty walking or sitting	Finding reasons to stay at school instead of going home

continually shaming, ridiculing, teasing, or shouting at the child; and isolating or scapegoating the child. Emotional neglect is the consistent failure of a parent or caregiver to provide a child with appropriate support, attention, or affection (Cates et al., 1995; Gillmer, 1992).

Abuse is rarely a single event but, rather, a pattern of behavior that is repeated over time. In addition, a specific type of abuse does not occur in isolation. Psychological maltreatment occurs in conjunction with physical abuse, physical neglect, and sexual abuse. There is growing consensus that psychological maltreatment is at the core of negative developmental outcomes for children. Not only does psychological maltreatment co-occur with other types of abuse, but also many of the negative short- and long-term effects of maltreatment are psychological in nature (Claussen & Crittenden, 1991).

Who Batters or Abuses?

Who is more likely to sexually abuse children? Risk factors include adult mental health issues or depression, a parental history of childhood abuse, and intimate partner violence (American Academy of Pediatrics, 2010).

As the statistics reveal, men are more likely to abuse a family member than are women. Those who abuse their partners or their children share some common characteristics; for example, most batterers have low self-esteem and tend to blame everyone else for their behavior. They are also typically extremely jealous and often use sex as their weapon of aggression and ultimate instrument of control. While violence is the way they express their anger or frustration, they underestimate or even deny that their behaviors are "really that violent" or harmful. Batterers have the need to control and dominate and they become master manipulators—they can manipulate their partner's weaknesses and their strengths.

There is a common misconception that family violence results from an argument that "got out of hand," then escalated into physical blows. Most often, this is not the case. Many abused women note that the violence appeared to have no trigger or cause, and appeared to come out of the blue. Another common misconception is that alcohol use or substance abuse is almost always associated with acts of family violence. In the 5.3 million cases of family violence in a 5-year period in the United States, 52.2 percent of the victims indicated that there was no drug or alcohol use by the family offender (Durose et al., 2005). While on the surface, domestic violence appears to be acts of physical, emotional, or sexual aggression against a victim, the central issues in family violence are not the acts of aggression at all. Rather, the central issues of domestic violence are *control and domination*—and are commonly perpetuated by the strongest against the weakest (McGoldrick, Broken Nose, & Potenza, 1999).

Family Characteristics

Why do parents abuse their children? The answer to this question is not simple. Early research sought to identify the personality characteristics of abusive parents, the social/environmental factors, the child characteristics, and the parent–child interaction patterns in an attempt to identify the risk factors of abuse. Recent theories emphasize abuse as complex and multidetermined. Interactions between environmental, interpersonal, parental, and child factors are the focus of recent research. As the knowledge of child maltreatment has grown, it has become clear that attempting to understand maltreatment as a single behavior is not useful. Numerous studies have indicated that multiple transactions among environmental forces, parental characteristics, and child characteristics make joint contributions to maladaptive parenting practices and child maltreatment. However, a few common characteristics of parents who have been found in numerous studies to inflict physical abuse, neglect, or sexual abuse can be found in Table 9.2.

One body of research provided a helpful discussion of family factors associated with child abuse and neglect from an ecological, or environmental, perspective (Baumrind, 1994).

TABLE 9.2 Characteristics of parents who abuse children.

PHYSICAL ABUSE

Intrapsychic disorders such as marital discord, drinking problems, mental illness	Low family interaction—emphasis on negative aspects
Family discord, poor spousal relationships	Intolerance
Modeling of aggressive behavior as preferred mode of interaction	Aversive behavior (mothers)
History of family violence	Multiple life stresses; economic problems
Low self-esteem, low family satisfaction (mothers)	Likelihood of emotional problems
Little understanding of child's needs	Likelihood of having been abused themselves as children

NEGLECT

Social disorganization	Withdrawal from environment (mothers)
Low family interaction; emphasis on negative aspects	Intellectual inadequacies
	Larger families
Environmental factors and parental inadequacies such as unemployment, low income, poor housing, separation, and divorce	Resistance to rehabilitation
	Inability to access support system
	Poor parenting skills
Psychic disorders—high stress, anxiety, depression	

SEXUAL ABUSE

Family disruption, psychopathology	Likelihood of alcohol and substance abuse
Perpetrators commonly males who live with and/or are related to child (stepfathers living in home five times more likely to abuse stepdaughters than biological fathers)	Intellectual inadequacies
	Parental illness
	Likelihood of mother having been sexually abused
History of parent-child problems	

The primary caregiving environment—the family—is embedded within many contexts within society that affect family processes. Economic stress is the most subtly harmful or destructive condition that contributes to the abuse of children: Poor families are more likely than more affluent families to be reported for abuse and neglect. The highest incidence of child neglect and the most severe physical injuries have been found in families living in the most extreme poverty. Thus, from an environmental perspective, not only the child but also the perpetrators are viewed to be victimized by poverty and prejudice. Other economic conditions, including unstable work and unemployment, are related to parents' emotional states and behaviors through their perceptions of economic pressure and limited resources to cope with pressure. Economic stress generates depression and demoralization, which in turn results in marital conflict and poor parenting. Abusive parents under economic stress are more likely to have the following attitudes and negative parenting techniques (Baumrind, 1994):

- Power-assertive and harsh discipline
- Little support, responsiveness, and affection
- Lack of involvement
- Rating their children as aggressive and hyperactive

There are environmental factors that buffer the negative effects of poverty. These include commitment, family support, and cohesive neighborhoods.

A widespread perception is that mothers primarily are responsible for child neglect, and trends support this—the highest incidence of neglect has been confirmed in low-income, marginalized, and mother-headed families. Unfortunately, focus on *who* abuses their children has been at the expense of an understanding of, and efforts to change, the social and economic contexts in which child neglect occurs. Therefore, child-welfare workers and scholars continue to dwell on the personal responsibility of parents, failing to address the social and economic factors related to child neglect (Swift, 1995).

Community Characteristics and Lack of Social Support

Child maltreatment is as much a function of community characteristics as of family characteristics (Coulton, Korbin, Su, & Chow, 1995). As we have seen so far, the most significant community indicators of abuse are poverty and unemployment. Other community variables include signs of lack of investment in communities, such as vacant housing, the childcare burden, including the high ratio of children to adults, and violent crime, drug trafficking, juvenile delinquency, and teen childbearing.

One study examined four primary factors of social support in relation to physical abuse of children by mothers: direct aid provided for caretaking; support for emotional needs and individual growth of the caretaker; education in and feedback about parenting efforts; and structural aspects of the support network (Moncher, 1995). The researcher concluded that the availability of concrete emotional support and lack of criticism from significant others were important components in the relationship between social isolation and abuse risk.

There is no question that abuse is harmful to children's well-being and health. The short- and long-term effects of abuse on children vary, depending on a number of factors: the specific type of abuse, the length and degree of abuse, and various mediating variables.

THE EFFECTS OF ABUSE ON CHILDREN

There is no one-size-fits-all effect or effects of child abuse on children because we cannot possibly account for all of the different individual and family factors that contribute to the violence. One researcher, however, noted that abused and neglected children often react to everyday events in ways that make no sense to casual observers (Gootman, 1996). For example, some become hyperactive when they have flashbacks to their trauma, while others regress academically when a theme emerges that is reminiscent of their trauma or holds intense personal meaning for them. They may flit from one activity to another or try to disrupt the classroom. Their hyperactivity may represent attempts to keep their minds busy so that frightening thoughts and images do not intrude.

Abuse is unpredictable—children never know what will trigger their parent or caregiver's aggression. Because of this, some child victims become hypervigilant, fearful, suspicious, and mistrustful—always on the lookout for potential dangers. They feel they must remain on guard so that feelings of helplessness and panic do not occur. Some abused children daydream frequently, becoming trancelike and appearing "spacey" and forgetful. Some read and do not seem to be processing what they are reading. Many dissociate or hypnotize themselves, separating their minds from their bodies to escape overwhelming thoughts, emotions, and sensations experienced during abuse. Children who are closely guarding family secrets also may exhibit severe learning problems.

Because of the behaviors abused children exhibit in school, many are mistakenly labeled learning disabled (LD), as having a behavioral disorder (BD), or as having attention-deficit/hyperactivity disorder (ADHD). The practices associated with managing and teaching children so labeled can be extremely detrimental to the treatment of abused children. Finding the source of the abused child's dysfunction often is blocked, and abused children are not provided with the compassion and skills they need to overcome the effects of maltreatment (Gootman, 1996).

The Effects of Physical Abuse and Neglect

Children may carry the scars of physical abuse forever, with the psychological scars being even more debilitating than the physical ones (Martin & Elmer, 1992). Numerous studies indicate that physically abused and neglected children suffer from a complex set of psychological, interpersonal, social, and intellectual deficits. The effects are both short and long term. Among these are problems reflecting the abused person's inability to deal in an effective way with feelings. These include a basic mistrust of self and others, followed by an inability to establish meaningful interpersonal relationships, ingrained feelings of low self-worth, and a sense of helplessness. Thus, it can be expected that such psychological impairment could create long-term difficulties in the more concrete tasks of living, such as obtaining and keeping a job, maintaining adult relationships, and successfully rearing children (Martin & Elmer, 1992).

Other research examined the differences in the expression of shame and pride in maltreated and nonmaltreated preschool children by presenting them with easy and difficult tasks in which their emotional responses could be observed (Alessandri & Lewis 1996). Failure on easy tasks produced more shame than failure on difficult tasks, and similarly, success with more difficult tasks produced more pride than success with easy tasks; maltreated girls exhibited more shame than abused boys and nonabused girls, and boys showed more pride than girls. In fact, girls showed more shame than both abused and nonabused boys. Overall, abused boys showed less emotional expression than both nonabused boys and both groups of girls. This study helps to show us that there are gender differences in the effects of abuse. This is important to understand because it helps those who work with children better identify those children who have possibly been victimized by family violence.

To better understand the long-term effects of physical abuse or neglect, other researchers studied a group of adult individuals who had been abused as children (Martin & Elmer, 1992). Not surprisingly, they found a range of variability of adaptation. For example, the adults had many deficits, especially in the economic sphere. Furthermore, some of the subjects showed evidence of cognitive delays, thought to be due to central nervous system damage suffered many years before; there were also a high proportion who had physical and cosmetic disfigurements. Severe emotional difficulties showed up in a variety of ways, such as through alcohol abuse. Although there was little incidence of aggressiveness, there were many signs of suspicion and resentment. Most, however, were more satisfied with their present lives than with their childhood experiences.

Of course, there are many factors that make some children more resilient to the effects of abuse than others. For example, one study noted that the effects of maltreatment on psychological functioning may be mediated by several important interactive variables, such as the overall quality of the parent–child relationship and the general socioeconomic condition of the family (Graziano & Mills, 1992). Mediating factors also include the type, duration, and severity of maltreatment; the child's developmental stage at the time maltreatment occurs; the completeness and soundness of the child's earlier development; and the degree to which development is disrupted by the maltreatment. Thus, an older child with a stable and healthy early development might suffer fewer and/or less severe psychopathological effects of abuse than a younger child with a tenuous developmental history, even if the abuse is the same.

The Effects of Child Sexual Abuse

The effects of CSA are often long term. Later on, those who are sexually victimized may turn to alcohol and drugs as coping mechanisms, and a sexually abused child/adolescent may run away or abuse others. As an adult, CSA survivors sometimes develop sexual and relationship difficulties, depression, or suicidal behaviors (Child Welfare Information Gateway, 2009). The younger the child at the age of abuse, the longer the CSA continues, and the closer the child's relationship with his or her abuser, the more significant the long-term emotional damage will be.

A number of studies give us insight into the potential lasting effects of CSA. These include:

- Clinical observations of sexually abused children indicate a variety of behavioral and emotional problems, including depression, guilt, learning difficulties, sexual promiscuity, runaway behavior, somatic complaints, sudden changes in behavior, phobias, nightmares, compulsive rituals, self-destructive behavior, or suicidal behavior (Banyard & Williams, 1996).
- They may display concentration problems; aggression; withdrawal; a characteristic personality style of being too nice, pleasant, or anxious to please; antisocial behavior; nervousness and anxiety; behavioral regression; self-esteem and body-image problems; fear; and symptoms of posttraumatic stress (Banyard & Williams, 1996).
- The majority of adults sexually abused as children report sexual problems in adulthood: frigidity, confusion about sexual orientation, promiscuity, decreased sex drive, sexual dissatisfaction, and other sexual disturbances (Beitchman, Zucker, Hood, DaCosta, & Akman, 1992).
- The highest rate of sexual disturbances has been found in victims of father–daughter incest, or abuse involving penetration. Abuse by stepfathers also is very traumatic. Abuse by a parent involves greater betrayal and loss of trust than abuse by others. Parental sexual abuse also is likely to reflect a significant level of family disturbance with little emotional support of the child and is likely to occur over a longer period of time and with greater frequency than abuse by others (Beitchman et al., 1992).

Helping a child heal from sexual abuse can be a difficult task, especially for nonabusing parents. They are often so overcome by feelings of shock, anger, sadness, and guilt that they are unable to be a stable source of support for their child (American Academy of Pediatrics, 2010). Organizations such as Safe Harbor, which serves more than 350,000 victims of violence each year, offer families individual and group counseling. Although the emotional scars are never fully removed or recovered from, counselors help to reduce some of the impact of the CSA. If a parent, caregiver, teacher, youth group leader, family friend, or community member suspects that a child has been sexually abused, they should immediately contact their local child protective agency or a pediatrician. Doctors, healthcare providers, and social services can help coordinate a treatment plan that includes medical treatment for physical injuries as well as counseling that addresses behavioral and emotional consequences.

The Effects of Family Abuse

The belief that abused children become abusive parents has been widespread. In fact, Baumrind (1994) stated that the most important predictor of maltreatment by a parent is prior abuse of the parent. The frequent explanation of intergenerational transmission of maltreatment comes from attachment theory: The child who is abused creates, at an early age, a model that best fits the reality that she experiences, and that model is resistant to other experiences that occur as she gets older—even positive ones. However, some researchers proposed that unqualified acceptance of this hypothesis is unfounded (Kaufman & Zigler, 1987). They reported that mediating factors affect the rate of intergenerational transmission of abuse. Some studies indicate that environmental factors (poverty, stress, and isolation), family structure, available social supports, and feelings about their abuse as children are related to the intergenerational transmission of abuse. Those who are poor, are isolated, and have fewer social supports are more likely to repeat the abuse with their children. Nonrepeaters more often reported a supportive relationship with one parent when growing up, had greater awareness of their history of being abused and vowed not to repeat the pattern, and had fewer current stressful life events. Those who are able to break the cycle of abuse are significantly more likely to have received emotional support from a nonabusive adult during childhood; to have participated in therapy during some period in their lives; and to have a nonabusive, stable, emotionally supportive, and satisfying relationship with a mate.

The child-abuse and -protection laws in all 50 states require certain professionals to report known and suspected incidents of child abuse and neglect. Included are teachers, childcare workers, doctors, nurses, social workers, and anyone who renders services to children under 18 years of age. These laws are aimed at protecting children and are not meant to punish those who neglect or abuse them but to rehabilitate them.

Reporting Abuse

To ensure the protection of children, reporters do not have to be certain that the child is abused or neglected; rather, a person must only have "cause to believe" or to "reasonably suspect" that abuse or neglect is occurring. The use of these terms affords legal protection to those who do report suspected cases. Reporters are immune from civil or criminal liability as long as the report is made in good faith.

Teachers are in a particularly strategic position to detect child abuse (Cates et al., 1995). Because children are required to attend school, teachers and other educators are faced with the responsibility of maintaining a protective and vigilant posture in relation to students' well-being. Since children will not report abuse directly, teachers need to be aware of specific behavioral and physical indicators that may indicate that abuse has occurred. A teacher who is equipped with knowledge of the symptoms of abuse and neglect and the characteristics of the child and family will be better able to determine whether an at-risk child is a victim of abuse. Teachers should make note of consistent behaviors or physical evidence, being aware that one incident may not be evidence of abuse.

Reports of suspected abuse and neglect should be made to the local departments of human services or to the police. It is the local child protection services division that ultimately receives and investigates reported cases. Individuals who work with children should make themselves aware of the symptoms of abuse so that they have a reasonable basis for reporting it.

Few people fail to report because they do not care about an endangered child. Instead, they may be unaware of the danger the child faces or of the protective procedures that are available (Besharov & Laumann, 1996). Others are not sure what constitutes abuse and neglect, do not know how or to whom to make a report, are reluctant to get involved for fear of prosecution by the child's parents, and lack confidence that a report will ultimately do any good.

Support for Abusive Parents

Each reported case is investigated by child welfare agencies, and decisions are made concerning the most appropriate way to assist the family. Since some abusive parents can be rehabilitated, it is important that a plan for this rehabilitation be developed as soon as possible. Some parents seek help on their own. Most organized services have been established to help the child and family after the abuse pattern has been established and the parent has been reported to the authorities. These services include supportive, supplementary, substitutive, and protective approaches. Most programs have focused on rehabilitating parents; few have been aimed at the abused child (Graziano & Mills, 1992).

In discussing strategies for rehabilitating neglectful parents, treatment programs must provide a wide array of intervention services that include hands-on assistance, as well as parent-skills development and social support (Martin & Walters, 1992). Home-health visitors have been found to be effective in providing services to prevent child neglect. Tangible aid in the areas of housing, healthcare, financial management, homemaking skills, nutrition, and transportation is also effective. Assisting the family in identifying and utilizing social support is important. The provision of parent education is also a clear need. Mental-health services for those parents suffering from depression and other problems must be provided.

Research suggests that the length of treatment should differ from family to family and that the outcomes of treatment will vary for families with different problems and patterns of change. Some families may not benefit from intervention and others may not need it. Some families may do well in one treatment program for a short length of time, whereas other families may require longer-term treatment in a different type of intervention program. In general, positive change in family functioning seems difficult to achieve and even harder to maintain.

Early interventions support families during the initial phases of the parent–child relationship, a period when families frequently face both their highest risk for physical abuse and/or neglect and their greatest opportunities for establishing lasting positive parent–child interaction patterns. Most early-intervention programs contain the following core principles: early identification and/or screening of families referred through a universalistic service system; initiation of supportive services during pregnancy or shortly after birth; voluntary participation; in-home service provision; case-management support; and provision of parenting education and guidance (Guterman, 1997).

Much more research needs to be done regarding programs for children victimized by all kinds of abuse. Clearly, the entire family must be involved if rehabilitation programs are to succeed.

We now turn our attention to one of the most visible and persistent social problems in the United States: homelessness. With the economic downturn that began in the United States in 2009, the number and diversity of homeless people continues to grow.

HOMELESS FAMILIES

Debate has occurred over how to define homelessness. Typically, **homelessness** refers to persons living in areas not designated as habitats (Dail, 1990). The United States Department of Housing and Urban Development (HUD) considers persons to be homeless if their nighttime residence is in public or private emergency shelters; in the streets, parks, subways, bus terminals, railroad stations, airports; under bridges or aqueducts; in abandoned buildings without utilities; in cars or trucks; or in any other public or private space that is not designated a shelter (Berger & Trembley, 1989). Sometimes those who are living temporarily in hotel rooms, as well as those residing in social- and health-service facilities without a permanent address, are defined as homeless. Although circumstances that lead to homelessness vary, it occurs when people are unable to acquire and/or maintain affordable housing.

Who Are the Homeless? What the Numbers Say

On any given night in the United States, nearly 700,000 people—roughly 22 out of every 10,000—are homeless (National Alliance to End Homelessness, 2010). Of these

- 37 percent are people in families
- 63 percent are individuals
- 20 percent of homeless individuals are veterans

The homeless population is quite diverse and includes homeless men, homeless women (with or without children), runaway youth, families, individuals who are employed, and the chronically mentally ill. Domestic violence is the precipitating factor for roughly one-half of homeless women seeking shelter (Steinbock, 1995). They are usually socially isolated and alienated from social-support systems, including the extended family. Others are victims of adverse economic conditions that may have been triggered by divorce, unemployment, or illness. And although it's still too early to determine the effects of the 2009 U.S. economic recession, experts estimate that approximately 1.5 million adults and children will be added to the homeless numbers over the next two years (National Alliance to End Homelessness, 2010).

Generally speaking, there are four categories of the homeless. *Homeless families* typically lose their homes because of some unforeseen or unmanageable financial crisis, such as the loss of a job, a medical emergency, a divorce, a car accident, or a death in the family. Almost always, the effect of the crisis is so severe that it prevents a family from being able to maintain their home. Today, about 85,000 families experience homelessness each night (National Alliance to End Homelessness, 2010). An estimated 50,000 *youth* experience homelessness every day. Many times homelessness among youth is the result of family disruption (such as divorce), neglect, or abuse. Some are chronic runaways, juvenile delinquents, or substance abusers. As noted earlier, *veterans* of the U.S. armed forces constitute 20 percent of the entire homeless population, or about 131,000 people (U.S. Department of Housing and Urban Development, 2010). Oftentimes, veterans have physical disabilities that prevent them from earning livable wages; they may also suffer from PTSD (post-traumatic stress disorder), a condition that makes it difficult for some veterans to adjust to civilian life. Sadly, this disorder often manifests itself in unsafe behaviors, such as substance use/abuse, and violence. *Chronic homelessness* refers to long-term or repeated experiences of homelessness; these individuals often suffer from a physical or mental disability (National Alliance to End Homelessness, 2010). While many people mistakenly believe this group represents the largest number of the homeless population, this is not so—they account for only about 20 percent of the homeless (U.S. Department of Housing and Urban Development, 2010).

As the gap between increasing housing costs and decreasing income widens for poor Americans, the homeless population continues to rise. Homeless mothers have been found to experience high prevalence of disruptive family events, including divorce, illness, and physical and/or sexual abuse. The vast majority are homeless for economic reasons—they were poor before becoming homeless, frequently struggling to pay bills. Many lived in neighborhoods characterized by violence, persistent unemployment, poor schools, and limited access to medical and social services. Although eviction or relationship problems sometimes cause homelessness for many single-parent households, the reality is that neither federal assistance nor minimum-wage earnings of these low-skilled women are sufficient to pay the rent, cover childcare, and meet healthcare and other living expenses. Such economic problems may increase feelings of hopelessness, dependency, and depression and contribute to family dysfunction (Anderson & Koblinsky, 1995).

Homelessness and Temporary Shelters

Other families are forced to settle for substandard housing conditions with major structural flaws, no heat or hot water, rodent infestation, and so forth, since decent housing is unaffordable. Frequently, the family has no alternative to the shelter system other than the streets. Long-term shelter has in some large cities, such as New York, most commonly been in welfare hotels or motels that provide private rooms, generally with private bathrooms but no kitchen or other cooking facilities. Usually beds are shared by two or more family members. There is no space for children to play, and not enough floor space for infants and toddlers to crawl. Many of these housing conditions are deplorable. Oftentimes shelters are found amid centers of pornography, drug trafficking, and prostitution. Drug-related violence often is high (Anderson & Koblinsky, 1995; Letiecq, Anderson, & Koblinsky, 1998). The trip to the local shelter is a family's final, desperate attempt to remain intact.

In general, emergency shelters provide from one night to several months of shelter. During the day, families are "on their own" to report to the welfare office, search for affordable housing, seek employment, or pursue education. Generally, cooking is not available, and thus parents must eat in a shelter cafeteria or find other ways to feed their families. Some research has found that as many as one-half of homeless preschoolers go to bed hungry several times a month. Emergency shelters often lack support services and restrict families to short stays.

In addition to shelter shortage, overcrowding of the existing shelters can lead to family separation, as some members of the family, usually fathers and older children, split off so that the rest of the family can stay together. Because of the lack of shelter space, the close physical arrangement of many family shelters leads to restrictions on the age and sex of clients. Forced to leave their families because of the restrictions, fathers and older children will go either to single-sex shelters, to relatives, or to the streets. This makes it difficult for homeless families to stay together. When shelters are full, families are threatened with charges of child neglect unless they can find alternative housing arrangements. If they are unable to, the children may be placed in foster care. These factors combine to threaten the unity and stability of homeless families.

In recent years, some cities have developed transitional-housing programs that offer families reduced-rent apartments for 1 to 2 years while parents complete school or job-training programs. Such programs may provide homeless families with supportive services such as child care, employment counseling, GED classes, job training, healthcare, and/or substance-abuse counseling (Anderson & Koblinsky, 1995; Letiecq et al., 1998).

Characteristics of Homeless Parents

Without shelter, homeless families have no place in which to conduct the daily activities necessary to function. Without an address, the homeless find it difficult to secure a job or obtain welfare benefits. They lack privacy and a place to keep possessions. In addition, the lack of shelter contributes over time to other problems, such as poor nutrition, poor physical and/or mental health, victimization, apathy, loneliness, and dejection. Families with minor children are in jeopardy of losing custody. Many families are alone, without knowledge of how and where to find a support system.

How does homelessness affect family relationships? One body of research explored mothers' perceptions of how homelessness and shelter life affected the relationships with their children (Lindsey, 1998). Results showed that the quality of parent–child relationships and the parental role are affected by homelessness, but not necessarily in negative ways—almost all of the mothers reported that relationships with their children became closer while living in a shelter. This closeness seemed to develop because of the amount of time they spent together and bonding during a time of crisis. Even though mothers became closer to their children, the almost constant interaction required by shelter life became a burden for some women; all but one of the mothers found it difficult to parent their children while in a shelter. Specifically, it was hard for them to be disciplinarians and to fulfill the provider/caretaker role because they were unable to meet their children's basic needs for shelter, food, safety, and emotional nurturance. Mothers tended to attribute disciplinary problems to shelter rules that prohibited corporal punishment and to interference of other residents.

Characteristics of Homeless Children

Most shelter children are younger than 5 years and show delays in language, social skills, gross and fine motor skills, and other characteristics that could lead to life-long emotional, social, and cognitive problems (Hunter, 1993). Furthermore, most children in shelters are unserved for primary health care, community health ties having been broken as the family relocated (Grant, 1990). The children who have been in shelters since infancy and who have experienced intervention programs display the fewest problems, but preschool children oftentimes exhibit signs of emotional disturbance and/or speech and language delay, frequently in combination. The health status and functional and behavioral characteristics of these preschool shelter children may be found in Table 9.3.

Another empirical study examined shelter children 4–10 years of age (Fox, Barrnett, Davies, & Bird, 1990). This data demonstrated that nearly all of the children showed some difficulties, from delays in verbal functioning to delays in motor abilities; others experienced emotional and behavioral problems.

When compared with other youth, homeless teens who reside at runaway shelters are found to have substantially more school and personal problems, especially more family difficulties (Kurtz,

TABLE 9.3 Characteristics of homeless children.

PRESCHOOL CHILDREN
- Under- or nonimmunized
- Chronic health conditions, such as frequent serious upper-respiratory problems, dehydration, and diarrhea
- Numerous functional and behavioral disorders, such as separation problems (characterized by hysterical crying, vomiting, and severe anxiety)
- Inappropriate physical pseudo-intimate relationships with adults unknown to them—indiscriminate friendliness
- Superficial relationships
- Little or lack of concern for classmates and teachers
- Sleep disturbances (try to avoid napping, have nightmares, unable to sleep because of noise, often have to sleep with parent)
- Signs of emotional disturbance—severe tantrums; dangerously aggressive and destructive behaviors; extreme withdrawal; mood swings; oppositional and manipulative behavior; lack of internalized behavior controls; dependent upon adults to structure immediate environment
- Very short attention span
- Random self-activity and absence of goal direction
- Restricted expressive language
- Delayed vocabulary development
- Articulation disorders
- Delayed cognitive development
- Immature motor skills
- Spatial difficulties

SCHOOL-AGE CHILDREN
- Depression and suicidal thoughts
- Intense anxiety
- Higher incidence of sleep problems, shyness, withdrawal, aggression (similar to behaviorally disordered children)
- Low self-esteem
- Nonattendance at school
- School failure and/or underachievement; special education
- Mental retardation or borderline retardation
- Impaired cognitive development (similar to that of abused children)

Jarvis, & Kurtz, 1991). Although the homeless youths received more services from shelters than nonhomeless youths, the prognosis for homeless teens is grim: Most lack a stable, supportive family to which they can return. Many are already victims of a fragmented child-welfare system that offers bleak alternative living arrangements.

Support for Homeless Families

In 1987, President Ronald Reagan signed the first major piece of federal legislation to deal with the needs of the homeless in a comprehensive manner—the Stewart B. McKinney Homeless Assistance Act. In the 1990s, Congress passed legislation that increased funds for shelters and housing, job training, health and counseling services, and education for homeless children and adults. However, it has been argued that changes in federal social policies have played a significant role in the rise in homelessness. Fewer families are qualifying for public assistance, and those who do receive drastic reductions. A large percentage of the homeless work full or part time, but low wages cannot provide for rent and other living expenses.

Clinical work with homeless families could be more effective if families that are more seriously affected by homelessness and who carry higher rates of emotional and behavioral symptoms could be identified (Danseco & Holden, 1998). These families should be targeted for more intensive intervention, such as psychotherapy for parents, child-management training, and intensive case-management services. The more resilient homeless families may need access to resources but less direct support and encouragement in their problem-solving efforts. Those families most at risk should be identified early and intervention efforts begun as soon as possible.

Shelters should be more family-friendly, allowing parents to have as much authority and control as possible over daily routines, because requiring families to leave the center during the day actually exacerbates parent–child conflicts (Lindsey, 1998); parenting classes should help parents learn appropriate disciplinary techniques. Policies preventing boys over a certain age from staying with the family should also be changed. Service providers should be particularly aware of emotional needs of parents and children and promote constructive interactions among shelter residents.

Finally, because homeless families differ on many dimensions (including family structure, family size, racial/cultural background, housing history, and pathways to homelessness), homeless policies must address the diversity of homeless-family life. Other family factors that need to be considered are extent of parental education, intergenerational interaction, family cohesion, family conflict, life stress, and amount of social support. Above all, policy must empower families to become self-sufficient, encourage involvement in parenting, recognize interdependency of family members, build social-support networks, and strengthen neighborhoods and communities.

Summary

Abusive parents and homeless parents represent families in high-risk situations, but the type and degree of risk are vastly different for each group.

Abusive parents pose considerable threats to the health, safety, and welfare of children. However, a number of parents who abuse or neglect their children are young, impoverished, socially isolated, unemployed, and/or victims of child abuse themselves. Considerable evidence supports the fact the abuse may be perpetuated from one generation to the next. Often, abusive parents make unrealistic demands on their children, and children try to comply to avoid being harmed. Our society has yet to find an effective system for the prevention of child abuse and neglect or for the rehabilitation of abusers. Clearly these issues need to be high priorities.

Encouragingly, federal leadership is stepping up to prevent and to end homelessness. Through the *Opening Doors* human service program, the federal government, along with local and state governments, and philanthropic and faith-based organizations hopes to end veteran and chronic homelessness by 2015, and to end children, family, and youth homelessness by 2020 (U.S. Interagency Council on Homelessness, 2010). This plan combines permanent housing with support services. It remains to be seen if this programming will be effective in reducing the numbers of the homeless in our country.

References

Alessandri, S. M., & Lewis, M. (1996). Differences in pride and shame in maltreated and nonmaltreated preschoolers. *Child Development, 67,* 1857–1869.

American Academy of Pediatrics (2010). *Safety and prevention: Sexual abuse.* Retrieved July 10, 2010, from www.healthychildren.org/English/safety-prevention/at-home/pages/Sexual-Abuse.aspx?nfstatus=401&nftoken.

Anderson, E., & Koblinsky, S. (1995). The need to speak to families. *Family Relations, 44,* 13–18.

Banyard, V., & Williams, L. (1996). Characteristics of child sexual abuse as correlates of women's adjustment: A prospective study. *Journal of Marriage and the Family, 58,* 853–865.

Baumrind, D. (1994). The social context of child maltreatment. *Family Relations, 43*(4), 360–369.

Beitchman, J., Zucker, K., Hood, J., DaCosta, G., & Akman, D. (1992). A review of the short-term effects of child sexual abuse. *Child Abuse and Neglect, 15,* 537–556.

Berger, P. & Tremblay, K. (1989, Fall). Homelessness: Strategies for education, advocacy, and research. *Journal of Home Economics,* pp. 27–32.

Besharov, D., & Laumann, L. (1996). Child abuse reporting. *Society, 33*(4), 40–47.

Catalan, S. (2004). *Criminal victimization, 2003.* Washington, DC: United States Department of Justice, Bureau of Justice Statistics. Retrieved April 4, 2009, from http://222.ojp.usdoj.gov/bjs/abstract/cv03.htm.

Cates, D., Markell, M., & Bettenhausen, S. (1995). At risk for abuse: A teacher's guide for recognizing and reporting child neglect and abuse. *Preventing School Failure, 39*(2), 6–10.

Centers for Disease Control and Prevention. (2009, February 8). 1 in 4 women, 1 in 9 men suffer intimate partner violence. Morbidity and Mortality Weekly Report.

Child Welfare Information Gateway, U.S. Department of Health and Human Services. (2009). *Child abuse and neglect.* Retrieved July 10, 2010, from http://www.childwelfare.gov/can.

Claussen, A., & Crittenden, P. (1991). Physical and psychological maltreatment: Relations among types of maltreatment. *Child Abuse and Neglect, 15,* 5–16.

Coulton, C., Korbin, J., Su, M., & Chow, J. (1995). Community level factors and child maltreatment rates. *Child Development, 66,* 1262–1276.

Dail, P. (1990). An essay on homelessness: American's gravest poverty. *Family Perspective, 24*(4), 419–430.

Danseco, E., & Holden, E. (1998). Are there different types of homeless families?: A typology of homeless families based on cluster analysis. *Family Relations, 47,* 159–165.

Durose, M. R., Harlow, C. W., Langan, P. A., Motivans, M., Rantala, R. R., & Smith, E. L. (2005). *Family violence statistics: Including statistics on strangers and acquaintances.* Washington, DC: Unites States Department of Justice, Bureau of Justice Statistics. Retrieved April 4, 2008, from www.ojp.usdoj.gov/bjs.

Finkelhor, D., Ormrod, R. K., & Turner, H. A. (2009). Lifetime assessment of poly-victimization in a national sample of children and youth. *Child Abuse and Neglect, 33,* 403–411.

Fox, S., Barrnett, J., Davies, M., & Bird, H. (1990). Psychopathology and developmental delay in homeless children: A pilot study. *Journal of the Academy of Adolescent Psychiatry, 29*(5), 733–735.

Gillmer, V. (1992). *A cry for action: Support for families in New Mexico.* Albuquerque: Task Force of the New Mexico Children, Youth, and Families Department.

Gootman, M. (1996). Child abuse and its implications for early childhood educators. *Preventing School Failure, 40,* 149–153.

Grant, R. (1990). The special needs of homeless children: Early intervention at a welfare hotel. *Topics in Early Childhood Special Education, 10*(4), 76–91.

Graziano, A., & Mills, J. (1992). Treatment for sexually abused children: When is a partial solution acceptable? *Child Abuse and Neglect, 16,* 317–228.

Guterman, N. (1997). Early prevention of physical child abuse and neglect: Existing evidence and future directions. *Child Maltreatment, 2*(1), 12–35.

Hunter, L. (1993). Sibling play therapy with homeless children: An opportunity in the crises. *Child Welfare, 62*(1), 65–74.

Kaufman, J., & Zigler, E. (1987). Do abused children become abusive parents? *American Journal of Orthopsychiatry, 57*(2), 186–191.

Kurtz, P., Jarvis, S., & Kurtz, G. (1991). Problems of homeless youth: Empirical findings and human service issues. *Social Work, 36*(4), 309–314.

Letiecq, B., Anderson, E., & Koblinsky, S. (1998). Social support of homeless and housed mothers: A comparison of temporary and permanent housing arrangements. *Family Relations, 47,* 415–421.

Lindsey, E. (1998). The impact of homelessness and shelter life on family relationships. *Family Relations, 47,* 243–252.

Martin, M., & Elmer, E. (1992). Batter children grown up: A follow-up study of individuals severely maltreated as children. *Child Abuse and Neglect, 16,* 75–87.

Martin, M., & Walters, J. (1992). Child neglect: Developing strategies for prevention. *Family Perspective, 26*(3), 305–314.

McGoldrick, M., Broken Nose, M. A., & Potenza, M. (1999). Violence and the family life cycle. In B. Carter & M. McGoldrick (Eds.), *The expanded family life cycle: Individual, family and social perspectives* (pp. 470–491). Boston: Allyn & Bacon.

Moncher, F. (1995, September). Social isolation and child-abuse risk. *Families in Society: The Journal of Contemporary Human Services,* pp. 421–433.

National Alliance to End Homelessness. (2010). *Snapshot of homelessness.* Retrieved July 15, 2010, from http://www.endhomelessness.org.

National Coalition Against Domestic Violence. (2008). *Battered women.* Retrieved February 27, 2009, from www.ncadv.org.

National Network to End Domestic Violence. (2007). *National Summary.* Retrieved February 27, 2009, from www.nnedv.org.

Steinbock, M. (1995). Homeless female-headed families: Relationships at risk. *Marriage and Family Review, 20*(1–2), 143–159.

Swift, K. (1995). An outrage to common decency: Historical perspectives on child neglect. *Child Welfare, 74*(1), 71–92.

U.S. Department of Health and Human Services, Administration on Children, Youth, and Families. (2009). *Child maltreatment: 2007.* Washington, DC: U.S. Government Printing Office. Retrieved July 14, 2010, from http://www.acf.hhs.gov/programs/cb/pubs/cm07/cm07.pdf.

U.S. Department of Health, Education, and Welfare, Office of the Human Development/Office of Child Development, Children's Bureau/National Center on Child Abuse and Neglect. (1975). *Child abuse and neglect: The problem and its management* (DHEW Publication No. OHD 75-30073). Washington, DC: Author.

U.S. Department of Housing and Urban Development. (2010). *Homelessness: Programs and the people they serve.* Retrieved July 16, 2010, from http://www.huduser.org/portal/publications/homelss/homelessness/contents.html.

U.S. Department of Justice. (2009). *Intimate partner violence in the United States: Bureau of Justice Statistics.* Retrieved February 27, 2009, from www.ojp-usdoj.gov/bjs.

U.S. Interagency Council on Homelessness. (2010). *Obama administration unveils national strategic plan to prevent and end homelessness.* Retrieved July 16, 2010, from http://www.ich.gov.

Welch, K. J. (2004). *Development: Journey through childhood and adolescence.* Boston: Allyn & Bacon.

Chapter 10

Parenting Children with Exceptionalities

An exceptional child, as labeled for education purposes, is one who is different in some way from a typical child. The term **exceptional children** includes those with special problems related to physical disabilities, sensory impairments, communicative disorders, emotional disturbances, learning disabilities, and mental retardation (or *intellectual disability*), as well as those who have special talents, or who are gifted. For the purposes of our study, we focus on those with deficits.

Most exceptional children require special education and related services if they are to reach their full potential of development. **Special education,** provided by the public school system and/or other institutions, refers to a wide range of educational and social services for people with disabilities (Gargiulo, 2005). Most often, this education is provided for those between the ages of 3 and 21. The education differs from traditional public schooling in that it provides special needs children with education that addresses their unique, individual differences.

A number of reasons have been identified why it is difficult to determine the number of exceptional children in a given category. These include (Hallahan & Kauffman, 2000):

- The definitions of disabilities often are ambiguous.
- The diagnosis of a condition may overlap with another condition or diagnoses may change over time.
- Many exceptional children remain unidentified.
- Parents often resist having their children identified as exceptional because of the stigma attached to its labeling

The number of unidentified—and therefore unserved—children is also not known, nor is the number who are misserved. Despite these limitations, we do know that, according to U.S. Department of Education data, approximately 600,000 children aged 3 to 5 receive special education services each year, and nearly 5.8 million students, ages 6 to 21, are served by special education annually (Gargiulo, 2005).

In this chapter, we examine some of the common types of children's exceptionalities, and we also explore challenges for families with exceptional children, as well as support for parents. Let's begin by first looking at parents' experiences when they learn that they have a child with disabilities.

HAVING A CHILD WITH DISABILITIES

Most parents plan for and expect healthy, happy babies. Birth defects, anomalies, and disabilities can range from barely noticeable, to life-threatening, to fatal. When an impairment is immediately obvious, it is traumatic for parents. No matter how severe the disability or defect, parents of infants with birth defects and physically and/or cognitively challenged babies mourn the loss of the healthy child they imagined they would bear.

At the Parents Encouraging Parents Conference, Roger and Ann Figard (personal communication, 1992) presented the *Loss and Grief Cycle* for parents of physically/cognitively challenged children (see Figure 10.1). As you can see, when parents are expecting a baby, they have a mental image or an idea of their perfect child-to-be. When parents have a baby that is born with disabilities, they come face to face with reality—a reality that does not align with their hoped-for image.

The initial reaction of parents may be one of disbelief, and the degree of disbelief is related to the degree of the visibility of the disability or anomaly. When parents receive the initial diagnosis of a disability, a dream is shattered, and they may begin to grieve for the loss of a healthy child and the expectations they held for the child. The birth of a child with disabilities into a family requires considerable adjustment on the part of family members.

Some experts believe that grieving is the process by which individuals can separate from a significant lost dream, and it begins spontaneously (Moses, 1983). According to Moses (1983), there are several states of grieving, which have no time limits. Notice how closely the states of

Pregnancy In pregnancy, the unknowns about the baby encourage a parent to hope and dream and fantasize about what the baby will be like.

The Fantasized, Hoped-For Child Often, the parents develop an idea or mental picture of the perfect child-to-be. This can include the sex of the child, talents, or other characteristics important to the parents.

Birth of a Challenged Child The parent is faced with the reality that the hoped-for child and the real child are not the same child.

Ideational Object Loss Unconsciously, the parent's mind recognizes the death of the dream of the hoped-for child and this moves the parent into a cycle of grief . . . letting go of the hoped-for child and accepting the real child.

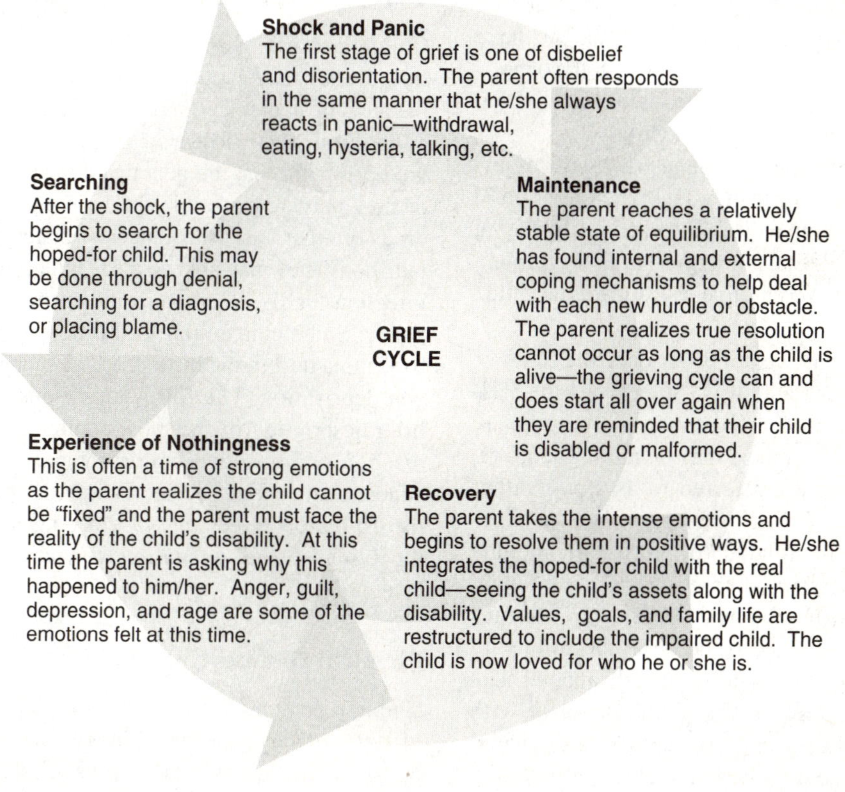

GRIEF CYCLE

Shock and Panic
The first stage of grief is one of disbelief and disorientation. The parent often responds in the same manner that he/she always reacts in panic—withdrawal, eating, hysteria, talking, etc.

Searching
After the shock, the parent begins to search for the hoped-for child. This may be done through denial, searching for a diagnosis, or placing blame.

Experience of Nothingness
This is often a time of strong emotions as the parent realizes the child cannot be "fixed" and the parent must face the reality of the child's disability. At this time the parent is asking why this happened to him/her. Anger, guilt, depression, and rage are some of the emotions felt at this time.

Maintenance
The parent reaches a relatively stable state of equilibrium. He/she has found internal and external coping mechanisms to help deal with each new hurdle or obstacle. The parent realizes true resolution cannot occur as long as the child is alive—the grieving cycle can and does start all over again when they are reminded that their child is disabled or malformed.

Recovery
The parent takes the intense emotions and begins to resolve them in positive ways. He/she integrates the hoped-for child with the real child—seeing the child's assets along with the disability. Values, goals, and family life are restructured to include the impaired child. The child is now loved for who he or she is.

FIGURE 10.1 Loss and grief cycle for physically challenged children.
When parents lose a child to death, or when they have a baby with birth defects, they experience a cycle of grief and loss.

Source: Roger and Ann Figard (1992), personal communication.

---

grieving Moses proposes correlate with Figard and Figard's Loss and Grief Cycle:

- *Denial:* The existence of, the permanence of, or the impact of the disability may be denied. Denial buys time for parents to gain the internal strength and the external supports necessary to cope. This requires (and uses up) enormous physical, emotional, and spiritual energy.
- *Anxiety:* A feeling of internal imbalance occurs. Anxiety facilitates the restructuring of attitudes concerning responsibility and serves as a mobilizer of energy.
- *Guilt:* This is the most disconcerting of all grief states. Normally, it is expressed in

three ways: (1) The parent feels that he or she has caused the disability; (2) the parent feels that having a child with a disability is a just or fair punishment for some specific or awful action committed in the past; or (3) the parent feels generalized or unspecified guilt because the disability exists.
- *Depression:* Self-anger, or anger turned inward, causes depression. If parents have the support needed to deal with the depression, it can help them to rework a definition of competence for their child.
- *Anger:* People have an internal sense of justice. The anger they feel when their child is born with a disability can be frightening and can result in aggression, overprotection, or overpunitiveness toward the child.

All parents do not experience the states of grieving in the same way. Sometimes the feelings overlap or occur simultaneously; some are intense, whereas others may be mild. Therefore, these findings are referred to as *states* rather than *stages*. Feelings that parents may experience that are related to depression include rejection, isolation, hopelessness, resentment, and antagonism (Wallace, 1992). Parents must generate new dreams; otherwise, the child with a disability will be nothing but a disappointment to them. Coping occurs simultaneously with grieving. Parents first conceptualize the worst before they deal with reality, and confrontation of reality is facilitated by the acceptance of both the child's and the parents' limitations (Moses, 1983).

There are also several variables that affect the degree and intensity of grief. For example, families from different cultures may grieve the loss of the hoped-for child in different ways—while a white, Western family may find certain milestone events to be very difficult (such as what would have been the first day of kindergarten or driver's education class), cultural attitudes in Korean families dictate a stiff upper lip and an attitude that almost ignores such events (University of Illinois at Chicago, 2002). Other variables, such as socioeconomic status, religious beliefs, the nature and visibility of the disability, the coping strategies of family members, the degree of marital stability, and the availability and use of support systems also affect how parents grieve their children's disabilities.

TYPES OF EXCEPTIONALITIES

Children may be born with one or more disabilities, or they may acquire disabilities later in life because of accident or disease. The causes of **congenital disabilities,** or those that children are born with, may be genetic or chromosomal, or they may be caused by prenatal exposure to drugs or other toxic substances or maternal malnutrition. They may also be the result of maternal infections or diseases before and/or during pregnancy. Some congenital disabilities are caused by trauma during the birth process, such as oxygen deprivation. The following discussion is a brief description of the most common types of disabilities for which children receive special educational services today. Table 10.1 provides the estimated percentage of those ages 6 to 21 receiving special-education services in each category.

Physical Disabilities

Children demonstrate a broad range and variety of types of physical disabilities. Children with physical disabilities may also have intellectual and/or learning disabilities, emotional disorders, communication disorders, or special gifts and talents. There is also a biologically or medically based category of disabilities. This includes such conditions as neurological impairments (e.g., cerebral palsy, epilepsy, spina bifida, polio, multiple sclerosis), musculoskeletal conditions (e.g., muscular dystrophy, rheumatoid arthritis, clubfoot, scoliosis, malformation of the hip, extremities, and heart), and accidents, diseases, and other conditions such as asthma, diabetes, rheumatic fever, tuberculosis, and hemophilia (Hallahan & Kauffman, 2000). Today, because of the epidemic of childhood obesity that is sweeping this country, some authorities are beginning to question

TABLE 10.1 Percent distribution of students 6–21 years olds served under Individuals with Disabilities Education Act, Part B, by type and time (regular school): Fall 2007.

Type of Disability	<21% of time	21–60% of time	>60% of time
Specific learning disabilities	59.0%	29.7%	9.2%
Speech/language impairments	86.7%	5.7%	4.5%
Intellectual disability (MR)	15.8%	27.6%	49.0%
Emotional/behavioral	37.3%	19.7%	24.2%
Multiple disabilities	12.9%	16.1%	45.2%
Hearing impairments	51.9%	17.6%	16.8%
Orthopedic impairment	50.0%	17.4%	24.5%
Visual impairment	60.1%	14.3%	12.9%
Autism	34.6%	18.2%	36.9%
Traumatic brain injury	43.9%	24.8%	22.5%
Developmental delay	61.6%	20.8%	16.2%

Source: Adapted from U.S. Department of Education, National Center for Education Statistics (2010). *Digest of Education Statistics, 2009* (NCES 2010-013), Chapter 2.

whether obese children should be considered as disabled, and if so, whether they should qualify for special-education services (National Center for the Dissemination of Disability Research, 2010).

Unlike learning disabilities and some forms of intellectual disability, physical disabilities are almost always visible; oftentimes, children require the use of prosthetic or adaptive devices to assist them in performing routine activities such as walking. We must be careful, however, not to stereotype or overgeneralize because many children with physical disabilities have no sensory or learning impairments and can learn to do most of the things that children without disabilities can do—they just do them in different ways. The more visible a physical disability is, the more likely the child is to experience insensitivity by society.

Intellectual Disability

Although the term mental retardation has been used for a number of decades, because of the stigma associated with the term, professionals and educators today prefer the term *intellectual disability*. Sometimes in empirical literature you may see the term presented as mental retardation/intellectual disability, or MR/ID, as a way to mark the transition in terminology (Sulkes, 2006).

Generally speaking, MR/ID is diagnosed when there is significantly subaverage intellectual functioning; this may be present from birth or early infancy (although most children don't develop noticeable symptoms until they are 2 to 3 years old); and the diagnosis is typically made after formal testing. Today, both intellectual functioning and adaptive skills are taken into consideration for diagnosis, and the lower-limit IQ score to be considered "normal" has been reduced to 70. The American Association of Mental Retardation classifies students with mental retardation by the degree of support they need to function as competently as they can.

MR/ID causes mild to substantial limitations in a person's day-to-day living, such as in a person's ability to (Sulkes, 2006):

- Communicate
- Live independently

Down syndrome, a condition in which the child has 47 chromosomes instead of the usual 46, results in symptoms that vary from person to person. These symptoms, including mental retardation/intellectual disability, can range from mild to severe.

- Take care of oneself (such as daily hygiene and nutrition)
- Make decisions
- Cope with multiple tasks at the same time
- Care for their personal health, safety, and well-being

Most individuals have mild limitations and are capable of functioning adequately in society with little or no assistance (Hallahan & Kauffman, 2000).

There are varying degrees of intellectual disability: mild, moderate, severe, and profound. For example, those with mild levels of MR/ID are able to develop social and communication skills, and can learn up to about a sixth-grade level; as an adult, they are usually self-supportive (Sulkes, 2006). Conversely, those with profound MR/ID experience extreme cognitive limitations, have poor motor skills, and may achieve only limited self-care. Today, about 3 percent of the U.S. population is thought to be affected by some degree of MR/ID, and about 1 percent are classified with profound cognitive limitations (Sulkes, 2006).

A common question that students ask is, What causes MR/ID? Is it preventable, such as by good maternal healthcare and nutrition? This is a somewhat difficult question to answer because it is thought that there are more than 250 causes of intellectual disability (Freund, 1994). We do know, however, that MR/ID is rarely caused by a single factor—typically there is a complex interaction of factors. These are grouped into four major categories: (1) socioeconomic and environmental factors, (2) injury, (3) infections and toxins, and (4) biological causes. *Down syndrome* (caused by a chromosomal abnormality) and *fetal alcohol syndrome* (caused by mothers' alcohol consumption during pregnancy) are two of the leading causes (Freund, 1994). Fragile X syndrome has been reported as the most common inherited form of mental retardation, especially for boys, since two-thirds of girls with Fragile X syndrome have IQs within the normal range.

Intellectual disability is usually not detectable at birth unless there is an obvious birth defect, such as an unusually large head (hydrocephaly), an unusually small head (microcephaly), or the physical characteristics of Down syndrome.

Learning Disabilities

Of all the categories of exceptional children, *learning disabled* is the most ambiguous and widespread. The *Individuals with Disabilities Education Act (IDEA)* is federal legislation that guides schools in providing special education services. IDEA defines **learning disabilities (LD)** as a disorder that causes an "imperfect ability" to use language, or to listen, think, speak, read, write, spell, or do mathematical calculations. LD also includes perceptual abilities, brain injury, and minimal brain dysfunction (Child Development Institute, 2010). It is estimated that today, 6 to 10 percent of the U.S. school-age population is learning disabled, and that they account for nearly 40 percent of the children enrolled in special education services; there are also about 6 million learning disabled adults (Child Development Institute, 2010).

As you can see, this is a very broad definition, and not all experts agree on the definition used by IDEA. For example, some experts focus on children's learning potentials versus what they are actually learning, their actual outcomes (Child Development Institute, 2010). These experts also note that oftentimes, learning disabled children show an uneven pattern of development, such as in their language or motor development. Unfortunately, researchers and educators still do not have a full grasp on what causes learning disabilities, although they have been able to identify some commonalities among these children. These are presented in Table 10.2.

So that you may gain an understanding of the variety of learning disabilities, in the sections that follow we briefly examine the characteristics of communicative disorders, hearing and vision impairments, emotional/behavioral disorders, and giftedness.

COMMUNICATIVE DISORDERS Speech is the vocal production of language, and language is the method of communication. Communication is either impaired or unsuccessful if the sender or the receiver cannot use the signals or symbols adequately. Communicative disorders affect either/both a child's ability to send/receive messages. These disorders have the potential to influence most aspects of a child's life, including social interaction. It is useful to distinguish between speech disorders and language disorders.

A **speech disorder** is an impairment of voice, articulation of speech sounds, and/or fluency (Hallahan & Kauffman, 2000):

- *Voice disorders* occur when there is an absence or an abnormal production of voice quality, pitch, loudness, resonance, and/or duration.

TABLE 10.2 What causes learning disabilities?

The Child Development Institute (2010) notes that, although there is no clear-cut scientific evidence about the origins of learning disabilities, there are a number of common observations among children who do exhibit learning disabilities. These include:

- Some children develop and mature at slower rates than children in the same age group, and may not be able to do the expected school work. This type of learning disability is referred to as a *maturity lag*.
- Some children with normal vision and hearing may misinterpret everyday sights and sounds because of an unexplained disorder of the nervous system.
- Injuries before birth (such as oxygen deprivation) or during early childhood may account for some later learning problems.
- Learning disabilities may be inherited, because they tend to run in families.
- Because boys mature more slowly than girls, learning disabilities are more common in boys.
- The incidence of learning disabilities is lower in Spanish and Italian speaking countries than in English speaking countries; some researchers believe learning disabilities are linked specifically to the English language.

- *Articulation disorders* are the abnormal production of speech sounds.
- *Fluency disorders,* the abnormal flow of verbal expressions, are characterized by impaired rate and rhythm that may be accompanied by struggle behavior.
- *Language disorder* is the impairment or deviant development of comprehension and/or use of a spoken, written, and/or other symbol system; it may involve the form, the content, and/or the function of language.

It is difficult to estimate the prevalence of communication disorders because they are widely varied and are often difficult to identify; they typically occur in tandem with other disabilities (such as MR/ID, learning disabilities, or sensory impairments). Experts estimate that nearly one-fourth of all children identified for special education receive services primarily for communicative disorders, and speech/language therapy is one of the most frequently provided services for children with other major disabilities.

HEARING IMPAIRMENTS There are two groups of hearing-impaired children: those who are deaf and those who have difficulty hearing. The distinctions between these two groups are not always clear, since different professionals define the conditions in different ways. In general, however, a child is considered deaf if he or she cannot process language information by auditory means, either with or without a hearing aid. A child has difficulty hearing if, with a hearing aid, he or she has enough residual hearing to process successfully language information through auditory means. Deafness also is categorized as *prelingual* (occurring at birth) or *postlingual* (occurring at some point after the development of speech and language). About 95 percent of the children who are identified as deaf are prelingually deaf; 9 out of 10 deaf children have hearing parents (Hallahan & Kauffman, 2000; Smith & Luckasson, 1992).

Severely hearing-impaired children have great difficulty in the comprehension and production of spoken language. It is more difficult for children who are prelingually deaf to speak than it is for children postlingually deaf because they have never had a spoken-language model—they are unable to receive feedback on the sounds they attempt to produce. Therefore, it is important for deaf children to be taught an effective communication system. Most educators use a total communication approach, which is a combination of oral production and manual production (sign language).

Deaf children are not necessarily intellectually deficient, but oftentimes their academic achievement suffers because so much of academic work—especially reading—depends on mastering the spoken language. Social interaction, too, is difficult for deaf children who have no way of communicating with their hearing peers unless the peers learn American Sign Language. This need for social interaction may be one reason why deaf individuals, both children and adults, seek to associate with other deaf individuals with whom they can communicate (Hallahan & Kauffman, 2000).

VISUAL IMPAIRMENTS/BLINDNESS Like hearing impairments, **visual impairments** fall into two categories: the blind and the partially sighted. As with hearing impairments, there is more than one definition of the categories. Children are declared *legally blind* if their visual acuity is 20/200 or less in the better eye, even with the use of glasses, or if their field of peripheral vision is extremely narrow. *Partially sighted* children have visual acuity between 20/70 and 20/200 in the better eye with glasses. Some definitions indicate that blind children must learn to read Braille or use aural methods such as tapes and records, whereas partially sighted children are able to read using glasses and/or magnification.

Visual impairment/blindness is one of the least prevalent disabilities in children. The most common visual problems, such as nearsightedness, farsightedness, and astigmatism, may be serious enough to cause significant impairment, but most can be corrected with glasses or contact lenses. Most of the visual impairments that affect children are due to prenatal causes, many of which are hereditary. Other causes include maternal prenatal infectious diseases such as syphilis and rubella—both of which are preventable (German measles) (Hallahan & Kauffman, 2000).

Children who are visually impaired are usually not significantly disabled in their ability to understand and use language, but their early language development may be restricted by the lack of visual experiences, making their language more self-centered. There is no evidence to suggest that blindness results in lower intelligence, but children who are blind rely more heavily on the senses of hearing and touch to perceive and learn about their world. Perhaps the greatest challenge for blind children is developing mobility skills that enable them to move about effectively. In addition, blind infants possess a limited range of behaviors for initiating and maintaining social interactions because of lack of contact and absence of smiling (Erwin, 1994; Hallahan & Kauffman, 2000; Smith & Luckasson, 1992).

EMOTIONAL/BEHAVIORAL DISORDERS It's particularly difficult to arrive at a definition for children who have extreme social-interpersonal or -intrapersonal problems. In the past, these children have been described as abusive, defiant, irritable, destructive, withdrawn, irresponsible, jealous, hostile, aggressive, and unpredictable. For a number of years, children have had labels attached to them—emotionally impaired, behaviorally impaired, socially/emotionally handicapped, emotionally disturbed, socially maladjusted, and so on. Currently, the term **emotional or behavioral disorders (EBD)** is accepted. Despite definition difficulties, however, most experts agree that children who fit this category demonstrate extreme behavior that is unacceptable within the social and cultural context and the problem is chronic rather than situational. Often the phrase "[the behavior] adversely affects educational performance" is added as a qualifier (Hallahan & Kauffman, 2000; Smith & Luckasson, 1992).

There are two types of disordered behavior: externalizing and internalizing (Achenbach, Howell, Quay, & Conners, 1991; Walker & Severson, 1990). **Externalizing behavior** consists of aggressive behaviors expressed outwardly toward others, such as aggression, acting out, or disruption. The most common behaviors of children being served by special education are externalizing; boys with these behaviors outnumber girls 5 to 1. **Internalizing behaviors** are expressed in a more socially withdrawn fashion and include anxiety and depression.

Several researchers have described other specific behaviors that represent the following dimensions: conduct disorder, socialized aggression, attention problems/immaturity, anxiety/withdrawal, psychotic behavior, and motor excess. Children may demonstrate several behaviors that represent more than one dimension. For example, a child might exhibit behaviors considered to be in the conduct-disorder dimension, such as disruption, temper tantrums, and fighting, and at the same time show motor-excess behaviors, such as inability to sit still and excessive talkativeness (Hallahan & Kauffman, 2000).

Dysfunctional family relationships, especially negative parent–child interactions, often are associated with behavioral disorders. The same is true for school experiences, which can influence a child's behavior in either negative or positive ways. Contextual factors, such as poverty, exposure to violence and drugs, and standards and expectations for behavior, are potential influencers. Very few children with emotional/behavioral disorders have high intelligence, and their ability to interact effectively with adults and peers is severely limited (Hallahan & Kauffman, 2000).

ATTENTION-DEFICIT/HYPERACTIVITY DISORDER Attention-Deficit/Hyperactivity Disorder (ADHD) is a behavioral disorder. It is characterized by chronic, impairing levels of attention, hyperactivity, or their combination (American Psychological Association, 2011). ADHD describes a set of symptoms in children reflecting excessive inattention or overactivity and impulsive responding, within the context of developmentally appropriate behavior for the child's age and gender group. Unable to sustain responses long enough to accomplish assigned tasks, these children show considerably less persistence than their peers.

Its prevalence is estimated at 3 to 5 percent of the child population, with boys outnumbering girls six to one. According to some sources, more than half of these children also meet the criteria for behavioral disorders, including such behaviors as extreme stubbornness, noncompliance, hostility, rule violations, aggressive acts, untruthfulness, and taking things from others without permission (Landau & McAnninch, 1993).

Professionals do not agree as to the causes of ADHD. To date, nearly 30 causes have been suggested, such as anxiety and depression, head trauma, and boredom. Many professionals believe the root is a biological cause and support the use of medication to help control the child's behavior (Reid, Maag, & Vasa, 1993). Probably the most commonly accepted cause is neurological dysfunction, which often is linked to hereditary factors (Hallahan & Kauffman, 2000). Other professionals support the use of behavior modification and/or social-skills training to improve the child's behavior.

DEVELOPMENTAL DELAYS **Developmental delays** describes children from 3 to 5 years of age who exhibit significant delays in one or more domains of physical, cognitive, communicative, social and emotional, and adaptive development; as a result of their delays they need special education and services. It is a useful category for ensuring early services. The label itself is an acceptable and nonjudgmental term that allows children access to services they need. The term also minimizes the possibility of inaccurate diagnosis in young children because of the wide variability in development.

GIFTEDNESS Giftedness is the only exceptionality not included in the category of disabilities. There is little agreement about the definition of giftedness, except that **gifted children** excel in some way(s) when compared with their peers; federal laws do not require special services for gifted students as they do for students with disabilities. Most states mandate programs for gifted students, and each state has its own definition of gifted. The most common features of these state definitions are general intellectual ability, specific academic aptitude, creative-thinking ability, advanced ability in the fine arts and performing arts, and leadership ability (Hallahan & Kauffman, 2000). A variety of educational models exist for gifted children, but research on the effectiveness of these models is sparse.

It is understandable that parents are perhaps fearful when they have a child who is diagnosed with exceptionalities, because as we have seen, such a reality dashes the dreams for the hoped-for child. It is important to remember, however, that despite a child's differences and variations from a "typical" child, exceptional children—with supportive, loving, encouraging environments—can (and do!) achieve their full developmental potentials.

A variety of other conditions place children at developmental risk or result in chronic illness or disability. We discuss these in the following section.

OTHER AT-RISK OR DISABLING CONDITIONS

While we cannot possibly account for every condition that may place a child at risk for acquiring an exceptionality, some conditions, determined by biological and/or environmental factors, can be prevented or at least mediated so they have a lesser effect. *Biological factors* include prematurity, neonatal and/or infant respiratory distress, and maternal prenatal substance use. *Environmental risks* include poverty, lack of nurturance, and poor parent–child interactions. Practitioners combine these two types of risks to determine the *actual risk* to a child (Thurman & Gonsalves, 1993). Let's briefly explore conditions that place children at risk, both biologically and environmentally.

Prematurity

Premature or **preterm** babies are those who are born before 37 weeks' gestation. The more preterm a baby is born, the more severe his or her health problems are likely to be. Today, one in every eight babies (about half a million annually) is born prematurely (Centers for Disease Control and Prevention, 2010c). In the United States, prematurity is the leading cause of death in newborns, and the second leading cause of infant death.

Babies who are born preterm are less active, initiate fewer interactions, and provide less feedback to their caregivers than babies who are born at term. Premature babies may also be at risk environmentally. Preterm neonatal behaviors such as maintaining less eye contact, averting their gaze, smiling less, using more unclear signals, and resisting cuddling may discourage inexperienced mothers from initiating interactions. If the preterm baby is born to a teenager, in addition to lacking experience, the teen may feel depressed, angry, scared, guilty, and incompetent, which will have significant impact on her interactions with her infant (Thurman & Gonsalves, 1993). Preterm babies may face lifelong problems that include intellectual disabilities, breathing/respiratory problems, cerebral palsy, vision and hearing loss, and feeding/digestion problems (Centers for Disease Control and Prevention, 2010a).

Babies who are extremely premature require care in a neonatal intensive care unit (NICU), sometimes for weeks, even months. This experience is stressful for parents and may result in distancing, creating a feeling of lack of control over the situation and the baby's fate. Parents often need help with ways to touch and hold their babies who are attached to wires, intravenous lines, and tubes (Krehbiel, Munsick-Bruno, & Lowe, 1991). Designing family-focused intervention becomes a challenge for medical staff.

Prenatal Substance Use

Prenatal substance use crosses all community, racial/ethnic, and socioeconomic groups. Children born to alcohol- and drug-using women and teens are at high risk for developmental, behavioral, and/or learning problems. Children of substance-abusing parents also are at greater risk for child abuse and neglect.

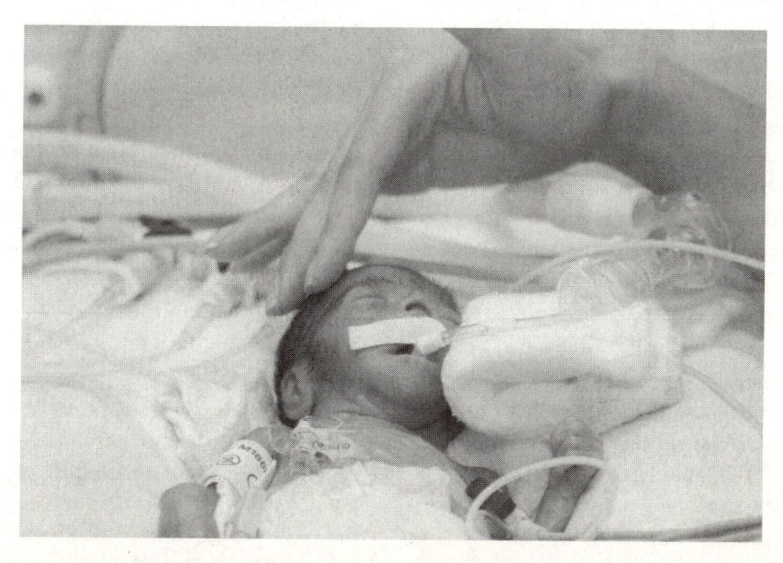

Pre-term infants often experience a wide range of physical difficulties, such as vision problems, that may later lead to learning disabilities.

Fetal alcohol spectrum disorders (FASDs) is a group of conditions that are seen in babies whose mothers drank alcohol during pregnancy. In addition to facial abnormalities and smaller-than-average body composition, a person with FASD may have ADHD, poor memory, difficulties with math, speech and language delays, MR/ID, poor reasoning and judgment skills, and vision or hearing problems (Centers for Disease Control and Prevention, 2010a). Demographers believe that there are at least six cases of FASD for every 1,000 live births in the United States (Centers for Disease Control and Prevention, 2010b).

Concern has also been expressed over the large numbers of women who use cocaine during pregnancy. Newborns of mothers who use cocaine experience tremors and irritability, in addition to sleeping and feeding difficulties. These babies may also exhibit a set of behaviors that influence the nature of the mother–infant relationship, and studies have found that these mothers may feel less than competent in interacting with their children. Oftentimes, these mothers divert their energy from interacting with their infants to finding their next "high"; they also tend to lead chaotic lives with little access to social-support networks, and are more depressed than their peers. Sadly, this leads to unresponsiveness, inattentiveness, and negative perceptions of the child (Gottwald & Thurman, 1994).

Not all children exposed to alcohol during the prenatal period are born with FASD, because both alcohol and drugs have differential effects on fetuses. As we have learned throughout our study together, the complex interaction of an array of biological and environmental factors determines developmental outcomes. What is indisputable, however, is that *FASD is 100 percent preventable.*

Parenting is challenging for all families, but families with exceptional children are faced with special challenges. There is no question that the caregiving demands associated with children with disabilities are substantially greater than those associated with children without disabilities.

CHALLENGES FOR FAMILIES WITH EXCEPTIONAL CHILDREN

Parents of children with disabilities experience significantly more stress in childrearing than other parents do (Floyd & Gallagher, 1997). In fact, there is considerable literature related to stress and coping in these families, and most of it supports the finding of increased stress. However, there is substantial variation in the nature and extent to which individual families report stress.

Stress and Family Environment

Research has identified several potential causes for increased stress in families with exceptional children. These include the increased caregiving demands, the need to feel normal, lack of information about their children's condition, uncertainty and disappointment about their children's future, severity/type of disability, increased financial burden, lack of available and appropriate childcare, single parenthood, and lack of support systems (Dyson, 1996; Freedman, Litchfield, & Warfield, 1995; Gottlieb, 1997; Judge, 1998). One study found that 23 percent of the mothers of young disabled children gave up paid employment to remain in the home to care for the children, and 41 percent of mothers declined offers of paid employment for the same reason (Trute, 1990). Another study of mothers with children with severe disabilities found that 62 percent never received help with household chores, and 60 percent never or only sometimes had babysitters for their disabled children. Furthermore, nearly one-third indicated they never received help in understanding the child's needs, and almost 19 percent reported that they never received information about available programs or services (Marcenko & Meyers, 1991).

Despite these stress-inducing conditions, families with disabled children appear to adapt remarkably well. For example, one study investigated two aspects of parental stress: stress resulting from the parent's perception of what the child brings to the parent–child relationship (referred to as child stress), and the impact of parenting this child on other aspects of the parent's life, such as spousal relationship and physical well-being (parent stress) (Innocenti, Huh, & Boyce, 1992). The results indicated that parents of children with disabilities reported significantly more stress than other parents and that the highest stress was related primarily to issues dealing directly with the child rather than to parent-related factors.

Interestingly, several studies indicate that the environments of families differ little between those with disabled children and those without. As assessed by the Family Assessment Measure in one study, the levels of organization and functioning are similar for the two types of families. The factors that are related to functioning in the families of children with disabilities include age of the child, number of children in the family, and marital adjustment. A key element in positive family adaptation is the level of emotional closeness between the two parents—as cohesion increased, family strength increased (Trute, 1990).

Another study included parents from 110 families, half with typically developing children and half with children with disabilities (Dyson, 1991). The investigator found strong evidence of stress in families with disabled children, but family groups did not differ in overall family functioning. Families with children with disabilities showed a distinct style of functioning along family dimensions. For example, these families emphasized achievement and moral/religious beliefs and valued set rules and procedures for operating family life more than families with typical children. Even though parents experienced stress, this stress did not necessarily predict family dysfunction.

COMPARISON OF MOTHERS AND FATHERS Few efforts have been made to explore the differences of family members in their perception of the effect of a child with disabilities; most research has focused on mothers.

One study, however, interviewed mothers and fathers of children with and without disabilities (Beckman, 1991). The results suggested that mothers and fathers clearly had different perceptions of the impact of their child on their lives—mothers reported more stress than fathers did. Mothers also reported more depression, more difficulties with their sense of competence, more restrictions of the parental role, more effects on their relationships with their spouses, and more effects on their health than fathers did; fathers reported more problems with attachment.

Another study included only fathers—20 fathers of autistic children, 20 fathers of children with Down syndrome, and 20 fathers of developmentally "normal" children (Rodrigue, Morgan, & Geffken, 1992). Although fathers of children with developmental disabilities reported more disruption in family planning and increased financial burden because of their disabled children, their reported levels of perceived parenting competence, marital satisfaction, and social support were comparable to those reported by fathers of developmentally normal children. Overall, fathers demonstrated healthy levels of psychological adaptation to rearing children with disabilities. It is important to point out, however, that all fathers in this study were white, middle- to upper-middle-class, and members of parent/advocacy support groups, making them a fairly select group. Fathers who had no access to support groups might have reported different experiences.

THE IMPACT OF SUPPORT The research is unequivocal about the positive impact of support on families of children with disabilities: The greater the level of social support, especially informal support, the lower the level of stress.

Spousal support seems especially critical. For example, mothers of children with disabilities have been reported to spend twice as much time in caretaking than mothers of children without disabilities (Innocenti et al., 1992), yet fathers don't always share the burden of caretaking. Several researchers have concluded that how well mothers of children with disabilities function with regard to depression, marital adjustment, and parenting appears to be related to their partners' capacity to be supportive, both instrumentally and expressively. There is no question that a strong and satisfying marital relationship with mutual support buffers the negative effect of children's behavior problems (Suarez & Baker, 1997).

Several other studies have noted the mediating effects of support on stress and family functioning. For instance, one report found that increased informal support was significantly associated with decreased stress, and fathers and mothers reported similar levels of informal support (Beckman, 1991). Formal support, however, was not significantly associated with lower stress levels, but fathers found formal support useful as a way of managing general life stress. Another body of research found that greater informal social support was associated with more positive parental emotional and physical well-being, decreased time demands, better-integrated family units, more frequent interactions with children, and perceptions of children's behavior as less troublesome (Trivette & Dunst, 1992). The researchers concluded that parent, family, and child functioning all are affected by role sharing within the family, and support from sources outside of the family.

Parent–Child Relationships

Throughout this book, we have discussed parent–child interactions in a variety of types of families. There are many elements or characteristics common to all families that facilitate positive outcomes. On the other hand, each family type has its particular challenges, and each family within those types has its unique characteristics. Families with children with disabilities share similar challenges, regardless of the type of disability. However, each type of disability brings with it additional special challenges, which are described briefly below.

PHYSICAL DISABILITIES The burden of care for a child with physical disabilities depends on the type and severity of the particular disability. When a child has severe neurological problems that prevent independent locomotion, she remains dependent on her parents long after the infancy stage. Lifting and transporting become more difficult as the child matures, and toilet learning and self-feeding may occur much later than usual. Parents may become socially isolated if they are reluctant or unable to take their disabled children to public places. This reluctance may be especially strong when the child's disability is extremely visible. Increased demands by children and fewer rewards to parents may cause angry feelings toward the child and subsequent guilt.

Many physical disabilities require the use of special equipment or prosthetic devices, which may create logistical problems. If the child has difficulty getting around, parents may be tempted to be overprotective and/or intrusive, doing things for the child that he may be able to do for himself if given time and patience and thereby encouraging unnecessary dependence. This dependence may be exacerbated if the child is unable to enter into extracurricular activities with his peers because of his physical limitations. Parents should be encouraged to nurture the child's self-concept and body image, focusing on his strengths.

MENTAL RETARDATION/INTELLECTUAL DISABILITY The initial diagnosis of mental retardation/intellectual disability (MR/ID) may be especially difficult for parents because they must accept that the child will be forever limited in intellectual development. During the early days and months of the child's life, parents are almost always able to get off to a good start with the child without the trauma associated with a diagnosed disability. These early positive patterns may make it easier for parents to cope with their grief at a later time. On the other hand, delayed diagnosis may be confusing and frustrating to parents if the cause of retardation is not known and if they perceive their roles in the child's optimal development as ambiguous or hopeless.

As the Loss and Grief Cycle illustrated for us at the beginning of this chapter, parents of children with intellectual disability experience recurring crises arising from their child's lack of typical developmental progression. The slowed rate of development and the discrepancy from the norm become a source for heightened stress. These crises are likely to occur at the age when children who are typically developing ordinarily would begin to walk and talk, begin regular kindergarten, experience the onset of puberty, and celebrate their 21st birthdays. Additionally, parents may experience a crisis when a younger sibling's development surpasses that of the MR/ID child.

Setting reasonable expectation levels for the disabled child's behavior and performance can be extremely difficult for parents. Parental warmth, nurturance, and acceptance, focusing on the child's total development, are important.

LEARNING DISABILITIES There is no "prototype" of a learning-disabled child—these children are characterized as much by their differences as by their similarities. Because of the diversity of characteristics, the lack of a visible disability, problems with definitions, and the difficulty in early identification, parents may perceive these children as lazy, stubborn, or unmotivated. Parents inadvertently may push the child beyond his capabilities, and he may respond with inconsistent behavior and frequent mood changes.

Unfortunately, many children with learning disabilities develop emotional/behavioral disorders, partly because their learning problems have led to repeated experiences of failure, and perhaps coupled with rejection by parents, teachers, and peers. These children have been found to have lower self-concepts, more anxiety, and lower peer acceptance than normally achieving children.

Children with learning disabilities need an abundance of affection, praise, and approval from parents and peers. Parents need to be supported in their efforts to provide as many successful experiences for these children as possible—even a series of small accomplishments. A partnership between parents and teachers to provide appropriate intervention while setting reasonable expectations can help these children lead more rewarding lives.

COMMUNICATIVE DISORDERS Children with communicative disorders are faced with major obstacles to social communication. An inability to convey their thoughts and feelings leads to frustration and, often, aggression.

For mildly impaired preschool children, normal language development can be facilitated by parents listening attentively and empathically, providing appropriate language models, encouraging children to use their communication skills appropriately, asking open-ended questions, and offering many opportunities for language learning. However, early intervention with children with communicative disorders is critical, and parental efforts may need to be augmented by the intervention of a speech therapist. Nonverbal children will require a specialist in language training to help them acquire functional language. Some children will require a system of augmentative or alternative communication, such as manual signing or utilization of communication boards or electronic devices.

HEARING IMPAIRMENTS/DEAFNESS Deafness usually is unexpected and may be difficult to detect in infants, especially by hearing parents. The average age for detection of congenital hearing loss has been reported to be 15 to 16 months of age. However, the increased practice of screening newborns who are at biological risk before they leave the hospital can result in much earlier diagnosis for many children.

Some researchers suggest that the full impact of deafness is not felt by parents until the preschool years, when the communication gap between deaf and hearing children becomes more evident (Meadow-Orlans, 1994). Experts report that frequent interaction with and positive feedback from family members can account for much of the impact of the deaf child's development of positive self-identity, especially in light of their risk for negative peer interactions (Gurlanick, Conner, Hammond, Gottman, & Kinnish, 1996; Spencer, 1996).

Some evidence suggests that deaf children are more impulsive than hearing children and often are rated by their mothers as being overly dependent, restless, fussy, and disobedient; thus, secure attachment from infant to mother may be compromised. Normal developmental milestones such as sitting and walking may occur later than expected, especially if the child is severely deaf.

Unless an effective early communication system is established, the child's cognitive abilities may be negatively impacted.

Undoubtedly, the biggest challenge facing the parents of deaf children is establishing an effective communication system. Hearing parents face a significant challenge in trying to unlearn habitual communication patterns and replace them with patterns more appropriate to the visual mode. Many experts advocate the use of deaf adults as models of effective sequential communicators (Bodner-Johnson, 1991).

VISUAL IMPAIRMENTS/BLINDNESS One of the most significant problems of parents with infants who are blind is the inability to establish eye contact. The infant's gaze is an important cue in sustaining reciprocal interactions with a caregiver, and it promotes positive social and emotional behaviors. Also, babies who are blind do not display the clearly differentiated facial expressions of sighted babies. They smile less often and often fail to smile even at the sound of the mother's voice, and the signals they give to their caregivers are more subdued. As a result, the inability of parents and other caregivers to interpret their babies' signals may lead to disruption in the bonding and attachment process. Research has shown that a blind child, during the second year, does not have a mental representation of the mother that can sustain her in the mother's absence.

Programs directed at supporting parents of children who are blind teach parents to provide many experiences that stimulate their young children's senses—hearing, touch, taste, smell, and movement. To develop communicative competence, parents learn to respond to all of the child's attempts to communicate by using alternative signals such as verbal response, soft touch, the imitation of vocalizations, and expanding on child utterances.

EMOTIONAL/BEHAVIORAL DISORDERS This exceptionality may be the most challenging of all for parents. It is often not clear with emotional/behavioral disorders whether children behave the way they do because of parents' behavior or if parents behave the way they do because of their children's behavior. In any event, the complex interactions of parents and children can cause the child's behavior either to improve or to deteriorate.

When young children do not respond well to usual disciplinary techniques, parents are likely to become angry, frustrated, and ineffective. Other parental behaviors associated with children with behavioral disorders include:

- Unreasonable or punitive discipline
- Emotional deprivation or rejection
- Severe marital conflict
- Requiring perfectionism
- Overindulgence
- Detachment
- Authoritarianism

When severely withdrawn children do not react or respond to parents' attempts to communicate and interact with them, parents may feel helpless, hurt, and guilty. Understandably, the negative feedback from the child affects the parent and causes him or her to respond in a negative manner, so that a vicious cycle of unhealthy behaviors—from child and parents alike—occurs. It is no wonder that many parents search avidly for a diagnosis to explain the child's behavior.

There are almost as many ways to deal with emotional/behavioral disorders as there are types of behaviors. Treatment often depends on the provided explanation of the behavior. For example, if a biological/medical model is accepted, parents are likely to use medication to regulate the child's behavior; if the behavior is explained through a psychoanalytic model, parents are likely to seek therapy to uncover the underlying causes of the behavior. If it is viewed through the behavioral lens, behavior modification techniques are likely to be used. Sometimes a combination of techniques is used. In any event, parents of children who are emotionally or behaviorally disordered need ample support to deal effectively with their children's behavior.

GIFTEDNESS Gifted children do not present the same types of challenges to parents presented by children with disabilities because most parents are happy to have a gifted child. However, some parents of gifted children may demonstrate behaviors that are on the opposite end of a continuum: they may fail to nurture the child's giftedness, not understanding his precocity, or they may exploit his exceptional traits and push him beyond reasonable limits. Oftentimes it is difficult for parents to find the right balance of nurturance and stimulation of giftedness and realistic expectations.

Parents of gifted children can learn to encourage original thinking, questioning, and experimentation without being overly demanding, treating the child as a normal member of the family. Providing a variety of reading materials and challenging experiences, avoiding interference with the child's work, and resisting the temptation to dominate or control the child's activities all are ways in which parents can nurture giftedness and encourage initiative and independence. To avoid conflict between gifted and nongifted siblings, the gifted characteristics of one sibling should not be overemphasized. All children should be encouraged to excel in the areas that are most congruent with their natural abilities and interests (Tuttle & Cornell, 1993).

Resilient Children

Resilience refers to a child's capacity to withstand stressors, overcome adversity, and achieve higher levels of self-mastery, self-esteem, and internal harmony. There is a continuum of potential resilience to counterbalance the vulnerability in children with disabilities (Poulsen, 1993). On the one end, children who are healthy, easy temperamentally, developmentally competent, and born into families that can provide positive relationships, appropriate expectations, and minimal environmental stress tend to develop sufficient self-regulation to respond to and recover from environmental challenges. Because they have acquired a repertoire of responses, they have the flexibility to respond in a manner consistent with the context and intensity of the situation. Resilient children experience smooth transitions and recover from stressful events in appropriate ways.

At the other end of the continuum are those children born at biological risk who are living in families overwhelmed by psychosocial and environmental circumstances and who often confront challenges that stress them beyond their capacity to cope. Children with difficult temperaments are more vulnerable to family stressors than those with easy temperaments. Unless vulnerable children receive identification and intervention early on, they will demonstrate negative developmental outcomes. If parents and other caregivers are not emotionally overwhelmed by their interpersonal and family lives, they can contribute to child resilience. Reassurance, encouragement, and appropriate developmental opportunities all help the child to learn resilience (Poulsen, 1993).

Research repeatedly shows that support for parents helps to mediate some of the stress experienced in rearing children with special needs. In the section that follows we take a look at contemporary ways in which support and empowerment help families cope with their children who have exceptionalities.

SUPPORT AND EMPOWERMENT FOR PARENTS WITH EXCEPTIONAL CHILDREN: BEST PRACTICES

Today, many more children with exceptionalities are being served at younger ages. Federal legislation promotes the idea of **family-centered support services,** a notion that embraces the idea that services should center on and be responsive to the needs of all family members as they relate to the child's development. An *Individualized Family Service Plan (IFSP)* is required, targeting the whole family, not just the child, for intervention. Principles for a family-centered philosophy include the recognition that the family is the constant in the child's life, and as such, recognize family strengths; a family-centered strategy also respects a family's choices regarding their desired outcomes for their child (Bruder, 1995).

Similar to family-centered services, **empowerment principles** allow families to control the direction and outcomes of support services (Turnbull, Turnbull, Erwin, & Soodak, 2006). They, too, promote family strengths and decision making. Below, we discuss several contemporary family support and empowerment strategies that promote children's and families' health and well-being. Unless otherwise noted, these strategies are adapted from the work of Barbara Van Haren, Director of Special Education for the Cooperative Extension Agency, Brookfield, Wisconsin, and Craig Fiedler, Professor of Special Education at the University of Wisconsin (2008).

Be Empathic and Foster Hope

As with any other type of family service, those of us who work with families and their exceptional children should be empathic and demonstrate understanding and compassion. When we display empathy for families, it allows us to approach families in judgment-free ways. When we are able to lay our judgments and personal opinions aside, we can then best put ourselves in the place of the families we are serving, and better understand the day-to-day challenges and frustrations they face. By showing empathy and understanding, we can then oftentimes be the voice of hope for parents and families. Careful not to be unrealistic of an exceptional child's future, we can be optimistic and hopeful for a child's continual progress.

Recognize Families as Experts and Enhance Their Self-Efficacy

As professionals who work with individuals and families, we oftentimes forget that we are not the experts—the parents and family members who interact with their exceptional child are the ones who best know the child. While we as service providers, educators, and family scientists might be able to help families identify their strengths and competencies, from time to time we must step out of our expert roles and allow families to see that they, indeed, "have what it takes" to help their child reach his or her developmental potentials. When we take a step back, families feel better supported and their strengths emerge—they feel empowered and motivated.

Enhance Family Access and Offer Family Networking

As our study has shown us, family support can come from a number of sources. Families who have accessible means of support, such as being able to place their exceptional child in the neighborhood school, are better able to build networks—both with other families who may share common ground and with families of children who do not have a child with disabilities. These family connections may assist parents in accessing new information, such as with parent-to-parent programs where matches are made between a "veteran" parent of a disabled child and a more experienced parent. Family connection networking may also help them to become more comfortable with the setting they have chosen to educate their child(ren). Schools can also serve as conduits between families and federal/state programming.

Encourage Effective Problem-Solving and Coping Skills

There are a number of processes involved in effective problem solving. First, families must be able to define the problem. As you saw in Chapter 5, this can be difficult because each of us assign different meanings to different situations. Next, families need to generate possible solutions; depending on the child's severity of disabilities, solutions will vary. Families then need to choose a solution or solutions, and they then need to implement the solution. Of course, these are difficult—if not impossible—steps without trained professionals guiding the way. Finally, parents must evaluate the effectiveness of their chosen solution(s). You can see why support and empowerment from service providers and educators are necessary to help parents and children alike. As a colleague of an exceptional child recently shared with us, "When we learned that our son was hearing impaired and cognitively delayed, we were devastated. I have my graduate degree in Special Education, and even still, when we first got the news I felt like I was being smothered. I looked at my husband and said, 'If we feel this helpless, imagine how families without an education in this feel.'"

Summary

Parents of children with exceptionalities face many challenges. The initial diagnosis of a disability in a child shatters a dream, and most parents experience a period of grieving for the loss of a healthy child. Overwhelming evidence suggests that parenting an exceptional child is stressful. The intensity and duration of stress vary, depending on a variety of child, family, professional, and cultural factors, and increased stress may surface at various times throughout the life cycle. However, most research suggests that with appropriate support, these families are little different from other families in healthy functioning and family environment.

Families of children with disabilities share many characteristics, but each disability brings its special challenges and rewards to parents.

Many children with disabilities demonstrate resilience—a remarkable capacity to adapt to stress and adversity and to achieve much higher levels of self-mastery and self-esteem than would be expected. Specific parental behaviors seem to contribute to a child's resiliency.

Early-intervention services for young children with disabilities and their families are mandated to implement a family-centered philosophy whereby parents are full partners in the decision making and in the assessment of and delivery of services to their children. Today, there are many family-centered support and empowerment strategies that professionals can use in their efforts to enhance the lives of exceptional children and their families.

References

American Psychological Association. (2011). *ADHD*. Retrieved May 9, 2011 from: http://www.apa.org/topics/adhd/index.aspx

Achenbach, T., Howell, C., Quay, H., & Conners, C. (1991). National survey of problems and competencies among four- to sixteen-year-olds: Parents' reports for normative and clinical samples. *Monographs of the Society for Research in Child Development, 56*(3), 1–120.

Beckman, P. (1991). Comparison of mothers' and fathers' perceptions of the effect of young children with and without disabilities. *American Journal on Mental Retardation, 95*(5), 585–595.

Bodner-Johnson, B. (1991). Family conversation style: Its effect on the deaf child's participation. *Exceptional Children, 57*(6), 502–509.

Bruder, M. (1995). The challenge of pediatric AIDS: A framework for early childhood special education. *Topics in Early Childhood Special Education, 15*(1), 83–99.

Centers for Disease Control and Prevention. (2010a). *Fetal alcohol spectrum disorders (FASDs)*. Atlanta, GA: Author. Retrieved August 12, 2010, from http://www.cdc.gov/ncbdd/fasd/index.html.

Centers for Disease Control and Prevention. (2010b). *Fetal alcohol spectrum disorders (FASDs): Data & statistics in the United States.* Atlanta, GA: Author. Retrieved August 12, 2010, from http://www.ncbi.nlm.nih.gov/pubmed/15095471.

Centers for Disease Control and Prevention. (2010c). *Prematurity*. Atlanta, GA: Author. Retrieved August 5, 2010, from http://www.cdc.gov/Features/PrematureBirth/.

Child Development Institute. (2010). *About learning disabilities*. Retrieved August 12, 2010, from http://www.childdevelopmentinfo.com/learning/learning_disabilities.html.

Dyson, L. (1991). Families of young children with handicaps: Parental stress and family functioning. *American Journal on Mental Retardation, 95*(6), 623–629.

Dyson, L. (1996). The experiences of families of children with learning disabilities: Parental stress, family functioning, and sibling self-concept. *Journal of Learning Disabilities, 29*(3), 280–286.

Erwin, E. (1994). Social competence in young children with visual impairments. *Infants and Young Children, 6*(3), 26–33.

Floyd, F., & Gallagher, E. (1997). Parental stress, care demands, and use of support services for school-age children with disabilities and behavior problems. *Family Relations, 46*(4), 359–371.

Freedman, R., Litchfield, L., & Warfield, M. (1995, October). Balancing work and family: Perspectives of parents of children with developmental disabilities. *Families in Society: The Journal of Contemporary Human Services,* 507–514.

Freund, L. (1994). Diagnosis and developmental issues for young children with Fragile X syndrome. *Infants and Young Children, 6*(3), 34–45.

Gargiulo, R. M. (2005). *Special education in contemporary society.* Florence, KY: Wadsworth.

Gottlieb, A. (1997). Single mothers of children with developmental disabilities: The impact of multiple roles. *Family Relations, 46*(1), 5–12.

Gottwald, S., & Thurman, K. (1994). The effects of prenatal cocaine exposure on mother–infant interaction and infant arousal in the newborn period. *Topics in Early Childhood Special Education, 14*(2), 217–231.

Gurlanick, M., Conner, R., Hammond, M., Gottman, J., & Kinnish, K. (1996). The peer relations of preschool children with communication disorders. *Child Development, 67,* 471–489.

Hallahan, D., & Kauffman, J. (2000). *Exceptional learners* (8th ed.). Boston: Allyn & Bacon.

Innocenti, M., Huh, K., & Boyce, G. (1992). Families of children with disabilities: Normative data and other considerations on parenting stress. *Topics in Early Childhood Special Education, 12*(3), 403–427.

Judge, S. (1998). Parental coping strategies and strengths in families of young children with disabilities. *Family Relations, 47*(3), 263–268.

Krehbiel, R., Munsick-Bruno, G., & Lowe, J. (1991). NICU infants born at developmental risk and the Individualized Family Service Plan/process (IFSP). *Children's Health Care, 20*(1), 26–32.

Landau, S., & McAnnich, C. (1993). Young children with attention deficits. *Young Children, 48*(4), 49–57.

Marcenko, M., & Meyers, J. (1991). Mothers of children with developmental disabilities: Who shares the burden? *Family Relations, 40*(2), 186–190.

Meadow-Orlans, K. (1994). Stress, support, and deafness: Perceptions of infants' mothers and fathers. *Journal of Early Intervention, 18*(1), 91–102.

Moses, K. (1983). The impact of initial diagnosis: Mobilizing family resources. In J. Mulick & S. Pueschel (Eds.), *Parent–professional partnerships in developmental disabilities services* (pp. 11–34). Cambridge, MA: Academic Guild.

National Center for the Dissemination of Disability Research. (2010). *Disparities in obesity and disability (Part 2): Developing research partnerships and collaborations* (PR#H1331060028). Retrieved August 12, 2010, from www.ncddr.org/webcasts/24/webcast_24030410.ppt.

Poulsen, M. (1993). Strategies for building resilience in infants and young children at risk. *Infants and Young Children, 6*(2), 29–40.

Reid, R., Maag, J., & Vasa, S. (1993). Attention deficit hyperactivity disorder as a disability category: A critique. *Exceptional Children, 60*(3), 198–214.

Rodrigue, J., Morgan, S., & Geffken, G. (1992). Psychosocial adaptation of fathers of children with autism, Down syndrome, and normal development. *Journal of Autism and Developmental Disorders, 22*(2), 249–262.

Smith, D., & Luckasson, R. (1992). *Introduction to special education: Teaching in an age of challenge.* Needham Heights, MA: Allyn & Bacon.

Spencer, P. (1996). The association between language and symbolic play at two years: Evidence from deaf toddlers. *Child Development, 67,* 867–876.

Suarez, L., & Baker, B. (1997). Child externalizing behavior and parents' stress: The role of social support. *Family Relations, 46,* 373–381.

Sulkes, S. B. (2006). *Mental retardation/intellectual disability.* Retrieved August 13, 2010, from http://www.merck.com/mmhe/sec23/ch285/ch285a.html.

Thurman, S., & Gonsalves, S. (1993). Adolescent mothers and their premature infants: Responding to double risk. *Infants and Young Children, 5*(4), 44–51.

Trivette, C., & Dunst, C. (1992). Characteristics and influences of role division and social support among mothers of preschool children with disabilities. *Topics in Early Childhood Special Education, 12*(3), 367–385.

Trute, B. (1990). Child and parent predictors of family adjustment in households containing young developmentally disabled children. *Family Relations, 39*(3), 292–297.

Turnbull, A. P., Turnbull, H. R., Erwin, E. & Soodak, L. (2006). *Families, professionals, and exceptionality: Positive outcomes through partnership and trust* (5th ed.). Columbus, OH: Merrill/Prentice Hall.

Tuttle, D., & Cornell, D. (1993). Maternal labeling of gifted children: Effects on the sibling relationship. *Exceptional Children, 59*(5), 402–410.

University of Illinois at Chicago. (2002). *The influence of culture on attitudes toward dying, death and grieving*. Retrieved July 20, 2010, from http://www.tneel.uic.edu/tneel-ss/demo/grief/frame1.asp.

Van Haren, B., & Fiedler, C. R. (2008). 20 ways to support and empower families of children with disabilities. *Intervention in School and Clinic, 43*(4), 231–235.

Walker, H., & Severson, H. (1990). *Systematic screening for behavior disorders (SSBD): A multiple gating procedure*. Longmont, CO: Sopris West.

Wallace, H. (1992). Perspective: Early steps in the care of disabled children being taken in some developing countries. *Infants and Young Children, 4*(3), v–viii.

Chapter 11
Alternatives to Biological Parenthood

Most people become parents by biologically bearing children, but a small percentage of individuals do not wish to or cannot achieve parenthood through the ordinary methods of reproduction. Adopting children is a desirable option for some, and others may wish to utilize one of the assisted-reproduction approaches. Others may elect to become foster parents. Each alternative has its appealing characteristics as well as its risks because there are legal, social, economic, and moral issues associated with each. This chapter explores the alternatives to biological parenthood.

THE EXPERIENCES OF ADOPTIVE PARENTS

Adoption provides a legal process that creates a parent–child relationship between individuals who are not biologically related (Schulman & Behrman, 1993). Adoption offers a means of providing a pregnant woman with an alternative home for her child, offers a solution for a couple who cannot have children of their own or who wish to complete their family, and it provides a child with a family.

In the United States today, adoption is characterized by a bit of a paradox. On one hand, there are large numbers of infertile couples urgently seeking babies for adoption to begin or to expand their families. On the other hand, nearly 134,000 children are waiting to be adopted (Child Welfare League of America [CWLA]; 2010). Most of these children are in foster care while permanent homes and families are being sought for them. In 2009, only 1 percent of babies born to unmarried women were placed for adoption (CWLA, 2010).

The numbers of waiting children are increasing steadily. The apparent contradiction arises from the fact that most people who wish to adopt are seeking healthy infants (usually white), whereas the children waiting to be adopted are predominantly older, are children of color, are members of sibling groups, and/or may have emotional, physical, or mental disabilities (children with "special needs") (Schulman & Behrman, 1993).

Experts speculate that the discrepancy between the number of couples seeking to adopt and the number of available healthy infants is the result of increased incidence of infertility among married couples and an absolute decrease in the number of infants placed for adoption. For example, each year in the United States, over 6 million couples face difficulties becoming pregnant and turn to adoption to begin or complete their families (American Adoptions, 2009). Also, today there is a tendency for married women to keep their babies, rather than place them for adoption (Fein, 1998).

Children may be adopted *formally* (a legal recognition of a parental relationship is made) or *informally* (someone—usually a family member—assumes responsibility for a child without obtaining legal recognition, which is very common among African American and Latino American families). Birth parents may relinquish their parental rights to an agency that in turn consents to adoption by specific adoptive parents; or birth parents may give consent directly to adoptive parents.

Historically, adoptions were either open or closed. In **open adoptions,** birth parents and adoptive parents know one another, exchange information, and often continue contact and communication over time, whereas in traditional **closed adoptions,** the identity of birth parents is not revealed to the adoptive parents or to the children. Open adoption became standard practice during the 1980s because of the belief that it facilitated healthy psychological development of both children and their adoptive parents.

Who Adopts?: Characteristics of Adoptive Parents

About 2 million adults—approximately 2 percent of the U.S. adult population—have adopted children (CWLA, 2010). Interestingly, more than twice the percentage of men (about 2.3 percent) have adopted a child compared to women (about 1.1 percent). People over the age of 30 (either currently married or formerly married) and who have either given birth or fathered a child are more likely to adopt than those who have never been married or who are without biological children (CWLA, 2010). Adoptive mothers tend to be older; about one-half of all adoptive mothers are between the ages of 40 and 44. Conversely, adoptive fathers tend to be younger, usually between the ages of 30 and 44 (CWLA, 2010). To date, about 100,000 never-married men and 73,000 never-married women have adopted children (CWLA, 2010).

Unrelated adoptions are more common among white women, whereas related adoptions appear to be somewhat more common among African Americans (Chadwick & Heaton, 1999). Latino women are much less likely to have ever adopted any child than are their African American or white counterparts. Also, women reporting higher levels of education or family income are significantly more likely to have adopted, especially unrelated children, whereas related adoptions are more common among those with lower levels of education and income (Chadwick & Heaton, 1999).

Adoptive and biological parents do not differ in levels of depression, overall health, levels of self-esteem, traditional attitudes toward family life, parents' acceptance of maternal employment, importance parents placed on desirable behaviors of children, frequency of parental discipline, involvement in children's activities, parents' perceptions of children's well-being, perceived behavior problems of children, prosocial behaviors exhibited by children, and educational expectations of their children (McKenzie, 1993). In contrast to earlier research using clinical samples, the researchers concluded that adoptive parents and biological parents were quite similar.

Intrafamily Adoptions

Intrafamily adoption occurs when someone adopts a stepchild, or with the adoption of a relatives child (such as an aunt legally adopting her nephew). One body of research explored issues considered in stepchild adoption (Ganong, Coleman, Fine, & McDaniel, 1998). This research estimated that 100,000 stepchildren are adopted by their stepparents every year. Although there are many similarities between stepparent/stepchild adoptions and unrelated adoptions, there also are contextual differences. Adoption by a stepparent requires the nonresidential parent to relinquish all legal ties to the child. He or she may do so voluntarily or be legally forced to do so. Termination of parental rights requires that the nonresidential parent be declared unfit and/or a judgment that termination is in the best interest of the child.

Gay and Lesbian Adoption

The landscape of gay and lesbian adoption continues to undergo rapid change. Currently, over 20 states in the United States allow gay and lesbian parents to legally adopt the biological child of their partner. Additionally, some states allow individual gays or lesbians to adopt, but they do not allow same-sex couples to adopt.

Generally, when considering any gay/lesbian adoption, today's courts are primarily interested in "the best interest of the child," and beliefs that lesbian and gay adults are not fit parents have no empirical foundation (among many others, Anderssen, Amlie, & Ytteroy, 2002; Patterson, 2000; Perrin, 2002). As such, a person's sexual orientation cannot be used as a factor in determining whether a homosexual individual or couple can adopt or foster-parent a child. Three states—Arkansas, New Hampshire, and Florida—prohibit gay and lesbian individuals and couples from being adoptive or foster parents. The American Civil Liberties Union (ACLU), a nonprofit, nonpartisan group that monitors the individual civil liberties of Americans spelled out in the Constitution, maintains that this is because these states adhere to "stereotypical" views that gays and lesbians are unfit to be parents.

Those opposed to the concept of same-sex adoption may believe that a female role model and a male role model are necessary in children's lives. Others claim that children who are reared by gay or lesbian parents might themselves grow

Today, more and more states are loosening their restrictions on same-sex couples being allowed to adopt children. Although some believe that both male and female role models are necessary for optimal child development, to date research does not bear out these concerns. Are you in favor of or opposed to same-sex adoption? Why or why not?

up to be homosexual, or that gay men might molest their children. Others are concerned that children of gay and lesbian parents will be teased ruthlessly and relentlessly by their classmates. Issues at the forefront of this discussion address gender identity and sexual orientation, as well as children's overall well-being:

- *Gender Identity:* In response to whether children need both a mother and a father in order to establish a solid gender identity, studies show that few differences in gender identity exist between children reared by same-sex parents and heterosexual parents (Golombok, Spencer, & Rutter, 1983; Green, 1978; Green, Mandel, Hotvedt, Gray, & Smith, 1986; Hoeffer, 1981).
- *Sexual Orientation:* Empirical studies reveal that being raised by homosexual parents does not increase the likelihood that the child will be gay or lesbian (Bailey, Bobrow, Wolfe, & Mikach, 1995; Bigner & Jacobson, 1989; Green, 1978).
- *Children's Well-Being:* Having gay or lesbian parents is less an indicator of the quality of the parent–child relationship than parenting styles are. Ultimately, it is the quality of parenting, not sexual orientation, that determines how children of same-sex parents fare (Lott-Whitehead & Tully, 1992; McCandish, 1987; Pennington, 1987).
- *Shared Parenting:* Lesbian and gay parents tend to divide childcare tasks and responsibilities relatively evenly, and report higher levels of satisfaction in their couple relationships than heterosexual couples do (Bos, van Balen, & van den Boom, 2004; Ciano-Boyce & Shelley-Sireci, 2002; Johnson & Connor, 2002).
- *Parenting:* Gay and lesbian parents possess better parenting skills than heterosexual couples do; this is reportedly due to greater levels of parent–child interaction and lower levels of physical punishment (Brewaeys & Van Hall, 1997; Flaks, Ficher, Masterpaqsqua, & Joseph, 1995).

Perhaps Sara Bonkowski (2003) best sums up the experience of same-sex adoption when she explains,

> Remember that a child needs the love and support of both parents. If one parent is gay or lesbian, in time the child will know and come to understand. Many of the concerns and worries that may be raised about homosexuality are concerns of adults; the concerns of a child are much simpler. If a gay or lesbian parent forms a caring paternal or maternal bond with his or her young child, by the time the child is old enough to understand homosexuality the child will know the parent and appreciate that Mom or Dad is, in every respect, a "good parent."

THE EXPERIENCES OF ADOPTED CHILDREN

Only a small percentage of the total population of children less than 18 years of age are adopted by nonbiologically related adults (Brodzinsky, 1993). However, because of the increase in international adoptions, this number is rising rapidly. Slightly more children in the United States are adopted by related than by unrelated adults, and more children with special needs are being adopted.

Children with Special Needs

Special needs is the term used to describe those children who, because of the presence of certain characteristics and conditions, are particularly difficult to place for adoption. The category includes older children; children with physical, mental, or emotional disabilities; and children who are part of a sibling group. Recently the term has become broader in meaning to include a child-welfare service that seeks permanent homes for children in foster care who will never be able to be reunited with their birth parents. Most of these children have experienced significant trauma in their young lives, including deprivation, physical and sexual abuse, abandonment, loss, and many moves in foster care. As a result, they are prone to emotional, behavioral, and learning problems. Once these children are adopted, they are very challenging to parent. Many of these children spend years waiting to be adopted.

Older children or children who have spent many years in foster care have a crucial need for adoptive parents. These youngsters have experienced emotional trauma, including multiple separations from their families while in foster care. Frequently they have experienced deprivation and abusive treatment. A majority have lived in families in which drugs, alcoholism, and violence were prevalent. Many are members of sibling groups, and most are boys (McKenzie, 1993).

Transracially Adopted Children

The term **transracial adoption** means the joining of racially different parents and children together in adoptive families (Silverman, 1993). Transracial adoption may be divided into two major categories: (1) the adoption of foreign-born children of a different race from the adopting American families, usually white, and (2) the adoption of American-born children of different race by American families, also usually white (Schulman & Behrman, 1993). In the United States, the term is sometimes reserved for the adoption of African American children by white families, but it includes also the adoption of Native American, Asian, and Hispanic children by white families (Silverman, 1993). Many refer to the adoption of foreign-born children as international adoption.

Constituting a very important part of the total adoption picture, *international adoption* provides an avenue for parents in the United States who want infants but are unable to adopt them. For other parents who are low on the list of potential eligible adopters, this avenue significantly increases the range of parenting choices. A single person, gay or lesbians (single or in a long-term partnership or marriage), or an over-40 couple are often precluded from adoption in the United States. Usually they can find at least some countries abroad where they can adopt. From the child's perspective, international adoption is also advantageous. For most of the homeless children of the world, international adoption represents the only realistic opportunity for permanent families of their own (Bartholet, 1993).

As a result of political pressure and rising nationalism, there has been growing hostility to international adoption in many countries that have previously been willing to free some of the homeless children for adoption by foreigners. The laws regulating adoption are varied among the "sending" countries, and numerous obstacles stand in the way of foreigners who wish to adopt. Aspects of the U.S. immigration laws pose additional obstacles in the path to the adoption of foreign-born children by American citizens (Bartholet, 1993).

Outcomes of Adoption

Historically, adoption has been viewed as a highly successful societal solution for the problems confronting children whose biological parents could not or would not provide for them. In fact, the literature is overwhelmingly supportive of the benefits of adoption for these children, particularly when we consider the alternative caregiving options available for them. For example, research indicates that adopted children fare much better than those youngsters who are reared in institutional environments or in foster care. Furthermore, adoptees develop significantly better than children who are reared by biological parents who are ambivalent about caring for them or who do not want them (Brodzinsky, 1993).

PSYCHOLOGICAL BENEFITS Considerable debate has arisen in the professional literature about the possibility of increased psychological risk in adopted children compared with nonadopted children. Although most adoptees are well within the normal range of development, as a group they are more vulnerable to various emotional, behavioral, and academic problems than their nonadopted peers living in intact homes with their biological parents (Bordzinsky, 1993). It must be noted, though, that the majority of studies documenting the increased risk of psychological and academic problems among adopted children have used samples that consist of children being seen in-clinic for various types of problems.

In one national study, the outcomes of adopted children were compared with those of biological children (Borders, Black, & Pasley, 1998). The researchers found adopted children to be self-confident and in control and to view their adoptive parents as nurturant, comforting, predictable, and positively concerned. Additionally, children had strong bonds with their adoptive parents and demonstrated positive psychological health, showing no differences from biological children in adjustment or prosocial behaviors. Just as their parents were similar to biological parents, adopted children were similar to biological children.

AGE DIFFERENCES Brodzinsky (1993) noted that there was substantial variability in the patterns of adjustment of adoptees, much of which is tied to such factors as age, gender, family structure and dynamics, and preplacement history. Most research has failed to find differences between adopted and nonadopted children in infancy, toddlerhood, and the preschool years. It is not until children are about 5 to 7 years of age that significant differences between these groups emerge. At this age, most children begin to understand the meaning and implications of being adopted. As children's knowledge of adoption deepens, so do their feelings of anxiety and confusion about their family status. Although the clinical literature suggests that adjustment difficulties for adoptees continue and perhaps even increase during adolescence, research data are sparse and contradictory on this issue.

GENDER DIFFERENCES Boys, adopted or nonadopted, tend to be more vulnerable than girls on a number of psychological variables, especially disruptive disorders and academic problems. In addition, some data suggest that the relative adjustment difficulties of adoptees compared with nonadoptees are greater for boys than for girls; however, at this point it is not possible to draw a firm conclusion regarding gender differences in adoption adjustment. Research on the ordinal position of the adopted child also has produced mixed results (Brodzinsky, 1993).

FAMILY CHARACTERISTICS Family communication patterns related to adoption are linked to the child's adjustment. It has been suggested that a more open "acknowledgment of difference" style of communication about adoption among family members ultimately facilitates healthier adjustment in adoptees than a closed, "rejection of difference" approach (Brodzinsky, 1993).

Acceptance of and satisfaction with adoptive parenthood, coupled with a warm and accepting attitude toward the child, are generally predictive of more positive adoption adjustment, compared with parental rejection of the child and parental dissatisfaction with adoptive parenthood. Problems in adopted children are more likely to be manifested when there are emotional problems in one or both of the adoptive parents and/or when there is a history of death or divorce within the adoptive family.

PREPLACEMENT HISTORY Preplacement history involves both the prenatal and the postnatal experiences of the child before entering the adoptive family. Adverse prenatal experiences such as heightened maternal stress, poor maternal nutrition, and inadequate medical care—as well as fetal exposure to alcohol, drugs, and other harmful agents—are linked to increased developmental problems in childhood.

Of all the postnatal risk factors, perhaps none has been investigated as frequently as age at placement. Numerous authors have argued that the older the child at the time of placement, the greater the chance of postplacement adjustment difficulties. Critical to any underlying increased psychological risk are the specific experiences the child encounters before adoption placement. Children who experience multiple changes in caretaking environments, as well as neglect and abuse, before being placed for adoption are significantly more likely to experience adjustment difficulties, including adoption disruption (Brodzinsky, 1993).

Children's Coping Strategies

The primary assumption of the **stress-and-coping model** of children's adoption adjustment is that children's adjustment to adoption is determined largely by how they view or appraise their adoption experience and by the type of coping mechanisms they use to deal with adoption-related stress (Brodzinsky, 1993). It is assumed that when children view adoption as stigmatizing, threatening, or involving loss, a pattern of negative emotions associated with stress (such as confusion, anxiety, sadness, embarrassment, and anger) is likely to be experienced. When children experience these emotions, they consider various coping options and eventually choose one or more to reduce their distress. They may choose to talk with a friend or a parent, or they may think about adoption in a new way so that it does not sadden or anger them. Other children may attempt to put all thoughts about adoption out of their minds or to avoid anything that reminds them of adoption. Although no one pattern of coping is necessarily associated with healthier adjustment, research generally suggests that overreliance on avoidance strategies often is tied to increased maladjustment patterns.

The way children view or appraise the experience of adoption is tied to many child-related characteristics, such as the child's level of cognitive development, temperament, self-esteem, sense of personal control, and interpersonal trust. Genetic, prenatal, and birth factors also affect how children appraise their adoptions. These biological factors influence children's well-being through their impact on cognitive, social, and emotional development. The way children view their adoption experience and cope with it may be tied to the feedback they receive about their adoptive status from society, from peers, and, most important, from the family in which they live.

In the last decade, adoption has become public, and increasingly children are told, even before they can fully understand, how they came to their families. Often the story is shared with family, friends, relatives, teachers, and sometimes strangers. Although adoption was once hidden, children today can belong to play groups consisting entirely of adopted children, buy storybooks about being adopted, go to summer camps for children adopted from particular foreign countries, and obtain treatment from therapists who specialize in adoption, should they need it (Fein, 1998).

ADULT ADOPTEES: THE SEARCH FOR BIRTH PARENTS

Numerous studies have focused on the search for birth parents by adult adoptees (Andersen, 1988; Pacheco & Eme, 1993). In the early 1950s adult adoptees began to express their needs and argue for their rights to obtain more knowledge about their backgrounds, and professionals studying adoption began to describe the adverse effects of the lack of this knowledge on adoptees, birth parents, and adoptive parents. All these forces led to changes in the adoption policies in most states (Schulman & Behrman, 1993).

Until the 1970s, adoption was shrouded in secrecy and stigma. Adoptive parents had little, if any, information about the birth parents of their adopted child, and most often children were told nothing about their adoptions. Over the last three decades, however, notable changes have occurred.

Adoption practices now lie on a continuum of openness, allowing for different levels of communication between adoptive families and birth parents (Mendenhall, Grotevant, & McRoy, 1996). In *confidential adoptions,* no communication between adoptive families and birth parents exists. In *fully disclosed,* or open, adoptions, adoptive families and birth parents maintain direct, ongoing communication. In *mediated adoptions,* communication is relayed through third parties without exchange of identifying information. Many adoptive families move along this continuum through their life cycle, and openness changes in response to one or more members' dissatisfaction with that current level. Research has shown that adopted children, during adolescence or early adulthood, often initiate searches for their birth parents.

Why do adults who were adopted in childhood search for their birth parents? Respondents in one study gave the following reasons for initiating a search for their birth parents: pregnancy or birth of a child of their own, medical or health concern, death of adoptive parents, engagement or marriage, and stress (Pacheco & Eme, 1993). Most adult adoptees who are asked why they initiated searches respond that they want more information on their medical history for the sake of their children or that they are interested in their genealogy and want to fill in their own histories.

The majority of adoptees who search do not do so because they have poor relationships with their adoptive parents (March, 1997; Pacheco & Eme, 1993). Rather, searching emerged from a need to fill the identity gaps created by secrecy in adoption. By gaining access to their birth mothers, they were able to form more cohesive identities based on complete knowledge of their genetic and genealogical roots. Concerns about the reactions of their adoptive parents often prevent adoptees from searching earlier. In fact, some adoptees even wait until their adoptive parents are dead, and others search without their adoptive parents' knowledge. If open adoption becomes more prevalent, the need for adult adoptees to search will diminish.

Some research indicates that only about one-half of adoptees tell their adoptive parents before they initiate searches for their birth parents. Interestingly, adoptees will often tell their fathers about their searches, but not their mothers. For example, one study found that more than 68 percent of the searchers had told their adoptive fathers about their searches, but 66 percent had not told their adoptive mothers (Lichtenstein, 1996). It appeared that adoptive families' discussion of adoption and adoptees' feelings that their adoptive parents were open to discussing adoption were important in decisions to reveal adoptee searches.

One study explored adult adoptees' reunions with their birth parents (Pacheco & Eme, 1993). The results indicated these reunions were rated as positive by 86 percent of the sample. Similarly, the majority of adoptees felt that the reunion improved their self-concept, self-esteem, emotional outlook, and ability to relate to others. Indeed, given the worst scenario about the reunion (rejection by the biological parent), every adoptee insisted that despite the stress involved, he or she would do it again if given the opportunity.

The principal element contributing to dissatisfaction seemed to be unrealistic expectations. Many of the adoptees found that their biological parents had an assortment of problems and needs they were not prepared to deal with, such as alcoholism, poverty, and illness. This led some to conclude that they had had a much better life than they would have had with their biological parents.

THE ADOPTION PROCESS

Each adoption agency may have its own policies and procedures, but generally there are seven steps to adoption. The process may take months, or a few years, depending on whether the couple or individual desires to adopt a newborn baby, or if they are waiting for a specific race/ethnicity.

Initial Information

To begin, each prospective adoptive parent must select an agency or a private organization through which to adopt. Couples may choose to adopt *domestically* (from the U.S.), or *internationally* (from abroad). For example, Angelina Jolie and Madonna chose to adopt their children from other countries. Many people believe that international adoptions cost far less than domestic adoptions, but this is not the case. According to the National Council for Adoption (2008), domestic and intercountry adoptions can range from $8,000 to $40,000; typically, adoptions fall in the $15,000 to 25,000 range. In the United States, the majority of international adoptions are from China (National Council for Adoption, 2008). Wait times also vary, depending on the country from which a couple adopts. In the United States, the average wait time is 1 to18 months; the average wait for a baby from China is 1 year, and most Russian adoptions take 6 to 12 months. For 2006, the U.S. Department of Citizenship and Immigration Services reported that slightly over one-half of the children adopted from China were 1 to 4 years old; over two-thirds of the children adopted from Russia were 1 to 4 years old.

Preparation

To be eligible for adoption, prospective parents must undergo a home study. The home study helps to ensure that the child is going to be placed in a loving, caring, nurturing home. During the study, a social worker interviews the couple and assesses such things as their relationship stability, their feelings about and readiness for becoming parents, and aspects about their daily lives. The social worker also checks the parents' health and income status; parents undergo a scrutinizing background check as well. Many adoption agencies and placement agencies are assigned a specialist who helps them through each stage of the adoption process.

The Family-in-Waiting

After the adoptive family has successfully completed all required documentation and have completed the home study, they are considered to be a family-in-waiting—they enter a somewhat unknown waiting period until a match occurs that results in a successful adoptive placement. This time frame varies for every adoptive family.

The Placement

After the couple is matched with a birth mother/couple, the adoptive couple works with the specialist until the baby is born or an older child is found. Placement typically occurs immediately after all of the paperwork is completed and filed. Perhaps one of the most intensely felt fear of adoptive parents is that the birth mother will change her mind; in reality, however, very few birth mothers decide to raise their babies after initiating the adoption process, but it is their right to do so. It is very important that a birth mom is not forced into her decision by others. Women who do change their minds about placing their children for adoption are typically under the age of 17, have no future plans, live with their parents, and have mothers who oppose the adoption (Adamec, 2004).

It's Final!

After the specified time frame has passed (this varies from state to state), and all of the documentation has been completed and filed with the court, a final court hearing is held and the adoption decree is awarded to the parents.

Adoption has long been a socially acceptable way of achieving parenthood. And although much has been learned about the effects of adoption procedures and the long-term outcomes of being adopted, there still are many social, ethical, and legal challenges in current adoption practice that require thoughtful attention and development of appropriate standards. Research should continue to investigate the long-term effects of adoption and identify all the variables that affect outcomes.

Many couples experience unexpected outcomes when they are unable to become pregnant, when they are infertile. For some couples, becoming pregnant represents grueling work and becomes a difficult and heart-wrenching challenge.

WHEN CONCEPTION FAILS: INFERTILITY

In the United States today, approximately 6.1 million women and over 2 million married couples are unable to conceive (Centers for Disease Control and Prevention, 2005a). **Sterility** refers to the absolute inability to reproduce, either because the woman has no uterus or ovaries, or the male has no testes or sperm production. No amount of medical intervention can help a sterile person reproduce. **Infertility** is the inability to conceive a baby after trying for a period of 1 year.

Women and Infertility

Approximately one-third of the problems associated with infertility are due to women's reproductive systems (American Society of Reproductive Medicine, 2006). Specifically, problems with the monthly release of an ovum from the ovary (ovulation) are responsible for most female infertility. Lack of ovulation may be due to *hormonal imbalances,* which refers to a decline in or an absence of the hormones estrogen and progesterone, which are necessary for pregnancy. Other causes for infertility may be a pituitary gland tumor (quite rare) or lifestyle habits such as poor nutrition (as in the case of anorexia or bulimia), stress, or even intense athletic training (U.S. Department of Health and Human Services, 2003). Once a woman reaches the age of 35, her ovaries' ability to produce eggs diminishes. As Figure 11.1 describes, a number of women who experience ovulation difficulties turn to egg donors to assist their fertility efforts.

Even when women successfully ovulate, the fertilized ovum may have difficulty reaching the uterus due to blocked or scarred fallopian tubes. This disorder, called **pelvic inflammatory disease (PID),** is primarily caused by untreated sexually transmitted infections (i.e., gonorrhea and chlamydia). PID renders 150,000 women per year infertile—making it the leading cause of infertility in young women (Centers for Disease Control and Prevention, 2009b). **Endometriosis,** a disease characterized by the buildup or migration of uterine tissue to other parts of the body (such as the ovaries or fallopian tubes), may also prevent the fertilized ovum from traveling through the fallopian tube to the uterus, or may prevent the fertilized ovum from becoming embedded in the uterine lining.

Men and Infertility

About one-third of fertility difficulties are due to male reproductive problems (American Society of Reproductive Medicine, 2006). Healthy, robust

Across college campuses, classified ads are seeking eggs—egg donors, that is. Calling for physically attractive women under the age of 29, fertility agencies are paying big bucks for eggs. Compensation for egg harvesting typically starts at $5,000, and skyrockets when high I.Q. and high SAT scores are combined with good looks and good personality traits. It is not uncommon for some fertility agencies to pay up to $20,000 when a donor has the right stuff. Compensation is even higher—up to $25,000—for Jewish and Asian donors, whose genetic material is high in demand. In the United States, it's illegal to be paid for body parts, but fertility experts claim that they are not compensating women for their eggs, per se, but for their time, effort, and discomfort.

Once approved for donation, the donor self administers by injection synthetic hormones that cause the woman's ovaries to produce many eggs—as many as a few dozen, instead of one, which is typical. Once the eggs are mature, ovulation is triggered by medication, and a needle through the vagina retrieves the eggs. The entire process can span up to six months.

1. In your opinion, should the harvesting and sale of human eggs be legal? Why or why not?
2. Do you think it's fair that only beautiful and intelligent women are sought after?
3. Would you, or anyone you know, sell your eggs for profit? Why or why not?

FIGURE 11.1 Eggs for Sale!
Source: Welch, *Family Life Now*, 2e. (2010). Boston: Allyn & Bacon. p. 337.

sperm are necessary in order for fertilization of the ovum to take place. There are two primary forms of infertility in men: *azoospermia,* which means that no sperm cells are produced, and *oligospermia,* which means that few sperm cells are produced. Sometimes these conditions are the result of a genetic disease, such as cystic fibrosis; sometimes they are the result of poor reproductive health. To produce an adequate number (at least 20 million sperm per milliliter of semen), the male must be healthy and lead a healthy lifestyle.

The American Society of Reproductive Medicine (ASRM) is an internationally recognized nonprofit medical organization that disseminates information, education, and standards in the field of reproductive health. According to the ASRM (2006), to improve fertility, men should consult with a physician about the proper vitamins and minerals that improve sperm function. In addition, men should limit alcohol intake and stop smoking, as alcohol lowers testosterone levels and smoking may cause the production of malformed, slow-moving sperm. Finally, men should keep their cool. For healthy sperm production, the testes must be cooler than the rest of the body—this is why nature designed the male's testicles to hang outside of the body. Males considering parenthood may want to avoid hot tubs, saunas, steam rooms, very hot baths, and placing laptop computers on their laps. Although folklore suggests men should wear boxers rather than briefs to promote the production of healthy sperm, to date no empirical evidence has been found to support such claims.

Treating Infertility

Each year, about 9 million American women receive infertility medical treatments of some kind (Centers for Disease Control and Prevention, 2009c). There are a variety of treatment options available, ranging from medication (fertility drugs to enhance ovulation) to surgery. Less invasive medical treatments include fertility drugs and donor insemination, often referred to as artificial insemination. In women, fertility drugs increase egg production. When fertility drugs are used, sometimes more than one egg is produced, which leads to multiple births, as in the case of this country's first set of septuplets. **Artificial insemination,** a popular fertility treatment used by both heterosexual and homosexual couples, is the medical process in which donor sperm is placed into the woman's vagina, cervix, or uterus by a syringe. Sperm are collected (through masturbation of the donor) and stored by medical facilities

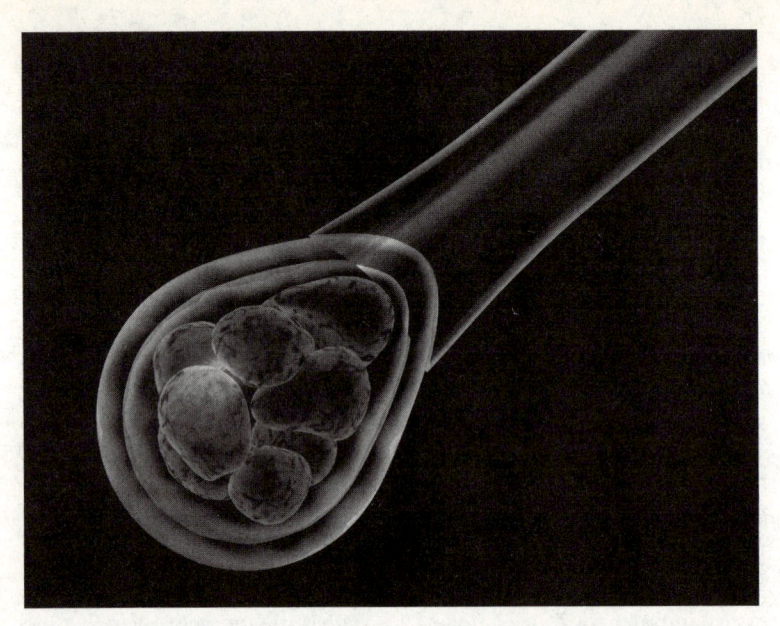

Today, infertile couples have a number of different assisted reproductive technology (ART) options available to them to help them to become biological parents. In IVF, for example, a woman's eggs are retrieved from her ovary; these eggs can be immediately fertilized, or frozen for later use.

called **sperm banks.** Sperm donors are typically paid $30–50 per specimen; a vial of sperm from a sperm bank costs about $350.

If these treatment options fail, there are other more invasive (and more costly) treatment options. The following are descriptions of **assisted reproductive technology (ART),** which are treatments that involve fertilization through the hands-on manipulation of the woman's ova and the male's sperm. In 2003, 48,000 babies were born in the United States as a result of ART (ASRM, 2006).

- **In vitro fertilization (IVF):** In infertile couples where a woman has blocked or absent fallopian tubes, or where the man has a low sperm count, IVF is typically used to help the couple conceive. IVF is a process whereby a woman's eggs are surgically removed from her ovary and mixed with a man's sperm in a laboratory culture dish. After about 40 hours in the culture dish, the eggs are examined to see if they were fertilized, and if they were, to see if cell division is taking place. If the balls of cells appear to be growing at a normal rate, the eggs (embryos) are placed within the uterus. This process bypasses the fallopian tubes. The average cost of IVF is $12,400 per attempt (ASRM, 2006).
- **Gamete intrafallopian transfer (GIFT):** This ART process also involves manually manipulating the sperm and eggs, but instead of fertilizing the eggs in a dish, the unfertilized eggs and the male's sperm are placed in the woman's fallopian tubes. This is designed to foster natural fertilization within the woman's fallopian tubes. Implantation rates are higher for this technique. The average cost of GIFT is approximately $10,000 per attempt (ASRM, 2006).
- **Zygote intrafallopian transfer (ZIFT):** Like IVF, this process requires the woman's eggs to be fertilized by the man's sperm in a laboratory culture dish. The

fertilized egg is then placed immediately in the woman's fallopian tubes, rather than in her uterus (as in IVF), allowing the conceptus to travel naturally to the uterus and implant. Implantation rates are not as high as GIFT implantation rates. The average cost of ZIFT is $10,000 per attempt (ASRM, 2006).
- **Surrogacy:** A woman may desire to have a biological child, but for medical reasons she cannot sustain a pregnancy. For these women, IVF is performed; rather than having the embryos implanted into her uterus, however, the embryos are implanted into a **surrogate mother,** who carries the pregnancy to term. Upon birth, the baby is given to the biological parents.

The Psychological Impact of Infertility

Infertility is distressing, frustrating, and depressing. Hoping, longing, and wishing month after month after month for a positive pregnancy test only to find out that the efforts failed yet again constitutes a life crisis for couples. The stress on finances and the stress on the marriage can lead to a breakdown of the couple's relationship. Fortunately, many support groups and infertility counseling organizations exist to help infertile women and couples navigate through the physical and emotional challenges infertility brings. Groups such as the National Infertility Association and the International Council on Infertility Information Dissemination offer psychological, psychosocial, and informational support for those experiencing infertility.

FOSTER PARENTHOOD

Another alternative to biological parenting is to become a foster parent. **Foster care** refers to placing a child in the temporary care of a family other than its own; it is sometimes referred to as *out-of-home-care.* Foster care is necessary when a child cannot remain safely in his or her own family of origin, such as because of abuse or neglect, or while the various steps of the adoption process are being completed. Foster care settings include nonrelative family homes, relative homes, group homes, emergency shelters, residential facilities, and preadoptive homes.

Foster care does not exist primarily for the benefit of adults who are seeking children but instead to substitute for, or supplement, families who do not, or cannot, adequately care for their children. Children are placed in foster care when a local social-services agency and the courts have determined that current parental care for the children has fallen below acceptable community standards and the children are at risk for harm (Barbell & Wright, 1999; Marcus, 1991).

The removal of a child from his or her biological parents is a serious step. It's difficult to imagine a greater intrusion into the lives of families by the government or society than that of separating children from their biological parents. The question arises as to what conditions would warrant this extreme action. In response, Congress passed the Adoption and Safe Families Act (ASFA), which was signed into law in late 1997. This new legislation authorized the Family Preservation and Family Support program, named it the Promoting Safe and Stable Families program, and modified and clarified a wide range of policies established under the Adoption Assistance and Child Welfare Act of 1980. States now have clearer guidelines for the safety of children and the decision-making process leading to permanency (Barbell & Wright, 1999).

Almost always, children enter foster care not as a result of their behavior (such as being a chronic runaway), but because of the actions of their parents. Children are removed from their family's home for a number of reasons, such as:

- Physical abuse
- Neglect
- Parent drug or alcohol abuse
- Sexual abuse
- Inadequate housing
- Inability to cope
- Parent's incarceration

- Child's disability
- Death of a parent
- Abandonment

Foster children range in ages from birth up to the age of 18, and come from diverse backgrounds.

The Children

At any point in time in the United States, there are an estimated 510,000 children in foster care, and an estimated 289,000 who are leaving "the system" (U.S. Department of Health and Human Services, 2009). As we just saw, placement settings vary, and Figure 11.2 illustrates for us the various placements of foster children. Today, almost one-half (46 percent) of foster children are placed with families they do not know or to whom they are not related. As the data shows us in Figure 11.3, there are racial/ethnic differences in the percentages of those children who are in foster care.

The preferred goal of any placement is permanency with caring parents (U.S. Department of Health and Human Services, 2009). Seen in Figure 11.4, nearly 50 percent have a goal of reunification with their parent(s) or primary caregiver(s); only about one-fourth have a goal of adoption. When children leave the foster care system (referred to as *exits*) slightly over one-half are reunited with their parents or caregivers.

EMOTIONAL EFFECTS ON CHILDREN Understandably, the process of placement itself, even if necessary to protect the child, is an additional source of distress for most children. During placement, children experience the loss of a familiar environment and the rupture of relationships in the family and the community. Along with the challenge to the child's identity as a member of his or her family of origin, the child also is likely to feel anxiety about other family members still at home and sometimes guilt at being in a more nurturant environment than other family members.

In the new home, there are additional issues and stresses, including adaptation to a new

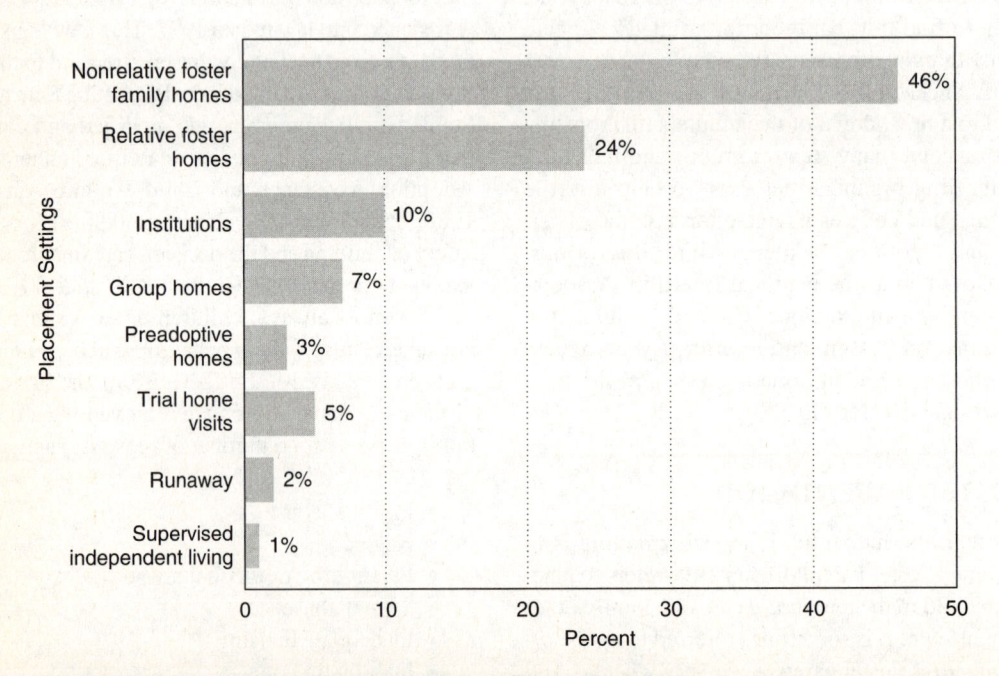

Placement Setting	Percent
Nonrelative foster family homes	46%
Relative foster homes	24%
Institutions	10%
Group homes	7%
Preadoptive homes	3%
Trial home visits	5%
Runaway	2%
Supervised independent living	1%

FIGURE 11.2 Placement settings for children in foster care: 2006.
Source: Based on data from U.S. Department of Health and Human Services (2009).

the foster home. The demand for rapid adjustment during a period of separation and loss may exacerbate existing problems for the child or contribute to the development of new emotional and behavioral problems (Rosenfeld et al., 1997).

Consideration of the emotional needs of foster children has focused on the issues arising as the immediate consequences of placement, blame, and loss. Children in foster care often blame themselves for their separation from their parents. Foster children need to grieve their losses, but they may be inhibited from doing so out of their fear that the expression of grief and anger will alienate the foster family. They may not feel the support and security necessary to open themselves to expression of loss. Instead, they may experience a "honeymoon" period with underlying distress before being able to grieve (Rosenfeld et al., 1997).

HEALTH EFFECTS ON CHILDREN Studies have shown that foster children have three to seven times more acute and chronic health conditions, developmental delays, and emotional adjustment problems than other poor children.

A number of researchers have addressed the health status of children in foster care (Altshuler & Gleeson, 1999; Rosenfeld et al., 1997; Zlotnick, Kronstadt, & Klee, 1998). For example, one

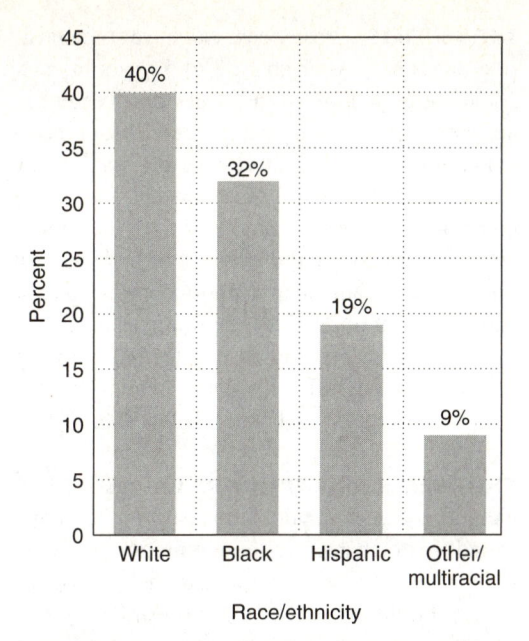

FIGURE 11.3 Race and ethnicity of children in foster care: 2006.

Source: Based on data from U.S. Department of Health and Human Services (2009).

context; possibly a poor match of personalities, resources, and needs between those of the foster family and those of the child; and, in the worst cases, retraumatization from abuse or neglect in

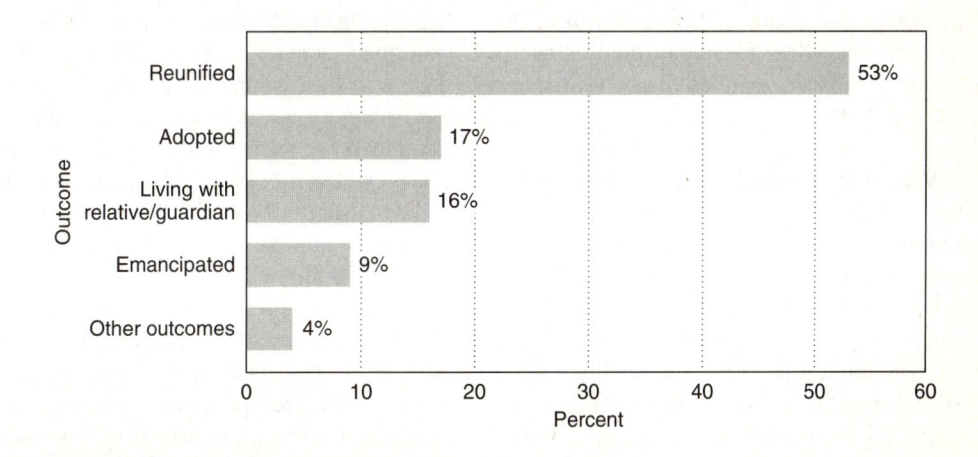

FIGURE 11.4 Outcomes for children exiting foster care.

Source: Based on data from U.S. Department of Health & Human Services (2009).

study showed that 60 percent of preschool foster children had developmental delays, 35 percent had chronic medical problems, 15 percent had birth defects, and 15 percent were of short stature. Many have lost parents to HIV, and increasing numbers are infected as well. Often, they have not received routine health care, have not been immunized, and continue to have unmet health needs after placement (Rosenfeld et al., 1997). Another study noted that 20 percent of all children in out-of-home care exhibit some type of disability and that 45 to 80 percent have some chronic or significant physical problem (Altshuler & Gleeson, 1999).

MENTAL HEALTH Foster children also have extensive mental health needs. Nearly one-half have some psychological disorder and more have behavior problems. On average, foster children have more than 14 risk factors (poverty, perinatal stress, mothers with little education, family discord or divorce, parental alcoholism, parental mental illness, and so forth). Also, young foster children are likely to blame themselves for their plight and feel that they are "throwaways" (Rosenfeld et al., 1997). Exacerbating these problems is the fact that most children in foster care do not receive the healthcare (including mental healthcare) they need, even after placement (Silver et al., 1999). Some research indicates lower rates of emotional disturbance for children living in kinship care than for those in nonrelative care (Altshuler & Gleeson, 1999).

BEHAVIORAL PROBLEMS Behavioral problems such as attention seeking, aggression, and delinquency are more common for foster children than for other children. Behavioral problems are linked with the number of placements, marital instability of biological parents, infrequent parental visits, abuse by biological parents, and the child's gender. Estimates of the prevalence of emotional disturbance (e.g., withdrawal, anxiety, depression, somatic complaints, difficulties with attachment) range from 25 to 96 percent.

THE BENEFITS Foster care can have some positive outcomes. After about 2 to 5 years in care, some children show significant improvement in academic achievement; many receive better medical care than before placement; and some show improvement in social development and social competence. The best predictor of a good long-term outcome is a child's ability to form at least one positive relationship with someone, not necessarily a parent or relative (Rosenfeld et al., 1997). Some research has shown that teens in kinship care function significantly better than their peers in nonrelative care (Altshuler & Gleeson, 1999).

CHILDREN'S PERCEPTIONS Gardner (1998) examined the perceptions of foster children and found that consistently these children related to their foster families rather than to their biological kin as "family." In fact, in their ideal family representations, biological parents and siblings were excluded, suggesting some level of disconnectedness from their biological families. Research has shown that foster children are satisfied with the care they receive from foster parents (e.g., Wilson & Conroy, 1999). Most children have reported that growing up in a foster family resembled growing up in one's own family. However, foster children are aware that their families are not like others. They often express the need for more background information about their biological parents, and 50 percent in some studies have described themselves as having no roots. Children who lose contact with siblings because of out-of-home placement lose contact with a source of support for resolving their grief over parental loss as well as the potential future support of adult siblings. Many foster children express the desire to see their siblings more often (Gardner, 1998).

Unfortunately, child well-being is not a variable in monitoring and evaluation. Growth and change in caseloads have placed considerable demand on the child welfare system; accountability, expedited permanency, managed care, and outcome-based contracting has redefined the policy environment for the system. Therefore, systematic measures of child well-being rarely are used to assess the current functioning of children while in foster care or changes in their functioning as a result of receiving services (Altshuler & Gleeson, 1999).

BOUNCING FROM FOSTER HOME TO FOSTER HOME Children with initial psychological problems experience more placement changes. Poor academic progress, poor adjustment in school and community, and emotional and behavior problems when discharged from foster care also have been found to be positively related to the number of changes in placement. Changes in placement may be necessary because of the child's feelings of insecurity and lack of attachment to his foster parents, leading to a deterioration in the relationship, progressing to the point at which daily disruptions cannot be tolerated by the foster parents, who then request that the child be transferred. Transfer also may be required because the caretaker decides not to continue as a foster parent because of the need to group siblings together, or because of the need for transfer to a longer-term placement when attempts at reunification have been unsuccessful.

The Foster Parents

People become foster parents for a number of reasons. Some indicate that they feel a sense of moral obligation, often based on religious beliefs. For others, becoming foster parents offers an alternative to adoption or an opportunity eventually to adopt a child. To many foster parents, these children fill a void created by the departure of their own children. A few enter the foster-parent program for the financial incentives offered by the agencies.

Foster parents are charged with enormous tasks because they must attempt to stabilize a child's life despite previous emotionally damaging experiences the child may have experienced. Foster parents should possess the same characteristics and skills that are desired in any parent providing care and treatment to promote the child's development physically, emotionally, intellectually, socially, and spiritually (Daly & Dowd, 1992). Thus, the foster care environment should be more than free from abuse and neglect and in compliance with legal and licensing guidelines—the foster parent should be dedicated and skilled in childcare. In addition, experts propose that foster parents should have positive values, good social skills, high energy, and good judgment (Daly & Dowd, 1992). In short, they must demonstrate the skills in parenting that one would want children to develop. In an effective, positive environment, caregivers are continually teaching new skills to children instead of focusing on problem behavior. Other research reports that successful child placement occurs when foster parents (Marcus, 1991):

- Have had prior foster parent experience
- When they function as loving, caring substitute parents
- When they are tolerant of children and allow them to function as individuals
- When their motives for becoming foster parents are altruistic
- When they allow children to bond with them
- When they provide reliability and stability

The best types of foster parents, then are those who are "psychological parents" to a child whose life has had no such person available in his family of origin. The reasons given by foster parents for dropping out of the system include lack of training, support, and respite care, and the increasing severity of problems presented by the children placed with them.

Foster Care and the Biological Parents

Numerous factors affect the child's length of stay in foster care and/or the ability to return to his or her parents. Oftentimes, the frequency of visitation by biological parents and the number of placements the child has had are associated with length of stay (Marcus, 1991). As seen in Figure 11.5, nearly one-half of the children in foster care stay for a period of 1 to 11 months (U.S. Department of Health and Human Services, 2009). Given this, the importance of the connectedness of the biological family to children in substitute, out-of-home care cannot be overlooked. But given the fact that most children are removed from their family homes due to some type of poor parenting (such as neglect or abuse or substance abuse by the parent), how do we help parents develop their capability for a continual role in their child/children's lives?

An empirical study proposed several ways to assist biological parents in improving their functioning in order to regain custody of their children. One approach is through programs and services that promote family and parent competencies and the provision of social support (Schatz & Bane, 1991). Probably the most widely used services for parents are therapeutic services that include mental health and alcohol/drug-related clinical therapy programs. Generally, parents are referred to a system outside the protective-service unit, with some therapeutically oriented intervention. The caseworker is responsible for management of the family in need. Other approaches and techniques include parent-support groups, family rights groups, parent-education groups, parent groupwork, social-support networking, and intensive treatment programs. The techniques and skills used to facilitate change in biological parents include contracting, communication skills, decision making, problem solving, behavior modification, and role modeling.

Training and self-help programs also provide assistance to biological parents. Self-help programs are designed to build on the strengths of families and to make available to all families the respect and resources needed for reunification. The major goal is to help parents learn to act responsibly on behalf of their children as quickly as possible. These programs include neighborhood parent-support groups, community networking, and group work with parents.

An empowerment-based approach is based on the belief that parents whose children are in out-of-home care must sustain involvement with and responsibility for their children if at all possible (Schatz & Bane, 1991). Biological parents must feel empowered in their roles as caregivers to preserve and possibly reunify their families. They must also become advocates for their children's needs, and they must believe that they can be good parents for their children while they are in substitute care. To accomplish these goals, the researchers provided parents with pertinent information, skill development, and social-support opportunities to increase their capacity to understand the steps necessary for maintaining responsible involvement with their children and

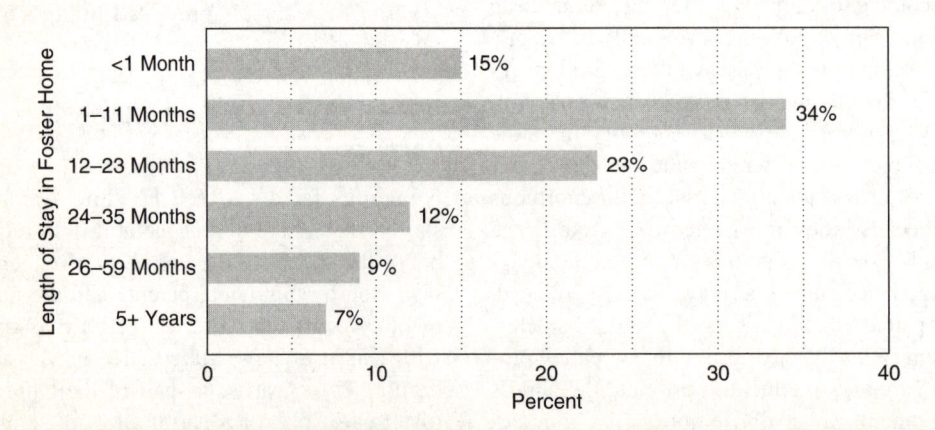

Length of Stay in Foster Home	Percent
<1 Month	15%
1–11 Months	34%
12–23 Months	23%
24–35 Months	12%
26–59 Months	9%
5+ Years	7%

FIGURE 11.5 Length of stay for children exiting foster care: 2006.
Source: Based on data from U.S. Department of Health & Human Services (2009).

achieving the necessary growth and development that would result in the family's reunification.

While parents are being rehabilitated, contacts with their children in foster care are encouraged. Visits between noncustodial parents and their children are crucial for successful reunification. Some visits are supervised because parents have abused or neglected their children. Oftentimes visits are difficult because parents overestimate how much they will be able to directly interact with their children. Parents also sometimes feel that they must compete with foster parents. Because of this, children may experience conflict of loyalties between the two families.

Summary

Adoption, various forms of assisted reproductive technology, and foster parenthood are potential alternatives to traditional biological childbearing. Adoption has long been a socially acceptable alternative, but with the number of available babies for adoption continuing to decline, adults are seeking other ways to achieve parenthood. With increased technology and acceptance of alternative lifestyles, in vitro fertilization, artificial insemination, and other forms of reproductive technology have become more popular. Foster parenthood has long been an alternative, and some couples choose either initially to become parents in this manner or to add children to the family by this approach.

Sadly, the foster care system has many disadvantages for both the parents and the children involved. As we have learned in this chapter, foster children have a range of psychological and other problems that make parenting extremely difficult, and unfortunately, the lack of permanence in placement precludes the development of lasting parent–child relationships and attachment. Yet for many parents and children, the foster care relationship can be extremely positive, and the development of the children can be facilitated.

More research is needed on each of these alternatives to parenthood, and particularly on the outcomes for children. Legal and social issues must be resolved so that both parents and children can benefit from their respective family situations.

References

Adamec, C. (2004). *The complete idiot's guide to adoption.* New York: Penguin.

Alschuler, S., & Gleeson, J. (1999). Completing the evaluation triangle for the next century. *Child Welfare, 78*(1), 125–148.

American Adoptions. (2009). *The steps to adoption.* Retrieved August 1, 2009, from www.americanadoptions.com.

American Society of Reproductive Medicine. (2006). *Infertility in women and in men.* Retrieved March 18, 2006, from www.asrm.org/patients/faqs.html#Q2.

Andersen, R. (1988). Why adoptees search: Motives and more. *Child Welfare, 67*(1), 15–19.

Anderssen, N., Amlie, C., & Ytteroy, E.A. (2002). Outcomes for children with lesbian or gay parents: A review of studies from 1978 to 2000. *Scandinavian Journal of Psychology, 43,* 335–351.

Bailey, J. M., Bobrow, D., Wolfe, M., & Mikach, S. (1995). Sexual orientation of adult sons of gay fathers. *Developmental Psychology, 31*(1), 124–129.

Barbell., K., & Wright, L., (1999). Family foster care in the next century. *Child Welfare, 78*(1), 3–14.

Bartholet, E. (1993). International adoption: Current status and future prospects. *The Future of Children: Adoption, 3*(1), 89–103.

Bigner, J. J., & Jacobsen, R. B. (1989). Parenting behaviors of homosexual and heterosexual fathers. *Journal of Homosexuality, 18*(1/2), 173–186.

Bonkowski, S. (2003). Gay and lesbian parenting. *Family Law Advisor.* Retrieved August 12, 2004, from www.divorcenet.com/il/ilart-15a.html.

Borders, L., Black, L., & Pasley, K. (1998). Are adopted children and their parents at greater risk for negative outcomes? *Family Relations, 47,* 237–241.

Bos, H. M. W., van Balen, F., & van den Boom, D. C. (2004). Experience of parenthood, couple relationship, social support, and child-rearing goals in planned lesbian mother families. *Journal of child Psychology and Psychiatry, 45,* 755–764.

Brewaeys, A., & Van Hall, E. V. (1997). Lesbian motherhood: The impact on child development and family functioning. *Journal of Psychosomatic Obstetrics and Gynecology, 18,* 1–16.

Brodzinsky, D. (1993). Long-term outcomes in adoption. *The Future of Children: Adoption, 3*(1), 153–166.

Centers for Disease Control and Prevention, Division of Vital Statistics. (2005a). Births: Preliminary data for 2004. *National Vital Statistics Report, 54*(8). Retrieved March 20, 2009, from www.cdc.gov/nchs/data/nvsr/nvsr54/nvsr54_08.pdf.

Centers for Disease Control and Prevention. (2009b). Division of STD Prevention (DSTDP). Retrieved January 10, 2009, from www.cdc.gov/std/.

Centers for Disease Control and Prevention. (2009c). Sexual and reproductive health of persons aged 10–24 years: United States, 2002–2007. *Morbidity and Mortality Weekly Report, 58*(SS06), 1–58. Retrieved August 1, 2009, from http://www.cdc.gov/mmwr/preview/mmwrhtml/ss5806a1.htm?s_cid=ss5806a1_e.

Chadwick, B., & Heaton, T. (Eds.). (1999). *Statistical handbook on the American family.* Phoenix, AZ: Oryx Press.

Child Welfare League of America. (2010). *The nation's children 2010.* Retrieved July 2, 2010, from www.cwla.org.

Ciano-Boyce, C., & Shelley-Sireci, L. (2002). Who is Mommy tonight?: Lesbian parenting issues. *Journal of Homosexuality, 43,* 1–13.

Daly, D., & Dowd, T. (1992). Characteristics of effective, harm-free environments for children in out-of-home care. *Child Welfare, 71*(6), 487–495.

Fein, E. (1998, October 25). Secrecy, stigma no longer clouding adoptions. *Tuscaloosa News,* p. A3.

Flaks, S., Ficher, I., Masterpaqsqua, F., & Joseph, G. (1995). Lesbians choosing motherhood: A comparative study of lesbian and heterosexual parents and their children. *Developmental Psychology, 31,* 104–114.

Ganong, L., Coleman, M., Fine, M., & McDaniel, K. (1998). Issues considered in contemplating stepchild adoption. *Family Relations, 47,* 63–71.

Gardner, M. (1998). Should children know donor parents? *Christian Science Monitor, 90,* p. B5.

Golombok, S., Spencer, A., & Rutter, M. (1983). Children in lesbian and single-parent households: Psychosexual and psychiatric appraisal. *Journal of Child Psychology and Psychiatry, 24,* 551–572.

Green, R. (1978). Sexual identity of 37 children raised by homosexual or transsexual parents. *American Journal of Psychiatry, 135,* 692–697.

Green, R., Mandel, J. B., Hotvedt, M. E., Gray, J., & Smith, L. (1986). Lesbian mothers and their children: A comparison with solo parent heterosexual mothers and their children. *Archives of Sexual Behavior, 15,* 167–184.

Hoeffer, B. (1981). Children's acquisition of sex-role behavior in lesbian-mother families. *American Journal of Orthopsychiatry, 51,* 536–544.

Johnson, S. M., & O'Connor, E. (2002). *The gay baby boom: The psychology of gay parenthood.* New York: New York University Press.

Lichtenstein, T. (1996). To tell or not to tell: Factors affecting adoptees' telling their adoptive parents about their search. *Child Welfare, 75*(1), 61–72.

Lott-Whitehead, L., & Tully, C. (1992). The family of lesbian mothers. *Smith College Studies in Social Work, 63,* 265–280.

March, K. (1997). The dilemma of adoption reunion: Establishing open communication between adoptees and their birth mothers. *Family Relations, 46,* 99–105.

Marcus, R. (1991). The attachments of children in foster care. *Genetic, Social, and General Psychology Monographs, 117*(4), 367–394.

McCandish, B. M. (1987). Against all odds: Lesbian mother family dynamics. In F. W. Bozett (Ed.), *Gay and lesbian parents* (pp. 23–36). New York: Praeger.

McKenzie, J. (1993). Adoption of children with special needs. *The Future of Children: Adoption, 31*(1), 62–76.

Mendenhall, T., Grotevant, H., & McRoy, R. (1996). Adoptive couples: Communication and changes made in openness levels. *Family Relations, 45,* 223–229.

National Council for Adoption. (2008). *Adoption facts and statistics.* Retrieved August 11, 2009, from http://www.adoptioncouncil.org/resources/facts_stats.html.

Pacheco, F., & Eme, R. (1993). An outcome study of the reunion between adoptees and biological parents. *Child Welfare, 72*(1), 53–64.

Patterson, C. J. (2002). Lesbian and gay parenthood. In M. H. Bornstein (Ed.), *Handbook of parenting, Volume 3: Status and social conditions of parenting* (pp. 255–274). Mahwah, NJ: Erlbaum.

Pennington, S. B. (1987). Children of lesbian mothers. In F. W. Bozett (Ed.), *Gay and lesbian parents* (pp. 58–174). New York: Praeger.

Perrin, E. C. (2002). *Sexual orientation in child and adolescent health care.* New York: Kluwer Academic/Plenum Press.

Rosenfeld, A., Pilowsky, D., Fine, P., Thorpe, M., Fine, E., Simms, M., et al. (1997). Foster care: An update. *Journal of American Adolescent Psychiatry, 36*(4), 448–457.

Schatz, M., & Bane, W. (1991). Empowering the parents of children in substitute care: A training model. *Child Welfare, 70*(6).

Schulman, I., & Behrman, R. (1993). Overview and major recommendations. *The Future of Children: Adoption, 3*(1), 4–16.

Silver, J., DiLorenzo, P., Zukoski, M., Ross, P. Amster, B., & Schlegel, D. (1999). Starting young: Improving the health care and developmental outcomes of infants and toddlers in the child welfare system. *Child Welfare, 78*(1), 148–183.

Silverman, A. (1993). Outcomes of transracial adoption. *The Future of Children: Adoption, 3*(1), 104–118.

U.S. Department of Health and Human Services. (2003, June 17). *Researchers identify a possible cause of infertility in some women with endometriosis.* National Institute of Child Health and Human Development. Retrieved August 1, 2009, from http://www.nichd.nih.gov/news/releases/infertility.cfm.

U.S. Department of Health and Human Services. (2009). *The AFCARS Report: Preliminary FY 2006 estimates as of January 2008* (14). Retrieved July 10, 2010, from www.acf.hhs.gov/programs/cb/systems/afcars/about.htm.

Wilson, L., & Conroy, J. (1999). Satisfaction of children in out-of-home care. *Child Welfare, 78*(1), 53–69.

Zlotnick, C., Kronstadt, D., & Klee, L. (1998). Foster care children and family homelessness. *Child Welfare, 88*(9), 1368–1370.

Chapter 12

Alternatives for Childcare and Early Education

Parents need alternatives for caring for their children for a variety of reasons, including their need for temporary relief from continual responsibility for childrearing, the desire to provide opportunities for the child to interact with peers, and/or so that the child can receive cognitive stimulation. But, as you saw in Chapter 8, today more than half of married couples in the United States are dual-earners—not surprisingly, then, the primary reason that increasing numbers of parents seek alternative care and education is that mothers work outside of the home. According to the National Association of Child Care Resource and Referral Agency (NACCRRA, 2010b), today over 11 million children under the age of 5 spend an average of 36 hours per week in the care of someone other than their mother.

Historically, childcare was considered a service for working parents, whereas early childhood education, or preschool, was intended for educational or enrichment purposes for those children whose families could afford it. Recently, however, early childhood professionals have begun to emphasize that all programs for young children should be of the same quality. The terms **care** and **education,** then, are meant to refer to programs that provide both early care and education, whether they are on a half-day or a full-day basis and whether they occur in centers, homes, schools, or churches.

Along with the economic crisis that swept the U.S. in 2009 came the increasing difficulty or impossibility for young families to live on one income. There is no question that childcare and early education programs are becoming a widespread necessity for a diversity of families. This chapter discusses the different alternatives for childcare and early education available for parents today, as well as self-care and after-school programs for school-age children. As we conclude, we examine the age-old question: Is alternative childcare or early education harmful to a child's development?

TYPES OF CARE AND EDUCATION

In the United States, weekly childcare arrangements vary by the child's age and by the type of care they receive. As Figure 12.1 illustrates, anywhere from about one-fourth to nearly 60 percent of children from the ages of under 1 year to 5 years receive no childcare from anyone other than their parents (U.S. Department of Health and Human Services, 2009). But nearly two-thirds (60 percent) of America's children do require some type of childcare arrangement because of their parents' employment (U.S. Department of Health and Human Services, 2009).

The most important priority of working parents is finding alternative care for their children that is not only safe, but that also promotes the children's health, well-being, and development. Contemporary parents have a number of childcare and early education alternatives available to them, and each alternative has its advantages as well as its disadvantages. The range of available alternatives is affected by geographic factors, family income, and personal belief systems.

Caregiver in the Home

Many families with young children find that a single caregiver who comes into the home can best meet their needs for the care of the child. These caregivers may consist of fathers, other relatives, and nonrelatives (such as a nanny). We saw in Chapter 8 that many dads are leaving the workforce today so they can care for their children while their wives work outside the home.

As the number of two-parent professional families continues to grow, the number of persons seeking full-time, often live-in, care in their own home increases. In fact, over the last 15 years, several nanny-training programs have been established throughout the United States. It should be emphasized, however, that a very small percentage of families are economically able to employ a full-time nonrelative as a caregiver. Other advantages and disadvantages of this type of alternative care are presented in Table 12.1.

Family Childcare

Family childcare provides care for children in the homes of the providers, who include both relatives and nonrelatives. For example, you saw in

Under 1 year

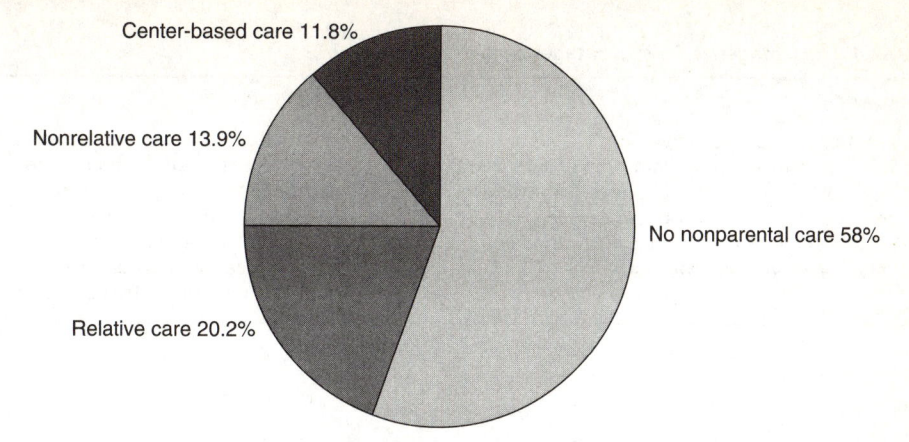

- Center-based care 11.8%
- Nonrelative care 13.9%
- Relative care 20.2%
- No nonparental care 58%

1-2 years

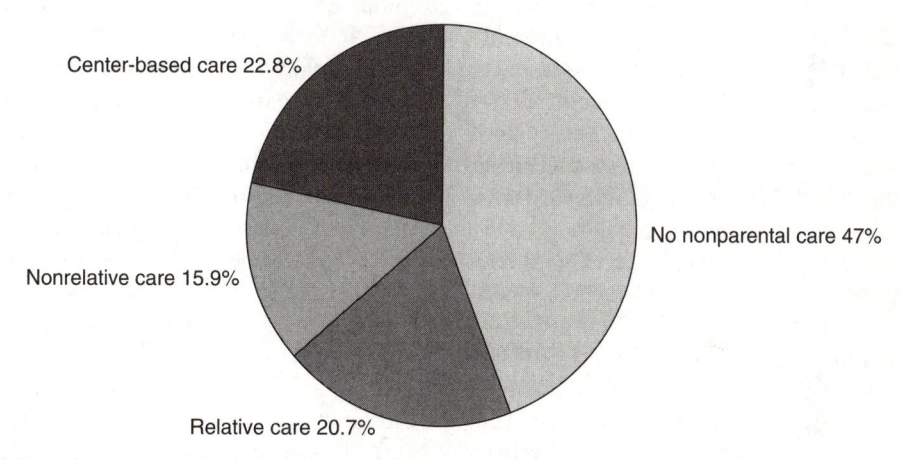

- Center-based care 22.8%
- Nonrelative care 15.9%
- Relative care 20.7%
- No nonparental care 47%

3-5 years

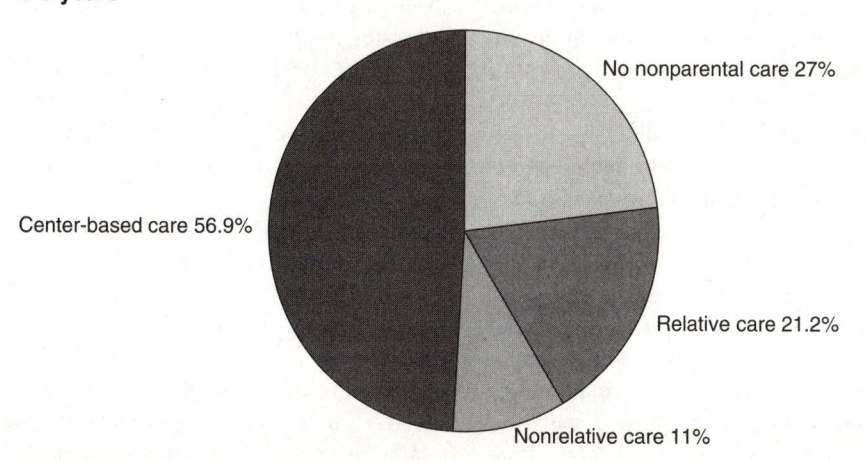

- No nonparental care 27%
- Center-based care 56.9%
- Relative care 21.2%
- Nonrelative care 11%

FIGURE 12.1 Weekly childcare arrangements by age.

Source: Based on data from U.S. Department of Health and Human Services, Health Resources and Services Administration, Maternal and Child Health Bureau, *Child Health USA 2008–2009*. Rockville, Maryland: U.S. Department of Health and Human Services, 2009.

TABLE 12.1 Advantages and disadvantages of caregiver in home.

ADVANTAGES	DISADVANTAGES
Parent can choose caregiver	Finding alternative care when caregiver is ill
Child can remain in familiar home environment	Minimum or no supervision of caregiver
Opportunities for adult-child interactions are greater than in center-based care	Potential loneliness and isolation of caregiver
	Lack of experiences with peers
Children can continue to play with familiar peers in own neighborhood	Limited toys and equipment
	Limited educational experience
	More expensive than other types of care

Chapter 4 that today about three in 10 grandparents are responsible for raising their grandchildren (U.S. Census Bureau, 2008). Referred to as *participatory caretaking* and *voluntary caretaking,* contemporary grandparents (particularly African American/Black Caribbean grandparents) play an active role in their grandchildren's day-to-day care. Figure 12.1 shows us that today, about 20 percent of children ages under 1 to 5 years are cared for by their relatives while their parents work.

Securing relatives to care for the child outside the child's home may have several advantages: the preexisting relationship between the child and the caregiver; the greater likelihood of a relative being loving to the child, thus providing a higher quality of emotional care; and the possibility of less expense for the parents.

STATE REGULATIONS Up to about 16 percent of children under the age of 5 who require alternate care are cared for by nonrelatives in a situation where a caregiver provides care for a few children in her home (see Figure 12.1) (U.S. Department of Health and Human Services, 2009). Most states require that family childcare homes be licensed, certified, registered, or otherwise approved. Regulations relate to the maximum number of children, by age, who may be cared for, as well as health and safety standards. Some states also have regulations relating to the activities provided for the children, equipment, nutrition, discipline, and so on. The specified adult-child ratio and maximum number of children vary from state to state, but the ratio is approximately six children to one adult. This number may or may not include the caregiver's own children. A variation of the family childcare home that may be found in some states is the *minicenter* or group childcare home. In this arrangement, approximately 12 children compose the group, but the center is located in a caregiver's home, and at least two adults must supervise the group.

In spite of the prevalence of family childcare and its potential for meeting the growing needs for childcare, family childcare homes have been largely invisible to public scrutiny. Despite state regulations, the majority of family childcare homes operate outside the formal regulatory system. It has been estimated that 80 percent of family childcare homes are unregulated (Hofferth, West, & Henke, 1994).

QUALITY OF CARE Not surprisingly, the conditions in these homes range from quality care to inadequate or intolerable care. In 2009, two-thirds of the states in the United States received "failing" grades by the NACCRRA's (2010b) regulations and oversight standards. The NACCRRA 2009 report also indicated that some states inspect childcare homes as infrequently as once every 5 or 10 years. To date, only nine states require comprehensive background checks

Today, about 16 percent of families turn to nonrelative care for their children. Oftentimes, this care is provided in someone's home, by a licensed childcare provider.

for family childcare providers. There is also no mandatory minimum education requirement—nearly one-third of childcare providers have less than a high school diploma, and 20 states do not even require that providers have a high school diploma (NACCRRA, 2010b).

CHILDREN'S EXPERIENCES Obviously, responsibility falls on the parent for selecting a quality family childcare home. When parents are considering family childcare, both the advantages and the disadvantages should be considered Very little is known about the kinds of experiences that are provided for the children and the consequences of those experiences on the child's development. The difficulties in locating family childcare homes, the reluctance of caregivers to be observed, the self-selection of caregivers and childcare families, the high turnover, and the changing composition of homes have contributed to the problems of research on family childcare.

To add to these difficulties, the U.S. economic downturn and dramatic rise in unemployment caused a sharp decrease in the number of childcare options available for working parents. For example, the survey of local Child Care Resource and Referral Agencies (CCR&Rs) indicated that nearly one-half (45 percent) of the nation's communities experienced declines in the number of family childcare homes in 2008 (NACCRRA, 2010a).

Recently, a variety of types of support for family childcare has emerged. Family childcare associations are now being organized at the local, regional, state, and national levels. The National Association for Family Day Care has established a voluntary accreditation system for family childcare homes; more than 30,000 family childcare providers have earned a Child Development Associate credential; the Child and Adult Care Food Program provides services to regulated family childcare homes; childcare resource and referral systems in every state maintain up-to-date listings of family childcare providers; a variety of corporations sponsor family childcare networks; and training and technical assistance is provided by a variety of organizations. These increasing support systems are providing ways to reduce the isolation and invisibility of family childcare and, ultimately, have the potential for significant impact on the quality of the care provided (Kontos, Howes, & Galinsky, 1996).

RESEARCH ON FAMILY CHILDCARE Although family childcare is widely used as alternative care for children, especially those younger than age 3, it is the least researched form of childcare in the United States. A few earlier studies, however, help us to better understand this alternative childcare option.

- Mothers who say that the educational features of childcare are important in their choice of care are more likely to choose center-based than family childcare (Johansen, Leibowitz, & Waite, 1996). However, mothers who value their child's knowing the caregiver more often choose family childcare.
- Family childcare users emphasize the childrearing philosophy of the provider and the homelike nature of the setting. Social support from the caregivers is an important indicator of parents' satisfaction (Britner & Phillips, 1995). Agreement on childrearing philosophies is a big factor in parents' satisfaction in family childcare.
- Most providers are uneducated mothers of young children with low levels of skills and limited attachment to the labor market. Licensed providers have more education and experience than unlicensed providers and exhibit other behaviors that indicate a stronger attachment to the profession of childcare; they provide a higher quality of care (Walker, 1992).
- Family childcare providers are less encouraging of autonomy in children and place less emphasis on the role of childcare in developing language and self-control skills, protecting children's health, supporting parents with their problems, and identifying children with special needs; they expect earlier development of some language and social skills and later development of some motor skills (Todd & Deery-Schmitt, 1996).

One study examined the interrelationships of multiple levels of the family childcare system in an attempt to gain a better understanding of this type of family childcare (Kontos, 1994). The "typical" caregiver in this study was in her mid-30s, had received some education past high school, had been caring for children in her home for 7 years, and had specialized training that was limited to workshops and conferences. Average ratings of the quality of the home environments were just above adequate; caregivers engaged in high-level interactions with the children during only 8 percent of the observation time.

These results speak to the need for parents to select a family childcare home carefully, especially since many parents of infants and toddlers prefer this form of care. The considerations should include the background and experience of the caregiver; the background and characteristics of others living in the home; the attitudes of the caregiver; and the number, age, and sex of the children served, since these factors seem to influence the quality of the program provided. It is likely that these caregivers are not sufficiently trained to provide a stimulating environment.

If family childcare homes are to provide rich and stimulating environments for young children, caregivers need specialized training, the number of children should be small, and models and supports should be provided. Caregivers need assistance in utilizing everyday interactions, basic care, and household routines as opportunities to facilitate the children's development. Parents need to be educated to select family childcare homes that are licensed or registered and those in which the strengths of caregivers and programs offered match objectives parents have for their children's care.

Center-Based Care and Education

As shown in Figure 12.1, nearly 60 percent of children between the ages of 3 and 5 receive center-based care (U.S. Department of Health and Human Services, 2009). A comprehensive study conducted by the National Center for Education Statistics (Hofferth et al., 1994) found the following variables to be related to whether children were in center-based programs:

- Three- and 4-year-old children in low-income and lower-middle-income households were less likely than their counterparts in upper-middle-income to high-income households to be enrolled in a center-based program.

Research consistently shows that high-quality childcare programs are beneficial in a number of ways for African American children.

- Children who had mothers with less education were less likely than those with mothers who had attended or graduated from college to participate in center-based programs.
- Preschool children whose mothers were younger than age 20 when they were born and children from larger families (four or more members) were less likely than children of older mothers and children from smaller families to be enrolled in center-based programs.

Center-based care and education generally is more expensive than family childcare, but less expensive than care in the child's own home by a single caregiver. Such care is not cheap—the price of care in a center ranges between $4,500 and nearly $16,000 per year, at least as much as college tuition at a public university (NACCRRA, 2010b). For a family to receive state childcare assistance, they cannot make over $35,000 per year for a family of three (NACCRRA, 2010b). Clearly, this type of childcare is unaffordable for many of today's families. In a weakened economy, the out-of-reach cost associated with high-quality childcare places even more stress on today's families.

The cost of center-based care is based on a number of variables: geographic area of the country, metropolitan as opposed to rural location, educational level and salaries of staff, whether the center is accredited, whether the center is non-profit or for-profit, and so forth. When parents are considering center-based care and education as an alternative, they need to consider both the advantages and the disadvantages (see Table 12.2).

INFANT CARE: DIFFERENT DECADES, DIFFERENT ISSUES

It's a long-debated question, and even today it's a hot-button issue: Does placing infants in care outside of the home harm the parent–child bond? Before the mid-1960s it was believed harmful to separate an infant from his or her mother, and few infants were placed in child-care centers. A number of studies in the 1970s, however, supported the idea that the separation of the mother and infant as a result of child-care was not harmful to mother–infant attachment (among many, Kagan, Kearsley, & Zelazo, 1978; Moskowitz, Schwarz, & Corsini, 1977). The studies of the 1970s are oftentimes referred

TABLE 12.2 Advantages and disadvantages of center-based care and education.

ADVANTAGES	DISADVANTAGES
A greater likelihood that:	*A chance that:*
The center will be licensed or regulated	There will be less flexibility in schedules for individual differences in children
The child will receive continual supervision	
The staff will be trained	There will be less adult-child interaction
The caregiver will not experience isolation	There will be multiple caregivers rather than a single, primary one
The caregivers will always be available	
The child will experience stability of place and routine	The children will be exposed to caregiver's and other children's diseases and/or infections
A wider variety of equipment, materials, activities, and programs will be available	There will be larger groups of children
	The child will have less space
An educational component will be provided	

to as the *first wave* of research on the developmental consequences of early childcare (Belsky, 1990); this wave focused primarily on comparing young children in home care with those in high-quality, university-based, infant-care centers. The studies were conducted to determine whether extensive and routine nonparental care initiated in the first years of life necessarily undermined children's psychological development. A comprehensive review of this first wave of empirical studies revealed that parents have little cause for concern, particularly with regard to socioemotional development, defined in terms of the affective bond between child and mother (Belsky, 1990).

The second wave of research focused on identifying childcare factors and processes that affected the development of children. This research was remarkably successful in identifying social structural features of care—particularly group size, adult–child ratios, and caregiver/teacher training—that systematically relate to the daily processes in the early childhood setting, such as the quantity and quality of time adults spend interacting with children and the extent of focused attention and aimless wandering that children engage in. The findings indicated that when group size is large, ratios are poor, and caregivers/teachers are untrained or unsupervised, individual attention to children is secondary to coping with overextended resources. As a result, both quality of care and child well-being are compromised (Belsky, 1990).

With the third wave of research in the 1980s, the issue of the impact of infant care resurfaced, and the debate among professionals at an international level continued throughout the 1990s. The crucial issue, once again, was whether infants with extensive early nonmaternal care were more likely than other infants to be insecurely attached to their parents. The debate was sparked by an analysis of data from two longitudinal studies in which children's attachment was measured by using Ainsworth's Strange Situation at 12 to 13 months of age (Belsky & Rovine, 1988). The investigators claimed that the data revealed that infants who experienced more than 20 hours of nonmaternal care per week displayed more avoidance of their mothers on reunion and were more likely to be classified as "insecurely attached" than infants with fewer than 20 hours of nonmaternal care. The researchers concluded that certain factors contribute to the development of insecurity: being male, being "fussy" or "difficult" (as described by mothers), having mothers with limited interpersonal sensitivity, having mothers with less satisfaction with certain aspects of their marriages, and having mothers with a strong career orientation.

Since the publication of this study, however, many researchers have conducted studies and have found evidence to refute its conclusions (Field, 1991; Field, Masi, Goldstein, Perry, & Parl, 1988; Howes & Hamilton, 1992a, 1992b; Howes, Rodning, Galluzzo, & Myers, 1988; Richters & Zahn-Waxler, 1988). In general, these studies found few, if any, differences in security of attachment between infants in childcare and infants reared by their mothers.

On the basis of these and other studies, the investigators concluded first that most children with significant childcare experience are secure with both their mothers and their teachers, but the relationships of childcare children with their mothers constitute their most consistent adult relationships. The question was once again raised concerning the effects of the interactive influences of the family and childcare. It now appears that infant childcare *per se* has no impact on the security of infants' attachment to their parents. However, the quality of infant care has become an issue of grave concern for both parents and professionals. Poor or substandard infant childcare can have serious long-term consequences for children's development, and high-quality care that is sensitive and responsive can facilitate the development of children, especially those who are at risk.

Clearly the issue of nonmaternal care for infants is a complex one. Recent studies have begun to focus on the quality of the caregiving environment as a variable, and although more longitudinal studies are being conducted, there still exists a need for sophisticated, well-designed, and tightly controlled research. It is unproductive to focus on whether it is good or bad for infants to be in childcare—the real issue is how we can improve the quality of care so that it enhances optimal development.

QUALITY EARLY CARE AND EDUCATION

The issue of what constitutes quality care and education is a complex one, and the difficulty of defining quality is compounded by the diverse opinions of parents, policymakers, caregivers, and advocacy groups. Each group has a distinct philosophy about what early care and education should accomplish for children and families.

Quality may be defined in relation to the services offered and the educational, social, health, and physical activities provided for the children. The climate of the classroom—such as caregiver/teacher behavior, the social structure, and the interaction patterns of the adults and the children—is of primary concern to others. Some experts and parents are concerned about the developmental changes in children as a result of childcare experiences, and others combine several or all of these factors in describing quality programs.

Assisting Parents in Selecting Quality Programs: Licensure

Parents have few, if any, resources available to assist them in selecting quality programs. One of the first criteria that parents can apply in their search for quality childcare is *licensing*. States have assumed the responsibility for licensing, certifying, or registering family childcare homes, minicenters, and early childhood centers. This licensing requirement is designed to protect children in group situations. States enact laws to provide for minimum standards that programs or homes must meet to provide services. A licensing law assigns a state agency to be responsible for developing and enforcing these minimum standards. Most states require licensing of childcare centers and some type of regulation for family childcare homes. States continually revise their regulations, and the minimum requirements, the types of care covered, and the enforcement practices vary considerably from state to state.

Most states have *minimum standards* that relate to the building and grounds, the personnel and staffing, and the services for and care of the children. Before a center is approved for licensing and begins operation, the facility is usually inspected by the licensing agency and is reinspected from time to time thereafter for renewal of the license. Many states encourage agency personnel to suggest to parents that they visit and observe in a variety of centers to determine which one best meets their needs. Sometimes parents are encouraged to contact a local childcare association or resource and referral agency for information. These procedures, however, are not very helpful to parents. It cannot be assumed that parents will visit even one center before enrolling the child; many make arrangements over the telephone.

Assisting Parents in Selecting Quality Programs: Important Factors to Consider

A number of other factors speak to the quality of a childcare facility. First, small groups of children provide the best care situation. Groups of 15 or fewer children as opposed to 25 or more children (3 to 6 years of age), with correspondingly small numbers of (but at least two) caregivers/teachers, are associated with higher frequencies of desirable child and caregiver behaviors and with higher gains by the children. Other advantages of smaller groups include (U.S. Department of Health, Education, and Welfare, 1978):

- Lead teachers in smaller groups engage in more social interaction with the children, such as questioning, responding, instructing, praising, and comforting, than did teachers in larger groups.
- Children in smaller groups show higher frequencies of behaviors such as considering/contemplating, contributing ideas, giving opinions, persisting at tasks, and cooperating than did children in larger groups.
- Fewer numbers of children per adult, as well as small groups, are associated with less stress on infants and staff. One adult per three or four children is optimal.

Staff specialization in child-related fields, not necessarily formal education, is also linked to quality care. Teachers who have training in child development and early childhood education tend to engage in more social interactions with the children than do teachers without training. Greater education and specialization of caregivers is also associated with higher staff interaction with children, more teaching of language, and more nurturance/touching of children.

Other research has shown consistently that childcare classrooms with a limited number of children per teacher, a relatively small group size, and teachers with strong educational backgrounds and specialized training in early childhood encourage teachers to interact with children in sensitive, nurturing, and intellectually stimulating ways (Phillipsen, Burchinal, Howes, & Cryer, 1997). Early childhood center directors also affected the quality of services. For example, one study found that overall quality is higher in infant-toddler classrooms in centers with moderately experienced directors (Phillipsen et al., 1997). In preschool classrooms, quality is higher when teachers have more education, a moderate amount of experience, and earn higher wages.

Not surprisingly, in both infant/toddler and preschool classrooms, higher quality is found in states with the most stringent regulations and in nonprofit centers. Results suggest that more stringent regulations for teacher education and experience and adult–child ratios have a substantial impact on childcare quality.

Assisting Parents in Selecting Quality Programs: Income and Childcare Quality

The National Institute of Child Health and Human Development Early Childcare Research Network (1997) found that the quality of care that infants experience is related to a wide range of family, economic, and child characteristics. For example, infants at the lowest and the highest income levels receive higher-quality care than those in the middle. This finding is due to the fact that the *actual* cost of childcare rather than the cost *paid by the parents* predicts quality. Therefore, upper-income parents and those low-income parents who receive subsidies have greater access to quality care than middle-income parents who do not qualify for subsidies.

There is increasing agreement among both researchers and policymakers that high-quality early childhood programs can improve some of the negative consequences of growing up in poverty. However, one study found that the quality of care provided to large proportions of low-income children is highly variable—and on some key indices barely adequate (Phillips, Voran, Kisker, Howes, & Whitebook, 1994). Generally speaking, centers that serve predominantly high-income families provide higher quality care than centers serving less-advantaged populations—the teachers are oftentimes better trained and more stable, are better compensated, are more sensitive, and provide more developmentally appropriate environments. Interestingly, the most uniformly poor quality of care, ranging from teacher training to the appropriateness of the activities in the classroom, is found in centers that served primarily middle-class children; however, in the area of teacher–child interaction, low-income children often experience the lowest quality.

The State of Union: Overall Quality of U.S. Childcare

Unfortunately, the overall quality of childcare in the United States is mediocre at best. A study of childcare in four states found that the health and welfare of infants and toddlers is only minimally met, with mean scores on a classroom environmental rating scale falling below the average (Phillipsen et al., 1997). The study noted a lack of warm, supportive relationships with caring adults—that is, little holding, cuddling, and talking to, and little use of toys that encourage development. Quality for preschool-age children is only somewhat better—a level considered mediocre by most professionals. In general, the level of quality required to support children's development is not being met by most centers.

The most comprehensive study of childcare in the 1990s was the Cost, Quality, and Outcomes Study (1999). This study documented that the quality of childcare occurring in typical settings in the United States is well below what the early childhood profession recognizes as high quality. The average scores on scales rating quality for preschool classrooms were in the medium range. The National Childcare Staffing Study (1997) also found that the quality of most of the centers they studied was barely adequate. These results are alarming in light of growing research that links quality to both short- and long-term positive outcomes in children.

There have been several attempts, all unsuccessful, to implement national standards for the quality of early care and education programs. In the absence of such standards, the National Association for the Education of Young Children has developed a set of standards as well as developmentally appropriate practices for programs serving children birth through age 8. Centers may seek to become accredited voluntarily by first undergoing an extensive self-study and finally submitting to evaluation by a national team. If the program meets all the requirements, then it may become accredited. Increasing numbers of centers are becoming involved in the accreditation process, a recognized mechanism for distinguishing high-quality centers.

The data thus far strongly suggest that quality care does make a difference. These findings underscore the need for widespread advocacy for quality care. Most parents believe that they are equipped to select quality care for their children, despite some evidence that suggests that parents actually do little observation and investigation of programs before enrolling their children.

In an attempt to provide parent education dealing with the variables that contribute to high-quality programs, the federal Childcare and Development Block Grant (CCDBG) mandates a consumer-education program as a condition of funding to states. Most states have produced brochures, checklists, or guidelines that help parents select quality early care and education programs; these aids often include information about the different types of care available. This information is widely distributed in state and local government agencies, doctors' offices, and sometimes supermarkets.

After more than a decade of lowering the minimum standards for programs, an increasing number of states are revising their standards upward. A sound regulatory process that guarantees that children will not be in substandard care, along with aggressive distribution of parent and public information about the importance of quality care, will go a long way toward changing the current face of early care and education.

EFFECTS OF EARLY CARE AND EDUCATION

As we noted earlier, parents and experts have been concerned for years with the effects of childcare on children. In the sections that follow, we explore the effects on children's cognitive, emotional, and social development.

Effects on Cognitive Development

Based on studies of the effects of childcare on cognitive development conducted in the 1970s and the early 1980s, it was concluded that for most middle-class children who attend centers that meet legal guidelines for quality, childcare does not have adverse effects on children's intellectual development. For economically disadvantaged children, however, childcare may have enduring positive effects because it appears that quality childcare experiences may positively impact poor test scores typically associated with high-risk populations after 18 months of age.

During the 1990s research on the effects of childcare on specific aspects of child development exploded. For example, one study noted that the opportunities for learning provided by nonmaternal care for children of low socioeconomic status may be as good as or better than those provided by their own homes (Caughy, DiPietro, & Strobino, 1994). Specifically, childcare participation of children from impoverished environments is related to their subsequent development of better mathematics and reading skills. The relationship is strongest for reading recognition performance if participation begins before the child's first birthday. The type of childcare is also related to math skills—children who attend center-based care or an early childhood program in a school have better math skills than those cared for in their own homes or in family childcare.

A different study found that preschool experience is associated with a large boost in IQ for African American/Black Caribbean children, and for both white and African American children, center/preschool experience is related to higher verbal IQs (Burchinal, Ramey, Reid, & Jaccard, 1995). Furthermore, experience in high-quality structural childcare settings appears to be particularly beneficial to intellectual development in African American children. In another study with black infants, the investigators found that the quality of infant care is positively related to tests of cognitive development, language development, and communication skills (Burchinal, Roberts, Nabors, & Bryant, 1996).

Perhaps the most definitive relationships between early care and education and cognitive development were demonstrated by the Cost, Quality, and Outcomes Study (1999), a study that focused on the impact of higher-quality care and education on children. The children involved in this study were followed through the end of second grade. This study's findings reveal that:

- Children who attend quality childcare centers perform better on both math and language measures, as well as on thinking and attentional skills.
- Children most at risk (i.e., those children whose mothers had less education) are more sensitive to the negative effects of poor quality and receive more benefits from high quality.
- All children benefit from high-quality programs, even though children from less-advantaged homes may benefit more than others.

Effects on Emotional Development

In the earlier section on infant care, the question of the quality of attachment of infants in childcare to their mothers was discussed. This question continues to be debated in the literature. Part of the difficulty lies with the assessment of attachment.

The most common type of measurement is the Strange Situation, in which a mother and her child are together in a strange room with toys; a stranger enters, the mother leaves, and finally the mother returns. The child's behavior, toward both the mother and the environment, is rated in each condition. Several studies using this approach have found that children are more likely to interact with their mothers than with their caregivers, and when confronted with a problem-solving task all children who requested help turned to their mothers. Neither the age of entry into childcare nor the length of time in care appeared to affect the mother–child attachment bond. Additional evidence indicates that infants can develop a discriminating attachment relationship toward a familiar caregiver. However, this relationship does not supersede the child's emotional bond with his or her mother. Children continue to express preference for their mothers.

The NICHD Early Childcare Research Network (1997) included approximately 1,200 mothers and their infants in nine states. This study supported the validity of the Strange Situation as a measure of attachment. In addition, the researchers found no significant differences in attachment security related to childcare participation. However, children who received less sensitive and responsive caregiving in childcare as well as less sensitive and responsive care from their mothers have the highest rates of insecurity. The authors concluded that childcare by itself is neither a risk nor a benefit for the development of infant–mother attachment. However, the *quality* of childcare may have an impact.

Effects on Social Development

Research during the 1980s provided some evidence suggesting that children who entered childcare before the age of 2 years are more likely than children who entered later to interact with peers in both positive and negative ways. Later research made close connections between relations with adults and relations with peers.

One study discovered that children who were more secure with their teachers were more competent with their peers than children insecure with teachers (Howes et al., 1992). These researchers noted that children do not become competent with peers merely through extended contact and experience but that by the provision of materials and the organization of the classroom the teacher can provide a context for the acquisition of peer social skills. They further noted that children who have daily contact with stable peer groups from fairly young ages appear most socially competent with peers. This study concludes that the quality of the early childhood program, including the adult–child relationship, influences the way in which social development is affected.

A Swedish study followed children from 6 weeks to 4 years of age who had been in childcare for more than 10 hours per week (Hagekull & Bohlin, 1995). This body of research revealed that differences in the quality of care are related to children's socioemotional development both concurrently and over time. In this study, high quality was defined in terms of appropriate levels of stimulation, effective and suitable discipline measures, good physical arrangements, and a warm emotional climate between children and between children and adults. Results revealed that mere exposure to childcare had some beneficial effects on acting-out behaviors for boys, and the better the quality of childcare, the more positive the emotions of children at home. The authors concluded that good-quality childcare has general effects on positive emotional expressions. Additionally, high-quality childcare seems to offset negative effects on children from less-advantaged homes, and boys seemed to gain more than girls from the experience of high-quality childcare.

In another study, Volling and Feagans (1995) examined the effects of infant childcare on children's social development by including family, child, and childcare characteristics. Across all measures of social competence, children's social functioning was related to multiple factors—family environment, quality of care, temperament, and so on. For example, children tended to engage in nonsocial activities with peers and less positive interactions with adults when group size was large and there were more children per adult, a finding consistent with other research. Children enrolled in more hours of center care per week also engaged in less nonsocial play and more friendly interactions with peers. However, children who entered care later during their first year were less likely to interact negatively with peers.

An interesting finding related to family characteristics emerged: When families stressed independence in male children, those boys tended to engage in less friendly interactions with their peers. The researchers concluded that it was the quality of the childcare environment rather than the childcare experience (e.g., hours, age at entry) that has the more pronounced effects on children's social outcomes. They also determined that temperamentally vulnerable children may be at risk for social difficulties when placed in low-quality programs, and high-quality programs may actually serve to protect these children from negative social outcomes.

Taken together, research seems to suggest that early care and education can have beneficial effects on children's social development.

However, the quality of care that children experience is the key to potential benefits.

PARENTAL SATISFACTION WITH CHILDCARE

The National Childcare Survey (Hofferth, Brayfield, Deich, & Holcomb, 1991) found that parents' level of satisfaction with childcare is quite high—96 percent of parents surveyed indicated that they are either "very satisfied" or "satisfied" with their current care arrangements. Nevertheless, slightly more than one-quarter indicated that they would prefer an alternative type of care for their youngest child, and quality was the reason most often mentioned for desiring a change. Forty-nine percent of parents desiring a change preferred center-based early care and education.

Consistent with other research, parental satisfaction with both center-based and family childcare is high overall (Britner & Phillips, 1995). On structural aspects of quality (such as health and safety, group size) and the quality of interactions between adults and children (adult warmth, attention to children), parents using center-based and family childcare are equally satisfied (Britner & Phillips, 1995). Although parents rated quality as more important than convenience in selection of care arrangements, they may have perceived quality on the basis of realistic options, given cost, hours, and location. Most parents in the study viewed both types of care as a source of extensive informational and emotional support.

Even with a sample of middle-class, educated parents who should be reasonably well-informed consumers, parents do not appear to match the care they selected for their infants and preschoolers to their childcare values (Cryer & Burchinal, 1997). Although the parents indicated that they value the same aspects of care that early childhood professionals find important, parents overestimated the quality of their children's programs on the aspects they valued the most highly. This suggests that, possibly, parents rate the quality of programs according to their hopes and desires—not reality. This data suggests that "imperfect information" may hinder parents from demanding the aspects of high-quality childcare they believe to be important for their children.

In light of the proliferation of early childhood programs that are only barely adequate in quality, it is puzzling that such a high percentage of parents are satisfied with their current arrangements. It may be that parents overinflate their satisfaction responses because they cannot accept consciously that their children are spending considerable amounts of time in less-than-adequate environments. It may be too that parents are poorly informed about what constitutes quality and the importance of quality in early care and education for optimal developmental outcomes.

THE FUTURE

Substandard environments for our most vulnerable citizens cannot be tolerated. If the United States works to meet the need for early care and education services, several considerations should be taken into account. Quality cannot be conceived of as the be-all-end-all answer for a troubled society; however, there is enough evidence to date that quality really matters, both in the short and the long terms. Early care and education appear to be a good option, serving variously as substitute care while parents work or participate in vocational or educational programs, as well as substitute care for children whose parents are physically or mentally disabled. Alternative care is also beneficial as a provider of enriching, stimulating, and developmental activities for children, especially children from less-than-adequate homes, and as an alternative to institutionalization for children living in dangerous home situations.

Parents seem to provide the best key for quality control and must be involved in the decision-making process. Educating parents must be an ongoing process accomplished by community and professional groups. There is a need for diversity of models and creative approaches to early care and education. Standardized equipment, buildings, and curricula are not necessary. Standardized children are not what society needs.

Credentialing of all early childhood personnel is seen by many as a way of increasing professionalism in the field and one way to contribute to quality programs. Indeed, research confirms the connection between teacher preparation and quality. Sadly, few incentives for personnel exist in most states. Low wages are paid, and only a small percentage of agencies have agreed to include credentials as a recognition of achievement.

Head Start has attempted through the Child Development Associate (CDA) program to recognize achievement of caregivers/teachers through training and credentialing, and new regulations have increased the educational requirements for teachers. The National Association for the Education of Young Children (NAEYC) has implemented a National Institute for Professional Development and is working with individual states to develop a career lattice for all early childhood personnel—whether they work in family childcare, childcare centers, public school programs, or Head Start—with recognized credentials at varying levels. These efforts will ultimately result in a group of trained individuals who understand the developmental needs and learning styles of young children and who will provide high-quality programs that do more than provide babysitting or custodial care.

Continued research on early care and education from an ecological perspective is also needed, as is research that focuses on the broader effects of childcare rather than on the consequences of childcare and its direct effects on the child. More also needs to be known about the differential consequences of center-based care, family childcare, and care in the home. The issue of quality needs continuing attention. What is "good enough" for children and their families? Where is the demarcation between what is harmful, innocuous, and beneficial in early care and education? To what extent should early childhood programs provide comprehensive services to families? What is the most effective and efficient way of educating parents about the importance of quality care and education?

OTHER PRESCHOOL PROGRAMS

Nursery schools, play groups, parent-cooperative programs, and drop-in centers also provide alternatives for care and education for young children. Most of these programs serve parents who are interested in occasional childcare, and they do not meet the needs of working parents. These programs provide opportunities for children to interact socially with peers, and educational activities usually are provided. They also give parents some respite from continual childcare:

- *Drop-in childcare centers* are likely to be provided by for-profit companies and may be located in shopping malls, in bowling alleys, and even in prisons.
- In *parent cooperatives,* parents perform designated roles and responsibilities for running the program, often in lieu of a portion of tuition.
- Sometimes parents get together and form *play groups,* another alternative for nonworking parents. These groups primarily provide opportunities for children to play together under the supervision of adults. Some are formalized and meet at the same location at designated times. Most often, mothers alternate in the supervision.

In all these programs, appropriate activities, materials and toys, and warm, caring adults should be provided if children are to benefit.

Head Start was created by the Economic Opportunity Act of 1964 to "interrupt the cycle of poverty" for America's poor families. It provides comprehensive child development and support services for young children, mostly beginning at age 3, and their families. As Figure 12.2 shows us, a number of family services are provided, including parenting and health education, crisis intervention services, housing assistance, and ESL (English as a Second Language) services. As seen in Figure 12.3, Head Start serves an ethnically diverse population. In 2009, slightly over 1 million children and about 10,000 pregnant women

Percent of families who received:

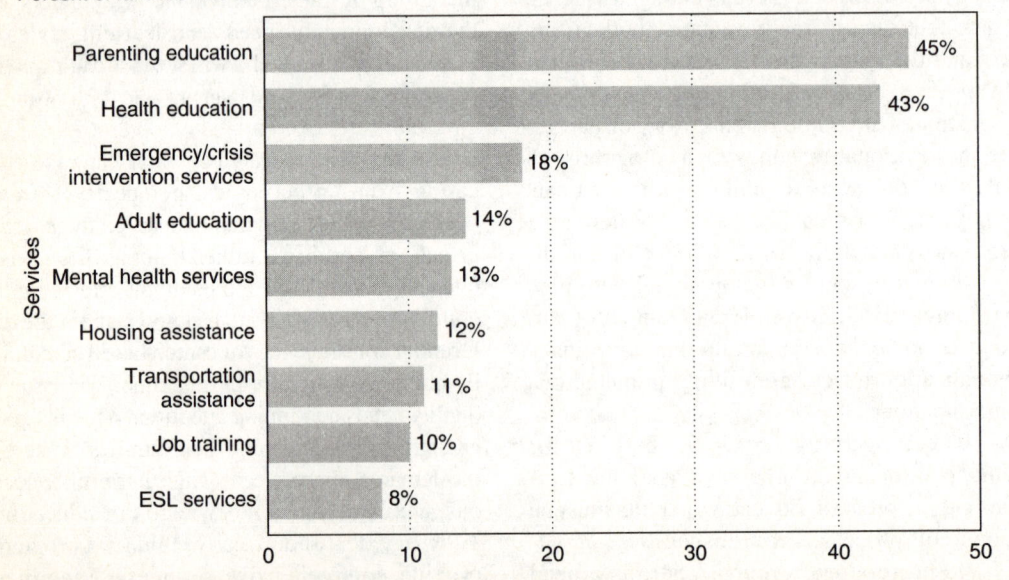

Services	Percent
Parenting education	45%
Health education	43%
Emergency/crisis intervention services	18%
Adult education	14%
Mental health services	13%
Housing assistance	12%
Transportation assistance	11%
Job training	10%
ESL services	8%

FIGURE 12.2 Head Start family services, by service provided.
Source: Based on data from Center for Law and Social Policy (2010).

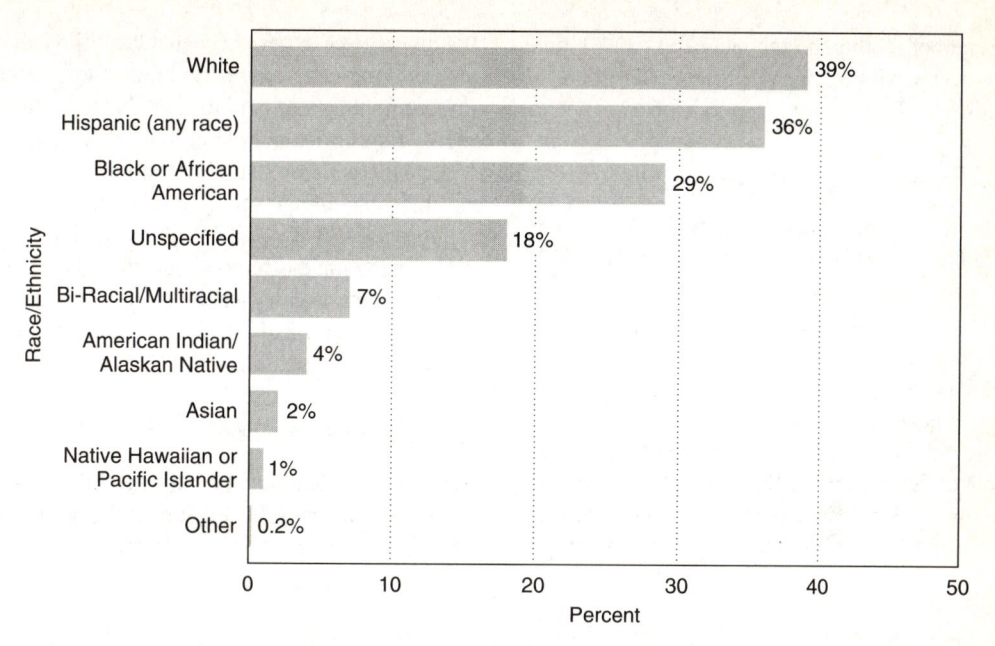

FIGURE 12.3 Head Start services, by race and ethnicity.
Source: Based on data from Center for Law and Social Policy (2010).

Race/Ethnicity:
- White: 39%
- Hispanic (any race): 36%
- Black or African American: 29%
- Unspecified: 18%
- Bi-Racial/Multiracial: 7%
- American Indian/Alaskan Native: 4%
- Asian: 2%
- Native Hawaiian or Pacific Islander: 1%
- Other: 0.2%

were enrolled in Head Start programs; about 92 percent of Head Start participants are served in center-based facilities (Center for Law and Social Policy, 2010). Family structures vary, with 57 percent of enrollees residing in single-parent families and 43 percent from two-parent families (Center for Law and Social Policy, 2010), at least one parent is employed in 70 percent of Head Start participants.

SCHOOL-AGE CHILDREN IN SELF-CARE

Research points to the increasing number of school-age children who are without direct adult supervision for some portion of the day (Creighton, 1993; Kay, 1999; Larkin, 1998/99; Miller, 1999; Turvett, 1995). These children have for years been referred to as latchkey children. The term **latchkey** was based on the practice of children wearing house keys on chains around their necks, so they could let themselves into their homes after school. More recently, to avoid the negative connotations of *latchkey* and its association with unsupervised children, the label *self-care* emerged (Powell, 1987).

Self-care children are those school-age children who are old enough to care for themselves for limited periods of time, and yet young enough to require adult supervision most of the time. Although an absolute age range cannot be established, it has been suggested that these are children between the ages of 6 and 13 who spend time alone or with a younger sibling on a regular basis (Turvett, 1995). Although this phenomenon has created considerable anxiety for professionals and parents, little research has been conducted on the outcomes of this arrangement.

Children under self-care are not only children of working parents but also are those left in charge of themselves while parents are away from home engaged in other activities. The largest percentage of children are in self-care in the afternoons after school. A smaller percentage are alone in the mornings before school, and a small number are in self-care at night. Increasing numbers of mothers in the labor force and single parents contribute to the growing numbers of children under their own supervision.

Readiness for Self-Care

Although all parents expect their children to accept increasing responsibilities as they develop, the decision to use a self-care arrangement involves a considerable increase in responsibility. When are children ready to care for themselves? The decision is obviously not an easy one for parents to make.

A particular age is certainly not the criterion. Some children develop faster than others and can assume responsibility for themselves earlier than others. Family and community circumstances, the diversity of experiences that the child has had as he or she develops, parental attitudes toward protecting the child, and the state's legal requirements for child supervision must be considered. Most experts agree that children under 10 (some say 12) years of age should not be left alone on a regular basis (Kay, 1999; Willwerth, 1993). Several experts have offered suggestions for parents to use in determining when children are ready to assume the responsibility for self-care; these are presented in Table 12.3.

Effects of Self-Care

Several viewpoints exist regarding children under their own supervision. For example, some view self-care arrangements as expecting children to

TABLE 12.3 Determining child's readiness for self-care.

PHYSICALLY

The child must be able to:

Control her body to the degree that she will not injure herself as she moves through the house

Manipulate the locks on the doors

Safely operate any accessible equipment to which he has access

EMOTIONALLY

The child must be able to:

Be comfortable enough to be alone for the required period of time without undue fear

Cope with boredom

Follow important established rules without testing them

Handle the usual and the unexpected events without excessive fear or anxiety

Avoid a pattern of withdrawn, hostile, or self-destructive behavior

SOCIALLY

The child should:

Be able to solicit, if needed, help from friends, neighbors, or other designated persons

Understand the role of, and call on when needed, the appropriate community resources—police, fire department, rescue squads, and so forth

Be able to maintain friendships with peers and adults

Be able to resolve sibling conflicts

Sources: Miller, A. (1999). They're home alone. *Newsweek, 134*(22), 105–107; Willwerth, J. (1993). "Hello? I'm home alone." *Time, 141*(9), 46–48.

assume adult-like responsibilities too soon. This pressure on children to grow up too soon can lead to unnecessary stress, with negative outcomes in such areas as achievement and socioemotional development. Yet, increasingly, families must face limited choices regarding childcare options. It is questionable whether some families can afford the luxury of childhood. Although most parents who use after-school programs approve of them, poor families are unable to afford them.

What are the effects of self-care situations on children? Are latchkey children at risk? The research has not kept pace with the growing public use of the self-care arrangement and parents' and professionals' concerns about it. There is limited research, though. For example, some studies have found that children can benefit from their new independence if they are emotionally ready and well prepared. One key factor is how the child feels about the situation (Miller, 1999). Whereas some children see themselves as independent and capable, others might perceive the use of self-care as abandonment and rejection. Many children find that being alone is frightening and boring. On the other hand, studies have shown that children in self-care are not necessarily worse off than other children with respect to self-esteem and behavior in school (Willwerth, 1993). In the best self-care situations, children feel that parents know what they are doing even when they are not present. It is those children who have no rules or expectations, who just "hang out," who are likely to get into trouble (Turvett, 1995). Chances are high that these children will experience substance abuse, sexual activity, truancy, and poor academic performance (Creighton, 1993; Larkin, 1998/99; Rueter, 1998).

Another study examined relationships between types of after-school care (self-care, mother care, and other adult care) in a predominantly low-income, minority, urban sample (Vandell & Ramanan, 1991). These results suggested that self-care is associated with some behavior problems. Specifically, mothers of children in self-care rated their children as more hyperactive and headstrong than mothers of other children rated theirs. However, when family income and family emotional support for the child were controlled, most of the apparent differences in child functioning associated with type of after-school care dissipated. Still, a small number of children who were in self-care and living below the poverty line were reported by their mothers to have significantly more behavior problems when compared with those children in other adult care. One study attempted to examine the long-term effects of self-care by gathering data from university students who were former "latchkey" children (Woodard & Fine, 1991). No differences were found between students who as children had been in self-care and those in mother care in the areas of personality traits, emotional adjustment, cognitive development, and academic performance.

It appears that a number of factors potentially influence the effects of the self-care arrangement—the age level of the child and her unique strengths and weaknesses, the context of the setting in which self-care takes place, family characteristics, and the geographic location (rural as opposed to urban or inner city). Future research must continue to focus on how the character of the parent–child relationship might mediate the effects, the important quality-of-life indicators in the neighborhood and community, the developmental processes of children and the indicators of readiness for self-care, and the child's need for and conception of privacy.

Families of Children in Self-Care

Research on families of children in self-care is sparse, partly because parents may define a self-care arrangement in different ways and perhaps partly because parents may not report accurately the extent to which they use self-care for fear of jeopardizing their children's welfare or of being ostracized socially (Coleman, Robinson, & Rowland, 1993). Contrary to the belief that self-care arrangements are used only by families that have no other choice, one study found that higher-income and white families were more likely to use self-care arrangements for their school-age children than were less affluent or minority families. Another study found that families using self-care were diverse, with diverse incomes. The majority of children were in grades 4 through 9; time alone each week varied; and most parents were satisfied or very pleased with the arrangement. Parents, especially those with younger children, expressed a need for some kind of after-school care for their children. Not all the parents in the study worked full time. The study also showed that there is a discrepancy between most parents' perceptions of their children's satisfaction with self-care and their own feelings about it (Coleman et al., 1993).

Other studies have examined parents' viewpoints regarding self-care arrangements. Even though parents often report positive benefits their children receive from the latchkey experience, most choose self-care for their children with concern, guilt, ambivalence, and uncertainty. Several factors have been found to affect parental satisfaction with self-care, such as whether or not the arrangement is voluntarily undertaken, whether the child is a boy or a girl, and whether the amount of time the child has to spend alone is excessive.

The reasons cited by some parents for using self-care vary—transportation problems, the expense of childcare, the refusal of children to participate in formal school-age childcare programs, and the belief that the child is old enough to care for him- or herself. Other research has not found the cost of after-school programs to be the major barrier to their use (Powell, 1987). In fact, some of the better-educated parents who could well afford to pay for after-school programs do not use them. Low-income parents do, however, seem to be more sensitive to cost factors.

After-School Programs

It is projected that more and more parents will be making a decision regarding after-school childcare. Being able to assess the available options is important for parents. The overriding question with regard to programs for school-age children should not be whether harm or risk has been prevented, but instead whether the child's development has been enhanced. The energies and commitment of program designers should be directed toward this end. Coaches, counselors, and mentors might provide sports and supervised activities, help with schoolwork, or provide enrichment programs (Reuter, 1998).

One study documented significant positive effects for low-income children who attended formal after-school programs (Posner & Vandell, 1994). The children who attended these programs were exposed to more learning opportunities than children in other forms of care, and they spent more time in academic activities and enrichment lessons and less time watching TV and engaging in unstructured activities than children in other forms of care.

In this study, activities were more structured and included intensive one-on-one academic work with teachers and working on cooperative projects with peers and other adults. Children's academic grades and conduct were improved when they spent time in one-on-one academic work with an adult, but these measures dropped when children spent time in unorganized outdoor activities. For the children in self-care (third graders), the more time without adult supervision was directly related to children's antisocial behaviors. The authors concluded that formal after-school programs are one way to alleviate some of the negative effects of urban poverty on children. Other studies have demonstrated that high school students involved in organized activities, as compared with noninvolved students, have higher self-esteem, grades, and educational aspirations, lower delinquency rates, and greater sense of control over their lives.

Today, more and more parents are faced with a decision regarding after-school care for their school-age children. A growing number of children are left at home in their own care or "hang out" on their own. Parents and professionals have ambivalent feelings about self-care, and research provides conflicting results about its effects. Future efforts need to be directed toward investigating the mediating variables that affect the outcomes. Attention should be focused also on providing a variety of quality options from which parents can choose.

Summary

Our contemporary, complex society requires a variety of alternatives for early care and education that support and supplement parents' roles and responsibilities because an available family member who helps with childcare or who intervenes in a crisis is no longer an option for many American families during their childrearing years. We have presented several options in this chapter for parents who need part-time or full-time care for their children, or for those parents who simply wish to provide additional stimulation for their children.

Although alternatives for parents clearly exist in the United States, our society by no means fully meets the needs of America's families. In fact, childcare in the United States is put to shame by comprehensive systems in many other nations. We still have a long way to go before all parents are truly provided with alternatives for early care and education that are acceptable, are affordable, and represent high quality.

References

Belsky, J. (1990). Parental and nonparental child care and children's socioemotional development: A decade in review. *Journal of Marriage and the Family, 52*(4), 885–903.

Belsky, J., & Rovine, M. (1988). Nonmaternal care in the first year of life and the security of infant–parent attachment. *Child Development, 59*(1), 157–167.

Britner, P., & Phillips, D. (1995). Predictors of parent provider satisfaction with child day care dimensions: A comparison of center-based and family child day care. *Child Welfare, 74*(6), 1135–1168.

Burchinal, M., Ramey, S., Reid, M., & Jaccard, J. (1995). Early child care experiences and their association with family and child characteristics during middle childhood. *Early Childhood Research Quarterly, 10,* 33–61.

Caughy, M., DiPietro, J., & Strobino, D. (1994). Daycare participation as a protective factor in the cognitive development of low-income children. *Child Development, 65*(2), 457–471.

Center for Law and Social Policy. (2010). *Child care and early education: Head Start/Early Head Start.* Retrieved July 12, 2010, from http://www.clasp.org/issues/topic?type+child_care_and_early_education&topic=0010.

Coleman, M., Robinson, B., & Rowland, B. (1993). A typology of families with children in self care: Implications for school-age child care programming. *Child and Youth Care Forum, 22*(1), 43–53.

Cost, Quality, and Outcomes Study. (1999). The children of the cost, quality, and outcomes study go to school. Retrieved from http://www.fpg.unc.edu/~NCEDL/PAGES/cqes.htm.

Creighton, L. (1993). Kids taking care of kids. *U.S. News and World Report, 115,* 26–32.

Cryer, D., & Burchinal, M. (1997). Parents as child care consumers. *Early Childhood Research Quarterly, 12,* 35–58.

Field, T. (1991). Quality infant day-care and grade school behavior and performance. *Child Development, 62*(4), 863–870.

Field, T., Masi, W., Goldstein, S., Perry, S., & Parl, S. (1988). Infant day care facilitates preschool social behavior. *Early Childhood Research Quarterly, 3*(4), 341–359.

Hagekull, B., & Bohlin, G. (1995). Day care quality, family and child characteristics and socioemotional development. *Early Childhood Research Quarterly, 10,* 505–526.

Hofferth, S., Brayfield, A., Deich, S., & Holcomb, P. (1991). *National child care survey, 1990.* Washington, DC: Urban Institute Press.

Hofferth, S., West, J., & Henke, R. (1994). *Access to early childhood programs for children at risk.* Washington, DC: U.S. Department of Education, OERI, National Center for Education Statistics.

Howes, C., & Hamilton, C. (1992a). Children's relationships with caregivers: Mothers and child care teachers. *Child Development, 63*(4), 859–866.

Howes, C., & Hamilton, C. (1992b). Children's relationships with child care teachers: Stability and concordance with parental attachments. *Child Development, 63*(4), 867–678.

Howes, C., Rodning, C., Galluzzo, D., & Myers, L. (1988). Attachment and child care: Relationships with mother and caregiver. *Early Childhood Research Quarterly, 3*(4), 403–416.

Johansen, A., Leibowitz, A., & Waite, L. (1996). The importance of child-care characteristics to choice of care. *Journal of Marriage and the Family, 58,* 759–772.

Kagan, J., Kearsley, R., & Zelazo, P. (1978). *Infancy, its place in human development.* Cambridge: Harvard University Press.

Kay, M. (1999, March). When is a child ready to stay home alone? *Family Life,* p. 94.

Kontos, S. (1994). The ecology of family day care. *Early Childhood Research Quarterly, 9*(1), 87–110.

Kontos, S., Howes, C., & Galinsky, E. (1996). Does training make a difference to quality in family child care? *Early Childhood Research Quarterly, 11,* 427–445.

Larkin, E. (1998/99). The intergenerational response to childcare and after-school care. *Generations, 22*(2), 33–37.

Miller, A. (1999). They're home alone. *Newsweek, 134,* 105–107.

Moskowitz, D., Schwarz, J., & Corsini, D. (1977). Initiating day care at three years of age: Effects on attachment. *Child Development, 48,* 1271–1276.

National Association of Child Care Resource and Referral Agencies. (2010a). *Child care centers and family child care homes across the nation are on the decline and vacancy rates on the rise.* Retrieved July 12, 2010, from www.naccrra.org.

National Association of Child Care Resource and Referral Agencies. (2010b). *Parents and the high cost of child care: 2010, Executive summary.* Retrieved July 12, 2010, from http://www.naccrra.org/docs/Cost-Report%20_073010_ExecSumm-final.pdf.

National Child Care Staffing Study. (1997). *Who cares?: Child care teachers and the quality of care in America.* Washington, DC: Center for the Child Care Workforce.

National Institute of Child Health and Human Development. (1997). The effects of infant child care on infant–mother attachment security: Results of the NICHD study of early child care. *Child Development, 68*(5), 860–879.

Phillips, D., Voran, M., Kisker, E., Howes, C., & Whitebook, M. (1994). Child care for children in poverty: Opportunity or inequity? *Child Development, 65*(2), 472–492.

Phillipsen, L., Burchinal, M., Howes, C., & Cryer, D. (1997). The prediction of process quality from structural features of child care. *Early Childhood Research Quarterly, 12,* 281–303.

Posner, J., & Vandell, D. (1994). Low-income children's after-school care: Are there beneficial effects of after-school programs? *Child Development, 65*(2), 440–456.

Powell, D. (1987). After-school care. *Young Children, 42*(3), 62–66.

Richters, J., & Zahn-Waxler, C. (1988). The infant day care controversy: Current status and future directions. *Early Childhood Research Quarterly, 3*(3), 319–336.

Rueter, T. (1998). An after-school haven needed. *Christian Science Monitor, 90,* 15.

Todd, C., & Deery-Schmitt, D. (1996). Factors affecting turnover among family child care providers: A longitudinal study. *Early Childhood Research Quarterly, 11,* 351–376.

Turvett, B. (1995). The latchkey solution. *Good Housekeeping, 221,* 217–220.

U.S. Census Bureau (2008). *Current Population Survey, 2007 Annual Social and Economic Supplement.* Retrieved August 8, 2009, from www.census.gov/population/www/socdemo/hh-fam.html.

U.S. Department of Health and Human Services, Health Resources and Services Administration, Maternal and Child Health Bureau. (2009). *Child Health USA 2008-2009.* Rockville, Maryland: U.S. Department of Health and Human Services.

U.S. Department of Health, Education, and Welfare, Office of Human Development Services, Administration for Children, Youth, and Families. (1978). *National day care study: Preliminary findings and their implications.* Cambridge, MA: Abt Associates.

Vandell, D., & Ramanan, J. (1991). Children of the national longitudinal survey of youth: Choices in after-school care and child development. *Developmental Psychology, 27*(4), 637–643.

Volling, B., & Feagans, L. (1995). Infant day care and children's social competence. *Infant Behavior and Development, 18,* 177–188.

Walker, J. (1992). New evidence on the supply of child care: A statistical portrait of family providers and an analysis of their fees. *Journal of Human Resources, 27*(1), 40–69.

Willwerth, J. (1993). "Hello? I'm home alone…" *Time, 141,* 46–48.

Woodard, J., & Fine, M. (1991). Long-term effects of self-supervised and adult-supervised child care arrangements on personality traits, emotional adjustment, and cognitive development. *Journal of Applied Developmental Psychology, 12*(1), 73–85.

GLOSSARY

A Campaign for Forgiveness: A foundation that supports scientific studies that deepen understanding of forgiveness and how reconciliation takes place.

acculturation: The adoption of mainstream values, languages, and practices.

acting out: A post-divorce effect in which children and adolescents externalize their feelings about the divorce, typically through aggressive misbehaviors, noncompliance, disobedience, delinquency, increased absences from school, and increased aggressiveness.

active listening: When we actively listen, we become connected to another person so we not only hear what they are saying, but understand what they are feeling.

adoption: A legal process that creates a parent–child relationship between individuals who are not biologically related.

African Heritage Theory: Based on the assumption that certain African traits have been retained by blacks and are evidenced in kinship patterns, marriage, sexuality, childbearing, and so forth.

alimony: A monetary payment, typically paid monthly, paid by one spouse to the other during and after the divorce proceedings.

anal stage: During Freud's anal stage (ages 1–3), the focus of the sensual energy is associated with toilet training, particularly with respect to the anus.

antinatalism: An ideology that discourages childbearing.

artificial insemination: The medical process by which donor sperm is placed by syringe into the woman's vagina, cervix, or uterus.

assertive discipline: A structured behavioral management approach designed to help teachers, educators, and parents to positively influence a child's behaviors.

assisted reproductive technology (ART): Treatments that involve fertilization through the manipulation of the woman's ova and the male's sperm.

attachment: Best described as an emotional or affectional bond that ties or binds the child to the parent or primary caregiver.

attachment theory: John Bowlby's attachment theory describes enduring patterns of interpersonal relationships from cradle to grave. With the premise that all newborns must be nurtured in order to survive, Bowlby observed that they form a type of bond—an attachment—with their caregivers. From this close affectional and emotional bond, children derive a sense of security, a trusting sense that the world is a safe place to be.

attained SES: Refers to the parents' socioeconomic status.

attention-deficit/hyperactivity disorder (ADHD): A behavior disorder characterized by chronic, impairing levels of attention, hyperactivity, or their combination. Symptoms reflect excessive inattention or overactivity and impulsive responding, within the context of developmentally appropriate behavior for the child's age and gender group.

authoritarian parents: Parents who exert authority and control over their children, but without being responsive, warm, or affectionate; imposing rigid rules of behavior that must be obeyed without question. Parent–child communication is very low.

authoritative parents: Parents who are responsive while expecting certain behavior of their children. Parents do not use shame, withdraw love, or impose guilt to control behavior. They set clear but flexible boundaries for their children's behavior, encourage parent–child communication, and use a balance of power and reason.

autonomy: A person's desire to self-rule, or one's will; independence.

autonomy granting: Permissive parents allowing their children age-appropriate independence and self-governing.

autonomy versus shame and doubt: The second stage in Erikson's theory of psychosocial development (occurring from about ages 1–3), in which the child develops a sense that he or she can control muscles, impulses, self, and environment. However, the caregivers reinforce a sense of shame and doubt if they are impatient and do for the child what he or she is capable of doing him- or herself.

balance: In terms of work and family, the positive psychological state we achieve through regularly meeting our own, others', and work-related needs.

basic budgets: The amount of money families need to manage at the most basic level; it must cover costs associated with housing, food, transportation, childcare, healthcare, clothing, personal care items, school materials, and taxes.

batterer: A person who commits family violence.

bicultural socialization: A process wherein both the aspects of a different culture and/or heritage and America are integrated.

binuclear family: The separate, distinct households that form after marital separation or divorce.

blue-collar workers: Individuals holding jobs in the service sector, such as sales, office, production, and transportation.

boomerang generation: A term used to describe adult children who are coresidents with their parents.

bullying: A power differential in which one or more youth use aggressive strategies repeatedly to dominate and cause harm to others of lower status.

care: Refers to programs that provide both early care and education. Can be on a half-day or full-day basis and can occur in centers, homes, schools, or churches.

caregiver: The term refers to the person or persons responsible for providing primary care of the infant or young child.

caregiver burden: Caregiving responsibilities impose a burden of physical and emotional wear and tear on caregivers.

caregiving: Reflects dependence on another person for any activity essential for daily living, including instrumental activities (such as laundry, meal preparation, and certain aspects of healthcare). Caregiving encompasses assistance beyond the aid provided to physically and psychologically healthy parents.

caregiving career: Those years caregivers commit to tending to dependent children, aging parents, and eventually, dependent spouses.

child sexual abuse (CSA): Any sexual activity the child cannot consent to. The sexual contact is often achieved through force, trickery, or bribery and involves an imbalance in age, size, power, and knowledge. Sexual contact can include fondling of the breasts, buttocks, or genitals; vaginal, anal, or oral intercourse; exhibitionism; forced masturbation or forced viewing of masturbation; obscene gestures or comments; prostitution; or any other sexual activity that is harmful to the child's mental, emotional, or physical welfare.

child support: Whether married or divorced, parents must provide financially for any of their children under 18 years old.

childfree by choice: Independent of social or physiological restrictions, some people make the choice to have no children.

childless/childfree: A couple may consider themselves childless if they are unable to conceive or bear of their own or adopt children. Some couples remain childfree as a deliberate choice.

classical conditioning: John B. Watson's (1878–1958) theory that people make associations between two events. For example, babies open their mouths and smack their lips when their parent puts them in a highchair, or when their parent opens a jar of baby food.

closed adoptions: An adoption in which the identity of birth parents is not revealed to the adoptive parents or to the children.

closed responses: A parent's communication that denies the child a right to his or her feelings by demonstrating the listener's unwillingness to accept and understand.

cognitive theories: These theories focus on how children think and how they understand their world. The focus of childhood development is centered on children's thinking and reasoning, not on personality development.

cohabiting: Cohabiting couples are unmarried partners who live together in a single household.

collectivist cultures: Cultures that define their identity in terms of the relationships individuals hold with others, which takes priority over individual needs; group membership is important.

communication: The process of making and sharing meanings.

companionate relationship: A relationship in which grandparents enjoy warm, loving, and nurturing relationships with their grandkids, though they are happy to send them home when it is time.

conditional forgiveness: The type of forgiveness used when people want relational repair, but they want to make it very clear that repeating certain behaviors will not be tolerated.

confirming messages/responses: Types of communication characterized by recognition of the other person, relevant dialogue, and acceptance; all of these show a willingness to be involved in the relationship.

congenital disabilities: Those disabilities that children are born with, and may be genetic or chromosomal, or they may be caused by prenatal exposure to drugs or other toxic substances or maternal malnutrition.

contact hypothesis: The idea that negative stereotypes (prejudices) about other groups exist because of the lack of contact and interaction between groups.

coparenting: The way parents negotiate their child-rearing beliefs and share in everyday parenting responsibilities. It is the support parents provide to one another in the raising of their children.

cross-sex friendships (CSF): Friendships between opposite-sex peers.

crude birthrate: The number of childbirths per 1,000 women, per year.

cultural variant: An approach that views black families as culturally unique systems. Also referred to as the African Heritage Theory.

custody: Refers to who is responsible for the children's financial, physical, and emotional well-being.

cyberbullicide: Describes suicides that are influenced by online harassment and aggression.

cyberbullying: Bullying that takes place in an electronic format (such as texting, email, Twitter, or Facebook).

developmental delays: Describes children from 3–5 years of age who exhibit significant delays in one or more domains of physical, cognitive, communicative, social and emotional, and adaptive developments.

diminished parenting: Refers to the new relationship between parent and children in the first few years following a divorce.

direct forgiveness: Family members or intimate partners clearly, plainly, and directly tell the offender that he or she is forgiven.

discipline: Refers to one receiving instruction from another. A system of discipline should imply a broad positive system of guidance of a young child, with particular methods of punishment being only a minor aspect of that total discipline system.

disorganized attachment type: This attachment type describes infants who do not fit into any of the three major classifications. This attachment is considered to be a risk factor for aggressive behavior, as well as concurrent and subsequent psychopathology.

dispenser of wisdom: A relationship in which the grandparent offers information and advice to their grandchildren—often whether it is asked for or not.

diverse: In the United States, it refers to people's differences in age, gender, race, ethnicity, culture, sexual orientation, and religion.

diversity: The broad spectrum of demographic and philosophical differences among groups within a culture.

domestic violence: Violence perpetrated against family members by a person who is related to the victim either biologically or legally, such as by marriage or through adoption.

dual-earner couples: Couples in which both spouses are actively engaged in the workforce.

education: Refers to programs that proved both early care and education, on either a half-day or full-day basis, in centers, homes, schools, or churches.

emotional abuse: When the parent (or adult caregiver) inflicts damage on the child through behaviors other than physical or sexual.

emotional or behavior disorders (EBD): Children who fit this category demonstrate extreme behavior that is unacceptable within the social and cultural context and the problem is chronic rather than situational.

empathy: The capacity to understand another's circumstances or situation, and the ability to feel or express emotional concern for another person.

empowerment principles: Promote family strengths and decision making, and allow families to control the direction and outcomes of support services.

empty nest: The home with no children after children have grown and left.

endometriosis: A disease characterized by the buildup or migration of uterine tissue to other parts of the body (such as the ovaries or fallopian tubes).

ethnicity: This refers to a social construction that is used to identify groups of people (commonly races) who share common cultural traits, such as religion, customs, language, and dress.

exceptional children: A term used to describe those children with special problems related to physical disabilities, sensory impairments, communicative disorders, emotional disturbances, learning disabilities, and mental retardation (or intellectual disability), as well as those who have special talents or who are gifted.

extended family: The family unit where two or more generations of close family relatives live together in one household.

externalizing behaviors/difficulties: Commonly referred to as *acting out,* children and adolescents externalize their feelings about the divorce, typically through aggressive misbehaviors, noncompliance, disobedience, delinquency, increased absences from school, and increased aggressiveness.

familism: Emphasizes the importance of family life and close, interdependent relationships among the person, the family, and the community, often stressing the importance of extended family.

Family and Medical Leave Act (FMLA): Under the Family and Medical Leave Act (FMLA), federal and state employees and those who work for employers with 50 or more employees are able to take up to 12 weeks of unpaid leave to care for an ill child, parent, or spouse, or for one's own serious illness, without fear of losing their job, benefits, or status.

family childcare: Provides care for children in the homes of the providers, who include both relatives and nonrelatives.

family-centered support services: An idea promoted by federal legislation that embraces the idea that services should center on and be responsive to the needs of all family members as they relate to the child's development.

family cohesion: The extent to which family members feel emotionally close and bonded to one another.

family law: In the United States, family law establishes policies and regulations to protect the rights and well-being of all family members and ensure that married or divorced couples fulfill their obligations to each other and to their children. Specific family laws vary from state to state.

Family Life Cycle: Comprised of multiple entrances and exits from the family of origin.

family meeting: Formal or informal regular family discussions that provide structure and organization to the family system and allow for meaningful conversation.

family policy: Refers to governmental goals and/or programs that seek to support and strengthen families.

family projection process: Stresses that the appeal of having children is the result of finding a way to satisfy one's individual unmet needs from childhood.

family values: Usually refers to a society's paradigm or viewpoint that expects its members to adhere to perceived proper social roles, such as marrying and having children, remaining monogamous and faithful to the marriage partner, and opposing same-sex relationships, marriages, and parenting by gay and lesbian partners.

family violence: A common term for domestic violence.

family well-being: Includes psychological health; high levels of self-esteem, sense of power, and internal locus of control; good physical health; low behavior/conduct problems; good social support; high marital quality and stability; and good parent–child relationships.

feminization of poverty: A term that reflects the impact of divorce on mothers and their children, and the increasing numbers of unmarried women having children.

fertility rate: The average number of live births per woman, in a given population, per year.

fetal alcohol spectrum disorders (FASD): A group of conditions that are seen in babies whose mother drank alcohol during pregnancy. A person with FASD may have facial abnormalities, smaller-than-average body composition, ADHD, poor memory, difficulties with math, speech and language delays, MR/ID, poor reasoning and judgment skills, and vision or hearing problems.

fictive kin: People who are not biologically related but who fulfill a family role.

forgiveness: A deliberate process that transforms a strong desire for revenge into a positive response.

formal grandparenting: A relationship in which grandparents see their role along common, traditional lines. These grandparents babysit every now and then and indulge their grandchildren on occasion, but when it comes to childrearing and discipline, they play a "hands-off" role; they are content to leave that aspect of parenting to the parents.

foster care: Refers to placing a child in the temporary care of a family other than its own; sometimes referred to as *out-of-home care*.

fun seeker: A relationship in which grandparents have a relationship with their grandchildren that is characterized by informal, spontaneous playfulness.

gatekeepers: Divorced mothers who deny visitation, make it difficult for fathers to see their children, and intend not to share parenting with the fathers of their children.

gender typing: The process of developing the behaviors, thoughts, and emotions associated with a particular gender.

generativity: The seventh stage of Erikson's eight Stages of Man theory, generally occurring during middle age.

genital stage: From ages 12 and beyond, or the genital stage, people develop mature sexual interests in the opposite sex, according to Freud's psychoanalytic theory.

ghetto poor: Refers to inner-city residents, primarily either black or Hispanic, living at or below the poverty line.

gifted children: There is little agreement about the definition of giftedness, except that gifted children excel in some way(s) when compared with their peers. Though federal laws do not require special services for gifted students, most states mandate programs for gifted students, with each state employing it's own definition of gifted.

grandparent visitation laws: Laws that grant grandparents legal standing to petition for legally enforceable visitation with their grandchildren—even over parental objections, existing in all 50 states.

Growing Together: A program geared toward single, at-risk teenage mothers, teaching positive behaviors such as setting goals; seeking help in the family, school, and community; and developing pride in themselves and their new role as parents. It focuses on practical methods to help teen moms cope with their own needs and those of their infants.

Head Start: A program of the U.S. Department of Health and Human Services, providing comprehensive education, health, nutrition, and parenting education/involvement services to low-income children and their families.

home visitation: A strategy for service delivery bringing various services to a family rather than requiring the family to come to the service provider(s). Programs primarily target pregnant women and/or families with children up to 3 years of age.

homelessness: Refers to persons living in areas not designated as habitats.

hooking up: Physical or sexual interaction with the absence of commitment or affection.

household work: The work associated with staying at home in order to nurture one's children.

ideal–actual gap: The term used to describe the discrepancy of the father's perceived involvement in parenting as much higher than the level of involvement reported by the mothers

identity: An individual's sense of who he or she is.

incest: Occurs when the forms of abuse are inflicted on a child by a relative such as a parent, grandparent, uncle, aunt, sister, or brother.

indirect forgiveness: Family members or intimate partners communicate this type of forgiveness by nonverbal displays (such as a hug, a smile, or eye contact) and by acting as though the transgression never happened.

individualistic cultures: In these cultures, individual goals are more important than the goals of the group. Individuals define their identity or sense of self by way of personal attributes (wealth, social status, education level, marital status, etc.).

individuation: The process of adolescents forming an identity that is separate from that of their family of origin.

industry: A feeling developed by a child's competencies meeting with success, when the child receives support and approval from parents, peers, and teachers.

industry versus inferiority: The fourth stage of Erikson's theory of psychosocial development, beginning around age 6 and ending about age 11. The child believes he or she is capable and able to do meaningful tasks, including taking on projects and tasks because of a basic interest in doing them and works to complete them to achieve satisfaction from the results.

inferiority: A child's persistent sense of inadequacy or a feeling that he or she is of lower status than others.

infertility: The inability to conceive a baby after trying for a period of 1 year.

initiative: A child's sense that she can accomplish anything before her. This sense of ability depends to a considerable extent on how parents respond to her self-initiated activities.

initiative versus guilt: Erikson's third stage of psychosocial development, beginning in the latter part of the third year and continuing until about the sixth year, after the child has attained proficiency in walking and feeding himself. The child now directs his attention toward increasing participation in his social environment.

insecure-avoidant attachment type: This attachment type describes infants who tend to be relatively independent of their parents and display little proximity seeking (the tendency to reduce distance from the attachment figure in times of distress).

insecure-resistant attachment type: This attachment type describes infants who tend to be distressed by separation from the parents and seek contact during reunion, but appear to be inconsolable.

integrity versus despair: The final stage of Erikson's eight Stages of Man theory.

intensive mothering: Term coined by Sharon Hays to reflect the mothering roles and expectations that have been evolving since the 1980s, when women flooded the workplace.

intensive mothering ideology: The Western cultural belief that a mother should give herself unconditionally, and focus all of her time, energy, money, love, support, and every other resource she has on raising her children.

intergenerational ties: The relationships between family members across multiple generations.

internalizing behaviors/difficulties: Internalizing difficulties result in emotional problems such as worry, feelings of unhappiness, anxiety, depression, distress, guilt, and poor self-concept.

interrole conflict: Occurs when we take on (or have assigned to us) many roles simultaneously.

intimate partner violence (IPV): Violence perpetrated against a relationship partner.

intrafamily adoptions: Occurs when someone adopts a stepchild, or with the adoption of a relative child, such as an aunt legally adopting her nephew.

involved relationship: Some grandparents assume the role of parents as they are involved in the everyday rearing of their grandchildren.

job autonomy: Occurs when employees are allowed a high degree of independence and self-direction.

job complexity: Occurs when jobs are challenging and stimulating at the same time.

job status: Refers to a type or kind of job that offers some kind of prestige in an organization or community.

joint custody: Parents share in the decision making on behalf of their children. They may also share the physical custody of their children.

kinship care: A situation in which grandparents provide a living environment for their grandchildren.

latchkey: The practice of children wearing house keys on chains around their necks, so they could let themselves into their homes after school.

latency stage: According to Freud, at about ages 7–11, sensual energies subside for a time.

learning disabilities (LD): A disorder that causes an "imperfect ability" to use language, or to listen, think, speak, read, write, spell, or do mathematical calculations, and may also include perceptual abilities, brain injury, and minimal brain dysfunction.

learning theories: Theories that emphasize the role of the environment, such as the home, school, community, and peers, in shaping a child's development.

legal custody: Refers to which parent has the right to make decisions about how the child is reared, such as decisions concerning education or religion.

logical consequences: Consequences that are assigned by the parent to express the reality of the social order, not of the person. For example, a child who disturbs the rest of the family at mealtime is given the choice to settle down or to leave the table.

market alternative cost method: Estimates the value of household labor by looking at what it would cost in the current market to pay someone to do the household labor the mother performs.

maternal gatekeeping: When women's socialization—and the inherent cultural notion that she will always be the better parent—makes it difficult for her to relinquish her traditional roles.

motherese: The special speech register adults use when talking to children, consisting of short simple sentences, frequent repetitions, high pitch and exaggerated pitch contours, and emphasis on the here and now.

mothering: A process whereby someone performs the relational and logistical work of caring for others.

multiple mothering: A practice that involves aunts, cousins, close friends, and fictive kin who provide mothers with a range of modeling and tangible support.

multiracial: Individuals of any combination of races (white, African American/Black Caribbean, Asian, Native American/Alaska Native, Pacific Islander, Hispanic, and "any other race") and ethnicities.

narcissistic entitlement: A sense of being entitled to, or deserving, only the good things in life; a pride-related barrier to forgiveness.

natalism: An ideology that embraces childbearing.

National Extension Parent Education Model: An overview of parenting essentials developed by a group of extension specialists to assist parent educators in developing and focusing their parent-education efforts.

Native American/Alaskan Native (NA/AN): The aboriginal peoples of the United States and their descendants, and who maintain tribal affiliation or community attachment.

natural consequences: Consequences that occur naturally from a child's behavior, such as a child who refuses to eat goes hungry.

neglect: The omission of the parent(s) to provide for normal growth and development of children.

New World experience: Attributes distinctiveness to American culture rather than to African traditions.

nuclear family: The nuclear family consists of a biological father, a biological mother, and their biological or adopted children.

nurturance: Affectionate care and attention.

open adoptions: An adoption in which the birth parents and adoptive parents know one another, exchange information, and often continue contact and communication over time.

open responses: A parent's communication with the child that acknowledges the child's right to his or her feelings by demonstrating that the listener both accepts and understands the feelings and the message.

operant conditioning: B. F. Skinner believed that children learn behaviors through a series of rewards and punishments called *operant conditioning*.

opportunity cost method: Attempts to value household work by asking, "What would a person be paid in wage labor for 1 hour of household work?"

oral stage: During Freud's oral stage (from birth to about age 1), the focus of sensual energy is the mouth and the tongue; the emphasis for personality development is thus centered on breastfeeding.

overtime: The hours a person works beyond his or her normal 40-hour per week schedule.

parent education: A variety of experiences to educate individuals who plan to become parents in the future, as well as to assist persons who are already parents to be more effective in their roles.

parent–child relationship: Refers to the emotional and physical connection between a parent and his or her child; it includes attributes such as emotional cohesion (closeness), parental influence on the child's development, attachment, and parental investment in the child's well-being.

parenting: The process or state of being a parent. This process includes nourishing, protecting, and guiding a child through the course of his or her physical, social, emotional, and intellectual development.

Partners for Fragile Families: A curriculum developed to address young fathers' real experiences, offering support, information, and motivation on issues involving parenthood, relationships, sexuality, job skills, and becoming self-sufficient.

patriarchal family structure: This family form includes the father figure, his wife, and his children. Everyone in the family is considered to be under the authority of the patriarch, the father.

pelvic inflammatory disease (PID): Even when women are able to successfully ovulate, the fertilized ovum may have difficulty reaching the uterus due to blocked or scarred fallopian tubes. This disorder is caused by untreated sexually transmitted infections (i.e., gonorrhea and chlamydia).

permissive parents: Also referred to as *indulgent parents,* permissive parents demonstrate high levels of warmth, affection, and responsiveness toward their children, and also show adequate to high levels of parent–child communication. This parenting style does not place high demands on children, nor do parents attempt to control their children's behavior; children's behavior is mostly self-regulated.

persistently poor: Populations with a continuous poverty rate of 30 percent or higher.

phallic stage: According to Freud, during the phallic stage (ages 3 to 6), children are intensely interested in the physical differences between men and women.

physical abuse: The parent (or caregiver) inflicts physical injury on the child through beating, whipping, branding, scalding, shaking, or even torture, and is often the most reported form of abuse.

physical custody: The legal right to have a child live primarily with one parent, who becomes the custodial parent.

poverty line: The estimated minimum income necessary for a family to meet basic needs, such as food, shelter, clothing, and other essentials.

poverty rate: The percentage of people with incomes below the published poverty line.

preadolescence: A period of transition between childhood and adolescence, roughly spanning the years between 9–13.

premature/preterm: A baby born before the 37th week of pregnancy.

primary divorce stressors: Provisions such as custody arrangements, visitation, and child support.

pronatalism: An ideology that embraces childbearing.

psychoanalytic theory: Championed by Sigmund Freud, this theory focuses on the personality development of children.

psychosexual stages: In Freud's view, development takes place through a series of psychosexual stages, in which sensual energy or satisfaction is focused on one particular part of the body.

punishment: Used to decrease the likelihood that a behavior will be repeated.

quality: Defined in relation to the services offered and the education, social, health, and physical activities provided for the children.

Quiverfull movement: A pronatalist belief in which couples are motivated to have many children because of a desire to be obedient to what they believe are commands in the Bible.

race: Refers to a group of people who are distinguished from another group of people, typically by their skin color, ancestry, or genetics.

racial/ethnic socialization: The way in which families teach children about the social meanings of their race/ethnicity.

racism: A belief system that holds that race accounts for differences in human character and/or availability; it results in discrimination and prejudice based on someone's race or ethnic background.

reciprocity: The degree of positive or negative involvement at given points during interaction.

reflective listening: A form of active listening in which we pay close attention to a person's verbal and emotional messages, and respectfully acknowledge their perspective.

reframe: To view the issue from another perspective.

remote relationship: Remote relationships are characterized by the distant grandparent who has little or no contact with grandchildren and is only involved on occasional holidays or birthdays.

residual tasks: Bill paying, yard work, and chauffeuring children.

resilience: Refers to a child's capacity to withstand stressors, overcome adversity, and achieve higher levels of self-mastery, self-esteem, and internal harmony.

resource dilution hypothesis: A theory that contends parents' finite resources become diluted when spread over a larger number of children.

responsivity: Refers to the degree to which mothers respond to their baby's cries, how affectionate and tender they are, how positive their behaviors are, and how often they interfere in their baby's ongoing behaviors.

revolving door syndrome: A term coined to describe the returning of young adult children to the home of their parents after previously leaving the home to live on their own.

rewards: Used to reinforce behavior and increase the likelihood that the behavior will occur again; the benefits (the payback, profit, or compensations) exchanged in a social relationship.

routine housework: House cleaning, meal preparation, grocery shopping, cleaning up after meals, and laundry.

sandwich generation: A term describing being in the middle of two generations—parenting adolescent or younger children while at the same time caring for aging parents.

second shift: Hochschild's term for the burden of the dual responsibilities of wage earner and housekeeper.

secondary divorce stressors: The "fallout" associated with divorce, including depression and greater risks for health problems.

secure attachment type: This attachment type describes infants who use their parents as a secure base from which to explore the novel environment. These infants seek comfort from their parents when distressed and typically continue to develop healthily, both cognitively and emotionally.

self-care: Children who are school-age and old enough to care for themselves for limited periods of time, and yet young enough to require adult supervision most of the time.

self-help skills: This is the first area in which a parent can provide learning experiences for the toddler. It is necessary that parents pick up on the child's cues of a desire for independence, despite the fact that the toddler's coordination may not be equal to that desire. The parent creates opportunity for the child to begin engaging in developmentally appropriate independent tasks.

self-righteousness: The inability to see one's own potential for doing wrong or hurting another person; a pride-related barrier to forgiveness.

sensitivity: Refers to the mother's ability to perceive the infant's signals accurately and the ability to respond to them promptly and appropriately.

SES of origin: The term used when describing a child's family's socioeconomic status.

shared care: A childcare arrangement in which parents share a babysitter or nanny.

shared legal custody: Both parents have an equal say in a child's upbringing.

shift work: Working nonstandard hours or working a schedule other than the typical Monday–Friday workweek.

single-parent family: A household with one parent, with no parenting partner or spouse.

social identity: Refers to whether the goals of a society/culture emphasize the advancement of the group's interests *(collectivist)* or individual interests *(individualistic)*.

social learning theory (SLT): Bandura's theory that children acquire behaviors and personality traits by observing others. An offshoot of the traditional behaviorism theory, this theory addresses the roles of reward and punishment and it goes a step further to include an individual's realm of cognition—the role of observation—in the process of learning.

social welfare: Programs developed in an effort to improve the living quality of the poor, funded by federal and state resources, originally proposed in federal legislation by President Lyndon B. Johnson.

socialization needs: Another base goal of parenting is to meet the socialization needs of children, which encompasses ensuring they become productive, contributing members of society.

sociocultural theories: Theories maintaining that children's development does not occur by stages but through direct interaction with culture, which shapes their values, goals, and expectations.

socioeconomic status (SES): The government's measure of a family's relative economic and social ranking within a community.

sole custody: One parent is the primary parent—legally, physically, or both legally and physically.

special education: A wide range of educational and social services for people with disabilities, most often provided for those between the ages of 3 and 21.

speech disorder: An impairment of voice, articulation of speech sounds, and/or fluency.

sperm bank: Storage place for sperm retrieved from donors used for artificial insemination procedures.

spousal support: Today, alimony is more commonly referred to as spousal support.

stepfamily: A stepfamily is formed when, after the death, divorce, or separation of one parent, the other parent marries again. A stepfamily is also formed when a never-married parent marries.

sterility: The absolute inability to reproduce, either because the woman has no uterus or ovaries or the male has no testes or sperm production.

strain-based conflict: Occurs when the demands in one domain make it difficult to perform effectively in another domain.

stress-and-coping model: A model of children's adoption adjustment suggesting that a child's adjustment to adoption is determined largely by how he or she views or appraises the adoption experience and by the types of coping mechanisms they use to deal with adoption-related stress.

surrogate mother: A woman who carries the fetus of another couple.

survival needs: The provision of food, shelter, safety, security, and love—a base goal of parenting.

synchrony: Reciprocal, mutually rewarding interactions between mother and baby.

Systemic Training for Effective Parenting (STEP): A program founded on healthy family communication and promoting a democratic family atmosphere. Quality and effective parenting is fostered through encouragement, mutual respect, discipline consistent with behavior, firm limits, offering choices, making suggestions, and joint decision making by parents and children.

temporal influences: Influences such as the passage of time and the child's age at the time of divorce that may play a role in children's long-term adjustment to their parent's divorce.

theory of maternal role attainment: The process through which a woman, through pregnancy and after the birth of her child, continues to construct an "ideal" image of herself as mother, and adopts roles that support this ideal image.

time-based conflict: Takes place when demands from the work domain and the family domain vie for a parent's time and attention.

transactional: The dynamic process whereby our exchanges with others simultaneously affect and are affected by our intimate relations.

transracial adoptions: The joining of racially different parents and children together in adoptive families. These may be divided into major categories: (1) the adoption of foreign-born children of a different race from the adopting American families, usually white, and (2) the adoption of American-born children of a different race by American families, also usually white.

trust versus mistrust: The first of the stages of the life cycle and the psychosocial development of the ego described by Erik Erikson. Trust is developed by the baby when care is consistent and accepting. If the child receives inconsistent, inadequate, and rejecting care, he or she develops a basic mistrust, or attitude of fear and suspicion toward the world in general and toward people in particular.

uninvolved parents: Parents who are typically low in responsiveness, warmth, and affection. They are also low in parental control or demands. Both parents reject and neglect their children.

visual impairments: These impairments fall into two categories: the blind and the partially sighted. Children are declared legally blind if their visual acuity is 20/200 or less in the better eye, even with the use of glasses or if the field of peripheral vision is extremely narrow. Partially sighted children have visual acuity between 20/70 and 20/200 in the better eye with glasses.

warmth: Refers to a parent's emotional expression of love.

white collar occupations: Professional occupations such as attorneys, bankers, and doctors.

work–family spillover/crossover: Occurs when a spouse carries the emotional events and tensions of one environment to the other.

working poor: Refers to those people who are working but who continue to remain below the poverty threshold for their family size.

zone of proximal development: The term developed by Vygotsky to refer to the small area just beyond a child's demonstrated level of development that a child can move toward with adult guidance.

AUTHOR INDEX

A

Achenbach, T., 247
Adamec, C., 270
Adams, G., 68
Adkins, V., 103
Adler, A., 123
Administration for Children and Families, 55
Administration for Children, Youth, and Families, 292
Afable-Munsuz, A., 147
Ahrons, C., 173–174, 179–180, 183
Ainsworth, M. D., 36, 37, 38
Airies, E. J., 75, 76
Akman, D., 229
Alan Guttmacher Institute, 78, 79–80
Aldous, J., 99
Alessandri, S. M., 228
Al-Fadhli, H. M., 5
Allegretto, S., 198, 201
Allen, L., 146
Allison, P. D., 176
Allport, G. W., 76
Alpern, D., 189
Alsaker, F., 84
Altschuler, S., 275, 276–277
Amato, P., 18, 160, 161, 170, 174, 176, 179, 185, 199, 204
Amato, R. P., 49
American Academy of Pediatrics, 223, 224, 229
American Academy of Pediatrics, Committee on Psychosocial Aspects of Child and Family Health, 118
American Adoptions, 262
American Community Survey, 146
American Psychological Association, 247
American Social Health Association, 80
American Society of Reproductive Medicine, 270–273
Amlie, C., 263
Andersen, R., 268
Anderson, E., 232, 233
Anderson, J., 75
Anderson, L. S., 30
Anderson, S. A., 132, 166, 185, 186
Anderssen, N., 263
Aquilino, W., 72, 98, 99, 170
Arab American Institute, 154, 200
Archenback, T., 247
Arditti, J., 170, 180
Arendell, T., 13
Arnold, L. B., 9
Arnold, S., 17
Artazcoz, L., 205
Atienza, A. A., 111

Atkinson, A., 96, 97
Atwater, E., 66, 67
Aunola, K., 20
Avison, W., 169
Axelson, L., 99

B

Baca Zinn, M., 200
Bahr, S., 82, 83
Bailey, D. C., 133
Bailey, J. M., 264
Bailey, S., 175
Baird, L. S., 204
Baker, B., 252
Bakermans-Kranenburgy, M. J., 38
Baldwin, A., 167
Baldwin, C. P., 167
Bandura, A., 34
Bane, W., 278
Bank, B. J., 74
Bank, L., 170
Banks, J. A., 138
Banyard, V., 167, 169, 229
Barbarin, O. A., 146
Barbell, K., 273
Barbour, C., 102, 139
Barbour, N. H., 102, 139
Barnes, G., 82, 83
Barnett, R. C., 211
Barratt, M., 170
Barrnett, J., 234
Bartholet, E., 266
Basow, S. A., 75
Bates, J., 63, 160
Baum, F., 10–11
Baum, N., 175, 181
Bauman, K., 81, 82, 83
Baumeister, R., 134–135
Baumrind, D., 43, 47, 48, 49, 225, 226, 229
Baxter, J., 32, 209
Baydar, N., 107
Beach, S. R. H., 132, 133
Beale, B., 105–106
Beaman, J., 169
Bearinger, L. H., 81
Bearman, P., 77–78, 81
Beccia, P. J., 204

Author Index

Becker, P. T., 30
Beckman, P., 251, 252
Bee, H., 49, 109
Behnke, A. O., 202
Behrman, R., 54, 262, 265, 268
Beitchman, J., 229
Bell, S. M., 36
Belsky, J., 14–15, 18–19, 20, 38, 43, 44, 47, 290
Benach, J., 205
Benasich, A., 16
Bengtson, V., 104
Berger, P., 231
Berkowitz, D., 7
Berndt, T. S., 74
Bernstein, J., 202
Besharov, D., 222, 230
Besser, A., 14
Bettenhausen, S., 223
Beutell, N. J., 206–207
Bianchi, S. M., 31–32
Bickley, P., 170
Bigner, J. J., 264
Billings, L. S., 132
Bird, H., 234
Bishaw, A., 156
Black, K., 79
Black, L., 266
Black, M., 81
Blair, S. L., 209
Blake, F. G., 30
Blake, J., 8
Blakeslee, S., 178
Blanchard-Fields, F., 104
Blehar, M. C., 37
Bleske-Rechek, A., 75
Bloir, K., 171
Blum, R. W., 81
Boak, A. Y., 49
Bobrow, D., 264
Bodner-Johnson, B., 254
Boellstorff, T., 154
Bogenschneider, K., 73, 82, 83
Bohannan, P., 174
Bohlin, G., 295
Boisjoly, J., 76
Bokker, P., 175
Bonach, K., 174
Bonkowski, S., 265
Booth, A., 170, 199
Booth, C., 64
Booth, K., 167, 169
Borders, L., 266
Borquez, J., 160
Borrell, C., 205
Bos, H. M. W., 7, 264

Bost, K. K., 18
Bowen, M., 6
Bowlby, J., 18, 37
Boyce, G., 251
Boyd, D., 49, 109
Brady, S. S., 78–79
Braver, S., 174, 175
Brayfield, A., 296
Brazelton, T. B., 16, 39, 42
Brewaeys, A., 264
Bridges, L., 18–19
Brindis, C. D., 147
Brinton, M., 169
Britner, P., 288, 296
Brody, E. M., 109, 110
Brody, G., 20
Brodzinsky, D., 265, 266, 267
Broken Nose, M. A., 225
Broman, C. L., 49
Brommel, B. J., 119
Bronstein, P., 64
Brooks, D., 7, 12
Brooks, R., 67
Brooks-Gunn, J., 16, 49, 107
Brott, A. A., 176
Brown, G. G., 18
Brown, T. N., 155
Bruckner, H., 77–78
Bruder, M., 255
Bryant, D., 294
Buehler, C., 172
Buhrmester, D., 74
Bumpus, M. F., 204
Burchinal, M., 292, 294, 296
Buriel, R., 148
Burleson, B. R., 74
Burr, W. R., 125
Burton, L., 106
Burton, S. J., 178
Buss, D. M., 75
Byers, K., 169
Bylund, C. L., 119
Bynum, R., 82

C

Cable, S., 201
Cabrera, N., 18
Campaign for Forgiveness Research, A, 132
Campbell, M. E., 76
Campbell, N., 9
Campbell, R., 8
Campbell, S. B., 20
Canary, D. J., 121
Canter, L., 126
Canter, M., 126

Capaldi, D., 81
Carlson, A., 6
Carlson, C., 176
Carnelley, K. B., 132
Carson, D., 152, 153
Carson, J. L., 18
Carter, B., 30, 95
Cartwright, C., 176, 178
Cartwright, R., 10
Cassidy, C. M., 30
Casta-eda, D. M., 138
Castellino, D. R., 12
Catalan, S., 221
Cates, D., 223, 225, 230
Caughy, M., 294
Cavanaugh, J. C., 104
Ceballo, R., 160
Cebalo, R., 50
Center for Law and Social Policy, 299
Centers for Disease Control and Prevention, 2–3, 5, 77, 80–81, 221, 249, 250, 270, 271, 272
Chadwick, B., 263
Chao, W., 169
Chapman, J., 68
Charnov, E. L., 16, 18
Chase-Lansdale, P. L., 47–48
Chatters, L., 170
Cheah, C. S. L., 49
Chen, A., 49
Cherlin, A., 48, 104, 176, 180
Chess, S., 16, 30–31
Child Development Institute, 245
Children's Bureau/National Center on Child Abuse and Neglect, 222
Child Trends, 142, 145–146, 148, 149
Child Welfare Information Gateway, 228–229
Child Welfare League of America, 262–263
Cho, Y., 138
Chow, J., 227
Chuang, S. S., 18
Ciano-Boyce, C., 264
Clark, E. M., 67
Clarke-Stewart, K., 15, 22
Clark-Lempers, D. S., 74
Claussen, A., 225
Claxton, A., 210
Clemns, A., 99
Coard, S. I., 155
Cody, M. J., 121
Cohen, T. F., 31
Colbert, K., 170
Coleman, M., 175, 187, 201, 263, 301, 302
Coll, C., 159
Coltrane, S., 209, 210

Conger, K., 82
Conger, R., 19, 73, 82, 131, 160, 169, 174
Congressional Caucus on Women's Issues, 168–169
Congressional Research Service, 200
Connell, C. M., 49
Connell, J., 18–19
Conner, R., 253
Conners, C., 247
Conroy, D. E., 30
Conroy, J., 276
Conway, J., 111, 112
Conway, S., 111, 112
Cook, P., 189
Cooksey, E., 180
Cookston, J. T., 175
Coontz, S., 142
Corbett, M., 168
Cornell, D., 255
Cornell, J. L., 77
Corns, K., 30
Corsini, D., 289
Cortes, I., 205
Cost, Quality, and Outcomes Study, 293, 294
Coughlin, C., 70
Coulton, C., 227
Craig, P., 180
Creasey, G., 104, 105
Creighton, L., 299, 301
Criddle, M., 175
Crimmins, E. M., 101
Crittenden, P., 225
Crnic, K., 19, 43
Crockenberg, S. C., 14
Crosby, L., 81
Crouter, A. C., 202, 204
Crowe, P. A., 74
Cryer, D., 292, 296
Cudaback, D., 127
Cummings, E. M., 198
Current, L. R., 211

D

Dacey, J., 177
DaCosta, G., 229
Dail, P., 152, 231
Daire, A., 109
Daly, D., 277
Danseco, E., 235
Darlington, J., 176
Davies, L., 169, 170
Davies, M., 234
Davila, J., 132, 133
Davis, D. A., 154
Davis, E. C., 179
Davis, J., 78

Author Index

Davis, K. K., 203, 204
Davis, S. S., 154
Davis-Kean, P., 17
Day, R., 18, 50–51, 63
DeBarros, K. A., 94
Deery-Schmitt, D., 288
Defrain, J., 204
Deich, S., 296
Deinhart, R., 175
DeLusé, S. R., 175
Denny, G., 175
Dent, C. W., 48
Dew, J., 198
DeWolff, M., 38, 39
Diener, E., 176
Di Filippo, L., 103
Dilworth-Anderson, P., 106
Dinkmeyer, D., 50, 123, 124, 125–126
Dion, K. K., 139
Dion, K. L., 139
DiPietro, J., 294
Dittus, P., 81
Division of Vital Statistics, 270
Dodge, K., 63, 160
Doherty, W., 17, 82
Dolich, C., 76
Donahoo, S., 167
Dornbusch, S., 49, 72
Douvan, E., 95–96
Dowd, T., 277
Dreikurs, R., 50, 123
Drew, L. M., 146
Driscoll, A., 169
Driver, D., 106
Druley, J. A., 111
Drummet, A. R., 201
Dubow, E., 15
Duck, S., 75
Dumka, L., 149
Duncan, G. J., 76
Dunne-Bryant, A., 174
Dunphy, D. C., 65–66, 67, 74
Dunst, C., 252
Duran-Aydingtug, C., 180
Durbin, M., 49
Durex, 77
Durose, M. R., 221, 225
Dvorak, D. M., 178
Dyk, P. H., 211
Dykeman, C., 153
Dyson, L., 251

E

Eamon, M. K., 48
Eccles, J., 76, 160
Eddy, L., 109

Edin, K., 169
Eiden, R., 30, 39
Eisenberg, M. E., 81
Elder, G., 103, 105, 160, 174
Elmer, E., 228
Eme, R., 268, 269
Emery, R. E., 176, 181, 185, 190
Emick, M., 104, 107
Emper, N., 201
Endresen, I. M., 84
Engler, J. N., 178
Ennett, S., 83
Enright, R., 133
Ensminger, M. E., 48
Erikson, E., 33, 35–37, 44, 52, 67, 73
Eron, L., 15
Erwin, E., 247, 256
Eskew, R. W., 95–96
Eyre, L., 211
Eyre, R., 211
Ezell, M. E., 155

F

Fagan, J., 18
Farley, R., 175
Farmer, T. W., 83, 84–85
Farrell, M., 82, 83
Feagans, L., 296
Feigelman, S., 81
Fein, E., 262, 268
Feldman, S. S., 81
Felner, R., 160
Fergusson, L. R., 5
Fernandez-Dols, J. M., 138
Ferron, J., 159
Fetrow, R., 170
Ficher, I., 264
Fiedler, C. R., 256
Field, T., 291
Fields, J. M., 167
Figard, A., 240, 241
Figard, R., 240, 241
Figueiredo, B., 21
Fincham, F. D., 132, 133, 176, 177
Fine, M., 263, 301
Fingerman, K. L., 100, 101–102
Finkelhor, D., 224
First, J., 131
Flaks, S., 264
Flay, B. R., 48
Fleming, W. C., 151
Flewelling, R., 82
Flor, D., 20
Floyd, F., 250
Folk, K., 170
Fonagy, P., 38

Fong, T. P., 150
Forehand, R., 81
Forgatch, M., 170
Forum on Child and Family Statistics, 168
Foshee, V. A., 49
Fowler, F., 49
Fox, N., 30, 38
Fox, S., 234
Foy-Watson, S., 155
Francis, C., 190
Franco, N., 68
Franks, M. M., 111
Freedman, R., 250
Freedman-Doan, C. R., 49
Freud, S., 32–33
Freund, L., 244
Friel, L. V., 179
Frisen, A., 84, 85
Frodi, A. M., 18
Frodi, M., 18
Frosch, C., 20
Fuligni, A. J., 155
Fuller-Thomson, E., 106
Fung, H., 150
Furman, W., 74
Furstenberg, F., 104, 176, 177, 180, 204–205

G

Gable, S., 19
Galbraith, J., 81
Galinsky, E., 287
Gallagher, E., 250
Galluzzo, D., 291
Galvin, K. M., 119, 120, 121
Ganong, L., 175, 187, 263
Garbers, B., 133
Gardner, M., 276
Gargiulo, R. M., 240
Garrett, P., 159
Gartrell, D., 126
Garwick, A., 152
Gates, G. J., 144
Gattai, F., 106
Gatz, M., 110
Gauthier, A. H., 8
Ge, X., 160
Gecas, V., 71
Gee, E., 97, 98
Gefken, G., 251
Genovese, T. A., 190
Gerson, M. J., 6, 7
Giarrusso, R., 104
Gibbs, J., 62
Gilbreth, J. G., 179
Giles-Sims, J., 51
Gilliland, J., 189

Gillmer, V., 223, 225
Girniss-Brown, D., 15
Glasgow, K., 72
Glass, J. C., 106
Gleeson, J., 275, 276–277
Glendinning, A., 49
Goddard, W., 127
Goeke-Morey, M. C., 198
Gohm, C. L., 176
Goldberg, W., 167
Goldscheider, C., 98
Goldscheider, F., 98
Goldstein, S., 291
Golombok, S., 264
Gomby, D., 54
Gonsalves, S., 248, 249
Gonzales, N. A., 47–48, 148
Goodman, M. R., 174
Gootman, M., 227–228
Gordon, V., 81
Gorman, J., 150–151
Gottfried, A., 166
Gottfried, A. E., 166
Gottlieb, A., 250
Gottman, J., 207, 253
Gottwald, S., 250
Graham, L., 186
Grall, T. S., 179, 180–181, 187
Grant, R., 233
Gray, J., 264
Graziano, A., 228, 230
Greeley, S., 152
Green, J., 37
Green, L., 78
Green, R., 264
Greenberger, E., 167
Greene, B., 146, 147
Greenhaus, J. H., 206–207
Grey, I., 50
Grief, G., 172
Griffin, K. W., 49
Griffin, W., 175
Grogan-Kaylor, A., 48
Gross, D., 45
Grossmann, K., 44
Grosswald, B., 203
Grotevant, H., 268
Gurlanick, M., 253
Gustafson, G., 37
Guterman, N., 231

H

Ha, J., 110
Haddoc, S. A., 211
Hagekull, B., 295
Hale-Benson, J., 146

Hall, J. H., 133
Hallahan, D., 240, 242, 244, 245, 246, 247, 248
Hallman, M., 175
Halmesmaki, E., 20
Halpern-Felsher, B., 77–79
Hamill, S., 167
Hamilton, C., 291
Hammer, J., 110
Hammer, L., 206
Hammond, M., 253
Hamner, T., 87
Hanisch, K. A., 204–205
Hannum, J. W., 178
Hansford, S. L., 74
Hanson, S. L., 79
Hao, L., 169
Harold, G., 73
Harris, K. M., 81
Harris, V. W., 208
Harrison, T. W., 76
Hartill, L., 9
Harvard Family Research Project, 49
Hashima, P., 160, 161
Haverkamp, B., 109
Hayen, A., 158
Hayford, S. R., 9
Haynes, M., 32, 209
Hays, S., 13
Hayslip, B., 104, 107
He, W., 94, 102, 108
Head, M. R., 204
Heaton, T., 263
Hellerstedt, W. L., 152
Hendry, L. B., 49
Henke, R., 286
Henley, K., 175
Henriksen, L., 49
Heron, R. L., 178
Hetherington, E. M., 49, 174, 175, 176, 184
Hewitt, B., 32, 209
Hinderlie, H. H., 178
Hinduja, S., 84
Hirsch, J. S., 81
Hitz, R., 126
Hochschild, A., 209
Hodgson, L., 105
Hoeffer, B., 264
Hoff, T., 78
Hofferth, S., 17, 18, 286, 288, 296
Hoffman C., 110
Hoffman, J., 82
Hoffman, L., 132
Hoffman, L. W., 5
Hoffman, M., 62
Hoffman, M. L., 5
Holcomb, P., 296

Holden, E., 235
Holden, G., 15
Hood, J., 229
Hotvedt, M. E., 264
Howell, C., 247
Howes, C., 287, 291, 292, 293, 295
Huang, L., 150
Huebner, A., 73
Huesmann, R., 15
Hughes, D., 155
Huh, K., 251
Hui Liang, C., 150
Hunneycutt, T. L., 106
Hunter, A., 103
Hunter, L., 233
Hurwicz, M., 110
Huston, A., 159
Huynh, V. W., 155
Hwang, C. P., 18

I

Iglesias, A., 18
Ingegneri, D. G., 101
Ingersoll-Dayton, B., 110
Ingoldsby, E. M., 176, 177–178
Innocenti, M., 251
Isabella, R., 38

J

Jaccard, J., 81, 294
Jackson, C., 49
Jackson, K., 149
Jacobsen, R. B., 264
Jacobvitz, D. B., 14
James, D., 96, 97
Jarvis, S., 234–235
Jayakody, R., 170
Jayaratne, T., 160
Jobe, R. L., 133
Johansen, A., 288
Johnson, C. L., 100
Johnson, D. R., 199
Johnson, F. L., 75, 76
Johnson, J., 128
Johnson, K., 102, 103, 106, 107
Johnson, M. D., 21
Johnson, R., 82
Johnson, S. M., 264
Johnson, T., 138, 139
Johnson-Mallard, V., 81
Jones, A., 143
Jones, J., 81
Jones, R., 77
Jonsson, A. K., 84
Joseph, G., 264
Judge, S., 250

K

Kachadourian, L. K., 133
Kagan, J., 289
Kaiser Family Foundation, 81
Kalgee, L., 81
Kalil, A., 160
Kalter, N., 189
Kaplan, G., 174
Kaplan, H. B., 49
Kauffman, J., 240, 242, 244, 245, 246, 247, 248
Kaufman, G., 103
Kaufman, J., 229
Kay, A. C., 67
Kay, M., 299, 300
Kearsley, R., 289
Kelley, D., 133–134
Kelley, M., 150
Kelly, J. B., 174, 175, 176, 184, 185, 188, 190
Kennell, J., 14, 37–38
Kenny, M., 178
Kenote, T., 152
Ketsetzis, M., 68
Kheshgi-Genovese, Z., 190
Kids Count, 148
Kiger, G., 208
Kim, J. E., 49
King, V., 105, 176
Kinnish, K., 253
Kisker, E., 293
Klaus, M., 14, 37–38
Klaus, P. H., 37–38
Kleban, M. H., 110
Klee, L., 275
Kleparchuk, C., 8
Klerman, L. V., 79–80
Klotz, M., 169
Kluwer, E. S., 21
Knight, G. P., 148
Knutson, J., 133, 134
Koblewski, P., 104, 105
Koblinsky, S., 232, 233
Kochanska, G., 15
Koeske, G., 174
Kohlhepp, K. A., 95–96
Kontos, S., 287, 288
Kooken, K., 138
Korbin, J., 227
Koslowski, B., 39
Kotchick, B., 81
Kouneski, E., 17
Kouneski, M., 17
Krasnow, A., 20
Krause, A., 109
Krehbiel, R., 249
Kreider, R. M., 167
Kremer, M., 76
Kretchmar, M. D., 14
Krevans, J., 62
Krieger, N., 198, 199
Kronstadt, D., 275
Kropp, R. Y., 77
Kruk, E., 186
Kuczynski, L., 15
Kuhn, B. R., 125
Kulesa, P., 138
Kulka, R. A., 95–96
Kupperbusch, C., 138
Kurtz, G., 234–235
Kurtz, P., 234–235
Kuttler, A. F., 75

L

LaFromboise, T., 152–153
LaGreca, A. M., 75
Lamb, M. E., 16, 18
Lamborn, S., 49
Lambourne, R., 68
Lamb-Parker, F., 49
Landau, S., 248
Lansford, J. E., 48
Larkin, E., 299, 301
Larson, C., 54
Larson, N. C., 79
Larson, R., 74
Larzelere, R. E., 125
Laub, J., 161
Laumann, L., 222, 230
Lawler, J. A., 133
Lawson, K., 5, 6
Lazarovici, L., 201–202
Leerkes, E. M., 14
Lees, N., 201
Lehr, R., 175, 179
Lehrman, G., 79
Leibowitz, A., 288
Lein, L., 169
Leite, R. W., 175
Lemme, B., 96, 109, 110, 111
Lempers, J. D., 74
Lenton, A. P., 75
Leo, B., 49
Lerner, R., 2, 12
Lesane-Brown, C. L., 155
Letiecq, B., 232, 233
Levine, J. A., 16, 18
Levitt, M., 68
Levy, D. M., 76
Lewis, J. M., 176, 178
Lewis, M., 228
Lewit, E., 54
Li, B., 82
Lichtenstein, T., 268

Author Index

Lichter, D., 209
Lin, C., 150
Lin, J., 202
Lincoln, D., 158
Lindberg, L. D., 77, 78
Lindgren, H. G., 122
Lindsey, E., 233, 235
Lino, M., 6
Litchfield, L., 250
Little Soldier, L., 154
Litvin, S. J., 110
Liu, W., 150
Loewinger, S., 138
Lorenz, F., 82, 160, 174
Lott-Whitehead, L., 264
Loudoun, R., 204
Low, K., 152–153
Lowe, J., 249
Lowrey, C., 210
Luckasson, R., 246, 247
Luskin, F., 133
Lutz, K. F., 30
Lynch, J., 174
Lynch, V., 15

M

Maag, J., 248
Macartney, S., 97
MacDermid, S. M., 202
MacKay, H., 10
MacMillan, P., 175, 179
MacRae, H., 100
Madden-Derdich, D., 180
Magnuson, S., 13
Main, M., 39
Maio, G. R., 132, 134
Majidi-Ahi, S., 146
Makes Marks, L. F., 151, 152
Mandel, J. B., 264
Mangelsdorf, S. C., 20
Manning, W. D., 143
Manusov, V., 121
Marcenko, M., 250
March, K., 269
Marcoen, A., 18
Marcos, A., 82
Marcus, R., 273, 277
Markell, M., 223
Markham, M., 175
Markman, L. B., 49
Marks, N., 110
Marmaros, D., 76
Marsh, H. W., 167
Marsiglio, W., 7, 18
Martin, M., 223, 228, 230

Martin, S. P., 11–12
Martinez, E., 149
Martire, L. M., 111
Masi, W., 291
Masterpaqsqua, F., 264
Matsumoto, P., 138
Mattingly, M. J., 31–32
Maughn, S., 82
McAlpine, D., 169
McAndrew, F. T., 67
McAnnich, C., 248
McBride, B. A., 18, 31
McCandies, T., 146
McCandish, B. M., 264
McClun, L. A., 49
McCracken, C., 50–51, 63
McDaniel, K., 263
McDonald, P. F., 10
McGee-Banks, C. A., 138
McGhie, A., 37
McGoldrick, M., 30, 95, 225
McHale, J., 20
McHale, S. M., 203, 204
McIntyre, A., 178
McIntyre, M. D., 178
McKay, G., 50, 123
McKendry, P. C., 175
McKenzie, J., 263, 265
McKim, M., 54
McKinney, M. H., 12
McLanahan, S., 167, 169, 176
McLeod, J. D., 48
McLoyd, V., 159, 160, 161
McNulty, J. K., 133
McQuillan, K., 9
McRoy, R., 268
McWilliams, P., 140–141
Meadow-Orlans, K., 253
Medina, S., 13
Melby, J., 19, 82
Mendelson, M. J., 67
Mendenhall, T., 268
Mercer, R. T., 13, 14
Merlo, R., 10
Merolla, A. J., 134
Merrell, K. W., 49
Merriwether-de-Vries, C., 106
Meyers, J., 250
Michael, S. T., 132
Mikach, S., 264
Miles, J. C., 175
Milkie, M. A., 31–32
Miller, A., 299, 300, 301
Miller, K., 81
Miller, M., 143

Miller, P., 150
Miller-Tutzauer, C., 82
Mills, G., 31
Mills, J., 228, 230
Minkler, M., 106, 107
Mitchell, B., 97, 98
Miyashita, K., 20
Moen, P., 207
Moncher, F., 227
Monsour, M., 75
Monthly Labor Review, 199
Moore, H., 158
Moran, G., 37, 38
Morgan, P., 142–143
Morgan, S., 251
Morgan, S. P., 9
Morgan-Lopez, A. A., 148
Morris, A. M., 7
Morris, A. S., 49
Moses, K., 240, 241, 242
Moskowitz, D., 289
Moss, E., 64
Mounts, N., 49
Mui, A., 110
Mulder, C., 48
Munsick-Bruno, G., 249
Musatti, T., 106
Myers, D. G., 138, 139
Myers, L., 291
Myers-Wall, J., 127
Mykyta, L., 97

N

Nabors, L., 294
Nash, M., 41
National Alliance to End Homelessness, 231–232
National Association of Child Care Resource and Referral Agencies (NACCRRA), 284, 286–287, 289
National Campaign to Prevent Teen Pregnancy, 78–79
National Center for the Dissemination of Disability Research, 243
National Child Care Staffing Study, 293
National Coalition Against Domestic Violence, 220, 221
National College Health Assessment, 81
National Council for Adoption, 269
National Council on Aging (NCOA), 109, 110
National Institute of Child Health and Human Development, 293, 295
National Network to End Domestic Violence, 219
National Organization on Adolescent Pregnancy, Parenting, and Prevention, 80
National Vital Statistics Report, 3

Neal, M., 110
Needle, R., 82
Neighbour, R. H., 94–95
Nelson, J., 153
Neto, F., 138
Neubaum, E., 20
Neugarten, B. L., 104
Nevid, J. S., 10
Ng'Andu, N., 159
Noelker, L., 109–110
Noh, E. R., 2
Nonnemaker, J. M., 48
Nurmi, J. E., 20

O

O'Connor, E., 264
O'Donnell, L., 76
Office of Child Development, 222
Office of Child Support Enforcement, 182, 183
Office of Human Development Services, 292
Office of the Human Development, 222
Ogata, K., 20
Oishi, S., 176
Olson, S., 167, 169
Olweus, D., 84
O'Neil, R., 167
Orell, L., 87
Ormrod, R. K., 224
Oswald, D. L., 67

P

Pacheco, F., 268, 269
Padgett, D., 146
Papp, L. M., 198
Parent, S., 64
Parish, T. S., 176
Park, K., 10
Parke, M., 187
Parke, R., 18, 108
Parke, R. D., 176
Parks, P., 54
Parl, S., 291
Parziale, J., 188, 189
Parziale, J. B., 188, 189
Pasley, K., 175, 266
Patchin, J. W., 84
Patterson, C. J., 263
Patterson, G., 170
Paul, E. L., 66
Peay, L., 49
Pederson, D., 37, 38
Penning, M. J., 95–96
Pennington, S. B., 264
Perren, S., 84
Perrin, E. C., 263

Perry, S., 291
Perry-Jenkins, M., 202, 210
Persson, C., 84
Peteron, G., 50–51
Peterson, G., 63
Peterson-Hickey, M., 152
Pettigrew, T. F., 76
Pettit, G., 63, 160
Pew Research Center, 10
Pew Research Forum, 121
Phares, V., 73
Phillips, D., 288, 293, 296
Phillipsen, L., 292, 293
Piaget, J., 34, 40, 42
Piferi, R. L., 133
Pinquart, M., 101
Pirog, M., 169
Pittman, L. D., 47–48
Pleck, E. H., 16, 17
Pleck, J. H., 16, 17, 18, 31, 176
Plunkett, J. W., 189
Pok, A. Y. H., 200
Popenoe, D., 143
Posner, J., 7, 302
Potenza, M., 225
Poulsen, M., 255
Powell, D., 299, 302
Pratt, C., 109
Presser, H. B., 203
Pridham, K. A., 30
Priel, B., 14
Prinstein, M. J., 75
Prinz, R. J., 49
Pruchno, R., 102, 103, 106, 107

Q

Qu, L., 10
Quay, H., 247
Quillian, L., 76
Quinlivan, J. A., 79

R

Radziszewska, B., 48
Raffaelli, M., 82
Ramanan, J., 301
Ramey, S., 294
Ramirez, O., 149
Ramisetty-Mikler, S., 131
Rao, N., 20
Raphel, S., 105
Rasmussen, H. N., 132
Rathus, S. A., 10
Read, J. G., 154
Reckase, M. D., 49
Reed, M., 181

Reeder, H. M., 75
Reid, M., 294
Reid, R., 248
Reiss, D., 49
Renk, K., 73
Repetti, R. L., 202
Resnick, M. D., 81
Reynolds, G. P., 105–106
Rezac, S., 179
Rhodes, K. L., 152
Ricardo, I., 81
Richards, M. H., 74
Richardson, J. L., 48
Richters, J., 291
Riesch, S. K., 30
Riley, P. J., 208
Ripple, C., 49
Ritter, P., 72
Rivers, C., 211
Roach, M., 170
Roberts, J. E., 294
Robinson, B., 301
Robinson, J. P., 31–32
Robson, M., 189
Roche, K. M., 48
Rocissano, L., 15
Rodgers, R. H., 173–174, 180
Rodke-Yarrow, M., 15
Rodning, C., 291
Rodrigue, J., 251
Roehling, P. V., 207
Roek, K., 106, 107
Rogers, A., 199
Rogers, S. J., 13
Romer, D., 81
Roosa, M., 149
Rose-Kransor, L., 64
Rosen, E., 76
Rosenbaum, J. E., 77–78
Rosenfeld, A., 275, 276
Rosenthal, D. A., 81
Rotundo, E. A., 17
Rousseau, D., 64
Rovine, M., 15, 290
Rowland, B., 301
Rowland, D., 10
Rubenfeld, K., 75
Rubin, K., 49, 64
Rubin, L., 74
Rubin, R., 13
Rueter, M., 131
Rueter, T., 301, 302
Rutter, M., 264
Ryan, B., 68
Rybak, A., 67

S

Sabatelli, R. M., 132, 166, 185, 186
Sacerdote, B., 76
Saenz, D., 148
Saintonge, J., 64
Saisto, T., 20
Salary.com, 205
Sales, E., 174
Salmela-Aro, K., 20–21
Samaniego, R. Y., 47–48
Sameroff, A. J., 167
Sampson, R., 161
Sandbert, J., 17
Sandefur, G., 176
Sanders, G., 107–108
Sangupta, M., 94
Santelli, J. S., 77, 81
Savin-Williams, R. C., 74
Scalora, M., 108
Schaffer, D., 170
Schatz, M., 278
Scheuerer-Englisch, H., 44
Schlosser, E., 199
Schlossman, S., 22
Schoppe, S. J., 20
Schoppe-Sullivan, S. J., 18
Schulman, I., 262, 265, 268
Schwarz, C., 71
Schwarz, J., 289
Scott, M., 175
Scully, P. A., 102, 139
Seccombe, K., 5
Seff, M., 71
Segatto, B., 103
Seifer, R., 167
Severson, H., 247
Sexuality Information and Education Council of the United States (SIECUS), 77
Seymour, T., 190
Shaffer, P., 133
Shapiro, J. R., 174
Shavitt, S., 138
Shaw, D. S., 176, 177–178
Shelley-Sireci, L., 264
Shin, N., 18
Shtarkshall, R. A., 81
Shucksmith, J., 49
Sieburg, E., 120–121
Sieving, R. E., 81
Silberman, S., 132
Silva, P., 68
Silver, C., 17
Silver, J., 276
Silverman, A., 265
Silverstein, M., 104

Simons, R., 19, 160, 169, 170
Sirolli, A., 148
Skinner, B. F., 34
Slade, A., 15
Small, S., 73
Smeriglio, V., 54
Smetana, J., 72, 150
Smith, C., 127
Smith, D., 246, 247
Smith, D. M., 144
Smith, J. C., 5
Smith, L., 264
Smith, P. K., 146
Smock, P. J., 143
Snipp, C. M., 200
Snyder, C. R., 132
Soerensen, S., 101
Solbere, M. E., 84
Solomon-Fears, C., 2, 3, 4, 166, 167
Solot, D., 143
Somary, K., 102
Somers, C. L., 82
Soodak, L., 256
Spence, R., 189
Spencer, A., 264
Spencer, P., 253
Stanley, S. M., 176, 177
Steele, A., 79
Steele, H., 38, 39
Steele, M., 38
Steffens, P., 190
Stein, C., 110
Steinberg, L., 47–48, 49, 72
Steinbock, M., 231
Stepfamily Association of America, 187–188
Stephens, M. A. P., 111
Stevens, D. P., 208
Stewart, S. D., 176
St. Laurent, D., 64
Stone, G., 175
Stoolmiller, M., 81
Straus, M., 51, 72
Stricker, G., 102
Strobino, D., 294
Strohschein, L., 8–9, 190
Su, M., 227
Su, S., 82
Suarez, L., 252
Sugarman, D., 51
Suh, E., 138
Sulkes, S. B., 243–244
Supple, K., 98, 99
Survey of Army Families IV, 201
Swain, C., 81
Swarr, A., 74

Swensen, C. H., 95–96
Swift, K., 227
Szinovacz, M. E., 102

T

Taffel, R., 32
Tan, L. H., 79
Tanner, J. L., 179
Tanner-Smith, E. E., 155
Taylor, R., 146, 170, 199
Taylor, R. L., 200
Terry, P. A., 12
Teti, D., 30
Theisen, C., 12–13
Thomas, A., 16, 30–31
Thomas, G., 132
Thomas, M., 158
Thomas, R., 131
Thompson, C., 206
Thompson, L., 98, 99, 100
Thompson, L.Y., 132
Thompson, R., 108
Thorne, B., 75
Thurman, K., 250
Thurman, S., 248, 249
Tillitski, C., 172
Tinsley, B., 108
Todd, C., 288
Townsend, A. L., 111
Travers, J., 177
Trembley, K., 231
Triandis, H., 138
Trivette, C., 252
Troll, L., 101
Tropp, L. R., 76
Troyer, L., 72
Trute, B., 250, 251
Trygstad, D., 107–108
Tsay, J., 73, 82
Tschann, J. M., 77
Tseng, H., 150
Tucker, S., 45
Tully, C., 264
Turnbull, A. P., 256
Turnbull, H. R., 256
Turner, H. A., 224
Turner, L. H., 119–120
Turner, P., 87
Turvett, B., 299, 301
Tuttle, D., 255

U

Umberson, D., 99–100
University of Illinois at Chicago, 242

U.S. Bureau of Labor Statistics, 199, 200, 210
U.S. Census Bureau, 4, 102, 105, 106, 139–149, 151, 154, 157, 166–169, 171, 176, 182, 183, 187, 199, 205, 206, 286
U.S. Department of Education, 55
U.S. Department of Health, Education, and Welfare, 222, 292
U.S. Department of Health and Human Services, 55, 83–86, 143, 167, 172, 179, 228–229, 270, 274–275, 277, 284, 286, 288
U.S. Department of Housing and Urban Development, 232
U.S. Department of Justice, 219, 221
U.S. Department of Labor, 198
U.S. Economic Research Service, 158
U.S. Interagency Council on Homelessness, 236

V

van Balen, F., 7, 264
Vandell, D., 301, 302
van den Boom, D. C., 7, 264
Van Hall, E. V., 264
Van Haren, B., 256
Van Ijzendoorn, M., 38, 39
Varcoe, K. P., 201, 202
Vasa, S., 248
Veenstra, R., 84
Veevers, J. E., 11
Velkoff, V. A., 94
Ventura, J., 181
Veroff, J., 95–96
Verschueren, K., 18
Villarruel, F. A., 12
Volling, B., 15, 296
Voran, M., 293
Voydanoff, P., 204–205
Vuchinich, S., 70
Vygotsky, L., 34, 53

W

Wade, N. G., 133
Wagner, R., 170
Waite, L., 288
Walker, A., 98, 99, 100, 109, 110
Walker, H., 247
Walker, J., 288
Wall, G., 17
Wall, S., 37
Wallace, A., 155
Wallace, H., 242
Wallace, R., 109–110
Wallace, S. G., 78
Wallerstein, J., 176, 178, 186, 188

Walters, J., 223, 230
Warfield, M., 250
Warshak, R., 189
Waters, E., 37
Watkins, C. E., 85
Watson, J. B., 34
Way, W., 131
Webber, L., 75
Webster, B. H., 156
Weinstein, E., 76
Weinstein, K. K., 104
Weiss, L., 71
Welch, K. J., 219
West, J., 286
West, L., 75
West, M., 15
West, R., 119–120
Weston, R., 10
Whitbeck, L., 19
White, K. M., 66
White, L., 100, 179
White, L. K., 13
Whitebook, M., 293
Whitehead, B. D., 143
Wickrama, K. A. S., 174
Wigle, S. E., 176
Wilbur, J., 172
Wilbur, M., 172
Wiley, A., 150
Williams, K., 174
Williams, L., 229
Willwerth, J., 300, 301
Wilson, C., 2
Wilson, L., 276
Wilson, P., 128
Windle, M., 82
Wolfe, M., 264
Woodard, J., 301
Wooden, M., 10
Woodworth, S., 43
Wright, J. V., 105–106
Wright, L., 273
Wu, M., 82
Wu, Z., 95–96

Y

Yamaguchi, K., 5
Yau, J., 150
Yellowbird, M., 200
Yeung, W. J., 17, 18
Ying, Y., 150
Yodanis, C., 72
Youngblade, L., 15
Younger, J. W., 133
Ytteroy, E.A., 263

Z

Zahedi, A., 154
Zahn-Waxler, C., 291
Zelazo, P., 289
Ziemba, S. J., 211
Zigler, E., 229
Zimmer, C., 155
Zimmerman, T. S., 211
Zlotnick, C., 275
Zucker, K., 229
Zvonkovic, A., 175

SUBJECT INDEX

Note: Page references with *f* indicate figures; those with *t* indicate tables.

A

Aboriginal peoples. *See* Native American/Alaska Native (NA/AN) families
Abusers. *See* Batterers/abusers
Accessibility, in father involvement, 18
Accident-proofing the home, 43*t*
Acculturation, 103
Acting out, 176
Active listening, 122–123
    definition of, 122
    poor listening styles, 122*t*
    reframing, 123
Adler, Alfred, 123
Adolescents, 71–86. *See also* Divorce, children of
    adolescents' perceptions of parents, 73
    autonomy, developing, 74
    bullying, 83–86
    friendships, 74–76
    identity, establishing, 73
    individuation, developing, 73–74
    parent-adolescent conflict, 72–73
    parenting styles, 71–72
    in poverty, 160–161
    preadolescence, 70–71
    sexual behaviors, 76–82
    social welfare, 160–161
    substance use, 82–83
Adopted children, 265–268
    adoption process, 269–270
    adoptive parents, 262–265
    adult adoptees, 268–269
    age differences, 266
    children's coping strategies, 267–268
    experiences of, 265
    family characteristics, 267
    gender differences, 266–267
    outcomes of, 266–267
    preplacement history, 267
    psychological benefits, 266
    with special needs, 265
    stress-and-coping model, 267
    transracially, 265–266
Adoption, definition of, 262
Adoption and Safe Families Act (ASFA), 273
Adoption Assistance and Child Welfare Act, 273
Adoption process, 269–270
    family-in-waiting, 269
    final court hearing, 270
    initial information, 269
    placement, 269–270
    preparation, 269
Adoptive parents, 262–265
    characteristics of, 262–263
    experiences of, 262
    gay and lesbian adoptions, 263–265
    intrafamily adoptions, 263
Adult Attachment Inventory (AAI), 38–39
Adult children, 95–102
    as adoptees, 268–269
    empty nest, developmental tasks associated with, 95–96, 96*t*
    extended family experiences, 102
    intergenerational ties, 100–101
    living at home, 96–99
    living away from home, 99–100
    parent-adult child relationship in late adulthood, 101–102
African American/Black Caribbean families, 145–147
    characteristics of, 146, 147*t*
    multiple mothering in, 146
    parent-child interactions, 147
    patterns, 146–147
African heritage theory, 146
After-school programs, 302
Aging stage, 95
Ainsworth, Mary, 37
Alcohol use in adolescence, 82–83
Alimony, 181
American Civil Liberties Union (ACLU), 263
American Society of Reproductive Medicine (ASRM), 271
Anal stage of development, 32
Anger, 190, 242
Antinatalist, 8
Anxiety, 241
Arab American families, 154
Articulation disorders, 246
Artificial insemination, 271–272
Asian American families, 149–151
    parent-child interactions, 150
    patterns, 149–150
Assisted reproductive technology (ART), 272
At-risk or disabling conditions, other, 248–250
    prematurity, 249
    prenatal substance abuse, 249–250
Attachment, 14
    across generations, 38–39
    biological and environmental factors in, 38
    child-caregiver, 14, 37–38, 39
    definition of, 37

Subject Index

father-child, 18
in infants, 37–38
in middle childhood, 64–65
mother-child, 14
types, 38
Attachment theory, 37–38
Attained SES, 198
Attention-deficit/hyperactivity disorder (ADHD)
in abused children, 227–228
definition of, 247
in exceptional children, 247–248
Authoritarian parents, 48, 71, 72
Authoritative parents, 48–49, 71–72
Autonomy
in adolescence, developing, 74
definition of, 74
granting, 48
job, 202
vs. shame and doubt, 36t, 42–44
in toddlerhood, 42–43
Azoospermia, 271

B

Balance, 208
Bandura, Albert, 34
Basic budget, 201
Batterers/abusers, 225
attitudes and negative parenting techniques of, 226
characteristics of, 226t
control and domination, 225
identifying, 225
misconceptions about, 225
mothers *vs.* fathers as, 227
Baumrind, Diana, 47. *See also* Parenting styles
Behavior, correcting. *See* Correcting behavior
Behavioral control, 47
Behavioral disorders (BD). *See also* Emotional or behavioral disorders (EBD)
in abused children, 227–228
in exception children, 247, 254
Belonging, sense of, 67
Bicultural socialization, 146
Binuclear family, 173–174
coparenting in, 179–181
definition of, 173
Binuclear Family study, 179–180
Biological father/stepmother stepfamily, 188t
Biological mother/stepfather stepfamily, 188t
Biological parenthood, alternatives to, 261–279
adopted children, 265–268
adoption process, 269–270
adoptive parents, 262–265
adult adoptees, 268–269
foster parenthood, 273–279
infertility, 270–273

Bird's nest, 184
Birthrates
among all age groups, 5f
crude, 3
outside of marriage, 3–4
teen, in developed countries, 4f
to unmarried women, 145f
Blended families, 187. *See also* Stepfamilies
Blue-collar workers, 199
Boomerang generation, 97
Bowlby, John, 37
Brain development, 40–41
electrical activity, 40–41
hearing, 41
touching, 41
vision, 41
Bullying, 83–86
bullied, 84–85
bullies, 84
cyberbullicide, 84
cyberbullying, 84
definition of, 83
direct, 83–84
indirect, 84
parent's role in preventing, 85–86
Phoebe Prince story, 83
school intervention, 85
suicidal ideation linked with, 83, 84

C

Care, definition of, 284
Caregiver burden, 110
Caregivers
adult children's losses and needs, 111–112
adult daughters as caregivers, 109–110
adult sons as caregivers, 110
autonomy *vs.* shame and doubt, 42–44
characteristics of, 110
child-caregiver attachment, 14, 37–38, 39
cognitive impairments, 111
definition of, 30
of elderly parents, 109–111
experiences, factors affecting, 30
in the home, 284, 286t
parents' losses and needs, 111
physical behaviors, problematic, 111
physical punishment administered by, 51t
reciprocity, 39, 40
rewards associated with, 111
stimulation provided by, 41
stressors associated with, 110–111
toilet learning and, 45
Caregiving, definition of, 109. *See also* Caregivers
Caregiving career, 109
Cement child, 187

Center-based care and education, 288–289, 290t
Chapter I programs, 86–87
Child abuse
    acts of omission/commission, 222–223
    batterers/abusers, 225
    child-abuse and -protection laws, 230
    child sexual abuse (CSA), 223–225
    community characteristics, 227
    definition of, 222
    effects of, 227–229
    emotional abuse, 225
    family characteristics, 225–227, 226t
    neglect, 223
    physical abuse, 223
    reporting, 230
    signs and symptoms of, 224t
    social support, 227
    statistics, 221–222
    types of, by percent of total abuse, 222f
Child-abuse and -protection laws, 230
Child and Adult Care Food Program, 287
Childbearing, 2–5
    among teenagers, 3
    among unmarried parents, 3–4
    delayed, 11–12
    pregnancy at different ages, 4–5
Childbearing stage, 94
Childcare and Development Block Grant (CCDBG), 294
Childcare and early education
    alternatives to, 283–303
    caregiver in the home, 284, 286t
    center-based care and education, 288–289
    early and prolonged out-of-home, 14
    effects of, 294–296
    family childcare, 284–288
    future of, 297
    infant care, 289–291
    licensing in, 291–292
    parental satisfaction with, 296–297
    preschool programs, other, 298–299
    quality, 291–294
    school-age children in self-care, 299–302
    single-parent mothers, 169
    types of, 284–289
    weekly childcare arrangements by age, 285f
Child Care Resource and Referral Agencies (CCR&Rs), 287
Child custody, 183–184
    bird's nest, 184
    joint custody, 183
    physical custody, 183
    sole custody, 183
Child development
    ages and stages of, 33t
    brain, 40–41
    delays in, 248
    empty nest, tasks associated with, 95–96, 96t
    mother's knowledge of, 16
    theories, 32–35
Child Development Associate credential, 287
Child Development Associate program (CDA), 297
Child development theories, 32–35
    cognitive, 34
    learning, 33–34
    psychoanalytic, 32–33
    sociocultural, 34
Childfree-by-choice, 10–11
Childless/childfree families, 142–143
Childrearing practices, 62–63, 63t
Children. *See also* Adolescents; Infants; Middle childhood; Preschoolers; Toddlers
    development, mother's knowledge of, 16
    with disabilities (*See* Exceptional children)
    of divorce, 177–181
    homeless, 233–235, 234t
    language development, 15
    perceived value of, 5–6
    in poverty, 160, 167–169, 168f
    socialization needs of, 12
    in stepfamilies, 189–190
Child sexual abuse (CSA), 223–225
    abusers, 224, 226t
    definition of, 223
    effects of, 228–229
    incest, 224, 229
    signs and symptoms of, 224t
Child stress, 250–251
Child support, 181–183
    collection of, 182
    court guidelines, 182
    definition of, 181
    who pays, 182–183
Chronic homelessness, 232
Classical conditioning, 34
Clinton, Bill, 159
Cliques, 66
Closed adoption, 262
Cluttered nest, 97
Coercive control, 72
Cognitive development, 33t, 294–295
Cognitive development model, 131
Cognitive theories, 34
Cohabitating families, 120, 143, 144f
Collectivist cultures, 120, 138–139
Commitment, in PPI, 6
Communication, 118–123
    acceptance, 121
    active listening, 122–123
    co-construction of meanings in, 119
    in cohabitating families, 120
    confirming messages/responses, 120–121

Subject Index

cornerstones of, 120–123
definition of, 119
family meetings, 122
family stories, 119*f*
in gay and lesbian families, 120
interconnecting family relationships, 118–120
in nuclear families, 120
as a process, 119
recognition, 121
in single-parent families, 120
in stepfamilies, 120
symbols involved in, 120
time devoted to, 121–122
as a transaction, 119
Communicative disorders, 245–246, 253
Communities of Color Teen Pregnancy Prevention Act of 2007, 80
Companionate relationship, 104
Competence, sense of, 67
Complex stepfamily, 188*t*
Conditional forgiveness, 134
Confidential adoptions, 268
Confirming messages/responses, 120–121
Conflict
　in adult children living at home, 98
　parent-adolescent, 72–73
　and transition to parenthood, 20–21
Congenital disabilities, 242
Contact hypothesis, 76
Contemporary families, 145–161
　African American/Black Caribbean families, 145–147
　Arab American families, 154
　Asian American families, 149–151
　cohabitating families, 143, 144*f*
　government's role in family policies, 155–161
　identities, children learning about, 154–155, 156*f*
　Latino American families, 147–149
　Native American/Alaska Native (NA/AN) families, 151–154, 152*f*
　poverty, 156–161
　social welfare, 158–161
Contemporary parents, strategies for, 117–135
　communication, 118–123
　correcting behavior, 125–127
　forgiveness, 132–135
　parenting models, 127–132
　Systematic Training for Effective Parenting (STEP), 123–125
Continuity, in PPI, 6
Control
　coercive, 72
　inductive, 72
Control, parental, 47
Coparenting, 19–20
　definition of, 19–20

strategies, 20
styles, 20*t*
Corporal punishment, 48, 51, 72
Correcting behavior, 125–127. *See also* Parenting models
　assertive discipline, 126–127
　hostile responses, 126
　logical consequences, 125–126, 125*t*
　natural consequences, 125–126, 125*t*
　nonassertive responses, 126
　phenomenological approach, 131
Cost, Quality, and Outcomes Study, 293, 294–295
Countertransition, 102
Credentialing of early childhood personnel, 297
Cross-sex friendships (CSFs), 75
Crowds, 66
Crude birthrate, 3
Crying in infants, 35–37
Cultural contexts of parenting, 138–139
　collectivist cultures, 120, 138–139
　individualistic cultures, 139
　social identity, 139
Cultural variant, 146
Custody, 183. *See also* Child custody
Cyberbullicide, 84
Cyberbullying, 84

D

Dating violence/teen violence, 221
Decision to become a parent, 5–7
　appeal of parenthood, 6–7
　gay men and lesbians, 7
　perceived value of children, 5–6
Delayed childbearing, 11–12
Denial, 241
Depression, 242
Developmental delays, 248
Diminished parenting, 179
Direct bullying, 83–84
Direct forgiveness, 134
Discipline
　correcting behavior in contemporary families, 125–127
　definition of, 50
　inductive, 50
　vs. punishment, 50
　spanking, 50–51
　through natural and logical consequences, 50
Disorganized attachment, 38
Dispenser of wisdom, 104
Diverse, 138
Diversity, 138
Divorce, 173–185
　aftermath of, 173–181
　binuclear family, 173–174, 179–181
　child custody, 183–184
　children of, 177–181

332 Subject Index

Divorce (*Continued*)
   child support, 181–183
   divorced dads, 175–176
   divorced moms, 174–175
   emotional challenges, 186–187
   financial challenges, 185
   former spouse relationships, 174
   gatekeepers, 175
   grandparenting of adult children, 104
   legal aspects of, 181–184
   living, loving, and parenting, 184–185
   negative effects of, 176–177
   parenting roles, 185–186
   residential challenges, 185
   spousal support, 181
Divorce, children of, 177–181
   acting out, 176
   adaptation to, 177–178
   coparenting, 179–181
   custodial parent-child relationship, 178–179
   by developmental stage, 177*t*
   externalizing difficulties, 176
   internalizing difficulties, 176
   noncustodial parent-child relationship, 179
   passage of time, 178
   separation from attachment figure, 178
   socioeconomic status (SES), 177, 180
Domestic adoption, 269
Domestic violence, 219–221. *See also* Family violence
Doubling up, 97
Down syndrome, 244
Dreikurs, Rudolf, 123
Drop-in childcare centers, 298
Drug use in adolescence, 82–83
Dual-earner couples, 198–200. *See also* Working families
   blue-collar workers, 199
   definition of, 198
   family well-being, 202–203
   partnership, striving for, 211
   racial/ethnic differences in, 198–200, 202
   taking pride in, 212–213
   white-collar workers, 199

E

Early Childhood Initiative, 55
Earning potential, 182
Economic Opportunity Act of 1964, 298
Education
   definition of, 284
   early, 289–291
   parent, 21–23
   special, 240
Educational neglect, 223
Effective talking, 124–125
El amor de madre (motherly love), 149

Elastic nest, 97
Elderly parents, 108–112. *See also* Caregivers
Elementary and Secondary Education Act, 86–87
Emotional abuse, 225
   batterers/abusers, 224*t*, 225
   definition of, 225
   signs and symptoms of, 224*t*
Emotional development, 33*t*, 295
Emotional neglect, 223
Emotional or behavioral disorders (EBD), 247, 254
Emotional violence, 220
Emotional women, childless, 10
Empathy, 67, 256
Empowerment principles, 256
Empty nest
   definition of, 95
   developmental tasks associated with, 95–96, 96*t*
   as revolving door syndrome, 97
Endometriosis, 270
English as a Second Language (ESL), 298
Enrichment, in PPI, 6
Erikson, Erik, 33. *See also* Psychosocial development theory
ESL. *See* English as a Second Language (ESL)
Ethnic groups. *See* Race and ethnicity
Ethnicity, definition of, 145. *See also* Race and ethnicity
Exceptional children
   family challenges, 250–255
   family support and empowerment strategies, 255–257
   number of, identifying, 240
   parenting, 239–257
   special education, 240
Exceptional children, parenting of, 239–257
   at-risk or disabling conditions, other, 248–250
   family challenges, 250–255
   having a child with disabilities, 240–241
   Loss and Grief Cycle, 240–242, 241*f*, 252–253
   types of exceptionalities, 242–248, 243*t*
Exceptionalities, 242–248, 243*t*
   Attention-Deficit/Hyperactivity Disorder (ADHD), 247–248
   causes of, 245*t*
   communicative disorders, 245–246, 253
   congenital disabilities, 242
   developmental delays, 248
   emotional/behavioral disorders, 247, 254
   gifted children, 248, 255
   hearing impairments/deafness, 246, 253–254
   intellectual disabilities, 243–244, 252–253
   learning disabilities (LD), 245–248, 253
   mental retardation/intellectual disability (MR/ID), 243–244, 252–253
   physical disabilities, 242–243, 252
   visual impairments/blindness, 246–247, 254
Expanded Family Life Cycle, The (Carter and McGoldrick), 95
Extended family, 102

Extended kin, 101
Externalizing behavior, 247
Externalizing difficulties, 176

F

Faker, 122*t*
Familism, 3, 147–148
Family and Child Experiences Survey (FACES), 55
Family and Medical Leave Act (FMLA), 207
Family as launching ground stage, 94
Family Assessment Measure, 251
Family-centered support services, 255
Family challenges of exceptional children, 250–255
    environment, 251
    mothers and fathers compared, 251
    parent-child relationships, 252–255
    resilient children, 255
    stress, 250–251
    support, impact of, 251–252
Family childcare, 284–288
    children's experiences, 287
    definition of, 284, 286
    quality of care, 286–287
    research on, 287–288
    state regulations, 286
Family cohesion, 208
Family deficit model, 167
Family Education Association, 123
Family form in history, 140–142
Family-in-waiting, 269
Family law, 181
Family life cycle, 94–95
    normative/non-normative changes in, 218
Family meetings, 122
Family policies, 155–161
    definition of, 158–161
    poverty, 156–161
    social welfare, 158–161
Family Preservation and Family Support program, 273
Family projection process, 6–7
Family size, 7–12
    childfree-by-choice trend, 10–11
    delayed childbearing, 11–12
    ideal, 8*f*
    Quiverfull (QF) Movement, 9–10
    resource dilution hypothesis, 8–9
Family support and empowerment strategies, 255–257
    coping skills, 256–257
    empathy, 256
    family access, enhancing, 256
    family networking, 256
    hope, 256
    impact of, 251–252
    problem-solving skills, 256–257
    self-efficacy, enhancing, 256

Family values, 140
Family violence, 218–231
    batterers/abusers, 225
    child abuse, 221–222
    community characteristics, 227
    control and domination, 225
    dating violence/teen violence, 221
    domestic violence, 219–221
    effects of, 229–230
    environmental factors in, 226–227
    family characteristics, 225–227, 226*t*
    murders, 221
    by race and ethnicity, 220*f*
    reporting, 230
    shelters, 221*f*
    statistics, 221–222
    victims of, 220–222
Family well-being, 202–203
Family with adolescents stage, 94
Father absence, 17
Fathering, 16–19
    of adolescents, 73
    attachment, 18
    of exceptional children, 251
    factors that influence, 17*t*
    father involvement, 17–18
    ideal-actual gap, 32
    in patriarchal family structure, 16
    as playmate and socializer, 18–19
    reciprocal nature of, 19
    zone parenting *vs.* man-to-man parenting, 9
Feminization of poverty, 158
Fertility rate, 3
Fetal alcohol spectrum disorders (FASDs), 250
Fetal alcohol syndrome, 244
Fictive kin, 100–101
Filial piety, 150
Finances
    in adult children living at home, 99
    in adult children living away from home, 100
    divorce challenges, 185
    earning potential, 182
    economic pressures and parenting, 159–160
    in grandparenting, 106
    of service men and women, 201
Financial Fitness program, 201
Fluency disorders, 246
Food stamps, 159
Forgiveness, 132–135
    barriers and benefits, 134–135
    Campaign for Forgiveness Research, 132
    communicating, 133–134
    conditional, 134
    definition of, 132
    direct, 134

Forgiveness (*Continued*)
   indirect, 134
   individual level of, 132
   interpersonal level of, 133
   intrapersonal level of, 132
   relationship level of, 132, 133
Forgotten fifth, 158
Formal adoption, 262
Formal grandparenting role, 104
Foster care, 273–279
   age of children in, 274
   behavioral problems, 276
   benefits of, 276
   biological parents, 277–279
   children's perceptions of, 276–277
   definition of, 273
   emotional effects on children, 274–275
   foster parents, 277
   goal of, 274
   health effects on children, 275–276
   length of stay in, 278*f*
   mental health, 276
   placement changes, 277
   placement settings, 274*f*
   race and ethnicity, 274, 275*f*
   reasons for removing child from home, 273–274
Freud, Sigmund, 32–33
Friendships
   in adolescence, 74–76
   chumships, 65, 67
   contact hypothesis in, 76
   cross-sex friendships (CSFs), 75
   culture/ethnicity, 76
   empathy in, 67
   gender differences in, 74–75
   in middle childhood, 65–67
   in preadolescence, 70–71
   romantic relationships, 74
   stages of development, 65–67
Fully disclosed adoptions, 268
Fun seeker, 104

G

Gamete intrafallopian transfer (GIFT), 272
Gatekeepers, 175
Gay and lesbian adoptions, 263–265
Gay and lesbian families, 143–145
   communication in, 120
   decision to become parents, 7
Gender differences
   in adopted children, 266–267
   in domestic partner violence, 220*f*
   in friendships, 74–75
   in grandparenting experiences, 103
   in household chores, 209

   in intimacy levels of elderly and adult children, 101
   in learning disabilities, 245*t*
Generativity stage of development, 98–99
Generativity *vs.* stagnation, 36*t*
Genital stage of development, 32–33
Ghetto poor, 158
Gifted children, 248, 255
Goodness of fit, 31, 39
Grandchildren, 107
Grandparenting, 102–108
   characteristics of, 103–104
   experiences, 103–104
   in family childcare, 286
   financial status in, 106
   geographical distance, 101, 103
   grandchildren, 107
   grandparents as parents, 105–107
   grandparent visitation laws, 108
   health, 106
   marital status of adult children, 101, 104
   passage to, 102
   in racial and ethnic groups, 101–102, 103, 104
   roles, 104–105
   service programs for, 107
   social support, diminished, 107
   stepgrandparenting, 107–108
Grieving states, 240–242
   anger, 242
   anxiety, 241
   degree and intensity of, 242
   denial, 241
   depression, 242
   guilt, 241–242
Gross income, 182
Growing Together, 128–129
Guilt, 189, 241–242

H

Head Start, 55, 159, 297, 298–299
Head Start Impact Study, 55
Healthcare Reform, 97
Hearing, development of, 41
Hearing impairments/deafness, 246, 253–254
Hedonist women, childless, 10
High-risk families, parenting in, 217–236
   family violence, 218–231
   homeless, 231–235
HIV/AIDS, 80–81, 276
Homelessness, 231–235
   categories of, 232
   children, characteristics of, 233–235, 234*t*
   definition of, 231
   parents, characteristics of, 233
   population of, 231–232
   support for, 235

Subject Index   **335**

temporary shelters for, 232–233
Home visitation, 54–55
Hooking up, 78
Hormonal imbalances, 270
Household chores, 208–210
    division of, 209
    residual tasks, 209
    routine housework, 209
    second shift, 209
Housing assistance, 159

I

Ideal-actual gap, 32
Idealistic women, childless, 11
Identities
    establishing, 73
    racial/ethnic, 154–155, 156f
    social, 139
Identity *vs.* role, 36t
Incest, 224, 229. *See also* Child sexual abuse (CSA)
Indirect bullying, 84
Indirect forgiveness, 134
Individualistic cultures, 139
Individualists, 139
Individuals with Disabilities Education Act (IDEA), 245
Individuation, developing, 73–74
Induction, 63t
Inductive control, 72
Indulgent parents, 48
Industry, developing sense of, 67
Industry *vs.* inferiority, 36t, 67
Infants, 30–42
    attachment, 37–38
    brain development, 40–41
    childcare and early education, 289–291
    child development theories, 32–35
    crying, 35–37
    divorce, 177t
    environment, 37
    fetal alcohol spectrum disorders (FASDs), 250
    fetal alcohol syndrome, 244
    goodness of fit, developing, 31, 39
    parent-child interaction, 31
    parent-infant relationship, 30–31
    parenting involvement with, 31–32
    premature or pre term babies, 249
    prenatal substance abuse, 249–250
    reciprocity, developing, 39–40
    stimulation, 41–42
    survival needs, 12
    synchrony, developing, 31, 39
    temperaments of, 30–31
    trust, establishing, 35–37
    visual impairments/blindness, 254
Inferiority, 67

Infertility, 270–273
    egg donors, 270, 271f
    men, 270–271
    psychological impact of, 273
    sterility, 270
    treating, 271–273
    women, 270
Informal adoption, 262
Initiative
    vs. guilt, 36t, 52–53
    in preschoolers, developing sense of, 52–53
Insecure-avoidant attachment, 38
Insecure-resistant attachment, 38
Instrumental costs, in PPI, 6
Integrity *vs.* despair, 36t, 99, 108
Intellectual disabilities, 243–244, 252–253
Intellectual learning of toddlers, 45–46
Intellectual listener, 122t
Intensive mothering, 13
Intensive mothering ideology, 13
Interaction, in father involvement, 18
Intercourse, sexual, 76–77, 77f
Intergenerational ties, 100–101
Internalizing behavior, 247
Internalizing difficulties, 176
International adoption, 265–266, 269
Inter-role conflict, 206
Interrupter, 122t
Intimacy levels of elderly and adult children, 101–102
Intimacy *vs.* isolation, 36t
Intimate partner violence (IPV), 220–221
Intrafamily adoptions, 263
In vitro fertilization (IVF), 272
Involuntary caretaking role, 105–106
Involved relationships, 104
Isolation, in PPI, 6

J

Job autonomy, 202
Job complexity, 202
Job status, 202
Johnson, Lyndon B., 55, 158, 159
Joint-biological stepfamily, 188t
Joint custody, 183
Judge and jury listener, 122t

K

Kinship care, 105

L

Language development
    mothering, 15
    parent's role in, 46
    in toddlers, 46
Language disorder, 246

Latchkey, 299
Latency phase of development, 32
Latino American families, 147–149
    characteristics of, 148*t*, 149
    familism in, 147–148
    generation status in, 148
    parent-child interactions, 148–149
    patterns, 148
Learning disabilities (LD)
    in abused children, 227–228
    definition of, 245
    in exceptional children, 245–248, 253
Learning experiences
    in-home, 69–70
    middle childhood, 68–70
    out-of-home, 68–69
    preschool, 53–54
Learning theory, 33–34
Legal custody, 183
Legally blind, 246
Leisure time, 210
Lenient parents, 48
Lesbians as parents. *See* Gay and lesbian families
Licensing in childcare, 291–292
Limited caretaking role, 105
Limits for toddlers, setting, 43–44
Logical consequences, 125–126, 125*t*
Loss and Grief Cycle, 240–242, 241*f*, 252–253
Love withdrawal, 63*t*
Loyalty conflicts, 189–190

M

Market alternative cost method, 205
Maternal gatekeeping, 32
Maternal responsivity, 38
Maternal sensitivity, 38
Maturity lag, 245*t*
Mediated adoptions, 268
Medicaid, 159
Medicare, 159
Mental retardation/intellectual disability (MR/ID), 243–244, 252–253
Middle childhood, 62–71
    attachment, 64–65
    childrearing practices, 62–63, 63*t*
    friendships and chumships, 65–67
    learning experiences, providing, 68–70
    preadolescence, 70–71
    school adjustment, 63–64
    self-concept, building, 67–68
    sense of industry, developing, 67
Middle years stage, 95
Mid-life squeeze, 109
Misbehavior, goals of, 123–124
Mixed co-parenting, 20*t*

Money Sense program, 201
Monotropy, 14
Mothering, 13–16
    attachment, 14
    characteristics of, positive, 15*t*
    child development knowledge, 15
    compliance, 15
    definition of, 13
    of exceptional children, 251
    intensive, 13
    language development, 15
    maternal gatekeeping, 32
    maternal involvement, 14–15
    reciprocal nature of, 16
    transition to, 13–14
Multiple mothering, 146
Multiracial families, 143–161
    African American/Black Caribbean, 145–147
    Arab American, 154
    Asian American, 149–151
    cohabitating, 143, 144*f*
    identities, children learning about, 154–155, 156*f*
    Latino American, 147–149
    Native American/Alaska Native (NA/AN), 151–154, 152*f*
    poverty, 156–161
Multiracial individuals, 145. *See also* Multiracial families
Mutual child, 187
Mutuality, 39

N

Narcissistic entitlement, 134
Natalism, 7
National Association for the Education of Young Children (NAEYC), 297
National Childcare Staffing Study, 293
National Childcare Survey, 296
National Congress of Mothers, 86
National Extension Parent Education Model, 127–128, 128*t*
National Institute for Professional Development, 297
National Survey of Family Growth (NSFG), 143
Native American/Alaska Native (NA/AN) families, 151–154
    characteristics of, 152*f*, 152*t*
    matrilineal lines, 151
    parent-child interactions, 153–154
    patrilineal lines, 151
    patterns, 151–153
    uterine descent, 151
Natural consequences, 125–126, 125*t*
Neglect
    batterers/abusers, 226*t*
    definition of, 223
    educational, 223
    effects of, 228
    emotional, 223
    physical, 223

signs and symptoms of, 224*t*
types of, by percent of total abuse, 222*f*
New World experience, 146
NICHD Early Childcare Research Network, 295
Nonmarital births, 3–4
Nontraditional parents, 48
Nuclear families, 139–145
    childless/childfree families, 142–143
    cohabitating families, 143, 144*f*
    communication in, 120
    definition of, 140
    family configurations, 141*f*
    family form in history, 140–142
    gay and lesbian families, 143–145
    single-parent families, 142
    stepfamilies, 143
Nurturance in parenting, 46

O

Obama, Barack, 55, 80, 97
Oligospermia, 271
One-child policy in China, 3
Open adoption, 262
Operant conditioning, 34
Opportunity cost method, 205
Oral sex, 77–78
Oral stage of development, 32
Out-of-home care. *See* Foster care
Overtime, 204

P

Pairing/marriage stage, 94
Parent-child interaction
    dimensions of childrearing in, 47
    during infancy, 31, 37, 42
    during toddlerhood, 43, 44, 46
Parent-child relationships
    custodial, 178–179
    definition of, 30
    exceptional children, 252–255
    noncustodial, 179
    parent-adolescence, 71–86
    parent-adult child, 93–112
    parent-infant, 30–42
    parent-middle childhood, 62–71
    parent-preschool, 46–54
    parent-toddler, 42–46
Parent cooperatives, 298
Parent education, 21–23
    concept of, 22
    early efforts in (1920s–1950s), 22
    future of, 23
    mothers benefiting from (1980s), 22
    rebirth of (1960s–1970s), 22

    social changes addressed by (1990s), 22–23
    term, use of, 22
Parenthood
    alternatives to biological, 261–279
    appeal of, 6–7
    conflict and transition to, 20–21
Parenting
    behaviors, determinants of, 21*t*
    contemporary, diversity and change in, 137–161
    definition of, 12
    exceptional children, 239–257
    of exceptional children, 239–257
    in high-risk families, 217–236
    responsibilities, 12–13
    rewards and costs associated with, 6
    in single-parent families, 166–187
    in stepfamilies, 187–190
    work, 197–214
    zone *vs.* man-to-man, 9
Parenting, changing nature of, 29–56, 61–88
    adolescence, 71–86
    infancy, 30–42
    later life, 93–112
    middle childhood, 62–71
    preschoolers, 46–54
    toddlerhood, 42–46
Parenting in perspective, 1–23
    childbearing trends, 2–5
    decision to become a parent, 5–7
    family size, 7–12
    parent education, 21–23
    process of parenting, 12–21
Parenting models, 127–132
    cognitive development model, 131
    differences among, 129–130
    Growing Together, 128–129
    limitations of, 130–131
    National Extension Parent Education Model, 127–128, 128*t*
    outcomes and effectiveness of, 131–132
    Partners for Fragile Families, 128
    similarities among, 129
    strengths of, 130
Parenting process, 12–21
    conflict and transition to parenthood, 20–21
    coparenting, 19–20
    fathering, 16–19
    mothering, 13–16
Parenting programs
    Chapter I, 86–87
    developing, 55*t*
    family literacy, 55
    Head Start, 55
    home visitation, 54–55
    impediments to success of, 54–55

Parenting programs (*Continued*)
  for parents of adolescents, 87
  for parents of infants, toddlers, and preschoolers, 54–56
  for parents of school-age children, 86
Parenting styles
  adolescence, 71–72
  authoritarian, 48, 71, 72
  authoritative, 48–49, 71–72
  ethnic group differences in, 49–50
  permissive, 48
  of preschoolers, 47–50
  uninvolved, 47–48
Parents
  contemporary, strategies for, 117–135
  grandparents as, 105–107
  homeless, 233
Parents and Teachers Association (PTA), 86
Parents as Teachers program, 54
Parents Encouraging Parents Conference, 240
Parent's Handbook, The (Dinkmeyer, McKay, and Dinkmeyer), 123
Partially sighted, 246
Participatory caretaking, 105, 286
Partners for Fragile Families, 128
Patriarchal family structure, 16
Patriarchy, 140
Peer group formation, 65–67
Pelvic inflammatory disease (PID), 270
Perceived support, in PPI, 6
Perceptions of Parenting Inventory (PPI), 6
Permanent alimony payments, 181
Permissive parents, 48
Persistently poor, 158
Phallic stage of development, 32
Phenomenological approach, 131
Physical abuse, 223
  batterers/abusers, 225, 226*t*
  definition of, 223
  effects of, 228
  signs and symptoms of, 224*t*
Physical custody, 183
Physical disabilities, 242–243, 252
Physical neglect, 223
Physical violence, 219
Piaget, Jean, 34
Play groups, 298
Postlingual deafness, 246
Poverty, 156–161
  adolescents in, effects on, 160–161
  children in, effects on, 160
  in contemporary families, 156–161
  economic pressures and parenting, 159–160
  factors leading to, 158
  feminization of, 158
  ghetto poor, 158
  parenting behaviors, 159–161
  persistently poor, 158
  by race, 157*f*
  rural poor, 158
  single-parent mothers, 167–169, 168*f*
  socioeconomic status (SES), 158
  urban poor, 158
  working poor, 157–158
Poverty line, 156
Poverty rate, 156
Power assertion, 63*t*
PPI. *See* Perceptions of Parenting Inventory (PPI)
Practical women, childless, 11
Preadolescence, 70–71
  characteristics of, 70
  definition of, 70
  family experiences, 70
  friendships, 70–71
Pregnancy. *See also* Birthrates; Teenage pregnancy
  at different ages, 4–5
  fertility rate, 3
  relationship quality during, 21
Prelingual deafness, 246
Premature or pre term babies, 249
Prenatal substance abuse, 249–250
Preschoolers, 46–54
  discipline and punishment, 50–51
  divorce, 177*t*
  homeless, 234*t*
  initiative, developing sense of, 52–53
  learning experiences, providing, 53–54
  nurturance in, 46
  self-concept, developing, 52
  styles of parenting, 47–50
  warmth in, 46–47
Preteens, divorce and, 177*t*
Primary divorce stressors, 174
Prince, Phoebe, 83
Problem-solving skills, for parents of exceptional children, 256–257
Promoting Safe and Stable Families program, 273
Pronatalism, 7
Psychoanalytic theory, 32–33
Psychosexual stages of development, 32
Psychosocial development theory
  autonomy *vs.* shame and doubt, 36*t*, 42–44
  generativity *vs.* stagnation, 36*t*
  identity *vs.* role, 36*t*
  industry *vs.* inferiority, 36*t*
  initiative *vs.* guilt, 36*t*, 52–53
  integrity *vs.* despair, 36*t*, 108
  intimacy *vs.* isolation, 36*t*
  trust *vs.* mistrust, 35–37, 36*t*
PTSD (post-traumatic stress disorder), 232
Punishment
  corporal, 48, 51, 72
  definition of, 50

Subject Index   339

    vs. discipline, 50
    in learning theory, 34
    physical, 50–51, 51*t*
Punitive parenting, 48

Q

Quiverfull (QF) Movement, 9–10

R

Race, definition of, 145. *See also* Race and ethnicity
Race and ethnicity. *See also* Multiracial families
    acculturation in, 103
    authoritarian parenting, 48
    in custodial mothers, 179
    differences in parenting styles, 49–50
    domestic partner violence, 220*f*
    in dual-earner couples, 198–200
    extended family experiences in, 102
    family childcare, 286
    fertility rates, 3
    foster care, 274, 275*f*
    friendships in, 76
    grandparenting style, 103, 104
    Head Start services, 299*f*
    intergenerational ties in, 100–101
    intimacy levels of elderly and adult children in, 101–102
    nonmarital births, 3
    teen pregnancies in, 80
    transracial adoption, 265–266
    in unemployment, 204–205, 205*f*
    uninvolved parenting, 47–48
Racial/ethnic identities, 154–155, 156*f*
Racial/ethnic socialization, 155
Racism, definition of, 154–155. *See also* Race and ethnicity
Reciprocity
    caregiver, 39, 40
    definition of, 39
    in fathering, 19
    in mothering, 16
    parent-infant, developing, 39–40
Reflective listening, 122–123, 124
Reframing, 123
Rehabilitative alimony payments, 181
Remote relationships, 104
Replacement level of fertility, 3
Research on family childcare, 287–288
Residual tasks, 209
Resilience, 255
Resilient children, 255
Resource dilution hypothesis, 8–9
Responsibility, in father involvement, 18
Responsivity, maternal, 38
Revolving door syndrome, 97
Rewards, 34

Risk and protective factor model, 167
Romantic relationships, 74
Routine housework, 209
Rural poor, 158

S

Safe Harbor, 229
Sandwich generation, 108–109
School adjustment, 63–64
School-age children stage, 94
School-aged children
    divorce, 177*t*
    homeless, 234*t*
    in self-care, 299–302
Secondary divorce stressors, 174
Second shift, 209
Secure attachment, 38
Secure-avoidant attachment, 38
Self-care, school-aged children in, 299–302
    after-school programs, 302
    definition of self-care, 299–300
    effects of, 300–301
    families of children in, 301–302
    latchkey, 299
    readiness for, 300
Self-centered listening styles, 122
Self-concept
    in middle childhood, 67–68
    in preschoolers, 52
Self-conscious listener, 122*t*
Self-help skills of toddlers, 45
Self-righteousness, 134
Sensitivity, maternal, 38
Service men and women, 200–201
    deployment, preparing for, 201
    financial difficulties, 201
SES of origin, 198
Sexual behaviors in adolescence, 76–82
    consequences of, 78–81, 79*f*
    hooking up, 78
    oral sex, 77–78
    parental influences on, 81–82
    sexual intercourse, 76–77, 77*f*
    sexually transmitted infections (STIs), 78, 80–81
    teenage pregnancy, 78–80
Sexually transmitted infections (STIs), 78, 80–81
Sexual violence, 220
Shared legal custody, 183
Shelters
    for abuse victims, 221*f*
    for homeless, 232–233
Shift work, 203–204
Simple expansions of utterances, 15
Single-parent families, 166–187
    communication in, 120
    coparenting, 179–181

Single-parent families (*Continued*)
  custodial parent-child relationship, 178–179
  deficits *vs.* strengths in, 166–167
  definition of, 166
  diminished parenting, 179
  divorce, 173–185
  models of, 167
  noncustodial parent-child relationship, 179
  nuclear, 142
  single-parent fathers, 170–173
  single-parent mothers, 167–170
Single-parent fathers, 170–173
  parenting by, 172–173
  vs. single-parent mothers, 171
  social factors resulting in, 171
  stress in, 171–172
Single-parent mothers, 167–170
  childcare, 169
  coping strategies, 169–170
  health issues, 169
  parenting by, 170
  poverty, 167–169, 168*f*
  vs. single-parent fathers, 171
Skinner, B. F., 34
Social development, early childcare and, 295–296
Social identity, 139
Socialization needs of children, 12
Social learning of toddlers, 45–46
Social learning theory, 34
Social stage of development, 33*t*
Social welfare, 158–161
  children, 160
  economic pressures and parenting, 159–160
  parenting behaviors, 159–161
  programs, 159
Sociocultural theory, 34
Socioeconomic status (SES)
  attained, 198
  definition of, 54, 158
  of divorced families, 177, 180
  of origin, 198
  poverty, 158
  program success, 54
  teenage pregnancy, 79–80
  working families, 198
Sole custody, 183
Special education, 240
Special needs children, adopted, 265
Speech disorder, 245–246
Sperm banks, 272
Spousal support, 181
State regulations in family childcare, 286
Stay-at-home dads, 205–206
Stay-at-home moms, 205

STEP. *See* Systematic Training for Effective Parenting (STEP)
Stepfamilies, 187–190
  challenges for children, 189–190
  characteristics of, 187–189
  communication in, 120
  definition of, 187
  negative connotations of term, 187
  nuclear, 143
  vs. nuclear families, 188–189, 188*t*
  types of, 187, 188*t*
Stepfamilies, children in, 189–190
  anger, 190
  guilt, 189
  loss of power and control, 189
  loyalty conflicts, 189–190
Stepgrandparenting, 107–108
Stepsiblings, 187
Sterility, 270
Stimulation of infant
  hearing, 41
  parents' roles of providing, 42
  touching, 41
  visual, 41
Strain-based conflict, 207
Strange Situation, 38, 290–291, 295
Stress
  abusive parents, 226
  in caregiving, 110–111
  divorce stressors, 174
  in families with exceptional children, 250–251
  marital conflict, 204
  in single-parent fathers, 171–172
Stress-and-coping model, 267
Substance use in adolescence, 82–83
Suicide linked with bullying, 83, 84
Supervised visitation, 183
Supportive co-parenting, 20*t*
Surrogacy, 273
Surrogate parents, 104, 273
Survival needs of infants, 12
Synchrony, 31, 39
Systematic Training for Effective Parenting (STEP), 123–125. *See also* Correcting behavior
  effective talking, 124–125
  misbehavior, goals of, 123–124
  open responses, 124
  reflective listening, 124

T

Teenage pregnancy, 78–80
  birthrates, 4*f*, 78
  childbearing trends among, 3
  impact on mother, 79–80

interventions, 80
issues caused by, 78–79
Temper tantrums, 44
Temporal influences, 178
Temporary Assistance for Needy Families (TANF), 159
Theory of maternal role attainment (MRA), 13–14
Time, valuing, 213
Time-based conflict, 206
Toddlers, 42–46
    accident-proofing the home, 43t
    autonomy in, developing, 36t, 42–44
    divorce, 177t
    intellectual learning, 45–46
    language development, 46
    limits for, setting, 43–44
    parenting involvement with, 31–32
    self-help skills, 45
    social learning, 45–46
    temper tantrums, 44
    toilet learning, 45
Toilet learning, 45
Touching, development of, 41
Traditional families. *See* Nuclear families
Transracial adoption, 265–266
Triangular Theory of Balancing Work and Family, 208f
Trust
    crying, 35–37
    establishing in infants, 35–37
    vs. mistrust, 35–37, 36t
Tweens. *See* Preadolescence

U

Unconscious, role of, 33
Unemployment, 204–205
Unexpected Legacy of Divorce, The (Wallerstein), 178
Uninvolved parents, 47–48
Unmarried parents, childbearing trends among, 3–4
Unsupportive co-parenting, 20t
Urban poor, 158
U.S. household configurations, 141f
Uterine descent, 151

V

Verbal input, 15
Verbal prodding, 15
Veterans, homeless, 232
Vision, development of, 41
Visual impairments/blindness, 246–247, 254
Voice disorders, 245
Voluntary caretaking, 105, 286
Vygotsky, Lev, 34

W

Warmth, 46–47
War on Poverty, 55, 158
Watson, John B., 34
Welfare and Medicaid Reform Act of 1996, 159
White-collar workers, 199
Women in the middle, 109–110
Work-family spillover/crossover, 207–208
Working families, 198–214
    balance in, 208
    basic budget, 201
    childcare, 201
    dual-earner couples, 198–200
    Family and Medical Leave Act (FMLA), 207
    family cohesion, 208
    family fun, prioritizing, 212
    family health, 208
    family well-being, 202–203, 204f
    focus, 212
    household chores, 208–210
    income requirements, 202
    inter-role conflict, 206
    job autonomy, 202
    job complexity, 202
    job status, 202
    leisure time, 201
    meaning from work, deriving, 211
    productive, 212
    saying no, 213
    service men and women, 200–201
    simple living, 213
    socioeconomic status (SES), 198
    stay-at-home dads, 205–206
    stay-at-home moms, 205
    strain-based conflict, 207
    strategies for, 211–213
    time, valuing, 213
    time-based conflict, 206
    today's, picture of, 201–202
    unemployment, 204–205
    valuing family, 211
    work boundaries, 211
    work-family spillover/crossover, 207–208
    work hours, 203
Working poor, 157–158
Worth, sense of, 67

Z

Zone of proximal development, 53–54
Zygote intrafallopian transfer (ZIFT), 272–273

PHOTO CREDITS

Page 1	Andres Rodriguez/Fotolia LLC	Page 165	Toblerone/Fotolia LLC
Page 2	Nicolas Turchin/Fotolia LLC	Page 173	iceteastock/Fotolia LLC
Page 16	Blend Imagés/Fotolia LLC	Page 180	Blend Images/Fotolia LLC
Page 29	OrangePeel Photography	Page 197	TheSupe87/Fotolia LLC
Page 31	Vladimir Mucibabic/Fotolia LLC	Page 200	elswarro/Fotolia LLC
Page 35	Jim Parkin/Fotolia LLC	Page 212	Andrey Armyagov/Fotolia LLC
Page 61	Aramanda/Fotolia LLC	Page 217	Photosani/Fotolia LLC
Page 65	Tjui Tjioe/Fotolia LLC	Page 218	Benjamin Haas/Fotolia LLC
Page 81	Cheryl Casey/Fotolia LLC	Page 223	TheFinalMiracle/Fotolia LLC
Page 93	Renáta Sedmáková/Fotolia LLC	Page 239	Blend Images/Fotolia LLC
Page 97	i love images/Fotolia LLC	Page 244	Tomasz Markowski/Fotolia LLC
Page 101	Lisa F. Young/Fotolia LLC	Page 249	reflektastudios/Fotolia LLC
Page 117	Rido/Fotolia LLC	Page 261	Thomas Perkins/Fotolia LLC
Page 118	Crashoran/Fotolia LLC	Page 264	Anton Gvozdikov/Fotolia LLC
Page 121	Ned White/Fotolia LLC	Page 272	Dmitry Knorre/Fotolia LLC
Page 137	TheFinalMiracle/Fotolia LLC	Page 283	Gennadiy Poznyakov/Fotolia LLC
Page 139	kleberestorilio/Fotolia LLC	Page 287	michaeljung/Fotolia LLC
Page 144	Arrow Studio/Fotolia LLC	Page 289	Vibe Images/Fotolia LLC